MW00380965

"Biblical illiteracy is rampant in the church today, resulting in part from the decline (or absence!) of expository preaching from the pulpit. Pastors often don't have sufficient training in the exegesis of Scripture, or have forgotten much of what they learned in seminary. The Big Greek Idea series is a helpful tool to remedy this situation. This series provides a comprehensive analysis of the meaning and function of Greek words, phrases, and clauses in the New Testament books. Highly recommended for those who want to sharpen their Greek skills and become better interpreters and expositors of God's Word."

—Mark L. Strauss,
University Professor of New Testament,
Bethel Seminary San Diego

"Herb Bateman and Aaron Peer have provided their readers with a rich feast of Greek grammar and theology. What a wonderful (and extensive!) handbook for students and pastors as they study and teach through the Johannine epistles!"

—Robert L. Plummer,
Founder and Host of "Daily Dose of Greek,"
Professor of New Testament Interpretation,
The Southern Baptist Theological Seminary

"As preachers who proclaim God's Word, we want to understand the text as best as we can. Herb Bateman and Aaron Peer put the deep grammatical and lexical technicalities of a critical commentary in understandable and usable format. It is a wonderful bridge between the critical scholar and the pastor/teacher."

—Calvin Pearson,
Associate Pastor at Crossroads Baptist Church, The Woodlands, TX ,
Adjunct Professor at Dallas Seminary,
Southwestern Seminary, Anderson University, and Grace School of Theology

BIG
GREEK
IDEA
SERIES

John's Letters

An Exegetical Guide
for Preaching
and Teaching

Herbert W. Bateman IV • Aaron C. Peer

Kregel
Academic

John's Letters: An Exegetical Guide for Preaching and Teaching
© 2018 by Herbert W. Bateman IV and Aaron C. Peer

Published by Kregel Academic, an imprint of Kregel Publications, 2450 Oak Industrial Dr. NE, Grand Rapids, MI 49505-6020.

All rights reserved. No part of this book may be reproduced, stored in a retrieval system, or transmitted in any form or by any means—electronic, mechanical, photocopy, recording, or otherwise—without written permission of the publisher, except for brief quotations in printed reviews.

The Hebrew font, NewJerusalemU, and the Greek font, GraecaU, are available from www.linguist-software.com/lgku.htm, +1-425-775-1130.

Nestle-Aland, Novum Testamentum Graece, 28th Revised Edition, edited by Barbara and Kurt Aland, Johannes Karavidopoulos, Carlo M. Martini, and Bruce M. Metzger in cooperation with the Institute for New Testament Textual Research, Münster/Westphalia, © 2012 Deutsche Bibelgesellschaft, Stuttgart. Used by permission.

The translation of the New Testament portions used throughout the commentary is the authors' own English rendering of the Greek.

Scripture quotations marked NET are from the NET Bible® copyright ©1996–2006 by Biblical Studies Press, LLC (www.bible.org). Scripture quoted by permission. All rights reserved.

Scripture quotations marked NLT are from the Holy Bible, New Living Translation, copyright © 1996, 2004, 2007 by Tyndale House Foundation. Used by permission of Tyndale House Publishers, Inc., Carol Stream, Illinois 60188. All rights reserved.

ISBN 978-0-8254-4546-0

Printed in the United States of America

18 19 20 21 22 / 5 4 3 2 1

Dedicated to our wives:
Cindy Ann Bateman & Shannon Peer

Contents

      John identifies himself as an authoritative representative of Jesus, who witnessed Jesus's life and ministry firsthand and now proclaims that earthly ministry, in order that fellowship might be shared among all who hear the message about Jesus and in order that true happiness might become a reality for many people.

      John's message about God's perfection (either in morality or in love) serves as the basis that separates self-righteous and self-promoting "Christians" from those whose lifestyle demonstrates that they are friends with God, spiritually self-aware, and supported by Jesus.

      Assurance of a relationship with God is grounded in a persistent observance of God's expectation to love others, whereby extending love to others in everyday life situations eliminates other people's excuses for not following Jesus, and contrasts with those who hate believers, thereby demonstrating that they have no spiritual awareness of God.

relationship with God that is in stark contrast to those who lack love because they have no relationship with God.

John, based upon the awareness of God's love, underscores the obligation for mutual love within the community of believers that in turn verifies the presence of God's Spirit, the belief that Jesus is the Messiah, and a mutual bond with God.

After asserting that God is love, John now asserts that all those who love have a mutual bond with God that results in confidence before God (rather than fear of punishment), reveals God's initiation of love, speaks of misguided love, and expects anyone who truly loves God to love all others who also have a bond with God.

John underscores that anyone who believes in Jesus is part of God's family, is aware of their love for God and others, and exhibits their love for God in their persistence in living out God's expectations as victorious people of faith.

Success in this self-centered world system comes to all those who believe in God's Messiah Jesus, whose life and death—along with the Spirit—verifies his messiahship, through whom God has promised an endless relationship for anyone who believes in Jesus.

Before expressing his exhortation to avoid turning from Jesus, God's Messiah, John closes, in summary fashion, with a restatement about belief in Jesus's messiahship that results in an awareness of an endless relationship with God, a confidence and awareness that God listens to personal needs and the interventions for others, an awareness of God's preservation and protection from the Devil, and an awareness of the bond that exists with God through God's Messiah, Jesus.

Second John

Due to John's affection for his readers, he asks them to comply with God's expectation to love fellow believers and beware of false teachers.

Third John

The basis for John's exhortation to imitate people who have a relationship with God, like Demetrius, is founded on Demetrius's
relationship with God and his reputation with God's people.

John ends his letter with expressed unwillingness to discuss the issue
of supporting itinerant preachers in writing, an expressed desire to
visit Gaius and speak with him in person, and closing greetings.

Preface to the Series

The Big Greek Idea Series: An Exegetical Guide for Preaching and Teaching is a grammatical-*like* commentary with interlinear-*like* English translations of the Greek text that provides expositional-*like* commentary to guide a pastor and teacher in their sermon and teaching preparations. Every volume of this series has a threefold audience in mind: the busy pastor, the overworked professor of an academic institution, and the student with demanding Greek professors.

WHY PASTORS, PROFESSORS, AND STUDENTS

First and foremost, the Big Greek Idea Series is for the busy *pastor* who desires to use their Greek text in their sermon preparation. Most preachers who have earned a Masters of Divinity degree and who have taken some New Testament Greek have not had a lot of exposure in studying books of the New Testament in Greek. If they were fortunate, they may have studied two New Testament books in Greek. Furthermore, many preachers who desire to work in the Greek New Testament do not have the luxury to study and work in the Greek on their own in any great detail. They need a tool to guide them in their use of New Testament Greek in their sermon preparation. This series is meant to be that tool.

> THE BIG GREEK IDEA: A GUIDE FOR PREACHING AND TEACHING was *written for* three groups of people:
> 1. the busy *pastor*,
> 2. the overloaded *professor*,
> 3. and the *student* with a demanding New Testament Greek professor.

Second, the Big Greek Idea Series is for the overloaded *professor* of an academic institution. Institutional demands are high and expectations at times appear overwhelming. On the one hand, many academies expect faculty to teach Greek exegesis with minimal time to prepare, forgetting that such courses differ from courses requiring only English language aptitude. On the other hand, students anticipate a great deal of explanation from those who teach them. Often the professor is merely one step ahead of their students. This tool is intended to streamline class preparation and perhaps even serve as a required or recommended textbook to help take a load off the professor.

Finally, the Big Greek Idea Series is for the *student* with demanding Greek professors. What a student puts into a course is what a student will get and retain from a course. Students who have professors with great expectations are blessed, though the student may feel cursed (at the time). This tool will provide answers that will impress your professor, but more importantly provide information that will build confidence in handling the Greek New Testament. The Big Greek Idea Series will be a tool students will use in ministry long after the course is over.

WHAT CAN BE EXPECTED

Each volume of the Big Greek Idea Series features one or more New Testament books in Greek. It is a series for people who have studied basic New Testament Greek grammar and intermediate Greek syntax and grammar. Each volume provides an introduction that features information crucial for understanding each New Testament book while making minimal assumptions about the reader's capabilities to work in the New Testament Greek text. After the introduction, the volume has three distinct features.

First, each featured New Testament book is broken into units of thought. The units open with a big Greek idea. Professors sometimes refer to the big Greek idea as the exegetical idea of a passage. The big Greek idea is followed by a summary overview underscoring verbs and key transitional and structural markers. The section closes with a simple outline for the unit.

Second, the Nestle-Aland 28th edition Greek text is broken into independent and dependent clauses that reveal visually the coordination and subordination of thought based upon key structural markers. Verbs and key structural markers are often in bold and always underlined. Under each Greek clause is an original English translation. The interlinear-*like* English translations of the Greek helps readers spot the words they know and those they do not.

Finally, each unit closes with an analysis of the clausal outline. It explains the various contemporary author's syntactical understanding of clausal relationships, their semantical rendering of all Greek verbs, verbals, and key structural markers, and an interpretive translation of the text. Interspersed throughout this closing section are grammatical, syntactical, semantic, lexical, theological, and text-critical nuggets of information. They are expositional-*like* commentary to enhance an understanding of selected issues that surface in the text.

HOW TO USE THE SERIES

The Big Greek Idea Series has the potential for a threefold usage.

First, use it as a grammatical commentary because it is a grammatical-*like* commentary. Every volume represents the early stages of Bible study in New Testament Greek. Identifying clauses is a first step typically practiced in exegesis. Yet, every independent and dependent Greek clause has a corresponding explanatory discussion that underscores the grammatical, syntactical, and semantic functions of their respective Greek structural markers that are underlined and often in **bold** print for easy interpretation. Unlike computer programs that present a New Testament Greek text with English translations and parsing capabilities, the Big Greek Idea Series discusses syntax and semantic options important for exegesis yet not available with computer programs . . . but I'm sure that too will change.

Second, use it as an interlinear because it has an interlinear-*like* presentation of the Nestle-Aland 28th edition of the Greek New Testament text with a corresponding English translation. Yet, the Big Greek Idea Series offers far more than a traditional interlinear. The Greek text is presented in a clausal outline format that provides the twenty-first-century reader a visual of the biblical author's flow of thought. More importantly, it causes a person to *slow down* and *look at the text* more closely.

- What does the text say . . . not what *I* remember about the text.
- What does it mean . . . not what *I* want it to mean.
- What do we need to believe . . . not *my* theological pet peeves.
- How should we then live for God . . . not according to *my* preconceived ideas.

Third, use it as a commentary because interwoven throughout every volume are expositional-*like* nuggets. Expositional-like nuggets are comments that underscore a grammatical, syntactical, semantic, lexical, theological, or text-critical issue. Typical of any expositional commentary, if time is taken to discuss an issue, it's probably important and warrants some special attention. Similarly, the expositional-*like* nuggets point the reader to important interpretive issues.

Yet, the Big Greek Idea Series is not meant to replace current commentaries. Commentators generally begin commentary preparation on the clause level, but a publisher's page restriction often makes it difficult to visualize clausal parallels, co-ordination, and subordination of thought. Descriptions are at

> THE BIG GREEK IDEA: A GUIDE FOR PREACHING AND TEACHING FEATURES
> 1. Units of Thought
>   *Big Greek Idea*
>   *Summary Overview*
>   *Outline*
> 2. Clausal Outlines
>   *Clausal Relationships Visualized*
>   *Structural Markers Identified*
>   *English Translation Provided*
> 3. Explanations
>   *Syntax Explained*
>   *Semantical Decisions Recognized*
>   *Interpretive Translation Justified*
>   *Expositional Comments Provided*

times ambiguous and perhaps even ignored, due to the difficulty in presenting a syntactical situation. This tool cannot hide ambiguities and difficulties of coordination or subordination of thought, because clauses are clearly reproduced and explained for readers to evaluate a contemporary author's decisions. Thus, the Big Greek Idea Series is meant to complement critical commentaries like Baker's Exegetical Commentary, Word Biblical Commentary, Anchor Bible, and others.

I trust the Big Greek Idea Series will be a rewarding tool for your use in studying the New Testament.

HERBERT W. BATEMAN IV
SERIES EDITOR

Authors' Acknowledgments

English grammar is not the most exciting subject to study and learn, and yet grammar and syntax are vital skills for interpreting the Bible, whether in an English translation or a Greek New Testament text. Consequently, I'm indebted to several people who throughout my training emphasized the importance of grammar and syntax for interpreting the Bible.

While at Cairn University, Janice Okulski required all her students to create a grammatical diagram for the NIV translation of Philippians, and Dr. McGormick expected his students to structurally outline an English translation of Galatians in order to trace Paul's train of thought. Special attention was always given to connecting words like "so that" (= result), "in order that" (= purpose), "therefore" (= inferential), "because" (= reason), and so on. Both professors prepared me for later study in the Greek New Testament, and to them I owe a great debt of gratitude. And though Professors Okulski and McGormick provided a sound foundation for studying the English Bible, Dallas Theological Seminary expanded that groundwork when I began working in the New Testament Greek text.

While at Dallas Theological Seminary, Darrell Bock, Buist Fanning, John Grassmick, and other New Testament faculty members were instrumental in teaching me skills of translation, syntax, and exegesis. Naturally, skills take time to master, and shortcuts were later developed while teaching others how to learn and work in the New Testament Greek text.

Later as a professor, my pedagogical skills were challenged and eventually sharpened as I was learning how to help students study and learn Greek. Several works resulted in those efforts: *A Workbook for Intermediate Greek: Grammar, Exegesis, and Commentary on 1–3 John* and *Interpreting the General Letters* in Kregel's Handbooks for Greek New Testament Exegesis. Another benefit that comes with teaching is having students whom you teach—and then getting out of their way so that they can move beyond you and your abilities. Aaron Peer is one of those students. Writing a technical work like this one is not an easy task to complete while pastoring. Yet his commitment and steadfastness to this project is to be commended, and for which I am truly grateful.

Consequently, I am indebted to three groups of people who have shaped this book *John's Letters*: two undergraduate professors from Cairn University, the New Testament department at Dallas Theological Seminary, and the numerous students whom I have tutored and taught for over twenty years, especially my coauthor and friend, Aaron C. Peer.

Yet my greatest indebtedness is to my wife, Cindy Ann Bateman, who, when I stepped away from the lectern in 2013, said to me: "Go reinvent yourself." *John's Letters* in the Big Greek Idea Series is just one of the by-products that has come from listening to my wife. She has been a great support in all of my new adventures. Thank you, Cindy.

HERBERT W. BATEMAN IV

The road to completing a detailed work such as this one cannot be done alone, nor can it be done without opportunity costs.

So first, I am thankful for my coauthor, Herb Bateman. This series was his brainchild, and he has worked many hours to see his vision come to fruition. I first met Herb on my first day of Greek back in 1997. Our first relationship was a teacher-student one, and I was grateful for the knowledge and wisdom that he imparted to me as a young college student. Two years later our relationship changed from teacher-student to boss-employee. I began to work for him as a teacher's assistant, and then with him as we taught New Testament Greek together. Our next professional relationship was as coauthors. This is the fourth work that we have pored over and created together, and amazingly he still wants to work with me on future projects. I am deeply indebted to his mentorship and friendship throughout the years. He has taught me more than I could ever give him credit for here.

Second, there have been opportunity costs involved in this project. I have sacrificed time that I could have spent in extra hours in my ministry at Charter Oak Church in Churubusco, Indiana. They have graciously allowed me to use some of my time to further develop my academic skills and to produce works such as this one. I am grateful to them for sticking beside me and allowing me to minister to them for the past fourteen years.

Finally, I have perhaps sacrificed time on this project that I could have spent with my wonderful wife and six children. I hope that I have not been too distracted. I thank Shannon, Caleb, Josiah, Rachel, Jada, Sarah, and Alex for bearing with me as I typed away and edited for many hours. Without the unswerving support of my wife, Shannon, I would not be able to accomplish much of anything. I cherish her very much and am forever grateful for her unconditional love.

AARON C. PEER

Charts and Sidebars

Abbreviations

BIBLE TRANSLATIONS

CNT	*Comprehensive New Testament*
ESV	*English Standard Version*
GNT	*Good News Translation*
KJV	*King James Version*
NASB	*New American Standard Bible*
NET	*New English Translation.* First Beta ed. Biblical Studies Press, 2001.
NIV	*New International Version*
NLT	*New Living Translation*
NRSV	*New Revised Standard Version*
WEB	*World English Bible*

GENERAL ABBREVIATIONS

BECNT	Baker Exegetical Commentary on the New Testament
BHGNT	Baylor Handbooks to the Greek New Testament
BLG	Biblical Languages: Greek
EEC	Evangelical Exegetical Commentary
HeTr	Helps for Translators
HNTE	Handbook for New Testament Exegesis
HThKNT	Herders theologischer Kommentar zum Neuen Testament
JBL	*Journal of Biblical Literature*
LCL	Loeb Classical Library
LEC	Library of Early Christianity
MT	Hodges, Zane C., and Arthur L. Farstad. *The Greek New Testament According to the Majority Text.* 2nd ed. Nashville: Nelson, 1985.
NA[28]	Aland, Kurt, et al. *Novum Testamenum Graece.* 28th ed. Stuttgart: Deutsche Bibelgesellschaft, 2012.
NTL	New Testament Library
OTM	Oxford Theological Monographs
PNTC	Pillar New Testament Commentaries
RP[2005]	Robinson, Maurice A., and William G. Pierpont. *The New Testament in the Original Greek: Byzantine Textform*, 2005. Southborough, MA: Chilton, 2005.
SBL	Holmes, Michael W. *The Greek New Testament SBL Edition*, Atlanta, GA: Society of Biblical Literature; Bellingham, WA: Logos Bible Software, 2010.
SBLDS	Society of Biblical Literature Dissertation Series

SP	Sacra Pagina
SubBi	Subsidia Biblica
TNTC	Tyndale New Testament Commentaries

TECHNICAL ABBREVIATIONS

ca.	circa
C.E.	Common Era (equivalent to A.D.)
cf.	*confer*, compare
ed(s).	editor(s)
e.g.	*exempli gratia*, for example
esp.	especially
ET	English translation
etc.	*et cetera*, and the rest
H	Hebrew
i.e.	*id est*, that is
lit.	literally
n(n).	note(s)
s.v.	sub verbo, under the word
v(v).	verse(s)

APOCRYPHA, PSEUDEPIGRAPHA, AND APOSTOLIC FATHERS

1 Macc	First Maccabees
2 Macc	Second Maccabees
3 Macc	Third Maccabees
4 Macc	Fourth Maccabees
Barn.	Epistle of Barnabas
Did.	The Didache, or Teaching of the Twelve Apostles
Jdt	Judith
Jub.	Jubilees
Odes Sol.	Odes of Solomon
Pr Azar	Prayer of Azariah
Pss. Sol.	Psalms of Solomon
Sib. Or.	Sibylline Oracles
Sir	Wisdom of Jesus the Son of Sirach (Ecclesiasticus)
T. Benj.	Testament of Benjamin
T. Gad	Testament of Gad
T. Isaac	Testament of Isaac
T. Jud.	Testament of Judah
T. Reu.	Testament of Reuben
Tob	Tobit
Wis	Wisdom of Solomon

ANCIENT WRITINGS

Apoc. Ab.   Apocalypse of Abraham

Const. ap.   Constitutiones apostolicae (Apostolic Constitutions)

Dead Sea Scrolls
    CD   The Cairo Genizah copy of the Damascus Document
    1Q28   1QS Rule of the Community
    1Q36   1Q Hymns
    1QM   War Scroll

Dionysius of Halicarnassus
    Comp.   *De compositione verborum*

Euripides
    Iph. Taur.   Iphigeneia at Tauris

Eusebius
    Hist. eccl.   *Historia ecclesiastica (Ecclesiastical History)*

Herodotus
    Hist.   *The History of Herodotus*

Ignatius
    Rom.   *To the Romans*
    Smyrn.   *To the Smyrnaeans*

Irenaeus
    Haer.   *Adversus haereses (Against Heresies)*

Josephus
    A.J.   *Antiquitates judaicae*
    C. Ap.   *Contra Apionem*
    Vita   *Vita (The Life)*
    B.J.   *Bellum judaicum*

Papyri
    P. Michel   Terentianus to Tiberianus
    Ant.   Antinoe Papyrus

Philo
    Cher.   *De cherubim (On the Cherubim)*

Det.	*Quod deterius potiori insidiari soleat (That the Worse Attacks the Better)*
Flacc.	*In Flaccum (Against Flaccus)*
Her.	*Quis rerum divinarum heres sit (Who Is the Heir?)*
Ios.	*De Iosepho (On the Life of Joseph)*
Leg.	*Legum allegoriae (Allegorical Interpretation)*
Mos.	*De vita Mosis (Life of Moses)*
Opif.	*De opificio mundi (On the Creation of the World)*
Post.	*De posteritate Caini (On the Posterity of Cain)*
Praem.	*De praemiis et poenis (On Rewards and Punishments)*
Prob.	*Quod omnis probus liber sit (Every Good Person Is Free)*
Sacr.	*De sacrificiis Abelis et Caini (On the Sacrifices of Abel and Cain)*
Sobr.	*De sobrietate (On Sobriety)*
Somn.	*De somniis (On Dreams)*
Spec.	*De specialibus legibus (Special Laws)*
Virt.	*De virtutibus (On the Virtues)*

Plato

Euthyd.	*Euthydemus*
Leg.	*Leges*
Resp.	*Respublica*
Soph.	*Sophista*

Plutarch

Adul. am.	*De Adulatore et Amico (How to Tell a Flatterer from a Friend)*

Polybius

Hist.	*History*

Socrates (ca. 440 c.e.)

Hist. eccl.	Historia ecclesiastica (Ecclesiastical History)

Sophocles

Oed. tyr.	*Oedipus tyrannus*

PERIODICAL, REFERENCE, AND SERIAL

Bateman[1] Bateman IV, Herbert W. 2008. *A Workbook for Intermediate Greek: Grammar, Exegesis, and Commentary on 1–3 John.* Grand Rapids: Kregel.

Bateman²   Bateman IV, Herbert W., Darrell L. Bock, and Gordon Johnston. 2012. *Jesus the Messiah: Tracing the Promises, Expectation, and Coming of Israel's King.* Grand Rapids: Kregel.

Bateman³   Bateman IV, Herbert W. 2015. *Jude.* Evangelical Exegetical Commentary. Bellingham, WA: Lexham.

Bateman⁴   Bateman IV, Herbert W. 2013. *Interpreting the General Letters: An Exegetical Handbook.* Handbooks for Exegesis. Grand Rapids: Kregel.

Baugh   Baugh, S. M. 1999. *A First John Reader: Intermediate Greek Reading Notes and Grammar.* Phillipsburg: NJ: P&R Publishing.

BDAG   Danker, Frederick W., Walter Bauer, William F. Arndt, and F. Wilbur Gingrich. 2000. *A Greek–English Lexicon of the New Testament and Other Early Christian Literature.* 3rd ed. Chicago: University of Chicago Press.

BDF   Blass, Frederich, Albert Debrunner, and Robert W. Funk. 1961. *A Greek Grammar of the New Testament and Other Early Christian Literature.* Chicago: University of Chicago Press.

Brown   Brown, Raymond E. 1982. *The Epistles of John.* AB 30. Garden City, NY: Doubleday.

Bullinger   Bullinger, E. W. 1986. *Figures of Speech Used in the Bible: Explained and Illustrated.* Grand Rapids: Baker.

Carson   Carson, D. A. 1996. *Exegetical Fallacies.* 2nd ed. Grand Rapids: Baker.

Comfort   Comfort, Philip Wesley. 2015. *A Commentary on the Manuscripts and Text of the New Testament.* Grand Rapid: Kregel.

Culpepper   Culpepper, R. Alan. 1998. *The Gospel and Letters of John.* Nashville: Abingdon.

Culy   Culy, Martin M. 2004. *I, II, III John: A Handbook on the Greek Text.* BHGNT. Waco, TX: Baylor University Press.

EDNT   Balz, Horst, and Gerhard Schneider. 1990–1993. *Exegetical Dictionary of the New Testament.* 3 vols. Grand Rapids: Eerdmans.

GJohn	Gospel of John
HJS	Hass, C., Marinus de Jonge, and Jan L. Swellengrebal. 1972. *A Translator's Handbook on the Letters of John*. HeTr 13. London: United Bible Societies.
L&N	Louw, Johannes P., and Eugene A. Nida, eds. 1989. *Greek-English Lexicon of the New Testament: Based on Semantic Domains*. 2nd ed. New York: United Bible Societies.
Lieu	Lieu, Judith. 2008. M. *I, II, III John: A Commentary*. NTL. Louisville: Westminster John Knox.
M	Mounce, William D. 2003. *Basics of Biblical Greek Grammar*. 3rd ed. Grand Rapids: Zondervan.
Metzger[1]	Metzger, Bruce M. 1994. A *Textual Commentary on the Greek New Testament*. 2nd ed. Stuttgart: Deutsche Bibelgesellschaft.
Metzger[2]	Metzger, Bruce M. 1992. *The Text of the New Testament: Its Transmission, Corruption, and Restoration*. 3rd enlarged ed. New York: Oxford University Press.
Moule	Moule, C. F. D. 1959. *An Idiom Book of the Greek New Testament*. 2nd ed. Cambridge: Cambridge University Press.
MM	Moulton, James Hope, and George Milligan. 1930. *The Vocabulary of the Greek Testament: Illustrated from the Papyri and Other Non-literary Sources*. Grand Rapids: Eerdmans.
Painter	Painter, John. 2002. *1, 2, and 3 John*. SP 18. Collegeville, MN: Liturgical.
Porter	Porter, Stanley E. 1994. *Idioms of the Greek New Testament*. 2nd ed. BLG 2. Sheffield: JSOT Press.
Schnackenburg	Schnackenburg, Rudolf. 1979. *Die Johannesbriefe*. 6th ed. HThKNT 13/3. Freiburg in Breisgau: Herder.
Smalley	Smalley, Stephen S. 1984. *1, 2, 3 John*. WBC 51. Waco, TX: Word.

Stott	Stott, John R. W. 1988. *The Epistles of John: An Introduction and Commentary*. 2nd ed. TNTC. Grand Rapids: Eerdmans.
Strecker	Strecker, Georg. 1996. *The Johannine Letters*. Edited by Harold Attridge. Translated by Linda M. Maloney. Hermeneia. Minneapolis: Fortress.
TDNT	*Theological Dictionary of the New Testament*. 1964–1976. Edited by Gerhard Kittel and Gerhard Friedrich. Translated by Geoffrey W. Bromiley. 10 vols. Grand Rapids: Eerdmans.
TLNT	Spiq, Ceslas. 1996. *Theological Lexicon of the New Testament*. Translated by James Ernest. 3 vols. Peabody, MA: Hendrickson.
Turner[1]	Turner, Nigel. 1963. *Grammar of New Testament Greek: Volume 3 Syntax*. Edinburgh: T&T Clark.
Turner[2]	Turner, Nigel. 1976. *A Grammar of New Testament Greek: Volume 4 Style*. Edinburgh: T&T Clark.
W	Wallace, Daniel B. 1996. *Greek Grammar Beyond the Basics: An Exegetical Syntax of the New Testament*. Grand Rapids: Zondervan.
WAC	Wise, Michael, Martin Abegg, and Edward Cook. 1996. *The Dead Sea Scrolls: A New Translation*. New York: HarperSanFrancisco.
Wen	Wenham, J. W. 1991. *The Elements of New Testament Greek*. Repr. with corrections. New York: Cambridge University Press.
Westcott	Westcott, Brooke Foss. 1966. *The Epistles of St. John: The Greek Text*. 3rd ed. 1892. Repr., Grand Rapids: Eerdmans.
Yarbrough	Yarbrough, Robert W. 2008. *1–3 John*. BECNT. Grand Rapids: Baker Academic.
Zerwick	Zerwick, Maximilian. 1963. *Biblical Greek: Illustrated by Examples*. Translated by Joseph Smith. SubBi 41. Rome: Pontifical Biblical Institute.

Introduction

John's Letters: An Exegetical Guide for Preaching and Teaching[1] guides pastors and teachers in their understanding of John's Greek structure, his use of Greek clauses, his Greek syntax, and his Greek writing style with this single intention: to underscore John's numerous big Greek ideas. Tracing the various big Greek ideas in John is possible by recognizing John's thought process evident in the coordination and subordination of the Greek clauses he employs within each of his letters. We do not assume that pastors and teachers remember everything learned during their initial study of New Testament Greek in their college or seminary classes. We strive to define and explain John's use of Greek in ways that help pastors and teachers recall what was once learned, refresh and expand an appreciation for John's presentation in Koine Greek, and underscore the value to engage the Greek text when preparing to preach and teach John's letters.

We construct the Greek words from John's letters in 232 independent clauses and 281 dependent clauses and arrange them into clausal outlines. Each clause is translated and then explained for interpretive recognition, comprehension, and communication. The clausal outlines represent an early stage in preparing to preach and teach the text.[2] All the clauses appear in Greek from NA[28] along with an interpretive translation for easy usage. The clausal outlines make it possible for pastors to visualize the relationship clauses have to one another in order to trace John's flow of thought and ultimately his big idea.

Number of Greek Words in John's Letters			
Letter	NA[28]	SBL	RP[2005]	MT
1 John 1	206	207	207	207
1 John 2	587	584	581	580
1 John 3	468	469	472	472
1 John 4	449	449	453	452
1 John 5	424	429	438	439
2 John	244	245	249	249
3 John	227	219	216	217

---

1. Portions of this work are excerpted from Bateman and Peer 2017; Peer and Bateman 2015; used by permission from the Cyber-Center for Biblical Studies.
2. For nine steps of exegesis, see Bateman (2013).

The Clausal Outline

The clausal outlines for John's letters are based on a variety of Greek clauses employed throughout John's letters. By nature, a Greek clause has a subject and a predicate, which may be a verb, a participle (ptc.), or an infinitive (inf.). They may be independent or dependent Greek clauses. Whereas independent clauses can stand alone, dependent clauses have a subordinate relationship to another clause.

Other terminology exists for this same process. Mounce (1996, xvi–xxiii) calls it "phrasing," Guthrie (Guthrie and Duvall 1988, 27–42) calls it "grammatical diagram," and MacDonald (1986, 145–52) calls it "textual transcription." While these other works tend to break sentences into clauses and phrases, *John's Letters* concentrates on the clause level. As you work your way through the clauses in John's three letters, you can expect the following:

1. Every clause reproduces the Greek text in the exact word order of NA^{28} even when syntax is less than clear. Every attempt is made to make sense of John's syntax regardless of the occasional lack of clarity.

2. Every Greek clause underscores the Greek words deemed as important structural markers. A structural marker is always a verb, which may be a verbal (ptc. or inf.). Other important structural markers are conjunctions, relative and demonstrative pronouns, and a select number of prepositional phrases that introduce clauses. Structural markers are always <u>underlined</u> and often in **bold** print. For instance:

   4:15a **<u>ὃς ἐὰν ὁμολογήσῃ</u>** (<u>ὅτι</u> Ἰησοῦς <u>ἐστιν</u> ὁ υἱὸς τοῦ θεοῦ),
   4:15a **<u>Whoever confesses</u>** (<u>that</u> Jesus <u>is</u> the Son of God),

   Although **<u>ὃς ἐὰν ὁμολογήσῃ</u>** are underlined and in bold type, ὅτι and ἐστιν are not—even though they too are important structural markers. They are not in bold often for visual purposes.

3. Every Greek structural marker serves to distinguish different types of independent and dependent clauses. The chart below summarizes the types of independent and dependent Greek clauses found in John's letters and the means by which they are introduced.

Types (Classifications) of Independent and Dependent Clauses[3]	
Three Types of Independent Clauses	Four Types of Dependent Clauses
Conjunctive clauses are introduced by simple connective (καί or δέ), contrastive conjunction (ἀλλά, δέ, πλήν), correlative conjunction (μέν...δέ, or καί...καί), explanatory conjunction (γάρ), inferential conjunction (ἄρα, διό, οὖν, or γάρ), or transitional conjunction (καί, δέ or οὖν).	Pronominal clauses are introduced by a relative pronoun (ὅς, ἥ, ὅ), a relative adjective (οἷος, *such as*; ὅσος, *as much/many as*), a relative adverb (ὅπου, *where*; ὅτε, *when*), or a demonstrative pronoun (οὗτος).
Prepositional clauses are introduced by "for this reason" (διὰ τοῦτο), "for this reason" (ἐπὶ τοῦτο), "as a result of this" (ἐκ τοῦτο), "why" (εἰς τίνα), or "in this" (ἐν τοῦτο).	Conjunctive clauses are introduced by a subordinate conjunction that denotes semantical concepts such as time (ὅτε, ὅτον), reason and cause (διό, ὅτι, ἐπεί), purpose and result (ἵνα, ὥστε), or comparison (καθώς, ὡς, ὡσεί, ὥσπερ); etc.
	Participial clauses are introduced by participles. Their objects may be a noun, pronoun, prepositional phrases etc.
Asyndeton clauses are not introduced by a conjunctive word or phrase.	Infinitival clauses are introduced by infinitives.

4. Every independent Greek clause (the main thought) is placed farthest to the left of the page. Dependent Greek clauses that directly modify a Greek word in another clause are either placed in parentheses or positioned under (or above if necessary) the word it modifies for easy identification. This positioning of a clause *visualizes* the *subordination* and *coordination* of John's basic grammatical and syntactical relationships, parallelisms, and emphases.

5. Every independent and dependent Greek clause has an interpretive English translation provided under the Greek text. Every translated structural marker is also <u>underlined</u> and often in **bold** print for easy recognition, use, and evaluation.

---

3.   W, 656–65. There is a difference between the chart above and Wallace. Whereas the pronominal clause represents both the relative and demonstrative pronoun in the chart on this page, Wallace limits the category to a relative pronoun.

One to Five Exemplified

An example of what to expect is nicely illustrated with a verse from 1 John 1:8.

^{1:8a} <u>ἐὰν εἴπωμεν</u> (ὅτι ἁμαρτίαν οὐκ <u>ἔχομεν</u>),
^{1:8a} <u>if we say</u>, ("<u>We have</u> no sin"),

^{1:8b} ἑαυτοὺς **πλανῶμεν**
^{1:8b} <u>we deceive</u> ourselves

^{1:8c} <u>καὶ</u> ἡ ἀλήθεια οὐκ <u>**ἔστιν**</u> ἐν ἡμῖν.
^{1:8c} <u>and</u> the truth <u>is</u> not in us.

1. The order of the Greek sentence is followed.

2. Every Greek clause underscores the Greek words deemed as important structural markers.

3. Every Greek structural marker distinguishes the different types of independent and dependent clauses. First John 1:8a has two dependent conjunctive Greek clauses, 1:8b is an independent asyndeton Greek clause, and 1:8c is an independent Greek conjunctive clause.

4. The independent clauses (1:8b and 1:8c) are placed to the extreme left. The two dependent conjunctive clauses of 1:8a are complex. On the one hand, the entire ἐὰν εἴπωμεν (ὅτι ἁμαρτίαν οὐκ ἔχομεν) is an adverbial dependent ἐάν clause that modifies the Greek verb πλανῶμεν, so the first word of the ἐάν clause is placed above the verb it modifies, πλανῶμεν. On the other hand, (ὅτι ἁμαρτίαν οὐκ ἔχομεν) is a dependent substantival ὅτι clause functioning as the direct object of the Greek verb εἴπωμεν. The entire ὅτι clause is placed in parentheses to visualize the clause's grammatical contribution to the dependent ἐάν clause. All structural markers are clearly identified.

5. Every Greek clause has a corresponding English translation and all the translated structural markers are identified for easy recognition.

6. Every independent and dependent Greek clause has a corresponding explanatory discussion that underscores the grammatical, syntactical, and semantic functions of their respective Greek structural markers that are <u>underlined</u> and often in **bold** print. Thus, not every word within a clause is discussed; ex-

planatory discussions major on the structural makers in order to underscore John's point. Yet if a structural marker is not in bold, it is often for easier visual distinctions.

> **Grammatical Function:** Grammatical function identifies the Greek *structural marker* as to whether it is pronominal, conjunctive, a verb, or verbal (ptc. or inf.). If the marker is a verb or verbal, it is parsed with an appropriate lexical meaning provided from BDAG. If it is pronominal or conjunctive, a lexical definition is also provided based upon BDAG.

> **Syntactical Function:** Syntactical function first draws attention to the independent or dependent clause's type. If a *dependent clause*, its syntactical function within a sentence is underscored. All clauses are identified as either substantival, adjectival, or adverbial, as well as the word or words the clause modifies.

> **Semantic Function:** Semantic functions are by nature interpretive suggestions whereby a Greek structural marker is explained based upon its literary context. Semantic interpretations employ the categories listed and defined in Wallace's *Greek Grammar Beyond the Basics* (1996), many of which are discussed in critical commentaries, and reflected in English Bible translations.[4]

7. Explanatory discussions about Greek structural markers are interspersed with commentary-*like* remarks identified as *nuggets*. Numerous text-critical, grammatical, syntactical, structural, theological, and lexical nuggets appear between clausal presentations that delve deeper into and expand on issues in order to advance your appreciation for John, his readers, and his message.

8. All independent and dependent Greek clauses are grouped into units of thought. While 1 John is broken into fifteen units of thought, 2 John has four units and 3 John has five units of thought.

9. Every unit opens with a structural overview that provides a synopsis for the unit's structure and each summary is followed with a "Big Greek Idea" statement.

10. An interpretive English translation of the Johannine Letters concludes *John's Letters: An Exegetical Guide for Preaching and Teaching.*

---

4. Because Wallace has a wide audience and is used as a textbook in many colleges and seminaries, we have intentionally chosen to employ his categories in the Big Greek Idea Series. Be aware, however that there are other approaches, e.g., Porter 1994; Fanning 1990; Campbell 2008.

All ten expectations are intended to help pastors and teachers recall and refresh their previous training in Greek, to expand a person's understanding of Koine Greek, and to encourage personal engagement with the Greek text. Hopefully the process in this book will increase confidence in understanding and appreciating John's letters for preaching and teaching them.

Yet *John's Letters* is not a guide for translation. There are works designed for that task (Bateman and Peer 2017; Peer and Bateman 2015; Culy 2004). This book is a grammatical-*like* commentary with interlinear-*like* English translations of the Greek text that provides expositional commentary-*like* comments to guide a pastor and teacher in their sermon and teaching preparations.

But before delving into examining the "Big Greek Idea" in John's letters, it may be helpful to pause, define, and illustrate the different types of Greek clauses typically found in the Johannine letters.

JOHANNINE INDEPENDENT CLAUSES

Independent Greek clauses are rather important in determining John's main thought in a given sentence. There are *three types of independent Greek clauses* found in the Greek New Testament: conjunctive, prepositional, and asyndetic. While all three types of independent clauses appear in 1 John, only the conjunctive and asyndetic independent clause occur in 2 and 3 John. The *independent prepositional clause* does not appear in John's latter two letters.

The first and most common type of independent Greek clause in John's letters is the *independent Greek conjunctive clause*. This clause is introduced by a Greek conjunction (καί, δέ, γάρ, ἀλλά, ἄρα, διό, οὖν, πλήν, ὅθεν). Sometimes the Greek conjunction starts the independent clause. Other times it appears in a postpositive position. The independent conjunctive clause dominates John's letters. In fact, independent conjunctive clauses appear in 1 John *at least* 93 times, 5 times in 2 John and 10 times in 3 John. Thus you can expect to interact with 108 independent Greek conjunctive clauses when studying the Johannine epistles. The following are a few representative samples worthy of mention.

1 JOHN

1:5a **καὶ** ἔστιν αὕτη ἡ ἀγγελία
1:5a **now** this is the gospel message

2:11a ὁ **δὲ** μισῶν τὸν ἀδελφὸν αὐτοῦ ἐν τῇ σκοτίᾳ ἐστὶν
2:11a **but** the one who persists in hating his (or her) brother (and sister) is in the darkness

²:¹⁸ᵈ **ὅθεν** γινώσκομεν ὅτι ἐσχάτη ὥρα ἐστίν
²:¹⁸ᵈ **Wherefore** we now know that it is the last hour

³:²⁴ᵃ **καὶ** ὁ τηρῶν τὰς ἐντολὰς αὐτοῦ ἐν αὐτῷ μένει
³:²⁴ᵃ **And** the one who persists in keeping his commandments abides
 with God

⁴:¹⁸ᵇ **ἀλλ᾽** ἡ τελεία ἀγάπη ἔξω βάλλει τὸν φόβον
⁴:¹⁸ᵇ **But** perfect love expels out fear

⁴:²⁰ᵈ ὁ **γὰρ** μὴ ἀγαπῶν τὸν ἀδελφὸν αὐτοῦ . . . , τὸν θεὸν . . . οὐ
 δύναται ἀγαπᾶν
⁴:²⁰ᵈ **For** the one who does not love his brother . . . is unable to love God

⁵:⁷ **ὅτι** τρεῖς εἰσιν οἱ μαρτυροῦντες, ⁸τὸ πνεῦμα καὶ τὸ ὕδωρ καὶ
 τὸ αἷμα
⁵:⁷ **For** the ones that testify are three, ⁸[*They are*] Spirit and the water
 and the blood.

2 John

⁵ᵃ **καὶ** νῦν ἐρωτῶ σε, κυρία
⁵ᵃ **And** now I ask you, lady

⁷ᵃ **ὅτι** πολλοὶ πλάνοι ἐξῆλθον εἰς τὸν κόσμον
⁷ᵃ **for** many deceivers have gone out into the world

3 John

³ᵃ ἐχάρην **γὰρ** λίαν
³ᵃ **for** I rejoiced greatly

⁸ᵃ ἡμεῖς **οὖν** ὀφείλομεν ὑπολαμβάνειν τοὺς τοιούτους
⁸ᵃ we, **therefore**, are obligated to support such people

¹⁴ᵃ ἐλπίζω **δὲ** εὐθέως σε ἰδεῖν,
¹⁴ᵃ **rather**, I hope to see you immediately,

Naturally, these Greek conjunctive clauses are independent because they contain a subject and predicate, present a complete thought, and can stand alone. While it is not evident above, in the pages to follow all independent clauses will be placed farthest to the left of the page because they are independent. Each of the independent clauses above begins with a Greek conjunction that makes some sort of connection with a previous clause or transitions to a new thought. Also, as you can see from the samples above, conjunctions sometimes appear in the postpositive position (1 John 2:11a; 4:20d; 3 John 3a, 8a, 14a) but not always (1 John 2:5a, 18d; 3:24a, 18b; 5:7; 2 John 5a, 7a).

The most frequent independent Greek conjunctive clauses in John's letters are those introduced with καί. Of the ninety-three conjunctive independent clauses in 1 John, 75 percent begin with "and" (καί). John's favored usage of "and" (καί) is as a coordinating conjunction, fifty-one times in 1 John and eight times in his other two letters (2 John 5a, 6a, 10d; 3 John 10g, 10h, 12b, 14b). Yet, καί is also interpreted twice as an ascensive (1 John 2:18c, 28a), three times as contrastive (1 John 2:20a; 4:3a; 5:17b), twice as emphatic (1 John 3:1c, 4b), once as explanatory (1 John 1:2a), seven times as inferential (1 John 1:4a; 2:11b, 3:13a, 19a, 22a; 4:11b, 16a), and four times as a transitional conjunction (1 John 1:5a; 2:3a, 25a, 27a).

Even though John's favored conjunction is καί, seven other Greek conjunctions appear in John's letters: ἀλλά, δέ, ὅτι, γάρ, πάλιν, ὅθεν, and οὖν. The following chart not only lists the Greek conjunction and where they appear in John's letters, it identifies how the conjunction has been interpreted semantically in our interpretive English translation for the Johannine Letters.

Conjunctions in John's Letters								
	καί	ἀλλά	δέ	ὅτι	γάρ	πάλιν	ὅθεν	οὖν
Ascensive The conjunction provides a point of focus "even"	1 John 2:18c, 28a							
Connective or **Coordinate** The conjunction adds an additional element to the discussion "and, also"	1 John 1:2b, 2c, 2d, 3b, 6d, 7d, 8c, 10c 2:2a, 2b, 4b, 10b, 11c, 17a, 20b, 24c, 27c, 27f 3:2b, 3a, 5a, 5c, 9c, 12c, 15b, 23a, 24a, 24b, 24c		1 John 1:3d 5:20a					

Conjunctions in John's Letters							
	καί	ἀλλά	δέ	ὅτι	γάρ	πάλιν	ὅθεν	οὖν
Connective or **Coordinate** The conjunction adds an additional element to the discussion "and, also"	4:3c, 4b, 5c, 7c, 7d, 12d, 14, 15c, 16b, 16e, 16f, 21a 5:1b, 3c, 4b, 6d, 8b, 11a, 11c, 14a, 16c, 20d **2 John** 5a, 6a, 10d **3 John** 10g, 10h, 12b, 12c, 14b							
Contrastive or **Adversative** The conjunction provides an opposing thought to the idea to which it is connected "but, yet"	**1 John** 2:20a 4:3a 5:17b	**1 John** 2:2c, 7b, 16b, 19b, 19e, 21c, 27e 3:18b 4:1b, 18b 5:6c, 18b **2 John** 12c **3 John** 9b, 13b	**1 John** 2:11a, 17b 3:12e **3 John** 14a			**1 John** 2:8a		
Emphatic The conjunction intensifies the discussion "indeed"	**1 John** 3:1c, 4b							
Explanatory Following verbs of emotion, the conjunction provides additional information "for"	**1 John** 1:2a			**1 John** 2:16a 3:11a 5:7 **2 John** 7a	**1 John** 4:20d 5:3a **3 John** 3a			
Inferential The conjunction signals a conclusion or summary of a discussion "therefore, thus"	**1 John** 1:4a 2:11b 3:13a, 19a, 22a 4:11b, 16a						**1 John** 2:18d	**3 John** 8a

Conjunctions in John's Letters								
	καί	ἀλλά	δέ	ὅτι	γάρ	πάλιν	ὅθεν	οὖν
Transitional	1 John 1:5a		1 John					
The conjunction moves the discussion in a new direction	2:3a, 25a, 27a		5:5a					
"now"								

The second type of independent Greek clause in John's first letter is the *independent Greek prepositional clause*. This clause is introduced by a Greek preposition (διὰ τοῦτο, εἰς τοῦτο, ἐπὶ τοῦτο, ἐκ τούτου, ἐν τούτῳ). While John refrains from using the independent prepositional clause in 2 and 3 John, there are *at least* twelve independent clauses in 1 John introduced with a Greek prepositional phrase. Five representative examples are worthy of mention.

1 JOHN

3:1d **διὰ τοῦτο** ὁ κόσμος οὐ γινώσκει ἡμᾶς
3:1d **For this purpose** the Son of God appeared

3:8c **εἰς τοῦτο** ἐφανερώθη ὁ υἱὸς τοῦ θεοῦ
3:8c **for this reason** the Son of God was revealed

4:5b **διὰ τοῦτο** ἐκ τοῦ κόσμου λαλοῦσιν
4:5b **Therefore** they speak regularly from the world's perspective

4:9a **ἐν τούτῳ** ἐφανερώθη ἡ ἀγάπη τοῦ θεοῦ ἐν ἡμῖν
4:9a **By this** the love of God was made known among us

4:13a **Ἐν τούτῳ** γινώσκομεν ὅτι ἐν αὐτῷ μένομεν καὶ αὐτὸς [μένομεν] ἐν ἡμῖν
4:13a **By this** we know that we remain in God and he [*remains*] in us

Like the independent Greek conjunctive clauses, these Greek prepositional clauses are independent because they contain a subject and predicate, present a complete thought, and can stand alone. In the pages that follow, all independent prepositional clauses will be placed farthest to the left of the page because they too are independent.

While one of these independent Greek prepositional clauses concludes John's thought (1 John 4:5b), more often John's use of "by this" (ἐν τούτῳ) and "for this reason" (διὰ τοῦτο, εἰς τοῦτο) raises a rather significant interpretive challenge. To what does the prepositional phrase refer? So whenever an independent Greek prepositional clause appears, we always ask: Does "by this" (ἐν τούτῳ) or "for this reason" (διὰ τοῦτο, εἰς τοῦτο) conclude a preceding statement or does it point forward to the statement that follows? More will be said about interpreting these sorts of clauses when we discuss "Johannine Style and Vocabulary."

The third type of independent Greek clause is the *independent Greek asyndeton clause*. This clause has neither an introductory Greek conjunction nor an opening Greek prepositional phrase. Yet it too is an independent clause with only a verb as its structural marker. It appears at least 112 times in John's letters. In 1 John, there are at least 86 examples of the independent Greek asyndeton clause. In 2 John, there are at least 11 examples (vv. 1a, 3, 4a, 6e, 7e, 8a, 9a, 9c, 10c, 12b, 13) and 15 examples in 3 John (vv. 1a, 2a, 4a, 5a, 9a, 10b, 10e, 11a, 11b, 11c, 12a, 13a, 15a, 15b, 15c). Of these, a few are worthy of mention because they exemplify what to expect when studying John's letters. There is but one structural marker, the verb, which is <u>underlined</u> and in **bold** print.

1 John

2:1d παράκλητον **ἔχομεν** πρὸς τὸν πατέρα, Ἰησοῦν Χριστὸν δίκαιον
2:1d **we have** an advocate with the Father, Jesus who is the Christ, the righteous one

2:15a Μὴ **ἀγαπᾶτε** τὸν κόσμον μηδὲ τὰ ἐν τῷ κόσμῳ
2:15a **Do** not **love** the world nor the things in the world

4:12a θεὸν οὐδεὶς πώποτε **τεθέαται**
4:12a No one **has seen** God at any time

4:16d Ὁ θεὸς ἀγάπη **ἐστίν**,
4:16d God **is** love,

5:1a (Πᾶς ὁ πιστεύων [ὅτι Ἰησοῦς ἐστιν ὁ Χριστὸς]) ἐκ τοῦ θεοῦ **γεγέννηται**,
5:1a (everyone who *persists in* believing [that Jesus is the Christ]) **has been fathered** by God,

5:12b (ὁ μὴ ἔχων τὸν υἱὸν τοῦ θεοῦ) τὴν ζωὴν οὐκ **ἔχει**.
5:12b (the one who does have the Son of God) does not **have** this life.

2 John

³ **ἔσται** μεθ᾽ ἡμῶν χάρις ἔλεος εἰρήνη παρὰ θεοῦ πατρός . . .
³ Grace, mercy, and peace **will be** with us from God, who is the Father

^{7c} οὗτός **ἐστιν** ὁ πλάνος καὶ ὁ ἀντίχριστος.
^{7c} This one **is** the deceiver and the Antichrist.

^{8a} **βλέπετε** ἑαυτούς
^{8a} **Watch** yourselves.

3 John

^{5a} Ἀγαπητέ, πιστὸν **ποιεῖς**
^{5a} Beloved, **you** *continually* **demonstrate** faithfulness

^{11a} Ἀγαπητέ, μὴ **μιμοῦ** τὸ κακὸν
^{11a} Beloved, **do** not **imitate** that which is bad

^{15c} **ἀσπάζου** τοὺς φίλους κατ᾽ ὄνομα.
^{15c} **Greet** the friends [there] by name.

Once again, these Greek asyndeton clauses are independent clauses because they contain a subject and predicate, present a complete thought, and can stand alone. In the pages that follow, they too will be placed farthest to the left of the page because they are independent. Yet they differ from one another. To begin with, seven express John's expectation: "do not love the world" (1 John 2:15a), "watch out" (βλέπετε) for false teachers (2 John 8a), "imitate" (μιμοῦ) in this case whom not to imitate, namely, people who refuse to support God's servants (3 John 11b), and "greet" (ἀσπάζου) other believers (3 John 15c).

In 1 John, two speak of a generic person: "Everyone" (5:1a) or "the one who" (4:12b). First John 5:1a, however, warrants a few additional comments. First, "everyone who persists in believing (that Jesus is the Christ)" (πᾶς ὁ πιστεύων [ὅτι Ἰησοῦς ἐστιν ὁ Χριστὸς]) is the subject of the governing verb "has been fathered" (γεγέννηται) and placed in parentheses.

^{5:1a} (Πᾶς ὁ πιστεύων [ὅτι Ἰησοῦς ἐστιν ὁ Χριστὸς]) ἐκ τοῦ θεοῦ
γεγέννηται,
^{5:1a} (everyone who *persists in* believing [that Jesus is the Christ]) **has
been fathered** by God,

Second, whenever a ὅτι clause functions substantivally as the direct object of a verb or in this case a verbal "the one who believes" (ὁ πιστεύων), you can expect the entire ὅτι clause to appear in parentheses so that you can visualize its grammatical contribution as a direct object. In this case, the entire ὅτι clause provides the "what" is believed, namely, "that Jesus is the Christ." Finally, the πᾶς + the participle is a generic reference applicable to any person. John is making a timeless theological point. Anyone who believes that Jesus is the Messiah has a relationship with the Father.

Other independent Greek asyndeton clauses state a simple fact: "we have an advocate" (1 John 2:1d), "no one has seen God" (1 John 4:12a), or "God is love" (1 John 4:16b). Still others are descriptive in that they equate (ἐστίν) false teachers to an antichrist (2 John 7c), and "reveal" (ποιεῖς) a person's faithfulness (3 John 5a). The frequent independent Greek asyndeton clause has been considered a stylistic feature in John's letters (Turner[2], 133). More will be said about the Greek asyndeton clause when we discuss "Johannine Style and Vocabulary."

In summary, independent Greek clauses are rather important in determining John's main thought of a given sentence. There are 232 independent clauses in John's letters. While the *independent Greek asyndeton clause* dominates John's letters with 112 occurrences, following closely behind are the *independent Greek conjunctive clauses* appearing 108 times in John's three letters. The *independent Greek prepositional* clause occurs merely 12 times and only in 1 John.

The chart below identifies where the 232 independent Greek clauses appear in John's three letters.

Independent Clauses in John's Letters			
Chapter	Conjunctive Independent Clauses	Prepositional Independent Clauses	Asyndeton Independent Clauses
First John			
1	2a, 2b, 2c, 2d, 3b, 3d, 4a, 5a, 6d, 7d, 8c, 10c		6c, 7c, 8b, 9b, 10b
2	2a, 2b, 2c, 3a, 4b, 7b, 8a, 10b, 11a, 11b, 11c, 16a, 16b, 17a, 17b, 18c, 19b, 19e, 20a, 20b, 21c, 24c, 25a, 27a, 27c, 27e, 27f, 28a	5c	1a, 1d, 4a, 5b, 6a, 7a, 7d, 9, 10a, 12, 13a, 13b, 14a, 14b, 14c, 15a, 15c, 18a, 19a, 19d, 21a, 22a, 22c, 23a, 23b, 24a, 26, 27i, 29b
3	1c, 2b, 3a, 4b, 5a, 5c, 9c, 11a, 12c, 12e, 13a, 15b, 18b, 19a, 22a, 23a, 24a, 24b, 24c	1d, 8c, 10a, 16a	1a, 2a, 2c, 4a, 6a, 6b, 7a, 7b, 8a, 9a, 10b, 14a, 14c, 15a, 17d, 18a, 21b
4	1b, 3a, 3c, 4b, 5c, 7c, 7d, 11b, 12d, 14, 15c, 16a, 16b, 16e, 16f, 18b, 20d, 21a	5b, 6d, 9a, 10a, 13a, 17a	1a, 2b, 4a, 5a, 6a, 6b, 6c, 7a, 8a, 12a, 12c, 15b, 16d, 18a, 19a, 20c

Independent Clauses in John's Letters			
Chapter	Conjunctive Independent Clauses	Prepositional Independent Clauses	Asyndeton Independent Clauses
5	1b, 3a, 3c, 4b, 5a, 6c, 6d, 7, 8b, 11a, 11c, 14a, 16c, 17b, 20a, 20d	2a	1a, 6a, 6b, 8a, 9b, 10a, 10b, 12a, 12b, 13a, 15c, 16b, 16d, 16e, 17a, 18a, 19a, 20e, 21
Second John			
1	5a, 6a, 7c, 10d, 12c	none	1a, 3, 4a, 6c, 7c, 8a, 9a, 9b, 10c, 12b, 13
Third John			
1	3a, 8a, 9b, 10g, 10h, 12b, 12c, 13b, 14a, 14b,	none	1a, 2a, 4a, 5c, 9a, 10b,10f, 11a, 11b, 11c, 12a, 13a, 15a, 15b, 15c

Throughout the *John's Letters: An Exegetical Guide for Preaching and Teaching*, independent Greek clauses will appear to the extreme left of the page with their verbs <u>underlined</u> and often in **bold** print. Yet just as there are different types of independent clauses, there are various types of dependent clauses in John's letters worthy of introduction because they expand John's initial thoughts expressed in his independent clauses.

JOHANNINE DEPENDENT CLAUSES

There are *four types of dependent Greek clauses*: (1) Greek pronominal clauses are introduced by a relative pronoun (ὅς, ἥ, ὅ), relative adjective (οἶος, *such as*; ὅσος, *as much/many as*), relative adverb (ὅπου, *where*; ὅτε, *when*), or sometimes a demonstrative pronoun (οὗτος), (2) Greek conjunctive clauses are introduced by a subordinate Greek conjunction (ἵνα, ὅτι, καθώς, εἰ, ἐάν etc.), (3) Greek participial clauses are introduced by a participle, and (4) Greek infinitival clauses are introduced by certain infinitives or infinitives with a preposition (e.g., διά, μετά, εἰς + infinitive). Regardless of its type, dependent clauses generally modify a word or possible concept in another clause.

Procedurally, *the type of dependent clause* is first identified, and then the relationship of the dependent Greek clause to words in other clauses (i.e., the *syntactical function*) is determined. The syntactical function of a Greek clause may be *adverbial, adjectival,* or *substantival*. Once the syntactical relationship of a dependent clause is determined, it is positioned in the outline for easy identification. If *adverbial*, the first word of the dependent clause is positioned under the Greek verb it modifies; if *adjectival*, the first

Steps for Identifying Dependent Clauses
1. Take note of the type of dependent clause it is.
2. Be aware of the clause's syntactical function.
3. Identify the verb, noun, or pronoun the clause modifies.

word of the dependent clause is positioned under the Greek noun or pronoun it modifies; if *substantival*, the clause is often placed in parentheses.

The first type of dependent Greek clause is the *dependent Greek pronominal clause.* There are *at least* thirty-four examples of the dependent Greek pronominal clause in John's letters. Naturally all begin with a Greek pronoun. In 1 John, there are twenty-eight dependent pronominal clauses, four in 2 John (1b, 1c, 5d, 8b), and five in 3 John (1b, 5b, 6a, 6b, 10c). Of these, twenty-seven relative pronouns (33 percent) are *adjectival* and thirteen function *substantivally*. In the samples below, the *adjectival* relative clause is positioned under or just above the noun or pronoun it modifies. All *substantival* relative clauses functioning as either the subject or direct object of a clause are placed in parentheses. All relative pronouns are <u>underlined</u> and often in **bold** print along with their respective verbs.

1 John

4:6c (<u>ὃς</u> οὐκ <u>ἔστιν</u> ἐκ τοῦ θεοῦ) οὐκ **ἀκούει** ἡμῶν.
4:6c (<u>whoever</u> <u>is</u> not from God) **does** not **listen** to us.

4:15a <u>**ὃς ἐὰν ὁμολογήσῃ**</u> (ὅτι Ἰησοῦς <u>ἐστιν</u> ὁ υἱὸς τοῦ θεοῦ),
4:15a **Whoever professes** (that Jesus <u>is</u> the Son of God),

|

4:15b ὁ θεὸς ἐν αὐτῷ **μένει**
4:15b God **remains** in him (or her)

2 John

1a Ὁ πρεσβύτερος ἐκλεκτῇ κυρίᾳ καὶ τοῖς τέκνοις αὐτῆς,
1a The Elder, to the elect lady and her children

|

1b <u>**οὓς**</u> ἐγὼ **ἀγαπῶ** ἐν ἀληθείᾳ καὶ οὐκ ἐγὼ μόνος
1b **whom** I **love** in truth and not I alone

8a **βλέπετε** ἑαυτούς
8a **Watch** yourselves,

|

8b **ἵνα** μὴ **ἀπολέσητε** (<u>ἃ</u> <u>εἰργάσασθε</u>)
8b **in order that** you **do** not **lose** (<u>what</u> <u>you</u> worked for),

3 John

^{1a} Ὁ πρεσβύτερος Γαΐῳ τῷ ἀγαπητῷ,
^{1a} The Presbyter, to Gaius the beloved,

|

^{1b} **ὃν** ἐγὼ **ἀγαπῶ** ἐν ἀληθείᾳ.
^{1b} **whom I love** in truth.

These Greek pronominal clauses are representative of what to expect in John's letters. The pronominal clause that dominates John's three letters is the Greek relative clause (ὅς, ἥ, ὅ). They are unable to stand alone and thereby are dependent clauses. Yet they contribute grammatically to the sentence either as a subject or direct object of a clause (substantival) or as a modifier of a noun or pronoun within another clause (adjectival).

On the one hand, there are two *substantival* relative clauses in the examples above. In 1 John 4:6c the relative clause "whoever is not from God" (ὃς οὐκ ἔστιν ἐκ τοῦ θεοῦ) functions grammatically as the subject of the independent clause. In 2 John 8b, "what you worked for" (ἃ εἰργάσασθε) is the direct object of the negated verb "you do not lose" (μὴ ἀπολέσητε) in the dependent ἵνα clause. Consequently, both relative clauses are placed in parentheses so that you can visualize the grammatical function of the relative clause within their respective clauses.

On the other hand, there are three examples whereby relative clauses function *adjectivally*. In 1 John 4:15a, the entire relative clause "whoever professes (that Jesus is the Son of God)" (ὃς ἐὰν ὁμολογήσῃ [ὅτι Ἰησοῦς ἐστιν ὁ υἱὸς τοῦ θεοῦ]) modifies the object of a prepositional phrase, which is a pronoun, "*him*" (αὐτῷ). The very first word of the Greek relative clause is positioned above αὐτῷ ("him"). Several other items are worth highlighting. First, the relative clause is complex because of the conjunctive ὅτι clause. It too is dependent, but functions *substantivally* as the direct object of the verb "professes" (ὁμολογήσῃ). The entire ὅτι clause is placed in parentheses to visualize its grammatical contribution as the direct object within the dependent relative clause.

^{4:15a} **ὃς ἐὰν ὁμολογήσῃ** (ὅτι Ἰησοῦς ἐστιν ὁ υἱὸς τοῦ θεοῦ),
^{4:15a} **Whoever professes** (that Jesus is the Son of God),

|

^{4:15b} ὁ θεὸς ἐν αὐτῷ **μένει**
^{4:15b} God **remains** in him (or her)

Second, the relative pronoun ὅς agrees in number (singular) and gender (masculine) with "him" (αὐτῷ). Third, "whoever" (ὅς) appears in the nominative case because it functions as the subject of the relative clause. Finally, John's use of "whoever" (ὅς ἐάν) triggers a general reference that targets any person. It presents a gnomic or timeless truth about any person who confesses that Jesus is the "Son of God" (= "the Christ" or "the Messiah"; Bateman[2], 2012, 303–25).

Similarly in 3 John 1a, the relative clause follows the basic rules of gender and number agreement (masculine and singular) for both the relative pronoun (ὅν) and the noun it modifies "Gaius" (Γαΐῳ). In this case, the relative clause reveals information about John's sincere emotional regard for Gaius. In both cases, the relative dependent clause modifies and thereby provides additional information about the noun "Gaius" in the previous clause.

However in 2 John 1a, the relative clause "whom I love in truth" (οὓς ἐγὼ ἀγαπῶ ἐν ἀληθείᾳ) modifies "lady and her children" (κυρίᾳ καὶ τοῖς τέκνοις αὐτῆς). While it too serves to clarify information about the "lady and her children" (κυρίᾳ καὶ τοῖς τέκνοις αὐτῆς), namely, that they are individuals of another local church that the elder loves in truth, this relative pronoun breaks the basic rules of gender and number agreement because sense agreement (*construction ad sensum*) supersedes syntactical agreement. So although οὓς is neuter and plural, the sense of the clause agrees with "lady and her children," which is feminine (κυρίᾳ) and neuter (τοῖς τέκνοις) and plural. Thus, John uses a neuter plural pronoun to reference a group of people, the elect lady and her children, rather than just her children, as syntactical agreement would suggest. This sort of construction appears often in the John's letters.

> ## The Relative Pronoun
>
> ### Regular Usage
>
> A relative pronoun usually agrees in number and gender with its antecedent and thereby links the noun or pronoun to the dependent relative clause to describe, clarify, or restrict its antecedent.
>
> ### Unusual Usage
>
> Sometimes the relative pronoun's gender does not match its antecedent because sense agreement supersedes syntactical agreement (*construction ad sensum*).
>
> Other times the case of the relative pronoun is attracted to that of its antecedent. Often referred to as "attraction" or "direct attraction."

The second type of dependent Greek clause is the *dependent Greek conjunctive clause*. There are *at least* 173 examples of dependent Greek conjunctive clauses in John's letters. In 1 John alone, there are *at least* 152 dependent Greek clauses, 39 (26 percent) of which are embedded in an independent or dependent Greek clause and appear in parentheses. In 2 John, there are 14. In 3 John there are 7. The following are a few representative samples worthy of mention. The Greek conjunctions with their respective verbs are <u>underlined</u> and in **bold** print for easy recognition.

1 John

1:8a **ἐὰν εἴπωμεν** (ὅτι ἁμαρτίαν οὐκ ἔχομεν),
1:8a **if we say**, ("We have no sin"),

|

1:8b ἑαυτοὺς πλανῶμεν
1:8b we deceive ourselves

2:19c **εἰ** γὰρ ἐξ ἡμῶν **ἦσαν**,
2:19c for you see **if they had been** of us,

|

2:19d μεμενήκεισαν ἂν μεθ' ἡμῶν·
2:19d they would have remained with us;

2:19e ἀλλ' [ἐξῆλθαν]
2:19e but [*they did go out*],

|

2:19f **ἵνα φανερωθῶσιν** (ὅτι οὐκ εἰσὶν πάντες ἐξ ἡμῶν).
2:19f **so that it would be shown** (that they all are not of us).

3:1d διὰ τοῦτο ὁ κόσμος οὐ γινώσκει ἡμᾶς
3:1d For this reason, the world does not know us,

|

3:1e **ὅτι** οὐκ **ἔγνω** αὐτόν.
3:1e **that** it (= world) did not **know** him.

2 John

4a Ἐχάρην λίαν
4a I rejoiced greatly,

|

4b **ὅτι εὕρηκα** ἐκ τῶν τέκνων σου περιπατοῦντας ἐν ἀληθείᾳ,
4b **because I have found** some of your children walking in truth,

|

4c **καθὼς** ἐντολὴν **ἐλάβομεν**
παρὰ τοῦ πατρός
4c **just as we have received** the
command from the Father.

12c ἀλλὰ ἐλπίζω γενέσθαι πρὸς ὑμᾶς καὶ στόμα πρὸς στόμα λαλῆσαι,
12c but I hope to come to you and to speak face-to-face,

|

12d **ἵνα** ἡ χαρὰ ἡμῶν **ᾖ πεπληρωμένη**.
12d **in order that** our joy **might be complete**.

3 John

⁴ᵃ μειζοτέραν τούτων οὐκ ἔχω χαράν,
⁴ᵃ <u>I have</u> no greater joy than this,

             |

      ⁴ᵇ **ἵνα ἀκούω** τὰ ἐμὰ τέκνα ἐν τῇ ἀληθείᾳ <u>περιπατοῦντα</u>.
      ⁴ᵇ *namely* **that I hear** my children <u>are continually walking</u> in
      the truth.

Like the dependent Greek pronominal clauses, these Greek conjunctive clauses are unable to stand alone and thereby are dependent clauses. Of these examples, five are clearly adverbial, three are adjectival, and two are substantival. The first word of the adverbial and adjectival conjunctive clauses is positioned either under or above the word it modifies. The substantival clauses are placed in parentheses.

On the one hand, there are a variety of dependent Greek conjunctive clauses that function adverbially with rather significant interpretive contributions. The adverbial dependent conjunctive ὅτι clause in 2 John 4b modifies the verb "rejoice" (ἐχάρην). It provides the *reason* why John is rejoicing. The three ἵνα clauses also contribute to the verbs they modify.

In 1 John 2:19f, the ἵνα clause provides the *results* of those who left the church, namely, that it would be revealed that they were not believers. The verb "They did go out" [ἐξῆλθαν] is *italicized* and in brackets because

> **Ellipsis Defined**
>
> An ellipsis is the omission of a word or any element of the Greek language that renders a sentence to be "ungrammatical," yet the missing element or word is from the context.

it is understood to be an ellipsis in the Greek text. Yet context determines the verb's presence. The substantival conjunctive ὅτι clause is also dependent and placed in parentheses because it functions as the direct object of "it would be shown" (φανερωθῶσιν) and thereby part of the ἵνα clause. Although φανερωθῶσιν is a third person plural passive, we translate it as an impersonal singular in English.

²:¹⁹ᵉ ἀλλ' [*ἐξῆλθαν*]
²:¹⁹ᵉ but [*they did go out*],

     |

    ²:¹⁹ᶠ**ἵνα φανερωθῶσιν** (ὅτι οὐκ εἰσὶν πάντες ἐξ ἡμῶν).
    ²:¹⁹ᶠ *so* **that it would be shown** (<u>that</u> they all <u>are</u> not of us).

In 2 John 12d, the ἵνα clause provides John's *intention*, namely, that John's joy might be complete. In 3 John 10a, the ἵνα clause *clarifies* joy, namely, that John's readers are living for Jesus. Finally, two are conditional clauses. In 1 John 1:8a, the Greek conjunction ἐάν ("if") introduces a dependent adverbial clause. Similarly in 1 John 2:19c, the Greek conjunction εἰ ("if") introduces a dependent adverbial clause. The latter two clauses (ἐάν and εἰ) are conditional clauses. They convey a conditional idea in Greek: ἐάν (a third class condition) presents something as uncertain of fulfillment, but still likely, and εἰ (a first class condition) presents an assumption of truth for the sake of an argument (W, 690–99). All of these clauses are *visibly adverbial* because the first word of the clause appears either immediately above or below the verb they modify. The conjunction along with its verb are clearly <u>underlined</u> and in **bold** print.

On the other hand, there are three adjectival dependent conjunctive clauses: one ὅτι clause (1 John 3:1e), one καθώς clause (2 John 4c), and one ἵνα clause (3 John 4b). They are adjectival because the entire clause modifies a noun or pronoun in the previous clause. In 1 John 3:1e, the ὅτι clause modifies the prepositions "for this reason" (διὰ τοῦτο). In 2 John 4c, "just as" (καθώς) modifies the direct object in the previous clause "walking" (περιπατοῦντας), and in 3 John 4a "namely that" (ἵνα) modifies "this" (τούτῳ). Once again, every conjunction is clearly <u>underlined</u> and in **bold** print. As it was for independent Greek conjunctive clauses, John uses dependent Greek conjunctions to connect additional elements or ideas to his thought process. Thus, conjunctions are extremely important for tracing and explaining John's flow of thought in all his letters.

The third type of dependent Greek clause is the *dependent Greek participial clause*. There are at least sixty-five dependent Greek participial clauses in John's letters. The most prominent dependent Greek participial clause is the substantival whereby sixty participial clauses function either as the subject or as an adjective and thereby contributing to another clause. There are, however, only five adverbial participles found in John's letters, none of which appear in 1 John; all five adverbial participial clauses appear in 2 and 3 John. The following examples are worthy of mention with all participles <u>underlined</u> and in **bold** print, and at times placed in parentheses for easy grammatical identification.

1 John

2:9 (**ὁ λέγων** ἐν τῷ φωτὶ <u>εἶναι</u> καὶ τὸν ἀδελφὸν αὐτοῦ **μισῶν**) ἐν τῇ σκοτίᾳ <u>ἐστὶν</u> ἕως ἄρτι.

2:9 (**The one who claims** <u>to be</u> in the light yet <u>persists in hating</u> his [or her] brother [and sister]) <u>is</u> still in the darkness until now.

3:4a (Πᾶς **ὁ ποιῶν** τὴν ἁμαρτίαν) καὶ τὴν ἀνομίαν <u>ποιεῖ</u>,

3:4a (Everyone **who makes** it a practice to sin) also <u>practices</u> lawlessness

4:16e καὶ (**ὁ μένων** ἐν τῇ ἀγάπῃ) ἐν τῷ θεῷ <u>μένει</u>

4:16e and (**the one who abides** in love) <u>abides</u> in God

2 JOHN

⁷ᵃ ὅτι πολλοὶ πλάνοι ἐξῆλθον εἰς τὸν κόσμον,
⁷ᵃ <u>For</u> many deceivers <u>have gone out</u> into the world,

      ⌐————┐
      ⁷ᵇ **οἱ** μὴ **ὁμολογοῦντες** (Ἰησοῦν Χριστὸν **ἐρχόμενον** ἐν σαρκί)·
      ⁷ᵇ **the ones who do** not **confess**, ("Jesus, who is the Christ, **has come**
      in the flesh").

    ⁹ᵃ (πᾶς **ὁ προάγων** καὶ μὴ **μένων** ἐν τῇ διδαχῇ τοῦ Χριστοῦ) θεὸν
    οὐκ **ἔχει**·
    ⁹ᵃ (Everyone **who goes on ahead** and **does** not **remain** in the teaching
    about Christ) <u>does</u> not <u>have</u> God.

      ¹²ᵃ Πολλὰ **ἔχων** ὑμῖν γράφειν
      ¹²ᵃ *Although* **I have** many things to write to you,

        |
¹²ᵇ οὐκ <u>ἐβουλήθην</u> [*γράφειν*] διὰ χάρτου καὶ μέλανος
¹²ᵇ <u>I do</u> not <u>wish</u> (*to write*) by means of pen and ink,

3 JOHN

³ᵃ <u>ἐχάρην</u> γὰρ λίαν
³ᵃ <u>For</u> <u>I rejoiced</u> greatly

    |
    ³ᵇ **ἐρχομένων** ἀδελφῶν καὶ **μαρτυρούντων** σου τῇ ἀληθείᾳ,
    ³ᵇ ***when*** the brothers **came** and **testified** to your truth,

These examples are representative of what to expect when translating dependent participial clauses in John's letters. As was the case for the Greek pronominal and Greek conjunctive dependent clauses, these Greek participial clauses cannot stand alone. They are dependent.

First and foremost, there are Greek participial clauses that function substantivally as the subject of a verb (1 John 2:9; 3:4a; 4:16e; 2 John 9a). They are placed in parentheses in order to visualize the contribution the dependent Greek participial clause makes to the independent clause. Furthermore, they all present a gnomic statement that identifies an eternal truth that tends to refer to any person. In 2 John 7b, however, "the ones who do not confess Jesus Christ has come in the flesh" (οἱ μὴ ὁμολογοῦντες Ἰησοῦν Χριστὸν ἐρχόμενον ἐν σαρκί) modifies "deceivers" (πλάνοι). This entire substantival Greek participial clause functions like an adjective and is placed immediately below the word it modifies, "deceivers" (πλάνοι). The adjectival clause tells us something more specific about the deceivers.

Finally, there are times when the dependent Greek participial clause is adverbial, or at least appears adverbial, modifying a verb. In 2 John 12a, "*Although* I have many things to write to you" (πολλὰ ἔχων ὑμῖν γράφειν) modifies the negated "I do not wish" (οὐκ ἐβουλήθην). Yet in 3 John 3b, the participles, "*when* the brothers came" and "testified to your truth" (ἐρχομένων ἀδελφῶν καὶ μαρτυρούντων σου τῇ ἀληθείᾳ), only appear to be adverbial because they are positioned under a verb. Nevertheless, they are really genitive absolutes. Genitive absolutes are participles in the genitive that tend to have a very loose grammatical connection with another clause (W, 654–55). Yet, the first word of these participial clauses is placed directly under the verb they modify. The examples above are just some of the participle clauses found in John's three letters, but there are several other types of participles in his letters. Some of those examples are noted in the following chart.

Excursus on the Participle

Participles are very important Greek verbals. Yet not all participles identify dependent participial clauses.

1. There are times when ***participles serve as a verb*** within a clause due to an article taking on the force of a relative clause. In 2 John 2a, the article τὴν has the force of a relative pronoun and is translated "which." Thus the participle "remains" (μένουσαν) has taken on *the force of the verb* for the dependent clause.

   2a διὰ τὴν ἀλήθειαν **τὴν μένουσαν** ἐν ἡμῖν

   2a because the truth **which remains** in us

2. In 2 John 12d, John joins the participle "complete" (πεπληρωμένη) with the verb "might be" (ᾖ). This sort of construction is called ***a periphrastic construction*** in which the participle is called a periphrastic participle "because it is in a *round-about* way of saying what could be expressed by a single verb" (W, 647). Together, "might be complete" (πεπληρωμένη ᾖ) *functions as the governing verb* for the dependent conjunctive ἵνα clause and therefore both the participle and the finite verb are underlined and in bold.

   12d ἵνα ἡ χαρὰ ἡμῶν **ᾖ πεπληρωμένη**.

   12d in order that our joy **might be complete**.

3. There are times when ***participles serve as an adjective.*** In 2 John 4b, "Walking in truth" (περιπατοῦντας ἐν ἀληθείᾳ) is functioning adjectivally as *an object-complement double accusative* to an implicitly understood accusative "some" (τίνας). The assumed particle "some" (τίνας) is the object of the verb "I have found" (εὕρηκα), and the participle "walking" (περιπατοῦντας) is an object-complement functioning adjectivally to "some" (τίνας).

   4b ὅτι εὕρηκα ἐκ τῶν τέκνων σου περιπατοῦντας ἐν ἀληθείᾳ,

   4b because I have found some of your children walking in truth,

> 4. There are times when participles serves as an ***indirect discourse***. In 2 John 7b, the negated participle "the ones who do not confess" (οἱ μὴ ὁμολογοῦντες) is a verbal noun of communication followed by an indirect discourse statement (W, 646). The anarthrous participle "has come" (ἐρχόμενον) is in the accusative case and functions as an indirect discourse participle for a verb of communication. Like other indirect discourse statements, it too is placed in parentheses.
>
> 7b οἱ μὴ ὁμολογοῦντες Ἰησοῦν Χριστὸν <u>ἐρχόμενον</u> ἐν σαρκί·
>
> 7b the ones who do not confess (Jesus Christ <u>has come</u> in the flesh).
>
> Thus participles are very important for understanding and interpreting the Johannine letters.

The fourth type of dependent Greek clause is the *dependent Greek infinitival clause*. There are six dependent Greek infinitival clauses in John's letters. And even some of these may be questionable. While there are no adverbial dependent infinitival clauses, there are a few dependent Greek infinitival clauses that appear to function substantivally (1 John 2:6a, 9; 2 John 12a; 3 John 2, 13a). The Greek substantival infinitives below are <u>underlined</u> and are in **bold** type, with their respective clauses placed in parentheses for easy identification.

1 John

2:6a ὁ λέγων (ἐν αὐτῷ **μένειν**) <u>ὀφείλει</u> . . . καὶ αὐτὸς περιπατεῖν.
2:6a The one who says (<u>that he</u> [= God] **abides** in him [or her]) <u>must</u> . . . also himself (or herself) *persist in* living.

2:9 ὁ λέγων (ἐν τῷ φωτὶ **εἶναι**) καὶ τὸν ἀδελφὸν αὐτοῦ μισῶν ἐν τῇ σκοτίᾳ <u>ἐστὶν</u> ἕως ἄρτι.
2:9 The one who says (**to be** in the light) and yet *persists in* hating his (or her) brother (and sister) <u>is</u> still in the darkness until now.

2 John

12a Πολλὰ <u>ἔχων</u> (ὑμῖν **γράφειν**)
12a *Although* <u>I have</u> many things (**to write** to you),

|

12b οὐκ <u>ἐβουλήθην</u> [γράφειν] διὰ χάρτου καὶ μέλανος
12b <u>I do</u> not <u>wish</u> (*to write*) by means of pen and ink,

3 John

²ᵃ Ἀγαπητέ, περὶ πάντων <u>εὔχομαί</u> (σε **εὐοδοῦσθαι** καὶ **ὑγιαίνειν**),
²ᵃ Beloved, in all respects <u>I pray</u> (that you **are prospering** and that you **are well**),

$$|$$
²ᵇ <u>καθὼς</u> <u>εὐοδοῦταί</u> σου ἡ ψυχή.
²ᵇ <u>just as</u> your soul <u>is prospering</u>.

¹³ᵃ Πολλὰ <u>εἶχον</u> (**γράψαι** σοι),
¹³ᵃ <u>I had</u> many *more things* (**to write** to you)

These dependent Greek infinitival clauses are all substantival. Like the other dependent clauses, Greek infinitival clauses cannot stand on their own. They have dependent relationships with other clauses. In 1 John 2:6a, the Greek infinitive clause "that he (= God) abides in him (or her)" (ἐν αὐτῷ μένειν) *functions as the direct object* of the participle of communication: "the one who says" (λέγων). Similarly in 1 John 2:9, the Greek infinitival clause "to be in the light" (ἐν τῷ φωτὶ <u>εἶναι</u>) is the direct object of "the one who claims" (ὁ λέγων).

In 3 John 2a, the compound Greek infinitival construction "that you are prospering and that you are well" (σε εὐοδοῦσθαι καὶ ὑγιαίνειν) is placed in parenthesis because the compound infinitival clause *functions as the direct object* of the verb "I pray" (εὔχομαί) and is thereby a contributing part of the independent clause. Thus, the dependent infinitival clause in 3 John provides the content of John's prayer for Gaius. Finally in 2 John 12a and 3 John 13a, the Greek infinitives "to write" (γράφειν and γράψαι) *function as epexegetical infinitives*. Thus, the infinitives appear to qualify "the many *more things*" (πολλά) John wishes to write.[5]

Some of these examples identify yet another type of Greek infinitive, namely, a *complementary infinitive*. For instance, in the very first example represented below, 1 John 2:6a, employs a complementary infinitive. The main verb of the independent clause that is <u>underlined</u> and in **bold** print, "must" (ὀφείλει), cannot stand alone; it needs a helping verb to complete the verb's thought. That helper is the shaded infinitive "*persist in* living" (<u>περιπατεῖν</u>).

²:⁶ᵃ ὁ λέγων (ἐν αὐτῷ μένειν) **<u>ὀφείλει</u>** . . . καὶ αὐτὸς περιπατεῖν.
²:⁶ᵃ The one who says (that he [= God] abides in him [or her]) **is obligated** . . . also himself (or herself) *persist in* living.

---

5. Although some commentators suggest that γράφειν is a complementary infinitive to ἔχων (2 John 12a) and that γράψαι is a complementary infinitive to εἶχον (3 John 13a), "I have" (ἔχω) is not a typical "helper" verb. πολλά ("the many *more things*") is the direct object of the main verb "I have" (ἔχω).

Similarly in 2 John 12c, the main verb that is <u>underlined</u> and in **bold** print below, "I hope" (ἐλπίζω), cannot stand alone; it too needs a helping verb to complete its thought. In this verse, it has two helpers: "to come" (γενέσθαι) and "to speak" (λαλῆσαι). Both are underlined.

> ^{12c} ἀλλὰ **ἐλπίζω** <u>γενέσθαι</u> πρὸς ὑμᾶς καὶ στόμα πρὸς στόμα <u>λαλῆσαι</u>,
> ^{12c} but **I hope** <u>to come</u> to you and <u>to speak</u> face-to-face

More will be said about John's use of the complementary infinitive when discussing "Johannine Style and Vocabulary."

In summary, there are four types of dependent Greek clauses: pronominal, conjunctive, participial, and infinitival. These dependent clauses are extremely important because they provide additional information about the independent clause that helps trace John's flow of thought. The most frequent type of dependent Greek clause in John's letters is the ***dependent Greek conjunctive clauses*** with *at least* 171 examples. Another dependent Greek clause commonly found in John's letters is the ***dependent Greek pronominal clauses*** with *at least* 34 examples.

Included in these calculations are the frequent appearances of καί with an elliptical relative pronoun or a conjunction within a bracket. For instance in 1 John 2:14d and 2:14e have two elliptical ὅτι conjunctions in [*brackets*] and *italic*.

> ^{2:14c} **<u>ἔγραψα</u>** ὑμῖν, νεανίσκοι, (<u>ὅτι</u> ἰσχυροί <u>ἐστε</u>
> ^{2:14c} **I have written** to you, young people, (<u>that</u> you <u>are</u> strong,
>
> > |
> > ^{2:14d} καὶ [<u>*ὅτι*</u>] ὁ λόγος τοῦ θεοῦ ἐν ὑμῖν μένει
> > ^{2:14d} and [*that*] the word of God <u>abides</u> in you
> >
> > |
> > ^{2:14e} καὶ [<u>*ὅτι*</u>] <u>νενικήκατε</u> τὸν πονηρόν).
> > ^{2:14e} and [*that*] <u>you have conquered</u> the Evil One).

There are at least eighteen occurrences. Five are καί plus an elliptical relative pronoun (1:1e, 5b; 3:17b, 17c; 4:3e). Thirteen are καί plus an elliptical conjunction: eight καί [ὅτι] dependent clauses (1:5e; 2:14d, 14e; 3:16c, 19b, 20c, 22c; 4:10d), three καί [ἵνα] dependent clauses (1:9d; 2:28d; 3:23c), one καί [ἐάν] dependent clause (4:20b), and one καί [ὅταν] dependent clause (5:2a).

While there are many participles in the John's letters, there are very few adverbial participles. Nevertheless, John's letters have an abundance of substantival participles. Yet that is not the case for the Greek infinitival clause because there are a minimal number of Greek infinitival clauses in John's letters.

The following chart lists the types of dependent clauses in John's letters, their syntactical function, and their semantical category is identified as we have interpreted them.[6]

Syntactical Function		Four Types of Dependent Clauses and Verbal Usage in John's Letters
Substantival Clauses	Pronominal	Relative Pronoun Clause: **1 John 2**:24a, 24b; **4**:6c
		Relative Pronoun Direct Object: **1 John 1**:1a, 1b, 1c, 1d, 1e, 3a; **2 John** 8b
		Relative Pronoun Epexegetical: **1 John 2**:25b
		Indefinite Relative Pronoun Clause: **1 John 3**:22a, 24c; **5**:15b; **3 John** 5b
	Conjunctive	ὅτι Direct Object: **1 John 1**:6a, 8a, 10a; **2**:3a, 4a, 5c, 12, 13a, 13b, 14a, 14b, 14c, 14d, 14e, 18b, 18d, 19f, 21e, 22b, 29a, 29b; **3**:2c, 5a, 5c, 14a, 15b, 19a, 19b, 24c; **4**:3d, 13a, 14, 15a, 20a; **5**:1a, 2a, 5b, 13b, 15a, 15c, 18a, 18b, 18c, 19a, 19b, 20a, 20b; **3 John** 12c
		ὅτι Appositional: **1 John 1**:5d, 5e
		ἵνα Appositional: **1 John 3**:8d, 11c, 23b, 23c; **4**:21b; **5**:3b; **2 John** 6b, 6e; **3 John** 4b
		καθώς: **3 John** 3c
		ἵνα Direct Object: **1 John 5**:16c;
		εἰ Direct Object: **1 John 3**:13a
	Participial	Subject: **1 John 2**:4a, 6a, 9 (2x), 10a, 11a, 17b, 23b; **3**:7b, 8a, 10c, 14c, 24a; **4**:6b, 8a, 16e, 18d, 20d, 21b; **5**:5b, 7, 10a, 10b, 12a, 12b, 18b;
		2 John 1c, 9b, 11
		Predicate nominative: **1 John 5**:5a, 6a, 6d
		Appositional: **1 John 2**:22c; **5**:13a, 16c; **3 John** 9b
	Infinitive	Direct Objects: **1 John 2**:9; **2 John** 10d; **3 John** 2 (2x)
		Epexegetical **2 John** 12a; **3 John** 13a
Adjectival Clauses	Pronominal	Relative Pronoun Clause: **1 John 1**:2e, 5b, 5c; **2**:7c, 7e, 8b, 25b, 27b; **3**:11b, 24d; **4**:2c, 3b, 3d, 3e, 16c, 20e, 20f; **5**:10d, 14b, 15d; **2 John** 1b, 1c, 5d;
		3 John 1b, 6a, 6b, 10c
		Indefinite Relative Pronoun Clause: **1 John 2**:5a; **4**:15a
	Conjunctive	ὅτι Epexegetical: **1 John 1**:5d; **3**:1e, 16b, 16c, 20a, 20b, 20c; **4**:9b, 10b, 10c, 10d, 13c; **5**:9d, 11b, 11c, 14c
		ἵνα Epexegetical: **1 John 2**:27d; **3**:1b; **2 John** 5e
		ὅταν Epexegetical: **1 John 5**:2b, 2c
		καί Epexegetical: **1 John 3**:10c
	Participial	ptc. with πᾶς: **1 John 2**:23a, 29b; **3**:3a, 4a, 6a, 6b, 9a, 10b, 15a; **4**:7c, 7d; **5**:1a, 1b, 4a, 18a; **2 John** 9a
		Attributive: **2 John** 7b
	Infinitive	none

---

6. Technically, examples of a conjunctive clause that functions adjectivally do not exist (at least, to my knowledge). However, the epexegetical and appositional semantical occurrences of the ὅτι and ἵνα appear to be the closest facsimile to an adjectival clause and thereby are identified in this chart as being *like* an adjective.

Syntactical Function	Four Types of Dependent Clauses and Verbal Usage in John's Letters	
Adverbial Clauses	Pronominal	none
	Conjunctive	ὅτι + Indicative Mood Clauses: **1 John 2**:8c, 8d, 11d, 21b, 21d, 21e; **3**:2e, 8b, 9b, 9d, 12d, 14b, 22b, 22c; **4**:1d, 4c, 7b, 8b, 17c, 18c, 18d, 19b; **5**:4a, 6e, 9c, 10c; **2 John** 4b
		ἵνα + Subjunctive Mood Clauses: **1 John 1**:3c, 4b, 9c, 9d; **2**:1b, 19f, 28b, 28d; **3**:5b; **4**:9c, 17b; **5**:13b, 20c; **2 John** 8b, 8c, 12d; **3 John** 8b
		καθώς; ὡς: **1 John 1**:7b; **2**:6b, 18b, 27g, 27h; **3**:2f, 3b, 7b, 12a, 23d; **4**:17d; **2 John** 4c, 5b, 5c, 6d; **3 John** 2b
		γάρ: **2 John** 11; **3 John** 7a
		ὅθεν: **1 John 2**:18d
		εἰ (first class condition): **1 John 2**:19c; **4**:1c, 11a; **5**:9a; **2 John** 10a, (10b)
		ἐάν (third class condition): **1 John 1**:6a, 6b, 7a, 8a, 9a, 10a; **2**:1c, 3b, 15b, 24b, 29a; **3**:21a; **4**:12b, 20a; 20b; **5**:15a, 16a; **3 John** 10a
		εἰ μή: **1 John 2**:22b; **5**:5b
		ἐάν Temporal: **1 John 2**:28c, 3:2d
		ἐάν Indefinite: **1 John 5**:14d
	Participial	Temporal: **3 John** 7b
		Causal: **3 John** 10e
		Means: **3 John** 10d, 10e
		Concessive: **2 John** 12a
		Genitive Absolute: **3 John** 3b
	Infinitival	None

JOHANNINE STYLE AND VOCABULARY

Every author of the Greek New Testament has a writing style that exhibits features readily repeated or perhaps even unique to their letters. Speaking very simplistically, the author of Hebrews likes chiastic structures, Peter somewhat idiomatically employs Greek imperatival participles, Jude favors the use of adjectival Greek participles, and the adverbial Greek participle abounds in Paul. The authors of Hebrews, Peter, Jude, and Paul often appeal to the Old Testament either by direct quotation or allusion. The authors of Hebrews, Peter, Jude, and Paul are at times difficult to read due to their complex writing styles. Although there are other stylistic issues that could be listed for each of these authors, the point to be made here is that John also exhibits several stylistic features worth highlighting.

For instance, John seldom appeals to the Old Testament. Evidence of Hebraic, Aramaic, and Semitic style have been evaluated in the Johannine epistles and the conclusion has been drawn that the author was Jewish (Turner[2], 135–37). Furthermore, John's writing style is very simplistic in comparison to the other letters of the New Testament. In fact, the style "is one of extreme simplicity all through," says Turner, "with some monotony of construction" (Turner[2], 135). Our focus, however, is to underscore John's stylistic features pertaining to his repetitive use of certain Greek clauses and constructions that seem to permeate his letters.

John's Style

First, there is the substantival dependent Greek participial clause. It is a stylistic feature that warrants special attention due to its repetitive appearance. On the one hand, there is the typical substantival Greek participle like "the one who does" (ὁ ποιῶν) and "the one who keeps" (ὁ τηρῶν) versus "the one who does not love" (ὁ μὴ ἀγαπῶν) and "the one who does not have" (ὁ μὴ ἔχων). Or like the two examples below from 1 John 5:12 where the substantival participial clauses not only serve as the subject of the independent clause and are placed in parentheses, they also divide people into one of two categories: those who have eternal life and those who do not.

> 5:12a (ὁ ἔχων τὸν υἱὸν) **ἔχει** τὴν ζωήν·
> 5:12a (The one who has the Son) **has** the life;
>
> 5:12b (ὁ μὴ ἔχων τὸν υἱὸν τοῦ θεοῦ) τὴν ζωὴν οὐκ **ἔχει**.
> 5:12b (the one who does not have the Son of God) does not **have** the life.

On the other hand, there is the informal Greek construction "everyone" (πᾶς) + the Greek article (ὁ) + a Greek participle. This construction occurs sixteen times in 1 John (2:23a, 29b; 3:3a, 4a, 6b [2x], 9a, 10b, 15a; 4:7c, 7d; 5:1a, 1b, 4a, 18a). John's fondness of this type of substantival participial clause also serves to divide people into one of two categories: "everyone who does this" as opposed to "everyone who does the opposite." Furthermore, these generic utterances nearly always involve a gnomic idea. John often provides theologically driven timeless truths throughout his letter by way of these substantival participles, as is evident in the following example.

> 5:1a (Πᾶς ὁ πιστεύων [ὅτι Ἰησοῦς ἐστιν ὁ Χριστὸς]) ἐκ τοῦ θεοῦ **γεγέννηται**
> 5:1a (Everyone who persists in believing [that Jesus is the Christ]) **has been fathered** by God

The πᾶς plus the ὁ πιστεύων creates a gnomic statement that identifies an eternal truth: any person who believes the teaching about the messiahship of Jesus has a relationship with God; those who don't, do not have that relationship. So the repetitive appearance of this sort of dependent participial clause not only functions as the subject of another clause, it often underscores John's dualistic manner of discussing people, presenting issues, and articulating his theological position.

Second, there is the frequent use of the independent Greek prepositional clause "in this" (ἐν τούτῳ). It occurs fourteen times in 1 John (2:3, 4, 5 [2x]; 3:10, 16, 19, 24; 4:2, 9, 10, 13, 17; 5:2). It is, as Raymond Brown declares, "a frequent and most troublesome Johannine idiom" (Brown, 248). To what does the prepositional phrase refer? Whenever the prepositional phrase appears, we always ask this question: Does "in this" (ἐν τούτῳ) refer to the preceding statement (anaphoric) or to the statement that follows (cataphoric)? John does appear, however, to follow a specific syntactical pattern that helps us answer our question.

In cases where "this" (τούτῳ) is modified by a subordinate clause that begins with "that" (ὅτι + indicative mood clause), "in order that" (ἵνα + subjunctive mood clause), "if" (ἐαν + subjunctive mood clause), "whenever" (ὅταν), or "from" (ἐκ),

> **Clues for Interpreting τοῦτο as Cataphoric**
>
> ὅτι + indicative mood clause
> ἵνα + subjunctive mood clause
> ἐαν + subjunctive mood clause
> ὅταν clause
> ἐκ clause

then the prepositional phrase "in this" (ἐν τούτῳ) is cataphoric. These sorts of subordinate clauses generally define the demonstrative pronoun. For example, 1 John 4:10a begins with a prepositional phrase "in this" (ἐν τούτῳ) followed by several dependent ὅτι conjunctive clauses that clarify how to interpret "this" (τούτῳ). Love is clearly defined in the three ὅτι clauses.

4:10a **ἐν τούτῳ** ἐστὶν ἡ ἀγάπη,
4:10a In this is love,

    |

4:10b οὐχ **ὅτι** ἡμεῖς **ἠγαπήκαμεν** τὸν θεόν,
4:10b not **that we have loved** God,

    |

4:10c ἀλλ᾽ **ὅτι** αὐτὸς **ἠγάπησεν** ἡμᾶς
4:10c but **that he loved** us

    |

4:10d καὶ [*ὅτι*] **ἀπέστειλεν** τὸν υἱὸν αὐτοῦ ἱλασμὸν περὶ τῶν ἁμαρτιῶν ἡμῶν.
4:10d and [*that*] **he sent** his Son to be the atoning sacrifice for our sins.

First John 4:10a begins with "in this is love" (ἐν τούτῳ ἐστὶν ἡ ἀγάπη). To what does "this" (τούτῳ) refer? According to our grammatical rule above, "this" (τούτῳ) is cataphoric, pointing forward to the three dependent Greek ὅτι claus-es. So, John first states what love is not. He then, in two statements, tells us what love is. The third [ὅτι] is an ellipsis and therefore assumed from the context. Thus, it appears in [*brackets*] and *italic*. This is an extremely important rule to remember when interpreting "this" (οὗτος) in 1 John.

Third, there is the appositional use of the dependent Greek conjunctive ἵνα clause. Semantic rendering of a ἵνα clause as appositional after a demonstrative pronoun is not only repetitive, it tends to be a unique characteristic of John because the appositional use of ἵνα seldom appears in the New Testament. Wallace considers it to be idiomatic within John's writings (W, 675). There are at least six occurrenc-es in 1 John (3:8d, 11c, 23b, 23c; 4:21b; 5:3b). For example, the ἵνα clause in 5:3b defines the demonstrative pronoun "this" (αὕτη) in 5:3a.

> 5:3a **αὕτη** γάρ ἐστιν ἡ ἀγάπη τοῦ θεοῦ,
> 5:3a For <u>this</u> is the love *for* God,
>
> |
>
> 5:3b **ἵνα** τὰς ἐντολὰς αὐτοῦ τηρῶμεν·
> 5:3b <u>*namely*</u> **that** we keep his commandments

Once again, this sort of dependent conjunctive clause is extremely important for interpreting the Greek demonstrative pronoun "this" (αὕτη), as was noted above under "The Frequent Use of the Greek Prepositional Clause."

Fourth, there is frequent use of the independent Greek asyndeton clause. This too is another stylistic feature that permeates John's letters. As they were identified above, there are at least eighty-five examples in 1 John, nine in 2 John, and fifteen in 3 John. The repetitive appearance of asyndeton clauses is attributed to Aramaic influences (Turner[2], 136). The simple and repeated use of "I *now* write to you" (γράφω ὑμῖν) or "I have written to you" (ἔγραψα ὑμῖν) exemplifies both John's simplicity and repetitiveness (1 John 2:12–14).

Fifth, there is a repetitive use of three conjunctions to introduce independent and dependent clauses. The repetitive use of καί abounds, beginning with the ninety-three independent clauses introduced with καί in 1 John alone, and with nearly a hundred introducing dependent clauses.

The uniform appearance of the substantival dependent conjunctive ὅτι clause as the direct object of a clause is undeniable.

And John's consistent use of ἐάν for uncertain fulfillment but still likely state-ments (a third class condition) is John's favored conditional clause throughout his first letter.

> **Repetitive Appearance of καί, ὅτι, and ἐάν in John's Letters**
>
> **Introducing Independent καί Coordinating Clauses**
>
> **1 John 1:**2a, 2b, 2c, 2d, 4a, 3b, 5a, 6d, 7d, 8c, 10c; **2:**2a, 2b, 3a, 4b, 10b, 11b, 11c, 17a, 18c, 20a, 20b, 24c, 27c, 27f, 28a; **3:**1c, 2b, 3a, 5a, 5c, 9c, 12c, 13a, 15b, 19a, 22a, 23a, 24a, 24b, 24c, 27a; **4:**3a, 3c, 4b, 5c, 7c, 7d, 11b, 12d, 14, 15c, 16a, 16b, 16e, 16f, 21a; **5:**1b, 3c, 4b, 6d, 8b, 11a, 11c, 14a, 16c, 17b, 20d ; **2 John** 5a, 6a, 10d; **3 John** 10g, 10h, 12b, 12c, 14b
>
> **Introducing Dependent Direct Object ὅτι Clauses**
>
> **1 John 1:**6a, 8a, 10a; **2:**3a, 4a, 5c, 12, 13a, 13b, 14a, 14b, 14c, 14d, 14e, 18b, 18d, 19f, 21e, 22b, 29a, 29b; **3:**2c, 5a, 5c, 14a, 15b, 19a, 19b, 24c; **4:**3d, 13a, 14, 15a, 20a; **5:**1a, 2a, 5b, 13b, 15a, 15c, 18a, 18b, 18c, 19a, 19b, 20a, 20b
>
> **Introducing Dependent ἐάν Clauses**
>
> **1 John 1:**6a, 6b, 7a, 8a, 9a, 10a; **2:**1c, 3b, 15b, 24b, 29a; **3:**21a; **4:**12b, 20a; **5:**15a, 16a; **3 John** 10a

Sixth, John likes the complementary Greek infinitive. While there are few infinitival clauses in John's letters, John often employs the use of the infinitive to complete a verb's thought: "I am able" (δύνομαι; 1 John 3:9a; 4:20d), "I wish" (βούλομαι; 2 John 12b), "I wish" (θέλω; 3 John 13b), "I hope" (ἐλπίζω; 2 John 12c; 3 John 14a), and "I ought" appears frequently (ὀφείλω; 1 John 2:6a; 3:16c; 4:11b; 3 John 8). All are followed by a complementary Greek infinitive.

JOHN'S VOCABULARY

There are some words in John's letters that are unique. They will not appear elsewhere in the New Testament. The following chart identifies nine *hapax legomena* in the Johannine letters.

		Hapax Legomena in John's Letters		
1 John	*Hapax Legomenon*	**English Translations**	**Lexical Form**	**Lexical Meaning**
1:5; 2:11	ἀγγελία	message	ἀγγελία	
2:2; 4:10	ἱλασμός	expiation, propitiation	ἱλασμός	expiation, propitiation
2:18, 22; 4:3	ἀντίχριστος	Antichrist	ἀντίχριστος	Antichrist
2:20, 27	χρῖσμα	anointing, unction	χρῖσμα	anointing, unction
5:4	νίκη	victory	νίκη	victory

Hapax Legomena in John's Letters				
2 John	*Hapax Legomenon*	**English Translations**	**Lexical Form**	**Lexical Meaning**
12	χάρτου	"paper" (Geneva Bishop KJV ASV NASB NRSV ESV NIV NET NLT CNT WEB)	χάρτης	
3 John	*Hapax Legomenon*	**English Translations**	**Lexical Form**	**Lexical Meaning**
9	ὁ φιλοπρωτεύων	"who loves preeminence" (Geneva Bishop KJV ASV) "who loves to be first" (NASB NIV NET CNT WEB) "who loves to be the leader" (NLT) "who likes to put himself first" (NRSV ESV)	φιλοπρωτεύω	"who loves to be first" BDAG, s.v., p. 1058
9 & 10	ἐπιδέχεται	Verse 9 "receive" (Geneva Bishop KJV ASV) "accept" (NASB CNT WEB) "acknowledge" (NRSV ESV NET) "refuses" (NLT) "will have nothing to do" (NIV) Verse 10 "receive" (Geneva Bishop KJV ASV NASB WEB) "refuses" (NRSV ESV NIV NET NLT) "stops" (CNT)	ἐπιδέχομαι	"receive" or "welcome" someone in a friendly manner BDAG, s.v. 1, p. 370
10	φλυαρῶν	"prating words" (Geneva KJV ASV) "accusing" (NASB NLT WEB) "gossiping" (NIV CNT) "talking nonsense" (ESV) "spreading charges" (NRSV) "bringing charges" (NET)	φλυαρέω	"talk nonsense (about)" or "disparage" BDAG, s.v., p. 1060

In summary, while there are very few Greek words that are *hapax legomena* in the Johannine letters, there are several stylistic features unique to, and deemed idiomatic of, John's writing style. There are two types of *independent* Greek clauses that John enjoys using: the independent Greek asyndeton and the independent Greek prepositional clause. While the asyndeton clause underscores John's repetitive simplistic style of writing, the prepositional clause involving the demonstrative pronoun "this" (οὖτος) reveals one of John's most troubling idiomatic features that challenges many contemporary interpreters.

Nevertheless, John's repetitive use of three conjunctions "and," "that," and "if" (καί, ὅτι, ἐάν) contribute to John's simplistic style of writing. The recurring appearance of these three conjunctions with the same tedious classification contributes to what Turner deems a "monotony of construction" (Turner[2], 135).

Finally, there are two *dependent* clauses that make a rather significant contribution to John's style. The first is John's idiomatic use of the appositional ἵνα clause that consistently defines John's repetitive use of the demonstrative pronoun "this" (οὖτος). The second is John's unrelenting use of the dependent Greek participial clause that not only serves as a subject of many clauses, but also discloses John's dualistic manner of distinguishing those who are followers of Jesus from those who are not. This latter feature corresponds nicely with John's regular use of the helping verb "I ought" (ὀφείλω).

Naturally, all English translations reflect interpretations. Consequently, numerous interpretive decisions are reflected throughout *John's Letters*, so when comparing our explanations with English translations and commentaries, remember to think critically. We take no offense if you differ with us. We do, however, take offense if you just accept at face value our interpretive interactions and renderings. Please engage and wrestle with John's letters and have fun.

First John

First John appears to be a letter written to a community of believers in the face of a crisis. People (or secessionists) had risen up within the church who were causing confusion about the person and mission of Jesus, as well as spawning unhealthy and perhaps even hostile relationships within the church. Thus 1 John has a twofold theological theme: *the humanity of Jesus* (his person and mission) and *living as a loving community*. Both themes appear in the letter as litmus tests for determining a person's relationship with God.

John opens his letter as an authoritative representative of Jesus and underscores his message about Jesus, who was indeed a living breathing human person (1:1–4). Yet he transitions (καί) from his proclamation about the humanity of Jesus to disclosing the *good news* (ἡ ἀγγελία) about God, which in turn serves as the basis for distinguishing between two types of people in the church: those who know God and those who do not (1:5–2:2). For John, the willingness to love others is the ultimate validation for determining a person's relationship with God (2:3–11). Yet John affirms (γράφω) his readers about their relationship with God before moving on to warn them

THE HUMANITY OF JESUS

The humanity of Jesus, introduced early in the prologue (1:1–2), provides the platform that undergirds John's more pointed proclamation that Jesus is the Christ (1:3; 2:22) who came in human flesh (4:2; cf., 2 John 1:7). Belief in the humanity of Jesus makes it possible for a person to have a relationship with God (2:22–25; 3:4–12). It underscores and foreshadows the importance of the eyewitness testimony about Jesus (4:14, 5:6–12). It prepares the way to speak of Jesus coming as Messiah that is tantamount to one's "relationship" (ἡ κοινωνία) with both Jesus and God (1:3; 2:23, 24; 4:15; 5:1, 20).

THE LOVE COMMAND

Living as a loving community, namely loving other believers, is John's second recurring theological theme. Those who share in the life from God are brought into a relationship with one another, which then becomes the basis for and obligation of mutual love for one another (2:10; 3:10, 11, 14, 18, 23; 4:7, 11, 12, 20, 21). One's relationship with God is demonstrated through obedience to God's command to love other believers, which in turn distinguishes a person's membership within God's community of true believers and their relationship with God (2:3–11; 5:1–4).

about the world: its negative behavior, its lack of acceptability, and its lack of durability (2:12–17). He then launches into a few emotive appeals (παιδία) to remain in Jesus (2:18–29) before closing out the first half of his letter with a somewhat sharp (ἴδετε) return to his theme about loving others (3:1–10).

As John launches into the second half of his letter (3:11–5:29), he begins it in a manner similar to the first half (1:5–3:10) in that he speaks about the *good news* (ἡ ἀγγελία). Whereas the good news in 1:5 was about God, here in 3:11 it is about love. John underscores this simple truth: love and hate are incompatible passions among followers of Jesus (3:11–17). He then makes an emotive appeal (τεκνία) not to love merely in what one says, but in what one does (3:18–24), before shifting somewhat abruptly (ἀγαπητοί) to his recurring theme about the humanity of Jesus. He makes it clear that teachings about Jesus as a human Messiah distinguish false teachings as a test of faith before returning to affirm (τεκνία) his readers of their heavenly origins (4:1–6). He then somewhat abruptly (ἀγαπητοί) returns to the theme of mutual love with first a calling to love (ἀγαπῶμεν) others because (ὅτι) God is love (4:7–10), to an expectancy (ὀφείλομεν . . . ἀγαπᾶν) to love as proof of their relationship (μένομεν) with God (4:11–16c). Advancing further the theme of love, John speaks of this eternal truth: God is (ἐστιν) love and those that live lives of love demonstrate that they have a relationship (μένει) with God (4:16d–21). John then moves to identify several timeless facts: anyone who believes (πᾶς ὁ πιστεύων) in Jesus identifies his paternal affiliation with God, loves God and other family members, obeys God's commandments, and has victory over the Evil One (5:1–4). John then underscores (δέ) what conquering power is: our faith. Faith in Jesus, who is the Christ, not only has made believers conquerors of the world's system, it has provided eternal life (5:5–12). John closes his letter (ἔγραψα) with a twofold epilogue: to build confidence in approaching God in prayer (5:15–17) and about God's protection of those who belong to him (5:18–20), followed by a command: don't worship idols (5:21).

1 John 1:1–4

Big Greek Idea: John identifies himself as an authoritative representative of Jesus, who witnessed Jesus's life and ministry firsthand and now proclaims that earthly ministry, in order that fellowship might be shared among all who hear the message about Jesus and in order that true happiness might become a reality for many people.

Structural Overview: John's opening four verses are an appraisal of those who proclaimed the message about Jesus. He begins by asserting that there were *eyewitnesses* (of whom John is an authoritative representative) of Jesus. They experienced (ἦν) firsthand in his earthly ministry: his words (ἀκηκόαμεν), his deeds (ἑωράκαμεν/ ἐθεασάμεθα), and his person (ἐψηλάφησαν; v. 1). Second, they proclaim (ἀπαγγέλλομεν) these revelations of Jesus's person, message, and work. Third, their intention (ἵνα) for proclaiming the message about Jesus is a shared (ἔχητε) partnership with God and Jesus (vv. 2–3). Finally, this proclaimed message about Jesus's life, message, and work is being written in order that (ἵνα) the happiness of John, the eyewitnesses, and his readers might be realized (ἦ πεπληρωμένη; v. 4).

Outline:
> A Testimony Is Provided by Eyewitnesses (vv. 1–3)
>> The personal testimony is all-encompassing (v. 1)
>> The personal testimony is shared (vv. 2–3a, b)
>> The intention for sharing the testimony is for fellowship (v. 3c, d)
> The Intention for Writing Is to Experience Shared Happiness (v. 4)

Clausal Outline for 1 John 1:1–4

1:1a (῾Ο ἦν ἀπ᾽ ἀρχῆς),
1:1a (**That which was** from the beginning)

1:1b (ὃ ἀκηκόαμεν),
1:1b (**which we have heard**)

1:1c (ὃ ἑωράκαμεν τοῖς ὀφθαλμοῖς ἡμῶν),
1:1c (**which we have seen** with our eyes)

1:1d (ὃ ἐθεασάμεθα)
1:1d (**which we have looked at**)

1:1e (καὶ [ὃ] αἱ χεῖρες ἡμῶν ἐψηλάφησαν περὶ τοῦ λόγου τῆς ζωῆς)
1:1e (**and** [*which*] our hands **have touched** about the word, which is life)

^{1:2a} <u>καὶ</u> ἡ ζωὴ **ἐφανερώθη**,
^{1:2a} <u>for</u> the life **was revealed**

^{1:2b} <u>καὶ</u> **ἑωράκαμεν**
^{1:2b} <u>and</u> **we have seen**

^{1:2c} <u>καὶ</u> **μαρτυροῦμεν**
^{1:2c} <u>and</u> **we** *now* **testify**

^{1:2d} <u>καὶ</u> **ἀπαγγέλλομεν** ὑμῖν τὴν ζωὴν τὴν αἰώνιον
^{1:2d} <u>and</u> **we** *now* **proclaim** to you eternal life

> ^{1:2e} **ἥτις ἦν** πρὸς τὸν πατέρα καὶ
> **ἐφανερώθη** ἡμῖν —
> ^{1:2e} **which was** with the Father and **was revealed** to us

^{1:3a} (**ὃ ἑωράκαμεν** καὶ **ἀκηκόαμεν**)
^{1:3a} (**that which we have seen** and **heard**)

^{1:3b} **ἀπαγγέλλομεν** καὶ ὑμῖν,
^{1:3b} **we** *now* **proclaim** to you also

> ^{1:3c} **ἵνα** καὶ ὑμεῖς κοινωνίαν **ἔχητε** μεθ᾽ ἡμῶν.
> ^{1:3c} **in order that** even **you may have** fellowship with us.

^{1:3d} καὶ ἡ κοινωνία δὲ ἡ ἡμετέρα [*ἐστιν*] μετὰ τοῦ πατρὸς καὶ μετὰ τοῦ υἱοῦ αὐτοῦ Ἰησοῦ Χριστοῦ.
^{1:3d} <u>And</u> *indeed* our fellowship [*is*] with the Father and with his Son, Jesus, who is the Christ.

^{1:4a} <u>καὶ</u> ταῦτα **γράφομεν** ἡμεῖς
^{1:4a} <u>Therefore</u> **we are writing** these *things*

> ^{1:4b} **ἵνα** ἡ χαρὰ ἡμῶν **ᾖ πεπληρωμένη**.
> ^{1:4b} **in order that** our joy **may be complete**.

Syntax Explained for 1 John 1:1–4

^{1:1a} ὅ: The Greek word ὅ is a neuter singular nominative from the relative pronoun ὅς, which means "that which" or "what" (BDAG, s.v. "ὅς" 1gγ, p. 727). Translations vary as to how to render the relative pronoun. Some translate it "what"

(NASB NRSV NET) others "that which" (KJV ASV ESV NIV CNT). **Syntactically,** ὅ introduces a dependent substantival relative clause. The entire relative clause functions as the direct object of "we now proclaim" (ἀπαγγέλλομεν) in verse 3b (cf. Moule, 34). It is placed in parentheses to show its dependence on the subsequent independent clause. It parallels four other relative clauses, which are considered headless, meaning they have no grammatical antecedent (Culy, 2). The relative pronoun is in the nominative case and thereby the subject of its verb "was" (ἦν).

ἦν: The Greek word ἦν is a third person singular imperfect active indicative from the verb εἰμί meaning "to be" or "to exist" (BDAG, s.v. "εἰμί" 1, p. 282). **Syntactically,** ἦν is the main verb of the first of four dependent relative clauses, "that which *was* from the beginning" (ὃ ἦν ἀπ᾽ ἀρχῆς). This clause serves as part of the compound direct object of the verb "we announce" (ἀπαγγέλλομεν). This relative clause is headless and has no apparent antecedent. The contextual antecedent of the pronoun seems to be the person and work of Jesus (see n. 1:1a above). The subject of the verb is the relative pronoun "that" (ὅ). **Semantically,** ἦν is a gnomic imperfect: "was" (cf. KJV NASB ESV NIV NLT etc.). John's timeless fact is this: Jesus has existed from the beginning of eternity (cf. John 1:1–14).

Syntactical Nugget: How are the first of four relative clauses in verse 1 to be understood? What or to whom is John referring? The referent could be "the word" in the phrase the "word of life." If this were true, we would expect a masculine pronoun in order to agree with the masculine gender of the "the word," but each of these pronouns is neuter and not masculine. The referent could also be "life" in the phrase "the word of life," but in that case we would expect a feminine pronoun for the same reason. It seems the relative clauses refer to the life and career of Jesus as a whole: his person, words, and deeds (cf. Bateman[1], Brown, 154–155). John tells his readers that he witnessed the incarnation and ministry of Jesus. Thus Jesus, who was from the beginning, whom our author heard, saw with his own eyes, and even touched, is the one about whom John wants to proclaim.

1:1b ὅ: The Greek word ὅ is a neuter singular accusative from the relative pronoun ὅς, meaning "which" (BDAG, s.v. "ὅς" 1gγ, p. 727). **Syntactically,** ὅ introduces a dependent substantival relative clause. The entire relative clause also functions as the direct object of "we now proclaim" (ἀπαγγέλλομεν) in verse 3b (cf. Moule, 34). It is placed in parentheses to show its dependence on the subsequent independent clause. It is the second of five relative clauses that are considered headless, which means it has no grammatical antecedent (Culy, 2). The relative pronoun is in the accusative case and thereby the direct object of its verb "we have heard" (ἀκηκόαμεν).

ἀκηκόαμεν: The Greek word ἀκηκόαμεν is first person plural perfect active indicative from the verb ἀκούω meaning "to hear" or "to exercise the faculty of hearing" (BDAG, s.v. "ἀκούω" 1bα, p. 37). **Syntactically,** ἀκηκόαμεν is the main verb of this second of four dependent relative clauses, "which *we have heard*" (ὃ ἀκηκόαμεν). The subject of the verb is an implied "we" embedded in the verb. It refers to the John and the eyewitnesses (W, 394–99; Brown, 158–61; Bateman[1], 160). **Semantically,** ἀκηκόαμεν is an extensive perfect: "we *have* heard" (cf. KJV NASB ESV NIV NET etc.). The focus is on the completed action upon which John's present testimony is based (W, 577). The point is that John and his associates had personal contact with Jesus and have heard what Jesus said firsthand; they now proclaim their experience to others.

Lexical Nugget: To whom does John refer when he says, "we have heard"? "We" can be understood one of three ways. First, it can be taken as an editorial plural (referring to just John). Second, it can be understood as an inclusive plural (referring to John and his audience). Finally, it could be an exclusive plural (referring to John and a larger group of eyewitnesses). The best option is to take this "we" as an exclusive plural referring to John and a group of eyewitnesses that he represents (W, 394–399; Brown, 158–61; Bateman[1], 160).

1:1c ὃ: The Greek word ὃ is a neuter singular accusative from the relative pronoun ὅς meaning "which" (BDAG, s.v. "ὅς" 1gγ, p. 727). **Syntactically,** ὃ introduces a dependent substantival relative clause. The entire relative clause also functions as the direct object of "we now proclaim" (ἀπαγγέλλομεν) in verse 3b (cf. Moule, 34). It is placed in parentheses to show its dependence on the subsequent independent clause. It is the third of five relative clauses that are considered headless, which means it has no grammatical antecedent (Culy, 2). The relative pronoun is in the accusative case and thereby the direct object of its verb "we have seen" (ἑωράκαμεν).

ἑωράκαμεν: The Greek word ἑωράκαμεν is first person plural perfect active indicative from the verb ὁράω meaning "to see" or "to notice" or "to perceive by the eye" (BDAG, s.v. "ὁράω" 1b, p. 719). **Syntactically,** ἑωράκαμεν is the governing verb of the third of four dependent relative clauses, "which *we have seen* with our eyes" (ὃ ἑωράκαμεν τοῖς ὀφθαλμοῖς ἡμῶν). The subject of the verb is an implied "we" and refers back to John and the eyewitnesses to Jesus's ministry. **Semantically,** ἑωράκαμεν is an extensive perfect: "we *have* heard" (cf. KJV NASB ESV NIV NET etc). The focus is on the completed action upon which John's present testimony is based (W, 577). Once again, the point is that John and his associates had personal contact with Jesus, but here he emphasizes what they saw Jesus do.

$^{1:1d}$ ὅ: The Greek word ὅ is a neuter singular accusative from the relative pronoun ὅς meaning "which" (BDAG, s.v. "ὅς" 1gγ, p. 727). **Syntactically,** ὅ introduces a dependent substantival relative clause. The entire relative clause also functions as the direct object of "we now proclaim" (ἀπαγγέλλομεν) in verse 3b (cf. Moule, 34). It is placed in parentheses to show its dependence on the subsequent independent clause. It is the fourth of five relative clauses considered headless, which means it has no grammatical antecedent (Culy, 2). The relative pronoun is in the accusative case and thereby the direct object of its verb "we have looked at" (ἐθεασάμεθα).

ἐθεασάμεθα: The Greek word ἐθεασάμεθα is first person plural aorist middle indicative from the verb θεάομαι meaning "to look at" or "to see" or "to have an intent look at something, to take something in with one's eyes" (BDAG, s.v. "θεάομαι" 1a, p. 445). **Syntactically,** ἐθεασάμεθα is one of the two governing verbs of the fourth of four dependent relative clauses, "which *we have looked at*" (ὅ ἐθεασάμεθα). The subject of the verb is an implied "we" and refers back to John and the group of eyewitnesses to the ministry of Jesus that he represents. **Semantically,** ἐθεασάμεθα is a consummative aorist: "we *have* looked at" (NASB NRSV NIV NET) or "we *have* looked upon" (KJV ESV CNT). The stress is on the cessation of an act (W, 559). Once again, John points to the personal contact that he and his associates had at one time with Jesus.

Grammatical Nugget: Why does John use two different tenses and verbs for sight? Each of the verbs in the opening four relative clauses (ἀκηκόαμεν, ἑωράκαμεν, ἐθεασάμεθα) are first person plurals. They all refer to John, the author of this letter, along with a group of eyewitnesses to the earthly ministry of Jesus whereby John's letter is given an air of authority. After having used the perfect tense twice, John now switches to the aorist tense. Why the shift? Contra Brown who believes the shift of tense is merely a stylistic variant (Brown, 296), Porter believes that John is not just trying to be stylistically diverse, but that the two aorist tense verbs actually offer supporting information to the perfect tense verbs (Porter, 229–30; cf. Culy, 3). The fact that they looked at Jesus and touched Jesus supports the idea that they were eyewitnesses to the ministry of Jesus. Why does John use two different verbs that mean sight? Commentators propose various shades of meaning between these two verbs. Yet Brown suggests it might be as simple as John having a preferred word for a given tense. He uses ὁράω in the perfect tense and θεάομαι in the aorist (Brown, 162). Yet what must be emphasized is this: John claims to know more about Jesus than those who appear to be wreaking havoc with the community to whom John is writing because unlike those who are stirring up doubt about Jesus, John knew Jesus personally (Culy, 3).

1:1e [ὅ]: The Greek word [ὅ] is a neuter singular accusative from the relative pronoun ὅς meaning "which" (BDAG, s.v. "ὅς" 1gγ, p. 727). **Syntactically,** [ὅ] introduces an elliptical dependent substantival relative clause. The entire relative clause also functions as the direct object of "we now proclaim" (ἀπαγγέλλομεν) in verse 3b (cf. Moule, 34). It is placed in parentheses to show its dependence on the subsequent independent clause. It is the fifth and final relative clause in this group of parallel clauses that are each considered headless, which means it has no grammatical antecedent (Culy, 2). The relative pronoun is in the accusative case and thereby the direct object of its verb "we have touched" (ἐψηλάφησαν).

ἐψηλάφησαν: The Greek word ἐψηλάφησαν is a third person plural aorist active indicative from the verb ψηλαφάω meaning "to touch" or "to handle" in quite a literal sense (BDAG, s.v. "ψηλαφάω" 1, p. 1097). **Syntactically,** ἐψηλάφησαν is one of the two governing verbs of the fourth of four dependent relative clauses, "which we have looked at and [which] our hands *have touched* about the word, which is life" (ὃ ἐθεασάμεθα καὶ αἱ χεῖρες ἡμῶν ἐψηλάφησαν περὶ τοῦ λόγου τῆς ζωῆς). The subject of the verb is an implied "we" and refers back to John and the group of eyewitnesses to the ministry of Jesus that he represents. **Semantically,** ἐψηλάφησαν is a consummative aorist: "we have touched" (KJV ASV NASB NRSV NIV). The stress, once again, is on the cessation of the action (W, 559). John underscores the personal contact that John and his associates had at one time with Jesus, his words.

Syntactical Nugget: Why is there a parenthetical statement in verse 1? Throughout verse 1, John piles up verbs to emphasize the importance of the historical eyewitness testimony to the person and work of Jesus (Brown, 163). The prepositional phrase "about the word of life" (περὶ τοῦ λόγου τῆς ζωῆς) is a parenthetical clarification related to the subject of the eyewitness testimony (cf. NET Bible note). It adds information about Jesus and his life and work. The genitive "of life" (τῆς ζωῆς), however, needs interpretation. On the one hand, this might be an objective genitive, "the word about life" (W, 116). If this is the case, then we are talking about the eyewitness testimony of the apostles to the life and work of Jesus. On the other hand, this might be an attributive genitive, "the living word," ascribing a quality to the word (W, 86). The message would then be about Jesus, who was the living word. This view is attractive because the troublemakers John was concerned about were denying the full humanity of Jesus. The best option, as it is presented in the clausal outline, is a genitive of apposition, "about the word, which is life" (W, 95). In this case the referent could either be personal (Jesus) or impersonal (the eyewitness testimony). John would be saying that the word is literally life itself. If the noun "word" (λόγου) is personal and an allusion to the title of Jesus given to him in John's Gospel (cf. 1:1–4; 14), then John could be suggesting that Jesus is life itself. This seems to fit the context of 1 John and forms an inclusion with 1 John 5:20 (cf. note 5:20e; see also John 11:25; 14:6). Thus John starts and ends with the assertion that Jesus is eternal life personified.

1:2a καί: The Greek word καί is a conjunction meaning "for" in this context (BDAG, s.v. "καί" 1c, p. 495). **Syntactically,** καί introduces a conjunctive independent clause "*for* the life was revealed" (καὶ ἡ ζωὴ ἐφανερώθη), which is providing additional information about the "the life." The entire verse is a parenthetical statement and thus shaded gray in the clausal outline. **Semantically,** καί is explanatory: "for" (KJV) and gives us some parenthetical explanation about "the life" (τῆς ζωῆς) (see Culy, 5; Bateman[1],162). This "life" is a personification of Jesus, an idea we find often in Johannine thought (John 11:25; 14:6; 1 John 5:20; Rev. 1:18; cf. Brown, 166).

ἐφανερώθη: The Greek word ἐφανερώθη is a third person singular aorist passive indicative from the verb φανερόω meaning "to reveal" or "to make known" or "to cause to become visible" (BDAG, s.v. "φανερόω" 1aβ, p. 1048). **Syntactically,** ἐφανερώθη is the governing verb of the conjunctive independent clause. The subject of the verb is "the life" (ἡ ζωή), which points to the relevance of Jesus's earthly life and ministry (cf. W, 327). **Semantically,** ἐφανερώθη is a consummative aorist: "was revealed" (NRSV NET NLT CNT cf. NIV). The stress again is on the cessation of the action (W, 559). In this opening clause within this parenthetical statement, John draws attention to the personal contact that John and his associates had at one time with Jesus. The idea that Jesus appeared on earth has far reaching implications for us today (cf. 1 Peter 1:20; Heb. 9:26; Brown, 167).

Grammatical Nugget: What is a Greek period? The first four verses of 1 John are one sentence called a period. We find these long sentences or periods throughout the New Testament (e.g., Heb. 1:1–4, Eph. 2:1–7 etc.). This particular period is especially difficult to translate because it is interrupted by parenthetical comments (v. 2; cf. Brown, 152). Despite this seemingly parenthetical interruption, however, the point is this: John tells his readers that he witnessed the incarnation and ministry of Jesus. Thus Jesus, who was from the beginning, whom our author heard, saw with his own eyes, and even touched, is the one about whom John wants to proclaim.

1:2b καί: The Greek word καί is a conjunction meaning "and" (BDAG, s.v. "καί" 1b, p. 494). **Syntactically,** καί introduces the conjunctive independent clause "*and* we have seen" (καὶ ἑωράκαμεν) that provides additional information about the "life." With one exception (NIV), translations tend to translate καί as "and" (KJV NASB ESV NET NLT). **Semantically,** καί is a coordinating conjunction that links two clauses together. In this clause, John adds further thought about "the life" (or Jesus).

ἑωράκαμεν: The Greek word ἑωράκαμεν is a first person plural perfect active indicative from the verb ὁράω meaning "to see" or "to notice" or "to perceive by the eye" (BDAG, s.v. "ὁράω" 1b, p. 719). **Syntactically,** ἑωράκαμεν is the governing verb of the conjunctive independent clause. The subject of the verb is an implied "we" and refers back to John and a group of eyewitnesses to the ministry of Jesus that he represents. **Semantically,** ἑωράκαμεν is a extensive perfect: "we *have* seen" (cf. NASB NRSV NIV NET NLT CNT). Returning to his use of the extensive perfect, the focus is on the completed action upon which his present preaching is based (W, 577). John points to Jesus's time on earth, when John and his associates saw him personally.

1:2c καί: The Greek word καί is a conjunction meaning "and" (BDAG, s.v. "καί" 1b, p. 494). **Syntactically,** καί introduces an independent conjunctive clause: "*and* we now testify" (καὶ μαρτυροῦμεν). **Semantically,** καί is a coordinating conjunction: "and" (KJV ASV NASB NRSV ESV NET NLT CNT). It provides additional information about John's firsthand experience (W, 671), which is evident with John's next verb.

μαρτυροῦμεν: The Greek word μαρτυροῦμεν is a first person plural present active indicative from the verb μαρτυρέω meaning "to declare" or "to bear witness to" or "to attest to something based upon personal knowledge" (BDAG, s.v. "μαρτυρέω" 1b, p. 618). **Syntactically,** μαρτυροῦμεν is the governing verb of the conjunctive independent clause. The assumed subject, "we," refers to John and the group of eyewitnesses he represents. **Semantically,** μαρτυροῦμεν is a progressive present: "we *now* testify" (cf. NLT). It describes something that is in progress (W, 518). John and his associates witnessed the ministry of Jesus firsthand, and they are now in the process of proclaiming Jesus's ministry to others.

1:2d καί: The Greek word καί is a conjunction meaning "and" (BDAG, s.v. "καί" 1b, p. 494). **Syntactically,** καί introduces a conjunctive independent clause "*And* we proclaim to you eternal life" (καὶ ἀπαγγέλλομεν ὑμῖν τὴν ζωὴν τὴν αἰώνιον). Most translations tend to translate καί as "and" (KJV NASB ESV NET NLT etc.). **Semantically,** καί is a coordinating conjunction that links two clauses together. This time, however, John adds a thought about "the life" (or Jesus) as "eternal."

ἀπαγγέλλομεν: The Greek word ἀπαγγέλλομεν is a first person plural present active indicative from the verb ἀπαγγέλλω meaning "to proclaim" or "to make something known publicly" (BDAG, s.v. "ἀπαγγέλλω" 2, p. 95). **Syntactically,** ἀπαγγέλλομεν is the governing verb of the independent conjunctive clause. The assumed subject, "we," refers to John and the other eyewitnesses whom he represents. **Semantically,** ἀπαγγέλλομεν is a progressive present: "we *now* proclaim" (cf. NASB ESV NIV NLT CNT). John describes his proclamation as something that is in progress (W, 518). The ministry of Jesus that John witnessed is currently being stated publicly to others.

Lexical Nugget: Why does John use two verbs (μαρτυροῦμεν and ἀπαγγέλλομεν) that essentially mean the same thing? The two verbs "we *now* testify" (μαρτυροῦμεν) and "we *now* proclaim" (ἀπαγγέλλομεν) have semantic overlap. The verb "we *now* testify" (μαρτυροῦμεν) seems to emphasize the fact that John and others were witnesses of the ministry of Jesus, while "we *now* proclaim" (ἀπαγγέλλομεν) emphasizes John's intention of informing the readers about what he has witnessed (Culy, 6).

1:2e ἥτις: The Greek word ἥτις is a feminine singular nominative from the relative pronoun ὅστις meaning "who" or "one who" (BDAG, s.v. "ὅστις" 3, p. 730). **Syntactically,** ἥτις introduces a compound adjectival relative clause, "*which* was with the Father and was revealed to us" (ἥτις ἦν πρὸς τὸν πατέρα καὶ ἐφανερώθη ἡμῖν; cf. KJV ASV NASB ESV NIV CNT). In this situation, ὅστις has taken the place of the simple relative pronoun and occurs quite often in New Testament Greek (BDAG, s.v. "ὅστις" 3, p. 730). The relative clause provides additional information about its antecedent "the life" (τὴν ζωήν), namely, that Jesus (eternal life) was with the Father prior to his being revealed on earth.

ἦν: The Greek word ἦν is a third person singular imperfect active indicative from the verb εἰμί meaning "to be" or "to exist" (BDAG, s.v. "εἰμί" 1, p. 282). **Syntactically,** ἦν is one of the governing verbs of the compound dependent relative clause "which *was* with the Father and was revealed to us" (ἥτις ἦν πρὸς τὸν πατέρα καὶ ἐφανερώθη ἡμῖν). The subject is the relative pronoun "which" (ἥτις). **Semantically** as it was the case in 1:1a, ἦν is an equative imperfect: "was" (cf. KJV NASB ESV NIV NLT etc.). Whereas John's point in 1:1a was that Jesus existed in eternity (cf. John 1:1–14), here John underscores that before his earthly ministry Jesus was in the presence of the Father.

ἐφανερώθη: The Greek word ἐφανερώθη is a third person singular aorist passive indicative from the verb φανερόω meaning "to reveal" or "to make known" or "to cause to become visible" (BDAG, s.v. "φανερόω" 1αβ, p. 1048). **Syntactically,** ἐφανερώθη is one of the governing verbs of the compound dependent relative clause "which was with the Father and *was revealed* to us" (ἥτις ἦν πρὸς τὸν πατέρα καὶ ἐφανερώθη ἡμῖν). The subject is the relative pronoun "which" (ἥτις). **Semantically,** ἐφανερώθη is a consummative aorist: "was revealed" (cf. NASB NET NLT CNT). The aorist underscores the cessation of an act: (W, 559). The emphasis on John's past association with Jesus further establishes his authority on the matters he is about to discuss (Culy, 7).

1:3a ὅ: The Greek word ὅ is a neuter singular accusative from the relative pronoun ὅς meaning "that which" or "what" (BDAG, s.v. "ὅς" 1gγ, p. 727). As was the case in 1:1a, translations vary. Some translate it "what" (NASB NRSV NIV NET NLT) others "that which" (KJV ASV ESV CNT). **Syntactically,** ὅ introduces a dependent substantival relative clause with two verbs, "*what* we have seen and heard" (ὅ ἑωράκαμεν καὶ ἀκηκόαμεν). Like the relative clauses that open verse 1, this relative clause is also functioning as the direct object of the verb "we proclaim" (ἀπαγγέλλομεν). The relative clause provides the content of what John and his associates proclaim, namely, Jesus's earthly ministry. This headless relative clause returns us to the opening group of relative clauses in verse 1, but now moves the discussion forward (Culy, 7).

ἑωράκαμεν: The Greek word ἑωράκαμεν is a first person plural perfect active indicative from the verb ὁράω meaning "to see" or "to notice" (BDAG, s.v. "ὁράω" A1b, p. 719). **Syntactically,** ἑωράκαμεν is one of the governing verbs of the substantival relative clause "what *we have seen* and heard" (ὅ ἑωράκαμεν καὶ ἀκηκόαμεν), which serves as the direct object of the verb "we proclaim" (ἀπαγγέλλομεν). The subject of the verb is an implied "we" and refers back to John and his associates. **Semantically,** ἑωράκαμεν is an extensive perfect: "we have seen" (cf. KJV ASV NASB ESV NIV NET CNT). The focus is on the completed action upon which John's present preaching is based (W, 577). Thus it underscores that John *was* an eyewitness of Jesus's ministry, a ministry he *now* announces to others.

ἀκηκόαμεν: The Greek word ἀκηκόαμεν is a first person plural perfect active indicative from the verb ἀκούω meaning "to hear" or "to have exercised the faculty of hearing" (BDAG, s.v. "ἀκούω" 1bα, p. 37). **Syntactically,** ἀκηκόαμεν is one of the governing verbs of the substantival relative clause "what *we have* seen and *heard*" (ὅ ἑωράκαμεν καὶ ἀκηκόαμεν). It serves as the direct object of the verb "we proclaim" (ἀπαγγέλλομεν). The subject of the verb is an implied "we" and refers back to John and his associates. **Semantically,** ἀκηκόαμεν is a extensive perfect: "we *have* heard" (cf. KJV ASV NASB ESV NIV NET CNT). The focus, once again, is on the completed action upon which John's preaching is based (W, 577). Thus it too underscores that John *was* an eyewitness of Jesus' ministry, a ministry he *now* announces to others.

1:3b ἀπαγγέλλομεν: The Greek word ἀπαγγέλλομεν is a first person plural present active indicative from the verb ἀπαγγέλλω meaning "to proclaim" or "to make something known publicly" (BDAG, s.v. "ἀπαγγέλλω" 2, p. 95). **Syntactically,** ἀπαγγέλλομεν is the main verb of the independent clause "that which we have seen and heard *we now proclaim* to you also" (ὅ ἑωράκαμεν καὶ ἀκηκόαμεν ἀπαγγέλλομεν καὶ ὑμῖν). The assumed subject, "we," refers to John and the group of eyewitnesses he represents. **Semantically,** ἀπαγγέλλομεν is a progressive present: "we *now* proclaim" (NASB ESV NIV NLT CNT). John restates his proclamation as something that is in progress (W, 518). Jesus *right now* is being proclaimed to those who will listen. Perhaps John is revealing the sequence of how tradition is passed along. Regardless, the ministry of Jesus was originally witnessed by some and now others are able to participate in that experience through the reception of those traditions (Brown, 170).

καί: The Greek word καί is a conjunction meaning "also" (BDAG, s.v. "καί" 2a, p. 495). **Syntactically,** καί introduces a conjunctive independent clause "we now proclaim to you *also*" (ἀπαγγέλλομεν καὶ ὑμῖν). **Semantically,** καί is a conjunctive marker to indicate an additive: "also" (ASV NASB ESV CNT). John stresses a key additional element of his message (W, 671) evident in the next clause.

1:3c ἵνα: The Greek word ἵνα is a conjunction meaning "that" or "in order that" or "to denote a purpose or goal" (BDAG, s.v. "ἵνα" 1aα, p. 475). **Syntactically,** ἵνα introduces a conjunctive dependent clause, "*in order that* you also may have fellowship with us" (ἵνα καὶ ὑμεῖς κοινωνίαν ἔχητε μεθ' ἡμῶν). This clause is adverbial and modifies the verb "we proclaim" (ἀπαγγέλλομεν). **Semantically,** ἵνα is rendered as a purpose: "in order that" or "that" (KJV; cf. W, 472). The entire conjunctive clause provides John's and the other eyewitnesses' intention for proclaiming Jesus, namely, that his readers become partners with them in their relationship with Jesus.

ἔχητε: The Greek word ἔχητε is a second person plural present active subjunctive from the verb ἔχω meaning "to have" or "to stand in a close relationship with someone" (BDAG, s.v. "ἔχω" 2a, p. 420). This verb is also in the subjunctive mood because it follows a ἵνα. **Syntactically,** ἔχητε is the governing verb of the adverbial dependent ἵνα clause. The subject is the emphatic personal pronoun "you" (ὑμεῖς) that refers to John's readers. **Semantically,** ἔχητε is a progressive present: "you may have" (cf. KJV NASB ESV NET etc.). It indicates the relationship John's readers can have with him *right now* through mutual belief in Jesus (W, 518). The fellowship that John describes is not just social interaction, but joint participation in the life and work of God (Culy, 8). John's concern is this mutual fellowship among believers, a concern he will develop throughout his letter.

1:3d καί: The Greek word καί is a conjunction, and when used with δέ could be translated "and also" or "but also" (BDAG, s.v. "καί" 2iγ, p. 496), though we render καί as 'indeed. **Syntactically,** καί introduces a conjunctive independent clause, "and *indeed* our fellowship is with the Father and His Son, Jesus, who is the Christ" (καὶ ἡ κοινωνία δὲ ἡ ἡμετέρα μετὰ τοῦ πατρὸς καὶ μετὰ τοῦ υἱοῦ αὐτοῦ Ἰησοῦ Χριστοῦ). **Semantically,** καί is emphatic: "indeed" (W, 673). It provides affirmation about the fellowship readers have with the author. The translations "indeed" (NET ESV NASB) or "truly" (KJV NRSV) not only indicates that fellowship exists between the reader and John, but also with both the Father and the Son. Take note that this is a conjunctive independent clause not because of καί but because of the next conjunction δέ.

δέ: The Greek word δέ is a conjunction meaning "and" (BDAG, s.v. "δέ" 5b, p. 213). **Syntactically,** δέ introduces a conjunctive independent clause. It appears in the postpositive position. **Semantically,** δέ is a coordinating connection with an emphatic καί: "*and* indeed" (NASB ESV NET). It provides more information about a person's fellowship with God the Father and Jesus, who is the Messiah.

[ἐστίν]: The Greek ellipsis ἐστίν is third person singular present active indicative from the verb εἰμί meaning "is" or is used "to describe a special connection between the subject and predicate" (BDAG, s.v. "εἰμί" 2b, p. 283). **Syntactically,** the elliptical [ἐστίν] is the main verb of the conjunctive independent clause (cf. KJV NASB ESV NIV NET etc.). The subject of the verb is "fellowship" (ἡ κοινωνία). **Semantically,** [ἐστίν] is an equative present: "is." John underscores the believer's fellowship as an ongoing relationship not just with John and his associates but also with God himself.

Lexical Nugget: What does κοινωνία mean? The term "fellowship" (κοινωνία) often references a concrete relationship such as a marriage (MM, 351; 3 Macc 4:6; Josephus, *A.J.* 304), a desire to reproduce (Philo, *Opif.* 152), or a partnership (MM, 351; Phil. 1:5; 4:15). On the other hand, the term can be used in more abstract ways, such as the relationship between the body and the soul (Philo, *Opif.* 138; cf. *Sacr.* 75), between people and the created order (Philo, *Cher.* 110), between people and other people (Acts 2:42; Philo, *Det.* 164–165; *Post.* 181), and between people and God (Phil. 2:1; 1 Cor. 1:9; 2 Cor. 6:14; Heb. 13:16; *EDNT* 1:303). Here in 1 John 1, "fellowship" (κοινωνία) is a mutual action or relationship between John and his readers, which also involves a mutual relationship with God. Strecker says, "The author of 1 John leaves no doubt of his conviction that the fellowship of believers founded by Christ must result in the undivided unity of the Christian community. In turn, it is a fact that no Christian fellowship is imaginable unless it is founded on participation in the Christ-event to which 1 John witnesses" (Strecker, 20). When believers who share a relationship with God are brought into a relationship with each other, that relationship becomes the basis for mutual love for each other (cf. Westcott, 12; Painter, 137). Therefore fellowship with God and fellowship with other believers are inseparable.

1:4a καί: The Greek word καί is a conjunction, which in this context means "therefore" (BDAG, s.v. "καί" 1bζ, p. 495). **Syntactically,** καί introduces a conjunctive independent clause, "*therefore* we are writing these things" (καὶ ταῦτα γράφομεν ἡμεῖς). John's reference to "we" is an actual "we" (v. 1; see W, 396). **Semantically,** καί is inferential and draws a conclusion from the previous discussion and is translated "therefore" or "thus" (NET). John is drawing a conclusion to his opening statements about his eyewitness pronouncements about Jesus's ministry.

γράφομεν: The Greek word γράφομεν is a first person plural present active indicative from the verb γράφω meaning "to write" or "to compose" as in the composition of a letter (BDAG, s.v. "γράφω" 2d, p. 207). **Syntactically,** γράφομεν is the main verb of the independent conjunctive clause. The assumed subject, "we," refers to John and his other eyewitness associates. The direct object "these *things*" is probably cataphoric and a reference to the entire letter, making this a purpose statement for the work (Culy, 9). **Semantically,** γράφομεν is a progressive present: "we are writing" (NRSV ESV NET NLT). John points out that he, along with others (ἡμεῖς), are currently writing this letter (W, 518). The pronoun ἡμεῖς is emphatic since technically it is not needed because the pronoun is already embedded in the verb (cf. W, 396). John's desire has compelled him ("therefore") to write this letter. His intention for writing his letter is found in the next ἵνα clause.

1:4b ἵνα: The Greek word ἵνα is a conjunction meaning "that" or "in order that" or "to denote a purpose or goal" (BDAG, s.v. "ἵνα" 1aα, p. 475). **Syntactically,** ἵνα introduces a conjunctive dependent clause, "*in order that* our joy may be complete" (ἵνα ἡ χαρὰ ἡμῶν ᾖ πεπληρωμένη). This clause is adverbial and modifies the verb "we write" (γράφομεν). **Semantically,** ἵνα is classified as purpose: "in order that" or "that" (KJV ASV CNT; cf. W, 472). The entire conjunctive ἵνα clause provides John's intention for writing, which is made clear with the next verb and verbal.

ᾖ πεπληρωμένη: The Greek word ᾖ is a third person singular present active subjunctive from the verb εἰμί that serves as an auxiliary verb (BDAG, s.v. "εἰμί" 11a, p. 285). The Greek word πεπληρωμένη is a nominative feminine singular perfect passive participle from the verb πληρόω meaning "to complete" or "to finish" or "to bring to completion that which was already begun" (BDAG, s.v. "πληρόω" 3, p. 828). **Syntactically,** ᾖ πεπληρωμένη is a perfect periphrastic construction functioning as the main verbal idea of the dependent adverbial ἵνα clause. This two-verb construction is "a *round-about* way of saying what could be expressed by a single verb" (W, 647). The subject of the periphrastic construction is "joy" (χαρά). **Semantically,** ᾖ πεπληρωμένη is an intensive perfect: "our joy may be complete" (cf. NRSV ESV NET CNT). The perfect is used to emphasize the results or present state produced by a past action, namely, joy (W, 574). John underscores his current joy as it pertains to his readers' shared communion with God.

1 John 1:5–2:2

Big Greek Idea: John's message about God's perfection (either in morality or in love) serves as the basis that separates self-righteous and self-promoting "Christians" from those whose lifestyle demonstrates that they are friends with God, spiritually self-aware, and supported by Jesus.

Structural Overview: John advances (καί) from an eyewitness accounting and aspiration (vv. 1–4) to an assessment of those who claim to have a relationship with God (1:5–2:2).

John opens with his *message* (ἔστιν αὕτη ἡ ἀγγελία) about God's purity (ἐστίν; v. 5). He then proceeds to *assess character traits* of two types of people. Whereas some people *claim* (ἐὰν εἴπωμεν) to have a relationship with God, other people (ἐὰν δέ) *live* a life that demonstrates they have *a relationship with God and others* (vv. 6–7). Whereas some people *claim* (ἐὰν εἴπωμεν) they do not sin, other people (ἐὰν [ἀλλά]) *confess their sin to God*, which results in God's pardon and purification (vv. 8–9). Whereas some people *claim* (ἐὰν εἴπωμεν) they have never sinned, John's intention (ἵνα) for writing this letter is so that followers of Jesus might not sin. But (καί) in the event that a follower of Jesus does sin (2:1), believers *know that through Jesus, forgiveness* of sin exists for all people (1:10–2:2).

So on the one hand John calls people who live contrary to their religiously correct statements, liars (v. 6c), deceivers (v. 8b), and slanderers (v. 10b). On the other hand, John describes those who strive to exhibit godly character to be people who have a relationship with God and other believers (v. 7c), who are forgiven (v. 9c, d), and whom Jesus supports before God (2:1d).

Outline:

> God's Perfection (v. 5)
> The Character Traits of People Are Diverse (1:6–2:2)
>> Behavioral traits expose a person's integrity and friendship with others (vv. 6–7)
>> Traits of spiritual self-awareness reveals a person's truthfulness (vv. 8–9)
>> Traits of self-righteousness depict a person's contempt for God and a misunderstanding of God's desire for an ongoing relationship with people through Jesus (1:10–2:2)

CLAUSAL OUTLINE FOR 1 JOHN 1:5–2:2

^{1:5a} <u>Καὶ</u> **ἔστιν** αὕτη ἡ ἀγγελία
^{1:5a} <u>Now</u> this **is** the gospel message

      |
     ^{1:5b} **ἣν ἀκηκόαμεν** ἀπ᾽ αὐτοῦ
     ^{1:5b} **which** <u>**we have heard**</u> from him (= Jesus)

      |
     ^{1:5c} <u>καὶ</u> [*ἣν*] **ἀναγγέλλομεν** ὑμῖν,
     ^{1:5c} <u>and</u> [*which*] **<u>we</u>** *now* **proclaim** to you

    |
   ^{1:5d} **ὅτι** ὁ θεὸς φῶς **ἔστιν**
   ^{1:5d} *namely* **that** God **is** light

    |
   ^{1:5e} <u>καὶ</u> [*ὅτι*] σκοτία ἐν αὐτῷ οὐκ **ἔστιν** οὐδεμία.
   ^{1:5e} <u>and</u> [*that*] in him there **is** no darkness at all.

   ^{1:6a} **Ἐὰν εἴπωμεν** (ὅτι κοινωνίαν <u>ἔχομεν</u> μετ᾽ αὐτοῦ)
   ^{1:6a} **If <u>we say</u>**, ("<u>We have</u> fellowship with him" [= God])

   |
   ^{1:6b} <u>καὶ</u> [*ἐὰν*] ἐν τῷ σκότει **περιπατῶμεν**,
   ^{1:6b} <u>yet</u> [*if*] **<u>we</u>** *persist on* **living** in the darkness,

  |
^{1:6c} **ψευδόμεθα**
^{1:6c} **<u>we lie</u>**

^{1:6d} <u>καὶ</u> οὐ **ποιοῦμεν** τὴν ἀλήθειαν·
^{1:6d} <u>and</u> **<u>we are</u>** not **practicing** the truth;

    ^{1:7a} **ἐὰν** δὲ ἐν τῷ φωτὶ **περιπατῶμεν**
    ^{1:7a} <u>but</u> **if <u>we</u>** *make it a point to* **live** in the light

      |
      ^{1:7b} **ὡς** αὐτός **ἔστιν** ἐν τῷ φωτί,
      ^{1:7b} **as** he (= God) **is** in the light,

  |
^{1:7c} κοινωνίαν **ἔχομεν** μετ᾽ ἀλλήλων
^{1:7c} **<u>we have</u>** fellowship with one another

^{1:7d} <u>καὶ</u> τὸ αἷμα Ἰησοῦ τοῦ υἱοῦ αὐτοῦ **καθαρίζει** ἡμᾶς ἀπὸ πάσης ἁμαρτίας.
^{1:7d} <u>and</u> the blood of Jesus, his Son, **<u>cleanses</u>** us from all sins.

^{1:8a} **ἐὰν εἴπωμεν** (ὅτι ἁμαρτίαν οὐκ <u>ἔχομεν</u>),
^{1:8a} **if** <u>we say</u>, ("<u>We have</u> no sin"),

       |

^{1:8b} ἑαυτοὺς **πλανῶμεν**
^{1:8b} **we deceive** ourselves

^{1:8c} <u>καὶ</u> ἡ ἀλήθεια οὐκ **ἔστιν** ἐν ἡμῖν.
^{1:8c} <u>and</u> the truth **is** not in us.

^{1:9a} **ἐὰν** [ἀλλὰ] **ὁμολογῶμεν** τὰς ἁμαρτίας ἡμῶν,
^{1:9a} [*But*] **if** <u>we confess</u> our sins,

       |

^{1:9b} πιστός **ἐστιν** καὶ δίκαιος
^{1:9b} **he (=God) is** faithful and righteous

       |

^{1:9c} **ἵνα ἀφῇ** ἡμῖν τὰς ἁμαρτίας
^{1:9c} **to pardon** our sins

       |

^{1:9d} <u>καὶ</u> [*ἵνα*] **καθαρίσῃ** ἡμᾶς ἀπὸ πάσης ἀδικίας.
^{1:9d} <u>and</u> **to declare** us **purified** from all unrighteousness.

^{1:10a} **ἐὰν εἴπωμεν** (ὅτι οὐχ <u>ἡμαρτήκαμεν</u>),
^{1:10a} **If** <u>we say</u> ("<u>We have</u> not <u>sinned</u>,")

       |

^{1:10b} ψεύστην **ποιοῦμεν** αὐτὸν
^{1:10b} **we make** him (= God) a liar

^{1:10c} <u>καὶ</u> ὁ λόγος αὐτοῦ οὐκ **ἔστιν** ἐν ἡμῖν.
^{1:10c} <u>and</u> his (= God's) word **is** not in us.

^{2:1a} Τεκνία μου, ταῦτα **γράφω** ὑμῖν
^{2:1a} My children, **I** *now* **write** these *things* to you

       |

^{2:1b} **ἵνα** μὴ **ἁμάρτητε**.
^{2:1b} **in order that you may** not **sin**.

^{2:1c} <u>καὶ</u> **ἐάν** τις **ἁμάρτῃ**,
^{2:1c} <u>But</u> **if** anyone **does sin**,

       |

^{2:1d} παράκλητον **ἔχομεν** πρὸς τὸν πατέρα, Ἰησοῦν Χριστὸν δίκαιον·
^{2:1d} **we have** an advocate with the Father, Jesus who is the Christ, the righteous one;

2:2a <u>καὶ</u> αὐτὸς ἱλασμός **ἐστιν** περὶ τῶν ἁμαρτιῶν ἡμῶν,
2:2a <u>and</u> he himself **is** the atoning sacrifice for our sins,

2:2b [αὐτὸς ἱλασμός <u>ἐστιν</u>] οὐ περὶ τῶν ἡμετέρων <u>δὲ</u> μόνον
2:2b <u>and</u> [he <u>is</u> the atoning sacrifice] not only for our sins,

2:2c <u>ἀλλὰ</u> <u>καὶ</u> [αὐτὸς ἱλασμός <u>ἐστιν</u>] περὶ ὅλου τοῦ κόσμου.
2:2c <u>But also</u> [he <u>is</u> the atoning sacrifice] for the whole world.

Syntax Explained for 1 John 1:5–2:2

1:5a Καί: The Greek word καί is a conjunction that may mean "and" (BDAG, s.v. "καί" 1bη, p. 495) or "now" (BDAG, s.v. "καί" 1e, p. 495). **Syntactically,** καί introduces an independent conjunctive clause: "*now* this is the message" (καὶ ἔστιν αὕτη ἡ ἀγγελία). **Semantically,** καί may be a connective of sentences and rendered "and" (e.g., kjv nasb esv niv etc.). Or καί may introduce something new and thereby it is transitional. In this case, καί is rendered "now" (net). Thus καί serves to show a slight shift in topic. John is now moving on to discuss the content of the gospel message.

ἐστίν: The Greek word ἐστίν is third person singular present active indicative from the verb εἰμί that means "is" or "to be in close connection with" (BDAG, s.v. "εἰμί" 2a, p. 283). **Syntactically,** ἐστίν is the main verb of the conjunctive independent clause. The subject of the verb is the demonstrative pronoun "this one" (αὕτη), due to the grammatical priority of pronouns (W, 42–43). **Semantically,** ἐστίν is an equative verb of identity. See the following "Syntactical Nugget."

Syntactical Nugget: How is John using the construction "is" (ἐστίν) with "this" (αὕτη)? In this instance, the demonstrative pronoun "this" (αὕτη) is cataphoric and points forward to an epexegetical ὅτι clause "that God is light." It is almost as if John is using these type of constructions to highlight his main points (Brown, 192). If that is true, then John wants his readers to know that they can have fellowship with the Father, the Son, and the followers of Jesus, but only if they walk in the light as God is in the light (Culy, 11).

1:5b ἦν: The Greek word ἦν is a feminine singular accusative from the relative pronoun ὅς meaning "which" or "that" (BDAG, s.v. "ὅς" 1a, p. 725). **Syntactically,** ἦν introduces a dependent adjectival compound relative clause, "*which* we have heard from him and [*which*] now we proclaim to you" (ἦν ἀκηκόαμεν ἀπ᾽ αὐτοῦ καὶ [ἦν] ἀναγγέλλομεν ὑμῖν). The entire relative clause modifies "the message" (ἡ ἀγγελία). **Semantically,** the relative clause is epexegetical: "which" (kjv asv). The entire clause provides the content of the message, which is clarified in the next verb.

ἀκηκόαμεν: The Greek word ἀκηκόαμεν is a first person plural perfect active indicative from the verb ἀκούω meaning "to hear" or "to hear something from someone" (BDAG, s.v. "ἀκούω" 1a, 1b, p. 37) or denote a body of authoritative teaching (BDAG, s.v. "ἀκούω" 3d, p. 38). **Syntactically,** ἀκηκόαμεν is one of the governing verbs of the compound relative clause. The subject of the verb is an implied "we" and refers back to John and his other eyewitness associates. **Semantically,** ἀκηκόαμεν is a extensive perfect: "we *have* heard" (KJV ASV NASB NRSV ESV NIV NET CNT). It focuses attention on a past action from which a present state emerges (W, 577; Culy, 10). What the eyewitnesses had heard from Jesus himself, John *now* proclaims to others (cf. NLT).

1:5c καὶ [ἦν]: The Greek word καί is a conjunction meaning "and" (BDAG, s.v. "καί" 1, p. 494). Syntactically, καί introduces a conjunctive independent clause (cf. KJV ASV etc.). Semantically, καί is a coordinating connective: "and" (cf. KJV NASB ESV NIV NET etc.). It adds an additional thought to the relative clause [ἦν] about what John has heard with what he now proclaims (W, 671) evident in the next verb.

ἀναγγέλλομεν: The Greek word ἀναγγέλλομεν is a first person plural present active indicative from the verb ἀναγγέλλω meaning "to proclaim" or "to announce" or "to provide information" (BDAG, s.v. "ἀναγγέλλω" 2, p. 59). **Syntactically,** ἀναγγέλλομεν is the second governing verb of the relative clause. The assumed subject, "we," refers back to John and his associates. **Semantically,** ἀναγγέλλομεν is a progressive present: "we *now* proclaim" or "we proclaim" (NRSV ESV). It describes that *right now* they are announcing this gospel message to the readers (W, 518).

1:5d ὅτι: The Greek word ὅτι is a conjunction meaning "that" (BDAG, s.v. "ὅτι" 2a, p. 732). **Syntactically,** ὅτι introduces a dependent compound conjunctive clause, "*that* God is light and in him there is no darkness at all" (ὅτι ὁ θεὸς φῶς ἐστιν καὶ σκοτία ἐν αὐτῷ οὐκ ἔστιν οὐδεμία). **Syntactically,** this ὅτι clause could be functioning in a number of different ways. It could be functioning adverbially giving us the reason for the announcement. We announce what we have seen and heard "*because* God is light." It could also be taken substantivally as the direct of object of the verb giving us the content of the announcement: "God is light'" (NET cf. NIV NLT). Finally, the clause could be functioning substantivally as an epexegetical ὅτι. It completes the idea of the demonstrative pronoun "this" (αὕτη; contra W, 459). The ὅτι + indicative provides the content of the message: "*namely,* that God is light" or "that" (KJV ASV NASB NRSV ESV CNT). This is consistent with how John uses ὅτι with the demonstrative pronoun throughout the letter. **Semantically,** ὅτι is epexegetical: "that." The specifics of this ὅτι clause are clarified with the verb.

ἐστίν: The Greek word ἐστίν is third person singular present active indicative from the verb εἰμί meaning "is" or "to be in close connection with" (BDAG, s.v. "εἰμί" 2a, 283). **Syntactically,** ἐστίν is one of the governing verbs of the conjunctive dependent epexegetical ὅτι clause. The subject of the verb is "God" (ὁ θεός). **Semantically,** ἐστίν is a gnomic present: "is (cf. kjv nasb esv niv net etc.)." It identifies a timeless fact about God. The εἰμί verb equates God with his abiding character. God is light. Thus, the content of the message is this: "God is light," or God is ethically pure as symbolized by light.

> **Lexical Nugget**: What does φῶς mean? In the LXX where the term "light" (φῶς) appears in the phrase "light of your face," "light" (φῶς) seems to be idiomatic of God smiling on or blessing his people (Pss. 4:6; 88[ET 89]:15). It is also used to speak of God's deliverance (Pss. 36[ET 37]:6; 96[ET 97]:11). Finally, it speaks of God's moral standards (Ps. 118[ET 119]:105; Isa. 2:5, 5:20; Sir 32:16). Here in 1 John 1:5, John provides no clue to what the metaphor means. Yet, two options exist. On the one hand, "light" may speak of truth or righteousness, and "darkness" of error or evil (Smalley, 19–20; Culy, 12). So perhaps, in 1 John 1:6–2:2 John addresses the ethical implications of God as light. On the other hand, "light" may parallel 4:8 and v. 16 where "God is love." First John 2:9–11 also equates light as love of fellow Christians and darkness as hatred. Thus, perhaps God's description as light in 1:5 is more of a metaphor for speaking of God's love (1 John 4:8, 16, cf. 2:9–11), and thereby serves as the basis to love others: "Love one another as I have loved you" (John 13:34). Within the Qumran community, the intention for living righteously was so that love might be extended to others (see 1Q28 I, 1–19; 5:25). So perhaps God's standard of conduct (i.e., light) emphasized in 1 John, which is based upon truth and righteousness, is that of love, and thereby the standard for believers: "Love one another" (3:11; John 15:12, 17).

1:5e καὶ [ὅτι]: The Greek word καί is a conjunction meaning "and" (BDAG, s.v. "καί" 1, p. 494). Syntactically, καί introduces a conjunctive independent clause (cf. kjv asv etc.). Semantically, καί is a coordinating connective: "and" (kjv nasb nrsv esv net nlt). It adds an additional thought to the [ὅτι] clause that completes the idea of the demonstrative pronoun "this" (αὕτη) evident in the next verb.

ἐστίν: The Greek word ἐστίν is third person singular present active indicative from the verb εἰμί meaning "is" or "to be in close connection with or with an equative function" (BDAG, s.v. "εἰμί" 2a, p. 283). **Syntactically,** ἐστίν is one of the governing verbs of the conjunctive dependent substantival clause functioning in apposition. The subject of the verb is "God" (ὁ θεός). **Semantically,** ἐστίν is a gnomic present presenting a timeless fact about God. There is no ethical impurity or darkness in God's nature.

1:6a Ἐάν: The Greek word ἐάν is a conjunction meaning "if" (BDAG, s.v. "ἐάν" 1ab, p. 267). **Syntactically,** ἐάν introduces a dependent conjunctive clause. The entire clause functions adverbially: "*if* we say, 'we have fellowship with him,' yet persist on living in darkness" (Ἐὰν εἴπωμεν ὅτι κοινωνίαν ἔχομεν μετ᾽ αὐτοῦ καὶ ἐν τῷ σκότει περιπατῶμεν), It modifies two verbs, "we are lying" (ψευδόμεθα) and "we are not practicing" (οὐ ποιοῦμεν). **Semantically,** ἐάν introduces a third class conditional clause: "if" (cf. KJV NASB ESV NIV NET etc.). It offers a hypothetical situation of probability (W, 696). The activity of ἐάν is expressed in the verb.

εἴπωμεν: The Greek word εἴπωμεν is a second person plural aorist active subjunctive from the verb λέγω meaning "to speak" or "to say" or "to express oneself orally" (BDAG, s.v. "λέγω" 1, p. 588). The verb is in the subjunctive mood because it follows ἐάν. **Syntactically,** εἴπωμεν is one of the governing verbs of the dependent ἐάν clause. The assumed subject, "we," refers to a hypothetical group of people who claim to have a relationship with a pure God, yet continue in impurity. **Semantically,** εἴπωμεν is a constative aorist: "we say." With one exception (NIV), most translations render εἴπωμεν as "we say" (e.g., KJV NASB ESV NET etc.). It views the action as a whole (W, 557). John speaks of a hypothetical situation whereby a person makes a claim. The specifics of that claim are evident in the ὅτι clause.

ὅτι: The Greek word ὅτι is a conjunction meaning "that" or "for" or as a marker of direct discourse and left untranslated (BDAG, s.v. "ὅτι" 3, p. 732). **Syntactically,** ὅτι introduces a dependent conjunctive clause: "*that* we have fellowship with him" (ὅτι κοινωνίαν ἔχομεν μετ᾽ αὐτοῦ). The clause functions substantivally as the direct object of the verb "we say" (εἴπωμεν). The entire clause is placed in parentheses in order to visualize its contribution to the independent clause. **Semantically,** ὅτι is direct discourse and it is not translated (ESV NET NIV CNT NLT), but rather quotation marks are employed to underscore the claim (W, 454). That claim is made clear in the rest of the clause.

ἔχομεν: The Greek word ἔχομεν is a first person plural present active indicative from the verb ἔχω meaning "I have" or "to stand in a close relationship to someone" (BDAG, s.v. "ἔχω" 2b, p. 420). **Syntactically,** ἔχομεν is the governing verb of the dependent substantival ὅτι clause. The assumed subject, "we," hypothetically refers to any Christian who claims to have a relationship with God yet lives in impurity. **Semantically,** ἔχομεν is a gnomic present: "we have" (cf. KJV NASB ESV NIV NET etc.). It underscores a generic statement that is true at all times (W, 523). John speaks of any person who claims to have fellowship (= a relationship) with God.

Grammatical Nugget: Why the chapter interruption in 2:2? John makes several hypothetical "If we claim…" statements (1:6, 8, 10) followed by the three correcting conditional statements introduced by "but if…" (1:7, 9; 2:1). Each are mitigated commands politely urging believers to change their behavior (Culy, 14, 16, 18). Why a new chapter division interrupts these claims is unknown. The New Testament text was initially divided into numbered verses by Stephanus and published in his fourth edition of the New Testament (1551). Folklore has it that Stephanus marked the verse division while journeying on horseback, and that some of the divisions deemed unwelcome by present-day scholars arose from the jogging of the horseback that bumped his pen into the wrong places. Although his son confirms that his father did indeed work on the text while on a journey from Paris to Lyons, in all probability the task was accomplished while resting at the inns along the road. (Metzger[2], 104). Regardless of the verse and chapter division, 1 John 1:5–2:2 is generally recognized as a single unit of thought. Thus, there is stylistic cohesiveness to 1 John 1:5–2:2 (see Brown, 230–42; Painter, 141–42; cf. Culy, 21).

1:6b καί [ἐάν]: The Greek word καί is a conjunction meaning "yet" (BDAG, s.v. "καί" 1bε, p. 494). **Syntactically,** καί introduces a conjunctive dependent clause. **Semantically,** καί is contrastive: "yet" (NASB NIV NET; cf. NLT). It reveals that the hypothetical claims contradict reality. That reality is evident in the rest of the clause.

περιπατῶμεν: The Greek word περιπατῶμεν is a first person plural present active subjunctive from the verb περιπατέω meaning "to go about" or "to walk around" or "to go here and there in walking" (BDAG, s.v. "περιπατέω" 1d, p. 803). This verb is in the subjunctive mood because it follows an ἐάν. **Syntactically,** περιπατῶμεν is one of the governing verbs of the dependent ἐάν clause. The assumed subject, "we," refers to a hypothetical group of people who claim to have a relationship with a pure God, yet continue in impurity. **Semantically,** περιπατῶμεν is a customary present: "we *persist on* living" (cf. NLT). It emphasizes the hypothetical pattern of behavior (W, 521). The pattern of behavior contradicts the claim to have a relationship with an ethical God. Their lifestyle is not in keeping with their claim.

1:6c ψευδόμεθα: The Greek word ψευδόμεθα is a first person plural present middle indicative from the verb ψεύδομαι meaning "to lie" or "to tell a falsehood" (BDAG, s.v. "ψεύδομαι" 1, pp. 1095–96). This middle verb is probably an example of the true or classical middle where the subject both does and receives the action of the verb (W, 419). **Syntactically,** ψευδόμεθα is the main verb of the independent clause. The assumed subject, "we," refers to the hypothetical person who claims to have a relationship God: "we lie" (ψευδόμεθα) or express a falsehood. **Semantically,** ψευδόμεθα is a gnomic present: "we lie" (cf. KJV NASB ESV NIV NET etc.). It underscores a generic statement that is true at all times (W, 523). John makes it clear that any person who says they have "fellowship" (= relationship) with God and yet lives in "darkness" (= morally impure lives) lies.

^{1:6d} καί: The Greek word καί is a conjunction meaning "and" (BDAG, s.v. "καί" 1b, p. 494). **Syntactically,** καί introduces a conjunctive independent clause. **Semantically,** some translations render καί as contrastive ("but" NET NLT; "yet" NIV), but it seems better to recognize the coordinating function of καί ("and" KJV ASV NASB CNT; cf. Culy, 15).

ποιοῦμεν: The Greek word ποιοῦμεν is a first person plural present active indicative from the verb ποιέω meaning "to do" or "to practice" or "to carry out an obligation of a moral or social nature" (BDAG, s.v. "ποιέω" 3b, p. 840). **Syntactically,** ποιοῦμεν is the main verb of the independent conjunctive clause, "and *we are* not *practicing* the truth" (καὶ οὐ ποιοῦμεν τὴν ἀλήθειαν). The assumed subject, "we," refers to the hypothetical Christian who claims to have a relationship with God. **Semantically,** ποιοῦμεν negated with οὐ is a gnomic present: "we are not practicing" (e.g., NASB ESV NET CNT). It underscores a generic statement that is true at all times (W, 523). John makes it clear that any person who says they have fellowship (= relationship) with God and yet lives in darkness (= morally impure lives) not only lies, but they are also active enemies of the truth (cf. 2:4, 22; 4:1, 20; Brown, 199).

^{1:7a} ἐάν: The Greek word ἐάν is a conjunction meaning "if" (BDAG, s.v. "ἐάν" 1aα, p. 267). **Syntactically,** ἐάν introduces a dependent conjunctive clause. The entire dependent clause, "*if* we live in the light" (ἐὰν . . . ἐν τῷ φωτὶ περιπατῶμεν), functions adverbially. It modifies the verb, "have" (ἔχομεν). **Semantically,** ἐάν introduces a third class conditional clause: "if" (cf. KJV NASB ESV NIV NET etc.). It offers a hypothetical situation of probability (W, 696). The activity of ἐάν is expressed in the verb.

δέ: The Greek word δέ is a conjunction meaning "but" or "rather" (BDAG, s.v. "δέ" 4a, p. 213). **Syntactically,** δέ is in the postpositive position and introduces the dependent adverbial conditional clause. **Semantically,** δέ is contrastive and introduces a second hypothetical situation or mitigated command (Culy, 16) that is expressed in the next verb.

περιπατῶμεν: The Greek word περιπατῶμεν is a first person plural present active subjunctive from the verb περιπατέω meaning "to walk" or "to live" or "to conduct one's life" (BDAG, s.v. "περιπατέω" 2a, p. 803). The verb is in the subjunctive mood, because it follows ἐάν. **Syntactically,** περιπατῶμεν is the governing verb of the dependent conjunctive ἐάν clause. The assumed subject, "we," refers to the hypothetical person who habitually lives a lifestyle of purity. **Semantically,** περιπατῶμεν is a gnomic present: "we live" (cf. NLT) or "we walk" (KJV ASV NASB NRSV ESV NIV NET CNT). It underscores a generic statement that is true at all times (W, 523). John speaks of any person who lives in "the light" (= a moral life or a life of loving others).

$^{1:7b}$ ὡς: The Greek word ὡς is a conjunction meaning "as" (BDAG, s.v. "ὡς" 3a, p. 1104). **Syntactically,** ὡς identifies the clause as a dependent conjunctive clause: "*as* he is in the light" (ὡς αὐτός ἐστιν ἐν τῷ φωτί; KJV ASV etc.). The entire ὡς clause functions adverbially modifying the verb "we walk" (περιπατῶμεν). **Semantically,** ὡς is a comparative marker for the believer whose character is to evidence moral purity, which is in keeping with God's moral character (cf. 1:5).

ἐστίν: The Greek word ἐστίν is third person singular present active indicative from the verb εἰμί meaning "is" or with reference to a condition or circumstance (BDAG, s.v. "εἰμί" 3c, p. 284). **Syntactically,** ἐστίν is the main verb of the dependent adverbial clause. The subject of the verb is the emphatic personal pronoun "he" (αὐτός). **Semantically,** ἐστίν is an equative verb of identity: "is" (cf. KJV NASB ESV NIV NET etc.). The statement parallels the earlier claim that "God is light," referring to his ethical purity and love for others (Culy, 16).

$^{1:7c}$ ἔχομεν: The Greek word ἔχομεν is a first person plural present active indicative from the verb ἔχω meaning "to have" or "to stand in a close relationship with someone" (BDAG, s.v. "ἔχω" 2b, p. 420). **Syntactically,** ἔχομεν serves as the main verb of the independent clause "*we have* fellowship with one another" (κοινωνίαν ἔχομεν μετ᾽ ἀλλήλων). The assumed subject, "we," refers to the hypothetical person who walks in moral purity. **Semantically,** ἔχομεν is a gnomic present: "we have" (cf. KJV NASB ESV NIV NET etc.). It underscores a generic statement that is true at all times (W, 523). John is saying that any believer who makes it a point to live a moral life has fellowship with other believers.

Theological Nugget: What does the inability to fellowship with other believers communicate? Based upon verse 6, it might be expected that John would say, "If we walk in the light . . . we have fellowship with God." But John says, "We have fellowship with one another." It seems a group of people are boasting of fellowship with God yet unwilling to fellowship with other Christians. Perhaps they have misunderstood God, Jesus, and the life of the believer (Painter, 144–45). Regardless, John teaches that a person cannot have fellowship with God and ignore fellowship with other Christians. *Fellowship with God and the love ethic are inseparable.* If we live in the light or the love of God, we must learn to fellowship with each other.

$^{1:7d}$ καί: The Greek word καί is a conjunction meaning "and" (BDAG, s.v. "καί" 1, p. 494). **Syntactically,** καί introduces a conjunctive independent clause (cf. KJV ASV etc.). **Semantically,** καί is a coordinating connective: "and" (cf. KJV NASB ESV NIV NET etc.). It adds additional thoughts about fellowship with other believers (W, 671) evident in the next verb.

καθαρίζει: The Greek word καθαρίζει is a third person singular present active indicative from the verb καθαρίζω meaning "to make clean" or "to *declare clean*" or "to purify through ritual cleansing" (BDAG, s.v. "καθαρίζω" 3bα, pp. 488–89). **Syntactically,** καθαρίζει is the governing verb of the independent καί clause: "and the blood of Jesus, his Son, *cleanses* us from all sins" (καὶ τὸ αἷμα Ἰησοῦ τοῦ υἱοῦ αὐτοῦ καθαρίζει ἡμᾶς ἀπὸ πάσης ἁμαρτίας). The subject is "the blood" (τὸ αἷμα). **Semantically,** καθαρίζει is a gnomic present: "cleanses us" (KJV ASV NASB NRSV ESV NET NLT CNT). It underscores a generic statement that is true at all times (W, 523). John makes it clear that any believer who makes it a point to live a moral life is purified from sin.

Syntactical Nugget: What does καθαρίζω mean? Elsewhere in the New Testament, καθαρίζω is used to describe the cleaning of a cup or dish (Matt. 23:25) or as a way to speak of a person having been cured of a disease (Matt. 8:2–3; cf. Philo, *Sobr.* 49). Here the idea of cleansing draws from the sacrificial practices of Israel, yet the emphasis is on the blood sacrifice of Jesus (cf. water and blood in 1 John 5:6 and John 19:34). Although the term is found only here and 1 John 1:9 in all of John's writings, its usage is similar to that of Hebrews 9:22, which uses the same verb to summarize the law as requiring the shedding of blood for all types of forgiveness. In contrast to the Old Testament, the one-time sacrifice of Jesus satisfies God's requirement for blood sacrifice and thus serves as a continual expiation of the believer's sins.

Theological Nugget: Is forgiveness of our sins dependent on our ethical behavior? Since "the blood of Jesus, his Son, cleanses us from all sins" is the apodosis of this third class conditional clause (if we make it a point to live in the light), does that mean that forgiveness of our sins is dependent on our ethical behavior? This idea seems to be in opposition to Paul's emphasis that justification is not a result of works. John is not worried as much about initial justification as he is about forgiveness of sins committed as a Christian. He is teaching us that when (ἐὰν δέ) a believer sins, the blood of Jesus covers those sins just as much as the ones they committed before their initial justification (Brown, 202).

1:8a ἐάν: The Greek word ἐάν is a conjunction meaning "if" (BDAG, s.v. "ἐάν" 1a, 1b, p. 267). **Syntactically,** ἐάν introduces a dependent conjunctive clause. The entire dependent clause "*if* we say, 'we have no sin'" (ἐὰν εἴπωμεν ὅτι ἁμαρτίαν οὐκ ἔχομεν) functions adverbially. It modifies two verbs, "deceive" (πλανῶμεν) and "is not" (οὐκ ἔστιν). **Semantically,** ἐάν introduces a third class conditional clause: "if" (cf. KJV NASB ESV NIV NET etc.). It offers a hypothetical situation of probability (W, 696). The activity of ἐάν is expressed in the next verb.

εἴπωμεν: The Greek word εἴπωμεν is a first person plural aorist active subjunctive from the verb λέγω meaning "to speak" or "to say" (BDAG, s.v.

"λέγω" 1, p. 588). The verb is in the subjunctive mood, because it follows ἐάν. **Syntactically,** εἴπωμεν is the main verb of the adverbial dependent clause. The assumed subject, "we," refers to a hypothetical person who claims to have no sin in their life. **Semantically,** εἴπωμεν is a constative aorist: "we say" (KJV ASV NASB NRSV ESV NET CNT with two exceptions NIV NLT). It describes an event as a whole (W, 557). John speaks of a hypothetical situation whereby a person makes a claim. The specifics of that claim are evident in the ὅτι clause.

ὅτι: The Greek word ὅτι is a conjunction meaning "that" or "for" or as a direct discourse marker left untranslated (BDAG, s.v. "ὅτι" 3, p. 732). **Syntactical-ly,** ὅτι introduces a dependent conjunctive clause: *that* we have no sin" (ὅτι ἁμαρτίαν οὐκ ἔχομεν). This clause functions substantivally as the direct object of the verb "say" (εἴπωμεν). The clause is placed in parenthesis in order to visualize its contribution to the independent clause. **Semantically,** ὅτι is the direct discourse marker whereby it is not translated (ESV NET NIV CNT NLT), but rather quotation marks are used to underscore the claim (W, 454). It highlights the hypothetical person's statement, which is made clear in the rest of the clause.

ἔχομεν: The Greek word ἔχομεν is a first person plural present active in-dicative from the verb ἔχω meaning "to have" or "to have an opinion about something" (BDAG, s.v. "ἔχω" 6, p. 421). **Syntactically,** ἔχομεν is the govern-ing verb of the dependent conjunctive ὅτι clause. The assumed subject, "we," refers to the hypothetical believer who claims to have no sin. **Semantically,** ἔχομεν is a gnomic present: "we have" (cf. KJV NASB ESV NIV NET etc.). It un-derscores a generic statement that is true at all times (W, 523). John speaks of any person who boasts: "I don't sin." What John thinks about such a person is clarified with the next verb.

1:8b πλανῶμεν: The Greek word πλανῶμεν is a first person plural present ac-tive indicative from the verb πλανάω meaning "to deceive" or "to lie" or "to stray from a specific way" (BDAG, s.v. "πλανάω" 1b, p. 821). **Syntactically,** πλανῶμεν is the governing verb of the independent clause. The assumed sub-ject, "we," refers to the hypothetical believer who claims to have no sin. **Se-mantically,** πλανῶμεν is a gnomic present: "we deceive" (KJV ASV NRSV ESV NIV CNT). It underscores a generic statement that is true at all times (W, 523). John makes it clear that any person who claims to be without sin is deceived.

Theological Nugget: Is the statement "we have no sin" a claim to have no sin (perfectionism) or a claim to not be guilty of sin (libertinism)? A survey of the epistle shows that the people with whom John was dealing were not perfectionistic. They were not claiming to have not sinned, but that their sin was not great enough to break off their intimacy with God. John sees this as a dangerous idea and actually a lie (Brown, 206).

^{1:8c}καί: The Greek word καί is a conjunction meaning "and" (BDAG, s.v. "καί" 1b, p. 494). **Syntactically,** καί introduces a conjunctive independent clause, "*and* the truth is not in us" (καὶ ἡ ἀλήθεια οὐκ ἔστιν ἐν ἡμῖν). **Semantically,** καί is connective (cf. KJV ASV etc.) and shows that the believer who claims to not have any sin is a liar and does not speak the truth. They have no connection with truth.

ἐστίν: The Greek word ἐστίν is third person singular present active indicative from the verb εἰμί meaning "is" or to have a special connection with someone or something (BDAG, s.v. "εἰμί" 2b, p. 283). **Syntactically,** ἐστίν is the main verb of the independent clause. The subject of the verb is "the truth" (ἡ ἀλήθεια). **Semantically,** ἐστιν is a gnomic present: "is" (cf. KJV NASB ESV NIV NET etc). It underscores a generic statement that is true at all times (W, 523). Anyone who claims to be without sin does not know the truth about themselves.

^{1:9a}ἐάν: The Greek word ἐάν is a conjunction meaning "if" (BDAG, s.v. "ἐάν" 1aα, p. 267). **Syntactically,** ἐάν introduces a dependent conjunctive clause. The entire dependent clause, "*if* we confess our sins" (ἐὰν ὁμολογῶμεν τὰς ἁμαρτίας ἡμῶν), functions adverbially. It modifies the verb "is" (ἐστίν). **Semantically,** ἐάν introduces a third class conditional clause: "if" (cf. KJV NASB ESV NIV NET etc.). It provides a fourth hypothetical situation (W, 698). The activity of ἐάν is expressed in the next verb.

[ἀλλά]: The Greek word ἀλλά is a conjunction that means "but" (BDAG, s.v. "ἀλλά" 2, p. 45). **Syntactically,** [ἀλλά] is elliptical and serves to introduce a conditional thought, "[*but*] if we confess our sins, he is faithful and righteous to pardon our sins and to *declare* us purified from all unrighteousness" (ἐὰν ὁμολογῶμεν τὰς ἁμαρτίας ἡμῶν πιστός ἐστιν καὶ δίκαιος ἵνα ἀφῇ ἡμῖν τὰς ἁμαρτίας καὶ καθαρίσῃ ἡμᾶς ἀπὸ πάσης ἀδικίας.). **Semantically,** [ἀλλά] is contrastive: "but" (NET NLT). It provides a counter claim to the opponents who were claiming that they had not sinned (W, 671). It contrasts a person who claims to be without sin with one who does not.

Grammatical Nugget: Why is there an elliptical ἀλλά? This elliptical ἀλλά is an example of a figure of speech called an anacoluthon, that is, the omission of a word. The conjunction is omitted, but a clear contrast is evident from the context (cf. NET NLT). Confession, not denial of sin, is a hallmark of the genuine believer's heart. This focus on wrestling with sin and repentance is a theme that often appears in Second Temple literature (Dan. 9:20; Prayer of Manasseh; Community Confessions: Prayer of Azariah; Mark 1:5; James 5:16).

ὁμολογῶμεν: The Greek word ὁμολογῶμεν is a first person plural present active subjunctive from the verb ὁμολογέω meaning "I confess" or "I admit" with a focus on an admission of wrongdoing (BDAG, s.v. "ὁμολογέω" 3c, p.

708). The verb is in the subjunctive mood because it follows ἐάν. **Syntactical-ly,** ὁμολογῶμεν is the governing verb of the adverbial dependent ἐάν clause. The assumed subject, "we," refers to any believer who chooses to confess their sin. **Semantically,** ὁμολογῶμεν is a gnomic present: "we confess" (KJV NASB ESV NIV NET etc.). It underscores a generic statement that is true at all times (W, 523). It seems to be focusing on verbally conceding that a sin has taken place (Culy, 18). John underscores a timeless truth about the person who confesses their sin evident in the next clause.

1:9b ἐστίν: The Greek word ἐστίν is third person singular present active indicative from the verb εἰμί meaning "is" or "to be in close connection with" (BDAG, s.v. "εἰμί" 2a, p. 283). **Syntactically,** ἐστίν is the governing verb of the independent clause: "He *is* faithful and righteous," (πιστός ἐστιν καὶ δίκαιος). The subject of the verb is an implied "he" referring to God who has the prerogative to forgive sins. **Semantically,** ἐστίν is a gnomic present: "is" (cf. KJV NASB ESV NIV NET etc.). It underscores a generic statement that is true at all times (W, 523). God, by his very nature, is faithful and righteous. Yet that timeless truth about God impacts the person who confesses their sin, which is clearly stated in the next ἵνα clause.

> **Lexical and Theological Nugget:** What does πιστός and δίκαιος mean? Whereas "faithful" (πιστός) tends to point to God as one who is credible and thereby can be depended upon, "righteous" (δίκαιος) tends to pertain to one who maintains high standards and thereby judges accordingly. It is assumed here in verse 9 that God is faithful, dependable, and credible (cf. Heb. 10:23; 1 Cor. 1:9; 10:13; 1 Peter 4:19). Thus the presentation of God as one who is credible becomes a prompting for faith or trust (cf. *EDNT* 3:97). In a similar manner, the Greco-Roman society assumed the deities were "just" and "righteous" (see BDAG, s.v. "δίκαιος" 1b, p. 246). So too was it assumed about God (John 17:25, 1 John 2:29, Rev. 16:5). Second Temple literature uses δίκαιος with reference to God's judgment of people and nations (2 Macc. 12:6, Pss. Sol. 9:2, Rev. 16:7; 19:2). Here in 1 John 1:9 individuals who confess their sins can depend on God to be *just* and thereby forgive wrongdoing because justice has already been carried out via the death of Jesus (v. 7). Thus God maintains, and is true to, his established standards (cf. *EDNT* 1:325).

1:9c ἵνα: The Greek word ἵνα is a conjunction meaning "that" but here is weakened and disappears altogether (BDAG, s.v. "ἵνα" 2c, p. 476). **Syntactically,** ἵνα introduces a dependent conjunctive clause, "*to pardon* our sins and *to declare* us purified from all unrighteousness" (ἵνα ἀφῇ ἡμῖν τὰς ἁμαρτίας καὶ καθαρίσῃ ἡμᾶς ἀπὸ πάσης ἀδικίας), functions adverbially. It modifies the verb "is" (ἐστίν). **Semantically,** ἵνα introduces a compound result clause: *resulting in* forgiveness and cleansing (cf. W, 473). While some translations seem to reflect *result* with "*will* forgive" (NRSV NIV CNT cf. NET) our translation follows the majority (KJV ASV NASB ESV NLT). Regardless of how it is translated, God's faithfulness and justice has results for those who confess their sins: they will be forgiven and cleansed because of Jesus's death (cf. Culy, 19). This is a grounds-conclusion construction in that the conjunction underscores a conclusion about the nature of God.

ἀφῇ: The Greek word ἀφῇ is a third person singular aorist active subjunctive from the verb ἀφίημι meaning "to cancel" or "to pardon" in that a person is released from a legal or moral obligation (BDAG, s.v. "ἀφίημι" 2, p. 156). The verb is in the subjunctive mood because it follows ἵνα. **Syntactically,** ἀφῇ is the governing verb of the dependent ἵνα clause. The assumed subject, "he," refers to our faithful and just God. **Semantically,** ἀφῇ is a gnomic aorist: "to pardon" or "to forgive" (KJV ASV NASB ESV NLT). It presents a timeless fact about God (W, 562). John makes it clear that God "pardons" all those who admit wrongdoing.

> **Lexical Nugget**: What does ἀφίημι mean? Like its noun form, ἀφίημι "has multiple shades of meaning" (see *TLNT* 1:238–44). In the LXX, it is used in connection with the sabbatical year where there were multiple types of religious "releases" (1) of *the land* from harvesting (translated "jubilee": Lev. 25:11–12; cf. Exod. 23:11), (2) of *Israelite slaves* (Lev. 25:10, 41; Jer. 34:8, 15, 17; cf. Polybius, *Hist.* 1.79.12; 1 Macc 10:34; Josephus *A.J.* 17.7.1 §185), (3) "return" of *property* held for debt (Lev. 25:13, 28, 31, 33), and (4) the "release," "remittance," or "discharge" of a *debt* (Deut. 15:1–2; 31:10; cf. Dionysys of Halicarnassus *Comp.* 26, 28, 34). The term, however, is rarely employed in the LXX and secular Greek to speak of the "forgiveness" of an offense (cf. "forgiven his guilt": Herodotus, *Hist.* 6.30; "acquit"; Plato, *Leg.* 9.869; Josephus *A.J.* 14.9.5 §185, *B.J.* 1.8.9 §214; "pardon"; Josephus, *B.J.* 1.24.4 §481). Yet to forgive an offense dominates New Testament usage. More often than most Jewish authors, Philo employs the term in a religious context to speak of the "liberation" of one's soul (*Her.* 273) and "remission" of sins (*Mos.* 2.147; *Spec.* 1.190, 215). Philo's latter usage is very similar to the New Testament in that "forgiveness" is almost always qualified as "forgiveness *of sins*" (Matt. 26:28; Mark 1:4; Luke 3:3; 12:47; Acts 5:31; 10:43; 13:38; 26:18; Col. 1:14; cf. Luke 1:77; Acts 2:38; Eph. 1:7; Heb. 10:18). Here in 1 John 1:9 it is used in an absolute sense to highlight the reality that divine "release" or "pardon" of an individual's or perhaps a community's offense is dependent upon a public confession (*TDNT* 1:509–12; *EDNT* 1:181–83).

[1:9d] καί: The Greek word καί is a conjunction meaning "and" (BDAG, s.v. "καί" 1bα, p. 494). **Syntactically,** καί introduces the second part of the compound dependent clause "*and* to declare us purified from all unrighteousness." (καὶ καθαρίσῃ ἡμᾶς ἀπὸ πάσης ἀδικίας). **Semantically,** καί is a coordinating connective that joins two dependent clauses (cf. KJV ASV etc.). John adds a further thought about the forgiveness of God.

καθαρίσῃ: The Greek word καθαρίσῃ is a third person singular aorist active subjunctive from the verb καθαρίζω that means "to make clean" or "to declare clean" as though through a ritual cleansing (BDAG, s.v. "καθαρίζω" 3b, pp. 488–89). The verb is in the subjunctive mood, because it follows ἵνα. **Syntactically,** καθαρίσῃ is the second governing verb of the compound adverbial dependent ἵνα clause. This verb is also in the subjunctive mood because it follows ἵνα. The assumed subject, "he" refers to our faithful and just God. **Semantically,** καθαρίσῃ is a gnomic aorist: "to declare purified" or "cleanse" (KJV ASV NASB NRSV ESV CNT NLT). It presents a timeless fact about God (W, 562). John makes it clear that God declares all those who admit wrongdoing as pure.

1:10a ἐάν: The Greek word ἐάν is a conjunction that means "if" (BDAG, s.v. "ἐάν" 1a, 1b, p. 267). **Syntactically,** ἐάν identifies the clause as a dependent conjunctive clause. The entire dependent clause, "*if* we say, 'we have not sinned'" (ἐὰν εἴπωμεν ὅτι οὐχ ἡμαρτήκαμεν), functions adverbially. It modifies the verbs "make" (ποιοῦμεν) and "is" (ἐστίν). **Semantically,** ἐάν introduces a third class conditional clause: "if" (cf. KJV NASB ESV NIV NET etc.). It provides a fourth hypothetical situation (W, 698). The activity of ἐάν is expressed in the next verb.

εἴπωμεν: The Greek word εἴπωμεν is a first person plural aorist active subjunctive from the verb λέγω meaning "to speak" or "to say" or "to express oneself orally" (BDAG, s.v. "λέγω" 1, p. 588). This verb is in the subjunctive because it follows ἐάν. **Syntactically,** εἴπωμεν is the governing verb of the adverbial dependent ἐάν clause. The assumed subject, "we," refers to a hypothetical person that makes the claim that they have never sinned. **Semantically,** εἴπωμεν is a constative aorist: "we say" (KJV ASV NASB NRSV ESV NET CNT with two exceptions NIV NLT). It describes an event as a whole (W, 557). John speaks of a hypothetical situation whereby a person makes a claim. The specifics of that claim are evident in the ὅτι clause.

ὅτι: The Greek word ὅτι is a conjunction that generally means "that" or "for" but here it is a direct discourse marker left untranslated (BDAG, s.v. "ὅτι" 3, p. 732). **Syntactically,** ὅτι introduces a dependent conjunctive clause "*that* we have not sinned" (ὅτι οὐχ ἡμαρτήκαμεν). This clause is functioning substantivally as the direct object of the verb "say" (εἴπωμεν). The clause is placed in parentheses in order to visualize its contribution to the independent clause. **Semantically,** ὅτι is direct discourse whereby it is not translated (ESV NET NIV NLT), but rather quotation marks are used to underscore the claim (W, 454). It highlights the hypothetical statement of a person, which is made clear in the rest of the clause.

ἡμαρτήκαμεν: The Greek word ἡμαρτήκαμεν is a first person plural perfect active indicative from the verb ἁμαρτάνω meaning "to sin" or "to commit a wrong doing" (BDAG, s.v. "ἁμαρτάνω" pp. 49–50). **Syntactically,** ἡμαρτήκαμεν is the governing verb of the substantival ὅτι clause. It is the direct object of the verb "we say" (εἴερσον). The subject of the verb is an implied "we" and refers to the person who claims to *have* no sin. **Semantically,** ἡμαρτήκαμεν is a gnomic perfect with an extensive force: "we *have* no sin" (KJV NASB ESV NIV NET etc.). It reveals a general truth with the focus on the decisive act of the verb (W, 580). John speaks of any person who boasts: "I have no sin." This claim goes further than the one in verse 8. Here it suggests that those who are in Jesus do not sin at all.

Theological Nugget: Where would a person get the idea of "I do no wrong"? Brown suggests that the original readers have mishandled the Gospel of John. They seem to believe it teaches that once someone becomes a disciple of Jesus, they receive the ability to not sin at all (John 3:18; 5:4). John rejects this idea as a perversion of the gospel. He wants his readers to know that sin will be a reality in their life. That does not mean he is encouraging sin, but that he is pointing to sin's solution, namely, the person and work of Jesus, the righteous one (Brown, 230–42).

1:10b ποιοῦμεν: The Greek word ποιοῦμεν is a first person plural present active indicative from the verb ποιέω meaning, "to make" or "to cause" or "to bring about" with a focus on causality (BDAG, s.v. "ποιέω" 2h, p. 840). **Syntactically,** ποιοῦμεν is the main verb of the independent clause: "*we make* him a liar" (ψεύστην ποιοῦμεν αὐτόν). The assumed subject, "we," refers to any person who claims to have not sinned. "Him" refers to God: "we make God out to be a liar." **Semantically,** ποιοῦμεν is a gnomic present: "we make" (cf. KJV NASB ESV NIV NET etc.). It underscores a generic statement that is true at all times (W, 523). John makes it clear that any person who claims to be sinless makes God out to be a liar.

1:10c καί: The Greek word καί is a conjunction meaning "and" (BDAG, s.v. "καί" 1b, p. 494). **Syntactically,** καί introduces a conjunctive independent clause. **Semantically,** καί is a coordinating conjunction: "and" (cf. KJV NASB ESV NIV NET etc.). It joins two independent clauses together (W, 671). So not only is the person a liar, he or she is also without God.

ἐστίν: The Greek word ἐστίν is third person singular present active indicative from the verb εἰμί meaning "is" or "to be in close connection with" (BDAG, s.v. "εἰμί" 2a, p. 283). **Syntactically,** ἐστίν is the main verb of the independent clause, "and his word *is* not in us" (καὶ ὁ λόγος αὐτοῦ οὐκ ἔστιν ἐν ἡμῖν). The subject of the verb is "his word" (ὁ λόγος αὐτοῦ). **Semantically,** ἐστίν is a gnomic present: "is" (cf. KJV NASB ESV NIV NET etc.). It presents a timeless fact (W, 562). John makes it clear that any person who claims to be sinless has no relationship with God.

2:1a γράφω: The Greek word γράφω is a first person singular present active indicative from the verb γράφω meaning "to write" or "to compose" with reference to composing a letter (BDAG, s.v. "γράφω" 2d, p. 207). **Syntactically,** γράφω is the main verb of the independent clause "my children, *I now write* these things to you" (τεκνία μου, ταῦτα γράφω ὑμῖν). The assumed subject, "I," refers to John. **Semantically,** γράφω is a progressive present: "I *now* write" or "I am writing" (NASB NRSV ESV NET NLT). It reveals an event occurring *right now* (W, 518). John gives emphasis to his current writing of the letter.

Lexical Nugget: What does τεκνία mean? The term is a familial term of endearment and the diminutive of τέκνον (a shortened, familiar form; e.g., "dad" is the diminutive of "father"). Although the two were probably interchangeable in common speech, in John's letters the two are used very differently. Whereas τέκνον may be used to refer to God's children in general (3:1, 2, 10; 5:2), τεκνία is a term of direct address that indicates John's relationship to those whom he considers his spiritual children (1 John 2:1, 12, 28; 3:7, 18; 4:4; 5:21). Here in 2:1, τεκνία clearly marks a break in the pattern of the fraudulent claims of some people. The diminutive illustrates the close relationship between John and those he is addressing. Note the single use of the same term in the John 13:33 when Jesus addresses his disciples at the Last Supper. This use of τεκνία illustrates the close relationship between the author and the community (Brown, 213–14; HJS, 41).

2:1b ἵνα: The Greek word ἵνα is a conjunction meaning "that" or "in order that" or "to denote a purpose or goal" (BDAG, s.v. "ἵνα" 1aα, p. 475). **Syntactically,** ἵνα introduces a dependent conjunctive clause: "*in order that* you may not sin" (ἵνα μὴ ἁμάρτητε). This clause is functioning adverbially, modifying the verb "I now write" (γράφω). **Semantically,** ἵνα introduces a purpose clause: "in order that" or "that" (KJV). Many translations, however, appear to render ἵνα as result (NASB NRSV ESV NIV NET NLT CNT). It indicates intention (cf. W, 472). John's intention is evident in the next verb.

ἁμάρτητε: The Greek word ἁμάρτητε is a second person plural aorist active subjunctive from the verb ἁμαρτάνω meaning "to sin" or "to 'transgress' against divinity," or "to commit a wrong" (BDAG, s.v. "ἁμαρτάνω" a, p. 49). It is in the subjunctive because it follows ἵνα. **Syntactically,** ἁμάρτητε is the governing verb of the adverbial dependent ἵνα clause. The assumed subject, "you," refers to the community to whom John is writing. **Semantically,** μὴ ἁμάρτητε is a constative aorist: "may not sin" (ASV NASB NRSV ESV NET CNT).

It describes sinning as an event as a whole (W, 557). John does not want his readers to sin period. This clause, just like the ἐάν clauses from chapter 1, serves as a mitigated command. John gently commands the readers not to sin.

2:1c καί: The Greek word καί is a conjunction meaning "and" or "but" (BDAG, s.v. "καί" 2c, p. 496). **Syntactically,** καί introduces the dependent conjunction clause: "*but* if anyone does sin" (καὶ ἐάν τις ἁμάρτῃ). The entire dependent clause is adverbial modifying "we have" (ἔχομεν). **Semantically,** καί is contrastive: "but" (NRSV ESV NIV NET CNT NLT). John denotes a contrast to the previous ἵνα clause.

ἐάν: The Greek word ἐάν is a conjunction meaning "if" (BDAG, s.v. "ἐάν" 1a, 1b, p. 267). **Syntactically,** ἐάν identifies the clause as a dependent clause. The entire dependent clause, "but *if* anyone does sin" (ἐάν τις ἁμάρτῃ) is functioning adverbially. It modifies the verb, "we have" (ἔχομεν). **Semantically,** ἐάν introduces a third class conditional clause of probability: "if" (cf. KJV NASB ESV NIV NET etc). The condition is uncertain of fulfillment but still likely (W, 696). The uncertain condition is expressed in the next verb.

ἁμάρτῃ: The Greek word ἁμάρτῃ is a third person singular aorist active subjunctive from the verb ἁμαρτάνω meaning "to sin" or "to 'transgress' against divinity," or "to commit a wrong" (BDAG, s.v. "ἁμαρτάνω" a, p. 49). **Syntactically,** ἁμάρτῃ serves as the governing verb of the dependent adverbial clause. The verb is in the subjunctive because ἐάν takes the subjunctive. The subject of the verb is the pronoun τις and refers to any believer who falls into sin. **Semantically,** ἁμάρτῃ is a gnomic aorist about "sin" (cf. KJV NASB ESV NIV NET etc.). John provides a generic or a timeless truth about the follower of Jesus and sin (W, 562). John underscores that sin happens in every believer's life, namely, that they do sin. But John does not leave the reader hanging. The resolution is found in the next clause.

2:1d ἔχομεν: The Greek word ἔχομεν is a first person plural present active indicative from the verb ἔχω meaning "I have" or "to have something at one's disposal" (BDAG, s.v. "ἔχω" 1c, p. 420). **Syntactically,** ἔχομεν is the main verb of the independent clause: "*we have* an advocate with the Father, Jesus who is the Christ, the righteous one" (παράκλητον ἔχομεν πρὸς τὸν πατέρα, Ἰησοῦν Χριστὸν δίκαιον). The assumed subject, "we," refers to John, his associates, and his readers. They have at their disposal an advocate. This advocate is Jesus who is with "the" (τόν) Father. The article is an article of *par excellence* (W, 223). **Semantically,** ἔχομεν is a gnomic present: "we have" (cf. KJV NASB ESV NIV NET etc.). It underscores a generic statement that is true at all times (W, 523). John speaks of any believer who sins. They have an advocate who intercedes for them. His name is Jesus who is both the Messiah and the one who is right with God.

Lexical Nugget: What does παράκλητον mean? The word, usually translated "advocate" (παράκλητον), is unique to John's writings. It first appears in John (14:16, 26, 15:26, 16:7) to describe the Holy Spirit as the "Paraclete." Here in 1 John 1:9, it refers to Jesus. Yet what does the term mean? In Philo, it speaks generally of a person who intercedes on behalf of another (*Ios.* 239, *Mos.* 2.234; *Spec.* 2.237, *Praem.* 166). On one occasion, however, the term implies "helper" or "counselor." Despite the fact that Philo argues that God has no παράκλητον (*Opif.* 23), John, on several occasions (14:16, 26; 15:26; 16:7), declares that the Holy Spirit is called a "counselor" (KJV, NIV), or a "helper" (NASB). Some translations render παράκλητον in John's Gospel as "advocate" (NET, NRSV). Brown simply transliterates the word (*paraklētos*). Here in 1 John 1:9, the context suggests that Jesus makes intercession in the sense of a legal advocate who is righteous. This idea is stressed elsewhere in the New Testament (Rom. 8:34; Heb. 7:25).

2:2a καί: The Greek word καί is a conjunction meaning "and" (BDAG, s.v. "καί" 1b, p. 494). **Syntactically,** καί introduces a conjunctive independent clause: "*and* he himself is the atoning sacrifice for our sins" (καὶ αὐτὸς ἱλασμός ἐστιν περὶ τῶν ἁμαρτιῶν ἡμῶν). **Semantically,** καί is a coordinating connector: "and" (KJV ASV NASB NRSV NET CNT). It adds further information about the person and work of Jesus on behalf of the believer. That additional information is found in the rest of the clause.

ἐστίν: The Greek word ἐστίν is third person singular present active indicative from the verb εἰμί meaning "is" or "to be in close connection with" (BDAG, s.v. "εἰμί" 2a, p. 283). **Syntactically,** ἐστίν is the main verb of the independent clause. The subject of the verb is the emphatic pronoun "he" (αὐτός). **Semantically,** ἐστίν is an equative present: "is" (cf. KJV NASB ESV NIV NET etc.). It underscores a generic statement that is true at all times (W, 523). John speaks of any believer who sins. They have an advocate who intercedes for them because of his atoning sacrifice (Culy, 23).

Lexical and Theological Nugget: What does it mean that Jesus is the ἱλασμός for sin? This noun appears in the New Testament only here and 1 John 4:10. Three interpretations are offered for the word: expiation (Painter, 158–59), propitiation (Strecker, 39n.17), and atonement. Yet "atonement" seems the best. In the third century, Origen recognized that the ritual of the Day of Atonement played a significant role in interpreting 1 John 2:1–2, since Leviticus 25:9 (LXX) renders the Hebrew "Day of Atonement" as τῇ ἡμέρᾳ τοῦ ἱλασμοῦ (cf. Heb. 9–10). It seems 1 John envisions a similar background. The concepts of ἱλασμός (e.g., blood, cleansing, the innocent victim, and the idea that the one who atones is himself in heaven continuing to cleanse) offer the basis of confidence for sinners (Brown, 221). So rather than propitiation, which implies a sacrifice that turns away the wrath of God, or expiation, which implies that the offender is purified of the sin that causes offense, the translation *"atonement"* or *"atoning"* best reflects John's usage.

$^{2:2b}$ δέ: The Greek word δέ is a conjunction meaning "and" (BDAG, s.v. "δέ" p. 213). **Syntactically,** δέ introduces an independent clause with an ellipsis: *"but (he is the atoning sacrifice) not only for our sins"* ([αὐτὸς ἱλασμός ἐστιν] οὐ περὶ τῶν ἡμετέρων δὲ μόνον). The position of δέ and the ellipsis makes for a difficult word-for-word rendering. **Semantically,** δέ is loosely connective and gives us some more information about the atoning work of Jesus. His sacrifice was not only for believers. We might even say "far as the curse is found" as the Christmas hymn puts it (Gen. 9:9–10, 12, 15–17; cf. Rom. 8:22)."

$^{2:2c}$ ἀλλὰ καί: The Greek word ἀλλά is a conjunction meaning "but" (BDAG, s.v. "ἀλλά" 2, p. 45). The Greek word καί is a conjunction meaning "also" (BDAG, s.v. "καί" 1f, p. 495). **Syntactically,** ἀλλὰ καί introduces an independent conjunctive clause with an ellipsis, *"but also (he is the atoning sacrifice) for the whole world"* (ἀλλὰ καὶ [αὐτὸς ἱλασμός ἐστιν] περὶ ὅλου τοῦ κόσμου). **Semantically,** ἀλλὰ καὶ is a coordinating contrastive with an adjunctive conjunction: "but also" (cf. KJV NASB ESV NIV NET etc.). Contrary (ἀλλά) to believing that Jesus is the atoning sacrifice for the sins of only believers, he is also (καί) the atoning sacrifice for the sins of the entire world.

1 John 2:3–11

Big Greek Idea: Assurance of a relationship with God is grounded in a persistent observance of God's expectation to love others, whereby extending love to others in everyday life situations eliminates other people's excuses for not following Jesus, and contrasts with those who hate believers, thereby demonstrating that they have no spiritual awareness of God.

Structural Overview: John transitions (καί) from his first litany of claims and contradictory lifestyles (1:5–2:2) to another list of claims to demonstrate that a true relationship with God is grounded in obedience to God's command to love (vv. 3–11).

John opens with a simple yet timeless truth of affirmation: People who obey (τηρῶμεν) God's command to love are mindful (γινώσκομεν) of their friendship with God (2:3). John once again enters into assessing several claims (ὁ λέγων) of people who profess to know God. Whereas some people claim (ὁ λέγων) to have a relationship with God, others demonstrate their relationship with God via their obedience (τηρῇ) in loving others and fulfilling the obligation to live a life of sacrifice (ὀφείλει . . . περιπατεῖν; vv. 4–6).

John then transitions (ἀγαπητοί) to update God's expectation to love. Whereas God's expectation to love is not new, an aspect of it is because (ὅτι) hatred is diminishing (παράγεται) and love is increasing (φαίνει; vv. 7–8). Whereas some people (ὁ λέγων) claim to love while being hateful, others comply with God's command and have a relationship (μένει) with God and become a blessing to others (σκάνδαλον . . . οὐκ ἐστίν; 9–10). They are contrasted (δέ) with those who hate followers of Jesus and have no spiritual awareness (v. 11).

Outline:

> Assurance of a Relationship with God Is Possible (v. 3)
> Character Traits of People Who Have a Relationship with God (vv. 4–6)
>> A person in relationship with God obeys God (vv. 4–5b)
>> A person in relationship with God lives a life of sacrifice (vv. 5c–6)
> God's Expectation Is to Love (vv. 7–11)
>> God's expectation to love is not new, but updated (vv. 7–8)
>> People who observe God's expectation to love are a blessing (vv. 9–10)
>> People who hate demonstrate their lack spiritual awareness (v. 11)

Clausal Outline for 1 John 2:3–11

^{2:3a} Καὶ ἐν τούτῳ **γινώσκομεν** (ὅτι ἐγνώκαμεν αὐτόν),
^{2:3a} Now by this **we know** (that we have known him [= God]),

    |
    ^{2:3b} **ἐὰν** τὰς ἐντολὰς αὐτοῦ **τηρῶμεν**.
    ^{2:3b} **if** we *persist in* **keeping** his commandments.

^{2:4a} ὁ λέγων (ὅτι Ἔγνωκα αὐτόν), καὶ τὰς ἐντολὰς αὐτοῦ μὴ τηρῶν, ψεύστης **ἐστίν**,
^{2:4a} The one who says ("I know him [= God]"), and who does not *persist in* keeping his commands, **is** a liar,

^{2:4b} καὶ ἐν τούτῳ ἡ ἀλήθεια οὐκ **ἔστιν·**
^{2:4b} and the truth **is** not in this person;

        ^{2:5a} **ὃς** δ' ἂν **τηρῇ** αὐτοῦ τὸν λόγον,
        ^{2:5a} But **whoever** *persists in* **keeping** his [= God's] word,

      |
^{2:5b} ἀληθῶς ἐν τούτῳ ἡ ἀγάπη τοῦ θεοῦ **τετελείωται**.
^{2:5b} truly, in this person, love for God **has been perfected**.

^{2:5c} ἐν τούτῳ **γινώσκομεν** (ὅτι ἐν αὐτῷ ἐσμεν)·
^{2:5c} By this, **we know** (that we are in him [= God]);

^{2:6a} (ὁ λέγων ἐν αὐτῷ μένειν) **ὀφείλει**
    . . . καὶ αὐτὸς **περιπατεῖν**.
^{2:6a} (The one who says that he [= God] abides in him [or her]) *is obligated*
    . . . also himself (or herself) to *persist in* **living**.

        |
      ^{2:6b} **καθὼς** ἐκεῖνος **περιεπάτησεν**
      ^{2:6b} **just as** that one [= Jesus] **lived**.

^{2:7a} Ἀγαπητοί, οὐκ ἐντολὴν καινὴν **γράφω** ὑμῖν,
^{2:7a} Beloved, **I write** no new commandment to you,

^{2:7b} ἀλλ' ἐντολὴν παλαιὰν [γράφω]
^{2:7b} but [*I now write*] an old commandment

    |
    ^{2:7c} **ἣν εἴχετε** ἀπ' ἀρχῆς·
    ^{2:7c} **which you have had** *as an obligation* from the beginning;

2:7d ἡ ἐντολὴ ἡ παλαιά **ἐστιν** ὁ λόγος
2:7d the old commandment **is** the word

|
2:7e **ὃν ἠκούσατε**,
2:7e **which you have heard**,

2:8b **ὅ ἐστιν** ἀληθὲς ἐν αὐτῷ καὶ ἐν ὑμῖν.
2:8b **which is** true in him [=Jesus] and in you.

2:8a πάλιν ἐντολὴν καινὴν **γράφω** ὑμῖν,
2:8a On the other hand, **I** *now* **write** to you a new commandment,

|
2:8c **ὅτι** ἡ σκοτία **παράγεται**
2:8c **because** the darkness **is passing away** *right now*

|
2:8d καὶ [*ὅτι*] τὸ φῶς τὸ ἀληθινὸν ἤδη **φαίνει**.
2:8d and [*because*] true light **is** *already* **shining**.

2:9 (ὁ λέγων ἐν τῷ φωτὶ εἶναι καὶ τὸν ἀδελφὸν αὐτοῦ μισῶν) ἐν τῇ σκοτίᾳ **ἐστὶν** ἕως ἄρτι.
2:9 (The one who claims to be in the light [= God] and yet *persists* in hating his [or her] brother [and sister]) **is** still in the darkness until now.

2:10a ὁ ἀγαπῶν τὸν ἀδελφὸν αὐτοῦ ἐν τῷ φωτὶ **μένει**,
2:10a [*In contrast to*] the one who *persists* in loving his [or her] brother [and sister] **abides** in the light,

2:10b καὶ σκάνδαλον ἐν αὐτῷ οὐκ **ἔστιν·**
2:10b and in him (or her), **there is** no cause for stumbling.

2:11a ὁ δὲ μισῶν τὸν ἀδελφὸν αὐτοῦ ἐν τῇ σκοτίᾳ **ἐστὶν**
2:11a But the one who *persists* in hating his (her) brother (and sister) **is** in the darkness

2:11b καὶ ἐν τῇ σκοτίᾳ **περιπατεῖ**
2:11b and *so* **he (or she)** *is* **walking** in the darkness

2:11c καὶ οὐκ **οἶδεν** (ποῦ ὑπάγει,)
2:11c and **he (or she) does** not **know** (where he [or she] is going),

|
2:11d **ὅτι** ἡ σκοτία **ἐτύφλωσεν** τοὺς ὀφθαλμοὺς αὐτοῦ.
2:11d **because** the darkness **has blinded** his (or her) eyes.

SYNTAX EXPLAINED FOR 1 JOHN 2:3–11

2:3a Καί: The Greek word καί is a conjunction that may mean "and" (BDAG, s.v. "καί" 1bη, p. 495) or "now" (BDAG, s.v. "καί" 1e, p. 495). **Syntactically,** καί introduces an independent conjunctive clause, "*Now* by this we know that we have known him," (καὶ ἐν τούτῳ γινώσκομεν ὅτι ἐγνώκαμεν αὐτόν). **Semantically,** καί can either be a simple connective or transitional. If this καί ("and") is a simple connective, it would add an additional thought to the discussion on the nature of sin (KJV ASV ESV NLT; Culy, 24). It seems more likely though that this καὶ is transitional (NRSV NET). John moves the discussion from God being light (1:5) and his three claims (1:6, 8, 10) and counterclaims (1:7, 9; 2:1) to how to know believers have fellowship with God.

ἐν τούτῳ: The Greek word ἐν is a preposition meaning "by" (BDAG, s.v. "ἐν" 5b, p. 328). The Greek word τούτῳ is declined as a dative singular neuter from the demonstrative pronoun οὗτος, meaning "this one" (BDAG, s.v. "οὗτος" 1bβ, p. 741). **Syntactically,** ἐν τούτῳ is a prepositional phrase that is part of an independent conjunctive clause, unlike other occurrences in 1 John (2:4, 5 [2x], 3:10, 16, 19, 24; 4:2, 9, 10, 13, 17; 5:2). **Semantically,** ἐν τούτῳ expresses means: "by this" (NASB ESV NET CNT). The clause can either be anaphoric, pointing back to the preceding discussion, or cataphoric, pointing forward. Usually the prepositional phrase is cataphoric if it is followed by a subordinating conjunction that is epexegetical to the demonstrative, "this" (τούτῳ; cf. Brown, 217), as in this case. The clause is explained in the subsequent ἐάν clause.

γινώσκομεν: The Greek word γινώσκομεν is a first person plural present active indicative from the verb γινώσκω meaning "to know" or "to know about" or "to arrive at a knowledge of someone" (BDAG, s.v. "γινώσκω" 1c, p. 200). **Syntactically,** γινώσκομεν is the main verb of the conjunctive independent clause. The subject of the verb is an implied "we" and refers to anyone who desires to have a relationship with God. **Semantically,** γινώσκομεν is a gnomic present: "we know" (ASV NASB ESV NET CNT NLT). It identifies something that is true at any time (W, 523). The content of what John's readers know is found in the next ὅτι clause.

ὅτι: The Greek word ὅτι is a conjunction meaning "that" or identifying content after a verb of mental perception (BDAG, s.v. "ὅτι" 1c, p. 731). **Syntactically,** ὅτι introduces a substantival dependent conjunctive clause: "*that* we have known him" (ὅτι ἐγνώκαμεν αὐτόν). The entire ὅτι clause functions as the direct object of the verb: "we know" (γινώσκομεν). The clause is placed in parentheses in order to visualize its contribution to the independent clause. **Semantically,** ὅτι is an indirect discourse marker: "that" (cf. KJV NASB ESV NIV NET etc.). The entire ὅτι clause provides the content of the verb "we know" (γινώσκομεν; W, 456), yet the specifics of that knowledge are found in the next verb.

ἐγνώκαμεν: The Greek word ἐγνώκαμεν is a first person plural perfect active indicative from the verb γινώσκω meaning "to know" or "to know about" or "to arrive at a knowledge of someone" (BDAG, s.v. "γινώσκω" 1c, p. 200). **Syntactically,** ἐγνώκαμεν serves as the governing verb of the substantival dependent ὅτι clause. The subject of the verb is an implied "we" embedded in the verb and refers to anyone who desires to have a relationship with God. **Semantically,** ἐγνώκαμεν is a gnomic perfect with extensive force: "we *have* come to know" (NASB EVS NIV contra the intensive rendering "we know": KJV ASV NRSV NLT CNT). Its gnomic force provides something that is envisioned as true on many occasions while focusing on the completed action of the past (W, 580). John identifies a timeless truth for a believer's confidence concerning their relationship with God, which is clarified in the next ἐάν clause.

2:3b ἐάν: The Greek word ἐάν is a conjunction meaning "if" (BDAG, s.v. "ἐάν" 1aα, p. 267). **Syntactically,** ἐάν identifies the clause as a dependent conjunctive clause. The entire dependent clause, "*if* we persist in keeping his commandments" (ἐὰν τὰς ἐντολὰς αὐτοῦ τηρῶμεν), functions adjectivally (epexegetically). It modifies the demonstrative pronoun, "by this" (ἐν τούτῳ). **Semantically,** ἐάν introduces a third class conditional clause: "if" (cf. KJV NASB ESV NIV NET etc.). The condition is uncertain of fulfillment but still likely (W, 696). This clause also serves as another mitigated command. John politely urges those who believe to not abuse God's grace, but to seek to keep God's commands, especially the command to love others (Culy, 25).

τηρῶμεν: The Greek word τηρῶμεν is a first person plural present active subjunctive from the verb τηρέω meaning "to keep," "to observe," or "to persist in obedience" (BDAG, s.v. "τηρέω" 3, p. 1002). It is a subjunctive because it follows ἐάν. **Syntactically,** τηρῶμεν serves as the governing verb of the dependent ἐάν clause that provides the content of the demonstrative pronoun, "this" (τούτῳ). The assumed subject, "we," refers to any believer who desires to have a relationship with God. **Semantically,** τηρῶμεν is a gnomic present with a customary present force: "we *persist in* keeping" or "we keep" (KJV ASV NASB ESV NIV NET CNT). It identifies something that is true at any time (W, 523). Followers of Jesus who obey God's commandments to love others can be assured of their relationship with God.

2:4a λέγων: The Greek word λέγων is a nominative masculine singular present active participle from the verb λέγω meaning "to maintain," "to declare," or "to proclaim as teaching" (BDAG, s.v. "λέγω" 2e, p. 590). **Syntactically,** λέγων is a substantival participle functioning as part of the compound subject of the compound verbs, "is" (ἐστίν) and "is" (ἐστίν). **Semantically,** λέγων is a gnomic present: "the one who says" (NASB NET) or "whoever says" (NRSV ESV). It introduces a generic person's statement that is true at any time (W, 615). John directs attention to people who make a claim, which is specified in the next ὅτι clause.

ὅτι: The Greek word ὅτι is a conjunction meaning "that" (BDAG, s.v. "ὅτι" 3, p. 732). **Syntactically,** ὅτι serves to introduce a dependent substantival ὅτι clause. "I know him" (ὅτι Ἔγνωκα αὐτόν) functions as the direct object of the substantival participle of speech, "saying" (λέγων). The entire clause is placed in parentheses in order to visualize its contribution to the independent clause. **Semantically,** ὅτι is classified as direct discourse providing the content of a hypothetical claim and is typically not translated. Instead, quotation marks appear (cf. NASB NRSV ESV NIV NET NLT CNT). Any person who claims to have a relationship with God, yet does not keep his commands, is a liar.

Ἔγνωκα: The Greek word ἔγνωκα is a first person singular perfect active indicative from the verb γινώσκω meaning "to know," "to know about," or "to arrive at a knowledge of someone" (BDAG, s.v. "γινώσκω" 1c, p. 200). **Syntactically,** ἔγνωκα is the governing verb of a dependent ὅτι clause that functions as the direct object of the substantival participle of speech "saying" (λέγων). It serves as part of the compound subject of the compound verbs "is" (ἐστίν) and "is" (ἐστίν). The subject of the verb is an implied "I" embedded in the verb and refers to any hypothetical individual who claims to have a relationship with God. **Semantically,** ἔγνωκα is a gnomic perfect with extensive force: "I *have* come to know" (NASB NRSV NET). Its gnomic force provides something that is envisioned as true on many occasions while focusing on the completed action in the past (W, 580). John is providing a timeless truth about anyone who says they have a relationship with God. That relationship is defined in the next verbal.

τηρῶν: The Greek word τηρῶν is a nominative masculine singular present active participle from the verb τηρέω meaning "to keep," "to observe," "to fulfill," or "to pay attention to," especially of law and teaching. The idea is "to persist in obedience" (BDAG, s.v. "τηρέω" 3, p. 1002). **Syntactically,** τηρῶν is a substantival participle functioning as part of the compound subject of the compound verbs, "is" (ἐστίν) and "is" (ἐστίν). **Semantically,** τηρῶν is a gnomic present with a customary present force: "I *persist in* keeping" or "I keep" (NASB ESV NET CNT; cf. KJV ASV). It presents a generic statement to describe something that is true at any time (W, 521, 615). Therefore, someone who claims to have a relationship with God yet refuses to keep his commands is problematic. That problem is made clear with the next verb.

ἐστίν: The Greek word ἐστίν is third person singular present active indicative from the verb εἰμί meaning "is" or "to be in close connection with"

(BDAG, s.v. "εἰμί" 2a, p. 283). **Syntactically,** ἐστίν serves as one of the main verbs of a compound independent clause. The subject of the verb is the compound participial clauses "*the one who says I know him* and *who does not persist in keeping his commands*" (ὁ λέγων ὅτι Ἔγνωκα αὐτόν, καὶ τὰς ἐντολὰς αὐτοῦ μὴ τηρῶν). **Semantically,** ἐστίν is a gnomic present with equative force: "is" (cf. KJV NASB ESV NIV NET etc.). It underscores a generic statement that is true at all times (W, 523). Any person who claims to have a relationship with God yet refuses to keep God's commands is equated with being a liar.

> **Grammatical Nugget:** How are the participles "keeping" (τηρῶν) and "saying" (λέγων) to be understood? The participles "keeping" (τηρῶν) and "saying" (λέγων) are substantival. They share an article "the" (ὁ) and are connected by καί: "and" (KJV ASV NASB).
>
> ὁ λέγων (ὅτι Ἔγνωκα αὐτόν), καὶ τὰς ἐντολὰς αὐτοῦ μὴ τηρῶν
>
> According to the Granville Sharp Rule, this means that these two substantives (λέγων and τηρῶν) should be read together with a high level of unity, having the same referent. Some translations render καί as "yet" or "but" (NRSV ESV NIV NET CNT), but the Granville Sharp Rule argues that this is not the case here. Instead, both participles should be taken substantivally and should retain a high level of unity (W, 275).

2:4b καί: The Greek word καί is a conjunction meaning "and" (BDAG, s.v. "καί" 1b, p. 494). **Syntactically,** καί introduces an independent conjunctive clause: "*and* the truth is not in this person" (καὶ ἐν τούτῳ ἡ ἀλήθεια οὐκ ἔστιν). **Semantically,** καί is a coordinating connective: "and." It adds to John's discussion about the person who claims to have a relationship with God. The prepositional phrase "in this *person*" (ἐν τούτῳ) is anaphoric, pointing back to the hypothetical person who claims to have a relationship with God and yet refuses to keep his commands. The details about John's additional thought are found in the rest of the clause.

ἐστίν: The Greek word ἐστιν is third person singular present active indicative from the verb εἰμί meaning "to be" or "to exist" (BDAG, s.v. "εἰμί" 1, 282). **Syntactically,** ἐστίν is one of the main verbs of a compound independent clause. The subject of the verb is the compound participial clauses: "the one who says that I know him and who does not *persist in* keeping his commands" (ὁ λέγων ὅτι Ἔγνωκα αὐτόν, καὶ τὰς ἐντολὰς αὐτοῦ μὴ τηρῶν). **Semantically,** ἐστίν is a gnomic present: "is" (cf. KJV NASB ESV NIV NET etc.). It underscores a generic statement that is true at all times (W, 523). A person who claims to have a relationship with God but does not follow his commands does not possess the truth. For a similar construction, refer back to 1 John 1:6, "we lie and do not practice the truth."

2:5a δ': The Greek word δέ is a conjunction meaning "but" and marks a contrast (BDAG, s.v. "δέ" 4a, p. 213). **Syntactically,** δέ is in the postpositive position and introduces a dependent indefinite relative clause: "*But* whoever persists in keeping his word" (ὃς δ' ἂν τηρῇ αὐτοῦ τὸν λόγον). **Semantically,** δέ is contrastive: "but" (KJV NASB ESV NIV NET etc.). It counters false claims (W, 671). The one who knows God is the one who desires to keep his commands, especially the command to love other believers.

ὃς...ἄν: The Greek word ὅς is a nominative masculine singular from the relative pronoun ὅς meaning "who" (BDAG, s.v. "ὅς" 1ja, p. 727). The Greek particle ἄν is untranslatable and serves to make a definite relative clause indefinite (BAGD, s.v. "ἄν" 1b, pp. 56–57; cf. W, 343). **Syntactically,** ὃς...ἄν introduces a dependent indefinite relative clause: "whoever" (NASB NRSV ESV NET CNT). It functions adjectivally modifying the demonstrative pronoun "this" (τούτῳ), clarifying it. For other instances of the indefinite relative clause in 1 John, see 3:17, 22; 4:15; 5:15; cf. 3 John 5.

τηρῇ: The Greek word τηρῇ is a third person singular present active subjunctive from the verb τηρέω meaning "to keep," "to observe," "to fulfill," "to pay attention to," especially of law and teaching. The idea is "to persist in obedience" (BDAG, s.v. "τηρέω" 3, p. 1002). This verb is in the subjunctive mood because it follows ἄν. **Syntactically,** τηρῇ is the governing verb of the dependent indefinite relative clause. The subject is the indefinite relative construction: "whoever." **Semantically,** τηρῇ is a gnomic present: "*persists in* keeping" or "keeps" (NASB ESV CNT; cf. KJV ASV). It introduces something that is true all the time (W, 523). The details of that timeless truth are revealed in the next clause.

2:5b τετελείωται: The Greek word τετελείωται is a third person singular perfect passive indicative from the verb τελειόω meaning "to make perfect" or "to finish" (BDAG, s.v. "τελειόω" 2eβ, p. 996). **Syntactically,** τετελείωται is the main verb of the independent clause: "truly, in this person, *our* love for God *has been perfected*" (ἀληθῶς ἐν τούτῳ ἡ ἀγάπη τοῦ θεοῦ τετελείωται). The subject of the verb is "the love of God" (ἡ ἀγάπη τοῦ θεοῦ). **Semantically,** τετελείωται is a gnomic perfect with extensive force: "*has been* perfected" (ASV NASB NET; cf. NRSV). Its gnomic force provides something that is envisioned as true on many occasions while focusing on the completed action of the past (W, 580). Wallace, however, considers τετελείωται as a futuristic perfect: "will be perfected" (W, 581). Regardless of the translation, when anyone keeps the word of God, their love for God is perfected.

Semantical Nugget: How is the genitive "of God" (τοῦ θεοῦ) with "the love" (ἡ ἀγάπη) to be interpreted? The genitive "of God" (τοῦ θεοῦ) with "the love" (ἡ ἀγάπη) could be interpreted one of three ways: (1) a subjective genitive, "God's love for us," (2) an objective genitive, "our love for God," or (3) a plenary genitive focusing on both objective and subjective aspects. The best option is to take this as an objective genitive (W, 121n.136). There is a direct correlation between our obedience to God and our love for him. If we love him, we desire to obey him. (For an extended discussion on this genitive, see Bateman[1], 214–15; see also Culy, 28.)

2:5c ἐν τούτῳ: The Greek word ἐν is a preposition meaning "by" (BDAG, s.v. "ἐν" 5b, p. 328). The Greek word τούτῳ is declined as a dative singular neuter from the demonstrative pronoun οὗτος meaning "this one" (BDAG, s.v. "οὗτος" 1bβ, p. 741). **Syntactically**, ἐν τούτῳ introduces an independent prepositional clause: "*by this*, we know that we are in him" (ἐν τούτῳ γινώσκομεν ὅτι ἐν αὐτῷ ἐσμεν). The construction, "by this" (ἐν τούτῳ) is common in 1 John (2:3, 4, 5 [2x]; 3:10, 16, 19, 24; 4:2, 9, 10, 13, 17; 5:2). **Semantically**, ἐν τούτῳ expresses means: "by this" (NASB ESV NET CNT). The clause can either be anaphoric, pointing back to the preceding discussion, or cataphoric, pointing forward. This one is anaphoric; it summarizes John's rebuttal (Culy, 29). The content of John's summary is evident in the next verb.

γινώσκομεν: The Greek word γινώσκομεν is a first person plural present active indicative from the verb γινώσκω meaning "to know" or "to know about" or "to arrive at a knowledge of someone" (BDAG, s.v. "γινώσκω" 1c, p. 200). **Syntactically**, γινώσκομεν is the main verb of the independent prepositional clause: "by this *we know* that we are in him" (ἐν τούτῳ γινώσκομεν ὅτι ἐν αὐτῷ ἐσμεν). The assumed subject, "we," refers to John and his readers who keep the word of God. **Semantically**, γινώσκομεν is a customary present: "we know" (ASV NASB NIV NET NLT CNT). It speaks of a pattern of behavior (W, 521). A believer who persists in obeying God's command can rest assured of something or know something; that something is made known in the next ὅτι clause.

ὅτι: The Greek word ὅτι is a conjunction meaning "that" (BDAG, s.v. "ὅτι" 1c, p. 731). **Syntactically**, ὅτι introduces a dependent conjunctive clause: "*that* we are in him" (ὅτι ἐν αὐτῷ ἐσμεν). It functions substantivally as the direct object of the verb "we know" (γινώσκομεν). The clause is placed in parentheses in order to visualize its contribution to the independent clause. **Semantically**, ὅτι is a marker of indirect discourse: "that" (KJV ASV NASB ESV NET CNT). It reveals John's thoughts (W, 456), which are evident in the rest of the clause.

ἐσμέν: The Greek word ἐσμέν is first person plural present active indicative from the verb εἰμί meaning "to be" or "to exist in a close relationship with someone" (BDAG, s.v. "εἰμί" 3b, p. 283). **Syntactically,** ἐσμέν is the governing verb of the dependent ὅτι clause. The clause functions as the direct object of the verb "we know" (γινώσκομεν). The subject of the verb is an implied "we" embedded in the verb and refers to any believer who desires to keep the words of God. **Semantically,** ἐσμέν is a gnomic present: "we are" (cf. KJV NASB ESV NIV NET etc.). It introduces something that is true all the time (W, 523). Followers of Jesus know they have a relationship with God when they persist in keeping God's commands.

2:6a λέγων: The Greek word λέγων is a nominative masculine singular present active participle from the verb λέγω meaning "to say," "to give expression to" or "to express oneself orally" (BDAG, s.v. "λέγω" 1aγ, p. 588). **Syntactically,** λέγων is a substantival participle that functions as the subject of the verb "ought" (ὀφείλει). **Semantically,** λέγων has a gnomic force: "the one who says" (NASB NET) or "whoever says" (NRSV ESV NIV). It presents a generic statement to describe something that is true any time (W, 523, 615). John directs attention to people who make a claim, which is specified in the next verb.

μένειν: The Greek word μένειν is a present active infinitive from the verb μένω meaning "to remain," "to continue," "to abide," or is used of someone who does not leave a certain realm or sphere (BDAG, s.v. "μένω" 1aβ, p. 631). **Syntactically,** μένειν is the direct object of the participle of communication: "the one who says" (λέγων). Since μένειν is not a structural marker, it is not underlined. **Semantically,** μένειν is an infinitive of indirect discourse: "that he abides" (KJV ASV NASB NRSV ESV), "resides" (NET), "walk" (NIV CNT), or "live" (NLT). It provides the content of the verbal of speech or completes the verbal of communication (W, 603). John draws attention to the person who makes it a practice to live like Jesus and thereby maintains a relationship with God.

ὀφείλει: The Greek word ὀφείλει is a third person singular present active indicative from the verb ὀφείλω meaning "to be obligated" or "to be under obligation to meet certain social and moral expectation" (BDAG, s.v. "ὀφείλω" 2aβ, p. 743). **Syntactically,** ὀφείλει is the main verb of the independent clause: "the one who says that he (= God) abides in him (or her) *is obligated . . .* also himself (or herself) to persist in living." (ὁ λέγων ἐν αὐτῷ μένειν ὀφείλει . . . καὶ αὐτὸς περιπατεῖν). The subject is the participial phrase, "the one who says that he abides in him" (ὁ λέγων ἐν αὐτῷ μένειν). It underscores an obligation of any person who claims to have a relationship with God. **Semantically,** ὀφείλει is a gnomic present: "we must" (NIV) or "we are obligated" or "we ought" (cf. KJV NASB ESV NET etc.). It is a generic statement to describe something that is true any time (W, 523). John underscores a believer's ongoing obligation. That obligation is revealed in the infinitive (περιπατεῖν).

περιπατεῖν: The Greek word περιπατεῖν is a present active infinitive from the verb περιπατέω meaning "to walk" or "to live" or "to conduct one's life as a habit of conduct" (BDAG, s.v. "περιπατέω" 2aγ, p. 803). **Syntactically,** περιπατεῖν is part of the main verb and underlined as a major structural marker. The pronoun, "they [singular]" (αὐτός) is not the subject of this infinitive, instead "they [singular]" (αὐτός) is resumptive and points back to the subject of "ought" (ὀφείλει; Culy, 30). **Semantically,** περιπατεῖν is a complementary infinitive: "to walk" (cf. KJV NASB ESV NIV NET etc.), completing the thought of the verb "ought" (ὀφείλει; cf. W, 598). The believer who claims to have a relationship with God is obligated to conduct one's life in a certain manner, which is made clear in the καθώς clause.

2:6b καθώς: The Greek word καθώς is a conjunction meaning "just as" or "even as" (BDAG, s.v. "καθώς" 2, p. 493). **Syntactically,** καθώς introduces a dependent conjunctive clause. The entire dependent clause, "*just as* that one lived" (καθὼς ἐκεῖνος περιεπάτησεν), functions adverbially modifying the verb "I must . . . persist in living" (ὀφείλει . . . περιπατεῖν). The clause is placed under περιπατεῖν to show subordination. **Semantically,** καθώς is comparative: "just as" (NRSV NET CNT), "as" (NASB NIV NLT), or "even as" (KJV ASV). It describes the way in which a believer who claims to have a relationship with God should live. They should live as "that one" (ἐκεῖνος), which is a technical term for Jesus (Brown, 261; cf. Culy, 30). The one who claims to have a relationship with God should conduct their lives in a manner similar to that of Jesus.

περιεπάτησεν: The Greek word περιεπάτησεν is a third person singular aorist active indicative from the verb περιπατέω meaning "to walk" or "to live" or "to conduct one's life as a habit of conduct" (BDAG, s.v. "περιπατέω" 2aγ, p. 803). **Syntactically,** περιεπάτησεν is the governing verb of the dependent adverbial clause. The subject of the verb is the emphatic demonstrative pronoun "that one" (ἐκεῖνος) and refers to Jesus himself. **Semantically,** περιεπάτησεν is a constative aorist: "he lived" or "he walked (KJV ASV NASB NRSV ESV NET CNT). It describes Jesus's manner of living as a whole (W, 557). Anyone who claims to have a relationship with God should live like Jesus did.

2:7a γράφω: The Greek word γράφω is a first person singular present active indicative from the verb γράφω meaning "to write" or "to compose" with reference to composing a letter (BDAG, s.v. "γράφω" 2d, p. 207). **Syntactically,** γράφω is the main verb of the independent clause: "Beloved, *I write* no new commandment to you" (Ἀγαπητοί, οὐκ ἐντολὴν καινὴν γράφω ὑμῖν). The assumed subject, "I," refers to John. **Semantically,** γράφω is a progressive present negated with οὐκ: "I am writing no new command" (NRSV ESV CNT) or "I am not writing a new command" (NRSV NIV NET NLT) or "I write no new command" (KJV). It describes something that is occurring right now (W, 518). John points out that what he is writing is not new.

2:7b ἀλλ': The Greek word ἀλλά is a conjunction meaning "but" or "rather" after a previous negative statement (BDAG, s.v. "ἀλλά" 1a, p. 44). **Syntactically,** ἀλλά identifies the clause as a conjunctive independent clause, "*but* I now write an old command" (ἀλλ' ἐντολὴν παλαιάν). **Semantically,** ἀλλά is contrastive: "but" (cf. KJV NASB ESV NIV NET etc.) or "rather" (NLT). John is about to counter what his readers may think with an elliptical clause.

[γράφω]: The elliptical Greek word γράφω is first person singular present active indicative from the verb γράφω meaning "to write" or "to compose" with reference to composing a letter (BDAG, s.v. "γράφω" 2d, p. 207). **Syntactically,** γράφω is the main verb of the independent contrastive clause. The subject of the verb is the assumed "I" that is embedded in the verb and refers to John. **Semantically,** γράφω is a progressive present: "I *now* write." It tells what John is currently doing (W, 518). John underscores that the command John is currently writing about is an old commandment.

2:7c ἥν: The Greek word ἥν is accusative singular feminine from the relative pronoun ὅς meaning "which" or "that" (BDAG, s.v. "ὅς" 1a, p. 725). **Syntactically,** ἥν introduces an adjectival relative clause: "*which* you have had *as an* obligation from the beginning" (ἥν εἴχετε ἀπ' ἀρχῆς). The entire clause modifies the noun "command" (ἐντολήν) This relative pronoun is in the accusative case because it serves as the direct object of the verb "we have had" (εἴχετε). Whether the relative pronoun is translated "that" (NASB ESV CNT) or "which" (KJV ASV NASB NIV NET), the entire clause underscores a commandment they have had from the beginning. It provides further information about the command.

εἴχετε: The Greek word εἴχετε is a second person plural imperfect active indicative from the verb ἔχω meaning "to have" or "to experience something in the sense of an obligation" (BDAG, s.v. "ἔχω" 7aδ, p. 421). **Syntactically,** εἴχετε is the governing verb of the dependent adjectival relative clause. The assumed subject, "you," refers to John's readers. **Semantically,** εἴχετε is a pluperfective imperfect: "you *have had* as an obligation" (cf. NASB NRSV NIV NET NLT; W, 549). In essence it is a command given previously to the writing of this short letter. God's command has been in their possession since that time, and they have been obligated to keep that divine expectation.

Lexical and Theological Nugget: What does "from the beginning" (ἀπ' ἀρχῆς) mean? John says that his readers have had this command from the beginning. Yet we must ask, the beginning of what? Some say that it refers to the beginning of an individual's relationship with Jesus (Brown, 265, 440), while others suggest it refers back to the teachings of Jesus while on earth (John 13:34) that essentially ushered in the apostolic message to love others (cf. Strecker, 104; Painter, 236). Culy seems to view this phrase more generally as a reference to truth that has been around for a long time (Culy, 32; cf. Smalley, 182; Yarbough, 34, 97, 197). It seems that since John addresses individuals, then their acquaintance with this command would have come at the beginning of their individual Christian journey. This prepositional phrase will appear again in 2:24 and 3:11.

2:7d ἐστίν: The Greek word ἐστίν is third person singular present active indicative from the verb εἰμί meaning "is" and has an equative function of identifying something with something (BDAG, s.v. "εἰμί" 2, p. 283). **Syntactically,** ἐστίν is the main verb of the independent clause "the old commandment is the word" (ἡ ἐντολὴ ἡ παλαιά ἐστιν ὁ λόγος). The subject of the verb is the noun "command" (ἡ ἐντολή). **Semantically,** ἐστίν is an equative present: "is" (cf. KJV NASB ESV NIV NET etc.). It equates the old command with the word.

2:7e ὅν: The Greek word ὅν is an accusative singular masculine from the relative pronoun ὅς meaning "who, which, that" (BDAG, s.v. "ὅς" 1a, p. 725). **Syntactically,** ὅν introduces an adjectival relative clause, "*which* you have heard" (ὅν ἠκούσατε), modifying the noun "word" (ὁ λόγος). The entire relative clause provides further information about the "word," which is found in its verb.

ἠκούσατε: The Greek word ἠκούσατε is a second person plural aorist active indicative from the verb ἀκούω meaning "to hear" or "to hear something from someone" (BDAG, s.v. "ἀκούω" 1a, 1b, p. 37) or to denote a body of authoritative teaching (BDAG, s.v. "ἀκούω" 3d, p. 38). **Syntactically,** ἠκούσατε is the governing verb of the relative clause. The subject of the verb is an implied "you" embedded in the verb, which refers to John's readers. **Semantically,** ἠκούσατε is a consummative aorist: "you *have* heard" (KJV NASB NRSV ESV NIV NET CNT). It describes a conclusion or cessation of an act as a whole (W, 559). John describes the "word" as a body of authoritative teachings that has been in the possession of his readers since they first came into the faith.

2:8a γράφω: The Greek word γράφω is a first person singular present active indicative from the verb γράφω meaning "to write" or "to compose" with reference to composing a letter (BDAG, s.v. "γράφω" 2d, p. 207). **Syntactically,** γράφω is the main verb of an independent clause "on the other hand I *now write* to you a new commandment" (πάλιν ἐντολὴν καινὴν γράφω ὑμῖν). The assumed subject, "I," refers to John. The adverb "again" (πάλιν) sets up a contrast. In this context πάλιν should be translated as "on the other hand" (BDAG, s.v. "πάλιν" 4, p. 753; cf. NASB NET), contrasting the old command that was received from Jesus, but has a new application in their lives today because they are living in a new era where hatred is losing and love is winning (Culy, 32). **Semantically,** γράφω is a progressive present: "I *now* write" or "I am writing" (NASB NRSV ESV NIV NLT CNT). It tells what John is currently doing (W, 518). John is *right now* writing a letter.

2:8b ὅ: The Greek word ὅ is a nominative singular neuter from the relative pronoun ὅς meaning "who, which, that" (BDAG, s.v. "ὅς" 1gβ, p. 727). **Syntactically,** ὅ introduces a dependent relative clause: "*which* is true in him and in you" (ὅ ἐστιν ἀληθὲς ἐν αὐτῷ καὶ ἐν ὑμῖν). In order to follow the Greek word order and our interpretation, the clause is placed above the independent clause in the clausal outline. This clause is difficult to interpret, with four options: (1) It seems natural to classify it as adjectival describing the new command, but it does not agree with the noun "command" (ἐντολήν) in gender. (2) It could be functioning substantivally in apposition to the entirety of the previous clause. In that case the new command would equal that which is true. (3) It could be functioning substantivally modifying the subsequent clause "because the darkness is passing away and the true light is already shining" (ὅτι ἡ σκοτία παράγεται καὶ τὸ φῶς τὸ ἀληθινὸν ἤδη φαίνει), telling us that this further statement is true. The best option, however, seems to be to take it (4) as an adjectival relative clause referring to the whole discussion that precedes (v. 7d, e). The specifics of the command are made known in the rest of the clause.

ἐστίν: The Greek word ἐστίν is a third person singular present active indicative from the verb εἰμί meaning "is" or "to show how something is to be understood" (BDAG, s.v. "εἰμί" 2c, p. 282). **Syntactically,** ἐστίν is the governing verb of the dependent relative clause. The subject of the verb is the relative pronoun "which" (ὅ). **Semantically,** ἐστίν is an equative present: "is" (cf. KJV NASB ESV NIV NET etc.). Through the relative clause, ἐστίν equates the command his readers have heard with Jesus. The command to love others is not new in time. It is true in both the life of Jesus and in the life of John's readers.

2:8c ὅτι: The Greek word ὅτι is a conjunction meaning "because" (BDAG, s.v. "ὅτι" 4a, p. 732). **Syntactically,** ὅτι introduces a dependent conjunctive clause: "*because* the darkness is passing away" (ὅτι ἡ σκοτία παράγεται). The decision that the adjectival relative clause (v. 8b) refers to the whole discussion that precedes it affects the interpretation of this ὅτι clause. This clause, then, is not providing the content of the "new commandment" (ἐντολὴν καινήν), but rather is functioning adverbially. Alternatively, it could modify the verb "is" (ἐστίν) and be translated "which is true because the darkness is passing away." If so, it would provide the reason why the command is true. However, the ὅτι clause is modifying the verb "write" (γράφω). **Semantically,** ὅτι is causal: "because" (cf. KJV NASB ESV NIV NET etc.). It provides the reason why John is writing to them (W, 460). That reason is rather groundbreaking and is expounded on in the clause's verb.

παράγεται: The Greek word, παράγεται, is a third person singular present passive indicative from the verb παράγω meaning "to pass away" or "to be going out of existence" (BDAG, s.v. "παράγω" 4b, p. 761). **Syntactically,** παράγεται is one of the governing verbs of the ὅτι clause. The subject is "the darkness" (ἡ σκοτία). **Semantically,** παράγεται is a progressive present: "is passing" (ASV NASB NRSV ESV NIV NET CNT) or "is disappearing" (NLT). It tells what is happening right now (W, 518). The first reason John is writing is to identify a change that is happening in the readers' situation. As God's kingdom advances, the darkness *right now* is going out of existence. The culmination of the ages has been set in motion, and in light of that fact, the readers should love one another (Culy, 34–35).

2:8d [ὅτι]: The Greek word ὅτι is a conjunction meaning "because" (BDAG, s.v. "ὅτι" 4a, p. 732). **Syntactically,** [ὅτι] is an ellipsis and serves to introduce the second part of the dependent clause: "and [*because*] the light is already shining" (καὶ [ὅτι] τὸ φῶς τὸ ἀληθινὸν ἤδη φαίνει). It too modifies the verb "write" (γράφω). **Semantically,** ὅτι is causal: "because." It provides the second reason why John is currently writing to them about the love command, which is evident in the next verb.

φαίνει: The Greek word φαίνει is a third person singular present active indicative from the verb φαίνω meaning "to shine" or "to produce light" (BDAG, s.v. "φαίνω" 1a, p. 1046). **Syntactically,** φαίνει is one of the compound governing verbs of the dependent conjunctive. The subject of the verb is "the light" (τὸ φῶς). **Semantically,** φαίνει is a progressive present: "is *already* shinning" (cf. NASB ESV NIV NET etc.) or "is shining *now*" (KJV). It tells what is happening right now (W, 518). It points out that *right now* (KJV) the kingdom of God is advancing. The second reason John writes is because the true light is already shining.

2:9 λέγων: The Greek word λέγων is a nominative masculine singular present active participle from the verb λέγω meaning "to say" or "to give expression to" or "to express oneself orally" (BDAG, s.v. "λέγω" 1aγ, p. 588). **Syntactically,** λέγων is a substantival participle functioning as part of the compound subject of the verb "is" (ἐστίν). **Semantically,** λέγων has a gnomic force: "the one who says" (NASB NET) or "whoever says" (NRSV ESV). It presents a generic statement to describe something that is true any time (W, 523, 615). John draws attention to people who make a claim that is specified in the next verb.

εἶναι: The Greek word εἶναι is a present active infinitive from the verb εἰμί meaning "to live in accordance with" (BDAG, s.v. "εἰμί" 3c, p. 284). **Syntactically,** εἶναι is the direct object of the participle of communication, "the one who says" (λέγων). Since εἶναι is not a structural marker, it is not underlined.

Semantically, εἶναι is an infinitive of indirect discourse: "anyone who claims *to be*" (NIV) or "the one who says *he is*" (NASB NET cf. CNT) or "whoever says *he is*" (NRSV ESV). It is providing the content of the verbal of speech or completing the verbal of communication (W, 603). The claim is that they live in accordance with the light (= God) or that they have a relationship with God.

μισῶν: The Greek word μισῶν is a nominative masculine singular present active participle from the verb μισέω meaning "to hate" or "to detest" or "to have a strong aversion to" (BDAG, s.v. "μισέω" 1a, p. 652). **Syntactically,** μισῶν is a substantival participle functioning as part of the compound subject of the verb "is" (ἐστίν). And although it is possible to interpret the participle with an adverbial temporal sense "while hating" (NRSV), most translations render the participle as substantival (e.g., KJV NASB ESV NIV NET). **Semantically,** μισῶν has a gnomic force: "the one who *persists* in hating." John provides another timeless reality (W, 523, 615). The person who has a continual strong aversion for another believer cannot have a relationship with a loving and pure God.

Lexical Nugget: What does John mean when he talks of people "hating" (μισέω) their brother? John uses the word "hate" (μισέω) five times in 1 John (2:9, 11; 3:13, 15; 4:20). The word is typically used to describe a strong aversion to someone or an act that should bring on hatred or contempt. For instance, having sexual intercourse with a close family member was viewed with abhorrence (Josephus, *A.J.* 3.7.1 §274). John uses the term "to hate" (μισέω) as an antonym for "love" throughout this letter. This becomes clear in 4:20 where John points out that anyone who claims to love God yet hates his brother is a liar. The hatred does not seem to be outright hostility though, but instead a complete lack of compassion (cf. 1 John 3:15–18; Culy, 35).

ἐστίν: The Greek word ἐστίν is third person singular present active indicative from the verb εἰμί meaning "is" and has an equative function of identifying something with something else (BDAG, s.v. "εἰμί" 2, p. 283). **Syntactically,** ἐστίν is the main verb of the independent clause: "the one who claims to be in the light and yet [BDAG, s.v. "καί" 1bη, p. 495] persists in hating his brother *is* still in the darkness until now" (ὁ λέγων ἐν τῷ φωτὶ εἶναι καὶ τὸν ἀδελφὸν αὐτοῦ μισῶν ἐν τῇ σκοτίᾳ ἐστὶν ἕως ἄρτι). The subject of the verb is the compound phrase "the one who claims to be in the light and yet persists in hating his brother" (ὁ λέγων ἐν τῷ φωτὶ εἶναι καὶ τὸν ἀδελφὸν αὐτοῦ μισῶν). **Semantically,** ἐστίν is equative with gnomic force: "is" (cf. KJV NASB ESV NIV NET etc.). John is elucidating the timeless truth (W, 523) that anyone who claims to have a relationship with God will not hate other believers, but instead will love them.

2:10a ἀγαπῶν: The Greek word ἀγαπῶν is a nominative masculine singular present active participle from the verb ἀγαπάω meaning "to love" or "to have a warm regard for and interest in another person" (BDAG, s.v. "ἀγαπάω" 1aα, p. 5). **Syntactically,** ἀγαπῶν is a participle functioning substantivally as the subject of the verb "remains" (μένει). **Semantically,** ἀγαπῶν has a gnomic force: "the one who loves" (NASB NET) or "whoever loves" (NRSV ESV NIV). John provides another timeless reality (W, 523, 615). The person who makes it a practice to love fellow believers abides in the light or has a relationship with God.

μένει: The Greek word μένει is a third person singular present active indicative from the verb μένω meaning "to remain" or "to stay" or "to remain in a certain realm or sphere" (BDAG, s.v. "μένω" 1aβ, p. 631). **Syntactically,** μένει is the main verb of the independent clause "the one who loves his brother *abides* in the light" (ὁ ἀγαπῶν τὸν ἀδελφὸν αὐτοῦ ἐν τῷ φωτὶ μένει). The subject is the participial phrase "the one who loves his brother" (ἀγαπῶν τὸν ἀδελφὸν αὐτοῦ). **Semantically,** μένει is a gnomic present with a customary present force: "abides" (KJV ASV NASB ESV CNT) or "lives" (NRSV NIV cf. NLT). John provides another timeless reality (W, 523, 615). The person who *persists* in loving other Christians lives in the light like God does.

2:10b καί: The Greek word καί is a conjunction that in this context means "and" (BDAG, s.v. "καί" 1b, p. 494). **Syntactically,** καί introduces an independent conjunctive clause, "*and* in him there is no cause for stumbling" (καὶ σκάνδαλον ἐν αὐτῷ οὐκ ἔστιν). **Semantically,** καί is a coordinating connective: "and" (cf. KJV NASB ESV NIV NET etc.). It provides additional information about the believer who loves his brother (W, 671). Such a believer is not a stumbling block.

Lexical Nugget: What is a stumbling block? This is the only time that this noun is used in Johannine literature. It normally refers to an obstacle that causes someone to trip. In John 6:61, the cognate verb is used to talk about Jesus's teaching being the cause for someone to stumble or trip. The idea here seems to be that a believer who loves his fellow Christians will not give another a cause or reason to fall away from the faith (Bateman[1], 235).

ἐστίν: The Greek word ἐστίν is third person singular present active indicative from the verb εἰμί meaning "there is" or "to show how something is to be understood" (BDAG, s.v. "εἰμί" 2cα, p. 283). **Syntactically,** ἐστίν is the main verb of the independent conjunctive clause. The subject of the verb is an implied "there" embedded in the third person singular verb. **Semantically,** ἐστίν is a gnomic present: "is" (cf. KJV NASB ESV NIV NET etc.). It presents another timeless truth (W, 523). Anyone who loves their fellow believer will not become a stumbling block to that believer's faith.

2:11a δέ: The Greek word δέ is a conjunction meaning "but" (BDAG, s.v. "δέ" 4a, p. 213). **Syntactically,** δέ is in the postpositive position introducing an independent conjunctive clause "*but* the one who persists in hating his brother is in the darkness" (ὁ δὲ μισῶν τὸν ἀδελφὸν αὐτοῦ ἐν τῇ σκοτίᾳ ἐστίν). **Semantically,** δέ is a marker of contrast: "but" (e.g., KJV NASB ESV NIV NET). It gives an opposing truth to the idea that the believer who loves has a relationship with God. The countertruth is that the one who hates their fellow believers does not have a relationship with God. They are in the darkness, not the light.

μισῶν: The Greek word μισῶν is a nominative masculine singular present active participle from the verb μισέω meaning "to hate" or "to detest" or "to have a strong aversion to" (BDAG, s.v. "μισέω" 1a, p. 652). **Syntactically,** μισῶν is a substantival participle functioning as the subject of the verb "is" (ἐστίν). **Semantically,** μισῶν is a gnomic present with a customary present force: "the one who hates" (NASB NET cf. CNT) or "whoever hates" (NRSV ESV NIV). It presents a generic statement to describe something that is true any time (W, 521, 615). Thus, the person who *persists* in hating other believers cannot possibly have a relationship with a loving and pure God.

ἐστίν: The Greek word ἐστίν is third person singular present active indicative from the verb εἰμί meaning "to be" or describes a special connection between subject and predicate (BDAG, s.v. "εἰμί" 2b, p. 282). **Syntactically,** ἐστίν is the main verb of the independent clause: "but the one who persists in hating their brother *is* in the darkness" (ὁ δὲ μισῶν τὸν ἀδελφὸν αὐτοῦ ἐν τῇ σκοτίᾳ ἐστίν). The subject of the verb is the substantival participial phrase "the one who hates their brother" (ὁ . . . μισῶν τὸν ἀδελφὸν αὐτοῦ). **Semantically,** ἐστίν is a gnomic present: "is" (cf. KJV NASB ESV NIV NET etc.). It presents another timeless truth (W, 523). Anyone who hates their brother cannot have a relationship with God.

2:11b καί: The Greek word καί is a conjunction that in this context means "and so" (BDAG, s.v. "καί" 1c, p. 494). **Syntactically,** καί introduces a conjunctive independent clause "*and so* they are walking in the darkness" (καὶ ἐν τῇ σκοτίᾳ περιπατεῖ). **Semantically,** καί is an inferential connective: "and so" (cf. NLT). It provides a conclusion about the believer who hates their brother. Such a believer is described with the next verb.

περιπατεῖ: The Greek word περιπατεῖ is a third person singular present active indicative from the verb περιπατέω meaning "to walk" or "to live" or "to go about here or there in imagery or nonliteral sense" (BDAG, s.v. "περιπατέω" 1d, p. 803). **Syntactically,** περιπατεῖ serves as the main verb of the independent conjunctive clause. The assumed subject, "he/she," refers to any believer who hates other Christians. **Semantically,** περιπατεῖ is a gnomic present with customary present force: "he is walking" or "walks" (cf. KJV NASB ESV NIV NET etc.). It presents a generic statement to describe something that is true any time (W, 521, 615). Any professing believer who persists in hating other Christians *lives* in darkness. Even though the verb is intended to convey the idea of lifestyle, it should be translated here as "walking" since it is part of an extended metaphor describing the one who hates their fellow believers (Culy, 37).

2:11c κaí: The Greek word καί is a conjunction meaning "and" (BDAG, s.v. "καί" 1b, p. 494). **Syntactically,** καί introduces a conjunctive independent clause, "*and* they do not know where they are going" (καὶ οὐκ οἶδεν ποῦ ὑπάγει). **Semantically,** καί is a coordinating connective: "and" (KJV ASV NASB NRSV ESV NET CNT). It shows that John is adding a further thought about the believer who hates their brother, made evident by the next verb.

οἶδεν: The Greek word οἶδεν is a third person singular perfect active indicative from the verb οἶδα meaning "to know," "to understand," "to recognize," or "to grasp the meaning of something" (BDAG, s.v. "οἶδα" 4, p. 694). **Syntactically,** οἶδεν is the governing verb of the independent conjunctive clause: "and *he does* not *know* where they are going" (καὶ οὐκ οἶδεν ποῦ ὑπάγει). The assumed subject, "he," refers to any believer who hates their fellow Christians. **Semantically,** the negated οἶδεν is a perfect with present force: "does not know" (οὐκ οἶδεν; e.g., KJV NASB ESV NIV NET). Some verbs, like οἶδα, appear almost exclusively in the perfect tense without the perfect's aspectual significance (W, 579–580). Believers who hate other believers fail to grasp their lives of darkness.

ποῦ: The Greek word ποῦ is a conjunction meaning "where" and is an interrogative reference with an implication of movement (BDAG, s.v. "ποῦ" 2b, p. 858). **Syntactically,** ποῦ introduces a dependent substantival clause, "*where* he is going" (ποῦ ὑπάγει). It is the direct object of the verb "know" (οἶδεν). The clause is placed in parentheses in order to visualize its contribution to the independent clause. **Semantically,** ποῦ has an adverbial force and functions locatively, describing the fact that the believer who is in the darkness has no idea in what direction they are heading (W, 676).

ὑπάγει: The Greek word ὑπάγει is a third person singular present active indicative from the verb ὑπάγω meaning "to go" or "to be moving in a certain direction" (BDAG, s.v. "ὑπάγω" 2b, p. 1028). **Syntactically,** ὑπάγει is the governing verb of the dependent substantival locative clause: "where *he is going*" (ποῦ ὑπάγει). The assumed subject, "he (singular)," refers to any believer who hates their fellow Christians. **Semantically,** ὑπάγει is a gnomic present with the force of a customary present: "he is going" (cf. KJV

NASB ESV NIV NET etc.). It presents a generic statement to describe something that is true any time (W, 521, 615). Anyone who claims to have a relationship with God yet hates their fellow Christians is not headed in the right direction, *namely,* they are not going to the Father as Jesus went to the Father (cf. John 7:33; 16:5).

2:11d ὅτι: The Greek word ὅτι is a conjunction meaning "because" (BDAG, s.v. "ὅτι" 4a, p. 732). **Syntactically,** ὅτι introduces an adverbial dependent clause: "*because the darkness has blinded their eyes*" (ὅτι ἡ σκοτία ἐτύφλωσεν τοὺς ὀφθαλμοὺς αὐτοῦ), modifying the verb "know" (οἶδεν). **Semantically,** ὅτι is a marker of causality: "because" (e.g., KJV NASB ES NIV NET). It provides the reason why the believer who hates other Christians does not know where he or she is going. The reason is clearly evident in the clause's verb.

ἐτύφλωσεν: The Greek word ἐτύφλωσεν is a third person singular aorist active indicative from the verb τυφλόω meaning "to be blind" or "to be deprived of sight" (BDAG, s.v. "τυφλόω," p. 1021). **Syntactically,** ἐτύφλωσεν is the governing verb of the adverbial dependent clause. The subject of the verb is "the darkness" (ἡ σκοτία). **Semantically,** ἐτύφλωσεν is a constative aorist: "*has* blinded" (KJV ASV ESV NIV NET CNT). It states an event as a whole (W, 557). Believers who hate other believers are blinded by their own immorality. This is a figurative usage of the word "blindness" that draws attention to those people whose hatred has led them to be spiritually blind.

Lexical Nugget: What does τυφλόω mean? Naturally the term is often used to refer to people who are physically blind or who are struck with physical blindness (of wilderness people: Josephus, *C. Ap.* 2.11, §132 of Zedekiah: Josephus, *A.J.* 10.8.2 §141). It is also used figuratively to refer to people who are unable to understand, whether that is because they (1) lack mental capacity (John 12:40), (2) are spiritually unperceptive (2 Cor. 4:4), or (3) are stuck in deliberate disbelief (1 John 2:11; of Apion: Josephus: *C. Ap.* 2.132, cf. 2:142; of judges Josephus, *A.J.,* 8.2.2 §30). In John 12:39–40, the Jewish leaders refuse to believe in spite of the sign-miracles that Jesus has performed, and this persistent disbelief leads to their inability to believe. John explains this willful blindness with the words of Isaiah 6:10, "Make the hearts of these people calloused; make their ears deaf and their eyes blind! Otherwise they might see with their eyes and hear with their ears, their minds might understand, and they might repent and be healed" (NET). The spiritual blinding is a direct response to their deliberate disbelief. Here in 1 John 2:11, darkness and hatred have caused the secessionists to become spiritually blind. We will also see later that the agents of this disbelief and the ones responsible for this spiritual blindness are the "Evil One" (2:13–14) and the "Antichrist" (2:18–22).

1 John 2:12–17

Big Greek Idea: John affirms his readers about their relationship with God, their resilience, and their triumph over the Devil before warning them about the world's negative behaviors, its lack of acceptability, and its imminent demise.

Structural Overview: John's mood shifts from one of assessment (2:3–11) to one of affection (2:12–17).

On the one hand, John affectionately (τεκνία) writes to **_affirm_** (γράφω . . . ὅτι) followers of Jesus about their relationship (ἀφέωνται/ἐγνώκατε) with God, their resilience (ἐγνώκατε/ἐγνώκατε), and their triumph (νενικήκατε/νενικήκατε) over the Devil (2:12–14).

On the other hand, John **_warns_** followers of Jesus not to develop an intimate relationship (μὴ ἀγαπᾶτε) with the world (2:15), because (ὅτι) the world and its negative behaviors will not last, in contrast (δέ) with followers of Jesus who will enter an eternity with God (2:16–17).

Outline:

> Followers of Jesus Are Affirmed (vv. 12–14)
>> Followers of Jesus have a relationship with God (vv. 13a, 14a)
>> Followers of Jesus have a resilient relationship with God (vv. 13b, 14b)
>> Followers of Jesus have triumph over the Devil (vv. 13b, 14c)
> Followers of Jesus Are Warned (vv. 15–17)
>> Don't get overly attached to this life and its system (v. 15)
>> Indulgence, sensual gratification, and vain confidence is not from God (v. 16)
>> This world's system and its ethical values will end (v. 17)

CLAUSAL OUTLINE FOR 1 JOHN 2:12–17

2:12 **Γράφω** ὑμῖν, τεκνία, (ὅτι <u>ἀφέωνται</u> ὑμῖν αἱ ἁμαρτίαι διὰ τὸ ὄνομα αὐτοῦ).

2:12 **I** _now_ **write** to you, children, (<u>that</u> for your benefit your sins <u>have been pardoned</u> because of his (= Jesus's) name).

2:13a **γράφω** ὑμῖν, πατέρες, (ὅτι <u>ἐγνώκατε</u> τὸν ἀπ᾽ ἀρχῆς).

2:13a **I** _now_ **write** to you, fathers, (<u>that</u> <u>you have known</u> the one [= Jesus] who is from the beginning).

2:13b **γράφω** ὑμῖν, νεανίσκοι, (<u>ὅτι</u> <u>νενικήκατε</u> τὸν πονηρόν).
2:13b **I** *now* **write** to you, young people, (<u>that</u> <u>you have overcome</u> the Evil One).

2:14a **ἔγραψα** ὑμῖν, παιδία, (<u>ὅτι</u> <u>ἐγνώκατε</u> τὸν πατέρα).
2:14a **I have written** to you, children, (<u>that</u> <u>you have known</u> the Father).

2:14b **ἔγραψα** ὑμῖν, πατέρες, (<u>ὅτι</u> <u>ἐγνώκατε</u> τὸν [πατέρα] ἀπ᾽ ἀρχῆς).
2:14b **I have written** to you, fathers, (<u>that</u> <u>you have known</u> the [*Father*] from the beginning).

2:14c **ἔγραψα** ὑμῖν, νεανίσκοι, (<u>ὅτι</u> ἰσχυροί <u>ἐστε</u>
2:14c **I have written** to you, young people, (<u>that</u> you <u>are</u> strong,

        |
       2:14d <u>καὶ</u> [<u>*ὅτι*</u>] ὁ λόγος τοῦ θεοῦ ἐν ὑμῖν <u>μένει</u>
       2:14d <u>and</u> [*that*] <u>the word of God</u> <u>abides</u> in you
        |
       2:14e <u>καὶ</u> [<u>*ὅτι*</u>] <u>νενικήκατε</u> τὸν πονηρόν).
       2:14e <u>and</u> [*that*] <u>you have conquered</u> the Evil One).

2:15a Μὴ **ἀγαπᾶτε** τὸν κόσμον μηδὲ τὰ ἐν τῷ κόσμῳ.
2:15a **Do** not **love** the world nor the things in the world.

    2:15b **ἐάν** τις **ἀγαπᾷ** τὸν κόσμον,
    2:15b **If** anyone *persists in* **loving** the world,
    |
2:15c οὐκ **ἔστιν** ἡ ἀγάπη τοῦ πατρὸς ἐν αὐτῷ·
2:15c the love of the Father **is** not in him (or her);

2:16a <u>ὅτι</u> πᾶν τὸ ἐν τῷ κόσμῳ, . . . οὐκ **ἔστιν** ἐκ τοῦ πατρὸς
2:16a <u>for</u> *this reason* all that is in the world . . . **is** not from the Father

         ἡ ἐπιθυμία τῆς σαρκὸς
         the flesh that desires

         καὶ ἡ ἐπιθυμία τῶν ὀφθαλμῶν
         and the eyes that desire

         καὶ ἡ ἀλαζονεία τοῦ βίου,
         and the boastful pride about one's life

2:16b <u>ἀλλὰ</u> [*πᾶν τὸ ἐν τῷ κόσμῳ*] ἐκ τοῦ κόσμου **ἐστίν**.
2:16b <u>but</u> [*all that is in the world*] **is** from the world.

$^{2:17a}$ <u>καὶ</u> ὁ κόσμος **παράγεται** καὶ ἡ ἐπιθυμία αὐτοῦ,
$^{2:17a}$ <u>And</u> the world **is *now* passing away**, and also its lusts,

$^{2:17b}$ ὁ <u>δὲ</u> ποιῶν τὸ θέλημα τοῦ θεοῦ **μένει** εἰς τὸν αἰῶνα.
$^{2:17b}$ <u>but</u> the one who does the will of God **remains** forever.

SYNTAX EXPLAINED FOR 1 JOHN 2:12–17

$^{2:12}$ Γράφω: The Greek word γράφω is a first person singular present active indicative from the verb γράφω meaning "to write" or "to compose" with reference to composing a letter (BDAG, s.v. "γράφω" 2d, p. 207). **Syntactically,** γράφω serves as the main verb of the independent clause: "*I now write*
to you, children" (γράφω ὑμῖν, τεκνία). The assumed subject, "I," refers to
John. **Semantically,** γράφω is a progressive present: "I *now* write" or "I write"
(KJV ASV NIV CNT) or "I am writing" (KJV ASV NIV NLT CNT). It tells what John
is currently doing (W, 518). John is *right now* writing a letter.

> **Lexical Nugget:** How does John use these three vocatives: children (τεκνία
> and παιδία), fathers (πατέρες), and young people (νεανίσκοι) in verses
> 12–17? Are these three different groups? On the one hand, John may be re-
> ferring to three different groups within the household of believers. If this
> were the case though, why wouldn't he also address women, as in the other
> household codes found in the New Testament? On the other hand, the first
> vocative "children" (τεκνία) may be a blanket word covering all members of
> the community, while the rest of the vocatives divide them into two groups:
> the young and the old or spiritually mature and spiritually young (Brown,
> 298–300). One final option is that this is a catchy rhetorical device that John
> uses to highlight common characteristics of a believer's experience at any age
> (Culy, 38–39) because every piece of data here could be applied to any believ-
> er regardless of their maturity or length of life.

ὅτι: The Greek word ὅτι is a conjunction meaning "that" (BDAG, s.v. "ὅτι"
1a, p. 731). **Syntactically,** ὅτι introduces a dependent conjunctive clause:
"*that* for your benefit your sins have been pardoned because of his (= Jesus's)
name" (ὅτι ἀφέωνται ὑμῖν αἱ ἁμαρτίαι διὰ τὸ ὄνομα αὐτοῦ). The entire
ὅτι clause is substantival, serving as the direct object of the verb, "I am writing" (γράφω). It is placed in parentheses in order to visualize its contribution
to the independent clause. **Semantically,** ὅτι is an indirect discourse marker: "that" (NET). It signals the content of what John is writing (W, 45). (See
Grammatical Nugget on verses 12–14.)

> **Grammatical Nugget:** What are the six parallel constructions in verses 12–14?
> Each begins with some form of the verb "I write" (γράφω or ἔγραψα) after

which follows a dependent ὅτι clause. The ὅτι clauses could be classified in one of two ways. On the one hand, they may all be adverbial, modifying the verb, "I write" (γράφω), giving us the reason why John is writing and translated as cause: "because" (KJV ASV NASB NRSV ESV NIV NLT CNT; cf. Culy, 29). On the other hand, the ὅτι clauses may be substantival serving as the direct object of the verb, "I am writing" (γράφω). In normal usage when a verb of communication is used followed by a ὅτι clause, the clause that follows functions as the direct object, explicating the content of the communication (BDAG, s.v. "ὅτι" 1a, p. 731; cf. NET). Yet there are exceptions in 1 John (cf. 2:8c, d).

ἀφέωνται: The Greek word ἀφέωνται is a third person singular perfect passive indicative from the verb ἀφίημι meaning "to forgive," "to cancel," "to pardon," or "to release someone from legal or moral obligation" (BDAG, s.v. "ἀφίημι" 2, p. 156). **Syntactically,** ἀφέωνται is the governing verb of the dependent ὅτι clause. The subject is the plural noun, "*your* sins" (αἱ ἁμαρτίαι). **Semantically,** ἀφέωνται is an extensive perfect: "*have been* pardoned" (NASB NIV NET NLT). John's emphasis is on the completed act of forgiveness in past time rather than the present results (W, 577). John underscores that his readers live in a state of forgiveness "because [διά + accusative] of his name."

Lexical Nugget: To whom does "his name" (τὸ ὄνομα αὐτοῦ) refer? "His name" is a figure of speech called a metonymy of adjunct, where John replaces a noun with an adjunct or characteristic of it (Bateman[1], 246). Here "his name" replaces the name of someone else. In 3 John 7 we see this same metonymy of adjunct. John's missionaries are said to have gone out "for the sake of *the name.*" It could be a reference to either God or Jesus. Here in 1 John 2:12 it is likely that Jesus is in view since he was just referred to as "that one" (ἐκεῖνος) in 2:6. The reason that our sins are pardoned is because of the work of Jesus.

2:13a γράφω: The Greek word γράφω is a first person singular present active indicative from the verb γράφω meaning "to write" or "to compose" with reference to composing a letter (BDAG, s.v. "γράφω" 2d, p. 207). **Syntactically,** γράφω is the main verb of the independent clause: "*I now write* to you, fathers" (γράφω ὑμῖν, πατέρες). The assumed subject, "I," refers to John. **Semantically,** γράφω is a progressive present: "I *now* write" or "I write" (KJV ASV NIV CNT) or "I am writing (KJV ASV NIV NLT CNT). It tells what John is currently doing (W, 518). John is *right now* writing a letter.

ὅτι: The Greek word ὅτι is a conjunction meaning "that" (BDAG, s.v. "ὅτι" 1a, p. 731). **Syntactically,** ὅτι introduces a dependent clause: "*that* you have known the one [= Jesus] who is from the beginning" (ὅτι ἐγνώκατε τὸν ἀπ' ἀρχῆς). The entire ὅτι clause is substantival and functions as the direct object of the verb, "I am now writing" (γράφω). It is placed in parentheses in order to visualize its contribution to the independent clause. **Semantically,** ὅτι is an indirect discourse marker: "that" (NET). It signals the content of what John is writing (W, 45). (See Grammatical Nugget on verses 12–14.)

ἐγνώκατε: The Greek word ἐγνώκατε is a second person plural perfect active indicative from the verb γινώσκω meaning "to know" or "to come to know" or "to have come to the knowledge of some person" (BDAG, s.v. "γινώσκω" 6aβ, p. 200). **Syntactically,** ἐγνώκατε is the governing verb of the dependent ὅτι clause. The subject of the verb is an implied "you [plural]" embedded in the verb and referring to the readers of this letter. **Semantically,** ἐγνώκατε is an extensive perfect: "you *have* known" (KJV NASB NIV NET CNT) John's emphasis is on the completed act of knowing someone in past time rather than the present results (W, 577). John's point is that this community has had—and continues to have—a personal knowledge of Jesus.

> **Syntactical Nugget**: How is the article τόν functioning? The construction "the one who is from the beginning" (τὸν ἀπ᾽ ἀρχῆς) has an article (τόν) preceding a prepositional phrase. In this case the article functions as a nominalizer, turning the prepositional phrase into a substantive, which in this case serves as the direct object of the verb "you have known" (ἐγνώκατε) (Culy, 40; cf. W, 231–36). This language is a reference to Jesus and links back to the previous description of him in the prologue of the book (1 John 1:1–4).

2:13b γράφω: The Greek word γράφω is a first person singular present active indicative from the verb γράφω meaning "to write" or "to compose" with reference to composing a letter (BDAG, s.v. "γράφω" 2d, p. 207). **Syntactically,** γράφω is the main verb of the independent clause: "*I now write* to you, young people" (γράφω ὑμῖν, νεανίσκοι). The assumed subject, "I," once again refers to John. **Semantically,** γράφω is a progressive present: "I *now* write" or "I write" (KJV ASV NIV CNT) or "I am writing (KJV ASV NIV NLT CNT). It tells what John is currently doing (W, 518). John is *right now* writing a letter.

ὅτι: The Greek word ὅτι is a conjunction meaning "that" (BDAG, s.v. "ὅτι" 1a, p. 731). **Syntactically,** ὅτι introduces a dependent clause: "*that* you have overcome the Evil One" (ὅτι νενικήκατε τὸν πονηρόν). The entire ὅτι clause is substantival and is functioning as the direct object of the verb, "I am writing" (γράφω). It is placed in parentheses in order to visualize its contribution to the independent clause. **Semantically,** ὅτι is an indirect discourse marker: "that" (NET). It signals the content of what John is writing (W, 45). (See Grammatical Nugget on verses 12–14.)

νενικήκατε: The Greek word νενικήκατε is a second person plural perfect active indicative from the verb νικάω meaning "to overcome" or "to vanquish" or "to overcome someone" (BDAG, s.v. "νικάω" 2a, p. 673). **Syntactically,** νενικήκατε is the governing verb of the dependent ὅτι clause. The subject of the verb is an implied "you [plural]" embedded in the verb and refers to the young believers among the intended recipients. **Semantically,** νενικήκατε is an extensive perfect: "you *have* overcome" (KJV ASV NASB ESV NIV CNT). John's emphasis is on the completed act of victory (W, 577). The "Evil One" (τὸν πονηρόν) occurs five times in the letter (2:13, 14; 3:12; 5:18, 19) and is a reference to Satan. While John assures the believer in 1 John 5:18–19 that while the Evil One rules the world and motivates the antichrists (Brown, 304), here the emphasis is that the Evil One cannot harm the young believer.

2:14a ἔγραψα: The Greek word ἔγραψα is a first person singular aorist active indicative from the verb γράφω meaning "to write" or "to compose" with reference to composing a letter (BDAG, s.v. "γράφω" 2d, p. 207). **Syntactically,** ἔγραψα is the main verb of the independent clause: "I *have written* to you, children" (ἔγραψα ὑμῖν, παιδία). The assumed subject, "I," refers to the author. **Semantically,** ἔγραψα is an epistolary aorist: "I *have* written" (KJV ASV NASB NET NLT). John underscores what he has just written (W, 563). John has just written to the "children" or "new believers"

> **Grammatical Nugget**: Why the tense shift from present to aorist? In the previous two verses, the progressive present tense "I now write" (γράφω) describes John's writing process. Yet here in verse 14, John shifts the tense to the aorist: "I have written" (ἔγραψα). Why? On the one hand, the present tense verbs, "I write" (γράφω), may serve as summary statements of the current letter, while the aorist tense verbs, "I have written" (ἔγραψα), are referencing a letter that John had previously written to them. On the other hand, the switch is merely for stylistic variation (Brown, 297). Interestingly, verse 14 is just part of a larger shift. All instances of γράφω before 2:14 are in the present tense, while all instances of γράφω from 2:14 on are in the aorist tense. Perhaps something bigger than stylistic variation seems to be going on (cf. Bateman[1], 251; Culy, 41).

ὅτι: The Greek word ὅτι is a conjunction meaning "that" (BDAG, s.v. "ὅτι" 1a, p. 731). **Syntactically,** ὅτι serves to introduce a dependent conjunctive clause "*that* you have known the Father" (ὅτι ἐγνώκατε τὸν πατέρα). The entire ὅτι clause is substantival and is functioning as the direct object of the verb "I have written" (ἔγραψα). It is placed in parentheses in order to visualize its contribution to the independent clause. **Semantically,** ὅτι is an indirect discourse marker: "that" (NET). It signals the content of what John is writing (W, 45). (See Grammatical Nugget on verses 12–14.)

ἐγνώκατε: The Greek word ἐγνώκατε is a second person plural perfect active indicative from the verb γινώσκω meaning "to come to know" or "to have come to the knowledge of some person" (BDAG, s.v. "γινώσκω" 6aβ, p. 200). **Syntactically,** ἐγνώκατε is the governing verb of the substantival dependent ὅτι clause. The subject of the verb is an implied "you [plural]" embedded in the verb and referring to the children among the intended recipients. **Semantically,** ἐγνώκατε is an extensive perfect: "you *have* known" (NET NLT; cf. CNT NRSV). John's emphasis is on the completed act of knowing someone in past time rather than the present results (W, 577). John's point is that members of this community whether interpreted as literal "children" or "children in the faith" (NLT) have had—and continue to have—a personal knowledge of God.

2:14b ἔγραψα: The Greek word ἔγραψα is a first person singular aorist active indicative from the verb γράφω meaning "to write" or "to compose" with reference to composing a letter (BDAG, s.v. "γράφω" 2d, p. 207). **Syntactically,** ἔγραψα is the main verb of the independent clause "*I have written* to you, fathers" (ἔγραψα ὑμῖν, πατέρες). The assumed subject, "I," refers to John once again. **Semantically,** ἔγραψα is an epistolary aorist: "I *have* written" (KJV ASV NASB NET NLT). John underscores what he has just written (W, 563). John has just written to the "fathers" or "mature believers."

ὅτι: The Greek word ὅτι is a conjunction meaning "that" (BDAG, s.v. "ὅτι" 1a, p. 731). **Syntactically,** ὅτι introduces a dependent conjunctive clause "*that* you have known the one who is from the beginning" (ὅτι ἐγνώκατε τὸν ἀπ᾽ ἀρχῆς). The entire ὅτι clause is substantival and is functioning as the direct object of the verb, "I have written" (ἔγραψα). It is placed in parentheses in order to visualize its contribution to the independent clause. **Semantically,** ὅτι is an indirect discourse marker: "that" (NET). It signals the content of what John is writing (W, 45). (See Grammatical Nugget on verses 12–14.)

ἐγνώκατε: The Greek word ἐγνώκατε is a second person plural perfect active indicative from the verb γινώσκω meaning "to come to know" or "to have come to the knowledge of some person" (BDAG, s.v. "γινώσκω" 6aβ, p. 200). **Syntactically,** ἐγνώκατε is the governing verb of the dependent ὅτι clause. The subject of the verb is an implied "you [plural]" embedded in the verb and refers to the senior members of his reading audience. **Semantically,** ἐγνώκατε is an extensive perfect: "you *have* known" (KJV NIV NET CNT). John's emphasis is on the completed act of knowing someone in past time rather than the present results (W, 577). John's point is that members of this community whether interpreted as literal "fathers" or "mature believers" (NLT) have had—and continue to have—a personal knowledge of God.

2:14c ἔγραψα: The Greek word ἔγραψα is a first person singular aorist active indicative from the verb γράφω meaning "to write" or "to compose" with reference to composing a letter (BDAG, s.v. "γράφω" 2d, p. 207). **Syntactically,** ἔγραψα is the main verb of the independent clause "*I have written* to you, young people" (ἔγραψα ὑμῖν, νεανίσκοι). The assumed subject, "I," refers to John. **Semantically,** ἔγραψα is an epistolary aorist: "I *have* written" (KJV ASV NASB NET NLT; cf. W, 563). John has just written to the "young people" or "young believers" among his recipients about how they are strong, how the word of God lives in them, and how they have victory over the Evil One.

ὅτι: The Greek word ὅτι is a conjunction meaning "that" (BDAG, s.v. "ὅτι" 1a, p. 731). **Syntactically,** ὅτι introduces a dependent conjunctive clause: "*that* you are strong, and the word of God abides in you and you have conquered the Evil One" (ὅτι ἰσχυροί ἐστε καὶ ὁ λόγος τοῦ θεοῦ ἐν ὑμῖν μένει καὶ νενικήκατε τὸν πονηρόν). The entire ὅτι clause is substantival and is functioning as the direct object of the verb, "I have written" (ἔγραψα). It is placed in parentheses in order to visualize its contribution to the independent clause. **Semantically,** ὅτι is an indirect discourse marker: "that" (NET). It signals the content of what John is writing (W, 45). (See Grammatical Nugget on verses 12–14.)

ἐστέ: The Greek word ἐστέ is second person plural present active indicative from the verb εἰμί meaning "to be" or describing a special connection between subject and predicate (BDAG, s.v. "εἰμί" 2b, p. 282). **Syntactically,** ἐστέ serves as the governing verb of the first part of the compound dependent ὅτι clause, "*you are* strong" (ἰσχυροί ἐστε). The subject of the verb is an implied "you [plural]" referring to the recipients of the letter, specifically the younger believers. **Semantically,** ἐστέ is an equative present: "are" (cf. KJV NASB ESV NIV NET etc.). It equates John's young believers with strength.

2:14d καί: The Greek word καί is a conjunction which in this context means "and" (BDAG, s.v. "καί" 1bα, p. 494). **Syntactically,** καί introduces a dependent conjunctive clause: "*and* [that] God's word abides in you" (καὶ [ὅτι] ὁ λόγος τοῦ θεοῦ ἐν ὑμῖν μένει). It is the second part of the compound ὅτι clause. **Semantically,** καί is connective and gives us additional information about these young believers. Not only are they strong, but they are strong because God's word lives in them.

[ὅτι]: The Greek word ὅτι in brackets is a conjunction meaning "that" (BDAG, s.v. "ὅτι" 1a, p. 731). **Syntactically,** [ὅτι] is an ellipsis and serves to introduce the second part of the compound dependent clause: "and [*that*] the word of God abides in you" (καὶ [ὅτι] ὁ λόγος τοῦ θεοῦ ἐν ὑμῖν μένει). The compound clause is substantival and functions as part of a compound direct object of the verb, "I have written" (ἔγραψα). **Semantically,** ὅτι is an indirect discourse marker: "that." It signals the content of what John is writing (W, 45). (See Grammatical Nugget on verses 12–14.)

μένει: The Greek word μένει is a third person singular present active indicative from the verb μένω meaning "to remain," "to continue," "to abide," or to describe someone who does not leave a certain realm or sphere (BDAG, s.v. "μένω" 1aβ, p. 631). **Syntactically,** μένει is the governing verb of the second part of the compound substantival dependent ὅτι clause: "and God's word *abides* in you" (καὶ ὁ λόγος τοῦ θεοῦ ἐν ὑμῖν μένει). The subject is the phrase, "the word of God" (ὁ λόγος τοῦ θεοῦ). **Semantically,** μένει is a customary present: "abides" (KJV ASV NASB NRSV ESV CNT), "resides" (NET), or "lives" (NIV NLT). John gives emphasis to the word of God that lives continually in young believers.

2:14e καί: The Greek word καί is a conjunction which in this context means "and" (BDAG, s.v. "καί" 1ba, p. 494). **Syntactically,** καί introduces a dependent conjunctive clause: "*and* [that] you have overcome the Evil One" (καὶ [ὅτι] νενικήκατε τὸν πονηρόν). It is the third part of the compound ὅτι clause. **Semantically,** καί is a connective and gives us additional information about young believers. Not only are they strong because God's word lives in them, but they also can have assurance that they have victory over the Devil because of the work of Jesus.

[ὅτι]: The Greek word ὅτι in brackets is a conjunction meaning "that" (BDAG, s.v. "ὅτι" 1a, p. 731). **Syntactically,** [ὅτι] is an ellipsis and serves to introduce the third part of the compound dependent clause: "and [*that*] you have conquered the Evil One" (καὶ [ὅτι] νενικήκατε τὸν πονηρόν). The compound clause is substantival and also functions as part of the compound direct object of the verb, "I have written" (ἔγραψα). **Semantically,** ὅτι is an indirect discourse marker: "that." It signals the content of what John is writing (W, 45). (See Grammatical Nugget on verses 12–14.)

νενικήκατε: The Greek word νενικήκατε is a second person plural perfect active indicative from the verb νικάω meaning "to overcome" or "to vanquish" or "to overcome someone" (BDAG, s.v. "νικάω" 2a, p. 673). **Syntactically,** νενικήκατε is the governing verb of the third part of the substantival dependent [ὅτι] clause. The subject of the verb is an implied "you [plural]" embedded in the verb and refers to the young people among the intended recipients. **Semantically,** νενικήκατε is an extensive perfect: "you *have* overcome" (KJV ASV NASB ESV NIV CNT). John's emphasis is on the completed act of victory (W, 577). John underscores how Jesus overcame the Evil One and that now these young believers currently live in victory.

2:15a ἀγαπᾶτε: The Greek word ἀγαπᾶτε is second person plural present active imperative from the verb ἀγαπάω meaning "to love" or "to have a high esteem for or satisfaction with something" (BDAG, s.v. "ἀγαπάω" 2b, p. 5).

Syntactically, ἀγαπᾶτε is the main verb of the compound independent clause: "do not *love* the world nor the things in the world" (Μὴ ἀγαπᾶτε τὸν κόσμον μηδὲ τὰ ἐν τῷ κόσμῳ). The subject of the imperative is an implied "you [plural]" and refers to the readers of John's letter. **Semantically,** the negated μὴ ἀγαπᾶτε is an imperative of prohibition that forbids an action: "do not love" (W, 487; cf. NASB ESV NIV NET CNT). John forbids his readers to hold the world or its sinful trappings in high esteem.

Semantical Nugget: What is the significance of a present imperative with μη? While a traditional understanding of the present imperative + μη was to command the cessation of an act that was already ongoing (cf. W, 724), tradition may not fit this context. The context reveals John's confidence about his reader's salvation and Christian life (vv. 12–14). He does it again in verses 20–21. It seems more likely that John is laying out a general principle for Christian living, "Do not love the world" (Bateman[1], 259). We also encounter another article + prepositional phrase construction, "the things of the world" (τὰ ἐν τῷ κόσμῳ). In this case the article is a nominalizer and turns the entire phrase into a substantive that serves as part of the compound direct object of the imperative "do not love" (μὴ ἀγαπᾶτε) (W, 231–36).

2:15b ἐάν: The Greek word ἐάν is a conjunction meaning "if" (BDAG, s.v. "ἐάν" 1aα, p. 267). **Syntactically,** the conjunction identifies the clause as a dependent clause. The entire dependent clause, "*if* anyone persists in loving the world" (ἐάν τις ἀγαπᾷ τὸν κόσμον), functions adverbially. It modifies the verb, "is" (ἐστίν). **Semantically,** ἐάν introduces a third class conditional clause of probability: "if" (cf. KJV NASB ESV NIV NET etc.). The condition is uncertain of fulfillment but still likely (W, 696). That uncertain condition is revealed in the next verb.

ἀγαπᾷ: The Greek word ἀγαπᾷ is third person singular present active subjunctive from the verb ἀγαπάω meaning "to love" or "to have a high esteem for or satisfaction with something" (BDAG, s.v. "ἀγαπάω" 2b, p. 5). The verb is in the subjunctive because ἐάν takes the subjunctive. **Syntactically,** ἀγαπᾷ is the governing verb of the dependent adverbial clause. The subject is the impersonal pronoun "anyone" (τις) and refers to anyone who loves the world and its trappings. **Semantically,** ἀγαπᾷ is a gnomic present with a customary present force: "*persists in* loving" or "loves" (cf. NASB ESV NIV NET). It underscores a timeless truth about people (W, 523). John emphasizes a point about anyone who has an infatuation with the world (cf. 2:16a). That point is driven home in the next clause.

2:15c ἐστίν: The Greek word ἐστίν is third person singular present active indicative from the verb εἰμί meaning "to be" or describing a special connection between subject and predicate (BDAG, s.v. "εἰμί" 2b, p.282). **Syntactically,** ἐστίν is the main verb of the independent clause: "the love of the Father *is* not in him" (οὐκ ἔστιν ἡ ἀγάπη τοῦ πατρὸς ἐν αὐτῷ). The subject of the verb is the phrase "the love of the Father" (ἡ ἀγάπη τοῦ πατρὸς). **Semantically,** ἐστίν is a gnomic present: "is" (cf. KJV NASB ESV NIV NET etc.). It underscores a timeless truth about God's relationship with anyone who loves the world (W, 523). The person infatuated with the world (cf. 2:16a) does not have a relationship with God.

2:16a ὅτι: The Greek word ὅτι is a conjunction meaning "for" or "for this reason" (BDAG, s.v. "ὅτι" 4, p. 733). **Syntactically,** ὅτι introduces an independent conjunctive clause, *"For this reason* all that is in the world, the flesh that desires the eyes that desire and the boastful pride about one's life is not from the Father" (ὅτι πᾶν τὸ ἐν τῷ κόσμῳ, ἡ ἐπιθυμία τῆς σαρκὸς καὶ ἡ ἐπιθυμία τῶν ὀφθαλμῶν καὶ ἡ ἀλαζονεία τοῦ βίου, οὐκ ἔστιν ἐκ τοῦ πατρός). The entire ὅτι clause, though adverbial of cause, appears to have a loose connection with the previous independent clause. **Semantically,** ὅτι is an explanatory conjunction, giving us some clarification about what the world is: "for" (cf. KJV NASB ESV NIV etc.) or "because" (NET). We find another article + prepositional phrase here "that is in the world" (τὸ ἐν τῷ κόσμῳ). The article in this instance serves as an adjectivizer that changes the phrase into an adjectival modifier, clarifying the substantival adjective "all" (πᾶν) (Culy, 44).

ἐστίν: The Greek word ἐστίν is third person singular present active indicative from the verb εἰμί meaning "to be" or is used "to describe a special connection between the subject and predicate" (BDAG, s.v. "εἰμί" 2b, p. 282). **Syntactically,** ἐστίν is the governing verb of the independent clause. The subject is the entire phrase, "all that *is* in the world" (πᾶν τὸ ἐν τῷ κόσμῳ). It further describes the flesh that desires, the eyes that desire, and the boastful pride about one's life. **Semantically,** ἐστίν is a gnomic present: "is" (cf. KJV NASB ESV NIV NET etc.). It underscores a timeless truth about God (W, 523). Human traits of indulgence, sensual gratification, and boastful overconfidence are not from God.

Semantical Nugget: How are the genitives "of the flesh" (τῆς σαρκός), "of the eyes" (τῶν ὀφθαλμῶν), and "of life" (τοῦ βίου) to be understood? This clause has three phrases that function as appositives, further naming "all that is in the world" (πᾶν τὸ ἐν τῷ κόσμῳ). Each phrase consists of a noun in the nominative followed by a noun in the genitive, "the lust of the flesh" (ἡ ἐπιθυμία τῆς σαρκός) better rendered as "the flesh that desires" (subjective genitive), "the lust of the eyes" (καὶ ἡ ἐπιθυμία τῶν ὀφθαλμῶν) better rendered as "the eyes that desire" (subjective genitive), and "the pride of life" (ἡ ἀλαζονεία τοῦ βίου) better rendered as "the boastful pride about one's life" (objective genitive). These phrases tell us that the nature of worldliness consists of human indulgence, sensual gratification, and boastful overconfidence.

2:16b ἀλλά: The Greek word ἀλλά is a conjunction meaning "but" after a previous negative statement (BDAG, s.v. "ἀλλά" 1a, p. 44). **Syntactically,** ἀλλά identifies the clause as an independent conjunctive clause: "*But* all that is in the world is from the world" (ἀλλὰ ἐκ τοῦ κόσμου ἐστίν). **Semantically,** ἀλλά is contrastive: "but" (KJV ESV NIV NET etc.). John emphasizes that the flesh that lusts, the eyes that lust, and the boastful pride about one's life are not from God, but from the self-centered world system.

ἐστίν: The Greek word ἐστίν is third person singular present active indicative from the verb εἰμί meaning "to be" or describing a special connection between subject and predicate (BDAG, s.v. "εἰμί" 2b, p. 282). **Syntactically,** ἐστίν is the main verb of the independent clause. The subject of the verb is an implied "all that is in the world." It refers back to the phrase earlier in the verse that describes the flesh that desires, the eyes that desire, and the boastful pride about one's life. **Semantically,** ἐστίν is a gnomic present: "is" (cf. KJV NASB ESV NIV NET etc.). It underscores a timeless truth about self-centeredness (W, 523). Self-centeredness is not from God, but instead it is from the world and its values.

2:17a καί: The Greek word καί is a conjunction that in this context means "and" (BDAG, s.v. "καί" 1bα, p. 494). **Syntactically,** καί introduces an independent conjunctive clause "*and* the world is now passing away, and also its lusts" (καὶ ὁ κόσμος παράγεται καὶ ἡ ἐπιθυμία αὐτοῦ). **Semantically,** καί is a coordinating connective: "and" (KJV ASV NRSV ESV NET NLT). John adds a further thought about the nature of the world system evident in the next verb.

παράγεται: The Greek word παράγεται is a third person singular present passive indicative from the verb παράγω meaning "to pass away" or "to disappear" or "to go out of existence" (BDAG, s.v. "παράγω" 4b, p. 761). **Syntactically,** παράγεται is the main verb of the independent clause. The subject is "the world" (ὁ κόσμος) and refers to the selfish lusts of the world system. **Semantically,** παράγεται is a progressive present: "is *now* passing away" (NASB ESV NET CNT cf. NLT) or "are passing" (NRSV). John underscores the *right now* reality that the world system is going out of existence (W, 518).

Lexical and Theological Nugget: What does κόσμος mean? The term κόσμος is used as a metonymy of subject, a figure of speech in which one noun is used for another noun closely associated with it. More specifically, κόσμος is used in place of the people who inhabit the world (1 John 2:2; 3:1; 4:1; 5:19) and their system of values. John uses κόσμος 103 times in his literature in both positive and negative ways (see HJS, 56–57). On the one hand, the world is the object of God's love (John 3:16) and of Jesus's saving mission (3:17; 12:46–47). The Samaritan believers regard Jesus as the savior of the world (4:42). These positive perspectives are echoed in 1 John 2:2 and 4:14. On the other hand, the world (its inhabitants and values) is hostile to Jesus and his mission (John 7:7; 15:18–19; 17:14–16). They don't recognize the true identity of Jesus (1:10; 17:25), his victory over them (16:33), and his coming judgment (9:39; 12:31). These negative perspectives are also echoed in 1 John (4:5: 5:4–5, 19). Here in 1 John 2:15 the world is viewed negatively. John urges believers not to set their affections on the world's negative values, which are destined for destruction, but instead to set their affection on God and his value system. Theologically, Culy argues that John is not trying to tell us that the world is currently passing away, but instead highlights a contrast between this world and the one to come. The present world and its system and values are destined for destruction, but those who belong to God will live forever (Culy, 45). Either way the point is clear. The wise reader of John will love God and not the world.

2:17b δέ: The Greek word δέ is a conjunction meaning "but" or "rather" (BDAG, s.v. "δέ" 4a, p. 213). **Syntactically,** δέ is in the postpositive position and introduces the independent conjunctive clause: "*but* the one who does the will of God remains forever" (ὁ δὲ ποιῶν τὸ θέλημα τοῦ θεοῦ μένει εἰς τὸν αἰῶνα). **Semantically,** δέ is a marker of contrast: "but" (cf. KJV NASB ESV NIV NET etc.).

μένει: The Greek word μένει is a third person singular present active indicative from the verb μένω meaning "to remain," "to continue," "to abide," or is used to describe someone who does not leave a certain realm or sphere (BDAG, s.v. "μένω" 1aβ, p. 631). **Syntactically,** μένει is the main verb of the independent clause. It is the subject of the phrase, "the one who does the will of God" (ὁ . . . ποιῶν τὸ θέλημα τοῦ θεοῦ). **Semantically,** μένει is a customary present: "remains" (NET), "abides" (KJV ASV ESV CNT) or "lives" (NASB NRSV NIV NLT). John points out that while the world and its lusts are currently passing away, the one who does God's will is never going to pass away.

1 JOHN 2:18–29

Big Greek Idea: John's description of the end (before Jesus comes), the many who are against Jesus, and the misguided who have left the church, leads to John's appeal to Jesus's followers to hold fast to the teaching about the humanity and messiahship of Jesus, warning about people who mislead followers of Jesus, and exhorting believers to remain in Jesus.

Structural Overview: After John affectionately (τεκνία) writes to affirm his readers (vv. 12–17), John shifts to underscore and reveal information about the misguided who have left the church (vv. 18–29).

After his somewhat emotive proclamation (παιδία . . . ἐστίν) about living in *the end times* (v. 18), John opens with a string of contrasts (ἀλλ᾽ and καί) between true followers of Jesus and a group of misguided people. The misguided left (ἐξῆλθαν) the church, they did not remain (μεμενήκεισαν), they were not followers of Jesus (ἵνα φανερωθῶσιν), and they did not experience (ἔχετε) the presence of God (vv. 19–20). John then explains (ὅτι) why he has written (ἔγραψα) about these contrasts: his readers know (οἴδατε) Jesus, God's human Messiah, in whom no lie exists (ἐστίν; v. 21).

John then expands on those who left the community (vv. 22–26). First, he describes (ἐστίν) all those who deny God's human Messiah to be the liar, the Antichrist, and people who do not have a relationship with God (vv. 22–23). Second, *John appeals* (μενέτω) to his readers to hold fast to the teaching of the eyewitnesses. Third, John encourages his readers to have confidence in God's promise (ἣν αὐτὸς ἐπηγγείλατο) of eternal life (vv. 24–25). Finally, John warns (ἔγραψα) about the many people who strive to mislead followers of Jesus (v. 26).

John closes with an *affirmation*, an *exhortation*, and a *reminder* (vv. 27–28). First, he draws attention to the presence (μένει) of God's Spirit within the community who confirms (διδάσκει) the truth about Jesus, God's human Messiah (v. 27). Second, John exhorts his readers to keep trusting (μένετε) God with an intention (ἵνα): to develop confidence for when Jesus returns (v. 28). Finally, John reminds (γινώσκετε) his readers who their Father is, God (v. 29).

Outline:

> There Are Signs of the Imminent End of Times (vv. 18–21)
>> Many people are against Jesus (v. 18)
>> Many misguided people have left the church (v. 19)
>> God is present in believers who know Jesus as Messiah (vv. 20–21)

An Appeal and Warning for Jesus's Followers Is Warranted (vv. 22–26)
 Descriptions of those who deny Jesus are unmistakable (vv. 22–23)
 An appeal to remain in Jesus until he returns is necessary (vv. 24–25)
 Warning about the many who strive to mislead others about Jesus is warranted (v. 26)
God's Presence and Right Living Determines Paternity (vv. 27–29)
 God's presence reminds believers that Jesus is God's Messiah (v. 27)
 An expectation is given to remain in Jesus until he comes again (v. 28)
 Living rightly determines paternity (v. 29)

CLAUSAL OUTLINE FOR 1 JOHN 2:18–29

2:18a Παιδία, ἐσχάτη ὥρα **ἐστίν**,
2:18a Children, **it is** the last hour,

> 2:18b καὶ **καθὼς ἠκούσατε** (ὅτι ἀντίχριστος ἔρχεται),
> 2:18b and **as you heard** (that the Antichrist is coming),

2:18c καὶ νῦν ἀντίχριστοι πολλοὶ **γεγόνασιν·**
2:18c even now many antichrists **have appeared**;

> 2:18d ὅθεν **γινώσκομεν** (ὅτι ἐσχάτη ὥρα ἐστίν).
> 2:18d whereby **we *now* know** (that it is the last hour).

2:19a ἐξ ἡμῶν ἐξῆλθαν,
2:19a **They went out** from us,

2:19b ἀλλ᾽ οὐκ **ἦσαν** ἐξ ἡμῶν·
2:19b but **they were** not of us;

> 2:19c **εἰ** γὰρ ἐξ ἡμῶν **ἦσαν**,
> 2:19c for *you see* **if they had been** of us,

2:19d **μεμενήκεισαν** ἂν μεθ᾽ ἡμῶν·
2:19d **they would have remained** with us;

2:19e ἀλλ᾽ [ἐξῆλθαν]
2:19e but [*they did go out*],

> 2:19f **ἵνα φανερωθῶσιν** (ὅτι οὐκ εἰσὶν πάντες ἐξ ἡμῶν).
> 2:19f **so that it would be shown** (that they all are not of us).

^{2:20a} <u>καὶ</u> ὑμεῖς χρῖσμα **ἔχετε** ἀπὸ τοῦ ἁγίου,
^{2:20a} <u>But</u> **you have** an anointing from the Holy One,

^{2:20b} <u>καὶ</u> **οἴδατε** πάντα.
^{2:20b} <u>and</u> **you know** all *things.*

^{2:21a} οὐκ **ἔγραψα** ὑμῖν
^{2:21a} **I have** not **written** to you
|
    ^{2:21b} **ὅτι** οὐκ **οἴδατε** τὴν ἀλήθειαν,
    ^{2:21b} **because you do** not **know** the truth,

^{2:21c} <u>ἀλλ'</u> [*ἔγραψα ὑμῖν*]
^{2:21c} <u>but</u> *rather* [*I have written to you*]
|
    ^{2:21d} **ὅτι οἴδατε** αὐτήν,
    ^{2:21d} **because you know** it,
|
    ^{2:21e} <u>καὶ</u> **ὅτι** [*οἴδατε (ὅτι*] πᾶν ψεῦδος ἐκ τῆς ἀληθείας οὐκ **ἔστιν**).
    ^{2:21e} <u>and</u> **because** [*you know (that*] every lie **is** not the truth).

^{2:22a} Τίς **ἐστιν** ὁ ψεύστης
^{2:22a} Who **is** the liar
|
    ^{2:22b} <u>εἰ μὴ</u> ὁ ἀρνούμενος (<u>ὅτι</u> Ἰησοῦς οὐκ **ἔστιν** ὁ Χριστός);
    ^{2:22b} <u>except</u> the one who *persists in* denying (<u>that</u> Jesus <u>is</u> the Christ);

^{2:22c} οὗτός **ἐστιν** ὁ ἀντίχριστος, (ὁ ἀρνούμενος τὸν πατέρα καὶ τὸν υἱόν).
^{2:22c} this **is** the Antichrist, (*namely,* the one who *persists in* denying the Father and the Son).

^{2:23a} (πᾶς ὁ ἀρνούμενος τὸν υἱὸν) οὐδὲ τὸν πατέρα **ἔχει**·
^{2:23a} (Everyone who *persists* in denying the Son) **does** not **have** the Father;

^{2:23b} (ὁ ὁμολογῶν τὸν υἱὸν) καὶ τὸν πατέρα **ἔχει**.
^{2:23b} (the one who *persists* in their confession of the Son) **has** the Father also.

^{2:24a} (ὑμεῖς <u>ὃ ἠκούσατε</u> ἀπ' ἀρχῆς) ἐν ὑμῖν **μενέτω**·
^{2:24a} **Let** (<u>what</u> <u>you</u> yourselves <u>have heard</u> from the beginning) **remain** in you;

2:24b **ἐὰν** ἐν ὑμῖν **μείνῃ** (ὃ ἀπ᾽ ἀρχῆς ἠκούσατε),
2:24b **if** (what you have heard from the beginning) **remains** in you,

2:24c καὶ ὑμεῖς ἐν τῷ υἱῷ καὶ ἐν τῷ πατρὶ **μενεῖτε**.
2:24c **you** also **will remain** in the Son and in the Father.

2:25a καὶ αὕτη **ἐστὶν** ἡ ἐπαγγελία
2:25a Now this **is** the promise

2:25b **ἣν** αὐτὸς **ἐπηγγείλατο** ἡμῖν, τὴν ζωὴν τὴν αἰώνιον.
2:25b **that he** (= God) himself **made** to us: eternal life.

2:26 Ταῦτα **ἔγραψα** ὑμῖν περὶ τῶν πλανώντων ὑμᾶς.
2:26 **I have written** these *things* to you concerning those who *persist in their attempt* to mislead you.

2:27a καὶ ὑμεῖς τὸ χρῖσμα . . . **μένει** ἐν ὑμῖν,
2:27a Now as for you, the anointing . . . **remains** *continually* in you.

2:27b **ὃ ἐλάβετε** ἀπ᾽ αὐτοῦ
2:27b **that you have received** from him (= God)

2:27c καὶ οὐ χρείαν **ἔχετε**
2:27c And **you have** no need

2:27d **ἵνα** τις **διδάσκῃ** ὑμᾶς·
2:27d **that** anyone **teach** you;

2:27e **ἀλλ᾽** . . . καὶ ἀληθές **ἐστιν**
2:27e **but** . . . *now* it (i.e., the anointing) **is** true

2:27f καὶ οὐκ **ἔστιν** ψεῦδος,
2:27f **and it is** not a lie,

2:27fg **ὡς** τὸ αὐτοῦ χρῖσμα **διδάσκει** ὑμᾶς περὶ πάντων,
2:27g **as** his (= God's) anointing *continually* **teaches** you about all things,

2:27h καὶ **καθὼς ἐδίδαξεν** ὑμᾶς,
2:27h **and just as he** (=God) *has* **taught** you,

2:27i **μένετε** ἐν αὐτῷ.
2:27i *make it a practice to* **remain** in him (= Jesus).

^{2:28a} <u>Καὶ νῦν</u>, τεκνία, **μένετε** ἐν αὐτῷ,
^{2:28a} <u>Even now</u>, children, *make it a practice to* **remain** in him (= Jesus),

> ^{2:28b} **ἵνα ... σχῶμεν** παρρησίαν
> ^{2:28b} **so that** ... **we may have** confidence

>> ^{2:28c} **ἐὰν φανερωθῇ**
>> ^{2:28c} **when he** (= Jesus) **appears**,

> ^{2:28d} <u>καὶ</u> [*ἵνα*] μὴ **αἰσχυνθῶμεν** ἀπ᾽ αὐτοῦ ἐν τῇ παρουσίᾳ αὐτοῦ.
> ^{2:28d} <u>and</u> [*so that*] **we may** not **shrink away** from him (= Jesus) at his coming.

^{2:29a} **ἐὰν εἰδῆτε** (ὅτι δίκαιός ἐστιν),
^{2:29a} **If you know** (<u>that he</u> [= Jesus] <u>is</u> righteous),

> ^{2:29b} **γινώσκετε** (<u>ὅτι</u> καὶ πᾶς ὁ ποιῶν τὴν δικαιοσύνην ἐξ αὐτοῦ γεγέννηται).
> ^{2:29b} **you** also **know** (<u>that</u> everyone who practices righteousness <u>has been fathered</u> by him [= God]).

SYNTAX EXPLAINED FOR 1 JOHN 2:18–29

^{2:18a} ἐστίν: The Greek word ἐστίν is third person singular present active indicative from the verb εἰμί meaning "it is" (BDAG, s.v. "εἰμί" 11d, p. 286). **Syntactically,** ἐστίν is the main verb of the independent clause: "Children, *it is* the last hour," (Παιδία, ἐσχάτη ὥρα ἐστίν). The subject of the verb is an implied "it," referring to the time at hand. **Semantically,** ἐστίν is an equative present: "is" that serves as an equative verb of identity. The last hour is now.

> **Grammatical Nugget:** How is "the last hour" (ἐσχάτη ὥρα ἐστίν) to be understood? The phrase "the last hour" (ἐσχάτη ὥρα ἐστίν) is a good example of Colwell's Rule which states, "Definite predicate nouns which precede the verb usually lack the article.... A predicate nominative which precedes the verb cannot be translated as an indefinite or a qualitative noun solely because of the absence of the article; if the context suggests that the predicate is definite, it should be translated as a definite noun" (W, 257). While it might be tempting to translate the phrase indefinitely as "*a* last hour," Colwell's Rule suggests that while there is no definite article, the idea is still definite: "*the* last hour" (cf. KJV NASB ESV NIV NET etc.).

^{2:18b} καὶ καθώς: The Greek word καί is a conjunction meaning "and" (BDAG,

s.v. "καί" 2i, p. 496). The Greek word καθώς is an adverbial conjunction meaning "just as" or "as" (BDAG, s.v. "καθώς" 1, p. 493). **Syntactically,** καὶ καθώς functions adverbially introducing a dependent conjunctive clause: "*and as* you heard that the Antichrist is coming" (καὶ καθὼς ἠκούσατε ὅτι ἀντίχριστος ἔρχεται). It modifies the verb "appeared" (γεγόνασιν). **Semantically,** καὶ καθώς together is comparative: "and as" (KJV ASV NRSV ESV NIV CNT). John is about to underscore a comparison about the appearance of false teachers (antichrists).

ἠκούσατε: The Greek word ἠκούσατε is second person plural aorist active indicative from the verb ἀκούω meaning "to hear" or "to receive news or information about something" (BDAG, s.v. "ἀκούω" 3, p. 38). **Syntactically,** ἠκούσατε is the main verb of the dependent καὶ καθώς clause. The subject of the verb is an implied "you" and refers to the readers of the letter. **Semantically,** ἠκούσατε is a constative aorist: "you heard" (ASV NASB NET). It views the event as a whole (W, 557). John refers to information the community received about an antichrist.

ὅτι: The Greek word ὅτι is a conjunction meaning "that" (BDAG, s.v. "ὅτι" 1b, p. 731). **Syntactically,** ὅτι introduces a dependent conjunctive clause: "*that* the Antichrist is coming" (ὅτι ἀντίχριστος ἔρχεται). The clause is placed in parentheses in order to visualize its contribution to the dependent καθώς clause. The clause is substantival and is functioning as the direct object of the verb, "you have heard" (ἠκούσατε). **Semantically,** ὅτι is an indirect discourse marker: "that" (cf. KJV NASB ESV NET). It reveals the content of what was heard (W, 456–58). More specifically, John discloses what believers were taught, which is clarified in the rest of the clause.

ἔρχεται: The Greek word ἔρχεται is a third person singular present middle indicative from the verb ἔρχμομαι meaning, "to come" or "to make an appearance before the public" (BDAG, s.v. "ἔρχμομαι" 1bβ, p. 394). **Syntactically,** ἔρχεται is the governing verb of the dependent conjunctive ὅτι clause. The subject is "the Antichrist" (ἀντίχριστος). **Semantically,** ἔρχεται is a futuristic present: "*shall* come" (KJV) or "is coming" (NASB NRSV ESV NIV NET NLT CNT). "The present tense describes an event *begun* in present time but completed in the future" (W, 537). John's readers have heard that Antichrist will come in the future.

Grammatical and Theological Nugget: Why is there no article before "Antichrist" (ἀντίχριστος)? While John refers to the knowledge of a coming eschatological figure called "*the* Antichrist," here the Greek word ἀντίχριστος is *anarthrous*. Why is it not articular? In narrative literature of John's world, it was common to introduce a character for the first time without the article, but then to add the article in every other time he is mentioned. This is John's first use of the term "Antichrist," but it appears again later with the definite article (1 John 2:22; 4:3; 2 John 7; cf. Culy, 48). Who is this coming Antichrist, and how does he relate to the many antichrists in the Christian community? Elsewhere in the New Testament, allusions to "The Antichrist" refers to a coming personality that will be against Christ at the consummation of the ages (Rev. 16:13, 19:20, and 20:10; cf. Deut. 13:1–5). He could be called a capital *A* Antichrist. The antichrists that were already present in John's community were those who were denying the incarnation of Jesus. John tells his readers that the spirit of the Antichrist who *will* come *already* exists in the false teaching of fraudulent teachers (Bateman[1], 271). We could call them lower case *a* antichrists.

2:18c καὶ νῦν: The Greek word καί is a coordinating conjunction meaning "even" (BDAG, s.v. "καί" 2b, p. 495). The Greek word νῦν is an adverb meaning "now" (BDAG, s.v. "νῦν" 1aα, p. 681). **Syntactically,** καὶ νῦν introduces an independent conjunctive clause: "*even now* many antichrists have appeared" (καὶ νῦν ἀντίχριστοι πολλοὶ γεγόνασιν). **Semantically,** καὶ νῦν is a temporal marker with the focus on the present moment: "and now" (BDAG, s.v. "νῦν" 1, p. 681; cf. NLT). While maintaining the present force, καὶ νῦν is ascensive: "even now" (KJV ASV NASB NIV) or "so now" (NRSV ESV NET). John is adding some additional information about those who left the church (antichrists) (W, 670–71).

γεγόνασιν: The Greek word γεγόνασιν is a third person plural perfect active indicative from the verb γίνομαι meaning "to come" or "to appear" or "to be present at a given time" (BDAG, s.v. "γίνομαι" 8, p. 199). **Syntactically,** γεγόνασιν is the main verb of the independent clause. The subject is the phrase "many antichrists" (ἀντίχριστοι πολλοί). **Semantically,** γεγόνασιν is an extensive perfect: "*have* come" (NRSV NIV CNT) or "have appeared" (NASB NLT). John's focus is on the completed act of knowing someone in past time rather than the present results: "is coming" (ESV NET; cf. W, 577). So not only is an antichrist coming in the future, he's here even now through fraudulent teachers who have infiltrated the community of believers.

2:18d ὅθεν: The Greek word ὅθεν is an adverbial conjunction meaning "from which" (BDAG, s.v. "ὅθεν" 1b, p. 692). **Syntactically,** ὅθεν introduces a dependent conjunctive clause. It is an adverbial conjunction clause: *whereby* we now know that it is the last hour" (ὅθεν γινώσκομεν ὅτι ἐσχάτη ὥρα ἐστίν), functioning adverbially and modifying the verb "have come" (γεγόνασιν). **Semantically,** ὅθεν is an inferential conjunction: "whereby" (KJV ASV; cf. ESV) or "from this" (NASB NRSV NET NLT) or "by this" (CNT). It provides a deduction about those who have left the church (W, 673; BDAG, s.v. "ὅθεν" 1b, p. 692) clearly evident in the rest of the clause.

γινώσκομεν: The Greek word γινώσκομεν is a first person plural present active indicative from the verb γινώσκω meaning "to know" or "to come to know about something" (BDAG, s.v. "γινώσκω" 1c, p. 200). **Syntactically,** γινώσκομεν is the governing verb of the dependent ὅθεν clause. The subject of the verb is an implied "we" embedded in the verb and refers to both John and the readers. **Semantically,** γινώσκομεν is a progressive present: "we *now* know" or "we know" (cf. KJV NASB ESV NIV NET etc.). It underscores something that is known *right now* (W, 518). The content of what is known is evident in the ὅτι clause.

ὅτι: The Greek word ὅτι is a conjunction meaning "that" after verbs of perception (BDAG, s.v. "ὅτι" 1c, p. 731). **Syntactically,** ὅτι introduces a dependent conjunctive clause: "*that* it is the last hour" (ὅτι ἐσχάτη ὥρα ἐστίν). The clause is substantival and is functioning as the direct object of the verb, "we know" (γινώσκομεν). The entire ὅτι clause is placed in parentheses in order to visualize its contribution to the independent clause. **Semantically,** ὅτι is an indirect discourse marker: "that" (KJV ASV NASB NRSV ESV NET NLT CNT). It provides the content of what John's readers now know (W, 456), which is made clear in the rest of the ὅτι clause.

ἐστίν: The Greek word ἐστίν is third person singular present active indicative from the verb εἰμί meaning "it is" (BDAG, s.v. "εἰμί" 11d, p. 286). **Syntactically,** ἐστίν is the governing verb of the dependent ὅτι clause. The subject of the verb is an implied "it" and refers to the time period that the readers currently find themselves in. **Semantically,** ἐστίν is an equative present: "is" (cf. KJV NASB ESV NIV NET etc.). It equates the current time period with the last hour. The verse ends the way it began with the phrase "it is the last hour" (ἐσχάτη ὥρα ἐστίν). This rhetorical device is called an *inclusio* or framing and it serves to heighten and stress the theme of the verse. Notice the "it is" in 2:18a and "it is" in 2:18d.

2:19a ἐξῆλθαν: The Greek word ἐξῆλθαν is a third person plural aorist active indicative from the verb ἐξέρχομαι meaning "to depart" or "to leave" or "to discontinue an association" (BDAG, s.v. "ἐξέρχομαι" 4, p. 348). **Syntactically,** ἐξῆλθαν is the main verb of the independent clause: "*they went out* from us" (ἐξ ἡμῶν ἐξῆλθαν). The subject of the verb is an implied "they" and refers to the false teachers or "antichrists" who had recently left their ranks. **Semantically,** ἐξῆλθαν is a constative aorist: "they went out" (cf. KJV NASB ESV NIV NET etc.) or "they *left*" (NLT). John states a historical fact (W, 557). A group of people left their religious community of faith. The prepositional phrase, "from us" (ἐξ ἡμῶν), has an emphatic position at the beginning of the verse that makes their leaving even more prominent (Culy, 48).

Theological Nugget: Why did a group of people leave the church? Why they left remains unknown. Nevertheless, their departure seems to have shaken the faith of this community. John seeks to reassure his readers that they themselves are not the problem. He tells them that their departure is actually proof that they are fraudulent and misguided people. They were never part of the true community in the first place.

2:19b ἀλλ᾽: The Greek word ἀλλά is a conjunction meaning "but" or "yet" (BDAG, s.v. "ἀλλά" 2, p. 44). **Syntactically,** ἀλλά identifies the clause as an independent conjunctive clause: "*but* they were not of us" (ἀλλ᾽ οὐκ ἦσαν ἐξ ἡμῶν). **Semantically,** ἀλλά is contrastive: "but" (cf. KJV NASB ESV NIV NET etc.). John provides the other side of the issue (BDAG, s.v. "ἀλλά" 2, p. 44). Even though a group of people was at one time part of their congregation, they never really belonged (cf. Brown, 174). Just because they were at their religious gatherings did not mean that they were really connected with the group.

ἦσαν: The Greek word ἦσαν is third person plural imperfect active indicative from the verb εἰμί meaning "to be" or "to be in close connection with" (BDAG, s.v. "εἰμί" 2a, p. 283). **Syntactically,** ἦσαν is the main verb of the independent clause. The subject of the verb is an implied "they" and refers back to the false teachers or the "antichrists" who had recently left the church. **Semantically,** ἦσαν is an ingressive imperfect: "were" (KJV ASV NASB ESV CNT) or "did not really belong" (NRSV NIV NET). It stresses the beginning of a past action of those who were not part of the community that was confirmed later after they left (W, 545–56). This clause serves as an identity marker for fraudulent misguided people. They were not really part of the church to begin with (Culy, 49).

2:19c εἰ γάρ: The Greek word εἰ is a conjunction meaning "if" (BDAG, s.v. "εἰ" 6e, p. 278). The second conjunction, γάρ is in the postpositive position meaning "for" or "you see" (BDAG, s.v. "γάρ" 2, p. 189). **Syntactically,** εἰ and γάρ introduce a dependent conjunctive clause: "*for if* they were of us" (εἰ γὰρ ἐξ ἡμῶν ἦσαν). The clause functions adverbially as the protasis of a conditional clause. It modifies the verb, "they would have remained" (μεμενήκεισαν). **Semantically,** εἰ γάρ introduces a second-class conditional clause: "for *you see* if" (cf. KJV ASV NASB NRSV ESV NIV CNT). Another possibility is "because if" (NET; cf. BDAG, s.v. "γάρ" 1b, p. 189). It assumes an untruth is given for the sake of an argument as a clarification or explanation for leaving (W, 694–96). That assumed untruth is evident in the rest of the clause.

ἦσαν: The Greek word ἦσαν is third person plural imperfect active indicative from the verb εἰμί meaning "to be" or "to be in close connection with" (BDAG, s.v. "εἰμί" 2c, p. 283). **Syntactically,** ἦσαν is the main verb of the independent clause. The subject of the verb is an implied "they" and refers back to the "antichrists" who had recently left the followers of Jesus. **Semantically,** ἦσαν appears to be a pluperfective imperfect: "they had been" (KJV ASV NASB NRSV ESV CNT) or "they had belonged" (NIV NET; cf. W, 549). This clause is the first part of John's thought. "If it were true that antichrists were part of the church" is completed with the next clause.

2:19d μεμενήκεισαν: The Greek word μεμενήκεισαν is a third person plural pluperfect active indicative from the verb μένω meaning "to remain" or "to stay" or "to remain in fellowship with someone" (BDAG, s.v. "μένω" 1b, p. 631). **Syntactically,** μεμενήκεισαν is the main verb of the independent clause that serves as the apodosis of the second-class condition. The subject is an implied "they" embedded in the verb and refers to the antichrists. **Semantically,** μεμενήκεισαν is an intensive pluperfect: "*would have* remained" (NASB NRSV NIV NET) or "*would have* continued" (KJV ASV ESV CNT) or "*would have* stayed" (NLT). John focuses on the results (W, 583). Had the antichrists been part of the community, they never would have left.

Semantical Nugget: How is the pluperfect μεμενήκεισαν to be understood? The pluperfect is not very common in the New Testament, only occurring eighty-six times, and of those at least sixteen times are in John's Gospel. It is slightly different than the perfect tense. While the perfect tense describes an action that was completed in the past but has effects into the present, the pluperfect describes an action that was completed in the past and that had ongoing effects, but those effects do not necessarily reach into the present (W, 583). The presence of the pluperfect ("would have remained"; μεμενήκεισαν) in verse 19 is a rather significant theological perspective. John argues that true believers never would have left to follow a false and misguided teaching. The very fact that a group of people left the community proves they were never true followers of Jesus.

2:19e ἀλλ': The Greek word ἀλλά is a conjunction meaning "but" or "yet" (BDAG, s.v. "ἀλλά" 2, p. 44). **Syntactically,** ἀλλά identifies the clause as an independent conjunctive clause: "*But* they did go out" (ἀλλ' [ἐξῆλθαν]). The elliptical verb ἐξῆλθαν is implied from the context. This combination of ἀλλά + ἵνα appears many times in the Gospel of John and almost always includes an elliptical verb (John 1:8, 31; 3:17; 9:3; 11:52; 12:9, 47; 13:18; 14:31; 15:25; 17:15). **Semantically,** ἀλλά is contrastive: "but" (cf. KJV NASB ESV NIV NET etc.). John provides the other side of the issue (BDAG, s.v. "ἀλλά" 2, p. 44).

2:19f ἵνα: The Greek word ἵνα is a conjunction meaning "that" (BDAG, s.v. "ἵνα" 2f, p. 476). **Syntactically,** ἵνα introduces a dependent conjunctive clause: "*so that* it would be shown that they are all not of us" (ἵνα φανερωθῶσιν ὅτι οὐκ εἰσὶν πάντες ἐξ ἡμῶν). The entire ἵνα clause is adverbial. It modifies the elliptical verb "they went out" ([ἐξῆλθαν]). **Semantically,** the entire ἵνα clause appears to have the force of a result infinitive: "that" (KJV ASV NRSV ESV NIV NET CNT) or "so that" (NRSV). The emphasis is on the *outcome* of their leaving. It showed that they were never part of the church.

φανερωθῶσιν: The Greek word φανερωθῶσιν is a third person plural aorist passive subjunctive from the verb φανερόω meaning "to disclose," "to show," "to make known," or "to cause to become known" (BDAG, s.v. "φανερόω" 2bβ, p. 1048). The verb is in the subjunctive mood because verbs in a ἵνα clause take the subjunctive. **Syntactically,** φανερωθῶσιν is the governing verb of the dependent adverbial result clause. The assumed subject, "they," refers to misguided people who have left the community. **Semantically,** φανερωθῶσιν is a constative aorist: "it would be known" (NASB) or "it would be shown." Perhaps the best rendering is "it proved" (NLT) or "they made it plain" (NRSV). John states a historical fact (W, 557), which is articulated in the next ὅτι clause.

ὅτι: The Greek word ὅτι is a conjunction meaning "that" after verbs of perception (BDAG, s.v. "ὅτι" 1c, p. 731). **Syntactically,** ὅτι serves to introduce a dependent conjunctive clause: "*that* they are not all of us" (ὅτι οὐκ εἰσὶν πάντες ἐξ ἡμῶν). The clause functions substantivally as the direct object of the verb, "it might be shown" (φανερωθῶσιν). The clause is placed in parentheses in order to visualize its contribution to the dependent ἵνα clause. **Semantically,** ὅτι is an indirect discourse marker: "that" (cf. KJV NASB ESV NIV NET etc.). The ὅτι provides the content of what has been shown.

εἰσίν: The Greek word εἰσίν is third person plural present active indicative from the verb εἰμί meaning "to be" as a way of denoting a close relationship with someone (BDAG, s.v. "εἰμί" 10, p. 285) or to have a close connection with (BDAG, s.v. "εἰμί" 2a, p. 283). **Syntactically,** εἰσίν is the main verb of the dependent ὅτι clause. The subject of the verb is an implied "they" referring to secessionists. **Semantically,** εἰσίν negated with οὐκ is equative: "are not" (ASV NASB ESV) or "were not" (KJV CNT). John says those people are not part of the community, simply based on their decision to leave it.

Grammatical and Theological Nugget: How is the particle "not" (οὐκ) being used? The particle "not" (οὐκ) could negate the adjective "all" ("not all of them are of us") or the verb "are" ("all of them are not of us"). If "not" (οὐκ) negates the adjective ("all," πάντες), John could be saying that there are some who left that are believers, while others are not. If the particle "not" (οὐκ) negates the verb ("are," εἰσίν), however, the idea would be that none were ever true believers. The negation's position before the verb, which is also before the adjective seems to suggest it is modifying the verb. Therefore, it seems that all, not just some who left, were never really followers of Jesus.

²·²⁰ᵃ καί: The Greek word καί is a conjunction meaning "but" (BDAG, s.v. "καί" 2c, p. 496). **Syntactically,** καί introduces an independent conjunctive clause: "*but* you have an anointing from the holy one" (καὶ ὑμεῖς χρῖσμα ἔχετε ἀπὸ τοῦ ἁγίου). **Semantically,** καί is contrastive: "but" (KJV NASB NRSV ESV NIV CNT NLT). It gives contrastive information about John's readers. Unlike those who left the community, John's readers have a special anointing from God that gives them assurance that they are "of us." This contrast is highlighted even more by the presence of the emphatic personal pronoun "you" (ὑμεῖς).

ἔχετε: The Greek word ἔχετε is a second person plural present active indicative from the verb ἔχω meaning "to have" or "to have something within oneself" (BDAG, s.v. "ἔχω" 1d, p. 420). **Syntactically,** ἔχετε is the main verb of the independent conjunctive clause. The assumed subject, "you," refers to the readers of the letter. **Semantically,** ἔχετε is a customary present: "you have" (cf. KJV NASB ESV NIV NET etc.). It points out that the readers have the continual presence of God in their life through this special anointing from the Holy One (W, 521).

Theological Nugget: What is the "anointing" (χρῖσμα) from God? This noun only occurs in the New Testament in this chapter (2:20, 27 [2x]). In other contexts, it normally refers to a physical anointing, such as pouring oil on prophets, priests, or kings to confirm their roles. John seems to be talking about a spiritual anointing rather than a physical one. For John, anointing is associated with the reader's correct belief about Jesus and their assurance that they are indeed part of the community. Similar language is used to talk about the Holy Spirit in John 2:20, 14:17, 26. The Holy Spirit is also seen as the instrument with which a believer is anointed in other parts of the New Testament as well (Acts 10:38; 2 Cor. 1:21–22; cf. Isa. 61:1 LXX). Thus, this anointing is a work of the Holy Spirit in the life of those who hold to a correct Christological confession (Culy, 51; Brown, 342–48).

²·²⁰ᵇ καί: The Greek word καί is a conjunction meaning "and" (BDAG, s.v. "καί" 2ba, p. 494). **Syntactically,** καί introduces an independent conjunctive clause: "*and* you know all things" (καὶ οἴδατε πάντες). **Semantically,** καί is a coordinating connective: "and" (cf. KJV NASB NIV ESV NET etc.). John's conjunctive clauses provide additional information about his readers, which is evident in the rest of the clause.

οἴδατε: The Greek word οἴδατε is a second person plural perfect active indicative from the verb οἶδα meaning "to know" or "to know about something" (BDAG, s.v. "οἶδα" 1b, p. 693). **Syntactically,** οἴδατε is the governing verb of the independent conjunctive clause. The assumed subject, "you," refers to the believers who have received an anointing from God. **Semantically,** οἴδατε is a perfect with present force: "you know all *things*" (KJV ASV). John underscores that all believers have an anointing from God, which enables them to know all things. Some verbs, like οἶδα, appear almost exclusively in the perfect tense without the perfect's aspectual significance (W, 579–80).

Text-Critical Nugget: Does the Greek text read πάντες or πάντα? On the one hand, some rather significant manuscripts (א B P Ψ 398 1839 1852 etc.) read πάντες (nominative) and are thereby translated: "*all things* you know" (NASB NET CNT; cf. Metzger[1], 641). On the other hand, other manuscripts (A C 33 81 322 etc.) read πάντα (accusative) and are thereby translated: "you know *all things*" (KJV ASV). The lack of a direct object for "you know" (οἴδατε) in the first textual reading has led some to believe that this harder reading is correct and that a scribe changed the nominative (πάντες) to an accusative (πάντα) to make better sense. Some translations add "the truth" at the end of "you *all* know" in order for their translation to make sense (NIV NLT). Nevertheless, the best reading is πάντα and thereby translated: "and you know *all things*."

2:21a ἔγραψα: The Greek word ἔγραψα is a first person singular aorist active indicative from the verb γράφω meaning "to write" or "to compose" some literary composition like a letter (BDAG, s.v. "γράφω" 2d, p. 207). **Syntactically,** ἔγραψα is a negated main verb of the independent clause "*I have* not *written* to you" (οὐκ ἔγραψα ὑμῖν). The assumed subject, "I," refers to John. **Semantically,** ἔγραψα is an epistolary aorist: "I have not written" (KJV ASV NASB NET; cf. 2:14a, 14b, 14c). John's stress is on what he has just written in *this* letter and the reader's full awareness of the truth. However, it is possible that John refers to another letter written earlier (W, 563).

2:21b ὅτι: The Greek word ὅτι is a conjunction meaning "because" or "since" (BDAG, s.v. "ὅτι" 4b, p. 732). **Syntactically,** ὅτι introduces a dependent conjunctive clause: "*because* you do not know the truth" (ὅτι οὐκ οἴδατε τὴν ἀλήθειαν). The clause is functioning adverbially. It modifies the verb, "I have written" (ἔγραψα). (See the Syntactical Nugget on verse 21.) **Semantically,** ὅτι is causal: "because" (KJV ASV NASB NRSV ESV NIV CNT NLT). It provides the reason why John is currently writing (W, 460), or in this case it provides a reason why he is "not" (οὐκ) writing to them, which is clarified in the next verb.

Syntactical Nugget: How are the three ὅτι clauses to be understood? Verse 21 has three ὅτι clauses, which are translated several ways. One rendering is to translate all three clauses as causal. It gives three different reasons why John is writing, "I did not write because . . . because . . . because . . ." (ASV NASB ESV NIV CNT NLT). A second rendering is to classify all three clauses as indirect discourse. It gives a summary content about what John is writing about,

"I did not write that . . . but that . . . and that . . ." (NET; Brown, 350). Finally, the first two clauses might be causal, giving two reasons why John is writing and then the third ὅτι clause as indirect discourse (KJV NRSV). The latter view has two additional options. The third ὅτι clause could be the direct object of the verb "I have written" ("I did not write because . . . but because . . . and that . . .") or as the direct object of an elliptical "you know" ("I did not write because . . . but because you know it and [you know] that . . ."). The presence of the καί seems to rule out the last option. The καί seems to connect the third ὅτι clause with the second ὅτι clause. The option of classifying all three as indirect discourse all serving as the direct object of "I have written" (ἔγραψα) seems to make little sense as well. Why would John be writing them to assure them of something of which they are already assured? See Culy, 53–54. The best option is that all three ὅτι clauses are causal. They provide three reasons why John is writing. The third ὅτι clause, however, has an elliptical indirect discourse "you know that" ("and [you know] that no lie comes from the truth"). (See 2:21d and 2:21e in the clausal outline.)

οἴδατε: The Greek word οἴδατε is a second person plural perfect active indicative from the verb οἶδα meaning "to know" or "to have information about something" (BDAG, s.v. "οἶδα" 1b, p. 693). **Syntactically,** οἴδατε serves as the governing verb of the dependent conjunctive clause. The assumed subject, "you," refers to the readers of the letter. **Semantically,** οἴδατε is a perfect with present force negated with οὐκ: "you do not know" (cf. KJV NASB ESV NIV NET etc.). Verbs like οἶδα appear regularly in the perfect tense without the perfect's aspectual significance (W, 579–80). It underscores the reason why John is not writing. It is not because they are unaware of the truth, but because they know it.

2:21c ἀλλ᾽: The Greek word ἀλλά is a conjunction meaning "but" or "but rather" (BDAG, s.v. "ἀλλά" 1a, p. 44). **Syntactically,** ἀλλά identifies the clause as an independent conjunctive clause: *But rather* [I have written]" (ἀλλ᾽ [ἔγραψα]). Elliptical verbs like "I have written" are not uncommon in John's writing (cf. 2:19; 2 John 5). **Semantically,** ἀλλά is a contrastive statement: "but rather" or "but" (cf. KJV NASB ESV NIV NET etc.). Because it follows a previous negative statement, John is underscoring that believers are not unaware of the truth, *instead* they know it.

[ἔγραψα]: This elliptical Greek word ἔγραψα is a first person singular aorist active indicative from the verb γράφω meaning "to write" or "to compose" some literary composition like a letter (BDAG, s.v. "γράφω" 2d, p. 207). The elliptical verb [ἔγραψα] is implied from the context. **Syntactically,** [ἔγραψα] is the main verb of the independent clause: "I have written to you" [ἔγραψα ὑμῖν]. The assumed subject, "I," refers to John. **Semantical-**

ly, ἔγραψα is a consummative aorist: "I *have* written" (KJV ASV NASB NET). John's stress is on what he has just written in *this* letter (W, 559).

2:21d ὅτι: The Greek word ὅτι is a conjunction meaning "because" or "since" (BDAG, s.v. "ὅτι" 4b, p. 732). **Syntactically,** ὅτι introduces a dependent conjunctive clause: "*because* you know it" (ὅτι οἴδατε αὐτήν). This ὅτι clause functions adverbially. It modifies the elliptical verb, "I have written" ([ἔγραψα]). (See the Syntactical Nugget on verse 21.) **Semantically,** ὅτι is causal: "because" (ASV NASB ESV NIV CNT NLT). It provides the second reason why John is writing (W, 460).

οἴδατε: The Greek word οἴδατε is a second person plural perfect active indicative from the verb οἶδα meaning "to know" or "to have information about something" (BDAG, s.v. "οἶδα" 1b, p. 693). **Syntactically,** οἴδατε serves as the governing verb of the dependent conjunctive clause. The assumed subject, "you," refers to the readers. **Semantically,** οἴδατε is a perfect with present force: "they know" (cf. KJV NASB ESV NIV NET etc.). The verb οἶδα appears regularly in the perfect tense with present force (W, 579–80). John is writing because his readers know the truth.

2:21e καί: The Greek word καί is a conjunction meaning "and" (BDAG, s.v. "καί" 1b, p. 494). **Syntactically,** καί introduces a dependent conjunctive clause: "*and* because [you know (that) every lie is not the truth)]" (καὶ ὅτι [οἴδατε ὅτι] πᾶν ψεῦδος ἐκ τῆς ἀληθείας οὐκ ἔστιν). **Semantically,** καί is a co-ordinating connector: "and" (cf. KJV NASB ESV NIV NET etc.). The clause provides additional information about the readers.

ὅτι: The Greek word ὅτι is a conjunction meaning "because" or "since" (BDAG, s.v. "ὅτι" 4b, p. 732). **Syntactically,** ὅτι introduces a dependent conjunctive clause: "*because* [you know (that) no lie is of the truth)]" (ὅτι [οἴδατε ὅτι] πᾶν ψεῦδος ἐκ τῆς ἀληθείας οὐκ ἔστιν). This ὅτι clause functions adverbially. It modifies the elliptical verb, "I have written" ([ἔγραψα]). (See the Syntactical Nugget on verse 21.) **Semantically,** ὅτι is causal: "because" (ASV NASB ESV NIV CNT NLT). It provides the third reason why John is writing. (See Syntactical Nugget on verse 21.)

ἐστίν: The Greek word ἐστίν is third person singular present active indicative from the verb εἰμί meaning "to be" or is used "to describe a special connection between the subject and predicate" (BDAG, s.v. "εἰμί" 2b, p. 283). **Syntactically,** ἐστίν is the governing verb of the dependent substantival clause. The elliptical phrase, "you know that" (οἴδατε ὅτι), is implied from the context. The subject of the verb is "every lie" (πᾶν ψεῦδος). **Semantically,** ἐστίν is a gnomic present: "is" (cf. KJV ASB NASB ESV NET CNT). It describes a general principle about a lie and a truth (W, 523): that there is no connection between a lie and the truth.

²:²²ᵃ ἐστίν: The Greek word ἐστιν is third person singular present active indicative from the verb εἰμί meaning "to be" or is used to show how something is to be understood (BDAG, s.v. "εἰμί" 2c, p. 283). **Syntactically,** ἐστίν is the main verb of the independent clause: "Who *is* the liar" (Τίς ἐστιν ὁ ψεύστης). The subject of the verb is the interrogative pronoun, "who" (τίς), due to the priority of pronouns (W, 43). **Semantically,** ἐστίν is a gnomic present: "is" (cf. KJV NASB ESV NIV NET etc.). It asks a generic question for identifying a liar (W, 523).

Lexical and Theological Nugget: Who is the "liar" (ψεύστης)? Unlike the other instances of this term in John's literature (John 8:44, 55; 1 John 1:10; 2:4; 4:20; 5:10), this occurrence may have a more specific referent in mind because of the definite article. Given that ψεύστης in John 8:44 and verse 55 references the Devil or people motivated by him, it is possible that John is referring to an eschatological figure like the Antichrist in this context. "The Liar" could even be another title for the Antichrist (2 John 7; cf. Brown, 351). A better possibility is that John is referring to the misguided people who have left the community. In 1 John 2:18–19, their departure is identified with the Antichrist because they foreshadow the work of the Antichrist who is yet to come. Their departure from the community is a sign of the inauguration of the last times, which are characterized by apostasy. It is clear that John is using the term polemically against community deserters (Brown, 351). They are considered liars because they were rejecting the true nature of Jesus as Messiah. John associates them with the career and message of the Antichrist.

²:²²ᵇ εἰ μή: The Greek word εἰ is an adverbial conjunction, which typically means "if" (BDAG, s.v. "εἰ," p. 277). The Greek word μή is an adverb, which typically means "not" (BDAG, s.v. "μή" 644). However, the construction εἰ + μή is a subcategory of the conditional conjunction that expresses a contrast or an exception, "but" or "except" (BDAG, s.v. "εἰ" 6iα, p. 278; s.v. "μή" 1aα, p. 644). **Syntactically,** εἰ μή introduces a dependent conjunctive clause. **Semantically,** εἰ μή points out a negative exception: "except" or "but" (KJV ASV NASB ESV NET CNT). It introduces John's answer to his interrogative statement. If anyone is a liar, it is the one who denies that Jesus is the Messiah.

ἀρνούμενος: The Greek word ἀρνούμενος is a nominative masculine singular present middle participle from the verb ἀρνέομαι meaning "to deny" or "to state that something is not true" (BDAG, s.v. "ἀρνέομαι" 2, p. 132). **Syntactically,** ἀρνούμενος is a substantival participle. **Semantically,** ἀρνούμενος is a gnomic present with customary force: "persists in denying" or "denies" (cf. KJV NASB ESV NIV NET etc.). It identifies a timeless fact for those who practice a pattern of behavior (W, 521, 615). John describes the person who continually denies that Jesus is the Christ. What is universally true about that person is clarified in the next ὅτι clause.

ὅτι: The Greek word ὅτι is a conjunction meaning "that" (BDAG, s.v. "ὅτι" 1a, p. 732). **Syntactically,** ὅτι introduces a dependent conjunctive clause: "*that* Jesus is not *the* Christ" (ὅτι Ἰησοῦς οὐκ ἔστιν ὁ Χριστός). This ὅτι clause functions substantivally as the direct object of the participle, "the one who persists in denying" (ὁ ἀρνούμενος). It is placed in parentheses in order to visualize its contribution to the independent clause. The article "the" (ὁ) before "Christ" (Χριστός) is a par excellence use that identifies Jesus as a Messiah who is in a class by himself (W, 223). There has never been nor will there ever be another Messiah like Jesus. **Semantically,** ὅτι is an indirect discourse marker: "that" (cf. KJV NASB ESV NIV NET etc.). John provides the explicit content of what the liars are denying (W, 456–58). They will not admit that Jesus is the Messiah.

ἔστιν: The Greek word ἔστιν is third person singular present active indicative from the verb εἰμί meaning "to be" or is used "to describe a special connection between the subject and predicate" (BDAG, s.v. "εἰμί" 2ca, p. 283). **Syntactically,** ἔστιν is the governing verb of the dependent ὅτι clause. In spite of the fact that "Christ [= Messiah]" (Χριστός) is articular and "Jesus" (Ἰησοῦς) is anarthrous, the subject of the verb is "Jesus" (Ἰησοῦς) due to word order (W, 44). Proper nouns are generally the subject (Culy, 55). **Semantically,** ἔστιν is an equative present: "is" (cf. KJV NASB ESV NIV NET etc.). John links Jesus to his rightful title. Jesus is the Christ (= Messiah).

2:22c ἔστιν: The Greek word ἔστιν is third person singular present active indicative from the verb εἰμί meaning "to be" or is used "to describe a special connection between the subject and predicate" (BDAG, s.v. "εἰμί" 2ca, p. 283). **Syntactically,** ἔστιν is the main verb of the independent clause: "this *is* the Antichrist, namely, the one who persists in denying the Father and the Son" (οὗτός ἐστιν ὁ ἀντίχριστος, ὁ ἀρνούμενος τὸν πατέρα καὶ τὸν υἱόν). The subject of the verb is the demonstrative pronoun "this one" (οὗτός) due to the priority of pronouns over articular nouns (W, 44). **Semantically,** ἔστιν is an equative present: "is" (cf. KJV NASB ESV NIV NET etc.). John links the one who denies the messiahship of Jesus to be against Christ (= the Antichrist).

ἀρνούμενος: The Greek word ἀρνούμενος is a nominative masculine singular present middle participle from the verb ἀρνέομαι meaning "to deny" or "to disclaim association with a person" (BDAG, s.v. "ἀρνέομαι" 3c, p. 132). **Syntactically,** ἀρνούμενος introduces a dependent participial clause. It could either be an adjective participle describing an attribute of one of these antichrists or a substantival participle functioning appositionally, further naming one of these antichrists. The entire participial clause in placed in parentheses to visualize its appositional contribution. Either way, the participle provides further information about these antichrists. **Semantically,** ἀρνούμενος is a gnomic present with customary force: "the one who persists in denying" or "denies" (cf. KJV NASB ESV NIV NET etc.). It identifies a timeless fact for those who practice a pattern of behavior (W, 521, 615). John underscores the identity of *anyone* who continually denies that Jesus is God's Messiah. That person is against Christ (= the Antichrist).

Lexical and Theological Nugget: What does ἀρνέομαι mean in this context? The verb is used nine times in John's writings (John 1:20; 13:38; 18:25, 27; 1 John 2:22 [2x], 23; Rev. 2:13; 3:8). In the Gospel, the majority of these refer to Peter's denial of Jesus (John 13:38; 18:25, 27). In this verse the word refers to the beliefs of those who left John's community of believers. What they deny is defined clearly for the first time. They were denying the messiahship of Jesus by questioning his humanity. John is asserting throughout his letter that Jesus's humanity is inseparable from his present exalted status as Messiah. There were numerous ideas about the Messiah that were proven wrong with the appearance of Jesus (Bateman[3], 322–25). John says that a person who denies Jesus's humanity is denying his messiahship and has no relationship with God.

2:23a ἀρνούμενος: The Greek word ἀρνούμενος is a nominative masculine singular present middle participle from the verb ἀρνέομαι meaning "to deny" or "to disclaim association with a person" (BDAG, s.v. "ἀρνέομαι" 3b, p. 132). **Syntactically,** ἀρνούμενος introduces a participial clause: "who persists in denying the Son" (ὁ ἀρνούμενος τὸν υἱόν). It is adjectival and modifies "everyone" (πᾶς). The entire πᾶς + participial clause is placed in parentheses to visualize its functioning together as the subject of the independent clause. **Semantically,** ἀρνούμενος is a gnomic present with customary force: "the one who persists in denying" or "denies" (cf. KJV NASB ESV NIV NET etc.). It identifies a timeless fact for those who practice a pattern of behavior (W, 521, 615). John underscores a timeless truth about the person who continually repudiates or disowns Jesus as Messiah, which is revealed in the next verb.

ἔχει: The Greek word ἔχει is a third person singular present active indicative from the verb ἔχω meaning "to have" or "to stand in a close relationship with someone" (BDAG, s.v. "ἔχω" 2b, p. 420). **Syntactically,** ἔχει is a negated main verb of the independent clause: "whoever persists in denying the Son *does not have* the Father" (πᾶς ὁ ἀρνούμενος τὸν υἱὸν οὐδὲ τὸν πατέρα ἔχει). The subject is the phrase "everyone who denies the Son" (πᾶς ὁ ἀρνούμενος τὸν υἱόν). **Semantically,** ἔχει is a gnomic present negated with οὐδέ: "does not have" (KJV ASV NET NLT). John underscores a timeless fact (W, 523): the one who persists in their denial of Jesus as Messiah cannot have a relationship with God.

Theological Nugget: What does it mean to "have the Father" or "not have the Father" (οὐδὲ τὸν πατέρα ἔχει)? In the Gospel of John, believers are said to *have* divine-like attributes, such as eternal life (3:16, 36), the word of God (5:38), the love of God (5:42), light (8:12; 12:35–36), peace (16:33), and joy (17:13). These divine attributes are a picture of what it means to "have God." That means having a relationship with God is closely related to remaining in God. Here in 1 John 2:23, it is related to the presence of God's anointing of the believer (1 John 2:20, 27). A similar idea appears in 2 John 9, where those who do not affirm the teachings about Jesus, particularly as it relates to his humanity, do not *have* God. Associating with God and remaining in God seem to be predicated on embracing the basics about the messiahship and humanity of Jesus (Brown, 370; Smalley, 116–17). The language of "having" expresses the presence or absence of a relationship between God and a person based upon the person's belief that Jesus was (and is) a human Messiah.

2:23b ὁμολογῶν: The Greek word ὁμολογῶν is a nominative masculine singular present active participle from the verb ὁμολογέω meaning "to confess" or "to profess an allegiance to someone publicly" (BDAG, s.v. "ὁμολογέω" 4b, p. 708). **Syntactically,** ὁμολογῶν functions substantivally as the subject of the verb, "has" (ἔχει). The entire participial clause is placed in parentheses to visualize its grammatical function as the subject of the independent clause. **Semantically,** ὁμολογῶν is a gnomic present with customary force: "the one who *persists in* their confession." It identifies a timeless fact for those who practice a pattern of behavior (W, 521, 615). John underscores a timeless truth about the person who continually confesses that Jesus is Messiah, which revealed in the next verb.

ἔχει: The Greek word ἔχει is a third person singular present active indicative from the verb ἔχω meaning "to have" or "to stand in a close relationship with someone" (BDAG, s.v. "ἔχω" 2b, p. 420). **Syntactically,** ἔχει is the main verb of the independent clause: "the one who persists in the confession of the Son *has* the Father also" (ὁ ὁμολογῶν τὸν υἱὸν καὶ τὸν πατέρα ἔχει). The subject of the verb ἔχει is the entire prepositional phrase: "whoever confesses the Son" (ὁ ὁμολογῶν τὸν υἱὸν). **Semantically,** ἔχει is a gnomic present: "has" (cf. KJV NASB ESV NIV NET etc.). John underscores a timeless fact (W, 523): the one who *persists in* their confession of Jesus as Messiah has a relationship with God.

Text-Critical Nugget: Why do the Byzantine Greek texts eliminate the clause "whoever persists in their confession of the Son also has the Father" (ὁ ὁμολογῶν τὸν υἱὸν καὶ τὸν πατέρα ἔχει)? Many of the best and earliest manuscripts, such as Sinaiticus (א) and Vaticanus (B, fourth century), include the clause, while most of the Byzantine manuscripts omit it. Normally the shorter reading is to be preferred, but that is not the case here. It is easy to see how a scribe might have accidentally skipped this section of text as he was copying. Both the first and second halves of this verse end with the same word (ἔχει) as well as the same string of words. Furthermore, it is easy to see how a scribe's eye could have skipped from one ἔχει to the other. This would have resulted in the omission of the second half of verse 23. This is known as a *homoeoteleuton*, from the Greek word that mean "same ending" (Metzger[1], 641; Brown, 354, Smalley, 92 n. d). For this reason the inclusion of the clause is the best reading.

2:24a ὅ: The Greek word ὅ is a neuter accusative singular from the relative pronoun ὅς meaning "that which" or "what" (BDAG, s.v. "ὅς" 1bα, p. 725). **Syntactically,** ὅ introduces a dependent relative clause: "*what* you yourselves have heard from the beginning" (ὑμεῖς ὃ ἠκούσατε ἀπ᾽ ἀρχῆς). The relative clause functions substantivally: "what you yourselves have heard" (NRSV ESV NIV ET NLT). It is the subject of the third person imperative "let . . . remain" (μενέτω): The entire clause is placed in parentheses to visualize its contribution to the independent clause.

ἠκούσατε: The Greek word ἠκούσατε is a second person plural aorist active indicative from the verb ἀκούω meaning "to hear" or "to hear something from someone" (BDAG, s.v. "ἀκούω" 1a, 1b, p. 37) or "to denote a body of authoritative teaching" (BDAG, s.v. "ἀκούω" 3d, p. 38). **Syntactically,** ἠκούσατε is the governing verb of the dependent relative clause. The subject of the verb within the relative clause is the emphatic pronoun "you" (ὑμεῖς), which refers to the readers/hearers of the letter. **Semantically,** ἠκούσατε is a consummative aorist: "you *have* heard" (KJV NIV NET). It describes a conclusion or cessation of an act as a whole (W, 559). John wants his readers to persist in their teaching about Jesus that they have had since the beginning of their faith journey as followers of Jesus (cf. 2:7).

μενέτω: The Greek word μενέτω is a third person singular present active imperative from the verb μένω meaning "to remain" or is used to describe someone who does not leave a relationship (BDAG, s.v. "μένω" 1aβ, p. 631). **Syntactically,** μενέτω is the main verb of the independent clause: "*Let remain* in you" (ἐν ὑμῖν μενέτω). The subject is "what you yourselves have heard from the beginning" (ὑμεῖς ὃ ἠκούσατε ἀπ᾽ ἀρχῆς). **Semantically,** μενέτω is an imperative of command: "let . . . remain" or "let . . . abide" (KJV ASV NASB NRSV ESV CNT). It assumes an *ongoing process*: "let *the teaching continually* remain in you" (W, 485). John expects his readers to persist in the teaching about Jesus, which they have had since the beginning of their Christian faith (see Theological and Lexical Nugget under 2:7).

2:24b ἐάν: The Greek word ἐάν is a conjunction meaning "if" (BDAG, s.v. "ἐάν" 1aβ, p. 267). **Syntactically,** the conjunction ἐάν identifies the clause as a dependent conjunctive clause. The entire dependent clause: "*if* what you have heard from the beginning remains in you" (ἐὰν ἐν ὑμῖν μείνῃ ὃ ἀπ' ἀρχῆς ἠκούσατε) functions adverbially. It modifies the verb, "you remain" (μενεῖτε). **Semantically,** ἐάν introduces a third class conditional clause of probability: "if" (cf. KJV NASB ESV NIV NET etc). The condition is uncertain of fulfillment but still likely (W, 696). John speaks of a probability for his readers that is clarified with the next verb.

μείνῃ: The Greek word μείνῃ is a third person singular aorist active subjunctive from the verb μένω meaning "to remain," "to abide," "to continue," or is used to describe someone who does not leave (BDAG, s.v. "μένω" 1aβ, p. 631). The verb is in the subjunctive because it is part of an ἐάν clause. **Syntactically,** μείνῃ is the governing verb of the dependent adverbial ἐάν clause. The subject is the substantival relative clause: "what you have heard from the beginning" (ὃ ἀπ' ἀρχῆς ἠκούσατε). **Semantically,** μείνῃ is a constative aorist: "remains" (KJV ESV NIV NET NLT). It views their belief as a whole or in a summary fashion (W, 257). The probability for John's readers is that if they remain in the correct teaching about Jesus, they will have an abiding relationship with God (Culy, 57).

ὃ: The Greek word ὃ is a neuter singular accusative from the relative pronoun pronoun ὅς meaning "that which" or "what" (BDAG, s.v. "ὅς" 1bα, p. 725). **Syntactically,** ὃ introduces a dependent relative clause: "*what* you have heard from the beginning" (ὃ ἀπ' ἀρχῆς ἠκούσατε). The entire clause functions as the subject of the verb "remain" (μείνῃ). The relative clause is placed in parentheses in order to visualize its substantival contribution to the dependent ἐάν clause. John reminds his readers of the message they heard about Jesus when they first came to the faith.

ἠκούσατε: The Greek word ἠκούσατε is a second person plural aorist active indicative from the verb ἀκούω meaning "to hear" or "to hear something from someone" (BDAG, s.v. "ἀκούω" 1a, 1b, p. 37) or "to denote a body of authoritative teaching" (BDAG, s.v. "ἀκούω" 3d, p. 38). **Syntactically,** ἠκούσατε is the governing verb of the dependent headless relative clause. The subject of the verb is an implied "you" embedded in the verb, which refers to the readers of the letter. **Semantically,** ἠκούσατε is a consummative aorist: "you *have* heard" (KJV). It describes a conclusion or cessation of an act (W, 559). John once again describes a body of authoritative teachings that has been in their possession since they first came into the faith (cf. 2:7).

2:24c καί: The Greek word καί is a conjunction meaning "also" and is not intended to coordinate or connect clauses (BDAG, s.v. "καί" 2a, p. 44). **Syntactically,** καί is part of the independent clause. It *does not* introduce an independent conjunctive clause. **Semantically,** καί is adjunctive: "also" (KJV ASV NASB NIV NET; cf. "too" ESV; W, 671). It underscores the abiding relationship the believer has with God provided they persist in the teachings about Jesus that they had accepted when they first heard them.

μενεῖτε: The Greek word μενεῖτε is a second person plural future active indicative from the verb μένω meaning "to remain," "to abide," "to continue," or is used to describe someone who does not leave (BDAG, s.v. "μένω" 1aβ, p 631). The future tense formative "σ" has dropped out because the stem of μένω ends in a liquid consonant (cf. M, 171; Wen, 104–5). **Syntactically,** μενεῖτε is the main verb of the independent clause: "you also *will remain* in the Son and in the Father" (καὶ ὑμεῖς ἐν τῷ υἱῷ καὶ ἐν τῷ πατρὶ μενεῖτε). The subject is the emphatic personal pronoun, "you" (ὑμεῖς), who are John's readers. **Semantically,** μενεῖτε is a predictive future: "you *will* remain" (KJV NET NLT). It speaks of something that will take place (W, 568). John underscores that when his readers remain in the correct teaching about Jesus, they will have an abiding or continual relationship with God.

Lexical and Theological Nugget: What does μένω mean in this context? There are three instances of μένω in verse 2:24. The first two usages refer to believers allowing the message about Jesus to *abide* in them. Within Johannine literature, John 15 provides a good model for understanding the meaning of *residing* or *abiding*. In John, remaining in the message about Jesus has results, *namely,* love being lived out in our lives. This love finds its basis in the love first shown by God to us (1 John 4:9–11). John is urging the community to *remain* in the correct teaching about Jesus as opposed to the misguided who have left the church and promote a fraudulent message about Jesus. Those who remain in the current teaching about Jesus will evidence love in their lives. The third usage of μένω in 2:24 refers to the permanence of one's relationship with God and Jesus. To reside in one is to reside in the other (cf. John 5:23; 15:9–10, 23; 17:3, 21). If John's readers continue to hold fast to the correct teaching about the nature of Jesus, then they *remain* in a loving relationship with both the Father and the Son.

2:25a καί: The Greek word καί is a conjunction that may mean "and" (BDAG, s.v. "καί" 1bη, p. 495) or "now" (BDAG, s.v. "καί" 1e, p. 495). **Syntactically,** καί introduces an independent conjunctive clause: "*now* this is the promise" (καὶ αὕτη ἐστὶν ἡ ἐπαγγελία). **Semantically,** καί may be a connective of sentences and rendered "and" (e.g., KJV NASB ESV NIV etc.) or it may introduce something new and thereby be transitional. In this case, καί is rendered "now" (NET) as it is in 1:5. John begins a new section about a continual relationship believers can have with God.

ἐστίν: The Greek word ἐστίν is third person singular present active indicative from the verb εἰμί meaning "to be" or can be used to show how something is to be understood (BDAG, s.v. "εἰμί" 2cα, p. 283). **Syntactically,** ἐστίν is the governing verb of the independent clause. The subject of the verb is the demonstrative pronoun "this" (αὕτη) because pronouns have priority over articular nouns (W, 41–42). The construction (demonstrative pronouns + εἰμί) occurs often in 1 John as John's way to highlight main ideas (Brown, 192). It points forward to the relative clause. **Semantically,** ἐστίν is an equative present: "is" (cf. KJV NASB ESV NIV NET etc.). The construction equates what God has promised with what is found in the next relative clause.

2:25b ἥν: The Greek word ἥν is an accusative singular feminine from the relative pronoun ὅς meaning "which" or "that" (BDAG, s.v. "ὅς" 2dδ, p. 726). **Syntactically,** ἥν introduces an adjectival relative clause: "*that* he (= God) himself promised to us, eternal life" (ἣν αὐτὸς ἐπηγγείλατο ἡμῖν, τὴν ζωὴν τὴν αἰώνιον). The entire clause modifies the demonstrative pronoun "this" (αὕτη). The relative pronoun ἥν is accusative because it functions as the direct object of the verb "he promised" (ἐπηγγείλατο). **Semantically,** the entire relative clause is epexegetical and the relative pronoun is rendered "that" (KJV ESV NET). It provides the content of the promise. God himself has promised the abiding believer eternal life.

ἐπηγγείλατο: The Greek word ἐπηγγείλατο is third person singular aorist middle indicative from the verb ἐπαγγέλλομαι meaning "to promise" (BDAG, s.v. "ἐπαγγέλλομαι" 1b, p. 356). **Syntactically,** ἐπηγγείλατο is the governing verb of the dependent relative clause. The subject is the emphatic personal pronoun, "he himself" and refers to God. **Semantically,** ἐπηγγείλατο is a constative aorist: "he made" or "he promised" (KJV NASB NIV NLT CNT). It describes the action as a whole (W, 557). John underscores God's promise of eternal life to his readers who remain in the truth about Jesus. The phrase "eternal life" (τὴν ζωὴν τὴν αἰώνιον) functions in apposition to the relative pronoun "that" (ἥν) identifying the content of the promise, which is eternal life.

Lexical and Theological Nugget: What is the ἐπαγγελία? The term is a simple declaration to do something with an obligation to carry out what is stated (BDAG, s.v. "ἐπαγγελία" pp. 355, 356). Although the term "promise" (ἐπαγγελία) appears often in the New Testament (Luke–Acts: 9x; Paul: 26x; Hebrews: 14x), it is used only here in Johannine literature. In Luke–Acts, the "promise of the Father" (Luke 24:49; Acts 1:4) is linked to the gift of the Holy Spirit (Acts 2:33, 39) and to the arrival of Jesus (Acts 7:17; 13:23, 32; 26:6). Luke uses "promise" to underscore Israel's salvation realized in the work of Jesus. For Paul, "promise" also highlights that God's promises to Israel are realized through Jesus (Rom. 4:13–14; Gal. 3:14) as well as to Gentile converts who are also recipients of Israel's promises (Gal. 4:28; Eph. 2:12; 3:6). In Hebrews, "promise" emphasizes that God makes promises and that the recipients of those promises are believers (1:14; 6:12, 17; 9:15). Some are fulfilled already and others are still to be realized (4:8; 11:10–40). Here in 1 John, the idea of *promise* is specifically defined. God has promised eternal life to those who remain in their confession about Jesus's humanity and messiahship. Thus John uses "promise" to speak exclusively of Jesus's incarnation and its effects on the community to be a community of love.

2:26 ἔγραψα: The Greek word ἔγραψα is a first person singular aorist active indicative from the verb γράφω meaning "to write" or "to correspond with someone in writing" (BDAG, s.v. "γράφω" 2c, p. 207). **Syntactically,** ἔγραψα is the main verb of the independent clause: "*I have written* these things to you concerning those who persist in their attempts to mislead you" (ταῦτα ἔγραψα ὑμῖν περὶ τῶν πλανώντων ὑμᾶς). The assumed subject, "I," refers to the author. **Semantically,** ἔγραψα is an epistolary aorist: "I *have* written" (KJV ASV NASB NET CNT; cf. 2:14a, 14b, 14c, 21a, 21c). John underscores what he has just written (W, 563) as a warning about those who are trying to lead them astray.

πλανώντων: The Greek word πλανώντων is a genitive masculine plural present active participle from the verb πλανάω meaning "to deceive" or "to mislead" or "to cause someone to go astray" (BDAG, s.v. "πλανάω" 1b, p. 821). **Syntactically,** πλανώντων is a substantival participle functioning as the object of the preposition, "about" (περί). **Semantically,** πλανώντων is a customary present: "those who *persist in their attempt* to mislead" (or "deceive"; cf. NASB ESV NET CNT). It describes a pattern of behavior (W, 521). John points out that there are those who are continually trying to deceive and lead people to believe misguided and fraudulent teachings about the nature of Jesus.

Lexical and Theological Nugget: What does πλανάω mean? This verb occurs thirty-nine times in the New Testament and has a wide range of usage. In 1 John, John uses πλανάω in various ways. First, πλανάω is used in 1 John 1:8 to indicate that the fraudulent people who left have *deceived* themselves into thinking that they are free from the effects of sin. John says that this belief separates them from the truth (cf. 2 Tim. 3:13). Second, πλανάω is used in admonitions not to be *deceived* about (1) unethical behavior (1 Cor. 6:9), (2) bad company (1 Cor. 15:33), (3) Jewish tradition (Gal. 6:7), and (4) the belief that something bad comes from God (James 1:16). In 1 John 3:7, John cautions his readers against being deceived about the nature of sin and righteousness. Third, πλανάω is used in connection with a mass *deception* that will occur in the end times. Jesus warns against those who will come and deceive (Mark 13:6; Matt. 24:5, 11, 24; Luke 21:8). The author of Revelation also speaks of a future deception by Satan (12:9; 20:3, 8, 10) and others (2:20; 13:4; 19:20). In 1 John 2:26, John may be linking πλανάω with those who left the church (2:18–19). He describes people in the "last hour" trying to *deceive* those who are followers of

Jesus. John wants his readers to stand up in the face of these sorts of deceptions that are manifested in the fraudulent antichrists of their day. Followers of Jesus can avoid misguided deceptions through the anointing of the Spirit that has been given to them and reaffirms them in what they have already been taught.

2:27a καὶ ὑμεῖς: The Greek word καί is a conjunction meaning "but" (BDAG, s.v. "καί" 1bη, p. 495) or "now" (BDAG, s.v. "καί" 1e, p. 495). **Syntactically,** καί serves to introduce an independent conjunctive clause: *"now as for you the anointing that you have received from him remains continually in you"* (καὶ ὑμεῖς τὸ χρῖσμα ὃ ἐλάβετε ἀπ' αὐτοῦ μένει ἐν ὑμῖν). **Semantically,** this construction (καί + the pendent nominative ὑμεῖς) is transitional: "now as for you" (NET; contra "but" KJV ESV NLT CNT). It serves to move the discussion in a slightly different direction. Many translations, however, translate καὶ ὑμεῖς "as for you" (ASV NASB NRSV NIV; see W, 51). It seems John turns his attention away from the deceivers and back to believers. The nature of John's turn of attention is evident in the next verb.

μένει: The Greek word μένει is a third person singular present active indicative from the verb μένω meaning "to remain," "to abide," "to continue," or is used to describe someone who does not leave (BDAG, s.v. "μένω" 1aβ, p. 631). **Syntactically,** μένει is the main verb of the independent clause. The subject is the noun, "the anointing" (τὸ χρῖσμα). **Semantically,** μένει is a customary present: "remains *continually*" (cf. NIV) or "lives *continually*" (NLT; cf. W, 521). John emphasizes that true believers are equipped with the constant presence of the Spirit.

2:27b ὅ: The Greek word ὅ is a neuter singular accusative from the relative pronoun ὅς meaning "which" or "that" (BDAG, s.v. "ὅς" 1a, p. 725). **Syntactically,** ὅ introduces an adjectival relative clause, *"that* you have received from him (=God)" (ὃ ἐλάβετε ἀπ' αὐτοῦ). The antecedent of this relative pronoun is the noun, "the anointing" (τὸ χρῖσμα). This relative clause provides additional information about the anointing, namely, that its origin is from God. Whether translated "which" (KJV ASV NASB CNT) or "that" (NRSV ESV NET), John highlights something about the anointing, which is revealed in the next verb.

ἐλάβετε: The Greek word ἐλάβετε is a second person plural aorist active indicative from the verb λαμβάνω meaning "to receive" or "to be a receiver" (BDAG, s.v. "λαμβάνω" 10c, p. 584–85). **Syntactically,** ἐλάβετε is the governing verb of the relative clause. The assumed subject, "you," refers to the readers. **Semantically,** ἐλάβετε is a consummative aorist: "you *have* received" (KJV NLT CNT). It emphasizes what believers have already received (W, 559). John reaffirms his readers about the Spirit they have received (2:18), namely, that God's Spirit remains in them.

2:27c κaί: The Greek word καί is a conjunction meaning "and" (BDAG, s.v. "καί" 1bα, p. 494). **Syntactically,** καί introduces an independent clause: "*and* you have no need" (καὶ οὐ χρείαν ἔχετε). **Semantically,** καί is a coordinating connective: "and" (cf. KJV NASB ESV NIV NET etc.). It gives us some additional information about the presence of the Spirit in the life of the believer.

ἔχετε: The Greek word ἔχετε is a second person plural present active indicative from the verb ἔχω meaning "to have" or "to have a need of something from someone" (BDAG, s.v. "ἔχω" 7aδ, p. 421). **Syntactically,** ἔχετε serves as the main verb of the independent clause. The subject is the implied "you" embedded in the verb and refers to the readers of the letter. **Semantically,** ἔχετε is a customary present negated with οὐ: "you have no" (NASB ESV NET). It speaks of a pattern of behavior (W, 521). John underscores that in addition to having the Holy Spirit, his readers have no needs. What they have no need of is revealed in the next clause.

2:27d ἵνα: The Greek word ἵνα is a conjunction meaning "that" (BDAG, s.v. "ἵνα" 2cα, p. 476). **Syntactically,** ἵνα introduces a dependent conjunctive clause: "*that* anyone teach you" (ἵνα τις διδάσκη ὑμᾶς). **Semantically,** ἵνα is an epexegetical "that" (KJV ASV ESV CNT) explaining how it is that believers have no need for a teacher because they have God's Spirit (Culy, 60), contra Wallace, who lists this ἵνα as an example of a result ἵνα (W, 473) functioning as an adverb modifying the verb, "have" (ἔχετε). If result, the believer's anointing from God results in having no need for a teacher: "so you have no need" (NRSV NLT). It seems better, however, to see this as an adjectival clause, describing the nature or content of the "need" (χρείαν) evident in the next verb.

διδάσκη: The Greek word διδάσκη is a third person singular present active subjunctive from the verb διδάσκω meaning "to teach" or "to provide instruction in a formal or informal setting" (BDAG, s.v. "διδάσκω" 2d, p. 241). The verb is in the subjunctive mood because ἵνα takes a subjunctive. **Syntactically,** διδάσκη is the governing verb of the dependent ἵνα clause. It modifies the noun, "need" (χρείαν). The subject is the pronoun "anyone" (τις). **Semantically,** διδάσκη is a customary present: "teach" (KJV ASV ESV CNT). John highlights that his readers, who have a Spirit anointing from God, do not need an instructor to aid them in distinguishing truth from error; they already know the truth about Jesus.

Theological Nugget: How is the "teaching" (διδάσκη) to be interpreted? It would be better to think of this teaching as "further" teaching. They have no need for a new instructor with "special teaching" or "special revelation." Later John will express the need for believers to test any new teaching for its accordance with the original gospel message (1 John 4:1–6; 2 John 9–10). But here the emphasis is on "remaining" in the teaching about Jesus as Messiah. Because of the continuous activity of the Spirit, the Johannine community has no need of any further teaching. This once again highlights John's dualism, his sharp distinction between true believers and the misguided fraudulent teachers who have left the church and presume to have a "special knowledge" about Jesus contra the truth about Jesus's humanity and messiahship found in the original proclamation of the gospel (1:1–4).

Excursus

The syntax for the clauses 27e to 27h is *very* difficult. There are at least three options from which to choose. *The first option* is the one presented in the clausal outline (cf. NET). But there are two other options worthy of discussion. Five clauses are disputed here: (1) "but as his anointing teaches you about all things" (ἀλλ᾽ ὡς τὸ αὐτοῦ χρῖσμα διδάσκει ὑμᾶς περὶ πάντων); (2) "and is true" (καὶ ἀληθές ἐστιν); (3) "and is no lie" (καὶ οὐκ ἔστιν ψεῦδος); (4) "and even as it taught you" (καὶ καθὼς ἐδίδαξεν ὑμᾶς); and (5) "but . . . remain in him" (ἀλλ᾽ . . . μένετε ἐν αὐτῷ).

Moving beyond the option in the clausal outline, *a second option* is to see one independent thought with two adverbial comparisons dependent on it, along with one parenthetical comment (seemingly NASB NRSV). John wants his readers in this case to remain in the truth about Jesus (5), just as God's anointing is currently teaching them about all things (1) and as it has indeed already taught them (3). The parenthetical comment (gray shading) would be describing this anointing: it is true (2) and is not a lie (3).

^{27e}**ὡς** τὸ αὐτοῦ χρῖσμα **διδάσκει** ὑμᾶς περὶ πάντων,
^{27e}**as** his anointing **teaches** you about all things,
|
^{27f}καὶ ἀληθές **ἐστιν**
^{27ef}and **it is** true

^{27fg}καὶ οὐκ **ἔστιν** ψεῦδος,
^{27g}and **it is** not a lie,

^{27h}καὶ **καθὼς ἐδίδαξεν** ὑμᾶς,
^{27h}and **just as he has taught** you,
|
²⁷ⁱ**ἀλλ᾽** . . . **μένετε** ἐν αὐτῷ.
²⁷ⁱ**but** . . . **remain** in him.

A *third option* is to see one independent thought with three adverbial comparisons dependent on it. In this case John wants his readers to remain in the truth about Jesus (5), just as God's anointing is currently teaching them about all things (1), just as that anointing is true (2) and not a lie (3), and just as it has already taught them (4).

^{27e}**ἀλλ'** . . . **μένετε** ἐν αὐτῷ.
^{27e}**but** . . . **remain** in him.

> ^{27f}**ὡς** τὸ αὐτοῦ χρῖσμα **διδάσκει** ὑμᾶς περὶ πάντων,
> ^{27f}**as** his anointing **teaches** you about all things,
>
> ^{27g}καὶ [ὡς] ἀληθές **ἐστιν** ^{27fg}καὶ οὐκ **ἔστιν** ψεῦδος,
> ^{27g}and as **it is** true ^{27g}and **it is** not a lie,
>
> ^{27h}καὶ **καθὼς ἐδίδαξεν** ὑμᾶς,
> ^{27h}and **just as he has taught** you,

Now let us resume the first option introduced in the clausal outline above, which sees two independent thoughts, each with its own adverbial comparison (NET). In this instance, John would first tell them that the anointing, which teaches them all things (1) is true (2) and is no lie (3). Then he tells them to remain in Jesus and the correct teaching about him (5), just as it was taught to them (4). See also Bateman[1], 308–9.

2:27e ἀλλ': The Greek word ἀλλά is a conjunction meaning "but" (BDAG, s.v. "ἀλλά" 3, p. 45). **Syntactically,** ἀλλά identifies the clause as an independent conjunctive clause: "*But* . . . now it is true and is no lie" (ἀλλ' . . . καὶ ἀληθές ἐστιν καὶ οὐκ ἔστιν ψεῦδος). The conjunction "but" (ἀλλά) before this independent clause indicates that the preceding statement in 2:27c–d is a settled matter (BDAG, s.v. "ἀλλά" 3, p. 45). **Semantically,** ἀλλά is a contrastive "but" (cf. KJV NASB ESV NIV NET etc.). It emphasizes that they do not need someone other than their anointing to help them distinguish between truth and error.

καί: The Greek word καί is typically a conjunction that means "and" or perhaps "now" (BDAG, s.v. "καί" 2c, p. 496). **Syntactically,** some translations appear to indicate that καί introduces an independent clause, "and it is true" (KJV ASV NASB NRSV ESV) or merely "is true" (NET NLT: cf. "is real," NIV). Yet it seems that while the conjunction ἀλλά introduces a contrastive independent clause, καί draws us back to the anointing of 2:27a (cf. NET). **Semantically,** καί is resumptive and need not be translated (NET NLT). It is, however, translated in the outline above as "now." John desires for his readers to know more about their anointing. (For a similar construction, cf. 1 John 2:18; John 6:5; Bateman[1], 309).

ἐστίν: The Greek word ἐστίν is third person singular present active indicative from the verb εἰμί meaning "to be" or shows how something is to be
understood (BDAG, s.v. "εἰμί" 2cα, p. 283). **Syntactically,** ἐστίν is the main
verb of the independent clause. The subject of the verb is an implied "it," referring to the anointing that was given to them by God. **Semantically,** ἐστίν
is equative: "is" (cf. KJV NASB ESV NIV NET etc.). John equates their anointing
(1 John 2:18) with truth.

2:27f καί: The Greek word καί is a conjunction meaning "and" (BDAG, s.v. "καί"
1b, p. 494). **Syntactically,** καί introduces an independent clause: "*and* it is not
a lie" (καὶ οὐκ ἔστιν ψεῦδος). **Semantically,** καί is a coordinating conjunction that connects two independent clauses: "but . . . now it is true" with "and
it is not a lie" (NET). The connective provides additional information about
the Spirit's anointing.

ἐστίν: The Greek word ἐστίν is third person singular present active indicative
from the verb εἰμί meaning "to be" or shows how something is to be understood
(BDAG, s.v. "εἰμί" 2cα, p. 283). **Syntactically,** ἐστίν is the main verb of the independent καί clause. The subject of the verb is an implied "it" that refers to the
Spirit's anointing that was given to them by God (2:18). **Semantically,** ἐστίν is
equative with a negating οὐκ: "is not" (cf. KJV NASB ESV NIV NET etc.). John adds
(καί) another fact about the Spirit's anointing: it is not a lie; it happened.

2:27g ὡς: The Greek word ὡς is a conjunction meaning "as" or marking a specific
function (BDAG, s.v. "ὡς" 3a, p. 1104). **Syntactically,** ὡς introduces a dependent clause: "*as* his (= God) anointing continually teaches you about all
things" (ὡς τὸ αὐτοῦ χρῖσμα διδάσκει ὑμᾶς περὶ πάντων). The entire
dependent clause functions adverbially. It modifies the two verbs "is" (ἐστίν)
and "is" (ἐστίν). **Semantically,** ὡς is comparative: "as" (cf. KJV NASB ESV NIV
NET etc.). John underscores a comparison evident with the next verb.

διδάσκει: The Greek word διδάσκει is a third person singular present active indicative from the verb διδάσκω meaning "to teach" or "to provide
instruction in a formal or informal setting" (BDAG, s.v. "διδάσκω" 2d, p.
241). **Syntactically,** διδάσκει is the governing verb of the dependent adverbial clause. It modifies the two verbs, "is" (ἐστίν) and "is" (ἐστίν). The
subject is the implied "it" embedded in the verb and refers to the Spirit's
anointing that they have received from God (2:18). **Semantically,** διδάσκει
is a customary present: "*continually* teaches" (cf. KJV NASB ESV NIV NET
etc.). It reveals a pattern of behavior (W, 521). John personifies the Spirit's
anointing as though it were a teacher. John's emphasizes that God's Spirit
continually acts like a teacher reminding them of the truth about Jesus.

2:27h καί: The Greek word καί is a conjunction meaning "and" (BDAG, s.v. "καί" 1bι, p. 494). **Syntactically,** καί introduces a dependent conjunctive clause: "*and* just as he (= God) has taught you" (καὶ καθὼς ἐδίδαξεν ὑμᾶς). **Semantically,** καί appears to introduce a parenthetical idea: "*and* just as he has taught" (cf. ESV NIV NLT) and thus the entire clause appears in a gray box. John is building upon the simple truth.

καθώς: The Greek word καθώς is a conjunction meaning "just as" (BDAG, s.v. "καθώς" 1, p. 493). **Syntactically,** καθώς is part of the dependent καί clause. The entire dependent clause: "and *just as* he (= God) has taught you" (καθὼς ἐδίδαξεν ὑμᾶς) functions adverbially modifying the verb "remain" (μένετε). **Semantically,** καθώς is comparative: "just as" (NSB NRSV ESV NIV NET CNT NLT) or "even as" (KJV ASV). John introduces a comparison with the preceding clause about the Spirit's continual teaching.

ἐδίδαξεν: The Greek word ἐδίδαξεν is a third person singular aorist active indicative from the verb διδάσκω meaning "to teach" or "to provide instruction in a formal or informal setting" (BDAG, s.v. "διδάσκω" 2d, p. 241). **Syntactically,** ἐδίδαξεν is the governing verb of the dependent adverbial clause. The subject is an implied "it" embedded in the verb and refers to the anointing that believers have received from God. **Semantically,** ἐδίδαξεν is a consummative aorist: "he *has* taught" (cf. KJV NASB ESV NIV NET etc.). It emphasizes the cessation of an act (W, 559). John compares the Spirit's current teaching (2:27g) with what the Spirit has already taught them in the past. There is a consistency in the Spirit's teaching.

2:27i μένετε: The Greek word μένετε is a second person plural present active imperative from the verb μένω meaning "to remain" or is used to describe someone who does not leave a certain realm (BDAG, s.v. "μένω" 1aβ, p. 631). **Syntactically,** μένετε is the main verb of the independent asyndeton clause: "*make it a practice to remain* in him" (μένετε ἐν αὐτῷ). **Semantically,** μένετε is an imperative of command: "make it a practice to remain" or "remain" (NET NLT) or "abide" (KJV ASV NASB NRSV ESV CNT). The command is an ongoing process (W, 485).

2:28a Καὶ νῦν: The Greek word καί is a conjunction meaning "even" (BDAG, s.v. "καί" 2bγ, p. 495). The Greek word νῦν is an adverb that means "now" as it pertains to a certain situation (BDAG, s.v. "νῦν" 2a, p. 681). **Syntactically,** καὶ νῦν introduces an independent conjunctive clause: "*Even now*, children, make it a practice to remain in him (= Jesus)" (καὶ νῦν, τεκνία, μένετε ἐν αὐτῷ). **Semantically,** καὶ νῦν is ascensive: "even now" (or "and now" KJV ESV NIV NET etc.). It summarizes the preceding discussion by adding a point of focus (W, 670–71). While some translations consider it as introducing a new section (NRSV NIV NET NLT), it seems John is closing out a section of his teaching here by giving the readers a proper application. A similar use of καὶ νῦν occurs in 2:18 as a conclusion of the ethical discussion of 2:12–17. Here in verse 28, John concludes his doctrinal discussion (2:18–27). The answer to both discussions is to abide in Jesus and the correct teaching about his nature (Culy, 62).

μένετε: The Greek word μένετε is a second person plural present active imperative from the verb μένω meaning "to remain" or is used to describe someone who does not leave a certain realm (BDAG, s.v. "μένω" 1aβ, p. 631). **Syntactically,** μένετε is the main verb of the independent clause. The subject is the implied "you" embedded in the verb and refers to John's readers. **Semantically,** μένετε is an imperative of command: "*make it a practice to remain.*" It assumes an ongoing process (W, 485). John exhorts his readers to continually maintain their relationship with Jesus.

2:28b ἵνα: The Greek word ἵνα is a conjunction meaning "that" or "so that" (BDAG, s.v. "ἵνα" 1a, 3, pp. 475, 477). **Syntactically,** ἵνα introduces a dependent conjunctive clause: "*so that* when he (= Jesus) appears, we may have confidence and so that we may not shrink away from him at his coming" (ἵνα ἐὰν φανερωθῇ σχῶμεν παρρησίαν καὶ μὴ αἰσχυνθῶμεν ἀπ᾽ αὐτοῦ ἐν τῇ παρουσίᾳ αὐτοῦ). The entire dependent clause functions adverbially. It modifies the verb "remain" (μένετε). **Semantically,** ἵνα is either result (BDAG, s.v. "ἵνα" 3, p. 477) or purpose-result (W, 473–74): "so that" (NET; perhaps NASB NRSV ESV NLT CNT). John presents the first of two purpose-result statements for those who remain in Jesus: the inner sense of confidence when Jesus returns.

σχῶμεν: The Greek word σχῶμεν is a first person plural aorist active subjunctive from the verb ἔχω meaning "to have" or "to experience an inner condition" (BDAG, s.v. "ἔχω" 7aβ, p. 421). The verb is in the subjunctive mood because it is part of a ἵνα clause. **Syntactically,** σχῶμεν is the governing verb of the first part of the dependent ἵνα clause. The subject is an implied "we" embedded in the verb and refers to John and his readers. John adds himself into this admonition by using the first person plural, giving the reader the impression that "we are all in this together" (Culy, 63). **Semantically,** σχῶμεν is a constative aorist: "we may have" (cf. KJV NASB ESV NIV NET etc). John views the possessing of an inner condition of "confidence" (παρρησίαν) or "courage" (NLT) as a whole (W, 557). The result of remaining in Jesus is confidence.

Lexical and Theological Nugget: What does John mean by "confidence" (παρρησίαν)? The Greek word "confidence" (παρρησία) carries the idea of safety and security in a person's relationship with Jesus, which occurs only by remaining in Jesus. In the Gospel of John, παρρησία often refers to the bold proclamations that Jesus made in his ministry (John 18:20) and his desire for straightforward, clear, and forthright teaching (John 7:26; 10:24; 11:14; 16:25,

29). In 1 John, however, the four usages focus on the idea of safety and security (2:28; 3:21; 4:17; 5:14). When discussing human relationships, παρρησία often is used to express *trust* or *security*, which is evident in the mutual confidence between two brothers (P. Michel 502.9, 12) and between a husband and a wife (Jos. *A.J.* 2.4.4 §52). In the LXX, *safety* exists for the poor (Ps. 11:6 [ET 12:5]) and for the repentant (Job 22:26) before God. Here in 1 John 2:28, John suggests that followers of Jesus can find security and assurance of their relationship with Jesus when they resolve to remain in the correct teachings about his nature.

2:28c ἐάν: The Greek word ἐάν is a conjunction meaning "when" or marking the prospect of an action in the future (BDAG, s.v. "ἐάν" 268.2). **Syntactically,** the conjunction ἐάν identifies the clause as a dependent clause. The entire dependent clause, "when he (= Jesus) appears" (ἐὰν φανερωθῇ) functions adverbially. It modifies the verb, "we might have" (σχῶμεν). **Semantically,** ἐάν is a temporal conjunction with a meaning similar to the adverb ὅταν (see ἐάν in John 12:32, 14:3). There is certainty about the believer who remains in Jesus: he or she will be able to stand before him with confidence.

φανερωθῇ: The Greek word φανερωθῇ is third person singular aorist passive subjunctive from the verb φανερόω meaning "to appear" or "to cause someone to become visible" (BDAG, s.v. "φανερόω" 1aβ, p. 1048). The verb is in the subjunctive mood because ἐάν takes its verb in the subjunctive. **Syntactically,** φανερωθῇ is the governing verb of the dependent ἐάν clause. The subject of the verb is an implied "he" embedded in the verb and refers to Jesus. **Semantically,** φανερωθῇ is a constative aorist: "he appears" (NASB ESV NIV NET CNT) or more pointedly, "he returns" (NLT). It points to a future event as a whole (W, 557). John underscores the certainty of the coming of Jesus and the confidence of his readers when Jesus returns.

2:28d καί: The Greek word καί is a conjunction meaning "and" (BDAG, s.v. "καί" 1b, p. 494). **Syntactically,** καί introduces a dependent conjunctive clause: "*and* so that we may not shrink away from him at his (= Jesus) coming" (καὶ [ἵνα] μὴ αἰσχυνθῶμεν ἀπ᾿ αὐτοῦ ἐν τῇ παρουσίᾳ αὐτοῦ). **Syntactically,** καὶ introduces the second part of a compound dependent ἵνα clause. **Semantically,** καί adds an additional purpose-result of remaining in the correct teaching about Jesus. Not only will remaining in Jesus result in confidence when Jesus appears, but it will have another result, which is evident in the [ἵνα] clause.

[ἵνα]: The Greek word ἵνα is a conjunction meaning "that" or "so that" (BDAG, s.v. "ἵνα" 1a, 3, pp. 475, 477). **Syntactically,** [ἵνα] is elliptical and introduces the second dependent clause, "and [*so that*] we may not shrink away from him at his coming" ([ἵνα] καὶ μὴ αἰσχυνθῶμεν ἀπ᾿ αὐτοῦ ἐν τῇ παρουσίᾳ αὐτοῦ). The clause functions adverbially modifying the verb "remain" (μένετε). **Semantically,** [ἵνα] is classified as either result (BDAG, s.v. "ἵνα" 3, p. 475) or purpose-result (W, 473–74): "so that" (NET; perhaps NASB NRSV ESV NLT CNT). John presents a second purpose-result, the details of which are defined with the next verb.

αἰσχυνθῶμεν: The Greek word αἰσχυνθῶμεν is a first person plural aorist passive subjunctive from the verb αἰσχύνω meaning "to shame" or "to experience shame or be disgraced before someone" (BDAG, s.v. "αἰσχύνω" 2, p. 30). The verb is in the subjunctive mood because it is part of a ἵνα clause. **Syntactically,** αἰσχυνθῶμεν is the governing verb of the elliptical dependent adverbial ἵνα clause. The assumed subject, "we," embedded in the verb refers to John and the readers of his letter. **Semantically,** μὴ αἰσχυνθῶμεν is a constative aorist: "not ashamed" (KJV ASV CNT) or "to be put to shame" (NRSV). It points to a future event as a whole (W, 557). John underscores the necessity for believers to cultivate a persistent relationship with Jesus so to avoid disgrace. This sense of shame before a God who judges is common elsewhere (see Isa. 1:24, 29; Rev. 6:15–17).

Lexical and Theological Nugget: What does αἰσχύνω mean? The Greek word αἰσχύνω occurs only five times in the New Testament (Luke 16:3; 2 Cor. 10:8; Phil. 1:20; 1 Peter 4:16; 1 John 2:28). Here in 1 John 2:28 it should be translated with a classical middle voice where the subject does the action and is also the recipient of the action of the verb, "be ashamed before him" (KJV) or "shrink back from him in shame" (NLT). If we remain in the correct teachings about the humanity and messiahship of Jesus, we can have confidence when Jesus comes, as opposed to shrinking from him in shame. We see this same *shame* before a judging God in other passages, such as Isaiah 1:24, 29 and Revelation 6:15–17. Avoiding cowering in shame at the coming of God seems to have become part of the eschatological expectation of early Christians.

2:29a ἐάν: The Greek word ἐάν is a conjunction meaning "if" or "to denote what is expected to occur under certain circumstances" (BDAG, s.v. "ἐάν" 1aα, p. 267; see the semantics of οἶδα below). **Syntactically,** ἐάν identifies the clause as a dependent conjunctive clause. The entire clause: "*if* you know that he (= Jesus) is righteous" (ἐὰν εἰδῆτε ὅτι δίκαιός ἐστιν) functions adverbially. It modifies the verb, "you know" (γινώσκετε). **Semantically,** ἐάν introduces a third class conditional clause: "if" (KJV NASB ESV NIV NET etc.). John is presenting a likely condition (W, 696). John speaks of a probability for his readers that is clarified with the next verb.

εἰδῆτε: The Greek word εἰδῆτε is second person plural perfect active subjunctive from the verb οἶδα meaning "to know" or "to have information about someone" (BDAG, s.v. "οἶδα" 1e, p. 693). The verb is in the subjunctive mood because it is part of a ἐάν clause. **Syntactically,** εἰδῆτε is the governing verb of the dependent conjunctive ἐάν clause. It is functioning adverbially, modifying the verb, "you know" (γινώσκετε). The assumed subject, "you," refers to the recipients of the letter. **Semantically,** εἰδῆτε is a perfect with present force: "you know" (cf. KJV NASB ESV NIV NET etc). What exactly is known is evident in the following ὅτι clause.

ὅτι: The Greek word ὅτι is a conjunction meaning "that" or identifies content after a verb of mental perception (BDAG, s.v. "ὅτι" 1c, p. 731). **Syntactically,** ὅτι introduces a dependent conjunctive clause: "*that* he (= Jesus) is righteous" (ὅτι δίκαιός ἐστιν). The entire clause is substantival. It functions as the direct object of the verb "you know" (εἰδῆτε). The clause is placed in parentheses in order to visualize its contribution to the dependent clause. **Semantically,** ὅτι is an indirect discourse marker: "that" (KJV NASB ESV NIV NET etc.). John discloses the content of the believer's knowledge found in the rest of the clause.

ἐστίν: The Greek word ἐστίν is third person singular present active indicative from the verb εἰμί meaning "to be" or "to be in close connection with someone" or it can be used in statements of identity (BDAG, s.v. "εἰμί" 2a, p. 283). **Syntactically,** ἐστίν is the governing verb of the dependent direct object clause. The subject of the verb is an implied "he." **Semantically,** ἐστίν is an equative present: "is." It equates Jesus with righteousness (cf. 2:1). A believer knows that Jesus is righteous and that those who are God's children are also righteous.

Grammatical Nugget: What is the problem with an implied subject for "is" (ἐστίν)? On the one hand, the implied "he" could refer to God the Father. God the Father is the pronoun at the end of the verse: "has been fathered by him" (ἐξ αὐτοῦ γεγέννηται). In the phrase, "has been fathered by him," αὐτός refers to God the Father because elsewhere in 1 John, it always refers to him (cf. 3:9; 4:7; 5:1, 4, 18). Furthermore, it is the Father who is called "the Righteous One" (δίκαιός) in 1 John 1:9. On the other hand, "he" could be Jesus. The "Righteous One" in 2:1 refers to Jesus. Furthermore, Jesus's return has been the recent focus of discussion in 2:28. Perhaps there is some purposeful Trinitarian ambiguity and thereby it may not be a case of either/or, but a case of both/and (Culy, 65). "Yet we have chosen to identify the implied subject "he" to be Jesus."

2:29b γινώσκετε: The Greek word γινώσκετε is second person plural present active indicative from the verb γινώσκω meaning "to know" or "to have come to the knowledge of a person" (BDAG, s.v. "γινώσκετε" 6c, p. 200). **Syntactically,** γινώσκετε is the main verb of the independent clause: "*you* also *know* that everyone who practices righteousness has been fathered by him" (γινώσκετε ὅτι καὶ πᾶς ὁ ποιῶν τὴν δικαιοσύνην ἐξ αὐτοῦ γεγέννηται). The assumed subject, "you," refers to the recipients of the letter. While this verb could be an imperative instead of an indicative, knowledge is rarely commanded in Johannine literature. Knowledge is more a result of one's status as a believer (Bateman[1], 315; Brown, 382–83). **Semantically,** γινώσκετε is a customary present: "you know" (KJV NASB ESV NIV NET). It speaks of a pattern of knowledge (W, 527). John's readers possess the knowledge that God is righteous, and they should also possess the knowledge that those who are righteous are his progeny.

ὅτι: The Greek word ὅτι is a conjunction meaning "that" or it can be used to identify content after a verb of mental perception (BDAG, s.v. "ὅτι" 1c, p. 731). **Syntactically,** ὅτι introduces a dependent conjunctive clause: "*that* everyone who practices righteousness has been fathered by him (= God)" (ὅτι καὶ πᾶς ὁ ποιῶν τὴν δικαιοσύνην ἐξ αὐτοῦ γεγέννηται). The entire clause is functioning substantivally as the direct object of the verb "you know" (γινώσκετε). The entire ὅτι clause is placed in parentheses in order to visualize its contribution to the independent clause. **Semantically,** ὅτι is an indirect discourse marker: "that" (KJV ASV NASB ESV NIV NET CNT). It provides the content of what the one who knows that God is righteous should also know (W, 454). The specific content of knowledge is clarified in the next verb.

γεγέννηται: The Greek word γεγέννηται is third person singular perfect passive indicative from the verb γεννάω meaning "to become the parent of" or "to exercise the role of a parental figure" (BDAG, s.v. "γεννάω" 1b, p. 193). **Syntactically,** γεγέννηται is the governing verb of the dependent ὅτι clause. The subject is "everyone" (πᾶς) and the participial clause "who practices righteousness" (ὁ ποιῶν τὴν δικαιοσύνην) that modifies "everyone" (πᾶς). **Semantically,** γεγέννηται is both a gnomic and an extensive perfect: "has been fathered" (NET) or "has been born" (NRSV ESV NIV). It is gnomic because of the generic subject (πᾶς) while extensive in that the focus is on the decisive relationship between the God and the believer (W, 580). This generic or proverbial force may also be rendered intensively: "is born" (KJV NASB CNT; cf. ASV) with an emphasis on the results of the present condition of the believer. Regardless of where one places the emphasis of the perfect, John's point is simply this: believers have been fathered by God in the past and that past event has continuing results in the present (cf. 3:9; 4:7; 5:1, 4, 18). The content of what is known about those who practice righteousness is this: they have an ongoing relationship with God.

Theological Nugget: What does it mean to be fathered by or born of God? This is a reoccurring theme throughout 1 John and may have its origin in Jesus's discussion with Nicodemus in John 3. Jesus suggested to the rabbi that in order to be a member of the faithful, he must be born again. Jesus makes it clear that this is not another physical birth, but a spiritual birth. Jesus suggests in John 3 and our author suggests here that receiving God's Spirit (i.e., being born of God) is a necessary requirement for obedience to the love commands of Jesus and membership in the community of faith.

1 John 3:1–10

Big Greek Idea: People identified as God's children, due to God's love, anticipate the return of Jesus and thereby imitate Jesus's self-sacrificing lifestyle (unlike those who don't), and are cautious to distinguish between those who imitate Jesus and those who imitate the selfish acts of the Devil whereby love is withheld from fellow children of God.

Structural Overview: Having made an emotive appeal to remain in Jesus (2:18–29), John returns (ἴδετε) to his theme of love (3:1–10). He begins with a simple assertion: God extended (δέδωκεν) love to Jesus followers that resulted (ἵνα) in their being *identified* (κληθῶμεν) *as God's children*, which in turn becomes the reason (διὰ τοῦτο) why people who do not follow Jesus question (οὐ γινώσκει) those who do (v. 1).

John then transitions (ἀγαπητοί) to a discussion about *being* (ἐσμέν) *a child* of God (vv. 2–6). First, God's children anticipate (ἐφανερώθη) being like Jesus when he comes back (αὐτῷ ἐσόμεθα/ἐὰν φανερωθῇ; v. 2). Building (καί) on this future expectation, God's children imitate Jesus (ἀγνίζει/καθώς; v. 3). Second, John speaks of self-serving selfish (ποιεῖ) people for whom Jesus came (οἴδατε/ἐφανερώθη) to die in order to (ἵνα) eliminate (ἄρη) selfishness (vv. 4–5). Finally, John makes a clear distinction between anyone (πᾶς) who makes it a practice to be selfless (οὐχ ἁμαρτάνει; like Jesus) and those who are selfish and do not have a relationship with God (οὐδὲ ἔγνωκεν; v. 6).

John closes with a *warning for God's children* (τεκνία) about two types of people in the world (vv. 7–8). First, John warns God's children not to be deceived (μηδεὶς πλανάτω; v. 7). Second, John distinguishes between one group of people who imitate Jesus (ἐστίν/καθώς) and those who imitate the Devil (ἐστίν). Third, the purpose (εἰς τοῦτο/ἵνα) for Jesus's coming (ἐφανερώθη) was to eliminate (λύσῃ) the selfish self-serving activities (v. 8). Finally, John distinguishes between two groups of people. Those who do not practice selfishness like Jesus (οὐ ποιεῖ) because their father is God (σπέρμα/γεγέννηται), and those who practice acts of self-serving selfishness against a fellow child of God and do (ἐστίν) know God (vv. 9–10).

Outline:

> God's children Are Loved, Celebrated, and Rejected (v. 1)
>> God's children experience divine love (v. 1a–b)
>> God's children are celebrated children (v. 1c)
>> God's children are rejected by the world (v. 1d–e)
> God's children Are Different (vv. 2–6)
>> God's children anticipate and imitate Jesus (vv. 2–3)

God's children differ from selfish self-serving people (vv. 4–5)

God's children differ from those who persist in wrongdoing (v. 6)

God's children are Warned (vv. 7–10)

God's children are to avoid being misinformed (v. 7)

God's children are to distinguish between imitators of Jesus and imitators of the Devil (v. 8)

God's children's paternity is evident in the absence of selfishness (vv. 9–10).

CLAUSAL OUTLINE FOR 1 JOHN 3:1–10

3:1a ἴδετε ποταπὴν ἀγάπην **δέδωκεν** ἡμῖν ὁ πατὴρ

3:1a Consider what sort of love the Father **has granted** to us

              |

3:1b **ἵνα** τέκνα θεοῦ **κληθῶμεν·**

3:1b**that we should be called** children of God;

3:1c καὶ **ἐσμέν** [τέκνα θεοῦ κληθωμεν].

3:1c *and so* **we** *really* **are** [*called children of God*].

3:1d διὰ τοῦτο ὁ κόσμος οὐ **γινώσκει** ἡμᾶς

3:1d For this reason the world does not **know** us,

    |

3:1e **ὅτι** οὐκ **ἔγνω** αὐτόν.

3:1e **that** it (= world) **did** not **know** him (= Jesus).

3:2a Ἀγαπητοί, νῦν τέκνα θεοῦ **ἐσμεν**,

3:2a Beloved, **we are** God's children,

3:2b καὶ οὔπω **ἐφανερώθη** τί ἐσόμεθα.

3:2b and what we will be (whenever [Jesus comes]) **has not been revealed**.

3:2c **οἴδαμεν** (ὅτι ... αὐτῷ ἐσόμεθα),

3:2c **We know** (that ... we will be like him [= Jesus]).

   |

3:2d **ἐὰν φανερωθῇ**

3:2d **when he appears**

                 |

3:2e **ὅτι ὀψόμεθα** αὐτὸν

3:2e **because we will see** him (= Jesus)

                     |

3:2f **καθώς ἐστιν**.

3:2f **as he is**.

3:3a <u>καὶ</u> (πᾶς ὁ ἔχων τὴν ἐλπίδα ταύτην ἐπ᾽ αὐτῷ) **ἁγνίζει** ἑαυτὸν
3:3a <u>And *so*</u> (everyone who has this hope in him [or her]) **purifies** himself
   (or herself)

   3:3b **καθὼς** ἐκεῖνος ἁγνός **ἐστιν**.
   3:3b **even as** he (= Jesus) **is** pure.

3:4a (Πᾶς ὁ ποιῶν τὴν ἁμαρτίαν) καὶ τὴν ἀνομίαν **ποιεῖ**,
3:4a (Everyone who practices sin) also **practices** lawlessness,

3:4b <u>καὶ</u> ἡ ἁμαρτία **ἐστὶν** ἡ ἀνομία.
3:4b *indeed* sin **is** lawlessness.

3:5a <u>καὶ</u> **οἴδατε** (ὅτι ἐκεῖνος ἐφανερώθη)
3:5a <u>And **you know**</u> (<u>that</u> he [= Jesus] <u>appeared</u>)

   3:5b **ἵνα** τὰς ἁμαρτίας **ἄρῃ**,
   3:5b **in order to take away** sin,

3:5c <u>καὶ</u> [*οἴδατε* (*ὅτι*] ἁμαρτία ἐν αὐτῷ οὐκ **ἔστιν**).
3:5c <u>and</u> [*you know* (*that*] in him (= Jesus) **there is** no sin).

3:6a (πᾶς ὁ ἐν αὐτῷ μένων) οὐχ **ἁμαρτάνει·**
3:6a (Everyone who makes it a practice to abide in him [= Jesus]) **does** not
   persist in **sin**;

3:6b (πᾶς ὁ ἁμαρτάνων) οὐχ **ἑώρακεν** αὐτὸν οὐδὲ **ἔγνωκεν** αὐτόν.
3:6b (everyone who *makes it a practice* to sin) **has** neither **seen** him (= Jesus)
   nor **known** him (= Jesus).

3:7a Τεκνία, μηδεὶς **πλανάτω** ὑμᾶς·
3:7a Children, **let** no one **mislead** you;

3:7b (ὁ ποιῶν τὴν δικαιοσύνην) δίκαιός **ἐστιν**,
3:7b (the one who practices righteousness) **is** righteous,

   3:7b **καθὼς** ἐκεῖνος δίκαιός **ἐστιν·**
   3:7b **even as** that one (= Jesus) **is** righteous;

3:8a (ὁ ποιῶν τὴν ἁμαρτίαν) ἐκ τοῦ διαβόλου **ἐστίν**,
3:8a (the one who practices sin) **comes from** the Devil,

   3:8b **ὅτι** ἀπ᾽ ἀρχῆς ὁ διάβολος **ἁμαρτάνει**.
   3:8b **because** the Devil *persists in* **sinning** from the *very* beginning.

3:8c εἰς τοῦτο **ἐφανερώθη** ὁ υἱὸς τοῦ θεοῦ,
3:8c For this purpose the Son of God **appeared**,

      3:8d **ἵνα λύσῃ** τὰ ἔργα τοῦ διαβόλου.
      3:8d *namely* **that he might destroy** the works of the Devil.

3:9a (Πᾶς ὁ γεγεννημένος ἐκ τοῦ θεοῦ) ἁμαρτίαν οὐ **ποιεῖ**,
3:9a (Everyone who has been fathered by God) **does** not **practice** sin,

      3:9b **ὅτι** σπέρμα αὐτοῦ ἐν αὐτῷ **μένει·**
      3:9b **because** God's seed **remains** in him;

3:9c καὶ οὐ **δύναται ἁμαρτάνειν**,
3:9c and **he** (or her) **is** not **able to persist in sin**,

      3:9d **ὅτι** ἐκ τοῦ θεοῦ **γεγέννηται**.
      3:9d **because he has been fathered** by God.

3:10a ἐν τούτῳ φανερά **ἐστιν** τὰ τέκνα τοῦ θεοῦ καὶ τὰ τέκνα τοῦ διαβόλου·
3:10a By this the children of God and the children of the Devil **are** made clear;

3:10b (πᾶς ὁ μὴ ποιῶν δικαιοσύνην) οὐκ **ἐστιν** ἐκ τοῦ θεοῦ,
3:10b (everyone who does not practice righteousness) **is** not of God,

      3:10c καὶ ὁ μὴ ἀγαπῶν τὸν ἀδελφὸν αὐτοῦ.
      3:10c *that is* the one who does not *persist in* loving his (or her)
      brother (or sister).

SYNTAX EXPLAINED FOR 1 JOHN 3:1–10

3:1a ἴδετε: The Greek word ἴδετε is second person plural aorist active imperative from the verb ὁράω meaning "to see" or "to be mentally or spiritually perceptive" or "to consider" (BDAG, s.v. "ὁράω" 4b, p. 720). **Syntactically,** ἴδετε serves as the governing verb of the independent clause: "*Consider* what sort of love the Father has granted to us" (ἴδετε ποταπὴν ἀγάπην δέδωκεν ἡμῖν ὁ πατήρ). The subject of the imperative is an implied "you" and refers to the readers. In this case the imperative clearly marks off the beginning of a new section and a new train of thought. **Semantically,** ἴδετε is an imperative of command: "behold" (KJV ASV) or "see" (NASB NRSV ESV NET NLT CNT) or "consider." It underscores the action as a whole (W, 485). John urges his readers to focus attention upon or to marvel at a great spiritual truth, specified in the next verb.

δέδωκεν: The Greek word δέδωκεν is third person singular perfect active indicative from the verb δίδωμι meaning "to give" or "to grant by formal action" generally of God (BDAG, s.v. "δίδωμι" 13, p. 242). **Syntactically,** δέδωκεν is the main verb of the independent clause. The subject of the verb is God "the Father" (ὁ πατήρ). The direct object, love (ἀγάπην), is qualified by the interrogative adjective: "what sort of" (ποταπήν). This interrogative is used to express both the quantity (how much) and quality (how great) of the love being described (Brown, 387). We also learn that this love comes from the Father. **Semantically,** δέδωκεν is an extensive perfect: "*has* given" (NRSV ESV NET CNT) or "has bestowed" (KJV ASV) or "has granted." It emphasizes the completed action (W, 577). John highlights a great theological truth: God has lavished his love on those who follow Jesus, love initiated by God the Father in the past and continuing even today.

3:1b ἵνα: The Greek word ἵνα is a conjunction meaning "that" (BDAG, s.v. "ἵνα" 2e, p. 476). **Syntactically,** ἵνα introduces a dependent conjunctive clause: "*that* we should be called children of God" (ἵνα τέκνα θεοῦ κληθῶμεν). The entire ἵνα clause is adjectival, modifying "what sort of love" (ποταπὴν ἀγάπην; Culy, 66). **Semantically,** the ἵνα clause is an epexegetical conjunction: "that" (KJV ASV NASB ESV NLT CNT). It provides the content of the "sort of love" given to believers (W, 456), which is defined in the next verb.

κληθῶμεν: The Greek word κληθῶμεν is first person plural aorist passive subjunctive from the verb καλέω meaning "to call" or "to identify by name" (BDAG, s.v. "καλέω" 1d, p. 503). The verb is in the subjunctive mood because it is part of a ἵνα clause. **Syntactically,** κληθῶμεν is the governing verb of the adverbial dependent clause. The subject of the verb is an implied "we" embedded in the verb and refers to anyone on whom God has lavished his love through Jesus. **Semantically,** κληθῶμεν is a constative aorist: "should be called" (KJV ASV NRSV ESV NIV NET CNT). John provides an overall description of the identity believers have when they receive God's love (W, 557). John's readers are God's children. The love indicates parentage that is from God. The word "child" is being used figuratively to describe the relationship of the believer to God the Father though faith in Jesus (see 2:29; 3:9; 4:7; 5:1, 4, and 18; also John 1:12 and esp. 11:52).

3:1c καί: The Greek word καί is a conjunction meaning "and so" or "indeed" or "to introduce a result that comes from what precedes" (BDAG, s.v. "καί" 1bζ, p. 495). **Syntactically,** καί introduces an independent clause, "*and so* we *really* are" (καὶ ἐσμέν). **Semantically,** καί is emphatic: "*and so*" with "*really*" (BDAG, s.v. "καί" 1bζ, p. 495; W, 673). Other translations add "and *such*" (ASV NASB ESV CNT) or "and *indeed*" (NET) to underscore the author's emphasis. We merely translate καί as "indeed" since John repeats a similar usage in verse 4b (cf. NET). Here John gives emphasis to a simple fact clarified in the next verb.

ἐσμέν: The Greek word ἐσμέν is first person plural present active indicative from the verb εἰμί meaning "to be" or "to be in close connection with someone" (BDAG, s.v. "εἰμί" 2a, p. 283). **Syntactically,** ἐσμέν is the main verb of the independent clause. The subject of the verb is an implied "we" referring to John and to the readers of his letter who have faith in Jesus. **Semantically,** ἐσμέν is an equative present: "we are" (cf. KJV NASB ESV NIV NET etc.). John affirms the special father/child relationship with God. The elliptical direct object "children of God" [τέκνα θεοῦ κληθωμεν] is implied from the previous clause. John's emphasis is that followers of Jesus are God's children.

> **Lexical and Theological Nugget**: Who are the "children of God" (τέκνα θεοῦ)? The noun τέκνον occurs ninety-nine times in the New Testament, but only four times in 1 John (3:1, 2, 10; and 5:2). The term τέκνον often speaks literally of a child (Luke 1:7) and of a child's relationship with its father and mother (Col. 3:20–21; Eph. 6:1). It is also used figuratively. On the one hand, Paul uses it to speak of Christians as God's children (Rom. 8:16; Phil. 2:15), and he uses the word "son" in a similar way (Rom. 9:26; 2 Cor. 6:18). On the other hand, John never refers to Christians as "sons," but he does use τέκνον to describe the believer's relationship with God. The term "Son" is used exclusively of Jesus. In the Gospel, John uses τέκνον to speak of believers becoming God's children (1:12) and of believers being chosen and called by their faith in Christ (11:52). In the same way, 1 John speaks of being born of God (2:29; 3:9; 4:7; 5:1, 4, 18), which results in being called God's *child* (3:1, 10; 5:2). Thus in John, τέκνον is a theological yet endearing term for describing a believer's relationship with God (Brown, 388–89).

3:1d διὰ τοῦτο: The Greek word διά is a preposition that references "the reason why something happens" (BDAG, s.v. "διά" B2a, p. 225). The Greek word τοῦτο is an accusative singular neuter from the demonstrative pronoun τοῦτο, which means "this one" (BDAG, s.v. "οὗτος" 1ba, p. 741). Together, the two Greek terms are translated "for this reason." **Syntactically,** διὰ τοῦτο is a prepositional phrase introducing an independent clause: "*For this reason*, the world does not know us" (διὰ τοῦτο ὁ κόσμος οὐ γινώσκει ἡμᾶς). This particular construction occurs frequently in the New Testament and is a very important structural marker in 1 John (3:1; 4:5). **Semantically,** διὰ τοῦτο can be anaphoric pointing back to the preceding discussion or cataphoric pointing forward. This construction points forward (cataphoric) to the ὅτι clause (contra Strecker, 87, who considers it an anaphoric construction). Thus the ὅτι clause is epexegetical to the demonstrative pronoun τοῦτο and provides its content (Culy, 67).

γινώσκει: The Greek word γινώσκει is third person singular present active indicative from the verb γινώσκω meaning "to know" or "to arrive at a knowledge of someone" (BDAG, s.v. "γινώσκω" 1b, p. 199). **Syntactically,** γινώσκει is the main verb of the independent clause. The subject of the verb is "the world" (ὁ κόσμος). **Semantically,** οὐ γινώσκει ἡμᾶς is a customary present: "did not know us" (cf. KJV NASB ESV NIV NET). It describes a pattern of behavior (W, 521). John underscores the world's lack of respect and misunderstanding of Jesus followers: the world system has never understood or respected God either, which is evident in the next clause.

3:1e ὅτι: The Greek word ὅτι is a conjunction meaning "that" after a preceding demonstrative pronoun (BDAG, s.v. "ὅτι" 2a, p. 732). **Syntactically,** ὅτι introduces the dependent adjectival clause: "*that* it (= world) did not know him" (ὅτι οὐκ ἔγνω αὐτόν). It modifies the demonstrative pronoun, "this" (τοῦτο). **Semantically,** ὅτι is classified as epexegetical to τοῦτο and therefore rendered "that" (ESV NIV CNT; contra an adverbial rendering of "because" KJV ASV NASB NRSV NET NLT; cf. BDAG, s.v. "ὅτι" 4a, p. 732). The entire ὅτι clause provides the content of the demonstrative pronoun "this" (τοῦτο). The specifics of John's content are evident in the next verb.

ἔγνω: The Greek word ἔγνω is third person singular aorist active indicative from the verb γινώσκω meaning "to know" or "to arrive at a knowledge of someone" or "to make an acquaintance with someone" (BDAG, s.v. "γινώσκω" 1b, p. 200). **Syntactically,** ἔγνω is the governing verb of the dependent adjectival clause. The subject of the verb is an implied "it" embedded in the verb and refers to the world system that does not understand God or his children. **Semantically,** ἔγνω is a constative aorist: "know" (cf. KJV NASB ESV NIV NET etc.). It summarizes knowledge as a whole (W, 557). John speaks of the world's general inability or unwillingness to understand God.

Theological Nugget: To whom does "him" (αὐτόν) refer? "Him" here in 1 John 3:1 is ambiguous. Did the world not know the Father (NLT; Brown, 392) or Jesus (NET; Painter, 218)? In John 1:10 the clause "and the world did not know him" is applied to Jesus, and in John 17:24 the phrase "the world does not know you" is also applied to the Father. Similarly in 1 John, John identified the world's failure to recognize Jesus (3:6) and to know God (4:8). Perhaps it is best not to take a hard stance either way. The phrase "the world" is a figure of speech (of subject) that references the inhabitants of the world. In John 16:3 and 8:19, Jesus says that the world has neither known the Father or himself. We find the same pattern in 1 John as well. We are told that the world fails to recognize Jesus (3:6) and does not understand God (4:8). Perhaps it is best to leave the referent ambiguous (Culy, 68). The world has not understood God (or Jesus) and they do not understand those who follow Jesus.

3:2a ἐσμέν: The Greek word ἐσμέν is first person plural present active indicative from the verb εἰμί meaning "to be" or "to be in close connection with"

(BDAG, s.v. "εἰμί" 2a, p. 283). **Syntactically,** ἐσμέν is the main verb of the independent clause, "Beloved, now *we are* God's children" (Ἀγαπητοί, νῦν τέκνα θεοῦ ἐσμεν). The subject of the verb is an implied "we," referring to both John and his readers who have put their faith in Jesus. **Semantically,** ἐσμέν is an equative present. John identifies or equates his readers with being God's children. The temporal adverb "now" (νῦν) adds emphasis to the statement that his readers are currently God's children, and sets up a contrast with the future indicatives (ἐσόμεθα) that are in the next clauses.

3:2b καί: The Greek word καί is a conjunction meaning "and" (BDAG, s.v. "καί" 1bγ, p. 494). **Syntactically,** καί introduces an independent conjunctive clause: "*and* what we will be (whenever [Jesus comes]) has not yet been revealed" (καὶ οὔπω ἐφανερώθη τί ἐσόμεθα). **Semantically,** καί is a coordinating connective that occurs with an expression of time (BDAG, s.v. "καί" 1bγ, p. 494). It introduces additional information about the reader's identity with Jesus, which is evident in the rest of the clause.

ἐφανερώθη: The Greek word ἐφανερώθη is a third person singular aorist passive indicative from the verb φανερόω meaning "to reveal" or "to cause to become visible publicly" (BDAG, s.v. "φανερόω" 1b, p. 1048). **Syntactically,** ἐφανερώθη is the main verb of the conjunctive independent clause. The subject of the verb is the entire interrogative clause "what we will be" (τί ἐσόμεθα). It refers to the mystery of the future for believers when Jesus returns. **Semantically,** ἐφανερώθη is a constative aorist negated with οὔπω: "*has* not yet *been* revealed" (passive, NET CNT) or "has not yet appeared" (NRSV ESV). It focuses on an event as a whole (W, 557). While our future life has not yet been revealed completely, readers know that they are children of God. The specifics about the future for followers of Jesus is somewhat clouded in mystery.

ἐσόμεθα: The Greek word ἐσόμεθα is first person plural future (middle) indicative from the verb εἰμί meaning "to be" or "to be in close connection with someone" (BDAG, s.v. "εἰμί" 2a, p. 283). **Syntactically,** ἐσόμεθα is the governing verb of the dependent conjunctive clause: "what *we will be*" (τί ἐσόμεθα). It functions as the subject of the verb, "has been revealed" (ἐφανερώθη). The subject of the verb is an implied "we" referring to both John and the readers of the letter. **Semantically,** ἐσόμεθα is a predictive future: "will be" (cf. KJV NASB ESV NIV NET etc.; W, 568). John tells his readers that their future identity at the return of Jesus has not yet been fully disclosed. John does not leave his readers hanging; the next clause helps clear up this mystery.

3:2c οἴδαμεν: The Greek word οἴδαμεν is first person plural perfect active indicative from the verb οἶδα meaning "to know" or "to have information about something" (BDAG, s.v. "οἶδα" 1e, p. 692). **Syntactically,** οἴδαμεν is the main verb of the independent asyndeton clause. The assumed subject, "we," refers to John and the readers of the letter. **Semantically,** οἴδαμεν is a perfect with present force: "we know" (cf. KJV NASB ESV NIV NET etc.). Verbs like οἶδα almost always appear in the perfect tense without the perfect's aspectual significance (W, 579–80). John underscores the mystery that surrounds the believer's identity when Jesus returns and yet they do know something about that mystery, which becomes even more evident in the next ὅτι clause.

ὅτι: The Greek word ὅτι is a conjunction meaning "that" (BDAG, s.v. "ὅτι" 1c, p. 731). **Syntactically,** ὅτι introduces a dependent conjunctive clause: "*that* when he appears, we will be like him (= Jesus) " (ὅτι ἐὰν φανερωθῇ ὅμοιοι αὐτῷ ἐσόμεθα). It functions as the direct object of the verb "we know" (οἴδαμεν). The clause is placed in parentheses in order to visualize its contribution to the independent clause. **Semantically,** ὅτι is an indirect discourse marker following a verb of perception: "that" (cf. KJV NASB ESV NIV NET etc.). John provides the content of information known in the rest of the ὅτι clause.

ἐσόμεθα: The Greek word ἐσόμεθα is first person plural future (middle) indicative from the verb εἰμί meaning "to be" or "to be in close connection with someone" (BDAG, s.v. "εἰμί" 2a, p. 283). **Syntactically,** ἐσόμεθα is the governing verb of the dependent substantival clause. The subject of the verb is an implied "we" referring to John and the readers of his letter. **Semantically,** ἐσόμεθα is a predictive future: "will be" (cf. KJV NASB ESV NIV NET etc.; W, 568). John describes the believer's future identity when Jesus returns, namely, that they will be "like him" (ὅμοιοι αὐτῷ). The pronoun "him" is once again problematic. Does "him" refer to the Father or Jesus? It seems in this case, it refers to Jesus due to his second appearing (contra BDAG, s.v. "ὅμοιος" a, p. 706). They know that even though they do not have all the facts, they do understand this much: followers of Jesus will one day be like the one they follow. That *time frame* is clarified in the next ἐάν clause.

Theological Nugget: What does John mean when he says that his readers will be "like him" (ὅμοιοι αὐτῷ)? The adjective ὅμοιοι means "of the same nature," "like," or "similar" (BDAG, s.v. " ὅμοιος" a, p. 706), and it frequently appears in the dative case as a dative of reference or respect (Baugh, 43–44). Here John uses the phrase to talk about the believer's transformation that will take place when Jesus comes again. When he returns, believers will become *like* him or more *similar* to him than they are now as a result of seeing him as he truly is. While John does not provide a great deal of specifics, followers of Jesus will see a resurrected Jesus (Acts 1:3, 11).

3:2d ἐάν: The Greek word ἐάν is a conjunction meaning "when" or it is used to underscore action in a point of time (BDAG, s.v. "ἐάν" 2, p. 268). **Syntacti-**

cally, ἐάν identifies the clause as a dependent conjunctive clause. The entire dependent clause: "*when* he appears" (ἐὰν φανερωθῇ) functions adverbially. It modifies the verb, "we will be" (ἐσόμεθα). **Semantically,** ἐάν is a temporal conjunction: "when" (NASB NRSV ESV NIV CNT NLT). It introduces a third class condition (W, 696). In this instance, like the usage in 1 John 2:28, the meaning approaches that of the adverb ὅταν (cf. John 12:32, 14:3). The idea here is not that Jesus's coming might or might not happen, but that when it happens, the believer can be assured that he will be like him (= Jesus).

ἐφανερώθῃ: The Greek word ἐφανερώθῃ is third person singular aorist passive subjunctive from the verb φανερόω meaning "to appear" or "to cause to become visible publicly" (BDAG, s.v. "φανερόω" 1aβ, p. 1048). The verb is in the subjunctive mood because ἐάν takes it verb in the subjunctive mood. **Syntactically,** ἐφανερώθῃ is the governing verb of the dependent adverbial clause. The subject of the verb is an implied "he" embedded in the verb and refers to Jesus. It is possible that the subject of this verb could be an implied "what we will be" (τί ἐσόμεθα), carried over from the previous instance of this verb in 3:1 (Brown, 393–94). Yet this seems unlikely because there are pronouns in the following phrases that seem to point to Jesus. Also, this verb is further explained by the following verb "we will see" (ὀψόμεθα). So the object of this verb is Jesus (αὐτόν) because Jesus's return is John's focus (Culy, 69). **Semantically,** ἐφανερώθῃ is a constative aorist: "he appears" (KJV NASB ESV NIV NLT CNT). It describes an event as a whole (W, 557). John speaks of what happens when Jesus returns.

3:2e ὅτι: The Greek word ὅτι is a conjunction meaning "because" (BDAG, s.v. "ὅτι" 4a, p. 732). **Syntactically,** ὅτι introduces a dependent conjunctive clause: "*because* we will see him (= Jesus)" (ὅτι ὀψόμεθα αὐτόν). The entire ὅτι clause is adverbial. It modifies the verb "we will be" (ἐσόμεθα). **Semantically,** ὅτι is causal: "because" (NASB ESV NET). John gives his readers the reason why they know that they will be like Jesus when he returns. It is because they will see Jesus firsthand and have a face-to-face encounter with him.

ὀψόμεθα: The Greek word ὀψόμεθα is first person plural future middle indicative from the verb ὁράω meaning "to see" or "to perceive someone by eye" or "to notice someone" (BDAG, s.v. "ὁράω" A1c, p. 719). **Syntactically,** ὀψόμεθα is the governing verb of the dependent adverbial clause. The subject of the verb is an implied "we" and refers back to John and the readers. **Semantically,** ὀψόμεθα is a predictive future: "we *will* see" (KJV NASB ESV NIV NET etc.). It emphasizes something yet to occur (W, 568). John emphasizes that his readers will one day have a face-to-face encounter with Jesus when he returns.

3:2f καθώς: The Greek word καθώς is a conjunction meaning "just as" or "as" (BDAG, s.v. "καθώς" 1, p. 493). **Syntactically,** καθώς introduces a conjunctive dependent clause. The entire dependent clause, "*as he is*" (καθώς ἐστιν) functions adverbially. It modifies the verb "we will see" (ὀψόμεθα). **Semantically,** καθώς is comparative: "as" (KJV NRSV ESV NIV NLT CNT) or "just as" (NASB NET). John makes a comparison about the way his readers will see Jesus when he returns.

ἐστίν: The Greek word ἐστίν is third person singular present active indicative from the verb εἰμί meaning "to be" or "to be in close connection with something" (BDAG, s.v. "εἰμί" 2a, p. 283). **Syntactically,** ἐστίν is the main verb of the dependent adverbial clause. The subject of the verb is an implied "he" referring to Jesus. **Semantically,** ἐστίν is an equative verb that serves to identify something about Jesus when he returns. John's readers will be like Jesus both inwardly and outwardly in their resurrection (1 John 3:7; 4:17; cf. Acts 1:3, 11).

3:3a καί: The Greek word καί is a conjunction meaning "and so" or is used "to introduce a result that comes from what precedes" (BDAG, s.v. "καί" 1bζ, p. 495). **Syntactically,** καί introduces a conjunctive independent clause: "*and so everyone who has this hope in him purifies himself (or herself)*" (καὶ πᾶς ὁ ἔχων τὴν ἐλπίδα ταύτην ἐπ' αὐτῷ ἁγνίζει ἑαυτόν). **Semantically,** καί is a coordinating connective: "and" (cf. KJV NASB ESV NIV NET etc.). It introduces additional information about the reader's identity when Jesus returns, which is evident in the rest of the clause.

ἔχων: The Greek word ἔχων is a nominative masculine singular present active participle from the verb ἔχω meaning "to have" or "to experience an emotion or inner possession" (BDAG, s.v. "ἔχω" 7aβ, p. 421). **Syntactically,** ἔχων introduces a participial clause: "who has this hope" (ὁ ἔχων τὴν ἐλπίδα ταύτην). The participle ἔχων is adjectival, modifying "everyone" (πᾶς). Together, they function as the subject of the verb "purifies" (ἁγνίζει). So the entire πᾶς + participial clause is placed in parentheses to visualize their grammatical function as the subject of the independent clause. **Semantically,** ἔχων is a gnomic present: "everyone" (ASV NASB ESV NIV NET CNT). The participle is being used in generic utterances (W, 615). John describes a timeless fact about people in general, which is clarified in the next verb.

ἁγνίζει: The Greek word ἁγνίζει is third person singular present active indicative from the verb ἁγνίζω meaning "to purify" or "to cause to be morally pure" (BDAG, s.v. "ἁγνίζω" 2, p. 12). **Syntactically,** ἁγνίζει is the main verb of the independent conjunctive clause. The subject is the entire phrase "everyone who has this hope in him" (πᾶς ὁ ἔχων τὴν ἐλπίδα ταύτην ἐπ' αὐτῷ). It refers to any person who believes in Jesus and is looking forward to physical transformation at his return. **Semantically,** ἁγνίζει is a gnomic present: "purifies" (cf. KJV NASB ESV NIV NET etc.). The verb is part of the generic statement that was introduced with the generic participle (W, 523–24). John underscores a timeless truth about possessing hope for a future transformation that affects the present desire to live an ethical lifestyle in the here and now (cf. Brown, 398).

Lexical and Theological Nugget: What is this ἐλπίδα that purifies the one who possesses it? Although ἐλπίδα apears fifty-three times in the New Testament, mostly in Paul (thirty-one times), this is the only occurrence of the noun in John's writings. "Hope" can be used in three main ways: (1) It can speak of looking forward to something good, such as returning home (Philo, *Spec.* 4:17; Polybius, *Hist.* 3.63.7), receiving a wage (Wis 2:22), reaping a harvest (Philo, *Virt.* 159; *Praem.* 129; 1 Cor. 9:10), or to being the father of many (Rom. 4:18). The related verb appears in 2 John 12 and 3 John 14 to indicate that John is looking forward to seeing the people to whom he is writing. (2) It can also speak of a desire to not become ill (2 Macc 3:29: Josephus, *B.J.* 1.657; *A.J.* 17.172), to not get shipwrecked (Acts 27:20), or to avert a disaster (Job 2:9 LXX). (3) Finally, it can speak of placing confidence in people or in earthly realities: the people of Shechem put their hope in Baal (Judg. 9:26 LXX; cf. 20:36); Hezekiah put his in Egypt and his horsemen (2 Kings 18:24 LXX); the Assyrians put theirs in their shields and spears; Israel in Bethel (Jer. 31:13 [ET 48:13] LXX) and Egypt (Ezek. 29:16 LXX); Paul in the Thessalonian church (1 Thess. 2:19); and the Colossians in Jesus (Col. 1:27). Of these options, the last one is favored. Believers can have confidence that at the return of Jesus they will be transformed to be like Jesus both inwardly and outwardly.

3:3b καθώς: The Greek word καθώς is a conjunction meaning "just as" or "as" or "even as" (BDAG, s.v. "καθώς" 1, p. 493). **Syntactically,** καθώς introduces a dependent conjunctive clause. The entire dependent καθώς clause, "*even as* he (= Jesus) is pure" (καθὼς ἐκεῖνος ἁγνός ἐστιν) functions adverbially. It modifies the verb "purifies" (ἁγνίζει). **Semantically,** καθώς is comparative: "even as" (KJV ASV) or "just as" (NASB NRSV NIV NLT CNT). John is making a comparison between Jesus and his readers, which is revealed in the rest of the καθώς clause.

ἐστίν: The Greek word ἐστίν is third person singular present active indicative from the verb εἰμί meaning "to be" or "to be in close connection with" (BDAG, s.v. "εἰμί" 2a, p. 283). **Syntactically,** ἐστίν is the governing verb of the dependent adverbial clause. The subject of the verb is the emphatic demonstrative pronoun "that one" (ἐκεῖνος) and refers to Jesus. **Semantically,** ἐστίν is an equative present: "he is" (cf. KJV NASB ESV NIV NET etc.). John states a theological truth that equates the purity of Jesus with the pure life that all those who follow Jesus are expected to live. In other words, imitate Jesus (cf. 2:6).

3:4a ποιῶν: The Greek word ποιῶν is a nominative masculine singular present active participle from the verb ποιέω meaning "to practice," "to do," "to commit," or "to carry out an obligation of a moral or social nature" (BDAG, s.v. "ποιέω"

3c, p. 840). **Syntactically,** ποιῶν is the first in a series of adjectival participles in this discussion on sin. The entire participial clause: *"who practices* sin" (ὁ ποιῶν τὴν ἁμαρτίαν) modifies the adjective "everyone" (πᾶς). It stands in contrast to the next participial clause: the "the one who practices righteousness" (ὁ ποιῶν τὴν δικαιοσύνην) from 2:29 (Brown, 398). John contrasts the one who is righteous and has been fathered by God with the one who habitually sins. The entire πᾶς + participial clause is placed in parentheses to visualize its grammatical function as the subject of the independent clause. **Semantically,** ποιῶν is a gnomic present: "everyone who practices" (ποιῶν; NASB ESV NET) or "commits" (KJV NRSV CNT). John presents a timeless maxim about people (W, 523). People who live a lifestyle of sin have a problem. That problem is disclosed in the next verb.

ποιεῖ: The Greek word ποιεῖ is third person singular present active indicative from the verb ποιέω meaning "to practice," "to do," "to commit," or "to carry out an obligation of a moral or social nature" (BDAG, s.v. "ποιέω" 3c, p. 840). **Syntactically,** ποιεῖ is the main verb of the independent asyndeton clause: "everyone who practices sin also *practices* lawlessness" (πᾶς ὁ ποιῶν τὴν ἁμαρτίαν καὶ τὴν ἀνομίαν ποιεῖ). The subject of ποιεῖ is the entire participial phrase, "everyone who practices sin" (πᾶς ὁ ποιῶν τὴν ἁμαρτίαν). The καὶ here is functioning adjunctively and should be translated as "also" (W, 671). **Semantically,** ποιεῖ is a gnomic present: "everyone who practices" (NASB ESV NET). John describes another timeless fact about people who live a lifestyle of sin: they also practice lawlessness.

3:4b καί: The Greek word καί is a conjunction meaning "and so" or indeed is used "to introduce a result that comes from what precedes" (BDAG, s.v. "καί" 1bζ, p. 495). **Syntactically,** καί introduces an independent conjunctive clause: *"indeed* sin is lawlessness" (καὶ ἡ ἁμαρτία ἐστὶν ἡ ἀνομία). **Semantically,** some translations interpret καί as explanatory: "for" (KJV NLT), or a coordinating connective: "and" (ASV NASB), "also" (ESV), but the best choice is an emphatic conjunction: "indeed" (NET), "in fact" (NIV) or "and so" along with "really." John links the gnomic truth about anyone who practices sins with another gnomic truth evident in the rest of the clause.

ἐστίν: The Greek word ἐστίν is third person singular present active indicative from the verb εἰμί meaning "to be" or "to be in close connection with" (BDAG, s.v. "εἰμί" 2a, p. 283). **Syntactically,** ἐστίν is the main verb of the independent conjunctive clause. The subject of the verb is the noun "sin" (ἡ ἁμαρτία). **Semantically,** ἐστίν is an equative present: "is" (cf. KJV NASB ESV NIV NET etc.). John equates sin with lawlessness. John's timeless fact is that sin is the same as lawlessness.

Theological Nugget: What is sin in 1 John 3:5? Three viewpoints have been asserted. Perhaps John is attacking the misguided who have left the church for living licentious lives because they thought the law had no significance in their lives (Wescott, 102). Brown argues that if that were the case, then why wouldn't John say "lawlessness is sin"? Instead he says that "sin is lawlessness" (399). Perhaps sin refers to those who left the church and were practicing the lawlessness that was expected to come before the end of the world (4 Ezra 5:1–12). This fits the eschatological context of 1 John 3:2–3 and also fits well with the assertion that the sins of the misguided were a sign of the Antichrist (2:18). Or perhaps sin is simply a reference to the willful ignoring of the command given by Jesus in John 13:34–35 and reiterated in 1 John 3:23. This is a major theme in 1 John as well as a specific charge leveled against the secessionists (2:9–11; 3:17). The best option is the last one. "Lawlessness" is a disregard for the expectation to love as set out in 1 John (Painter, 222). Therefore, John says refusing to love is both sin and an indication of lawlessness.

3:5a καί: The Greek word καί is a conjunction meaning "and" (BDAG, s.v. "καί" 1bγ, p. 494). **Syntactically,** καί introduces a conjunctive independent clause: "*and* you know that he (= Jesus) appeared" (καὶ οἴδατε ὅτι ἐκεῖνος ἐφανερώθη). **Semantically,** καί is a coordinating connective: "and" (KJV ASV NET NLT CNT; contra "but" NIV). John is about to link gnomic information about sin with the first coming of Jesus.

οἴδατε: The Greek word οἴδατε is second person plural perfect active indicative from the verb οἶδα meaning "to know" or "to have information about something" (BDAG, s.v. "οἶδα" 1e, p. 692). **Syntactically,** οἴδατε is the main verb of the independent conjunctive clause. The assumed subject, "you," refers to the readers of the letter. **Semantically,** οἴδατε is a perfect with present force: "you know" (cf. KJV NASB ESV NIV NET etc). This verb appears in the perfect tense without the perfect's aspectual significance (W, 579–80). John's readers are aware that Jesus came, which is spelled out in the next ὅτι clause.

ὅτι: The Greek word ὅτι is a conjunction meaning "that" (BDAG, s.v. "ὅτι" 1c, p. 731). **Syntactically,** ὅτι introduces a dependent conjunctive clause: "*that* he (= Jesus) appeared" (ὅτι ἐκεῖνος ἐφανερώθη). The entire clause functions as the direct object of the verb "you know" (οἴδατε). The clause is placed in parentheses in order to visualize its contribution to the independent clause. **Semantically,** ὅτι is an indirect discourse marker following a verb of perception: "that" (cf. KJV NASB ESV NIV NET etc). John provides the content of information known to his readers about Jesus.

ἐφανερώθη: The Greek word ἐφανερώθη is third person singular aorist passive indicative from the verb φανερόω meaning "to reveal" or "to appear" or

"to cause to become visible publicly" (BDAG, s.v. "φανερόω" 1aβ, p. 1048).
Syntactically, ἐφανερώθη is the governing verb of the dependent ὅτι clause.
The emphatic demonstrative pronoun "that one" (ἐκεῖνος = Jesus) functions
as the subject. In fact this particular demonstrative seems to refer to Jesus in the
Johannine epistles (see Theological Nugget below). **Semantically,** ἐφανερώθη
is a constative aorist: "he appeared" (NASB NIV NET CNT) or "came" (NLT). John
underscores the first coming of Jesus as a whole (W, 557). It is the event John
mentioned in 1:1–4 in order to reinforce his humanity. Jesus's intention for
coming is disclosed in the next ἵνα clause.

Theological Nugget: To whom does "that one" (ἐκεῖνος) refer: God or
Jesus? In verse 8 we come across an unambiguous parallel to our current
clause. In verse 8 we are told that the "Son of God . . . was revealed to destroy
the work of the Devil." This clause in verse 8 seems to be set in parallel to
the one that we are discussing, and in verse 8 the subject is unambiguously
Jesus. Therefore, it is safe to assume that the remote demonstrative here is
referring to Jesus as well (Bateman[1], 338).

3:5b ἵνα: The Greek word ἵνα is a conjunction meaning "in order that" or is used
"to denote purpose, aim, or goal" (BDAG, s.v. "ἵνα" 1aε, p. 475). **Syntactically,** ἵνα introduces a dependent conjunctive clause: "*in order* to take away sin"
(ἵνα τὰς ἁμαρτίας ἄρῃ). The entire ἵνα clause is adverbial. It modifies the
verb "he appeared" (ἐφανερώθη). **Semantically,** ἵνα is a purpose conjunction: "in order that" (NASB ESV). John provides the intention for Jesus's coming
(W, 472). The intention is evident in the clause's verb.

ἄρῃ: The Greek word ἄρῃ is third singular aorist active subjunctive from the
verb αἴρω meaning "to take away" or "to remove" (BDAG, s.v. "αἴρω" 3, p. 29).
The verb is in the subjunctive mood because it is part of a ἵνα clause. **Syntactically,** ἄρῃ is the governing verb of the dependent adverbial ἵνα clause. The
subject of the verb is an implied "he" and refers to Jesus. **Semantically,** ἄρῃ is
a constative aorist: "take away" (cf. KJV NASB ESV NIV NET etc.). John describes
Jesus's once-for-all sacrifice as an event as a whole (W, 557). The intention for
Jesus's coming into the world was to take away sins. Jesus removed the sins of
the world (2:2), he is the redeemer (1:29), he cleanses sin (1:7), and he provides atonement for sins (2:2; 4:10).

3:5c καί: The Greek word καί is a conjunction meaning "and" (BDAG, s.v. "καί" 1bα, p.
494). **Syntactically,** καί introduces an independent conjunctive clause, "*and* [you
know (that] there is no sin in him [= Jesus])" (καὶ [ὅτι] ἁμαρτία ἐν αὐτῷ οὐκ
ἔστιν). **Semantically,** καί is a coordinating connective: "and" (KJV ASV NASB NRSV
ESV NIV NET NLT CNT). It joins what John's readers know in the independent clause
of verse 5a and b about Jesus's first coming with additional knowledge about Jesus.

[οἴδατε (ὅτι]: The Greek word οἴδατε is second person plural perfect active indicative from the verb οἶδα meaning "to know" or "to have information about something" (BDAG, s.v. "οἶδα" 1e, p. 692). **Syntactically,** the elliptical [οἴδατε] is the main verb of the independent conjunctive clause. The assumed subject, "you," refers to the readers of the letter. The ὅτι clause is placed in parentheses in order to visualize its contribution to the independent clause. **Semantically,** οἴδατε is a perfect with present force: "you know." This verb appears in the perfect tense without the perfect's aspectual significance (W, 579–80). John's readers are aware about Jesus, which is spelled out in the elliptical [... (ὅτι] clause. It seems best to imply an elliptical ὅτι to make this clause parallel to the first.

ἐστίν: The Greek word ἐστίν is third person singular present active indicative from the verb εἰμί meaning "to be" or "to be in close connection with" (BDAG, s.v. "εἰμί" 2a, p. 283). **Syntactically,** ἐστίν is the governing verb of the dependent conjunctive clause introduced by an elliptical ὅτι. The subject of the verb is "there" embedded in the verb. **Semantically,** the negated (οὐκ) ἔστιν is a gnomic present: "there is no" (cf. KJV NASB ESV NIV NET etc.). John presents a timeless fact about Jesus. He is sinless.

Theological Nugget: What is significant about the expression: "in Jesus there is no sin"? This expression "in Jesus there is no sin" parallels John 7:18 where John says that there was no unrighteousness in him. In John's letters the sinlessness of Jesus is necessary for him to be an effective sacrifice for the sins of humankind (1 John 2:2; John 4:42). The misguided who have left the church were claiming to be without sin, but they were just deceiving themselves. Jesus was actually sinless when he came to earth, lived on earth, and ascended from earth.

3:6a μένων: The Greek word μένων is a nominative masculine singular present active participle from the verb μένω meaning "to remain," "to abide," "to continue," or is used of "someone who does not leave" (BDAG, s.v. "μένω" 1aβ, p. 631). **Syntactically,** μένων introduces a participial clause: "*who makes it a practice to abide* in him (= Jesus)" (ὁ ἐν αὐτῷ μένων). It functions as an adjectival participle that modifies "everyone" (πᾶς). Together they serve as the subject of the verb "sin" (ἁμαρτάνει). Thus, the entire πᾶς + participial clause is placed in parentheses in order to visualize its contribution to the independent clause. **Semantically,** μένων is a gnomic present: "everyone who . . . abide" or "resides" (NET) or "abides" (KJV ASV NASB NRSV ESV CNT) or "lives" (NIV; cf. NLT). John presents a timeless truth that is almost always true about any follower of Jesus (W, 523, 615 contra 524–25). That gnomic truth is disclosed in the next verb.

ἁμαρτάνει: The Greek word ἁμαρτάνει is third person singular present active indicative from the verb ἁμαρτάνω meaning "to sin" or "to commit a wrong"

(BDAG, s.v. "ἁμαρτάνω" a, p. 49). **Syntactically,** ἁμαρτάνει is the main verb of the independent asyndeton clause. The subject of the verb ἁμαρτάνει is the entire participial clause, "everyone *who makes it a practice to abide* in him (= Jesus) does not persist in sin" (πᾶς ὁ ἐν αὐτῷ μένων οὐχ ἁμαρτάνει). The rather lengthy subject refers to those who have an abiding relationship with Jesus. **Semantically,** the negated (οὐχ) ἁμαρτάνει is a gnomic present: "does not *persist* in sin." John once again speaks of a general or timeless fact (W, 523). Any follower of Jesus who continues to maintain correct teaching about Jesus's humanity and messiahship will not want to live a life of habitual sin.

3:6b ἁμαρτάνων: The Greek word ἁμαρτάνων is a nominative masculine singular present active participle from the verb ἁμαρτάνω meaning "to sin" or "to commit a wrong against God or God's commands" (BDAG, s.v. "ἁμαρτάνω" a, p. 49). **Syntactically,** ἁμαρτάνων introduces an adjectival participial clause: "*who makes it a practice to sin*" (ὁ ἁμαρτάνων). It modifies the "everyone" (πᾶς). Together they function as the subject of the compound verbs, "has seen" (ἑώρακεν) and "has known" (ἔγνωκεν). Thus the entire πᾶς + participial clause is placed in parentheses in order to visualize its contribution to the independent clause. **Semantically,** ἁμαρτάνων is a gnomic present: "everyone who . . . sin" John once again presents a timeless fact (W, 523, 615 contra 524–25). John is making a generic statement about anyone who lives a lifestyle of sin.

ἑώρακεν: The Greek word ἑώρακεν is a third person singular perfect active indicative from the verb ὁράω meaning "to see" or "to be mentally or spiritually perceptive" (BDAG, s.v. "ὁράω" 4b, p. 720). **Syntactically,** ἑώρακεν is the first verb in the independent asyndeton clause: "everyone who sins *has* neither *seen* him (= Jesus) nor known him (= Jesus)" (πᾶς ὁ ἁμαρτάνων οὐχ ἑώρακεν αὐτὸν οὐδὲ ἔγνωκεν αὐτόν). The subject of the verb is the phrase "everyone who sins" (πᾶς ὁ ἁμαρτάνων). **Semantically,** the negated οὐχ ἑώρακεν is rendered as a gnomic perfect with an extensive perfect force: "*has* neither seen" (KJV ASV NET; cf. "either seen" NASB NRSV ESV NIV). John's focus is on a generic subject where a decisive act of judgment has been carried out (W, 580). John focuses on people who persist in living lives of habitual sin.

ἔγνωκεν: The Greek word ἔγνωκεν is third singular perfect active indicative from the verb γινώσκω meaning "to know" or "to arrive at a personal knowledge of someone" (BDAG, s.v. "γινώσκω" 1b, p. 199). **Syntactically,** ἔγνωκεν is the second verb in the independent asyndeton clause: "everyone who sins has neither seen him nor *known* him" (πᾶς ὁ ἁμαρτάνων οὐχ ἑώρακεν αὐτὸν οὐδὲ ἔγνωκεν αὐτόν). The subject of the verb is the phrase "everyone who sins" (πᾶς ὁ ἁμαρτάνων). Like "has seen" (ἑώρακεν), "has known" (ἔγνωκεν) is **semantically** a gnomic perfect with an extensive force (KJV NRSV ESV NIV NET CNT). John's focus is on a generic subject where a decisive act of judgment has been carried out (W, 580). Any person who persists in living lives of habitual sin has not known Jesus (= is not saved).

3:7a πλανάτω: The Greek word πλανάτω is third person singular present active imperative from the verb πλανάω meaning "to deceive" or "to mislead" or "to cause someone to stray from a specific way via misleading or deceiving" (BDAG, s.v. "πλανάω" 1b, p. 821). **Syntactically,** πλανάτω is the main verb of the independent asyndeton clause: "Children, *let* no one *mislead* you" (Τεκνία, μηδεὶς πλανάτω ὑμᾶς). The subject is the indefinite pronoun "no one" (μηδείς). **Semantically,** πλανάτω is an imperative of prohibition that forbids an action: "do not be mislead" (W, 487; cf. "deceive" KJV NASB NRSV ESV NET NLT CNT; "lead astray" ASV NIV). The force of the present imperative is to "command an action as an ongoing process" (W, 485). The present tense imperative + μηδείς intensifies John's expectation. John forbids believers to succumb to misguided and fraudulent teaching about Jesus as Messiah and his command to love (Brown, 429).

> **Grammatical Nugget:** What is the significance of the third person imperative, πλανάτω? Although third person imperatives are difficult to translate because English only has second person imperatives, the most common way to translate a negated third person imperative is "let no one deceive you" or "let no third party deceive you." As with ἀγαπᾶτε in 2:15a, the negated present imperative should not be pressed to assume that John is urging his readers to stop something that they were already doing, as if the entire congregation were already deceived.

3:7b ποιῶν: The Greek word ποιῶν is a nominative masculine singular present active participle from the verb ποιέω meaning "to do" or "to practice" or "to carry out an obligation of a moral or social nature" (BDAG, s.v. "ποιέω" 3b, p. 840). **Syntactically,** ποιῶν introduces a dependent participial clause: "*the one who practices* righteousness" to be righteous (ὁ ποιῶν τὴν δικαιοσύνην). The entire participial clause is the subject of the verb "is" (ἐστίν) and is placed in parentheses to visualize its contribution to the independent clause. **Semantically,** ποιῶν is a gnomic present with a customary force: "the one who practices" (cf. NASB NET). John again shares a generic utterance (W, 521, 523). He describes anyone who makes it a habit to live a righteous lifestyle.

ἐστίν: The Greek word ἐστίν is third person singular present active indicative from the verb εἰμί meaning "to be" or "to be in close connection with" (BDAG, s.v. "εἰμί" 2a, p. 283). **Syntactically,** ἐστίν is the main verb of the independent asyndeton clause. The subject of the verb is the participial phrase "the one who practices righteousness" (ὁ ποιῶν τὴν δικαιοσύνην). **Semantically,** ἐστίν is an equative gnomic present: "is." John presents a timeless fact (W, 524). Anyone who lives righteously is equated with being a righteous person.

3:7c καθώς: The Greek word καθώς is a conjunction meaning "just as" or "even as" (BDAG, s.v. "καθώς" 1, p. 493). **Syntactically,** καθώς introduces a dependent conjunctive clause. The entire dependent clause, "even as he (= Jesus) is righteous" (καθὼς ἐκεῖνος δίκαιός ἐστιν), is functioning adverbially modifying the verb "is" (ἐστίν). **Semantically,** καθώς is comparative: "even as" (KJV ASV NLT) or "just as" (NASB NRSV NIV NET CNT). John makes a comparison about the person who is righteous; they are like Jesus.

ἐστίν: The Greek word ἐστίν is third person singular present active indicative from the verb εἰμί meaning "to be" or "to be in close connection with" (BDAG, s.v. "εἰμί" 2a, p. 283). **Syntactically,** ἐστίν is the governing verb of the dependent adverbial clause. The subject of the verb is the demonstrative pronoun "that one" (ἐκεῖνος) which is a reference to Jesus. **Semantically,** ἐστίν is an equative gnomic present: "he is" (cf. KJV NASB ESV NIV NET etc.). It presents a timeless fact (W, 524). Jesus is righteous. John underscores time and again that Jesus's life was characterized by righteousness. This is the third time that Jesus has been called righteous (cf. 2:1 and 2:29).

3:8a ποιῶν: The Greek word ποιῶν is a nominative masculine singular present active participle from the verb ποιέω meaning "to practice," "to do," "to commit," or "to carry out an obligation of a moral or social nature" (BDAG, s.v. "ποιέω" 3b, p. 840). **Syntactically,** ποιῶν introduces a dependent participial clause: *The one who practices sin* (ὁ ποιῶν τὴν ἁμαρτίαν). It is the subject of the verb ἐστίν and functions substantivally. It is set in contrast to the "the one who practices righteousness" (πᾶς ὁ ποιῶν τὴν δικαιοσύνην). The one who practices righteousness is contrasted with the one who practices sin. **Semantically,** ποιῶν is a gnomic present with a customary force: "the one who makes it a practice" (cf. NASB NET). John again shares a generic utterance (W, 521, 523). While the one finds his or her exemplar in Jesus, the other finds his or her exemplar in the deceiver. In very black and white terms, John leaves no room for middle ground. Behavior determines whether a person is a child of God or a child of the Devil.

ἐστίν: The Greek word ἐστίν is third person singular present active indicative from the verb εἰμί meaning "to come from" or "to have a point of derivation or origin" (BDAG, s.v. "εἰμί" 8, p. 285). **Syntactically,** ἐστίν serves as the main verb of the independent asyndeton clause. The subject of the verb is the participial phrase "the one who practices sin" (ὁ ποιῶν τὴν ἁμαρτίαν). **Semantically,** ἐστίν is an equative gnomic present intended to describe a point of origin: "comes from" (or "is of" KJV ASV NASB ESV NIV NET CNT). Anyone who persists in sin is of the Devil.

3:8b ὅτι: The Greek word ὅτι is a conjunction meaning "because" or "for" (BDAG, s.v. "ὅτι" 4a, p. 732). **Syntactically,** ὅτι introduces a dependent conjunctive clause:

"*because* the Devil persists in sinning from the very beginning" (ὅτι ἀπ᾿ ἀρχῆς ὁ διάβολος ἁμαρτάνει). The clause is adverbial, modifying the verb "is" (ἐστίν). **Semantically,** ὅτι is causal: "because" (NET) or "for" (KJV ASV NASB NRSV ESV). John is providing the reason for linking habitual sinners with the Devil.

ἁμαρτάνει: The Greek word ἁμαρτάνει is third person singular present active indicative from the verb ἁμαρτάνω meaning "to sin" or "to commit a wrong against God or God's commands" (BDAG, s.v. "ἁμαρτάνω" a, p. 49). **Syntactically,** ἁμαρτάνει is the governing verb of the dependent ὅτι clause. The subject of the verb is the proper noun "the Devil" (ὁ διάβολος). The Devil is a hostile spirit that stands against God and his work (Culy, 76). **Semantically,** ἁμαρτάνει is a customary present: "*persists in* sinning" (cf. KJV ASV). It speaks of a pattern of behavior (W, 521). But translations typically render the verb "has been sinning" (NRSV ESV NIV NET NLT) or "has sinned" (CNT). Regardless, the reason for linking habitual sinners with the Devil is because the Devil has a record of sinning since the very beginning of creation (Gen. 3:1, 4–5, 13).

Lexical and Theological Nugget: Who is "the Devil" (ὁ διάβολος)? The Greek word occurs thirty-seven times in the New Testament, yet only four times in 1 John, three of which are in this verse and one more which is in 3:10. On the one hand, ὁ διάβολος can be used as a common noun to describe a "slanderer" or someone who is "slanderous" (1 Tim. 3:11; Titus 2:3; Est. 7:4; 8:1 LXX). On the other hand, ὁ διάβολος is a proper noun, a title for a transcendent evil being. The Qumran community saw a sharp division between light and darkness and they believed there was a hostile spirit or angel of darkness called Belial whose reign was one of injustice (1Q28 IV, 19–20). He had destroying angels under his rule (1QM XIII, 10–13; cf. Jub. 14:31–33), he was created by God to exercise hostility and wickedness toward people (1QM XIII, 10–15), he lived in the hearts of those who followed him (1Q28 I, 10). The Qumran community stood against Belial and all who belonged to him (1Q28a II, 19) and cursed him at their annual covenant renewal (1Q28 I, 16–18, 2:19; 1QM XIV, 9–10). In 1 John 3:8, ὁ διάβολος is typically translated as "the Devil," and addresses a similar concern that we find in the Qumran community. Whom do you follow? John agrees with the Qumran community that there is no middle ground. You are either a follower of the Devil or a follower of God.

3:8c εἰς τοῦτο: The Greek word εἰς is a preposition meaning "for this reason" or "for this purpose" (BDAG, s.v. "εἰς" 4f, p. 290). The Greek word τοῦτο is an accusative singular neuter from the demonstrative pronoun οὗτος. **Syntactically,** εἰς τοῦτο is a prepositional phrase introducing an independent prepositional clause: "*For this purpose*, the Son of God appeared" (εἰς τοῦτο ἐφανερώθη ὁ υἱὸς τοῦ θεοῦ). This kind of prepositional construction occurs frequently in the New Testament and is a very important structural marker. **Semantically,** εἰς τοῦτο expresses a statement of purpose (BDAG, s.v. "οὗτος" 1b, p. 741) and is often translated: "for this purpose" (KJV NET). John provides the intention for Jesus's coming.

ἐφανερώθη: The Greek word ἐφανερώθη is third person singular aorist passive indicative from the verb φανερόω meaning "to reveal" or "to appear" or "to cause to become visible publicly" (BDAG, s.v. "φανερόω" 1aβ, p. 1048). **Syntactically,** ἐφανερώθη is the main verb of the independent clause introduced by a prepositional phrase. The subject of the verb is the phrase "the Son of God" (ὁ υἱὸς τοῦ θεοῦ). **Semantically,** ἐφανερώθη is a constative aorist: "he appeared" (NASB ESV NIV CNT). While the prepositional phrase could be anaphoric, pointing back to the preceding discussion, the ἵνα clause in 3:8d makes it cataphoric. John refers to the historical fact of Jesus's first advent as a whole (W, 557). The purpose behind the coming of Jesus appears in the ἵνα clause.

Lexical and Theological Nugget: Who is this "Son of God"? This is the first of seven instances of this title in 1 John (3:8; 4:15; 5:5, 10, 12, 13, 20). Does this phrase speak of Jesus's deity or his role as Messiah? The context suggests that John's focus is on the first coming of Jesus and his earthly lifestyle and ministry. So in light of context, the title "Son of God" is a reference to Jesus's messiahship (see Bateman[1], 348). Also, in the synoptic tradition, the high priest uses the title "Son of God" as a messianic title (Matt. 6:63; cf. Culy, 76). For a treatment of the title "son" in nonbiblical Jewish literature, see Bateman[2], 303–29.

3:8d ἵνα: The Greek word ἵνα is a conjunction meaning "that" (BDAG, s.v. "ἵνα" 2e, p. 476). **Syntactically,** ἵνα serves to introduce a conjunctive dependent clause: "*namely that* he might destroy the works of the Devil" (ἵνα λύσῃ τὰ ἔργα τοῦ διαβόλου). **Syntactically,** the ἵνα clause is substantival. It clarifies the demonstrative pronoun "this" (τοῦτο). **Semantically,** ἵνα is appositional: "*namely,* that" (KJV ASV). It provides the content of the demonstrative (contra W, 472; cf. 475). Since the prepositional phrase "For this purpose" (εἰς τοῦτο) is telic in nature, this clause underscores one of John's purposes for Jesus coming into the world. That purpose is described with the next verb.

λύσῃ: The Greek word λύσῃ is third person singular aorist active subjunctive from the verb λύω meaning "to destroy" or "to bring an end to" or "to do away with" (BDAG, s.v. "λύω" 4, p. 607). The verb is in the subjunctive mood because it is part of a ἵνα clause. **Syntactically,** λύσῃ is the governing verb of the ἵνα clause. The subject of the verb is an implied "he" embedded in the verb and refers to Jesus, who is the Son of God (= Messiah). **Semantically,** λύσῃ is a constative aorist: "he might destroy" (cf. KJV ASV) or "to destroy" (NASB NRSV ESV NET NLT). It describes an event as a whole (W, 557). John provides an overall picture about Jesus's activities: he abolished the Devil's work.

Lexical and Theological Nugget: What is the significance of John's dualism? In John's literature, everything is dualistic: light or darkness, righteousness or sin, and child of God or child of the Devil. We see that dualism on full display in these verses. The one who practices righteousness is of God, while the one who practices sin is from the Devil. John makes it clear: Jesus came and he destroyed the Devil's work. When a believer lies, hates, or murders, they are putting themselves on the side of one who has been defeated.

3:9a γεγεννημένος: The Greek word γεγεννημένος is a nominative masculine singular perfect passive participle from the verb γεννάω meaning "to become the parent of" or "to exercise the role of a parental figure" (BDAG, s.v. "γεννάω" 1b, p. 193). **Syntactically,** γεγεννημένος introduces a participial clause: "*who has been fathered* by God" (ὁ γεγεννημένος ἐκ τοῦ θεοῦ). It functions adjectivally and modifies the substantival "everyone" (πᾶς). Together they serve as the subject of the verb ποιεῖ. Thus the entire πᾶς + participial clause is placed in parentheses in order to visualize its contribution to the independent clause. John continues to contrast the behavior of those who have been fathered by God and those who belong to the Devil. **Semantically,** γεγέννηται is both a gnomic and extensive perfect: "has been fathered" (NET) or "has been born" (NRSV cf. NLT). It is gnomic because of the generic subject (πᾶς). It is extensive because the focus is on the decisive relationship between God the Father and the believer (W, 580). This generic or proverbial force may also be rendered as intensive: "is born" (KJV ASV NASB NIV; cf. ESV CNT) with an emphasis on the results of the present condition of the believer. Regardless of where one places the emphasis of the perfect, John's point is simply this: believers have been fathered by God in the past and that past event has continuing results in the present (cf. 2:29; 4:7; 5:1, 4, 18). The focus is on those who practice righteousness: they have had an ongoing relationship with God.

ποιεῖ: The Greek word ποιεῖ is a third person singular present active indicative from the verb ποιέω meaning "to practice," "to do," "to commit," or "to carry out an obligation of a moral or social nature" (BDAG, s.v. "ποιέω" 3c, p. 840). **Syntactically,** ποιεῖ is the main verb of the independent clause "everyone who is fathered by God does not practice sin" (πᾶς ὁ γεγεννημένος ἐκ τοῦ θεοῦ ἁμαρτίαν οὐ ποιεῖ). **Semantically,** the negated (οὐ) ποιεῖ is a gnomic present: "*does* not *practice*" (e.g. NASB ESV NLT CNT). John provides another timeless truth (W, 523). Anyone who is fathered by God has entered into a life-changing relationship with him, and it changes the way that person lives. He or she does not make it a practice to sin. John's reasoning is clearly stated in the next clause.

3:9b ὅτι: The Greek word ὅτι is a conjunction meaning "because" or "for" (BDAG, s.v. "ὅτι" 4a, p. 732). **Syntactically,** ὅτι introduces a dependent conjunctive clause: "*because* God's seed remains in him" (ὅτι σπέρμα αὐτοῦ ἐν αὐτῷ μένει). The clause is adverbial modifying the verb "does" (ποιεῖ). **Semantically,** ὅτι is causal: "because" (e.g. KJV NASB ESV NIV NET etc.). John provides the reason why the child of God will not sin (W, 460), which John discloses with the next verb.

μένει: The Greek word μένει is third person singular present active indicative from the verb μένω meaning "to remain," "to continue," "to abide," or it is said of someone who does not leave a certain realm or sphere (BDAG, s.v. "μένω" 1aβ, p. 631). **Syntactically,** μένει is the governing verb of the dependent adverbial clause. The subject is the noun, "seed" (σπέρμα). **Semantically,** μένει is a customary present: "remains" (e.g. KJV NIV). It provides a pattern of behavior (W, 527). The reason (ὅτι) a child of God will not sin is because God's seed remains in them.

Lexical and Theological Nugget: To whom does "God's seed" refer? God's seed here could be quasi-literal and refer to God's children as bearers of his image, yet this would then include both believers and nonbelievers. John, however, makes a clear distinction between the children of God and those who are not. It is better to interpret it metaphorically as either God's word (Matt. 13:3–9, 18–23; Luke 8:11; James 1:18; 1 Peter 1:23; see Westcott, 108; HJS, 85), God's Spirit (Ezek. 36:26–27; see Brown, 411; also Schnackenburg, 175), or God's nature (spiritual DNA, cf. Culy, 77; also Strecker, 175). All of these are emphases in 1 John. John speaks about God's word in 2:7–8, God's Spirit in 2:20, 27, and the expectation that believers live out God's nature of love and purity in 3:17, 4:7–8, and 16. Therefore, it is contextually unnecessary to exclude any of these ideas. When one believes in Jesus, they begin a different type of relationship with both the word of God and his Spirit, which begins to change them, so that they are reflecting the character of God in their daily lifestyle.

3:9c καί: The Greek word καί is a conjunction meaning "and" (BDAG, s.v. "καί" 1bα, p. 494). **Syntactically,** καί introduces an independent conjunctive clause: "*and* he is not able to persist in sin" (καὶ οὐ δύναται ἁμαρτάνειν). **Semantically,** καί is a coordinating connective of two independent clauses: "and" (KJV ASV NASB ESV NET CNT). John provides additional information about the one who is fathered by God. Culy suggests that while this clause is clearly a logical connective, it also has the force of a result clause and is closely related to the idea that God's seed remains in us (Culy, 78). This seems to be indicated in the NLT with a translation of καί as "so."

δύναται: The Greek word δύναται is third person singular present middle/passive indicative from the verb δύναμαι mean "to be able" or "to be capable of something" or "to have the capacity for something" (BDAG, s.v. "δύναμαι" c, p.

262). **Syntactically,** δύναται is the main verb of the conjunctive independent καί clause. The subject of the verb is an implied "they [singular]" embedded in the verb and refers to the one who is fathered by God. **Semantically,** the negated οὐ δύναται is a gnomic present: "they are *not* able" (NET) or "they cannot" (KJV ASV NASB ESV CNT). It speaks of a general truth about anyone (contra W, 524). Yet the verb demands a complementary verbal to clarify John's point, which is discussed next.

ἁμαρτάνειν: The Greek word ἁμαρτάνειν is a present active infinitive from the verb ἁμαρτάνω meaning "to sin" or "to commit a wrong" (BDAG, s.v. "ἁμαρτάνω" a, p. 49). **Syntactically,** ἁμαρτάνειν is part of the negated main verb of the independent καί clause: "he is *not* able to persist in sin" (οὐ δύναται ἁμαρτάνειν). **Semantically,** ἁμαρτάνειν is a complementary infinitive that completes the thought of the negated finite verb: "he is not able" (οὐ δύναται). It clarifies that the one who is fathered by God is incapable of habitual sin (W, 599). Any person (see πᾶς in 3:9a) who has this special father/child relationship with God through belief in Jesus cannot *persist* in sin.

Lexical and Theological Nugget: In what way is the believer incapable of sinning? Some focus on the continuous aspect of the present tense and thereby suggest that believers will sin, but they will not live in a state of habitual unrepentant sin of any kind. Others pair this passage up with the discussion on different types of sin (the sin that leads to death and sin that does not lead to death) found in 1 John 5:16–17. They talk about how believers might commit lesser sins but not the greater ones. The best option, however, is to think about this statement in light of the situation that John is addressing. John is concerned with a group of people who refuse to live out God's command to love and care for others, due to their erroneous views of Jesus. So their lifestyle is inconsistent with being parented by God. Therefore, those who live in such a way (habitual hate) cannot by definition have a relationship with God the Father. The sins of a follower of Jesus should never be deliberate, habitual, or entertaining.

3:9d ὅτι: The Greek word ὅτι is a conjunction meaning "because" or "for" (BDAG, s.v. "ὅτι" 4a, p. 732). **Syntactically,** ὅτι introduces a dependent conjunctive clause: "*because* he is born of God" (ὅτι ἐκ τοῦ θεοῦ γεγέννηται). The entire clause is adverbial. It modifies the verb "is able" (δύναται). **Semantically,** ὅτι is causal: "because" (e.g., KJV NASB ESV NIV NET). John provides the reason why believers are not able to sin (W, 460), which John discloses with the next clause.

γεγέννηται: The Greek word γεγέννηται is third person singular perfect passive indicative from the verb γεννάω meaning "to become the parent of" or "to exercise the role of a parental figure" (BDAG, s.v. "γεννάω" 1b, p. 193). **Syntactically,** γεγέννηται is the governing verb of the dependent ὅτι clause.

The subject is an implied "he" embedded in the verb and refers to the believer. **Semantically,** γεγέννηται is both a gnomic and extensive perfect: "has been fathered" (NET) or "has been born" (ESV CNT NIV cf. NRSV). It is gnomic because of the generic subject (πᾶς) mentioned in 3:9a while extensive in that the focus is on the decisive relationship between God and the believer (W, 580). Others translate the perfect as an intensive perfect: "is born" (KJV NASB CNT; cf. ASV NLT) with an emphasis on the results of the present condition of the believer. Regardless of where one places the emphasis of the perfect, John's point is that God has fathered believers in the past and that past event has continuing results in the present (cf. 2:29; 4:7; 5:1, 4, 18). Any person who has been born of God enters into a state where they do not habitually sin and hate, but rather are characterized instead by God's spiritual DNA.

Theological Nugget: What is the significance of the chiastic structure in 3:9? John's chiastic structure may be presented as

> A The one who is fathered by God
> B does not sin
> C because God's seed remains in him
> B' he is not able to *persist in* sin
> A' because he is fathered by God

The thrust of this chiastic pattern is that followers of Jesus are God's seed (C), who do not make it a practice to sin (B B') and are fathered by God (A A').

3:10a ἐν τούτῳ: The Greek word ἐν is a preposition meaning "by" (BDAG, s.v. "ἐν" 5b, p. 328). The Greek word τούτῳ is declined as a dative singular neuter from the demonstrative pronoun οὗτος meaning "this one" (BDAG, s.v. "οὗτος" 1bβ, p. 741). **Syntactically,** ἐν τούτῳ introduces an independent prepositional clause: "*By this* the children of God and the children of the Devil are made clear" (ἐν τούτῳ φανερά ἐστιν τὰ τέκνα τοῦ θεοῦ καὶ τὰ τέκνα τοῦ διαβόλου). The construction, "by this" (ἐν τούτῳ) appears often in 1 John (2:3, 4, 5; 3:16, 19, 24; 4:2, 9, 10, 13, 17; 5:2). **Semantically,** ἐν τούτῳ means: "by this" (NASB ESV NET CNT). The clause can either be anaphoric, pointing back to the preceding discussion, or cataphoric, pointing forward. In this context, ἐν τούτῳ points forward. After a lengthy discussion of how to tell the difference between someone fathered by God and someone who is not, John clarifies how to tell the difference: a person's lifestyle. The one whose life is characterized by hate and impurity cannot possibly have God's seed in him, whether that seed be defined as God's Spirit, Word, or nature.

ἐστίν: The Greek word ἐστίν is third person singular present active indicative from the verb εἰμί meaning "to be" or "to describe a special connection with" (BDAG, s.v. "εἰμί" 2b, p. 283). **Syntactically,** ἐστίν is the main verb of the independent clause. The subjects of the verb are the compound neuter plural nouns "children" (τέκνα) and "children" (τέκνα). In New Testament Greek, plural neuter nouns take a singular verb. **Semantically,** ἐστίν is an equative present: "are" (cf. KJV NASB ESV NIV NET etc.). It equates people as either children of God or children of the Devil. A person's parentage is *evident* (φανερά) in their lifestyle.

3:10b ποιῶν: The Greek word ποιῶν is a nominative masculine singular present active participle from the verb ποιέω meaning "to practice," "to do," "to commit," or "to carry out an obligation of a moral or social nature" (BDAG, s.v. "ποιέω" 3b, p. 840). **Syntactically,** ποιῶν introduces a participial clause: *"who does* not *practice* righteousness" (ὁ μὴ ποιῶν δικαιοσύνην). The participle ποιῶν functions adjectivally and modifies the substantival adjective "everyone" (πᾶς). Together they serve as the subject of the verb "is" (ἐστίν). Thus the entire πᾶς + participial clause is placed in parentheses in order to visualize its contribution to the independent clause. **Semantically,** ποιῶν is a gnomic present expressing a timeless maxim about anyone "who does not practice" (NASB NET) moral or socially accepted behavior (W, 523). Once again, John's point is very black and white, there is no middle ground. Your behavior exhibits that you are either a child of God or a child of the Devil.

ἐστίν: The Greek word ἐστίν is third person singular present active indicative from the verb εἰμί meaning "to be" or "to describe a special connection with" (BDAG, s.v. "εἰμί" 2b, p. 283). **Syntactically,** ἐστίν is the main verb of the independent clause. The subject of the verb is "everyone who does not practice righteousness" (πᾶς ὁ μὴ ποιῶν δικαιοσύνην). **Semantically,** ἐστίν is a gnomic present that identifies who is not a child of God. John states a timeless maxim. Anyone who practices unrighteousness does not have a relationship with God the Father.

3:10c καί: The Greek word καί is a conjunction meaning "that is" (BDAG, s.v. "καί" 1c, p. 495). **Syntactically,** καί introduces an independent conjunctive clause: *"that is* the one who persists in not loving his brother" (καὶ ὁ μὴ ἀγαπῶν τὸν ἀδελφὸν αὐτοῦ). The entire clause functions adjectivally. **Semantically,** καί is an explanatory conjunction: "that is" (W, 673). The clause then further defines the unrighteous person already described: "Everyone who does not practice righteousness, *that is,* the one who does not love his brother, is not from God."

Semantical Nugget: How should the Greek conjunction καί be understood? There are at least three ways to understand καί here: (1) It could be a coordinating conjunction giving us additional information. In that case we would imply another verb and prepositional phrase and set this clause as parallel to the one previous, "Everyone who does not practice righteousness is not from God, and everyone who does not love his brother [is not from God]" (cf. Culy, 79). (2) It could be a correlative conjunction expressing contrary relationships whereby καί is rendered "neither" (KJV ASV) or "nor" (NASB NRSV ESV NIV CNT). (3) It could be an explanatory conjunction, "that is" (W, 673). The clause, then, would further define the unrighteous person already described, "Everyone who does not practice righteousness, *that is*, the one who does not love his brother, is not from God." Yet this last option does not differ significantly from an epexegetical rendering (NET; BDF §394) or an appositional rendering (Smalley, 177, 181). The explanatory, epexegetical, or appositional options all convey the same idea. John equates unrighteous behavior with a refusal to love throughout the letter. The one who practices unrighteousness is the one who does not love.

ἀγαπῶν: The Greek word ἀγαπῶν is a nominative masculine singular present active participle from the verb ἀγαπάω meaning "to love" or "to have a warm regard for and interest in another person" (BDAG, s.v. "ἀγαπάω" 1aα, p. 5). **Syntactically,** ἀγαπῶν functions substantivally. The entire participial clause: "*the one who does* not *persists in loving* his brother" (ὁ μὴ ἀγαπῶν τὸν ἀδελφὸν αὐτοῦ) with καί is epexegetical. It provides further information about the one who is not from God. **Semantically,** ἀγαπῶν is a gnomic present with a customary present force: "the one who *persists* in not loving." It speaks of a generic person's pattern of behavior (W, 527, 615). Anyone who practices a lifestyle of habitual sin (= not loving) cannot possibly be fathered by God.

1 John 3:11–18

Big Greek Idea: John's message to love one another contrasts the selfish self-centered behavior of Cain that erupted into treating his brother poorly—an expectation to be anticipated from non-family members—with the selfless sacrificial love of Jesus that demands God's children love in what they say and in how they treat one another.

Structural Overview: Building (ὅτι) upon the first half of his letter (1:5–3:10), John launches into the second half (3:11–5:12) by underscoring that love and hate are incompatible passions among God's children (3:11–18). John opens with an exemplified *message* (ἐστὶν ἡ ἀγγελία), what it is and what it is not (vv. 11–13). First, the message is (ἵνα ἀγαπῶμεν) love one another other (v. 11a–c). God's family members, his children (vv. 1–10), are to demonstrate love within the family. Second, lest there be any confusion, John pauses to inform his readers what family love is not: it is not like (οὐ καθώς) Cain's love who killed (ἔσφαξεν) his brother Abel. Third, John makes clear the reason why (ὅτι) Cain killed his brother. He was a selfish self-centered (τὰ ἔργα αὐτοῦ πονηρὰ ἦν) person in contrast (δέ) to his brother, Abel (v. 12). John concludes (καί) with an application: anticipate (μὴ θαυμάζετε) being disliked by people who are not part of God's family.

John then expresses a child of God's *self-awareness* (οἴδαμεν/ἐγνώκαμεν; vv. 14–17). First, there is self-awareness (οἴδαμεν) about a new life (μεταβεβήκαμεν) within God's family: they love (ἀγαπῶμεν) their brothers and sisters in God's family (v. 14a–b). Second, John makes it clear that those who do not love family members are spiritually dead (μένει; vv. 14c–15). Third, there is self-awareness (ἐγνώκαμεν) about love. Just as Jesus lived a self-sacrificing life (ἔθηκεν), members of God's family are expected (ὀφείλομεν . . . θεῖναι) to live in a self-sacrificing manner (v. 16). John closes with a description of a person who does not have God's love (μένει): they have (ἔχῃ) possessions, they perceive (ἔχοντα) a need, and they do not help (κλείσῃ) meet the need (v. 17).

John closes with *an appeal* to God's children (τεκνία). John urges members of God's family not to love (μὴ ἀγαπῶμεν) merely in what they say but (ἀλλά) to love ([ἀγαπῶμεν]) in both what is said and what is done to one another (cf. James 2:14–19).

Outline:

Love within God's Family: What It Is and What It Is Not (vv. 11–13)
God's Family Members Are Aware of their Family (vv. 14–17)
God's Family Members Are Encouraged to Love (v. 18)

Clausal Outline for 1 John 3:11–18

^{3:11b} **ἣν ἠκούσατε** ἀπ᾿ ἀρχῆς
^{3:11b} **that you heard** from the beginning
|
^{3:11a} **Ὅτι** αὕτη **ἐστὶν** ἡ ἀγγελία . . . ,
^{3:11a} **For** this **is** the *gospel* message . . .
|
   ^{3:11c} **ἵνα ἀγαπῶμεν** ἀλλήλους
   ^{3:11c} *namely* **that we should love** one another;
     |
      ^{3:12a} οὐ **καθὼς** Κάϊν ἐκ τοῦ πονηροῦ **ἦν**
      ^{3:12a} not **as** Cain *who* **was** of the Evil One
        |
      ^{3:12b} καὶ **ἔσφαξεν** τὸν ἀδελφὸν αὐτοῦ·
      ^{3:12b} and *who* **brutally murdered** his brother (= Abel)

^{3:12c} καὶ χάριν τίνος **ἔσφαξεν** αὐτόν;
^{3:12c} and for what reason did **he** *brutally* **murder** him (= Abel)?
     |
      ^{3:12d} **ὅτι** τὰ ἔργα αὐτοῦ πονηρὰ **ἦν**,
      ^{3:12d} **because** his (= Cain's) deeds **were** evil,

      ^{3:12e} τὰ [ἔργα] **δὲ** τοῦ ἀδελφοῦ αὐτοῦ δίκαια [**ἦν**].
      ^{3:12e} **but** the [*deeds*] of his brother (= Abel) [*were*] righteous.

^{3:13a} [καὶ] μὴ **θαυμάζετε**, ἀδελφοί, (εἰ μισεῖ ὑμᾶς ὁ κόσμος).
^{3:13a} **And** *so,* **do** not **be surprised**, brothers and sisters, (that the world *persists in* hating you).

^{3:14a} ἡμεῖς **οἴδαμεν** (ὅτι μεταβεβήκαμεν ἐκ τοῦ θανάτου εἰς τὴν ζωήν),
^{3:14a} **We know** (that we have passed out of death into life),
  |
    ^{3:14b} **ὅτι ἀγαπῶμεν** τοὺς ἀδελφούς·
    ^{3:14b} **because** we *persistently* **love** *our* brothers (and sisters);

^{3:14c} (ὁ μὴ ἀγαπῶν) **μένει** ἐν τῷ θανάτῳ.
^{3:14c} (the one who does not *persist in* love) **abides** in death.

^{3:15a} (πᾶς ὁ μισῶν τὸν ἀδελφὸν αὐτοῦ) ἀνθρωποκτόνος **ἐστίν**,
^{3:15a} (Everyone who *persists in* hating his brother) **is** a murderer,

³:¹⁵ᵇ <u>καὶ</u> **οἴδατε** (ὅτι πᾶς ἀνθρωποκτόνος οὐκ <u>ἔχει</u> ζωὴν αἰώνιον ἐν
αὐτῷ μένουσαν).
³:¹⁵ᵇ <u>and</u> **you know** (that no murderer <u>possesses</u> eternal life abiding in him
[or her]).

³:¹⁶ᵃ <u>ἐν τούτῳ</u> **ἐγνώκαμεν** τὴν ἀγάπην,
³:¹⁶ᵃ <u>By this</u> **we know** love,

> ³:¹⁶ᵇ **ὅτι** ἐκεῖνος ὑπὲρ ἡμῶν τὴν ψυχὴν αὐτοῦ **ἔθηκεν·**
> ³:¹⁶ᵇ **that** that one (= Jesus) **gave up** his life for us;
>
> ³:¹⁶ᶜ <u>καὶ</u> [ὅτι] ἡμεῖς **ὀφείλομεν** ὑπὲρ τῶν ἀδελφῶν τὰς ψυχὰς
> **θεῖναι**.
> ³:¹⁶ᶜ <u>and</u> [*that*] **we are obligated** <u>to give up</u> our lives for our brothers
> (and sisters).

> > ³:¹⁷ᵃ **ὃς** δ' ἂν **ἔχῃ** τὸν βίον τοῦ κόσμου
> > ³:¹⁷ᵃ <u>but</u> **whoever** **possesses** the resources of
> > the world
> >
> > ³:¹⁷ᵇ <u>καὶ</u> [ὃς ἂν] **θεωρῇ** τὸν ἀδελφὸν
> > αὐτοῦ χρείαν ἔχοντα
> > ³:¹⁷ᵇ <u>and</u> [*whoever*] **perceives** his brother (or
> > sister) possessing a need
> >
> > ³:¹⁷ᶜ <u>καὶ</u> [ὃς ἂν] **κλείσῃ** τὰ σπλάγχνα
> > αὐτοῦ ἀπ' αὐτοῦ,
> > ³:¹⁷ᶜ <u>and</u> [*whoever*] **shuts off** his (or her)
> > heart against him (or her),

³:¹⁷ᵈ πῶς ἡ ἀγάπη τοῦ θεοῦ **μένει** ἐν αὐτῷ;
³:¹⁷ᵈ how does the love of God **remain** in him (or her)?

³:¹⁸ᵃ Τεκνία, μὴ **ἀγαπῶμεν** λόγῳ μηδὲ τῇ γλώσσῃ
³:¹⁸ᵃ Little children, **let us** not **love** with word or with tongue

³:¹⁸ᵇ <u>ἀλλὰ</u> [*ἀγαπῶμεν*] ἐν ἔργῳ καὶ ἀληθείᾳ.
³:¹⁸ᵇ <u>but</u> [*let us love*] in deed and truth.

SYNTAX EXPLAINED FOR 1 JOHN 3:11–18

³:¹¹ᵃ Ὅτι: The Greek word ὅτι is a conjunction meaning "for" (BDAG, s.v. "ὅτι"
4b, p. 732). **Syntactically,** ὅτι introduces the independent conjunctive clause:

"*For* this is the gospel message" (ὅτι αὕτη ἐστὶν ἡ ἀγγελία). While there remains a connection with the previous clause, the subordination is so loose that the translation "for" is best and thereby presented as an independent clause, though Brown presents it adverbially. **Semantically,** ὅτι is explanatory: "for" (KJV ASV NASB NRSV ESV NET CNT). John introduces a new section that builds on the previous one. It is almost as if John is using these type of constructions to highlight his main points (Brown, 192). He moves from how our parentage relates to our behavior to examine the life of love expected by God.

Grammatical Nugget: How is the ὅτι clause functioning? On the one hand, Culy understands this ὅτι clause to be functioning adverbially, giving the reason why we can discover someone's parentage by the way we treat one another. He then insists that the main break in structure occurs in verse 13 rather than here in verse 11 (Culy, 80). On the other hand, Yarbrough views the ὅτι as a loosely connected conjunction to what precedes (Yarbrough, 197; BDF §456; cf. Smalley, 180). So the unit begins in verse 9 and is broken out as verses 9–10, 11–12, and 13–18 (Yarbrough, 193–207). Yet it seems more reasonable to agree with Brown. Brown points out that John now moves into the second main section of his letter (the first section also beginning with a similar structure in 1 John 1:5 (Brown, 440; cf. Strecker, 104; Painter, 232).

ἐστίν: The Greek word ἐστίν is third person singular present active indicative from the verb εἰμί meaning "to be" or "to be in close connection with" (BDAG, s.v. "εἰμί" 2a, p. 283). **Syntactically,** ἐστίν is the main verb of the conjunctive independent ὅτι clause. The subject of the verb is the demonstrative pronoun "this" (αὕτη), due to the grammatical priority of pronouns (W, 42–43). **Semantically,** ἐστίν is gnomic. John is about to explain a timeless message (W, 523). The demonstrative pronoun "this" (αὕτη) points forward to an epexegetical ἵνα clause. But first there is a relative clause.

3:11b ἥν: The Greek word ἥν is accusative singular feminine from the relative pronoun ὅς meaning "that" (BDAG, s.v. "ὅς" 1a, p. 715). **Syntactically,** ἥν introduces an adjectival relative clause, "*that* you heard from the beginning" (ἣν ἠκούσατε ἀπ᾽ ἀρχῆς). It modifies the noun "message" (ἀγγελία). The relative pronoun is in the accusative case because it is the direct object of the verb "you heard" (ἠκούσατε). The relative clause provides further information about the message revealed in the next verb.

ἠκούσατε: The Greek word ἠκούσατε is a second person plural aorist active indicative from the verb ἀκούω meaning "to hear" or "to have exercised the faculty of hearing" (BDAG, s.v. "ἀκούω" 1a, p. 37). **Syntactically,** ἠκούσατε is the governing verb of the relative clause. The subject of the verb is an implied "you" embedded in the verb and refers to the recipients of the letter. **Se-**

mantically, ἠκούσατε is a constative aorist: "you heard" (KJV ASV NIV CNT). John merely speaks of the event as a whole (W, 557). John's readers have heard this message in the past and they are hearing it again. It is not a new message; believers are to love others (See Theological and Lexical Nugget under 2:7).

3:11c ἵνα: The Greek word ἵνα is a conjunction meaning "that" (BDAG, s.v. "ἵνα" 2e, p. 476). **Syntactically,** ἵνα introduces a conjunctive dependent clause: "*namely, that we should love one another*" (ἵνα ἀγαπῶμεν ἀλλήλους). The entire ἵνα clause is substantival. It clarifies the demonstrative pronoun "this" (αὕτη). **Semantically,** ἵνα is an appositional conjunction: "*namely, that*" (KJV ASV NASB ESV NLT CNT). It clarifies the demonstrative pronoun "this" (αὕτη). It is almost idiomatic within Johannine literature (W, 475). John's clarification is evident in the next verb.

ἀγαπῶμεν: The Greek word ἀγαπῶμεν is first person plural present active subjunctive from the verb ἀγαπάω meaning "to love" or "to have a warm regard for and interest in another" person (BDAG, s.v. "ἀγαπάω" 1aα, p. 5). The verb is in the subjunctive mood because it is part of a ἵνα clause. **Syntactically,** ἀγαπῶμεν is the governing verb of the conjunctive dependent clause. The subject of the verb is an implied "we" and refers to John and the readers of his letter. **Semantically,** ἀγαπῶμεν is a customary present: "we should love" (e.g., KJV NASB ESV NIV NET etc.). John speaks of a pattern of behavior (W, 527). The message the readers have heard since their conversion is that they *are to persist in loving others.*

Theological Nugget: How does John's "message" (ἀγγελία) in 3:11 differ from the one in 3:5? John's "message" (ἀγγελία) to love one another parallels 1 John 1:5. There the "message" (ἀγγελία) speaks of God as light. The subsequent discussion is then on how his followers should live ethical lives. Here in this parallel construction the content of the gospel is that believers are to love each other. Therefore, the gospel's ethical implications are that followers of Jesus are to imitate a God who is light and love by living ethically and justly (cf. 3:23b ἵνα).

3:12a καθώς: The Greek word καθώς is a conjunction meaning "just as" or "as" (BDAG, s.v. "καθώς" 1, p. 493). **Syntactically,** καθώς introduces a dependent conjunctive clause. The entire καθώς clause, "not *as* Cain" (οὐ καθὼς Κάϊν) functions adverbially. It modifies the verb "we love" (ἀγαπῶμεν). It is best to imply an elliptical verb and direct object from the previous clause to make the best sense of the author's flow of thought, "not as Cain [loved his brother]" (Culy, 81). **Semantically,** καθώς is comparative: "as" (KJV ASV NASB). Here opposites are compared. Believers, who are expected to love, are compared with Cain.

ἦν: The Greek word ἦν is third person singular imperfect active indicative from the verb εἰμί meaning "to be" or "to have a point of derivation or origin" (BDAG, s.v. "εἰμί" 8, p. 285). **Syntactically,** ἦν is the main verb of this conjunctive dependent clause "who *was* from the Evil One" (ἐκ τοῦ πονηροῦ ἦν). The subject is an implied "he" embedded in the verb, which refers to Cain. **Semantically,** ἦν is an equative imperfect: "*who* was" (KJV NASB NRSV ESV NET CNT). In this comparative, John shows Cain's close derivation or origin with the Evil One or the Devil.

3:12b καί: The Greek word καί is a conjunction meaning "and" (BDAG, s.v. "καί" 1bα, p. 494). **Syntactically,** καί introduces a dependent conjunctive clause: "*and* who brutally butchered his brother" (καὶ ἔσφαξεν τὸν ἀδελφὸν αὐτοῦ). **Semantically,** καί is a coordinating connective that adds some additional information about Cain: "and" (e.g., KJV NASB ESV NIV NET etc.).

ἔσφαξεν: The Greek word ἔσφαξεν is third person singular aorist active indicative from the verb σφάξω meaning "to butcher" or "to murder" (BDAG, s.v. "σφάξω," p. 979). **Syntactically,** ἔσφαξεν is the main verb of the conjunctive dependent clause, "and *who brutally butchered* his brother" (καὶ ἔσφαξεν τὸν ἀδελφὸν αὐτοῦ). The subject of the verb is an implied "he" embedded in the verb and refers to Cain. **Semantically,** ἔσφαξεν is a constative aorist: "*who brutally butchered*" ("murdered," cf. NRSV ESV NIV NET CNT). It describes Cain's action as a whole (W, 557). John provides a heightened sense of what Cain did with his chosen word for murder (σφάξω). It implies that Cain's murder of his brother Abel was exceptionally brutal and violent.

Theological Nugget: What is significant about John's mention of Cain? Although Genesis 4 never mentions that Cain actually belonged to the Evil One, his evil nature and origin are a constant refrain of Second Temple literature and even the New Testament. Cain is an example of moral corruption (T. Benj. 7:5), a narcissistic person (Philo, *Det.* 10:32), one under the influence of the adversary (Apoc. Ab. 24:5), filled with hatred and greed (Josephus, *A.J.* 1.52–62), and is an unbeliever (Jude 10–11; see an extensive discussion about Cain in Bateman[3], 262–49). Cain's murder of his brother is explained when we see that he partnered himself with the greatest murderer (John 8:44).

3:12c καί: The Greek word καί is a conjunction meaning "and" (BDAG, s.v. "καί" 1bα, p. 494). **Syntactically,** καί introduces an interrogative independent clause: "*and* for what reason did he brutally murder him" (καὶ χάριν τίνος ἔσφαξεν αὐτόν). The prepositional phrase χάριν τίνος appears rarely in the New Testament but is rendered "for the sake of what" or "for what reason" (BDAG, s.v. "χάριν," p. 1078; BDAG, s.v. "τίς" 1aβ, p. 1007; cf. Culy, 81) and introduces a question. **Semantically,** καί is a coordinating connective: "and" (cf. KJV NASB ESV NIV NET etc.). It introduces a clause with some additional information about Cain evident in the next verb.

ἔσφαξεν: The Greek word ἔσφαξεν is third person singular aorist active indicative from the verb σφάξω meaning "to butcher" or "to murder" (BDAG, s.v. "σφάξω," p. 979). **Syntactically,** ἔσφαξεν is the governing verb of the interrogative independent clause. The assumed subject, "he," refers to Cain. **Semantically,** ἔσφαξεν is a constative aorist: "he butchered" ("murder," NRSV ESV NIV CNT). John provides an overall picture of Cain's murder of his brother Abel as a whole with emphasis on the historical fact (W, 557). In questioning Cain's motivation, John underscores the motivation for Cain's murder of his brother Abel with the subsequent ὅτι clause.

3:12d ὅτι: The Greek word ὅτι is a conjunction meaning "because" (BDAG, s.v. "ὅτι" 4a, p. 732). **Syntactically,** ὅτι introduces a dependent conjunctive clause: "*because* his (= Cain) deeds were evil, but his brother's were righteous" (ὅτι τὰ ἔργα αὐτοῦ πονηρὰ ἦν, τὰ δὲ τοῦ ἀδελφοῦ αὐτοῦ δίκαια). The entire ὅτι clause functions adverbially, modifying the verb, "murdered" (ἔσφαξεν). **Semantically,** ὅτι is causal: "because" (cf. KJV NASB ESV NIV NET etc.). It provides the reason why Cain murdered his brother (W, 460).

ἦν: The Greek word ἦν is a third person singular imperfect active indicative from the verb εἰμί meaning "to be" or "to describe a special connection with someone" (BDAG, s.v. "εἰμί" 2b, p. 284). **Syntactically,** ἦν is the governing verb of the dependent adverbial clause. The subject is the nominal phrase "his deeds (= Cain)" (τὰ ἔργα αὐτοῦ). **Semantically,** ἦν is an equative imperfect: "were" (cf. KJV NASB ESV NIV NET etc.). Here John has a plural subject with a verb in the singular to describe Cain's collective works as a whole (W, 400). It underscores that "all" of Cain's deeds are evil and is one reason why he *brutally* butchered or *brutally* murdered his brother.

3:12e τὰ [ἔργα] δέ . . . [ἦν]: The Greek word δέ is a coordinating conjunction meaning "but" or is used to mark a contrast (BDAG, s.v. "δέ" 4a, p. 213). **Syntactically,** δέ is in the postpositive position. It introduces the second part of the dependent adverbial clause: "*But* the [deeds] of his brother (= Abel) [were] righteous" (τὰ [ἔργα] δὲ τοῦ ἀδελφοῦ αὐτοῦ δίκαια [ἦν]). To make sense of this clause, an elliptical "deeds" [ἔργα] is supplied along with an elliptical "were" [ἦν] implied from the first part of the compound sentence. **Semantically,** δέ is contrastive: "but" (NET; contra "and," e.g., KJV ESV NIV). John contrasts Abel's deeds with Cain's. While Cain practiced evil, his brother practiced righteousness. This difference made Cain envious, which provided him with his second motivation for *brutally* murdering his own brother.

Theological Nugget: What is significant about John's mention of Cain and family love? Ultimately, Cain's example is incompatible with God's expectation to love family members. Cain becomes a metaphor for the people of the world and representative of the misguided people who have left the church and gone out into the world (vv. 13–15; cf. 2:18–19, 4:1). He clearly represents those whose beliefs and behavior are evil, because they are of the Evil One (cf. 3:8, 10), while Abel represents the righteous who stand firm in their faith in God and their righteous deeds. This continues and even heightens the ethical dualism that we have seen so far in the epistle (Brown, 444), and which will continue to be expanded on as the letter unfolds.

3:13a [καί]: The Greek word καί is a conjunction meaning "and so" or "indeed" or "to introduce a result that comes from what precedes" (BDAG, s.v. "καί" 1bζ, p. 495). **Syntactically,** καί introduces an independent clause: "[*And so*] do not be surprised, brothers" ([καὶ] μὴ θαυμάζετε, ἀδελφοί). **Semantically,** καί is inferential and draws a conclusion: "and so" or "so" (NLT CNT) or "therefore" (NET). Many translations do not recognize the textual variant [καί] and leave it untranslated (KJV ASV NASB NRSV ESV NIV). Regardless, John is about to draw a conclusion evident in the next verb.

θαυμάζετε: The Greek word θαυμάζετε is a second person plural present active imperative from the verb θαυμάζω meaning "to be surprised" or "to be disturbed by something" (BDAG, s.v. "θαυμάζω" 1aγ, p. 444). **Syntactically,** θαυμάζετε is the main verb of the independent clause. The assumed subject, "you," refers to the readers/hearers. **Semantically,** θαυμάζετε is a customary present: "surprised" (NASB ESV NIV NET NLT). It speaks of a pattern of behavior (W, 521). John draws a conclusion for his readers. He tells then not to be disturbed or don't be surprised, a surprise evident in the direct object introduced with εἰ.

εἰ: The Greek word εἰ is a conjunction that in the context of this indirect question means "that" (BDAG, s.v. "εἰ" 2, p. 277–78). **Syntactically,** εἰ identifies the clause as a dependent conjunctive clause. The entire dependent clause, "*that* the world persists in hating you" (εἰ μισεῖ ὑμᾶς ὁ κόσμος), functions substantivally. It is the direct object of the verb (Smalley, 187). It is a content marker for the verb "surprised" (θαυμάζετε). **Semantically,** εἰ introduces the content: "that" (NRSV ESV). The contrast is evident in the next verb.

μισεῖ: The Greek word μισεῖ is a third person singular present active indicative from the verb μισέω meaning "to hate" or "to detest" or "to have a strong aversion to" (BDAG, s.v. "μισέω" 1a, p. 652). **Syntactically,** μισεῖ is the governing verb of the dependent substantival clause. The subject of the verb is the noun "the world" (κόσμος). It is possible to interpret εἰ adverbially: "if" (KJV ASV NASB NIV NET NLT CNT) and thereby it functions as the protasis of a conditional clause modifying "marvel" (θαυμάζετε). **Semantically,** μισεῖ is a customary present: "*persists in* hating" (cf. KJV NASB ESV NIV NET etc.). It speaks of a pattern of behavior (W, 521). The world's system is persistent in its opposition to God and his followers. Therefore followers of Jesus should not be surprised when it hates them as well (John 15:18; 17:14; cf. Brown, 445). Any believer who finds themselves as an object of the world's hate should not be surprised. The wicked have felt this way about the righteous ever since Cain and Abel.

Lexical Nugget: What does θαυμάζω mean? Even though this verb occurs forty-three times in the New Testament, it appears in John's Letters only here. The word contains the idea of wonder or astonishment. In John's Gospel the term is used to describe people's reactions to Jesus's actions and teachings (3:7; 4:27; 5:20, 28; 7:15, 21). In Revelation, the beast's followers are amazed at his miraculous recovery from his head wound (13:3). The same reaction is produced by the vision of the harlot (17:6, 7, 8). In this context, John says that believers should not be *surprised* when the world hates them. Just as Cain hated his brother because of the contrast between their attitudes and actions, believers should expect the same kind of treatment from the people of the world who also live by a different set of values.

3:14a οἴδαμεν: The Greek word οἴδαμεν is first person plural perfect active indicative from the verb οἶδα meaning "to know" or "to have information about something" (BDAG, s.v. "οἶδα" 1e, p. 693). **Syntactically,** οἴδαμεν is the governing verb of the independent asyndeton clause: "*We know* that we have passed out of death into life" (ἡμεῖς οἴδαμεν ὅτι μεταβεβήκαμεν ἐκ τοῦ θανάτου εἰς τὴν ζωήν). The subject is the emphatic pronoun "we" (ἡμεῖς), referring to both John and his readers. Since the pronoun is already assumed in the verbal ending, its presence here is emphatic (W, 321). John contrasts the murderous behavior of Cain and the world system that Cain represents with that of those who love others as a result of their relationship with Jesus. **Semantically,** οἴδαμεν is a perfect with present force. Some verbs, like οἶδα, almost exclusively appear in the perfect tense without the perfect's aspectual significance (W, 579). What exactly John's readers know appears in the ὅτι clause.

ὅτι: The Greek word ὅτι is a conjunction meaning "that" (BDAG, s.v. "ὅτι" 3, p. 732). **Syntactically,** ὅτι introduces a dependent clause: "*that* we have passed out of death into life" (ὅτι μεταβεβήκαμεν ἐκ τοῦ θανάτου εἰς τὴν ζωήν). The clause is substantival. It functions as the direct object of the verb of perception "we know" (οἴδαμεν). The clause is placed in parentheses in order to visualize its contribution to the independent clause. **Semantically,** ὅτι is an indirect discourse marker: "that" (cf. KJV NASB ESV NIV NET etc.). It provides the content of what believers know (W, 454) evident in the next verb.

μεταβεβήκαμεν: The Greek word μεταβεβήκαμεν is first person plural perfect active indicative from the verb μεταβαίνω meaning "to pass over" or "to move" or "to change from one condition to another" (BDAG, s.v. "μεταβαίνω" 2a, p.

638). **Syntactically,** μεταβεβήκαμεν is the governing verb of the dependent substantival clause. The assumed subject, "we," refers to John and his readers. **Semantically,** μεταβεβήκαμεν is an extensive perfect: "we *have* passed" (KJV ASV NASB NRSV ESV NIV CNT). John's focus is on the past event of conversion that clearly affects present behavior (W, 577). Believers can know that they have truly passed from death to eternal life because their behavior of love reflects the change. The change in status from death to life for the believer parallels the common Johannine theme of changing from darkness to light (John 3:19–21; 8:12; 12:35, 46; 1 John 2:9–11). Those who place their faith in Jesus no longer find themselves in darkness, death, and hatred, but have crossed over to light, life, and love. Believers who love fellow believers have changed their status from death to life.

3:14b ὅτι: The Greek word ὅτι is a conjunction meaning "because" or "for" (BDAG, s.v. "ὅτι" 4a, p. 732). **Syntactically,** ὅτι introduces a dependent conjunctive clause: "*because* we *persistently* love our brothers (and sisters)" (ὅτι ἀγαπῶμεν τοὺς ἀδελφούς). The clause is adverbial. It modifies the verb "we know" (οἴδαμεν). **Semantically,** ὅτι is causal: "because" (cf. KJV NASB ESV NIV NET etc.). John provides the reason why his readers know that they have changed from death to life. That reason is found in the rest of the clause.

ἀγαπῶμεν: The Greek word ἀγαπῶμεν is first person plural present active indicative from the verb ἀγαπάω meaning "to love" or "to have a warm regard for and interest in another person" (BDAG, s.v. "ἀγαπάω" 1aα, p. 5). **Syntactically,** ἀγαπῶμεν is the governing verb of the dependent adverbial clause. **Semantically,** ἀγαπῶμεν is a customary present: "we *persistently* love" (or "we love"; e.g., KJV NASB ESV NIV NET). John's point is that the believer makes it a habit to love their brothers and sisters (W, 521). The article before the definite plural direct object of this verb "the brothers" (τοὺς ἀδελφούς) could be just an individualizing article "*the* brothers (and sisters)," but context seems to suggest the article be translated like a possessive pronoun: "*your* brothers (and sisters)" (W, 215–16). In this way it is clear that where this love is shown most clearly is in how believers treat their fellow Christians.

Theological Nugget: What is the significance of exhibiting "love" to other believers? Followers of Jesus can have assurance of their status because of the love that they have and show to their brothers and sisters in Jesus. This parallels a similar statement of assurance made by Jesus in John 13:35: "by this all men will know that you are my disciples, if you have love for one another" (NASB). Love then becomes an indicator of what is in the believer's heart. It is an external signpost that points out that there is light and love within (Brown, 446).

3:14c ἀγαπῶν: The Greek word ἀγαπῶν is a nominative masculine singular present active participle from the verb ἀγαπάω meaning "to love" or "to have a warm regard for and interest in another person" (BDAG, s.v. "ἀγαπάω" 1aα, p. 5). **Syntactically,** ἀγαπῶν is a participle functioning substantivally as the subject of the verb "remains" (μένει). The entire participial clause is placed in parentheses to visualize its contribution to the independent clause. **Semantically,** the negated (μὴ) ἀγαπῶν is a gnomic present with the force of a customary present: "the one who does not *persist* in love" or "the one who does not love" (NET) or "whoever does not love" (NASB ESV), or "anyone who does not love" (NIV CNT NLT). John identifies a timeless fact about any person (W, 523, 615). Anyone who withholds love from others has not crossed over into eternal life, but remains in death.

μένει: The Greek word μένει is a third person singular present active indicative from the verb μένω meaning "to remain," "to continue," "to abide," or is used "of someone does not leave a certain realm or sphere" (BDAG, s.v. "μένω" 1aβ, p. 631). **Syntactically,** μένει is the main verb of the independent asyndeton clause. The subject is the participial phrase, "the one who does not love" (ὁ μὴ ἀγαπῶν). It refers to any believer who does not give of themselves for their fellow followers of Jesus. **Semantically,** μένει is a gnomic present: "abides" (KJV ASV NASB NRSV ESV CNT) or "remains" (NIV NET). It identifies a timeless fact (W, 523). It demonstrates that the one who refuses to love other believers "is still dead" (NLT). Death here is *not* physical death or the termination of one's life, but a type of spiritual death which encompasses condemnation and destruction (John 8:21–24). This future is not a cause of worry for those who love fellow believers.

3:15a μισῶν: The Greek word μισῶν is a nominative masculine singular present active participle from the verb μισέω meaning "to hate" " or "to detest" or "to have a strong aversion to" (BDAG, s.v. "μισέω" 1a, p. 652). **Syntactically,** μισῶν is an adjectival participle. It modifies the substantival adjective "everyone" (πᾶς). Together they serve as the subject of the verb "is" (ἐστίν), due to the grammatical priority of weightier phrases (Culy, 85). The entire πᾶς + participial clause is placed in parentheses in order to visualize its contribution to the independent clause. **Semantically,** μισῶν is a gnomic present with the force of a customary present: "everyone who *persists in* hating" (cf. NASB ESV NET) or "anyone who hates" (NIV NLT CNT). John identifies a timeless fact about any hateful person (W, 523, 615). In the rest of the clause he equates them with murderers.

ἐστίν: The Greek word ἐστίν is third person singular present active indicative from the verb εἰμί meaning "to be" or "to be in close connection with" (BDAG, s.v. "εἰμί" 2a, p. 282). **Syntactically,** ἐστίν is the main verb of the independent asyndeton clause. The subject of the verb is the participial phrase: "everyone who hates their brother: (πᾶς ὁ μισῶν τὸν ἀδελφὸν αὐτοῦ). **Semantically,** ἐστίν is a gnomic present: "is" (cf. KJV NASB ESV NIV NET etc.). It presents a timeless fact about those who hate other people (W, 523). Actions of hate are tantamount to murder. This is most likely hyperbole following the teachings of Jesus on anger and hate in the Sermon on the Mount (Matt. 5:21–22; see also John 8:44 where the Devil is also called a murderer).

Lexical Nugget: What does ἀνθρωποκτόνος mean? This word only appears three times in John's writings (John 8:44; 1 John 3:15 [2x]). It never occurs in the LXX or Koine Greek literature. It is seldom used in Classical Greek (MM, 43). Euripides, a writer of many Greek tragedies, uses ἀνθρωποκτόνος to describe those who literally take lives (*Iph. Taur.* 389). In John 8:44, the Devil is described as a murderer and involved with murder from the beginning. The Devil is a murderer in the sense that he is responsible for bringing death to Adam and Eve and by consequence to humanity at large. In 1 John 3:15, is John describing the misguided fraudulent teachers who left the church as literal murderers? Probably not! But their mistreatment was tantamount to murder, similar to the teaching of Jesus in the Sermon on the Mount (Matt. 5:21–22). This means that ἀνθρωποκτόνος is being used in a metaphorical sense (cf. T. Gad 4:6–7). The effect is stated (i.e., murder), but the cause is intended (hatred). Therefore, those who actively hate their fellow believers do not have eternal life and they demonstrate that their true father is the Devil.

3:15b **καί:** The Greek word καί is a conjunction meaning "and" (BDAG, s.v. "καί" 1bα, p. 494). **Syntactically,** καί introduces an independent conjunctive clause: "*and* you know that no murderer possesses eternal life abiding in him" (καὶ οἴδατε ὅτι πᾶς ἀνθρωποκτόνος οὐκ ἔχει ζωὴν αἰώνιον ἐν αὐτῷ μένουσαν). **Semantically,** καί is connective providing additional information about hateful murderers evident in the next verb and its direct object.

οἴδατε: The Greek word οἴδατε is a second person plural perfect active indicative from the verb οἶδα meaning "to know" or "to have information about something" (BDAG, s.v. "οἶδα" 1e, p. 693). **Syntactically,** οἴδατε is the main verb of the independent conjunctive clause. The assumed subject, "you," refers to the orthodox readers of the letter. **Semantically,** οἴδατε is a perfect with present force: "you know" (cf. KJV NASB ESV NIV NET etc.). Some verbs, like οἶδα, almost exclusively appear in the perfect tense without the perfect's aspectual significance (W, 579). What John's readers know appears in the ὅτι clause.

ὅτι: The Greek word ὅτι is a conjunction meaning "that" after verbs of perception (BDAG, s.v. "ὅτι" 1c, p. 731). **Syntactically,** ὅτι introduces the dependent conjunctive clause: "*that* no murderer possesses eternal life abiding in him" (ὅτι πᾶς ἀνθρωποκτόνος οὐκ ἔχει ζωὴν αἰώνιον ἐν αὐτῷ μένουσαν). It functions substantivally as the direct object of the verb of perception, "you know" (οἴδατε). The clause is placed in parentheses in order to visualize its contribution to the independent clause. **Semantically,** ὅτι is an indirect discourse marker: "that" (cf. KJV NASB ESV NIV NET etc.). It provides the content of what John's readers know (W, 454). John's readers are aware of people who claim to be believers yet continue to live in hatred of their brothers. What they know is found in the next verb.

ἔχει: The Greek word ἔχει is a third person singular present active indicative from the verb ἔχω meaning "to have" or "to possess" (BDAG, s.v. "ἔχω" 1a, p. 420). **Syntactically,** ἔχει is the governing verb of the dependent ὅτι clause. The subject is the nominal phrase "every murderer" (πᾶς ἀνθρωποκτόνος). **Semantically,** ἔχει is a gnomic present: "possesses" (contra "has": NASB ESV NIV NET CNT). The verb points to a timeless fact (W, 523). Anyone who habitually hates other believers has an eternal problem.

μένουσαν: The Greek word **μένουσαν** is an accusative singular feminine present active participle from the verb μένω meaning "to remain," "to continue," "to abide," or is used "of someone who does not leave a certain realm or sphere" (BDAG, s.v. "μένω" 1aβ, p. 631). **Syntactically,** μένουσαν is an adjectival participle modifying the noun "life" (ζωήν). We could also classify this participle as a double accusative or an object complement ("we know that every murderer does not have eternal life *to be* dwelling in him"). It seems more likely, however, to be adjectival, because of the grammatical agreement with the noun. **Semantically,** μένουσαν is a customary present: "abiding" (KJV ASV NASB NRSV ESV CNT), "residing" (NET) or just "in them" (NIV NLT). It reveals an ongoing state (W, 521). It suggests that people who hate fellow believers cut themselves off from both the present and future eternal life. This idea is in direct contrast to the ones who love their fellow believers and so have passed over from spiritual death to spiritual life (Culy, 85–86; cf. Brown, 447).

3:16a ἐν τούτῳ: The Greek word ἐν is a preposition meaning "by" (BDAG, s.v. "ἐν" 5b, p. 328). The Greek word τούτῳ is declined as a dative singular neuter from the demonstrative pronoun οὗτος, which means "this one" (BDAG, s.v. "οὗτος" 1bβ, p. 741). **Syntactically,** ἐν τούτῳ is a prepositional phrase introducing an independent prepositional clause "*By this* we know love" (ἐν τούτῳ ἐγνώκαμεν τὴν ἀγάπην). The construction, "by this" (ἐν τούτῳ) is common in 1 John (2:3, 4, 5 [2x]; 3:10, 16, 19, 24; 4:2, 9, 10, 13, 17; 5:2). **Semantically,** ἐν τούτῳ can either be anaphoric or cataphoric. Here it is cataphoric because of the epexegetical ὅτι clause. The ὅτι clause provides the content of the demonstrative pronoun.

ἐγνώκαμεν: The Greek word ἐγνώκαμεν is first person plural perfect active indicative from the verb γινώσκω meaning "to know" or "to have come to know" something (BDAG, s.v. "γινώσκω" 6aα, p. 200). **Syntactically,** ἐγνώκαμεν is the main verb of the independent clause. The subject of the verb is an implied "we" embedded in the verb and refers to John and his readers who live in love for other believers. **Semantically,** ἐγνώκαμεν is an intensive perfect: "we know" (NASB NRSV ESV CNT). It focuses attention on the present state that results from a completed event (W, 574). Those who believe have heard about the example of the self-giving life of Jesus and they truly know what love is all about.

3:16b ὅτι: The Greek word ὅτι is a conjunction meaning "that" (BDAG, s.v. "ὅτι" 2a, p. 732). **Syntactically,** ὅτι introduces the dependent adjectival clause: "*that* that one (= Jesus) gave up his life for us" (ὅτι ἐκεῖνος ὑπὲρ ἡμῶν τὴν ψυχὴν αὐτοῦ ἔθηκεν). It modifies the demonstrative pronoun, "this" (τοῦτο). **Semantically,** ὅτι is epexegetical: "that" (ASV NASB ESV NET CNT). The ὅτι clause explains or clarifies the demonstrative within the prepositional phrase (ἐν τούτῳ; W, 459). What is known is clearly stated with the verb of this ὅτι clause.

ἔθηκεν: The Greek word ἔθηκεν is a third person singular aorist active indicative from the verb τίθημι meaning "to take off" or "to give up" or "to remove" (BDAG, s.v. "τίθημι" 1bβ, p. 1003). **Syntactically,** ἔθηκεν is the governing verb of the dependent ὅτι clause. The subject of ἔθηκεν is the demonstrative pronoun "that one" (ἐκεῖνος) and refers to Jesus. **Semantically,** ἔθηκεν is a constative aorist: "he laid down" (KJV ASV NASB NRSV ESV NIV NET CNT) or "he gave up" (NLT). It explains the event of Jesus's death as a whole (W, 557). The phrase "give up his life" (τὴν (ψυχὴν αὐτοῦ ἔθηκεν) is idiomatic, meaning "to die voluntarily" or "to surrender" (L&N 23.113; cf. Culy, 87). It is used euphemistically as a kind way of expressing that Jesus died. Jesus (ἐκεῖνος) showed the ultimate form of love when he died voluntarily for others.

3:16c καί: The Greek word καί is a conjunction meaning "and" (BDAG, s.v. "καί" 1b, p. 494). **Syntactically,** καί introduces a conjunctive independent clause: "*and* [that] we are obligated to give up our lives for our brothers (and sisters)" (καὶ ἡμεῖς ὀφείλομεν ὑπὲρ τῶν ἀδελφῶν τὰς ψυχὰς θεῖναι). The article before "lives" (τὰς ψυχάς) should be translated with the possessive pronoun "our" (W, 215). **Semantically,** καί is a coordinating conjunction joining two dependent clauses together: "and" (KJV ASV NASB NRSV ESV NIV CNT), though some render καί as though it introduces a result from what Jesus did (NET NLT; cf. BDAG, s.v. "καί" 1bζ, p. 495). John began with Jesus showing what love is by giving up his personal interests and life for his followers (v. 16b), then adds that his followers should follow his example, which is evident in the next two words.

ὀφείλομεν: The Greek word ὀφείλομεν is first person plural present active indicative from the verb ὀφείλω meaning "to be obligated" or "to be under obligation to meet certain social and moral expectations" (BDAG, s.v. "ὀφείλω" 2aβ, p. 743). **Syntactically,** ὀφείλομεν is the main verb of the independent conjunctive clause. The subject is the emphatic personal pronoun "we" (ἡμεῖς). It refers to John and the readers of the letter. The pronoun does not need to be expressed, but its presence heightens the fact that believers should imitate the sacrifice of Jesus. **Semantically,** ὀφείλομεν is a customary present: "we are obligated" or "we are obligated" or "we ought" (cf. KJV NASB ESV NIV NET etc). While the word "we are obligated" indicates the believer's obligation, the customary present indicates an ongoing action (W, 521). John underscores a believer's ongoing obligation. That obligation is revealed by the infinitive (θεῖναι).

θεῖναι: The Greek word θεῖναι is an aorist active infinitive from the verb τίθημι meaning "to take off" or "to give up" or "to remove" (BDAG, s.v. "τίθημι" 1bβ, p. 1003). **Syntactically,** θεῖναι is part of the main verb of the clause, "we are obligated" (ὀφείλομεν). **Semantically,** θεῖναι is a complementary infinitive: "we ought to give up" (NLT) though most render the verb "to lay down" (cf. KJV NASB ESV NIV NET etc.). The infinitive completes the thought of the verb "we are obligated" (ὀφείλομεν; cf. W, 598, 664). The one who believes in Jesus ought to live for others.

Lexical Nugget: What does John mean when he says, "we ought to give up our lives" (ὀφείλομεν ὑπὲρ τῶν ἀδελφῶν τὰς ψυχὰς θεῖναι)? This is another figure of speech. This one is called a synecdoche and occurs where a greater, or in this case Jesus, is put in place of a lesser one. If believers are to follow the example of Jesus and give their lives, then surely they should be able to daily serve other believers through their words and actions (cf. Strecker, 115; Culy, 381). Therefore, John is describing an ethical obligation to serve other believers that comes with declaring one's relationship with God.

3:17a δ': The Greek word δέ is a conjunction meaning "but" (BDAG, s.v. "δέ" 4a, p. 213). **Syntactically,** δέ is in the postpositive position and introduces a dependent indefinite relative clause ὃς ἄν: "*But* whoever possesses the resources of the world and [whoever] perceives their brother (or sister) in need and [whoever] shuts off his (or her) heart against him (or her)" (ὃς δ' ἄν ἔχη τὸν βίον τοῦ κόσμου). It modifies the personal pronoun "them [singular]" (αὐτῷ). **Semantically,** δέ has adversative force: "but" (KJV ASV NASB ESV NET CNT) though some translations do not translate δέ (NRSV NIV NLT). John essentially questions how God's love can reside in a confessing follower of Jesus who has the resources to show compassion and yet does not love their brother.

ὃς . . . ἄν: The Greek ὅς is a masculine singular nominative from the relative pronoun ὅς followed by ἄν meaning "anyone" or "whoever" (BDAG, s.v. "ἄν" 1bβ, p. 56; s.v. "ὅς" 1jα, p. 727). **Syntactically,** ὅς introduces a dependent indefinite relative clause. The entire clause also functions adjectivally. It modifies "him (or her)" (αὐτῷ) in 3:17d. It is translated either as "anyone" (ESV NIV CNT) or "whoever" (KJV ASV NASB NET). Our interpretive translation at the end of this commentary will render "αὐτῷ" as "those who claim to follow Jesus"

ἔχῃ: The Greek word ἔχῃ is a third person singular present active subjunctive from the verb ἔχω meaning "to own" or "to possess," indicating that something is under one's control (BDAG, s.v. "ἔχω" 1aα, p. 420). The verb is in the subjunctive mood because it is part of an ἄν clause. **Syntactically,** ἔχῃ is the first governing verb of the compound relative clause. It modifies the personal pronoun "him (or her)" (αὐτῷ). The subject is the indefinite relative pronoun, "whoever" (ὅς . . . ἄν), which refers to anyone who professes Christ yet refuses to help those in need. **Semantically,** ἔχῃ is a gnomic present: "possesses" (contra "has"; cf. KJV NASB ESV NIV NET etc.). The verb points to a timeless fact (W, 523). Believers are expected to help others.

> **Lexical Nugget:** What does the word βίος mean? This noun occurs ten times in the New Testament, including twice in this letter (1 John 2:16; 3:17). Luke uses the word figuratively to speak of the *resources* needed to maintain life. The woman who had suffered from internal bleeding spent all *the resources* she had to live on in order to get well (Luke 8:43). A poor woman casts "all she had to live on" into the temple-offering box (Luke 21:4; Mark 12:44). The word is also used when the father divides up his *resources* between his sons in the parable of the prodigal son (Luke 15:12, 20). In each case there is no value judgment placed on the presence or lack of resources, instead the judgment is on how one uses their worldly wealth when others lack "the necessities of life" (βίος). The word "resources" (τὸν βίον; BDAG, s.v. "βίος" 2, p. 177) is used instead of the more specific word "riches" (πλοῦτον), which is rather interesting. The point is that while everyone has resources, not everyone is rich (Culy, 88). So, John expects fellow followers of Jesus to help people in need. If they don't, then John questions whether they have a relationship with God.

3:17b καί [ὅς ἄν]: The Greek word καί is a conjunction meaning "and" (BDAG, s.v. "καί" 1b, p. 494). **Syntactically,** καί introduces the second part of the indefinite relative clause: "*and* [whoever] perceives their brother (or sister) possessing a need" (καὶ [ὅς ἄν] θεωρῇ τὸν ἀδελφὸν αὐτοῦ χρείαν ἔχοντα). It modifies the personal pronoun "them [singular]" (αὐτῷ). **Semantically,** καί is a coordinating conjunction joining two dependent clauses together: "and" (cf. KJV NASB ESV NIV NET etc.). It provides some additional information about the one who possess worldly resources. The additional information is found in the rest of the clause.

θεωρῇ: The Greek word θεωρῇ is a third person singular present active subjunctive from the verb θεωρέω meaning "to see," "to observe," "to perceive," or "to observe something with sustained attention" (BDAG, s.v. "θεωρέω" 1, p. 454). The verb is in the subjunctive mood because it is part of an ἄν clause and thereby connected to the previous clause. **Syntactically,** θεωρῇ is the second verb of the indefinite relative clause. It modifies the personal pronoun "him (or her)" (αὐτῷ). The subject is the elliptical indefinite relative pronoun, "whoever" [ὃς ... ἄν]. It refers to anyone who professes Christ yet refuses to help those in need. **Semantically,** θεωρῇ is a gnomic present: "perceives," though most render it as "sees" (cf. KJV NASB ESV NIV NET etc.). John is about to make another timeless fact about anyone who sees another in need (W, 523).

ἔχοντα: The Greek word ἔχοντα is an accusative singular masculine present active participle from the verb ἔχω meaning "to own" or "to possess" (BDAG, s.v. "ἔχω" 1aα, p. 420). **Syntactically,** ἔχοντα is a double accusative, an object-complement to the direct object "need" (χρείαν), modifying the verb "whoever perceives" (θεωρῇ). **Semantically,** ἔχοντα is a gnomic present: "possesses" (contra "has"; cf. KJV NASB ESV NIV NET etc.). John continues to specify a timeless fact about anyone who sees a person in need.

3:17c καὶ [ὃς ἄν]: The Greek word καί is a conjunction meaning "and" (BDAG, s.v. "καί" 1b, p. 494). **Syntactically,** καί introduces the third part of the compound dependent indefinite relative clause, "*and* shuts off their heart against him (or her)" (καὶ κλείσῃ τὰ σπλάγχνα αὐτοῦ ἀπ' αὐτοῦ), modifying the personal pronoun "him (or her)" (αὐτῷ). **Semantically,** καί is a coordinating conjunction joining two dependent clauses together: "and" (KJV ASV NASB NET), though some (ESV NIV NLT CNT) render καί as though it introduces a surprising or unexpected event (cf. BDAG, s.v. "καί" 1bη, p. 495). Regardless, καί provides some additional information about the one who possess worldly resources.

κλείσῃ: The Greek word κλείσῃ is a third person singular aorist active subjunctive from the verb κλείω meaning "to close" or "to close one's heart against someone" (BDAG, s.v. "κλείω" 2, p. 547) or "shut down their intestines" (L&N 25.55). The verb is in the subjunctive mood because it is part of an ἄν clause. **Syntactically,** κλείσῃ is the third governing verb of the elliptical dependent indefinite relative clause, modifying the personal pronoun "him (or her)" (αὐτῷ). The subject is the elliptical indefinite relative pronoun, "whoever" [ὃς ... ἄν], which refers to anyone who professes to follow Jesus yet refuses to help those in need. **Semantically,** κλείσῃ is a gnomic aorist rendered various ways: "closes" (NASB ESV CNT), "has no pity" (NIV), "shows no compassion" (NLT), "refuses help" (NRSV), and "shut off" (KJV ASV NET). The gnomic aorist is rendered in the present tense presenting a timeless fact (W, 562). Regardless of how κλείσῃ is rendered the point remains the same: any person who shuts down their emotions and refuses to help others has a problem. This phrase goes further than just to say that they would not help, but that they shut down their natural instinct of compassion as well (Brown, 450).

Lexical Nugget: What does κλείσῃ τὰ σπλάγχνα αὐτοῦ mean? Literally the phrase could be translated as "they close their intestines." The noun "intestines" (σπλάγχνον) occurs eleven times in the New Testament, but only once in John's writings (*EDNT*, 3:265). First, the word is used of literal physical organs of humans and animals, such as the internal parts of a sacrificial animal (Philo, *Spec.* 1.216), the stomach, the heart, the lungs, the spleen, the liver, and the two kidneys (Philo, *Opif.* 118), and innards/intestines (Jos. *B.J.* 2.21.5 §612; Acts 1:18). The word is more often used figuratively to speak of human emotion. This is the usage that dominates the New Testament. In Paul, the followers of Jesus are expected to exercise the *compassion* (σπλάγχνον) of God through loving acts for fellow believers (Col. 3:12. cf. Luke 1:78), and by exercising selfless attitudes toward others (Phil. 2:1; cf. 5–11). In the same way, John uses the term here in 3:17 to reference a compassionate disposition that seeks to help others in tangible ways. Therefore, "to close one's intestines" (κλείσῃ τὰ σπλάγχνα), can be rendered as "closes his heart" (NASB), "shuts off his compassion" (NET), or "refuses [to] help" (NRSV; cf. NIV). It is a figure of speech that could be classified as a metonymy of subject where the subject ("intestines") is stated for an attribute ("compassion"). John's point is that anyone who claims to be a Christian yet refuses to demonstrate compassionate acts toward their fellow believer, is not exhibiting the character of God.

3:17d πῶς: The Greek word πῶς is a conjunction meaning "how" (BDAG, s.v. "πῶς" 1aδ, p. 901). **Syntactically,** πῶς introduces an independent interrogative clause, "*how* does the love of God remain in him (or her)" (πῶς ἡ ἀγάπη τοῦ θεοῦ μένει ἐν αὐτῷ). **Semantically,** πῶς introduces a rhetorical question expecting "no" for an answer. John contends that a person who has the means to help someone, yet refuses, can in no way have a relationship with the self-giving Christ.

μένει: The Greek word μένει is a third person singular present active indicative from the verb μένω meaning "to remain," "to continue," "to abide," or is used of someone or something that does not leave a certain realm or sphere (BDAG, s.v. "μένω" 1aβ, p. 631). **Syntactically,** μένει serves as the main verb of the independent interrogative clause. The subject is the nominal phrase "the love of God" (ἡ ἀγάπη τοῦ θεοῦ). **Semantically,** μένει is a customary present: "remain" (NET), "abide" (ASV NASB NRSV ESV), "in" (NLT CNT). It speaks of an ongoing state (W, 521). John's point is this: the love of God does not have a home in the heart of a person that refuses to show compassion to those in need.

3:18a ἀγαπῶμεν: The Greek word ἀγαπῶμεν is first person plural present active subjunctive from the verb ἀγαπάω meaning "to love" or "to cherish" or "to practice/express love" (BDAG, s.v. "ἀγαπάω" 3, p. 6). **Syntactically,** ἀγαπῶμεν is the main verb of the independent clause, "Children, *let us* not *love* in word or tongue" (τεκνία, μὴ ἀγαπῶμεν λόγῳ μηδὲ τῇ γλώσσῃ). **Semantically,** the negated (μὴ) ἀγαπῶμεν is a hortatory subjunctive: "let us not love" (cf. KJV NASB ESV NIV NET etc.). It functions as a first person imperative in the present tense indicating something that ought to be a regular practice (W, 465). Believers are to make it a practice *not* to love with mere words.

Lexical Nugget: How is the vocative "children" (τεκνία) to be understood? On the one hand, Brown suggests that this vocative marks a new section of the epistle (Brown, 439). He views the previous vocative "brothers" in 3:13 in the same way. On the other hand, it could just be a rhetorical device that John uses to summarize what has come before. Since there is a close thematic connection to the previous verses, perhaps verse 18 is a summary of the preceding discussion that began in verse 11 (Culy, 89; cf. Yarbrough, 205).

3:18b ἀλλά: The Greek word ἀλλά is a conjunction meaning "but" or "rather" (BDAG, s.v. "ἀλλά" 1a, p. 44). **Syntactically,** ἀλλά introduces the independent conjunctive clause: "*but* [let us love] in deed and truth" (ἀλλὰ ἐν ἔργῳ καὶ ἀληθείᾳ). It introduces the second part of the compound independent clause. It seems best to insert "let us love" (ἀγαπῶμεν) from the first part of the clause, in order to make the best sense out of this compound sentence. **Semantically,** ἀλλά, after the negative "let us not love" (μὴ ἀγαπῶμεν), is contrastive: "but" (cf. KJV NASB ESB NIV NET etc.). It contrasts love that loves with mere words with real love. John tells his readers what real love is in the rest of this clause.

[ἀγαπῶμεν]: The Greek word ἀγαπῶμεν is first person plural present active subjunctive from the verb ἀγαπάω meaning "to love" or "to cherish" or "to practice/express love" (BDAG, s.v. "ἀγαπάω" 3, p. 6). **Syntactically,** ἀγαπῶμεν is an elliptical verb functioning as the main verb of the second independent clause. **Semantically,** ἀγαπῶμεν is a hortatory subjunctive: "let us love" (cf. NLT). It functions as a first person imperative in the present tense indicating something that ought to be a regular practice (W, 464). In contrast to people who love in mere words, true love manifests itself regularly through selfless actions.

Lexical Nugget: How are the two sets of two datives in this context, "word nor speech" (λόγῳ μηδὲ τῇ γλώσσῃ) and "deed and truth" (ἔργῳ καὶ ἀληθείᾳ) to be understood? These pairs could be a figure of speech called a hendiadys (although the first pair might technically be a doublet). This particular figure of speech is when two ideas that are coordinate work together to form one thought. If we were to put these two pairs together, we would then come up with two single ideas. Therefore a good translation might be, "Children do not love *with words alone* but *with sincere actions*" (cf. Bateman[1], 389; Culy, 90–91; Brown, 451–52).

1 JOHN 3:19–24

Big Greek Idea: John's threefold method to affirm his assertions—that what a child of God believes about Jesus is true and that their confidence is reliable—is apparent in an untroubled conscience, compliance with God's expectations, and God's enduring presence.

Structural Overview: Having underscored the incompatibilities of love and hate within God's family and among God's children (vv. 11–18), John moves to affirm his readers (vv. 19–24).

John opens (καί) to affirm (γνωσόμεθα) God's children (ἐσμέν; cf. 3:1, 10) in a twofold manner (vv. 19–20). John first asserts that God's children are (ἐσμέν) correct in what they believe about Jesus (v. 19a). He then follows up with identifying an inward confidence (πείσομεν) that when doubts arise (καταγινώσκῃ) among God's children, God will intervene (ἐστίν/γινώσκει; vv. 19b–20).

John then transitions (ἀγαπητοί) to God's threefold method for developing assurance among God's children (vv. 21–24). First, there is (ἔχομεν) an untroubled conscience that results (ὃ ἐάν) in God's hearing, listening, and answering talks with God (λαμβάνομεν; vv. 21–22). Second, there is (ἐστίν) compliance with God's twofold (ἵνα) expectation: believe (πιστεύσωμεν) in Jesus, the Messiah, and persist in loving (ἀγαπῶμεν) others in God's family (v. 23). Finally, there is God's enduring presence (μένει) for those who keep his command, which is confirmed (γινώσκομεν) by the presence (ἔδωκεν) of God's Spirit (v. 24).

Outline:

> Belief in Jesus Is to be Done with Confidence (vv. 19–20)
> The Measurements of Assurance Are Threefold (vv. 21–24)
> > Assurance is evident in an untroubled conscience (vv. 21–22)
> > Assurance is evident in compliance with God's expectations (v. 23)
> > Assurance is evident in God's enduring presence (v. 24)

CLAUSAL OUTLINE FOR 1 JOHN 3:19–24

3:19a [Καὶ] ἐν τούτῳ **γνωσόμεθα** (ὅτι ἐκ τῆς ἀληθείας ἐσμέν),
3:19a [And so] by this **we _will_ know** (that _we are_ of the truth),

^{3:19b} (καὶ [ὅτι] ἔμπροσθεν αὐτοῦ <u>πείσομεν</u> τὴν καρδίαν ἡμῶν)
^{3:19b} (and [*that*] we *will* <u>convince</u> our heart before him [= God])

       ^{3:20a} **ὅτι ἐὰν καταγινώσκῃ** ἡμῶν ἡ καρδία,
       ^{3:20a} **that whenever** our heart **condemns** us,

       ^{3:20b} **ὅτι** μείζων **ἐστὶν** ὁ θεὸς τῆς καρδίας ἡμῶν
       ^{3:20b} **that** God **is** greater than our heart

       ^{3:20c} <u>καὶ [ὅτι] **γινώσκει** πάντα.</u>
       ^{3:20c} <u>and [*that*]</u> **he knows** all things.

     ^{3:21a} Ἀγαπητοί, **ἐὰν** ἡ καρδία μὴ **καταγινώσκῃ** ἡμῶν,
     ^{3:21a} Beloved, **if** our heart **does** not **condemn** us,

^{3:21b} παρρησίαν **ἔχομεν** πρὸς τὸν θεόν,
^{3:21b} **we feel** confident before God,

^{3:22a} <u>καὶ (ὃ ἐὰν αἰτῶμεν) **λαμβάνομεν** ἀπ᾽ αὐτοῦ,</u>
^{3:22a} <u>and *so*</u> (whatever we ask for) **we** *will* **receive** from him (= God),

       ^{3:22b} **ὅτι** τὰς ἐντολὰς αὐτοῦ **τηροῦμεν**
       ^{3:22b} **because we** *persist* **in keeping** his commandments

       ^{3:22c} <u>καὶ [ὅτι] τὰ ἀρεστὰ ἐνώπιον αὐτοῦ **ποιοῦμεν**.</u>
       ^{3:22c} <u>and [*because*]</u> **we** *persist* **in doing** *the things* that
        are pleasing in his sight.

^{3:23a} <u>καὶ αὕτη **ἐστὶν** ἡ ἐντολὴ αὐτοῦ,</u>
^{3:23a} <u>And</u> this **is** his (= God's) commandment,

   ^{3:23b} **ἵνα πιστεύσωμεν** τῷ ὀνόματι τοῦ υἱοῦ αὐτοῦ Ἰησοῦ
       Χριστοῦ
   ^{3:23b} *namely* **that we believe** in the name of his Son Jesus, who is the
    Christ

   ^{3:23c} <u>καὶ [ἵνα] **ἀγαπῶμεν** ἀλλήλους,</u>
   ^{3:23c} <u>and [*that*]</u> **we** *persist* **in loving** one another,

       ^{3:23d} **καθὼς ἔδωκεν** ἐντολὴν ἡμῖν.
       ^{3:23d} **just as he** (= Jesus) **gave** the (= God's) commandment to us.

³:²⁴ᵃ <u>καὶ</u> (ὁ τηρῶν τὰς ἐντολὰς αὐτοῦ) ἐν αὐτῷ **μένει**
³:²⁴ᵃ <u>And</u> (the one who *persists* in keeping his [God's] commandments)
    abides with him (= God).

³:²⁴ᵇ <u>καὶ</u> [*μένει*] αὐτὸς ἐν αὐτῷ·
³:²⁴ᵇ <u>and</u> this one (= God) [*abides*] with him (or her);

³:²⁴ᶜ <u>καὶ</u> ἐν τούτῳ **γινώσκομεν** (ὅτι <u>μένει</u> ἐν ἡμῖν),
³:²⁴ᶜ <u>And</u> by this **we know** (<u>that</u> he [=God] <u>abides</u> in us),
               |
           ³:²⁴ᵈ ἐκ τοῦ πνεύματος (<u>οὗ</u> ἡμῖν <u>ἔδωκεν</u>).
           ³:²⁴ᵈ by the Spirit <u>whom</u> <u>he has given</u> us.

SYNTAX EXPLAINED FOR 1 JOHN 3:19–24

³:¹⁹ᵃ [Καί]: The Greek word καί is a conjunction meaning "and so" (BDAG, s.v.
"καί" 1bζ, p. 495). **Syntactically,** καί introduces an independent conjunctive
clause: "[*and so*] by this we will know" ([καί] ἐν τούτῳ γνωσόμεθα). The
brackets around [καί] indicate that there is a textual problem. **Semantically,**
καί is an inferential connective: "and so." It provides a conclusion: the followers of Jesus who love through selfless action demonstrate something. That
something is evident in the rest of the clause.

> **Text-Critical Nugget:** Why is καί in brackets? Because some Greek texts do
> not include the conjunction, it has been placed in brackets. The UBS com-
> mittee had difficulty in deciding about inserting καί ("C" rating; Metzger[1],
> 643), so some translations reflect the presence of καί (KJV NRSV NET CNT)
> while others do not (NASB ESV NIV NLT). The earliest manuscript evidence is
> divided. Some of the earliest and best manuscripts have the conjunction pres-
> ent (Sinaiticus), while others omit it (Alexandrinus and Vaticanus). It could
> be as simple as the καί was omitted accidentally due to the similar ending of
> verse 18. A scribe's eye could have jumped from the "αι" ending of "truth"
> (ἀληθεία) to the iota in the next phrase, "by this" (ἐν τούτῳ). It could also be
> that a scribe omitted the conjunction intentionally due to its weak connective
> value. It is our opinion that the conjunction is original. It seems more likely
> that the conjunction would have been omitted because of its relatively weak
> connective value, rather than added into the text to strengthen a connection.

ἐν τούτῳ: The Greek word ἐν is a preposition meaning "by" (BDAG, s.v.
"ἐν" 5b, p. 328). The Greek word τούτῳ is declined as a dative singular
neuter from the demonstrative pronoun οὗτος meaning "this one" (BDAG,
s.v. "οὗτος" 1bα, p. 741). **Syntactically,** ἐν τούτῳ introduces an independent prepositional clause: "[and so] *by this* we will know" ([καί] ἐν τούτῳ

γνωσόμεθα). The construction, "by this" (ἐν τούτῳ) is very important in 1 John (2:3, 4, 5 [2x], 3:10, 16, 19, 24; 4:2, 9, 10, 13, 17; 5:2). **Semantically,** ἐν τούτῳ can either be anaphoric, pointing back to the preceding discussion, or cataphoric, pointing forward. Here the phrase is anaphoric and points back to the previous verse and its discussion on how to be assured that you belong to God (cf. BDAG, s.v. "οὗτος" 1bα, p. 741). Followers of Jesus have assurance by showing love with selfless action rather than just with empty words. Brown puts it this way, "The exterior deed shows the interior reality" (Brown, 454).

Semantical Nugget: How is τούτῳ to be understood? The usual rule is that the prepositional phrase is cataphoric if it is followed by a subordinating conjunction such as "that" (ὅτι + indicative mood clause), "in order that" (ἵνα + subjunctive mood clause), "if" (ἐάν + subjunctive mood clause), "whenever" (ὅταν), or "from" (ἐκ). They are either epexegetical or appositional (ἵνα) and provide the content of the demonstrative pronoun (τούτῳ). Although there is a ὅτι clause immediately following the clause, "that we are of the truth and we have assured our hearts before him" (ὅτι ἐκ τῆς ἀληθείας ἐσμέν), it is *not* functioning expexegetically. The ὅτι clause is substantival functioning as the direct object of "we will know" (γνωσόμεθα). Since there is no expexegetical clause that can explicate the content of the demonstrative pronoun, τούτῳ is anaphoric.

γνωσόμεθα: The Greek word γνωσόμεθα is first person plural future middle indicative from the verb γινώσκω meaning "to know" or "to arrive at a knowledge of someone or something" (BDAG, s.v. "γινώσκω" 1c, p. 199). **Syntactically,** γνωσόμεθα is the main verb of the independent clause. The subject of the verb is an implied "we" embedded in the verb and refers to John and his readers. **Semantically,** γνωσόμεθα is a predictive future: "we *will* know" (NASB NRSV NET) or "we shall know" (ASV ESV CNT). It indicates that something will take place (W, 568). Followers of Jesus who love in selfless action like Jesus will know something. That something is evident in the next content ὅτι clause.

ὅτι: The Greek word ὅτι is a conjunction meaning "that" (BDAG, s.v. "ὅτι" 1c, p. 731). **Syntactically,** ὅτι introduces the compound dependent conjunctive clause: "*that* we are of the truth" (ὅτι ἐκ τῆς ἀληθείας ἐσμέν). The entire ὅτι clause is substantival. It is the direct object of the verb "we will know" (γνωσόμεθα). The clause is placed in parentheses in order to visualize its contribution to the independent clause. **Semantically,** ὅτι is an indirect discourse marker: "we know *that*" (KJV ASV NASB NRSV ESV NIV NET). It provides the content of what the believer should know (W, 454–55). The specifics of the ὅτι clause are found in the next verb.

ἐσμέν: The Greek word ἐσμέν is first person plural present active indicative from the verb εἰμί meaning "to be" or "to be in close connection (with)" (BDAG, s.v. "εἰμί" 2b, p. 283). **Syntactically,** ἐσμέν is the governing verb of the dependent ὅτι clause. The subject of the verb is an implied "we" embedded in the verb and refers to John and his readers. **Semantically,** ἐσμέν is an equative present: "are" (cf. KJV NASB ESV NIV NET etc.). It equates a believer's selfless acts of love with being "of the truth" so that they can have assurance they have a relationship with God.

3:19b καὶ [ὅτι]: The Greek word καί is a conjunction meaning "and" (BDAG, s.v. "καί" 1bα, p. 494). **Syntactically,** καί introduces another dependent conjunctive clause: "*and [that] we will convince our heart before him(= God)*" (καὶ [ὅτι] ἔμπροσθεν αὐτοῦ πείσομεν τὴν καρδίαν ἡμῶν). The clause is placed in parentheses in order to visualize its contribution to the independent clause as well as view it as parallel to the previous ὅτι clause. **Semantically,** καί is a connective ("and") that introduces an additional thought about the assurance that we can have, namely, our faith is genuine. A ὅτι is inserted to make better sense of this compound clause.

> **Syntactical Nugget:** It is possible that this καὶ [ὅτι] clause is not the second part of a compound thought? Although this clause begins a new series of thoughts, the verb in the previous clause is future as is this one. So it seems they should be read together as parallel clauses (Culy, 92). John moves beyond God's greatness to God's knowing of all things. He underscores a basic theological axiom. Followers of Jesus, who take time to talk with God, can be assured that God is both great and omniscient. He knows our hearts (Acts 1:24; Luke 16:15) and he forgives those who repent (Prayer of Manasseh). All believers have an advocate sitting at the right hand of God: his name is Jesus (1 John 2:1).

πείσομεν: The Greek word πείσομεν is first person plural future active indicative from the verb πείθω meaning "to convince" or "to be so convinced that one puts confidence in something" (BDAG, s.v. "πείθω" 2b, p. 792). **Syntactically,** πείσομεν is the governing verb of the conjunctive dependent ὅτι clause. **Semantically,** πείσομεν is a predictive future: "we *will* convince" (NET) or "assure" (KJV ASV NASB CNT) or "reassure" (NRSV ESV). It indicates that something will take place (W, 568). When believers exhibit selfless acts of love for their fellow Christians, they have assurance that one day they will stand before Jesus confident in their relationship with God.

> **Lexical Nugget:** How is "we will convince our hearts" (πείσομεν τὴν καρδίαν ἡμῶν) to be understood? The difficulty of this phrase comes from the variety of acceptable translations for the verb "persuade" (πείθω), and the figurative use

of the noun "heart" (καρδία). The verb could be translated as convince, accept, believe, conform, submit, give in, or obey (*TLNT* 3:66), and the noun "heart" (καρδία). Since it never refers to the actual blood-pumping organ in John's writings, it is a figurative term. Here it seems to refer to a believer's conscience that governs their moral thoughts. This is an example of a figure of speech called a synecdoche, where a part of a person is used to represent the whole (i.e., face for presence, mouth for speaking, eye for vision, feet for swiftness). Here in 1 John 3:19–21, the heart (a part of a person) is used for a person's emotions, wishes, and desires. Therefore, John encourages the believer to exhibit sincere actions of love that allow their whole person be persuaded that they will have nothing to fear when they stand before God. The person whose heart does not condemn him or her is a blessed person (Sir 14:2).

3:20a ὅτι: The Greek word ὅτι is a conjunction meaning "that" (BDAG, s.v. "ὅτι" 1e, p. 731). **Syntactically,** ὅτι introduces a dependent conjunctive clause, "*that whenever our heart condemn us*" (ὅτι ἐὰν καταγινώσκη ἡμῶν ἡ καρδία). It functions adverbially to "is" (ἐστίν) in 20b. **Semantically,** the conjunctive ὅτι clause is epexegetical and modifies the entire previous clause: "and [*that*] we will assure our heart before him (= God)" (καὶ [ὅτι] ἔμπροσθεν αὐτοῦ πείσομεν τὴν καρδίαν ἡμῶν). Thus the entire clause that expresses a believer's emotional state is [bracketed] (cf. BDAG, s.v. "ὅτι" 1e, p. 731). This option parallels a subsequent usage in 1 John 5:14 where a conjunctive ὅτι clause modifies an entire preceding clause (see NET note for an extended discussion). John assures his readers that they belong to God ,which is clearly evident in the next conjunctive ὅτι clause (v. 20b).

Semantical Nugget: How should the ὅτι clause be rendered? The conjunctive ὅτι clause could be classified one of three ways with three different English translations: epexegetical ("that if"), adverbial ("because if"), or redivide the Greeks words ὅτι ἐάν into an indefinite relative clause ὅ τι ἐάν ("in whatever"). If epexegetical "that if our hearts condemn us" (NET), it could be giving us the content of the "by this" (ἐν τούτῳ) or could be explicating the noun "heart" (καρδίαν). We have already concluded in 3:19a that the prepositional phrase (ἐν τούτῳ) refers back to the previous context rather than pointing forward to an epexegetical clause. If adverbial "because if our hearts condemn us" (KJV ASV), it could be either modifying the verb "know" (γνωσόμεθα) giving us the reason that the believer knows, or the verb "persuade" (πείσομεν) providing us with the reason that the believer can have assurance. If an indefinite relative clause, the Greek letters would be redivided from ὅτι ἐάν to ὅ τι ἐάν and then translated as "whenever our hearts condemn us" (NRSV ESV NIV; cf. NASB). John, however, seems to use the indefinite relative clause "whatever" (ὅ ἐάν) elsewhere (3:22) and it is therefore part of John's style. Of all the options, the best is the epexegetical. Thus the conjunctive ὅτι clause modifies the entire previous clause: "and [*that*] we will assure our heart before him" (καὶ [ὅτι] ἔμπροσθεν αὐτοῦ πείσομεν τὴν καρδίαν ἡμῶν).

ἐάν: The Greek word ἐάν is a conjunction meaning "whenever" (BDAG, s.v. "ἐάν" 2, p. 268). **Syntactically,** the conjunction ἐάν is a conjunction marker of time for the dependent ὅτι clause: "that *whenever* our heart condemns us" (ἐὰν καταγινώσκη ἡμῶν ἡ καρδία). **Semantically,** ἐάν is a marker of the prospect of an action, namely, the heart or condemning conscience at any given point of time (cf. ESV, "for whenever"). It approaches closely the function of ὅταν. Since the believer has assurance of their standing before God due to their selfless acts, at any given point in time when their conscience brings doubt, believers can know that God is greater than their conscience.

καταγινώσκη: The Greek word καταγινώσκη is third person singular present active subjunctive from the verb καταγινώσκω meaning "to condemn" or "to convict" (BDAG, s.v. "καταγινώσκω," p. 515). The verb is in the subjunctive because it is the verb for the ἐάν clause. **Syntactically,** καταγινώσκη is the governing verb of the dependent epexegetical clause. The subject is the nominal phrase "our heart" (ἡμῶν ἡ καρδία) and is a metaphor for the believer's conscience. **Semantically,** καταγινώσκη is a conative present whereby the present tense portrays the subject (ἡμῶν ἡ καρδία) as desiring to do something, namely, condemn (W, 534). Whenever the believer's conscience (e.g., ἡμῶν ἡ καρδία) brings guilt, they can still have assurance of their faith because God is greater than their hearts.

3:20b ὅτι: The Greek word ὅτι is a conjunction meaning "that" (BDAG, s.v. "ὅτι" 1e, p. 731). **Syntactically,** ὅτι introduces a conjunctive dependent clause: "*that* God is greater than our heart" (ὅτι μείζων ἐστὶν ὁ θεὸς τῆς καρδίας ἡμῶν). It modifies the believer's emotional state, which is [bracketed] (cf. BDAG, s.v. "ὅτι" 1e, p. 731). Any semantical decision about this conjunctive ὅτι clause is dependent upon the decision made concerning the first ὅτι clause of verse 20a. Based upon our decision for the conjunctive ὅτι clause of verse 20a, this ὅτι clause is classified as epexegetical of verse 20a and thereby a technical (though ungrammatical) way to underscore God's knowing the depths of our heart (Brown, 457; Culy, 94). Believers should know by their selfless imitation of the love of Jesus that even if their consciences condemn them, God is greater than their hearts and knows everything about them. The NLT captures the author's core theological concern for verse 20 the best: "Even if we feel guilty, God is greater than our feelings."

Semantical Nugget: How should the ὅτι clause be rendered? If we assume that the first ὅτι is epexegetical, then this ὅτι would be classified as epexegetical:

"that God is greater than our heart" is epexegetical to "that whenever our heart condemns us" (see NET note). If we assume the first ὅτι is causal, then this ὅτι could also be causal, acting resumptively as well: "because if our hearts condemn us, *because* I repeat, God is greater than our hearts," or it could be indirect discourse following an elliptical verb "because if our hearts condemn us, *we know that* God is greater than our hearts" (KJV ASV; cf. NASB). Finally, if we redivide the first clause into an indefinite relative pronoun, then this second ὅτι would be classified as causal, "whenever our hearts condemn us; *for* God is greater than our hearts. All of these options are grammatically possible (NRSV NIV ESV). Yet the best option is to classify this ὅτι clause as epexegetical of verse 20a and thereby a technical (though ungrammatical) way to underscore God's knowing the depths of our heart (Brown, 457; Culy, 94).

ἐστίν: The Greek word ἐστίν is third person singular present active indicative from the verb εἰμί meaning "to be" or "to show how something is to be understood" (BDAG, s.v. "εἰμί" 2cα, p. 282). **Syntactically,** ἐστίν is the governing verb of this dependent conjunctive epexegetical ὅτι clause. The subject of the verb is the noun "God" (ὁ θεός). **Semantically,** ἐστίν is a gnomic present: "is" (cf. KJV NASB ESV NIV NET etc.). John reveals a timeless fact (W, 523): God is greater than our conscience.

3:20c καὶ [ὅτι] The Greek word καί is a conjunction meaning "and" (BDAG, s.v. "καί" 1b, p. 494). **Syntactically,** καί introduces a dependent conjunctive clause that links together two dependent clauses: "*and [that]* he knows all things" (καὶ [ὅτι] γινώσκει πάντα) is linked to "that God is greater than our heart." The elliptical [ὅτι] is inserted to visualize John's second reason why God answers a believer's prayer. **Semantically,** καί is a coordinating connector: "and" (KJV NASB ESV NIV NET etc.). It introduces additional information about God's awareness.

γινώσκει: The Greek word γινώσκει is third person singular present active indicative from the verb γινώσκω meaning "to have come to know" or "to know" or "to have come to the knowledge of something" (BDAG, s.v. "γινώσκω" 6aα, p. 200). **Syntactically,** γινώσκει is the governing verb of a dependent conjunctive epexegetical [ὅτι] clause. The subject of the verb is the noun "God" (ὁ θεός). **Semantically,** γινώσκει is a gnomic present: "he knows" (NRSV ESV NIV NLT CNT). John reveals a timeless fact about God (W, 523): God knows all things, including the heart of the believer. God's opinion is what matters.

3:21a ἐάν: The Greek word ἐάν is a conjunction meaning "if" (BDAG, s.v. "ἐάν" 1aα, p. 267). **Syntactically,** ἐάν identifies the clause as a dependent conjunctive clause. The entire clause, "Beloved, *if* our heart does not condemn us"

(Ἀγαπητοί, ἐὰν ἡ καρδία μὴ καταγινώσκῃ ἡμῶν), functions adverbially. It modifies the verb, "we have" (ἔχομεν). **Semantically,** ἐάν introduces the protasis of a third class condition: "if" (cf. KJV NASB ESV NIV NET etc.). The third class conditional clause has a level of uncertainly (W, 696). What is uncertain is made clear in the rest of the clause.

καταγινώσκῃ: The Greek word καταγινώσκῃ is third person singular present active subjunctive from the verb καταγινώσκω meaning "to condemn" or "to convict" (BDAG, s.v. "καταγινώσκω," p. 515). The verb is in the subjunctive because it is part of the ἐάν clause. **Syntactically,** καταγινώσκῃ is the governing verb of the dependent adverbial clause. The subject is "heart" (ἡ καρδία) and is a metaphor for the believer's conscience. **Semantically,** καταγινώσκῃ is a customary present: "*persistently* condemn" (W, 521) or "condemn" (KJV NASB ESV NIV NET etc.). In the probability that the believer's conscience does not bring guilt, they feel assured concerning their relationship with God.

Lexical Nugget: What does καταγινώσκω mean? The verb occurs three times in the New Testament (Gal. 2:11; 1 John 3:20, 21) and also four times in the LXX (Deut. 25:1; Prov. 28:11; Sir 14:2; 19:5). This verb is often used in situations of litigation in which military leaders (Josephus, *A.J.* 14.3.3 §46), judges (Deut. 25:1; Josephus *A.J.* 4.8.38 §287), or kings condemn people (Josephus, *A.J.* 8.2.2 §33; 10.7.2 §107). The term can also be used in contexts of self-condemnation (Sir 14:2; T. Gad 5:3). In this context, John is speaking of self-condemnation. Whether or not our personal conscience condemns us, it is God's opinion that truly matters.

3:21b ἔχομεν: The Greek word ἔχομεν is first person plural present active indicative from the verb ἔχω meaning "to have" or "to experience an inner condition" (BDAG, s.v. "ἔχω" 7aβ, p. 421). **Syntactically,** ἔχομεν is the main verb of the independent clause: "*we feel* confident before God" (παρρησίαν ἔχομεν πρὸς τὸν θεόν). The subject is an implied "we" embedded in the verb and refers to the readers who exhibit the selfless love of Jesus. The inner emotion experienced or felt is "confidence" (BDAG, s.v. "παρρησία" 3b, p. 781). **Semantically,** ἔχομεν is a gnomic present: "we feel" or "we have" (KJV NASB ESV NIV NET etc.). John discloses another timeless fact (W, 523): the believer whose conscience does not condemn feels confident before God. (For the first timeless fact, return to 3:20b.)

3:22a καί: The Greek word καί is a conjunction meaning "and so" (BDAG, s.v. "καί" 1bζ, p. 495). **Syntactically,** καί introduces an independent conjunctive clause: "*and so* whatever we ask for we will receive from him" (καὶ ὃ ἐὰν αἰτῶμεν λαμβάνομεν ἀπ' αὐτοῦ). **Semantically,** καί is a coordinating connector: "and" (KJV NASB ESV NIV NET etc.). It connects two clauses together.

Here John introduces a result that comes from the believer's confidence before God, which is fleshed out in the rest of the clause.

ὃ ἐάν: The Greek word ὃ is a neuter singular accusative from the relative pronoun ὅς meaning "what" (BDAG, s.v. "ὅς" 1jα, p. 727). The Greek word ἐάν is a conjunction meaning "ever" (BDAG, s.v. "ἐάν" 3, p. 268). Together ὃ ἐάν is translated "whatever." **Syntactically,** the Greek construction ὃ ἐάν is a dependent indefinite relative clause. The entire clause "whatever we ask" (ὃ ἐὰν αἰτῶμεν) is the direct object of the verb "we receive" (λαμβάνομεν). So the ὃ ἐάν clause is placed in parentheses in order to visualize its contribution to the independent clause. The rest of this clause is rather significant.

αἰτῶμεν: The Greek word αἰτῶμεν is first person plural present active subjunctive from the verb αἰτέω meaning "to ask," "to ask for" or "to ask for, with a claim on receipt of an answer" (BDAG, s.v. "αἰτέω," p. 30). The verb is in the subjunctive because it is part of the ἐάν clause. **Syntactically,** αἰτῶμεν is the governing verb of the dependent indefinite relative clause. The subject is an implied "we" embedded in the verb and refers to John and his readers. **Semantically,** αἰτῶμεν is an instantaneous present: "We ask for" or "we ask" (cf. KJV NASB ESV NIV NET etc.). The act of asking is completed at the moment of praying (W, 517). What is rather significant is the response evident in the next verb.

λαμβάνομεν: The Greek word λαμβάνομεν is first person plural present active indicative from the verb λαμβάνω meaning "to receive," "to get," "to obtain" or "to be a receiver" (BDAG, s.v. "λαμβάνω" 10c, p. 585). **Syntactically,** λαμβάνομεν is the main verb of the independent clause "And (whatever we ask for) *we will receive* from him" (λαμβάνομεν ἀπ᾽ αὐτοῦ). The phrase "from him" refers to God. **Semantically,** λαμβάνομεν is a futuristic present: "*will receive*" (NLT) or "we receive" (cf. KJV NASB ESV NIV NET etc.). John describes "an event that is *wholly* subsequent to the time of speaking" (W, 536). Followers of Jesus (= God's children) *will* receive whatever we ask of God.

Theological Nugget: What does it mean that God gives followers of Jesus what they ask? We find this theme of asking God for things other places in the New Testament (Mark 11:24; John 14:14–16; 16:13–26; see also James 1:5–6). Here "receive from him" is linked to the confidence that believers can have when they talk with God. A persistent lifestyle of love guarantees a confident conscience. This also seems to be a common theme throughout the New Testament (John 9:31; James 5:16; see Brown, 461). God will consider whatever the believer who is practicing a lifestyle of love asks for. So not only can believers have confidence before God when he appears (v. 2:28; cf. 3:2), but they can also have confidence now. Followers of Jesus know that God hears them, listens to them, and answers them when they talk with God.

3:22b ὅτι: The Greek word ὅτι is a conjunction meaning "because" (BDAG, s.v. "ὅτι" 4a, p. 732). **Syntactically,** ὅτι introduces a dependent conjunctive clause: "*because* we persist in keeping his commandments" (ὅτι τὰς ἐντολὰς αὐτοῦ τηροῦμεν). The entire clause functions adverbially. It modifies the verb, "we receive" (λαμβάνομεν). **Semantically,** ὅτι is causal: "because" (cf. KJV NASB ESV NIV NET etc.). It provides the reason why God considers the request of the believer (W, 460), which is highlighted in the next verb.

τηροῦμεν: The Greek word τηροῦμεν is first person plural present active indicative from the verb τηρέω meaning "to keep" or "to observe" or "to persist in obedience" (BDAG, s.v. "τηρέω" 3, p. 1002). **Syntactically,** τηροῦμεν is the governing verb of the compound dependent adverbial ὅτι clause. The subject of the verb is an implied "we" embedded in the verb and refers to John and his readers who follow Jesus's example of selfless love. **Semantically,** τηροῦμεν is a customary present: "we *persist* in keeping" or "we keep" (KJV ASV NASB ESV NET CNT) or "we obey" (NRSV NIV NLT). It describes a pattern of behavior (W, 521). The reason God answers a believer's prayer is because they *continually strive to obey* God in their life. The theme of keeping (τηρέω) God's commands first appeared in chapter 2 (vv. 3a, 4a, 5a).

3:22c καὶ [ὅτι]: The Greek word καί is a conjunction meaning "and" (BDAG, s.v. "καί" 1b, p. 494). **Syntactically,** καί introduces a dependent conjunctive clause that links together two compound dependent adverbial clauses: "*because* we persist in keeping his commands" (ὅτι τὰς ἐντολὰς αὐτοῦ τηροῦμεν) is linked to "and [*because*] we persist in doing the things that are pleasing to him" (καὶ [ὅτι] τὰ ἀρεστὰ ἐνώπιον αὐτοῦ ποιοῦμεν). The elliptical [ὅτι] is inserted to visualize John's second reason why God answers a believer's prayer. **Semantically,** καί is a coordinating conjunction that introduces additional information about why God answers prayer.

ποιοῦμεν: The Greek word ποιοῦμεν is first person plural present active indicative from the verb ποιέω meaning "to do" or "to bring about" or "to undertake or do something that brings about an event" (BDAG, s.v. "ποιέω" 2e, p. 840), **Syntactically,** ποιοῦμεν is the governing verb of the conjunctive dependent adverbial [ὅτι] clause. The subject of the verb is an implied "we" embedded in the verb and refers to John and his readers who follow Jesus's example of selfless love. **Semantically,** ποιοῦμεν is a customary present: "we *persist in* doing" or "do" (cf. KJV NASB ESV NIV NET etc.). It describes a pattern of behavior (W, 521). The prayers are answered for any believer who undertakes or makes it a practice to follow Jesus's example of selflessness.

Syntactical Nugget: Are the two clauses: "we persist in keeping his commands" (τὰς ἐντολὰς αὐτοῦ τηροῦμεν) and "we persist in doing what is pleasing in his sight" (τὰ ἀρεστὰ ἐνώπιον αὐτοῦ ποιοῦμεν) two distinct ideas or are they equivalent ideas? Westcott suggests that this is a "twofold aspect of right actions." It is both a work of obedience and a work of freedom (Westcott, 119). Smalley suggests that they represent "obedience and willing service" (Smalley, 205). On the other hand, it could be that these two phrases taken together are an example of a figure of speech called a synonymous parallelism, a common staple of Hebrew poetry where a second phrase poetically explains or identifies a first phrase. We see examples of these two phrases used in this way in the LXX. (1) The Exodus generation was expected to "do what is pleasing before God" and "keep his commands" (Exod. 15:26; cf. Tob 4:21). (2) Wisdom is described as understanding what is pleasing in God's sight and what is right according to God's commandments (Wis 9:9). (3) Hezekiah did what was pleasing to the Lord as he was commanded by God's prophet Isaiah (Sir 48:22; cf. Isa. 38:3). It seems John is using the two phrases in a similar way to get across a singular idea. Therefore, to keep God's love command is to do what is pleasing to God (Brown, 462).

3:23a καί: The Greek word καί is a conjunction meaning "and" (BDAG, s.v. "καί" 1b, p. 494). **Syntactically,** καί introduces a conjunctive independent clause: "*And this is his (= God's) commandment*" (καὶ αὕτη ἐστὶν ἡ ἐντολὴ αὐτοῦ). **Semantically,** καί is a marker that introduces additional information about the commandments of God with loose connections to the previous independent clause. The translation of καί appears in most translations as "and" (KJV ASV NASB NRSV ESV NIV NLT CNT), but at least one translation interprets καί as a transitional conjunction, "now" (NET). Nevertheless, John adds information about God's command.

ἐστίν: The Greek word ἐστίν is third person singular present active indicative from the verb εἰμί meaning "to be" or "to be in close connection with" (BDAG, s.v. "ἐστίν" 2a, p. 283). **Syntactically,** ἐστίν is the main verb of the independent conjunctive clause. The subject of the verb is the demonstrative pronoun "this" (αὕτη), due to the grammatical priority of pronouns (W, 42–43). **Semantically,** ἐστίν is a gnomic statement: "is" (cf. KJV NASB ESV NIV NET etc.). It reveals a timeless commandment (W, 523). This construction (αὕτη ἐστίν) occurs often in 1 John. It is a way John highlights his main ideas (Brown, 192). It is cataphoric in that what John says in the following ἵνα clauses is rather important because, while the theme of keeping (τηρέω) God's commands first appeared in chapter 2 (vv. 3a, 4a, 5a), John specifies what the command is via the next two ἵνα clauses.

3:23b ἵνα: The Greek word ἵνα is a conjunction meaning "that" (BDAG, s.v. "ἵνα" 2e, p. 476). **Syntactically,** ἵνα introduces a conjunctive dependent clause, "*namely, that* we will believe in the name of his Son, Jesus, who is the Christ, and persist in loving one another" (ἵνα πιστεύσωμεν τῷ ὀνόματι τοῦ υἱοῦ αὐτοῦ Ἰησοῦ Χριστοῦ καὶ ἀγαπῶμεν ἀλλήλους). The entire ἵνα clause is substantival. It modifies the demonstrative pronoun "this" (αὕτη). **Semantically,** ἵνα is an appositional conjunction: *"namely,* that" (KJV ASV NASB NRSV ESV NET CNT). It explains the demonstrative pronoun "this" (αὕτη). It is almost idiomatic within John's writings (W, 475). The explanation is found in the next verb.

πιστεύσωμεν: The Greek word πιστεύσωμεν is first person plural aorist active subjunctive from the verb πιστεύω meaning "to believe" or "to trust" or "to entrust oneself to an entity in complete confidence" (BDAG, s.v. "πιστεύω" 2aα, p. 817). "We believe" (πιστεύσωμεν) is in the subjunctive because ἵνα takes a subjunctive verb. **Syntactically,** πιστεύσωμεν is the governing verb of the dependent adjectival ἵνα clause. **Semantically,** πιστεύσωμεν is a constative aorist: "we believe" (cf. NASB ESV NET). Others render πιστεύσωμεν as "we should believe" (KJV ASV NRSV CNT), or "we must believe" (NLT) or "to believe" (NIV). The rendering "we believe" as a constative aorist, suggests that John views belief as an event that covers a multitude of actions (W, 557). John tells his readers that the first part of God's command is belief. God's command is that believers place their faith in Jesus and love one another (cf. 3:11c ἵνα). The actual object of belief is the "name of Jesus" (τῷ ὀνόματι τοῦ υἱοῦ αὐτοῦ Ἰησοῦ Χριστοῦ), which is in the dative case rather than the accusative. This is because the verb πιστεύω takes a direct object in the dative case. And yet there is another aspect to this command evident in the next clause.

Lexical and Text-Critical Nugget: What does it mean to "believe in the name of his Son Jesus, who is the Christ"? In John's letters it means to believe in his messiahship (1 John 2:22–23; 4:15; 5:1, 5) and his humanity (1 John 4:2; 2 John 7). So for John, in his letters, it seems that believing in the name of Jesus is acknowledging his position as God's Messiah and accepting the physical person of Jesus (Brown, 462). This belief is foundational to having assurance before God. No one can properly love their fellow believers unless this faith in Jesus exists first. This belief also moves beyond mere intellectual ascent and refers to putting one's *total* trust in Jesus (Culy, 97).

3:23c καὶ [ἵνα]: The Greek word καί is a conjunction meaning "and" (BDAG, s.v. "καί" 1b, p. 494). **Syntactically,** καί introduces a second dependent ἵνα clause: *"and [that]* we *persist in* loving one another" (καὶ [ἵνα] ἀγαπῶμεν ἀλλήλους). An elliptical [ἵνα] is inserted to visualize John's second substantival comment. **Semantically,** καί is a marker to indicate additional information about God's command. It links two content clauses together: *"that* we believe in the name of his Son, Jesus Christ and [*that*] we love one another." This second aspect of the command is underscored in the next verb.

ἀγαπῶμεν: The Greek word ἀγαπῶμεν is first person plural present active subjunctive from the verb ἀγαπάω meaning "to love" or "to have a warm regard for and interest in another" person (BDAG, s.v. "ἀγαπάω" 1aα, p. 5). The ἵνα is inserted to signal a second epexegetical clause; "we love" (ἀγαπῶμεν) is in the subjunctive because ἵνα requires the subjunctive. **Syntactically,** ἀγαπῶμεν is the governing verb of the dependent adjectival [ἵνα] clause. The subject is an implied "we" embedded in the verbal ending and refers to John and the believers who put their faith in the name of Jesus. **Semantically,** ἀγαπῶμεν is a customary present: "we persist in loving" or "love" (cf. KJV NASB ESV NIV NET etc.). It indicates a pattern of behavior (W, 521). Together the two ἵνα clauses emphasize two expectations: believers are to trust in Jesus's messiahship and continually love each other with sincere actions. When belief in Jesus and love for others are paired together, then the individual can have assurance before God. "The call to believe," according to Yarbrough, "is an ethical imperative" (Yarbrough, 214).

3:23d καθώς: The Greek word καθώς is a conjunction meaning "just as" or "as" (BDAG, s.v. "καθώς" 1, p. 493). **Syntactically,** καθώς introduces a dependent conjunctive clause. The entire dependent καθώς clause, "*just as* he (= Jesus) gave the (= God's) commandment to us" (καθὼς ἔδωκεν ἐντολὴν ἡμῖν) functions adverbially modifying the verb "we love" (ἀγαπῶμεν). **Semantically,** καθώς is comparative: "just as" (NASB NRSV ESV NET NLT CNT). Believers who trust in Jesus and continually love each other with sincere actions are compared with being obedient to God. When belief in Jesus and love for others are paired together, then the individual can have assurance when they stand before God.

ἔδωκεν: The Greek word ἔδωκεν is third person singular aorist active indicative from the verb δίδωμι meaning "to give" (BDAG, s.v. "δίδωμι" 8, p. 242) or "to command" where the translation of ἔδωκεν is determined by the object ἐντολήν (see BDAG, s.v. "δίδωμι" 17a, p. 243). **Syntactically,** ἔδωκεν is the main verb of the dependent adverbial καθώς clause. The subject is an implied "he" embedded in the verb and can either refer to the God the Father, or Jesus (See Theological Nugget below). **Semantically,** ἔδωκεν is a constative aorist: "he gave" (KJV ASV NET) or "he commanded" (NASB NIV NLT). It describes an event as a whole (W, 557). John points to multiple actions in the past that are ultimately summed up with the simple statement: God gave us *the* command.

Theological Nugget: Who gave the love command, God the Father or Jesus? John is, once again, ambiguous. Perhaps the ambiguity is intentional to speak of the Godhead in general (Painter, 250). But this seems unlikely due to John's frequent use of αὐτός for God the Father and ἐκεῖνος for Jesus in 1 John, though there are exceptions (cf. 2:12; 3:2). Two other options exist.

On the one hand in John's Gospel, Jesus commanded his disciples to love each other (13:34; 15:10, 12, 17). So Jesus seems to be the possible referent. On the other hand in 1 John, the commands come from God the Father (2:3, 4; 3:22, 24; 5:3; 2 John 2–4). The reason that God the Father is the referent is twofold. First, the demonstrative pronoun, "that one" (ἐκεῖνος), is *typically* used when Jesus is referred to in chapter 3 (vv. 2, 5, 7, 16; cf. 2:6). Second, contextually this command encompasses both love for others and belief in the Son. It would seem strange, *though not impossible*, that Jesus would issue the command to believe in his own name.

3:24a καί: The Greek word καί is a conjunction meaning "and" (BDAG, s.v. "καί" 1b, p. 494). **Syntactically,** καί introduces an independent conjunctive clause: "*and* the one who *persists in* keeping his (= God's) commands abides in him (= him)" (καὶ ὁ τηρῶν τὰς ἐντολὰς αὐτοῦ ἐν αὐτῷ μένει). While a translation of καί appears in some translations (KJV ASV NET), others leave καί untranslated (NASB NRSV ESV NIV NLT). **Semantically,** καί is a coordinating connective: "and" (KJV NASB ESV NIV NET etc.). It introduces some additional thoughts about the believer who keeps the commands of God.

τηρῶν: The Greek word τηρῶν is a nominative masculine singular present active participle from the verb τηρέω meaning "to keep" or "to observe" or "to persist in obedience" (BDAG, s.v. "τηρέω" 3, p. 1002). **Syntactically,** τηρῶν, "the one who persists in keeping," functions substantivally as the subject of the verb "remains" (μένει). The entire participial phrase is placed in parentheses to underscore its contribution to the independent clause. **Semantically,** τηρῶν is a gnomic present with a customary present force: "the one who *persists in* keeping" or "the one who keeps" (KJV ASV NASB ESV NET CNT) or "who obeys" (NRSV NIV NLT). John presents a timeless maxim about people (W, 521, 523). The timeless truth that exists for any person who "keeps" or "lives" a lifestyle of obedience is made clear with the next clause.

μένει: The Greek word μένει is third person singular present active indicative from the verb μένω meaning "to remain," "to abide," "to continue," or is used of "someone who does not leave" (BDAG, s.v. "μένω" 1aβ, p. 631). **Syntactically,** μένει is the main verb of the independent clause. The subject is the participial phrase, "the one who persists in keeping his (= God's) commandments" (ὁ τηρῶν τὰς ἐντολὰς αὐτοῦ). John speaks of the believer who persists in keeping God's commands. The referent, however, is ambiguous (see Theological Nugget 3:23d). **Semantically,** μένει is a gnomic present with a customary present force: "*continues to* remain" or "remains" (NLT). Some render μένει as "abides" (KJV ASV NASB ESV CNT) or "lives" (NIV). Regardless of how it is rendered, John once again shares a timeless truth (W, 521, 523). Anyone who persists in obedience concerning their belief in Jesus (ἵνα; v. 23b) and loves their fellow believers (ἵνα; v. 23c) has an enduring or guaranteed relationship with God. But there is yet another guarantee evident in the next clause.

^{3:24b} καί: The Greek word καί is a conjunction meaning "and" (BDAG, s.v. "καί" 1b, p. 494). **Syntactically,** καί introduces an independent conjunctive clause: "*and* this one (= God) [abides] with him (or her)" (καὶ [μένει] αὐτὸς ἐν αὐτῷ). **Semantically,** καί is a coordinating connective: "and" (KJV NASB ESV NIV NET etc.). It is a marker that introduces additional information about those who persist in keeping God's command. John adds to God's guaranteed relationship.

[μένει]: The Greek word μένει is third person singular present active indicative from the verb μένω meaning "to remain," "to abide," "to continue," or is used of "someone who does not leave" (BDAG, s.v. "μένω" 1aβ, p. 631). **Syntactically,** μένει is an ellipsis assumed from the previous clause and serves as the main verb of the independent conjunctive clause. The subject is the emphatic pronoun, "this one" (αὐτός), and refers to God. The pronoun is already embedded in the elliptical verb and therefore does not need to be explicitly stated. Its presence heightens the intimacy of the relationship between God and the follower of Jesus who loves others. **Semantically,** μένει is again a gnomic present with a customary present force: "*continues to* abide." John shares a timeless truth (W, 521, 523). So not only is God's relationship guaranteed with believers, a believer's relationship with God is guaranteed for anyone who follows his commands.

^{3:24c} καί: The Greek word καί is a conjunction meaning "and" (BDAG, s.v. "καί" 1b, p. 494). **Syntactically,** καί introduces a conjunctive independent clause, "*and* by this we know that God abides in us" (καὶ ἐν τούτῳ γινώσκομεν ὅτι μένει ἐν ἡμῖν). **Semantically,** καί is a coordinating connective: "and." While a translation of καί appears in some translations (NRSV NLT), others leave it untranslated (KJV ASV NASB ESV NIV). At least one translation renders it as a transitional καί similar to that found in 1:5a (NET). Regardless of the presence of καί, the point is that they can also be assured by the continual presence of the Spirit of God in their life.

ἐν τούτῳ: The Greek word ἐν is a preposition meaning "in" (BDAG, s.v. "ἐν" 5b, p. 328). The Greek word τούτῳ is declined as a dative singular neuter from the demonstrative pronoun οὗτος meaning "this one" (BDAG, s.v. "οὗτος" 1bα, p. 741). **Syntactically,** ἐν τούτῳ introduces an independent prepositional clause: "by this we know" (ἐν τούτῳ γινώσκομεν). As noted before, this prepositional construction occurs frequently in 1 John (2:3, 4, 5 [2x], 3:10, 16, 19, 24; 4:2, 9, 10, 13, 17; 5:2) and is an important structural marker. **Semantically,** ἐν τούτῳ can either be anaphoric, pointing back to a preceding discussion, or cataphoric, pointing forward. Since there is a prepositional phrase "by the Spirit" (ἐκ τοῦ πνεύματος) immediately following our current clause, the phrase is cataphoric and points forward to the prepositional phrase in 3:24d ἐκ τοῦ πνεύματος, which provides the content of the demonstrative pronoun, "this" (τούτῳ; Brown, 464; Culy, 98).

γινώσκομεν: The Greek word γινώσκομεν is first person plural present active indicative from the verb γινώσκω meaning "to know" or "to arrive at a knowledge of someone or something" (BDAG, s.v. "γινώσκω" 1c, p. 200). **Syntactically,** γινώσκομεν is the main verb of the independent clause. The subject of the verb is an implied "we" embedded in the verb and refers to John and his readers. **Semantically,** γινώσκομεν is a customary present: "we know" (cf. KJV NASB ESV NIV NET etc.). John's focus is on an ongoing awareness that believers have (W, 521). That awareness or knowledge is made clear in the next ὅτι clause.

ὅτι: The Greek word ὅτι is a conjunction meaning "that" or is used to identify content after a verb of mental perception (BDAG, s.v. "ὅτι" 1c, p. 731). **Syntactically,** ὅτι introduces a dependent conjunctive clause: "*that* he (= God) abides in us" (ὅτι μένει ἐν ἡμῖν). The entire ὅτι clause functions substantivally as the direct object of the verb, "we know" (γινώσκομεν; cf. W, 454). The clause is placed in parentheses in order to visualize its contribution to the independent clause. **Semantically,** ὅτι is an indirect discourse marker: "that" (cf. KJV NASB ESV NIV NET etc.; cf. W, 456). The entire ὅτι clause provides the content of the verb "we know" (γινώσκομεν). The specifics are found in the governing verb of this ὅτι clause.

μένει: The Greek word μένει is third person singular present active indicative from the verb μένω meaning "to remain," "to abide," "to continue," or is used of "someone who does not leave" (BDAG, s.v. "μένω" 1aβ, p. 631). **Syntactically,** μένει is the governing verb of the dependent substantival ὅτι clause. The subject is an implied "he" embedded in the verb and refers to God. **Semantically,** μένει is a customary present: "abides." It emphasizes an ongoing state (W, 521). While some render μένει as "abides" (KJV ASV NASB NRSV ESV CNT), others prefer "lives" (NIV NLT) or "resides" (NET). Regardless of how μένει is rendered, John underscores that his readers know that God abides in them. Note that in 3:24a, John speaks of Christians relating to God, but here as in 3:24b God is relating to Christians. The *source* of this awareness is made known in the next clause.

3:24d ἐκ: The Greek word ἐκ is a preposition meaning "from" or "of" or is used to denote origin (BDAG, s.v. "ἐκ" 3cβ, p. 297). **Syntactically,** ἐκ τοῦ πνεύματος is a prepositional phrase that functions adjectivally. It modifies the demonstrative pronoun, "this" (τούτῳ), which provides information or insight. **Semantically,** ἐκ indicates means: "by" (cf. KJV NASB ESV NIV NET etc.). It tells how believers know they have an abiding relationship with God (for the semantic categories of the preposition ἐκ, cf. W, 371–72). So the source of a believer's assurance is through the presence of God's Spirit in their lives, a point John underscores earlier in the letter (cf. 2:20, 27).

οὗ: The Greek word οὗ is a genitive singular neuter from the relative pronoun ὅς meaning "who" (BDAG, s.v. "ὅς" 1aα, p. 726). **Syntactically,** οὗ introduces a dependent adjectival relative clause: "*whom* he has given us" (οὗ ἡμῖν ἔδωκεν), which modifies its antecedent "the Spirit" (τοῦ πνεύματος). Technically, the relative pronoun should be in the accusative case, since it is the direct object of the verb "he gave" (ἔδωκεν); however, οὗ is in the genitive case. Sometimes a relative pronoun takes on the case of its antecedent rather than its grammatical case. This is called attraction and occurs over fifty times in the New Testament; it seems to be an idiomatic phenomenon with no linguistic impact (cf. BDAG, s.v. "ὅς" 1aα, p. 726; Culy, 99; W, 337–39). The relative clause gives us some additional information about the Spirit of God also evident in the next verb.

ἔδωκεν: The Greek word ἔδωκεν is third person singular aorist active indicative from the verb δίδωμι meaning "to give" or "to give something out" (BDAG, s.v. "δίδωμι" 2, p. 242). **Syntactically,** ἔδωκεν is the governing verb of the dependent adjectival relative clause. The subject of the verb is an implied "he" embedded in the verb and refers to God. **Semantically,** ἔδωκεν is a consummative aorist: "he *has* given" (KJV NASB NRSV ESV NET CNT). The stress is on the cessation of God's giving the Spirit because the act was already presented as having happened in 2:20, 27 (W, 559). John then draws attention once again to an event, namely, the time when God anointed his readers with his Spirit (2:20, 27). God himself gave us the Spirit.

1 JOHN 4:1–6

Big Greek Idea: John's expectation for followers of Jesus to be discerning in what to believe about Jesus's humanity and messiahship is balanced with an affirmation of divine protection from fraudulent and misguided teaching, as well as the ability of God's children to pay attention to truth and to distinguish between truth and deceit.

Structural Overview: John transitions (ἀγαπητοί) to another set of *expectations* (vv. 1–3) Rather (ἀλλά) than trusting any spirit (teaching; μὴ . . . πιστεύετε), followers of Jesus are to be discerning (δοκιμάζετε) in what they believe because (ὅτι) there are many misguided people in the world (ἐξεληλύθασιν) who promote fake and fraudulent information about God (v. 1). John then provides a helpful way to differentiate good and bad information (ἐν τούτῳ). He makes it clear (γινώσκετε) that teachings about Jesus as a human Messiah are in conflict (καί) with false teachings of the misguided people of the world (μὴ ὁμολογεῖ) about Jesus (vv. 2–3).

John's mood then shifts to a twofold *affirmation* (τεκνία; vv. 4–6). First as members of God's family, followers of Jesus are protected (νενικήκατε) because (ὅτι) God is greater than any misguided group of people of the world (εἰσίν; vv. 4–5b). Second, in contrast to the people who promote (λαλοῦσιν) and pay attention (ἀκούει) to ill-advised and mistaken teaching of the world (v. 5b–c), God's family pays attention to (ἀκούει) and distinguishes (γινώσκομεν) truth from deceit (v. 6).

Outline:

> Discernment Is Expected of Followers of Jesus (vv. 1–3)
>> Complacency is not an option (v. 1)
>> Teachings are to be compared (vv. 2–3)
> Affirmation Exists for Followers of Jesus (vv. 4–6)

CLAUSAL OUTLINE FOR 1 JOHN 4:1–6

4:1a Ἀγαπητοί, μὴ παντὶ πνεύματι **πιστεύετε**,
4:1a Beloved, **do** not **believe** every spirit,

4:1b ἀλλὰ **δοκιμάζετε** τὰ πνεύματα
4:1b **but test** the spirits

> 4:1c **εἰ** ἐκ τοῦ θεοῦ **ἐστιν**,
> 4:1c *to determine* **whether they are** from God,

>> 4:1d **ὅτι** πολλοὶ ψευδοπροφῆται **ἐξεληλύθασιν** εἰς τὸν κόσμον.
>> 4:1d **because** many false prophets **have gone out** into the world.

4:2a ἐν τούτῳ **γινώσκετε** τὸ πνεῦμα τοῦ θεοῦ·
4:2a By this **you know** the Spirit of God;

4:2b πᾶν πνεῦμα . . . ἐκ τοῦ θεοῦ **ἐστιν**,
4:2b every spirit . . . **is** from God,

        4:2c **ὃ ὁμολογεῖ** Ἰησοῦν Χριστὸν ἐν σαρκὶ ἐληλυθότα,
        4:2c **that** *repeatedly* **acknowledges** Jesus *to be* the Christ who has
          come in flesh,

4:3a καὶ πᾶν πνεῦμα . . . ἐκ τοῦ θεοῦ οὐκ **ἔστιν**·
4:3a but every spirit . . . **is** not from God;

        4:3b **ὃ** μὴ **ὁμολογεῖ** τὸν Ἰησοῦν [ἐν σαρκὶ ἐληλυθότα]
        4:3b **that** does not *repeatedly* **claim** Jesus [has come in the flesh]

4:3c καὶ τοῦτό **ἐστιν** τὸ [πνεῦμα] τοῦ ἀντιχρίστου,
4:3c and this **is** the *spirit* of the Antichrist,

    4:3d **ὃ ἀκηκόατε** (ὅτι ἔρχεται),
    4:3d *about* **which you have heard** (that it is coming),

    4:3e καὶ [ὃ] νῦν ἐν τῷ κόσμῳ **ἐστὶν** ἤδη.
    4:3e and [*which*] **is** now in the world already.

4:4a ὑμεῖς ἐκ τοῦ θεοῦ **ἐστε**, τεκνία,
4:4a **You** *yourselves* **are** from God, little children,

4:4b καὶ **νενικήκατε** αὐτούς,
4:4b and **you have overcome** them (= antichrists),

    4:4c **ὅτι** μείζων **ἐστὶν** (ὁ ἐν ὑμῖν) ἢ (ὁ ἐν τῷ κόσμῳ).
    4:4c **because** the one (= Spirit of God) who [*is*] in you **is** greater than
      the one (= spirit of the Antichrist) who [*is*] in the world.

4:5a αὐτοὶ ἐκ τοῦ κόσμου **εἰσίν**·
4:5a **They** (= antichrists) themselves **are** from the world;

4:5b διὰ τοῦτο ἐκ τοῦ κόσμου **λαλοῦσιν**
4:5b therefore **they speak** *regularly* from the world's perspective

4:5c καὶ ὁ κόσμος αὐτῶν **ἀκούει**.
4:5c and the world **listens** *regularly* to them.

4:6a ἡμεῖς ἐκ τοῦ θεοῦ **ἐσμεν·**
4:6a **We** ourselves **are** from God;

4:6b (ὁ γινώσκων τὸν θεὸν) **ἀκούει** ἡμῶν,
4:6b (the person who knows God) **listens** to us,

4:6c (ὃς οὐκ ἔστιν ἐκ τοῦ θεοῦ) οὐκ **ἀκούει** ἡμῶν.
4:6c (whoever is not from God) **does** not **listen** to us.

4:6d ἐκ τούτου **γινώσκομεν** τὸ πνεῦμα τῆς ἀληθείας καὶ τὸ πνεῦμα
τῆς πλάνης.
4:6d From this **we know** the spirit of truth and the spirit of deceit.

Syntax Explained for 1 John 4:1–6

4:1a πιστεύετε: The Greek word πιστεύετε is a second person plural present active imperative from the verb πιστεύω meaning "to believe" or "to consider something to be true and therefore worthy of one's trust" (BDAG, s.v. "πιστεύω" 1b, p. 816). **Syntactically,** πιστεύετε is the main verb of the independent clause: "Beloved, *do* not *believe* every spirit" (ἀγαπητοί, μὴ παντὶ πνεύματι πιστεύετε). The subject of the imperative is an implied "you" and directed at John's readers. In this case the vocative "beloved" (ἀγαπητοί) plus the imperative clearly marks off the beginning of a new paragraph and a new train of thought. John is stressing the responsibility that believers have to discern true teaching from false teaching (Culy, 100). This is the second of three vocatives of direct address (3:21 and 4:7). Here, it begins a new section. **Semantically,** the negated (μὴ) πιστεύετε is an imperative of prohibition (W, 487): "do *not* believe" (cf. KJV NRSV ESV NIV NET etc.). John forbids his readers to believe every spirit. Perhaps he is telling them not to be naïve. The present tense is meant to communicate that John's command is to be an ongoing process (W, 715). John's readers are to be persistent in discerning what to believe.

Theological Nugget: What does John mean when he says, "test the spirits"? In 1 John 3:24, the word πνεῦμα was used to refer to the Spirit of God and the true wisdom and knowledge that he provides for the believer. That idea is expanded here. Not every teaching that sounds spiritual comes from the Spirit of God. There are false spirits that spread error, which was evident in the life and teaching of the secessionists who were teaching untrue ideas about the nature of Jesus and stirring up hostility in the church. This dualism is not unique to John (cf. T. Jud., 20:1, 3; 1Q28 III, 17b–21; 1Q28 IV, 15–16). The point is that not every teaching that sounds spiritual comes from God. Therefore, believers need to learn how to practice discernment.

⁴:¹ᵇ ἀλλά: The Greek word ἀλλά is a conjunction meaning "but" (BDAG, s.v. "ἀλλά" 1a, p. 44). **Syntactically,** ἀλλά identifies the clause as a conjunctive independent clause: "*but* test the spirits" (ἀλλὰ δοκιμάζετε τὰ πνεύματα). It typically follows after a negative like "do not believe" (μὴ ... πιστεύετε). **Semantically,** ἀλλά is contrastive: "but" (cf. KJV NRSV ESV NIV NET etc.). The clause contrasts John's command against spiritually naïvety with another command.

δοκιμάζετε: The Greek word δοκιμάζετε is a second person plural present active imperative from the verb δοκιμάζω meaning "to put to the test" or "to make a critical examination of something to determine genuineness" (BDAG, s.v. "δοκιμάζω" 1, p. 255). This is the only time "test" (δοκιμάζω) is found in John's writings. It has the idea of evaluating or discerning what is true from what is false. **Syntactically,** δοκιμάζετε is the main verb of the conjunctive independent clause. The subject of the imperative is an implied "you" embedded in the verb and directed at John's readers. **Semantically,** δοκιμάζετε is an imperative of command: "test" (cf. KJV NRSV ESV NIV NET etc.). Believers are expected not to be spiritually naïve but to think critically about messages purported to be from God. Believers have a responsibility not to believe every teaching about Jesus, but to put those teachings to a test so that they do not fall into theological error about Jesus.

Theological Nugget: What does John mean when he says, "but test the spirits"? Throughout the Old Testament and into the Second Temple period, prophecy is linked dualistically to either the Spirit of God (2 Chron. 15:1; Ezek. 2:2; Mic. 3:8; Zech. 7:12) or a false or lying spirit (2 Kings 22:22–24). A non biblical work, the Testament of Judah, warns that "two spirits await the opportunity with humanity: the spirit of truth and the spirit of error" (20:1–3). Qumran literature also assumes that two heavenly forces influence human beings (cf. 1 Q28 III, 17b–21): the spirits of truth (principally Michael) and the spirits of falsehood (principally Belial). In fact, 1Q28 later says, "The character and fate of all humankind reside with the these spirits. All the hosts of humanity, generation by generation, are heirs to these spiritual divisions, walking according to their ways; the outworking of every deed inheres in these divisions according to each person's natural heritage" (IV, 15–16, WAC, 131). Therefore, just because someone claimed that their message was from God, didn't mean that it was. In the same way, the New Testament era prophets spoke "in the Spirit," claiming inspiration from God. In 1 Thessalonians 5:19–22, Paul warns of twin dangers or errors. The first would be to quench the Spirit, or not allow the true prophets to speak their message, since it was from God. So, Paul tells them to refuse to censor the prophets. The second was that just because someone claims to be speaking from the true Spirit of God, doesn't mean that they are. So, Paul tells the believer to test every claim and hold fast to what is true and to reject what is false. The same idea exists here in 1 John. Believers should not believe an idea just because someone claims a message is from God. They should use the anointing that God has given them to discern true teaching from error. Unfortunately, the fraudulent clothe their teaching about Jesus in spiritual language and claim inspiration from the Spirit of God, when in fact they are inspired by the spirit of the Antichrist. Interestingly, an early Christian work, the Didache, gives the opposite advice and tells the believer to refuse to evaluate those who claim to speak by the Spirit (cf. Did. 11.7).

4:1c εἰ: The Greek word εἰ is a conjunction meaning "whether" (BDAG, s.v. "εἰ" 5bα, p. 278). **Syntactically,** εἰ identifies the clause as a conjunctive dependent clause. The entire dependent clause, "to determine (lit. "if") they are from God" (εἰ ἐκ τοῦ θεοῦ ἐστιν) functions adverbially. It modifies the verb, "test" (δοκιμάζετε). Translated "whether" (KJV ASV) or "to see whether" (NASB NARSV ESV NIV CNT), if (εἰ) is a marker of an indirect question (BDAG, s.v. "εἰ" 5bα, p. 278; cf. Culy, 100). John exhorts or expects (δοκιμάζετε) his readers to test the spirits by asking the question, "Is the prophecy or teaching from God?"

ἐστίν: The Greek word ἐστίν is third person singular present active indicative from the verb εἰμί meaning "to be" or "to have a point of origin," that is, "to come from somewhere" (BDAG, s.v. "εἰμί" 8, p. 285). **Syntactically,** ἐστίν is the governing verb of the dependent adverbial conjunctive clause. The subject of the verb is an elliptical "the spirits" [τὰ πνεύματα] implied from the previous clause. The subject is plural and the verb is singular because neuter plural nouns always take a singular verb (W, 399–400). **Semantically,** ἐστίν is a verb of origin: "be from" or "are from" (cf. KJV NASB ESV NIV NET etc.). John expects believers to question the origin of a teaching or prophecy: Is it from God?

4:1d ὅτι: The Greek word ὅτι is a conjunction meaning "because" (BDAG, s.v. "ὅτι" 4a, p. 732). **Syntactically,** ὅτι introduces a dependent conjunctive ὅτι clause: "*because* many false prophets have gone out into the world" (ὅτι πολλοὶ ψευδοπροφῆται ἐξεληλύθασιν εἰς τὸν κόσμον). The entire clause functions adverbially. It modifies the verb "test" (δοκιμάζετε). **Semantically,** ὅτι is causal: "because" (cf. KJV ASV NASB NIV NET) or "for" (NRSV ESV NLT). John provides the reason why the believer should not believe every teaching or prophecy. It seems the necessity of discernment stems from the abundance of false teachers who have made their way throughout the world.

ἐξεληλύθασιν: The Greek word ἐξεληλύθασιν is third person plural perfect active indicative from the verb ἐξέρχομαι meaning "I go out" or "to move out of or away from an area" (BDAG, s.v. "ἐξέρχομαι" 1aᴊ, p. 348). **Syntactically,** ἐξεληλύθασιν is the governing verb of the dependent adverbial ὅτι clause. The subject of the verb is the nominal phrase "many false prophets" (πολλοὶ ψευδοπροφῆται). **Semantically,** ἐξεληλύθασιν is an extensive perfect: "*have gone out*" (NASB NRSV ESV NIV NET CNT). The focus is on the completed action of the false teachers (W, 577). They have rejected the true teachings of God and left the church. Their association with the world requires believers to discern and evaluate teaching. When comparing this verse with 2:29, there is a noted difference in tense. In 1 John 2:19, the aorist tense is used, while here it is a perfect. While John may be emphasizing the permanent departure of these false teachers, perhaps this is just an example of John's linguistic variety similar to that in chapter 1 where John vacillated between the aorist and perfect tenses for stylistic reasons (Brown, 490).

4:2a ἐν τούτῳ: The Greek word ἐν is a preposition meaning "in" (BDAG, s.v. "ἐν" 5, p. 328). The Greek word τούτῳ is declined as a dative singular neuter from the demonstrative pronoun οὗτος meaning "this one" (BDAG, s.v. "οὗτος" 1ba, p. 741). **Syntactically,** ἐν τούτῳ introduces an independent prepositional clause: "*by this* you know the Spirit of God" (ἐν τούτῳ γινώσκετε τὸ πνεῦμα τοῦ θεοῦ). The construction, "by this" (ἐν τούτῳ) is discussed several times in 1 John (2:3, 4, 5; 3:10, 16, 19, 24; 4:9, 10, 13, 17; 5:2 below). **Semantically,** ἐν τούτῳ means: "by this" (NASB ESV NET CNT). The clause can either be anaphoric, pointing back to the preceding discussion, or cataphoric, pointing forward. "This" (τούτῳ) is cataphoric to verses 2–3. The believer can know if a teaching is true or false by whether or not it confesses that Jesus is God in human flesh.

γινώσκετε: The Greek word γινώσκετε is a second person plural present active indicative from the verb γινώσκω meaning "to know" or "to know about" or "to arrive at a knowledge of someone or something" (BDAG, s.v. "γινώσκω" 1a, p. 199). **Syntactically,** γινώσκετε is the main verb of the independent clause. The subject of the verb is an implied "you" embedded in the verb and refers to John's readers. It is possible that this could be an imperative rather than an indicative (see KJV ASV). If an imperative, John exhorts his readers to test the prophets rather than suggesting a way in which they can discern teachings. Since the context seems to be a gentle reminder of something that they should already know, it is more likely to be an indicative. **Semantically,** γινώσκετε is a customary present: "know" (cf. KJV NASB ESV NIV NET etc.). John's focus is on the continual knowledge believers possess about a teaching's origin (W, 521). If from God, it will cohere with the teaching about Jesus espoused in John's letter. In this context John repeatedly contrasts the one Spirit of God (or God's Spirit; possessive genitive) with the spirits of the Antichrist. It is the Holy Spirit who animates those who belong to God (Culy, 101).

4:2b ἐστίν: The Greek word ἐστίν is third singular present active indicative from the verb εἰμί meaning "to be" or "to be in close connection (with)" (BDAG, s.v. "εἰμί" 2b, p. 283). **Syntactically,** ἐστίν is the main verb of the independent asyndeton clause "every spirit … *is* from God" (πᾶν πνεῦμα … ἐκ τοῦ θεοῦ ἐστιν). The subject of the verb is the nominal phrase "πᾶν πνεῦμα" along with the relative clause that amplifies it. **Semantically,** ἐστίν is a gnomic present: "is" (cf. KJV NASB ESV NIV NET etc.). John reveals a timeless truth (W, 523) about what followers of Jesus know about "the Spirit of God" or teaching of God. Anyone who provides *correct teaching* (πᾶν πνεῦμα) is speaking *from God*. The correct teaching is found in the next clause.

4:2c ὅ: The Greek word ὅ is nominative singular neuter from the relative pronoun ὅς, meaning "that" (BDAG, s.v. "ὅς" 1a, p. 725). **Syntactically,** ὅ introduces a dependent relative clause: "*who* repeatedly acknowledges Jesus to be the Christ who has come in flesh" (ὃ ὁμολογεῖ Ἰησοῦν Χριστὸν ἐν σαρκὶ ἐληλυθότα). The gender agreement with the noun "spirit" (πνεῦμα) reveals that the entire relative clause modifies "spirit" (πνεῦμα). This relative pronoun is in the nominative case because it is the subject of the verb "confesses" (ὁμολογεῖ). The relative clause then underscores a specific Christological teaching from God.

ὁμολογεῖ: The Greek word ὁμολογεῖ is third person singular present active indicative from the verb ὁμολογέω meaning "to acknowledge," "to claim," "to profess," or "to acknowledge something, ordinarily in public" (BDAG, s.v. "ὁμολογέω" 4b, p. 708). **Syntactically,** ὁμολογεῖ is the governing verb of the dependent relative clause. The subject of the verb is the relative pronoun "that" (ὅ). **Semantically,** ὁμολογεῖ is a gnomic iterative present: "*repeatedly claim*," "*repeatedly* acknowledges" (cf. NIV) or "claims" (NLT) or "confesses" (KJV ASV NASB NRSV ESV NET CNT). John speaks about anyone who repeatedly acknowledges a certain teaching about Jesus's humanity and messiahship can be assured that that teaching is from God.

ἐληλυθότα: The Greek word ἐληλυθότα is an accusative masculine singular perfect active participle from the verb ἔρχομαι meaning "to come" or "to make an appearance before the public" (BDAG, s.v. "ἔρχομαι" 1bα, p. 394). **Syntactically,** ἐληλυθότα is part of a double accusative object complement. "Jesus" (Ἰησοῦν) is the direct object of the verb "acknowledges" (ὁμολογεῖ). "Christ" (Χριστόν) is the first object complement. The participle "who has come" (ἐληλυθότα) is a second object complement. Thus translated: "that *repeatedly* acknowledges Jesus *to be* the Christ who has come in flesh." "In flesh" (ἐν σαρκὶ) is a figure of speech called a synecdoche where a part is used to reference the whole. Here the idea of flesh is used to indicate the full bodily incarnation of Jesus. John underscores that Jesus, as the Messiah, was human (cf. NET note on this verse). **Semantically,** ἐληλυθότα is an extensive perfect: "who *has* come" (cf. NASB NRSV ESV NIV NET CNT). John's focus is on the completed action upon which the present confession is based (W, 577). Thus the past action of Jesus's incarnation has present effects for those who put their faith in him. The correct Christological confession then involves the historical reality of Jesus's humanity and messiahship.

Syntactical Nugget: What is the connection between Ἰησοῦν and Χριστόν and ἐληλυθότα? On the one hand, it is possible that ἐληλυθότα is a simple object complement of the verb "repeatedly acknowledges" (ὁμολογεῖ) and its direct object "Jesus Christ" (Ἰησοῦν Χριστόν). If that is the case, it would be translated: "that repeatedly acknowledges Jesus Christ *as* having come in the flesh." On the other hand, Ἰησοῦν could be considered the direct object of ὁμολογεῖ with Χριστὸν ἐληλυθότα as an object-complement double accusative to Ἰησοῦν. An object-complement double accusative is a construction in which one accusative is the direct object of the verb and the other accusative complements the direct object (W, 182), which means that the confession specifies the fact that Jesus as Christ has come with a focus on the past action, "that repeatedly acknowledges Jesus *to be* the Christ who has come in flesh." (Culy, 101; cf. Brown, 492–93).

4:3a καί: The Greek word καί is a conjunction that can mean either "and" or "but" (BDAG, s.v. "καί" 1bε, p. 494). **Syntactically,** καί introduces an independent conjunctive clause: "but every spirit . . . is not from God" (καὶ πᾶν πνεῦμα . . . ἐκ τοῦ θεοῦ οὐκ ἔστιν). **Semantically,** καί is adversative: "but" (NIV NET NLT) even though some translations prefer "and" (KJV ASV NASB NRSV ESV CNT). John's contrastive καί heightens the Christological affirmative. Regardless of how one translates καί, it introduces a contrastive teaching (Brown, 494).

ἐστίν: The Greek word ἐστίν is third person singular present active indicative from the verb εἰμί meaning "is" or "to be in close connection (with)" (BDAG, s.v. "εἰμί" 2b, p. 283). **Syntactically,** ἐστίν is the main verb of the independent clause (but every spirit . . . *is* not from God" (καὶ πᾶν πνεῦμα . . . ἐκ τοῦ θεοῦ οὐκ ἔστιν). The subject of the verb is the nominal phrase "πᾶν πνεῦμα" along with the relative clause that amplifies it. **Semantically,** ἐστίν is a gnomic present: "is" (cf. KJV NASB ESV NIV NET etc.). John reveals a timeless truth about teaching (W, 523). Anyone who offers *incorrect teaching* (πᾶν πνεῦμα) is *not from God*. The specifics of that incorrect teaching is found in the next clause.

4:3b ὅ: The Greek word ὅ is nominative singular neuter from the relative pronoun ὅς, meaning "that" (BDAG, s.v. "ὅς" 1a, p. 725). **Syntactically,** ὅ introduces a dependent relative clause: "*that* does not repeatedly acknowledge Jesus to be the Christ [who has come in the flesh] (ὃ μὴ ὁμολογεῖ τὸν Ἰησοῦν [ἐληλυθότα]). The entire relative clause modifies the noun "spirit" (πνεῦμα).

The relative pronoun is in the nominative case because it is the subject of the verb "confesses" (ὁμολογεῖ). The use of the negative particle "not" (μή) with the indicative mood is grammatically unusual since it is typically used with subjunctive and imperatival moods (W, 469, 487). Culy suggests that the presence of "not" (μή) is an aberration and could be a Classical Greek hold-over that was used to express an assertion with no exceptions (Culy, 102). Regardless of which particle is used, the point remains the same: "every spirit" (= teaching and lifestyle; Yarbrough, 222) that refuses to present the correct belief about Jesus's humanity and does not love is not from God.

ὁμολογεῖ: The Greek word ὁμολογεῖ is third person singular present active indicative from the verb ὁμολογέω meaning "to acknowledge," "to claim," "to profess," or "to acknowledge something, ordinarily in public" (BDAG, s.v. "ὁμολογέω" 4b, p. 708). **Syntactically,** ὁμολογεῖ is the governing verb of the dependent relative clause. The subject of the verb is the relative pronoun "who" (ὅ). **Semantically,** ὁμολογεῖ is an iterative present: "repeatedly claim," *regularly claim*" (cf. NLT) or "acknowledge" (NIV) or "confess" (KJV ASV NASB NRSV ESV NET CNT). It speaks of something that happens on a regular basis (W, 520). Anyone ("every spirit") who repeatedly teaches against Jesus's humanity and messiahship and refuses to live a lifestyle of love reveals that they are not from God.

[ἐληλυθότα]: The Greek word ἐληλυθότα is an accusative masculine singular perfect active participle from the verb ἔρχομαι meaning "to come" or "to make an appearance before the public" (BDAG, s.v. "ἔρχομαι" 1bα, p. 394). **Syntactically,** ἐληλυθότα is an elliptical participle implied from the previous clause. As was the case in 4:2c, [ἐληλυθότα] is a substantival double accusative object complement. "Jesus" (Ἰησοῦν) is the direct object of the verb "claims" (ὁμολογεῖ). "Christ" (Χριστόν) is the first object complement, and the substantival participle, "having come" (ἐληλυθότα), is the second object complement: "that *regularly* claims Jesus who *has come* in flesh." The ellipsis has led many scribes to make explicit what was implied (ℵ Ψ and the Byzantine tradition, among others). **Semantically,** ἐληλυθότα is an extensive perfect: "who *has* come" (W, 577). Translations, however, tend to leave out translating the ellipsis (cf. NASB NRSV ESV NIV NET CNT). Regardless, John's focus is on those who do not acknowledge the historical reality of Jesus having come in the flesh as Messiah.

Text-Critical Nugget: Which Greek variant reading is correct: "annuls" (λύει) or "does not confess" (μὴ ὁμολογεῖ)? The first carries a sense of actively repudiating correct teaching about Jesus, while the second reading implies a passive rejection of the nature of Jesus. It was a debated verse among early church leaders. On the one hand, the Greek historian Socrates (ca. 440 C.E.) wrote that the λύει reading was original and that the Nestorians, who believed that Jesus had two separate natures, had amended the text (*Hist. eccl.* 7.32). The church fathers Irenaeus (ca. 180 C.E.), Clement, and Origen all support the variant reading λύει as well (although Origen also supports μὴ ὁμολογεῖ). The harder reading would be λύει, because a scribe would be more likely to create a parallel with the previous clause than to remove it. On the other hand, many argue in favor of the reading μὴ ὁμολογεῖ, believing that λύει reflects a second-century debate and the text was amended to argue against those who were dividing a divine Christ from an earthly Jesus (docetism). Brown argues, however, that this is unlikely because the term λύει doesn't play an important role in the second-century debates about Jesus's nature. It seems unlikely that a scribe immersed in these debates would have chosen to insert that particular word here. The major obstacle to adopting λύει is the external evidence doesn't support it. The manuscript evidence is virtually unanimous in favor of μὴ ὁμολογεῖ (א, A B Y 33 81 322 etc.) over λύει. The UBS committee had little difficulty in deciding in favor of μὴ ὁμολογεῖ (giving it an A rating; Metzger[1], 644).

4:3c καί: The Greek word καί is a conjunction meaning "and" (BDAG, s.v. "καί" 1bα, p. 494). **Syntactically,** καί introduces an independent conjunctive clause: "*and* this is the [spirit] of the Antichrist" (καὶ τοῦτό ἐστιν τὸ τοῦ ἀντιχρίστου). **Semantically,** καί is a coordinating conjunction. While some translate καί as "and" (KJV ASV NASB NRSV NET), others leave καί untranslated (ESV NLT CNT). It not only joins two independent clauses together, it also provides additional information about those who do not acknowledge the incarnation of Jesus.

ἐστίν: The Greek word ἐστίν is third singular present active indicative from the verb εἰμί meaning "to be" or "to be in close connection (with)" (BDAG, s.v. "εἰμί" 2b, p. 283). **Syntactically,** ἐστίν is the main verb of the independent conjunctive clause. The subject of the verb is the demonstrative pronoun "this one" (τοῦτο) due to the grammatical priority of pronouns (W, 43). While the definite article (τό) positioned before "of the Antichrist" (τοῦ ἀντιχρίστου) could indicate it is a substantival predicate nominative phrase (Culy, 103), it seems more likely that the article is anaphoric, modifying an elliptical "spirit" [πνεῦμα] (W, 217). Thus the article and the implied "spirit" [πνεῦμα] is the predicate nominative (cf. NASB NRSV ESV NIV NET CNT). **Semantically,** ἐστίν is an equative present: "is" (cf. KJV NASB ESV NIV NET etc.). The one who does not confess the humanity of Jesus who is Messiah (Χριστόν) has a close connection with the Antichrist.

Theological Nugget: Who is the Antichrist? Although it could be that these people are the Antichrist, the parallels in 2:18 negate this possibility. John merely points out that an adversative spirit drives the misguided, speaks through them, and carries functions similar to those of an anticipated Antichrist. This is also made clear by the use of the masculine plural personal pronoun "them" (αὐτούς) to reference the misguided who have left the church (2:19) in the next verse. Brown puts it this way, "The secessionists are not only a manifestation of evil; they manifest eschatological evil" (Brown, 496).

4:3d ὅ: The Greek word ὅ is accusative singular neuter from the relative pronoun ὅς meaning "which" (BDAG, s.v. "ὅς" 1bβ, p. 725). **Syntactically,** ὅ introduces a dependent relative clause: "*about which* you have heard is coming" (ὃ ἀκηκόατε ὅτι ἔρχεται). Some translations render ὅ as "which" (ESV NIV NET NLT) others "of which" (NASB NRSV CNT). Regardless, the entire clause is adjectival. It modifies the elliptical noun "spirit" (τὸ [πνεῦμα]) and provides additional information about the spirit of the Antichrist. He is the one whose coming had been predicted. The relative pronoun is in the accusative case because it is the direct object of the verb "you have heard" (ἀκηκόατε).

ἀκηκόατε: The Greek word ἀκηκόατε is a second person plural perfect active indicative from the verb ἀκούω meaning "to hear" or "to receive news or information about something" or "to learn something" (BDAG, s.v. "ἀκούω" 3e, p. 38). **Syntactically,** ἀκηκόατε is the governing verb of the dependent relative clause: "about which *you have heard* is coming" (ὃ ἀκηκόατε ὅτι ἔρχεται). The subject of the verb is an implied "you" embedded in the verb and refers to John's readers. **Semantically,** ἀκηκόατε is an extensive perfect: "you *have* heard" (KJV ASV NASB NRSV NIV NET CNT). The focus is on the completed action upon which John's present comment is based (W, 577). John's readers had heard that an antichrist was coming, resulting in a state of their expectation that continues to be relevant.

ὅτι: The Greek word ὅτι is a conjunction meaning "that" (BDAG, s.v. "ὅτι" 1b, p. 731). **Syntactically,** ὅτι introduces a dependent conjunctive clause: "*that* he is coming" (ὅτι ἔρχεται). The entire clause is substantival. It functions as the direct object of the verb "you have heard" (ἀκηκόατε). Thus the entire clause is placed in parentheses in order to visualize its contribution to the dependent relative clause. **Semantically,** ὅτι is an indirect discourse marker: "that" (NASB NRSV). The clause provides the content of the message that believers had received about the Antichrist (W, 456). Specifics are provided with the next verb.

ἔρχεται: The Greek word ἔρχεται is third person singular present middle indicative from the verb ἔρχομαι meaning "to come" or is used with a focus on an approach of a forerunner from John's perspective (BDAG, s.v. "ἔρχομαι" 1bβ, p. 394). **Syntactically,** ἔρχεται is the governing verb of the dependent conjunctive ὅτι clause. The subject of the verb is an implied "it" embedded in the verb and refers to "the spirit of the Antichrist" that the believers had heard was coming. **Semantically,** ἔρχεται is a *mostly* futuristic present: "it is com-ing" (NIV NET NLT). "The present tense describes an event *begun* in present time but completed in the future" (W, 537). This interpretation is validated in the next clause with "and [who] *now* is" (καὶ [ὃ] νῦν . . . ἐστίν). John un-derscores the immediacy or certain coming of false messiahs (cf. 1 John 2:18; Mark 13:6; Matt. 24:5; Luke 21:8).

4:3e καὶ [ὃ] νῦν: The Greek word καί is a conjunction meaning "and" (BDAG, s.v. "καί" 1bα, p. 494). Similarly, the Greek word νῦν is a conjunction, but it means "now" (BDAG, s.v. "νῦν" 1aα, p. 681). **Syntactically,** καὶ [ὃ] νῦν introduces a second conjunctive dependent relative clause, "*and* [which] is now in the world already" (καὶ [ὃ] νῦν ἐν τῷ κόσμῳ ἐστὶν ἤδη). The entire relative clause is ad-jectival. It modifies the elliptical noun "spirit" (τὸ [πνεῦμα]). **Semantically,** καὶ [ὃ] νῦν is a coordinating connection with temporal force: "and now" (NASB NRSV ESV NET) or "and indeed" (NIV). Together the two conjunctions provide addi-tional information about the spirit of the Antichrist with a focus on the imme-diate present. John's readers have heard that an antichrist figure was coming, but now he warns that the Antichrist's teachings are already present among them.

[ὃ]: The Greek word ὃ is nominative singular neuter from the relative pro-noun ὅς meaning "which" (BDAG, s.v. "ὅς" 1bβ, p. 725). **Syntactically,** [ὃ] introduces a dependent adjectival relative clause: "and [*which*] is now in the world already" (καὶ [ὃ] νῦν ἐν τῷ κόσμῳ ἐστὶν ἤδη). Like the previous rel-ative clause, it too modifies the elliptical noun "spirit" (τὸ [πνεῦμα]). This relative pronoun is in the nominative case because it is the subject of the verb "is" (ἐστίν). Due to the presence of καὶ [ὃ] νῦν, the relative clause reveals that Antichrist-like teachings are already present in the fraudulent teachings of the misguided who have left the church (2:19).

ἐστίν: The Greek word ἐστίν is third person singular present active indica-tive from the verb εἰμί meaning "to be" or "to be in close connection (with)" (BDAG, s.v. "εἰμί" 2b, p. 283). **Syntactically,** ἐστίν is the main verb of the second dependent adjectival relative clause. The subject of the verb is an im-plied relative pronoun "which" ([ὃ]). **Semantically,** ἐστίν is an equative pres-ent: "is" (cf. KJV NASB ESV NIV NET etc.). The people in John's churches, those who are spreading teachings against the humanity of Jesus the Messiah, have a close connection (ἐστίν) with the teachings of the forthcoming Antichrist.

Grammatical and Theological Nugget: What is the significance of the relative clauses in 4:1–3 that discusses two spirits in the relative clauses? The first rela-tive clause (4:2c) speaks of God's Spirit. People who teach that Jesus was human and is God's Messiah reveal that that their teaching is from God. The second relative clause (4:3b) provides a contrast. People who do not cohere with the idea that Jesus was human and is God's Messiah reveal that their teaching does not have its origin in God. The third relative clause (4:3d) reminds readers that there is a spirit of the Antichrist about whom they had been taught was coming. The final relative clause (4:3e) underscores the fact that this spirit of the Antichrist is already in the world and at work in the misguided teachings of people in John's day, namely, those who had left the church (2:19).

4:4a ἐστέ: The Greek word ἐστέ is second person plural present active indicative from the verb εἰμί meaning "to be" or "to be in close connection (with)" (BDAG, s.v. "εἰμί" 2b, p. 283). **Syntactically,** ἐστέ is the main verb of the independent asyndeton clause, "you, yourselves *are* of God" (ὑμεῖς ἐκ τοῦ θεοῦ ἐστε). The subject of the verb is the emphatic personal pronoun "you" (ὑμεῖς). While an explicit pronoun is not often seen as emphatic with a verb of being, here it is. It is set in stark contrast to the third person masculine pronoun that serves as the direct object of the next clause (Bateman[1], 434). John strengthens the distinction between those who belong to God and the misguided teachers who belong to the world system. John's stark dualism continues to typify his writing style. The lines are vividly drawn, and every human either belongs to God or to God's enemy. **Semantically,** ἐστέ is an equative present: "are" (cf. KJV NASB ESV NIV NET etc.). John once again underscores the close connection his readers have with God (cf. 3:1–2).

Syntactical Nugget: How is the preposition ἐκ to be understood? The phrase ἐκ τοῦ θεοῦ occurs sixteen times in John's writings: three times in the Gospel of John, twelve times in 1 John, and once in 3 John. Its best rendering in this context is to classify the preposition as source: *"from"* God. God is being identified as the source of something. When ἐκ τοῦ θεοῦ is used in connection with γεννάω, it has great significance in that it describes the believer's origin of new life (1 John 3:9; 4:7; 5:1, 4, 18). God is the *source* of life, visible through the believer's actions. The use of ἐκ τοῦ θεοῦ also expresses a strong dualism. In Johannine literature, one is either *from* God or *from* the Devil. The lines are clearly drawn and a decision must be made.

4:4b καί: The Greek word καί is a conjunction meaning "and" (BDAG, s.v. "καί" 1bα, p. 494). **Syntactically,** καί introduces a conjunctive independent clause: "*and* you have overcome them (= antichrists)" (καὶ νενικήκατε αὐτούς). **Semantically,** καί is a coordinating connector: "and" (KJV ASV NASB NRSV ESV NIV). It connects an additional idea about his readers' relationship with God (W, 671). They not only belong to God, but the καί signals that some additional information about his readers' status with God is yet to come.

νενικήκατε: The Greek word νενικήκατε is a second person plural perfect active indicative from the verb νικάω meaning "to conquer" or "to overcome" or "to overcome someone" (BDAG, s.v. "νικάω" 2a, p. 673). **Syntactically,** νενικήκατε is the main verb of the independent conjunctive clause. The subject of the verb is an implied "you" embedded in the verb and refers to John's readers. **Semantically,** νενικήκατε is an extensive perfect: "you *have* overcome" (cf. KJV NASB ESV NIV NET etc.). The focus is on the completed action upon which John's present comment is based (W, 577). John focuses attention on the past victory believers have over people of the world who spread information that is against Jesus and has continuing results in the present. The NLT captures the force of this clause the best: "You have already won a victory over those people."

Lexical and Theological Nugget: What does νικάω mean? The word νικάω occurs twenty-eight times in the New Testament. It occurs once in Luke (11:22) and three times in Romans (3:4; 12:21 [2x]). In John's writings, the idea of *victory* is a key theme. The idea of overcoming is an act demanded of believers and is not described as a work of Jesus. In his farewell discourse, Jesus told his disciples that he had overcome the world (John 16:33) through his messianic activity. Here Jesus's work becomes the model for believers to imitate. In other words, Jesus's life is connected to the life of John's readers. The idea is that followers of Jesus are to live out the victory of Jesus. Just as Jesus defeated the world system, the believer can also live in that same victory. John already told them in 2:13–14 that positionally they have already defeated the world through their belief in Jesus (cf. 1 John 5:13–14). They can now live out this victory by being faithful to Jesus and discerning true teaching from fraudulent teaching (cf. Culy, 103–4).

4:4c ὅτι: The Greek word ὅτι is a conjunction meaning "because" (BDAG, s.v. "ὅτι" 4a, p. 732). **Syntactically,** ὅτι introduces the dependent conjunctive clause: "*because* the one (spirit of the Antichrist) who [is] in you is greater than the one (Spirit of God) who [is] in the world" (ὅτι μείζων ἐστὶν ὁ ἐν ὑμῖν ἢ ὁ ἐν τῷ κόσμῳ). The entire clause functions adverbially. It modifies the verb "overcome" (νενικήκατε). **Semantically,** ὅτι is causal: "because" (KJV ASV NASB NIV NET CNT NLT) or "for" (NRSV ESV). John provides the reason why the believer has overcome the world. The details are defined in the next verb.

ἐστίν: The Greek word ἐστίν is third person singular present active indicative from the verb εἰμί meaning "to be" or "to be in reference to a condition" (BDAG, s.v. "εἰμί" 3c, p. 284). **Syntactically,** ἐστίν is the governing verb of the dependent conjunctive ὅτι clause. The subject of the verb is "the one in you" (ὁ ἐν ὑμῖν). The articles preceding both prepositional phrases are equivalent to relative pronouns in force (W, 213) and nominalize the phrases as subjective. The first functions as the nominative of the verb "is" (ἐστίν): "(the one who [is] in you) is" (NRSV ESV NIV NET). **Semantically,** ἐστίν is an equative present that is part of an explanation disclosing the Spirit in a believer (2:20, 27) to be greater than the spirits who are in the world (= spirit of the Antichrist). The NLT captures this interpretation: "because the *Spirit* who lives in you is greater than the *spirit* who lives in the world" (emphasis added).

4:5a εἰσίν: The Greek word εἰσίν is third person plural present active indicative from the verb εἰμί meaning "to be" or "to come from somewhere" or "to have a point of derivation or origin" (BDAG, s.v. "εἰμί" 8, p. 285). **Syntactically,** εἰσίν is the main verb of the independent asyndeton clause: "they (= antichrists) themselves *are* of the world" (αὐτοὶ ἐκ τοῦ κόσμου εἰσίν). The subject of the verb is the emphatic personal pronoun "they" (= antichrists) (αὐτοί). The presence of an explicit pronoun emphasizes the dualism that has been prevalent throughout the letter and in this section specifically. John distinguishes between those who are of the world and those who belong to God (Culy, 104). **Semantically,** εἰσίν is an equative present: "are" (cf. KJV NASB ESV NIV NET etc.). Those who are against Jesus are not from God and are equated with people of the world system.

Lexical Nugget: What does κόσμος mean? The word κόσμος here is a figure of speech called a metonymy of subject, where one noun is used in place of another noun closely associated with it. The word "world" is used not to refer to the physical universe, but to the values of the world that are antagonistic to God (1 John 2:15–16; see Theological and Lexical Nuggets in clauses 2:17a and 3:1e). This means that the subject "world" is substituted for the "values" of the world. Those who "speak from the world" offer no opposition to the world's perversions and value systems, instead they exhibit those same values. This is most likely alluding to 1 John 2:16 where John describes the world's values as "the flesh that desires," "the eyes that desire," and "the boastful pride of life" (2:15–16).

4:5b διὰ τοῦτο: The Greek word διά is a preposition meaning "therefore" (BDAG, s.v. "διά" B2a, p. 223). The Greek word τοῦτο is declined as an accusative singular neuter from the demonstrative pronoun οὗτος and means "this one" (BDAG, s.v. "οὗτος" 1ba, p. 741). **Syntactically,** διὰ τοῦτο introduces an independent prepositional clause: "*therefore* they regularly speak from the world's perspective *and* the world listens regularly to them" (διὰ τοῦτο ἐκ τοῦ κόσμου λαλοῦσιν καὶ ὁ κόσμος αὐτῶν ἀκούει). The prepositional phrase is common in 1 John (3:1; 4:5). **Semantically,** διὰ τοῦτο can either be anaphoric, pointing back to the preceding discussion, or cataphoric, pointing forward. The usual rule is that the prepositional phrase is cataphoric if it is followed by a subordinating conjunction. Since there is no subordinating conjunction it points back as a summary of the previous statements. People who speak against Jesus are animated by the spirit of the Antichrist and have their origin in the world system, which John builds upon in the next verb.

λαλοῦσιν: The Greek word λαλοῦσιν is third person plural present active in- dicative from the verb λαλέω meaning "to talk" or "to speak" or "to utter words" (BDAG, s.v. "λαλέω" 2aδ, p. 582). **Syntactically,** λαλοῦσιν is the main verb of the independent clause introduced by a prepositional phrase. The subject of the verb is an implied "they" embedded in the word and refers to the people who are against Jesus. **Semantically,** λαλοῦσιν is a customary present: "they speak *regularly*" (cf. KJV ASV NASB ESV NET NLT). It speaks of a pattern of teaching ma- terial (W, 521). People who are of the world system speak the world's language.

4:5c καί: The Greek word καί is a conjunction meaning "and" (BDAG, s.v. "καί" 1bα, p. 494). **Syntactically,** καί introduces an independent conjunctive clause: "*and* the world listens to them" (καὶ ὁ κόσμος αὐτῶν ἀκούει). **Semantical- ly,** καί is a coordinating connector: "and" (KJV ASV NASB NRSV ESV NIV NLT CNT). It connects an additional element about those who speak against Jesus's humanity and messiahship (W, 671). John builds upon his two previous state- ments about people who are part of the world's system (v. 5a) and who speak the world's language (v. 5b), which John builds upon further with the next verb.

ἀκούει: The Greek word ἀκούει is third person singular present active indic- ative from the verb ἀκούω meaning "to hear" or "to listen to" or "to have or exercise the faculty of hearing" (BDAG, s.v. "ἀκούω" 1c, p. 37). **Syntactically,** ἀκούει is the main verb of an independent conjunctive clause. The subject of the verb is the noun "world" (ὁ κόσμος). **Semantically,** ἀκούει is a customary present: "listens *regularly*" (NASB NRSV ESV NIV NET CNT NLT). John stress- es the continual receptivity that the people of the world's system have to the teachings against Jesus's humanity and messiahship (W, 521). John continues to build on his statement about people who are part of the world's system (v. 5a): they speaks the world's language (v. 5b) and the world's system is attracted to what they have to say (v. 5c).

4:6a ἐσμεν: The Greek word ἐσμέν is first person plural present active indica- tive from the verb εἰμί meaning "to be" or "to be in close connection (with)" (BDAG, s.v. "εἰμί" 2b, p. 283). **Syntactically,** ἐσμέν is the main verb of the independent asyndeton clause: "We ourselves *are* from God" (ἡμεῖς ἐκ τοῦ θεοῦ ἐσμεν). The subject of the verb is the emphatic personal pronoun "we" (ἡμεῖς). Again the explicit presence of the personal pronoun highlights the dualistic contrast between John and his readers (ἡμεῖς) and the misguided and fraudulent teachers (cf. Culy, 105). **Semantically,** ἐσμέν is a equative present: "are" (cf. KJV NASB ESV NIV NET etc.). In contrast to those teachers whose origin is from the world system, believers have their origin in God.

Grammatic and Theological Nugget: What is the significance of the per- sonal pronoun (ἡμεῖς)? The personal pronoun that appears to highlight the dualistic contrast between John and his readers (ἡμεῖς) and the misguided teachers is debated. On the one hand, some see it as a non distinct reference to John and the readers similar to the first personal plural throughout the letter. On the other hand, John could be using it as a distinct reference to himself and the group of official eyewitnesses who speak authoritatively for God, while the misguided teachers are aberrations. However the first person plurals in the rest of the verse are non distinct, so the personal pronoun "we" (ἡμεῖς) is most likely non distinct, placing an emphasis on the community being able to discern for themselves rather than always relying on a class of tradition bearers or eyewitness (Brown, 498–99).

4:6b γινώσκων: The Greek word γινώσκων is a nominative masculine singular present active participle from the verb γινώσκω meaning "to know" or "to know about" or "to arrive at a knowledge of someone or something" (BDAG, s.v. "γινώσκω" 1a, p. 199). **Syntactically,** ὁ γινώσκων and its object τὸν θεόν function substantivally as the subject of the verb "listens" (ἀκούει). The entire participial phrase is placed in parentheses to underscore its contribution to the independent clause. **Semantically,** γινώσκων is a gnomic present: "the person who knows God" or "whoever knows God" (NRSV ESV NIV NET CNT) or "those who know God" (NLT). The stress is on a timeless fact about those who claim to have a relationship with God (W, 523), which is defined with the following phrase.

ἀκούει: The Greek word ἀκούει is third person singular present active indicative from the verb ἀκούω meaning "to hear" or "to listen to" or "to have or exercise the faculty of hearing" (BDAG, s.v. "ἀκούω" 1c, p. 37). **Syntactically,** ἀκούει is the main verb of the independent asyndeton clause: "the person who knows God listens to us" (ὁ γινώσκων τὸν θεὸν ἀκούει ἡμῶν). The subject of the verb is the substantival participial phrase, "the person who knows God" (ὁ γινώσκων τὸν θεὸν). The "to us" is John and the eyewitnesses; ἡμῶν is in the genitive because ἀκούω takes a genitive for the thing or person heard or listened to. This string of asyndeton clauses (without conjunctions) creates a staccato effect that very powerfully illustrates another aspect of John's teaching style. **Semantically,** ἀκούει is a gnomic present: "listens" (NASB NRSV ESV NIV NET CNT NLT). John presents a timeless truth (W, 523): people who claim to know God will be receptive to the teaching about Jesus's humanity and messiahship.

Lexical Nugget: How should we understand ἀκούει ἡμῶν? Two options exist. On the one hand, terms like "hearing" and "listening" may be synonyms for obeying (Bullinger, 828). Jesus says, "The one who belongs to God, hears [ἀκούει] God's words" (John 8:47). The followers of Jesus hear God's word in the sense that they *listen to and respond to* it. That means that they *obey* it. If "hearing" is used for *obeying* in this context, then people whose source of life is

from God *obey* the message spoken by believers, while those whose source of
life is not from God refuse to *obey*. Second, "hear" may be a synonym for believing. In John 9:27 (cf. 12:38), a man who was formerly blind says to a group of
doubting religious leaders, "I told you already and you did not hear." "Hearing"
in that context refers to the religious leaders' unwillingness to *believe* the report
of the formerly blind man's testimony. If "hearing" means *believing*, then people
whose source of life is from God would *believe* the message spoken by believers,
while those whose source of life is not from God would refuse to *believe*. In both
cases, this is another example of a figure of speech called a metonymy, where the
verb "hearing" (ἀκούει) stands for *obeying* or *believing*.

4:6c ὅς: The Greek word ὅς is nominative singular masculine from the relative
pronoun ὅς meaning "the one who" (BDAG, s.v. "ὅς" 1bα, p. 725). **Syntactically,** ὅς introduces a dependent relative clause: "*whoever* is not of God" (ὃς
οὐκ ἔστιν ἐκ τοῦ θεοῦ). The relative pronoun (ὅς) is in the nominative case
because it is the subject of the verb "is" (ἐστίν). The entire clause functions as
the subject of the verb "listens" (ἀκούει) and is placed in parentheses in order
to visualize its contribution as the subject of the independent clause. Technically, this relative pronoun conceals a demonstrative pronoun and is called
an "embedded demonstrative" (W, 240). The clause demonstrates that anyone
whose origin is not from God will not be receptive to the teaching about Jesus.

ἐστίν: The Greek word ἐστίν is third person singular present active indicative from the verb εἰμί meaning "to be" or "to be in close connection (with)"
(BDAG, s.v. "εἰμί" 2b, p. 283). **Syntactically,** ἐστίν is the governing verb of
the dependent substantival relative clause. The subject of the verb is the relative pronoun "whoever" (NRSV ESV NIV NET). In order to heighten the implied
contrast, some translations insert "but" (NIV NET). Yet any inserted conjunction seems to take away from John's staccato effect (see 1:6b ἀκούει). **Semantically,** ἐστίν an equative present: is it points out that the one whose origin is
not from God is equated with a person who will not be receptive to the true
teaching about Jesus.

ἀκούει: The Greek word ἀκούει is third person singular present active indicative from the verb ἀκούω meaning "to hear" or "to listen to" or "to have or
exercise the faculty of hearing" (BDAG, s.v. "ἀκούω" 1c, p. 37). **Syntactically,**
ἀκούει is the main verb of the independent clause: "Whoever is not from God
does not *listen* to us" (ὃς οὐκ ἔστιν ἐκ τοῦ θεοῦ οὐκ ἀκούει ἡμῶν). The subject of the verb is the relative clause "whoever is not from God" (ὃς οὐκ ἔστιν
ἐκ τοῦ θεοῦ). **Semantically,** ἀκούει is a gnomic present: "listens" (NASB NRSV
ESV NIV NET NLT CNT). John continues to stress a timeless fact (W, 523): anyone who does not have an abiding relationship with God will not be receptive
to the true teaching about Jesus and his nature.

4:6d ἐκ τούτου: The Greek word ἐκ is a preposition meaning "from" or "of" or is a marker denoting origin (BDAG, s.v. "ἐκ" 3a, p. 296). The Greek word τούτου is declined as an genitive singular neuter from the demonstrative pronoun οὗτος meaning "this one" (BDAG, s.v. "οὗτος" 1bα, p. 741). **Syntactically,** ἐκ τούτου introduces an independent prepositional clause: *"from this* we know the spirit of truth and the spirit of deceit" (ἐκ τούτου γινώσκομεν τὸ πνεῦμα τῆς ἀληθείας καὶ τὸ πνεῦμα τῆς πλάνης). **Semantically,** ἐκ τούτου can either be anaphoric, pointing back to the preceding discussion, or cataphoric, pointing forward. Since there is no subsequent clause to further define ἐκ τούτου, it is anaphoric. It summarizes the previous statements (Culy, 106). On the one hand, some people are animated by the spirit of the Antichrist and have their origin in the world system, therefore they speak the world's language, and the world is attracted to their message. On the other hand, others are animated by the Spirit of God and have their origins in him, therefore, when they speak, those who belong to God listen to them. John concludes that believers can discern who those people are by observing who is attracted to their message.

γινώσκομεν: The Greek word γινώσκομεν is first person plural present active indicative from the verb γινώσκω meaning "to know" or "to know about" or "to arrive at a knowledge of someone or something" (BDAG, s.v. "γινώσκω" 1a, p. 199). **Syntactically,** γινώσκομεν is the main verb of the independent clause. The subject of the verb is an implied "we" embedded in the verb and refers to John and his readers of the letter. **Semantically,** γινώσκομεν is a customary present: "we know" (cf. KJV NASB ESV NET etc.; W, 521). John underscores that believers can continually assess the difference between individuals who are attracted to the message about Jesus's humanity and messiahship and those who are not.

1 John 4:7–10[1]

Big Greek Idea: John's reasoned expectation for followers of Jesus to exhibit mutual love is grounded in God's love, a divine paternity, and a personal relationship with God that is in stark contrast to those who lack love because they have no relationship with God.

Structural Overview: John transitions (ἀγαπητοί) to a new theme: mutual love. However, he seems to be developing the twofold themes of the commandment in 3:23 whereby John expands upon the ethical imperative of belief in Jesus and love for others. He began in 4:1–6 with expectations about believing balanced with affirmation. Here in verses 7–10, John expects readers to persist in mutual love (ἀγαπῶμεν). His reasoning (ὅτι) is because God is love. Love indicates one's paternity (γεγέννηται); and those who love have a relationship (γινώσκει) with God the Father (vv. 6–7).

In an apparent contrast, lack of love marks a nonexistent relationship (οὐκ ἔγνω) with God for a simple reason (ὅτι): God is love, a love that is documented (ἐφανερώθη) in Jesus's coming (ἀπέσταλκεν) with the intention (ἵνα) that all his readers live (ζήσωμεν) lives of love (vv. 8–9).

John closes with a definition of love (ἐστίν): where it began and what it is. Contrary (ἀλλ') to what may be believed, love did not begin (οὐχ ... ἠγαπήκαμεν) with the follower of Jesus, it began (ἠγάπησεν) with God. Love (ἀπέστειλεν) is sacrificing something for another person (v. 10).

Outline:

> Exhibiting Mutual Love Is Expected (v. 7a)
> Mutual Love Is Expected (vv. 7b–8)
> > Mutual love is expected because God is love (v. 7b)
> > God fathers loving children (v. 7c)
> > Loving children have a relationship with God (v. 7d–8)
> God Demonstrates His Love (vv. 9–10)

---

1. Determining the structural breaks for 1 John 4:7–5:4 is difficult. Further difficulty exists concerning whether 1 John 5:1 begins a new unit or not. Whereas Painter suggests that a new section begins at 5:1 because the focus has turned to Christology (Painter, 289), Brown disagrees, identifying 1 John 4:7–5:4a as one textual unit whose theme is love and commandments (Brown, 592; cf. Yarbrough, 233–79). Smalley agrees with Brown that a new section begins with 1 John 4:7 but concludes the section with 5:5, not 5:4a (Smalley, 232). The difficulty of 1 John is John's circular (some would say repetitive) structure. Whatever one's view of the structure of this section, the relationship between rebirth, obedience, and Jesus is particularly noteworthy. We consider 1 John 4:7–5:4 to be a single textual unit with several subunits: 4:7–10, 4:11–16a, 4:16b–19, 4:20–5:4.

Clausal Outline for 1 John 4:7–10

^{4:7a}Ἀγαπητοί, **ἀγαπῶμεν** ἀλλήλους,
^{4:7a} Beloved, **let us** *persist in* **love** *for* one another,

>
> ^{4:7b} **ὅτι** ἡ ἀγάπη ἐκ τοῦ θεοῦ **ἐστιν**,
> ^{4:7b} **because** love **is** from God,

^{4:7c} καὶ (πᾶς ὁ ἀγαπῶν) ἐκ τοῦ θεοῦ **γεγέννηται**
^{4:7c} and (everyone who loves) **has been fathered** by God

^{4:7d} καὶ ([πᾶς ὁ ἀγαπῶ]) **γινώσκει** τὸν θεόν.
^{4:7d} and ([*everyone who loves*]) **knows** God.

^{4:8a} ὁ μὴ ἀγαπῶν οὐκ **ἔγνω** τὸν θεόν,
^{4:8a} The person who does not love does not **know** God,

>
> ^{4:8b} **ὅτι** ὁ θεὸς ἀγάπη **ἐστίν**.
> ^{4:8b} **because** God **is** love.

^{4:9a} ἐν τούτῳ **ἐφανερώθη** ἡ ἀγάπη τοῦ θεοῦ ἐν ἡμῖν,
^{4:9a} By this the love of God **was made known** among us,

>
> ^{4:9b} **ὅτι** τὸν υἱὸν αὐτοῦ τὸν μονογενῆ **ἀπέσταλκεν** ὁ θεὸς εἰς τὸν κόσμον
> ^{4:9b} **that** God **sent** his one and only Son into the world

>
> > ^{4:9c} **ἵνα ζήσωμεν** δι᾽ αὐτοῦ.
> > ^{4:9c} **in order that** **we may live** through him (= Jesus).

^{4:10a} ἐν τούτῳ **ἐστὶν** ἡ ἀγάπη,
^{4:10a} By this **is** love,

>
> ^{4:10b} οὐχ **ὅτι** ἡμεῖς **ἠγαπήκαμεν** τὸν θεόν,
> ^{4:10b} not **that we loved** God,

>
> ^{4:10c} ἀλλ᾽ **ὅτι** αὐτὸς **ἠγάπησεν** ἡμᾶς
> ^{4:10c} but **that he loved** us

>
> ^{4:10d} καὶ [ὅτι] **ἀπέστειλεν** τὸν υἱὸν αὐτοῦ ἱλασμὸν περὶ τῶν ἁμαρτιῶν ἡμῶν.
> ^{4:10d} and [*that*] **he sent** his Son *to be* the atoning sacrifice for our sins.

Syntax Explained for 1 John 4:7–10

4:7a ἀγαπῶμεν: The Greek word ἀγαπῶμεν is first person plural present active subjunctive from the verb ἀγαπάω meaning "to love" or "to have a warm regard for and interest in another" person (BDAG, s.v. "ἀγαπάω" 1aα, p. 5). **Syntactically,** ἀγαπῶμεν is the main verb of the independent clause: "Beloved, let us *persist in love* for one another" (ἀγαπητοί, ἀγαπῶμεν ἀλλήλους). The subject of the verb is an implied "we" embedded in the word and refers to John and his readers. The noun that begins this sentence, "beloved" (ἀγαπητοί), is a vocative of direct address and introduces a new paragraph and train of thought. The pronoun, "one another" (ἀλλήλους), is a reciprocal pronoun. **Semantically,** ἀγαπῶμεν is a hortatory subjunctive and a customary present: "let us *persist in* love *for*" (cf. KJV NASB ESV NIV NET etc.). While the hortatory subjunctive urges John's readers, the customary present signals an urging that will occur on a regular basis (W, 464, 521). John urges believers to persist in their love for fellow believers.

4:7b ὅτι The Greek word ὅτι is a conjunction meaning "because" (BDAG, s.v. "ὅτι" 4a, p. 732). **Syntactically,** ὅτι introduces a dependent conjunctive ὅτι clause: "*because* love is from God" (ὅτι ἡ ἀγάπη ἐκ τοῦ θεοῦ ἐστιν). The entire clause is functioning adverbially modifying the verb, "let us love" (ἀγαπῶμεν). **Semantically,** ὅτι is causal: "because" (NRSV NET) or "for" (KJV ASV NASB ESV NIV CNT NLT; cf. W, 460). John provides the reason why believers should demonstrate love for each other, which is evident in the next verb.

ἐστίν: The Greek word ἐστίν is third person singular present active indicative from the verb εἰμί meaning "to be" or "to be in close connection (with)" (BDAG, s.v. "εἰμί" 2cα, p. 284). **Syntactically,** ἐστίν is the governing verb of the dependent adverbial ὅτι clause. The subject of the verb is the noun "love" (ἡ ἀγάπη). **Semantically,** ἐστίν is equative: "is" (cf. KJV NAS ESV NIV NET). John equates a believer's persistent love with God's love. All true love finds its origin in God (cf. 1:5; 3:10; 4:7–8, 16).

4:7c καί: The Greek word καί is a conjunction meaning "and" (BDAG, s.v. "καί" 1bα, p. 494). **Syntactically,** καί introduces an independent conjunctive clause that joins two independent clauses together: "*and* everyone who loves has been fathered by God" (καὶ πᾶς ὁ ἀγαπῶν ἐκ τοῦ θεοῦ γεγέννηται). **Semantically,** καί is a coordinating connector: "and" (KJV ASV NASB ESV NET). It introduces additional information (W, 671). While most translations translate καί, others leave it untranslated (NRSV NIV NLT). Nevertheless, John builds upon his statement about his expectation for believers to persist in love.

ἀγαπῶν: The Greek word ἀγαπῶν is a nominative masculine singular present active participle from the verb ἀγαπάω meaning "to love" or "to cherish" or "to have a warm regard for and interest in another" (BDAG, s.v. "ἀγαπάω" 1aα, p. 5). **Syntactically,** ὁ ἀγαπῶν functions substantivally. It is an adjectival participle. It modifies the substantival adjective "everyone" (πᾶς). Together they are the subject of the verbs "has been fathered" (γεγέννηται) and "knows" (γινώσκει). The entire πᾶς + participial clause is placed in parentheses in order to visualize its joint contribution to the independent clause. **Semantically,** ἀγαπῶν is a gnomic present: "everyone who loves" (KJV ASV NASB NRSV NIV NET CNT) or "whoever" (ESV) or "anyone" (NLT). This generic reference conveys a gnomic idea (W, 521, 615). John is describing any person who loves or does not love. John's thought is completed with the next verb.

γεγέννηται: The Greek word γεγέννηται is third person singular perfect passive indicative from the verb γεννάω meaning "to become the parent of" or "to exercise the role of a parental figure" (BDAG, s.v. "γεννάω" 1b, p. 193). **Syntactically,** γεγέννηται is the first of two main verbs in the independent conjunctive καί clause. The subject of γεγέννηται is the phrase "everyone who loves" (πᾶς ὁ ἀγαπῶν). **Semantically,** γεγέννηται is both gnomic and extensive perfect: "*has been* fathered" (NET) or "*has been* born" (ESV NIV). It is gnomic because of the generic subject (πᾶς) while extensive in that the focus is on the decisive relationship between God and the believer (W, 580). This generic or proverbial force may also be rendered as an intensive: "is born" (KJV NASB NRSV CNT; cf. ASV NLT) with an emphasis on the results of the present condition of the believer. Regardless of where one places the emphasis of the perfect, John's point is that God has fathered followers of Jesus in the past and that past event has continuing results in the present (cf. 2:29; 3:9; 5:1, 4, 18). The focus is upon those who practice righteousness: they have had an ongoing relationship with God.

4:7d καί: The Greek word καί is a conjunction meaning "and" (BDAG, s.v. "καί" 1bα, p. 494). **Syntactically,** καί introduces an independent conjunctive clause that joins two independent clauses together: "*and* everyone who loves knows God" (καὶ [πᾶς ὁ ἀγαπῶν] γινώσκει τὸν θεόν). **Semantically,** καί is a coordinating connector: "and" (KJV ASV NASB ESV NET). It introduces additional information undergirding John's urging to love others (W, 671). While many translations translate καί, others leave it untranslated (NRSV NIV NLT). John continues to build upon his statement about his expectation for believers to persist in love.

γινώσκει: The Greek word γινώσκει is third person singular present active indicative from the verb γινώσκω meaning "to know" or "to have come to the knowledge of a person" (BDAG, s.v. "γινώσκω" 6c, p. 200). **Syntactically,** γινώσκει is the main verb in the independent conjunctive καί clause. The subject is the elliptical phrase "everyone who loves" (πᾶς ὁ ἀγαπῶν). **Seman-**

tically, γινώσκει is a customary present: "know" or "knows" (cf. KJV NASB ESV NET etc.). It describes an ongoing state (W, 521). John once again stresses that people who demonstrate love for their fellow Christians show that they have an abiding knowledge of God and his nature.

4:8a ἀγαπῶν: The Greek word ἀγαπῶν is a nominative masculine singular present active participle from the verb ἀγαπάω meaning "to love" or "to cherish" or "to have a warm regard for and interest in another" (BDAG, s.v. "ἀγαπάω" 1aα, p. 5). **Syntactically,** ἀγαπῶν is a substantival participle ("the person who loves"). It functions as the subject of the verb "know" (ἔγνω). The participle is negated with μή. It is not placed in parentheses because it is not a participial clause. **Semantically,** ἀγαπῶν is a gnomic present negated with μή: "the person who does not love" (cf. KJV NASB ESV NIV NET etc.). John presents a timeless statement about people who refuse to love their brothers and sisters in Christ (W, 521). John underscores any person's neglect of affection (cf. 4:20d).

ἔγνω: The Greek word ἔγνω is third person singular aorist active indicative from the verb γινώσκω meaning "to know" or "to have come to the knowledge of a person" (BDAG, s.v. "γινώσκω" 6c, p. 200). **Syntactically,** ἔγνω is the main verb of the independent clause, "the person who does not love does not *know* God" (ὁ μὴ ἀγαπῶν οὐκ ἔγνω τὸν θεόν). The subject of the verb is the participial phrase: "The person who does not love" (ὁ μὴ ἀγαπῶν). **Semantically,** ἔγνω is a gnomic aorist negated with μή: "does not know" (cf. KJV NASB ESV NIV NET etc.). John speaks a timeless or general truth (W, 562): any person who claims to be a believer but refuses to demonstrate love, cannot possibly have a relationship with God (cf. 1 John 1:9–11).

4:8b ὅτι: The Greek word ὅτι is a conjunction meaning "because" (BDAG, s.v. "ὅτι" 4a, p. 732). **Syntactically,** ὅτι introduces the dependent clause, "*because* God is love" (ὅτι ὁ θεὸς ἀγάπη ἐστίν). The entire dependent clause functions adverbially. It modifies the verb of perception, "know" (ἔγνω). **Semantically,** ὅτι is causal: "because" (ESV NIV NET) or "for" (KJV ASV NASB NRSV NLT CNT; cf. W, 460). John underscores the reason why someone who claims to know God, yet refuses to love, does not have a relationship with God. How can anyone who refuses to imitate God's character truly have a relationship with him?

ἐστίν: The Greek word ἐστίν is third person singular present active indicative from the verb εἰμί meaning "to be" or "to be in close connection (with)" (BDAG, s.v. "εἰμί" 2ca, p. 282). **Syntactically,** ἐστίν is the main verb of the dependent adverbial ὅτι clause. The subject of the verb is the proper noun "God" (ὁ θεὸς). **Semantically,** ἐστίν an equative present: "is." John equates God with a qualitative noun "love" (ἀγάπη; cf. W, 245). By his very nature,

God is love. Love is but one description of God's character. He is also Spirit (John 4:24) and light (see 1:5). Similarly in 1 John, John describes God as light and love because he encourages believers to follow God's ethical demand for love which springs from his very character (Bateman[1], 454–55; Brown, 515). Here God is equated with love.

Theological Nugget: What does John mean when he says, "God is love" (ὁ θεὸς ἀγάπη ἐστίν)? First, all of the instances of ἀγάπη in 1 John appear with the definite article, except three instances. One of those instances occurs in 3:1 where the extent of the love (ποταπὴν ἀγάπην) that God has lavished on us is at issue. The other two instances (4:8, 16) use the statement "God is love" (ὁ θεὸς ἀγάπη ἐστίν). These are predicate nominative constructions where the predicate nominative is an anarthrous noun. This type of construction may suggest that a specific content is in view and not just a loving feeling. Second, the word order is also important: to say, "God is love" is not the same as saying its reverse, "love is God." The context highlights the idea that believers who act consistently in a loving and selfless manner are imitating God's character.

4:9a ἐν τούτῳ: The Greek word ἐν is a preposition meaning "by" (BDAG, s.v. "ἐν" 5b, p. 328). The Greek word τούτῳ is declined as a dative singular neuter from the demonstrative pronoun οὗτος meaning "this one" (BDAG, s.v. "οὗτος" 1bβ, p. 741). **Syntactically,** ἐν τούτῳ introduces an independent prepositional clause: *by this* the love of God is revealed in us" (ἐν τούτῳ ἐφανερώθη ἡ ἀγάπη τοῦ θεοῦ ἐν ἡμῖν). "By this" (ἐν τούτῳ) occurs frequently in 1 John (2:3, 4, 5; 3:10, 16, 19, 24; 4:2, 10, 13, 17; 5:2). **Semantically,** ἐν τούτῳ can either be anaphoric, pointing back to the preceding discussion, or cataphoric, pointing forward. Here "by this" is cataphoric pointing forward to the subordinating conjunctive clause (ὅτι . . . τὸν κόσμον). The content of "by this" is found in the ὅτι clause below in 4:9b.

ἐφανερώθη: The Greek word ἐφανερώθη is third person singular aorist passive indicative from the verb φανερόω meaning "to make known" or "to show" or "to cause to become known" (BDAG, s.v. "φανερόω" 2aβ, p. 1048). **Syntactically,** ἐφανερώθη is the main verb of the independent clause. It is a passive with an intransitive sense. The subject is the nominal phrase "the love of God" (ἡ ἀγάπη τοῦ θεοῦ). **Semantically,** ἐφανερώθη is a constative aorist: "was made known," "was manifested" (KJV ASV NASB ESV), or "was revealed" (NRSV NET CNT), or "showed" (NIV NLT). John stresses the cessation of a state (W, 559). God's great sacrificial love was shown to us through the historical coming of Jesus.

Syntactical Nugget: How should the prepositional phrase "among us" (ἐν ἡμῖν) be understood? It could be rendered one of three ways. First, it could be referentially as "for us" emphasizing that God's love has been directed at the believing community through the work of Jesus (KJV; cf. Brown, 516). Second, it might be taken as sphere: "in us" (NET) indicating God's presence within believers or locatively (2:20, 27). Finally, it may be rendered as "among us" indicating that God's love is revealed in the midst of the believing community (ESV NIV CNT; Culy, 107).

4:9b ὅτι: The Greek word ὅτι is a conjunction meaning "that" (BDAG, s.v. "ὅτι" 2a, p. 732). **Syntactically,** ὅτι introduces the dependent clause, "*that* God sent his one and only Son into the world" (ὅτι τὸν υἱὸν αὐτοῦ τὸν μονογενῆ ἀπέσταλκεν ὁ θεὸς εἰς τὸν κόσμον). The entire ὅτι clause is functioning adjectivally modifying the demonstrative pronoun "this" (τούτῳ). **Semantically,** ὅτι is epexegetical: "that" (ASV NASB ESV NET CNT). The ὅτι clause explains or clarifies the demonstrative, τούτῳ (W, 459). The way believers know the love of God is by looking back at the selfless giving of his Son, Jesus. This ὅτι clause is very important. The first indication of its importance is in explaining the demonstrative. The second is the direct object of this clause "the Son" (τὸν υἱόν). It is emphatic because it is at the beginning of the ὅτι clause. The final reason is that the verb tense switches from an aorist to a perfect tense. All of these factors point out that John fervently desires to proclaim to his readers that God sent Jesus into the world to give his life for all people (2:2; cf. John 3:16, Culy, 107–8).

ἀπέσταλκεν: The Greek word ἀπέσταλκεν is third person singular perfect active indicative from the verb ἀποστέλλω meaning "to send" or "to dispatch someone for the achievement of some objective" (BDAG, s.v. "ἀποστέλλω" 1aβ, p. 120). **Syntactically,** ἀπέσταλκεν is the governing verb of the dependent adjectival ὅτι clause. The subject is the proper noun "God" (ὁ θεός). **Semantically,** ἀπέσταλκεν is an intensive perfect: "sent" (KJV NRSV ESV NIV CNT). The emphasis is on the results of God's past action (W, 574). God dispatches Jesus into the world to achieve something specific. What he achieved is evident in the next clause.

Lexical and Theological Nugget: How should the adjective "one and only" (τὸν μονογενῆ) be translated? The traditional rendering "only begotten" (KJV ASV NASB CNT) focuses on the root meaning of the word. The root words are "only" (μόνος) and "begotten" (γεννάω). Unfortunately, it falls victim to the root fallacy, which equates the meaning of the word to a sum of its parts (Carson, 30–31). Although the adjective is often used to describe a sole physical child to a set of parents (Luke 7:12; 8:42; 9:38), it is also used in other ways. The author of Hebrews uses τὸν μονογενῆ to speak about the unique relationship between Abraham and Isaac. Ishmael was also a son of Abraham, so in what sense could Isaac be described as his "only begotten"? In that context it is clear that Isaac is the son of promise and that is what makes him the "only begotten." Therefore, the emphasis is on a unique status not on unique ancestry (BDAG, s.v. "μονογενής" 1, p. 658; Culy, 108). And while Jesus does have a special rela-tionship with God, the better rendering is "only" (NRSV ESV) or "one and only" (NIV NET NLT). John stresses that Jesus is "the only one of his kind or class" (BDAG, s.v. "μονογενής" 2, p. 658). God does not physically beget Jesus, nor is he the only child of God, but rather Jesus is the one of a kind "Son."

4:9c ἵνα: The Greek word ἵνα is a conjunction meaning "in order that" or "that" or "to denote purpose, aim, or goal" (BDAG, s.v. "ἵνα" 1aβ, p. 475). **Syntactical-ly,** ἵνα introduces the conjunctive dependent adverbial clause: "*in order that* we may live through him" (ἵνα ζήσωμεν δι᾿ αὐτοῦ). The entire ἵνα clause modifies the verb "sent" (ἀπέσταλκεν). **Semantically,** ἵνα indicates purpose: "in order that" or "that" (KJV ASV). It indicates God's intention behind his sending Jesus into the world (W, 472). That intention is found in the govern-ing verb of the ἵνα clause.

ζήσωμεν: The Greek word ζήσωμεν is first person plural present active sub-junctive from the verb ζάω meaning "to live" or is used "of the sanctified life of a child of God" or "to live in a transcendent sense" (BDAG, s.v. "ζάω" 2bβ, p. 425). The verb is in the subjunctive mood because ἵνα takes the subjunctive mood. **Syntactically,** ζήσωμεν is the governing verb of the dependent adver-bial ἵνα clause. The assumed subject, "we," refers to John and his readers. **Se-mantically,** ζήσωμεν is a customary present: "we might live" (KJV ASV NASB NRSV ESV NIV CNT). God's intention for sending Jesus into the world was so that believers might *continually* live (W, 521).

Lexical Nugget: What does John mean when he says, "*in order that* we may live"? Although life can have a variety of meanings, it seems this phrase re-fers to eternal life (NLT). John speaks elsewhere of God's purpose for sending Jesus into the world, namely, that anyone who believes in Jesus has eternal life (John 3:16–17). Jesus also promises his disciples that they will possess eternal life (John 5:24; 6:57; 11:25; 14:29). Therefore, the type of life that God offers through belief in his Son is eternal life (Brown, 518). God sent his Son *in order that* those who believe in him might have an eternal life with God.

4:10a ἐν τούτῳ: The Greek word ἐν is a preposition meaning "by" (BDAG, s.v. "ἐν" 5b, p. 328). The Greek word τούτῳ is declined as a dative singular neuter from the demonstrative pronoun οὗτος meaning "this one" (BDAG, s.v. "οὗτος" 1bβ, p. 741). **Syntactically,** ἐν τούτῳ is a prepositional phrase introducing an independent prepositional clause, "*by this* is love" (ἐν τούτῳ ἐστὶν ἡ ἀγάπη). "By this" (ἐν τούτῳ) occurs frequently in 1 John (2:3, 4, 5; 3:10, 16, 19, 24; 4:2, 9, 13, 17; 5:2). **Semantically,** ἐν τούτῳ can either be anaphoric, pointing back to the preceding discussion, or cataphoric, pointing forward. "By this" (ἐν τούτῳ) is cataphoric pointing forward to the two subordinating ὅτι clauses, "not *that* we loved God" (οὐχ ὅτι ἡμεῖς ἠγαπήκαμεν τὸν θεόν) and "but *that* he loved us and sent his Son to be the atoning sacrifice for our sins" (ἀλλ᾽ ὅτι αὐτὸς ἠγάπησεν ἡμᾶς καὶ ἀπέστειλεν τὸν υἱὸν αὐτοῦ ἱλασμὸν περὶ τῶν ἁμαρτιῶν ἡμῶν) in 4:10b and 4:10c and thereby providing the content of the demonstrative pronoun.

ἐστίν: The Greek word ἐστίν is third person singular present active indicative from the verb εἰμί meaning "to be" or "to be in close connection (with)" (BDAG, s.v. "εἰμί" 2ca, p. 284). **Syntactically,** ἐστίν is the main verb of the independent clause introduced by a prepositional phrase. The subject of the verb is the noun "love" (ἡ ἀγάπη). **Semantically,** ἐστίν is an equative present: "is" (cf. KJV NASB ESV NIV NET etc.). God is equated with love (see Theological Nugget in 4:8b). It introduces John's explanation about real love, which is spelled out in the next three clauses.

4:10b ὅτι: The Greek word ὅτι is a conjunction meaning "that" (BDAG, s.v. "ὅτι" 2a, p. 732). **Syntactically,** ὅτι introduces a dependent conjunctive clause: "not *that* we ourselves have loved God" (οὐχ ὅτι ἡμεῖς ἠγαπήκαμεν τὸν θεόν). It modifies the demonstrative pronoun "this" (τούτῳ). **Semantically,** ὅτι is epexegetical negated with οὐχ: "not that" (cf. KJV NASB ESV NIV NET etc.). The ὅτι clause explains or clarifies the demonstrative (W, 459). Real love is not evident in people reaching out for God, but in God reaching out to them.

ἠγαπήκαμεν: The Greek word ἠγαπήκαμεν is first person plural perfect active indicative from the verb ἀγαπάω meaning "to cherish," "to have affection for," "to love," or "to have a warm regard for and interest in another" (BDAG, s.v. "ἀγαπάω" 1ba, p. 5). **Syntactically,** ἠγαπήκαμεν is the governing verb of the dependent ὅτι clause. The subject is the emphatic personal pronoun "we" (ἡμεῖς). It refers to John and his readers. **Semantically,** ἠγαπήκαμεν is an intensive perfect: "we loved" (KJV ASV NASB NRSV NIV NLT). The emphasis is on the present state of a past action or in this case the lack of a past action (W, 574). So John's first explanation is presented in the negative: real love is not evident in a person's love for God.

Text-Critical Nugget: Which Greek textual variant ἠγαπήσαμεν or ἠγαπήκαμεν is correct? This textual problem is a grammatical issue. The manuscript evidence is equally divided over whether this verb is in the aorist tense: ἠγαπήσαμεν (ℵ, A, 048, 33, 81, 436 etc.) or the perfect tense: ἠγαπήκαμεν (B, Ψ, 322, 323, 945 etc.). The difference is just one letter. It seems more likely that a scribe would have changed the tense to the aorist, because of the abundance of other aorist verbs. Also, the presence of the perfect tense seems out of place, so it is the more difficult reading. Therefore, the perfect tense we loved (ἠγαπήκαμεν) is the preferred reading (see Brown, 518). The UBS committee had minimal difficulty in deciding in favor of ἠγαπήκαμεν (giving it a B rating; Metzger[1], 645).

4:10c ἀλλ᾽: The Greek word ἀλλά is a conjunction meaning "but" (BDAG, s.v. "ἀλλά" 1a, p. 44). **Syntactically,** ἀλλά introduces a conjunctive dependent clause: "*but* that God loved us and sent his Son to be the atoning sacrifice for our sins" (ἀλλ᾽ ὅτι αὐτὸς ἠγάπησεν ἡμᾶς καὶ ἀπέστειλεν τὸν υἱὸν αὐτοῦ ἱλασμὸν περὶ τῶν ἁμαρτιῶν ἡμῶν). This clause also modifies the demonstrative pronoun "this" (τούτῳ). **Semantically,** ἀλλά is contrastive: "but" (cf. KJV NASB ESV NIV NET etc.). It contrasts with the previous οὐχ ὅτι clause (W, 671). People did not love God first. The specifics of the contrast are evident in the ὅτι clause.

ὅτι: The Greek word ὅτι is a conjunction meaning "that" (BDAG, s.v. "ὅτι" 2a, p. 732). **Syntactically,** ὅτι is a dependent conjunctive clause: "*that* he loved us and sent his Son to be the atoning sacrifice for our sins" (ὅτι αὐτὸς ἠγάπησεν ἡμᾶς καὶ ἀπέστειλεν τὸν υἱὸν αὐτοῦ ἱλασμὸν περὶ τῶν ἁμαρτιῶν ἡμῶν). This clause also modifies the demonstrative pronoun "this" (τούτῳ). **Semantically,** ὅτι is epexegetical negated with ἀλλά: "but that" (cf. KJV NASB ESV NIV NET etc.). The ὅτι clause explains or clarifies the demonstrative (W, 459). Real love is exemplified in God's sending of his Son into the world to become its atoning sacrifice (2:2). John emphasizes here that a believer's love begins with God and not with mankind.

ἠγάπησεν: The Greek word ἠγάπησεν is third person singular aorist active indicative from the verb ἀγαπάω meaning "to cherish," "to have affection for," "to love," or "to have a warm regard for and interest in another" (BDAG, s.v. "ἀγαπάω" 1bα, p. 5). **Syntactically,** ἠγάπησεν is the governing verb of the second dependent conjunctive ὅτι clause. The subject is the emphatic personal pronoun "he" (αὐτός) referring to God. The contrast between the first person plural emphatic pronoun and this third person emphatic pronoun highlights the main idea here. Believers did not love God first. Instead, God reached out to ordinary human beings when they least deserved it. **Semantically,** ἠγάπησεν is a constative aorist: "he loved" (cf. KJV NASB ESV NIV NET etc.). The verb describes God's act of loving as a whole in a summary fashion without any specifics (W, 557). God loved ordinary people, which is in contrast to ordinary people loving God.

4:10d καί: The Greek word καί is a conjunction meaning "and" (BDAG, s.v. "καί" 1a, p. 494). **Syntactically,** καί introduces another part of the compound dependent adjectival ὅτι clause: "*and* he sent his Son to be the atoning sacrifice for our sins" (καὶ ἀπέστειλεν τὸν υἱὸν αὐτοῦ ἱλασμὸν περὶ τῶν ἁμαρτιῶν ἡμῶν). **Semantically,** καί is a coordinating connector of two dependent clauses: "and" (cf. KJV NASB ESV NIV NET etc.). It introduces additional information about God's love (W, 671). John builds upon his previous dependent ὅτι clause about God and his love. ·

ἀπέστειλεν: The Greek word ἀπέστειλεν is third person singular aorist active indicative from the verb ἀποστέλλω meaning "to send" or "to dispatch someone for the achievement of some objective" (BDAG, s.v. "ἀποστέλλω" 1bγ, p. 121). **Syntactically,** ἀπέστειλεν is the governing verb of the dependent ὅτι clause. The subject is also the emphatic personal pronoun "he" (αὐτός). We have here another double accusative object-complement construction. The direct object of the verb "sent" (ἀπέστειλεν) is the noun "Son" (τὸν υἱόν). The second accusative functions as the complement for the noun "atoning sacrifice" (ἱλασμόν). This type of construction is often translated with the words "to be." Therefore, we should translate this, "and he sent his Son *to be* the atoning sacrifice for our sins" (W, 182). **Semantically,** ἀπέστειλεν is a constative aorist: "he sent" or "sent" (cf. KJV NASB ESV NIV NET etc.). The verb describes God's act of sending Jesus into the world as a whole in a summary fashion without any specifics (W, 557). God showed his love for ordinary people when he sent Jesus into the world as an atoning sacrifice (cf. 1 John 2:2).

1 John 4:11–16c

Big Greek Idea: John, based upon the awareness of God's love, underscores the obligation for mutual love within the community of believers that in turn verifies the presence of God's Spirit, the belief that Jesus is the Messiah, and a mutual bond with God.

Structural Overview: Moving from his reasoned expectation for followers of Jesus to exhibit mutual love as grounded in God, a divine paternity, and personal relationship with God (4:7–10), John shifts attention to God's love and the Spirit that "indwells" believers (4:11–16c).[1] The transitional use of "beloved" (ἀγαπητοί) from verse 12 to verse 13 is a notable feature of John's writing style.

Based upon the assumption (εἰ) that God loves (ἠγάπησεν) followers of Jesus, John underscores a believer's duty (ὀφείλομεν) to love others in the community. Provided (ἐάν) a community of believers expresses mutual love (ἀγαπῶμεν), those acts of love not only reflect God's presence and his abiding relationship (μένει) within the community but also loves continual increase (τετελειωμένη; v. 12).

John then provides the first of three proofs or tests of God's presence and abiding relationship within a community of believers. The first proof is that God has given (δέδωκεν) followers of Jesus his Spirit (v. 13). The second proof or test of God's presence and abiding relationship with a community of followers of Jesus is that they believe (ὃς ἐὰν ὁμολογήσῃ) that Jesus is the Messiah (vv. 14–15). The final proof or test of God's presence and abiding relationship with a community of followers of Jesus is their having experienced (ἐγνώκαμεν) God's love (v. 16).

Outline:

> Followers of Jesus Are Obligated to Love Others (v. 11)
> Verifications of God's Love Are Threefold (vv. 12–16c)
> > God's Spirit is present (v. 12)
> > Belief in Jesus as Messiah is evident (vv. 14–15)
> > Familiarity with God and his love is evident (v. 16a–c)

---

1. There is a lack of agreement concerning where this next section begins and where it ends, so we must admit that there are other ways to divide this paragraph. For instance, Painter sees a new paragraph beginning in verse 13 (Painter, 227–77; cf. Stott, 167–71), while Smalley sees verses 11–16 together under the rubric "the inspiration of love" (Smalley, 236). Nevertheless, we agree with Brown that the ἐν τούτῳ in verses 17 cannot begin a new paragraph (Brown, 545–46). Consequently we see 4:7, 11, and 16d as beginning new units thought, each of which begins and ends with a reference to God's love.

Clausal Outline for 1 John 4:11–16c

^{4:11a}Ἀγαπητοί, **εἰ** οὕτως ὁ θεὸς **ἠγάπησεν** ἡμᾶς,
^{4:11a} Beloved, **if** God so **loved** us,

^{4:11b} καὶ ἡμεῖς **ὀφείλομεν** ἀλλήλους **ἀγαπᾶν**.
^{4:11b} *then* **we** ourselves **are obligated to love** one another.

^{4:12a} θεὸν οὐδεὶς πώποτε **τεθέαται·**
^{4:12a} No one **has seen** God at any time;

^{4:12b} **ἐὰν ἀγαπῶμεν** ἀλλήλους,
^{4:12b} **if we** *persist in* **loving** one another,

^{4:12c} ὁ θεὸς ἐν ἡμῖν **μένει**
^{4:12c} God **abides** in us,

^{4:12d} καὶ ἡ ἀγάπη αὐτοῦ **τετελειωμένη** ἐν ἡμῖν **ἐστιν**.
^{4:12d} and his love **is perfected** in us.

^{4:13a} Ἐν τούτῳ **γινώσκομεν** (ὅτι ἐν αὐτῷ μένομεν καὶ αὐτὸς [μένει] ἐν ἡμῖν)
^{4:13a} By this **we know** (that we remain in him (=God) and he [*remains*] in us),

^{4:13b} **ὅτι** ἐκ τοῦ πνεύματος αὐτοῦ **δέδωκεν** ἡμῖν.
^{4:13b} **that he has given** to us *a portion of* his (=God's) Spirit.

^{4:14} καὶ ἡμεῖς **τεθεάμεθα** καὶ **μαρτυροῦμεν** (ὅτι ὁ πατὴρ ἀπέσταλκεν τὸν υἱὸν σωτῆρα τοῦ κόσμου).
^{4:14} And **we have seen** and **we** *now* **testify** (that the Father sent the Son *to be* the savior of the world).

^{4:15a} **ὃς ἐὰν ὁμολογήσῃ** (ὅτι Ἰησοῦς ἐστιν ὁ υἱὸς τοῦ θεοῦ),
^{4:15a} **Whoever professes** (that Jesus is the Son of God),

^{4:15b} ὁ θεὸς ἐν αὐτῷ **μένει**
^{4:15b} God **remains** in him (or her),

^{4:15c} καὶ αὐτὸς [μένει] ἐν τῷ θεῷ.
^{4:15c} and he (or she) [*remains*] in God.

^{4:16a} καὶ ἡμεῖς **ἐγνώκαμεν**
^{4:16a} And *so* **we** ourselves **have come to know**

4:16b καὶ **πεπιστεύκαμεν** τὴν ἀγάπην
4:16b and **we have** *come to* **believe** the love

                            |

4:16c **ἣν ἔχει** ὁ θεὸς ἐν ἡμῖν.
4:16c **that** God **has** for us.

SYNTAX EXPLAINED FOR 1 JOHN 4:11–16c

4:11a εἰ: The Greek word εἰ is a conjunction meaning "if" or "since" (BDAG, s.v. "εἰ" 3, p. 278). **Syntactically,** εἰ identifies the clause as a dependent conjunctive clause. The entire clause, "Beloved, *if* God so loved us" (Ἀγαπητοί, εἰ οὕτως ὁ θεὸς ἠγάπησεν ἡμᾶς) functions adverbially. It modifies the verb, "we are obligated" (ὀφείλομεν). The word "so" (οὕτως) here seems to be a linguistic link to John 3:16 where we learn that God *so* loved the world that he gave his one and only Son. The noun "beloved" is a vocative of direct address and serves as a paragraph break. **Semantically,** εἰ is a marker of a cause: "since" (NRSV NIV NLT) or "if" (KJV ASV NASB ESV NET CNT). The rendering "since" appears appropriate because John has affirmed the truth of the protasis elsewhere in his letter, yet "if" is preferred to discourage the idea that John is lecturing (W, 694). What John affirms is evident in the accompanying verb.

ἠγάπησεν: The Greek word ἠγάπησεν is third person singular aorist active indicative from the verb ἀγαπάω meaning "to cherish," "to have affection for," "to love," or "to have a warm regard for and interest in another" (BDAG, s.v. "ἀγαπάω" 1bα, p. 5). **Syntactically,** ἠγάπησεν is the governing verb of the dependent adverbial εἰ clause. **Semantically,** ἠγάπησεν is a constative aorist: "loved" (cf. KJV NASB ESV NIV NET etc.). As in 4:10, ἠγάπησεν once again describes God's act of loving as a whole in a summary fashion without any specifics (W, 557). God loved ordinary people. He loved them enough that he gave Jesus to atone for their sins (1 John 3:10).

4:11b καί: The Greek word καί is a conjunction meaning "then" (BDAG, s.v. "καί" 1bδ, p. 494). **Syntactically,** καί introduces an independent conjunctive clause: "*then* we ourselves ought to love one another" (καὶ ἡμεῖς ὀφείλομεν ἀλλήλους ἀγαπᾶν). The entire clause functions as the apodosis of the first class condition. **Semantically,** καί introduces the apodosis of the preceding clause: "then" (NET). While many translations consider καί to be a continuative connective, "also" (KJV ASV NASB NRSV ESV NIV CNT), the presence of the previous εἰ clause favors the translation "then." So, based upon the assumption that God loved ordinary people, *then* some sort of conclusion is expected. That conclusion is found in the next two verses.

ὀφείλομεν: The Greek word ὀφείλομεν is first person plural present active indicative from the verb ὀφείλω meaning "to be obligated" or "to be under obligation to meet certain social and moral expectations" (BDAG, s.v. "ὀφείλω" 2ab, p. 743). **Syntactically,** ὀφείλομεν is the main verb of the independent conjunctive καί clause and is functioning as an apodosis. The subject is the emphatic personal pronoun "we" (ἡμεῖς) and refers to John and the readers of his letter. The presence of the pronoun is to emphasize the point that what God has done, we should imitate (Culy, 110). **Semantically,** ὀφείλομεν is a customary present: "we are obligated" or "we must" or "we ought" (cf. KJV NASB ESV NIV NET etc). While the word "ought" indicates the believer's obligation, the customary present indicates an ongoing action (W, 521). John underscores a believer's ongoing obligation. That obligation is revealed in the infinitive (ἀγαπᾶν).

ἀγαπᾶν: The Greek word ἀγαπᾶν is a present active infinitive from the verb ἀγαπάω meaning "to love" or "to have a warm regard for and interest in another" person (BDAG, s.v. "ἀγαπάω" 1aα, p. 5). **Syntactically,** it is part of the main verb. **Semantically**: ἀγαπᾶν is a complementary infinitive: "to love" (cf. KJV NASB ESV NIV NET etc.). The infinitive completes the thought of the verb "we are obligated" (ὀφείλομεν; cf. W, 598). Since God loved ordinary people enough that he gave Jesus to atone for their sins, then those who believe in him ought to show a similar kind of love to fellow believers.

4:12a τεθέαται: The Greek word τεθέαται is third person singular perfect middle indicative from the verb θεάομαι meaning "to see" or "to look at" or "to have an intent look at something" (BDAG, s.v. "θεάομαι" 1a, p. 445). **Syntactically,** τεθέαται is the main verb of the independent clause: "No one *has seen* God at any time" (θεὸν οὐδεὶς πώποτε τεθέαται). The subject of the verb is the indefinite pronoun "no one" (οὐδείς). **Semantically,** τεθέαται is a gnomic perfect: "has seen" (cf. KJV NASB ESV NIV NET etc). "No one" (οὐδείς) indicates a timeless truth about all people (W, 580). Unlike John's usage of this verb to describe his seeing Jesus (1 John 1:1), here John emphasizes that no one has seen God. So God must be made known in other ways.

Theological Nugget: What does John mean when he says that no one has seen God? He is most likely representing his Jewish theological tradition that asserted that God was not seen at Sinai, only heard (Deut. 4:10–12; Exod. 33:15–23). This does not deny the fact that something was indeed seen (Exod. 24:9–11; Deut. 34:7, 10; cf. Josephus, *A.J.* 3.5.3 §88). The statement seems out of place because John does not seem to be countering people who were claiming to have seen God. John does not elaborate on why he is making this point until verse 20 where he claims that if someone cannot love another person who is right in front of them, they cannot by definition love God who is invisible. Therefore, the succeeding group of clauses is closely tied to John's gnomic truth about God. What John says is this: no one sees God *except* through the behavior of the confessing community. When followers of Jesus love one another, they demonstrate the character of God. When people see the loving community of Jesus, they see God (cf. Brown, 520).

4:12b ἐάν: The Greek word ἐάν is a conjunction meaning "if" (BDAG, s.v. "ἐάν" 1aα, p. 267). **Syntactically,** ἐάν identifies the clause as a dependent conjunctive clause. The entire dependent ἐάν clause: "*if* we *persist in* loving one another" (ἐὰν ἀγαπῶμεν ἀλλήλους) functions adverbially. It modifies the verb "remains" (μένει) and the periphrastic construction "is perfected" (τετελειωμένη ... ἐστιν). **Semantically,** ἐάν introduces a third class conditional clause of probability: "if" (cf. KJV NASB ESV NIV NET etc). The condition is uncertain of fulfillment but still likely (W, 696). That uncertain condition is found in the next verb.

ἀγαπῶμεν: The Greek word ἀγαπῶμεν is first person plural present active subjunctive from the verb ἀγαπάω meaning "to love" or "to have a warm regard for and interest in another" person (BDAG, s.v. "ἀγαπάω" 1aα, p. 5). The verb is in the subjunctive mood because ἐάν takes the subjunctive. **Syntactically,** ἀγαπῶμεν is the governing verb of the dependent adverbial ἐάν clause. The subject of the verb is the implied "we" embedded in the verb and refers to John and his readers. The direct object of the verb is the reciprocal pronoun "one another" (ἀλλήλους). It indicates the type of love that is evidence of God's existence within the community. **Semantically,** ἀγαπῶμεν is a customary present: "we *persist in* loving" or "we love" (cf. KJV NASB ESV NIV NET etc.). The present tense underscores a pattern of behavior (W, 521). In the likelihood that a person persists in love toward other believers, a certain fact may be concluded. That fact is found in the next clause.

4:12c μένει: The Greek word μένει is third person singular present active indicative from the verb μένω meaning "to remain," "to abide," or "to continue," or is used of "someone who does not leave" (BDAG, s.v. "μένω" 1aβ, p. 631). **Syntactically,** μένει is the main verb of the independent clause: "God *abides* in us" (ὁ θεὸς ἐν ἡμῖν μένει). It is the first of two clauses that function as an apodosis of the third class ἐάν adverbial clause. The subject is the noun, "God" (ὁ θεός). **Semantically,** μένει is a customary present: "remains" or "abides" (ASV NASB ESV CNT) or "lives" (NRSV NIV NLT; cf. KJV) or "resides" (NET). The present tense underscores God's continual presence in the lives of those who love others (W, 521). The relationship between the protasis (adverbial ἐάν clause) and the apodosis (independent μένει clause) is an evidence-inference construction. When believers love each other, it is evidence that God and his love abide in them and in their community. And yet there is another apodosis in 4:12d.

^{4:12d} καί: The Greek word καί is a conjunction meaning "and" (BDAG, s.v. "καί" 1a, p. 494). **Syntactically,** καί introduces an independent conjunctive clause: "*and* his love is perfected in us" (καὶ ἡ ἀγάπη αὐτοῦ τετελειωμένη ἐν ἡμῖν ἐστιν). It too is an apodosis to the third class ἐάν adverbial clause. **Semantically,** καί is a coordinating connector: "and" (cf. KJV NASB ESV NIV NET etc). It introduces an additional element to John's inference drawn from a loving community of believers (W, 671) evident in the next verb.

τετελειωμένη . . . ἐστίν: The Greek word τετελειωμένη is a nominative singular feminine perfect middle participle from the verb τελειόω meaning "to perfect" or "to overcome an imperfect state" (BDAG, s.v. "τελειόω" 2eβ, p. 996). The Greek word ἐστίν is third person singular present active indicative from the verb εἰμί that acts as an auxiliary verb (BDAG, s.v. "εἰμί" 11a, p. 285). **Syntactically,** τετελειωμένη . . . ἐστίν is a perfect periphrastic construction where a participle and a verb of being work together to form a finite verbal idea. This two-verb construction is "a *round-about* way of saying what could be expressed by a single verb" (W, 647). The periphrasis is the main verb of the independent clause that is functioning as the second part of apodosis of the ἐάν clause. The subject is the nominal phrase "his love" (ἡ ἀγάπη αὐτοῦ). **Semantically,** τετελειωμένη . . . ἐστίν is an intensive perfect: "is perfected" (KJV ASV NASB NRSV ESV NET CNT). The perfect is used to emphasize the results or present state produced by a past action, namely, perfection (W, 574). When believers love one another, they are imitating the love of God, which is manifested and completed among them. They are in the process of overcoming their imperfect state and thereby being perfected. So not only can it be seen that God abides in a community of believers, but also that God's love is perfected among them.

Syntactical Nugget: How is the genitive pronoun "his" (αὐτοῦ) to be understood? The genitive pronoun "his" (αὐτοῦ) in the nominal phrase "his love" (ἡ ἀγάπη αὐτοῦ) modifying the articular noun "love" (ἡ ἀγάπη) can be a subjective genitive (God's love) or an objective genitive (love for God). The difference between the two is substantial. Are believers manifesting God's love when they love one another or are they manifesting their love for God. Since God is the subject of the previous clause (God lives in us), it seems likely that this should be taken as a subjective genitive (Brown, 521). Culy, however, suggests that it could be intentional ambiguity or "semantic density" on the part of John (Culy, 111), meaning that we shouldn't make a choice, because John is being ambiguous. Nevertheless, classifying "his" (αὐτοῦ) as a subjective genitive seems best. God's love is seen in the life of the believer when they love others. And this selfless imitation of God is evidence that God has an abiding relationship with believers (see 1 John 3:24; also 2:5, 20, 27). All of this is perhaps an answer to Jesus's prayer in John 17:23 that his followers might be perfected into one. Evidence of perfected love involves keeping God's word, caring for other believers, and imitating Christ's selflessness.

4:13a ἐν τούτῳ: The Greek word ἐν is a preposition meaning "by" (BDAG, s.v. "ἐν" 5b, p. 328). The Greek word τούτῳ is declined as a dative singular neuter from the demonstrative pronoun οὗτος meaning "this one" (BDAG, s.v. "οὗτος" 1bβ, p. 741). **Syntactically,** ἐν τούτῳ introduces an independent prepositional clause: "*by this* we know that we remain in him and he [remains] in us" (Ἐν τούτῳ γινώσκομεν ὅτι ἐν αὐτῷ μένομεν καὶ αὐτὸς ἐν ἡμῖν). "By this" (ἐν τούτῳ) occurs frequently in 1 John (2:3, 4, 5; 3:10, 16, 19, 24; 4:2, 9, 10, 17; 5:2). **Semantically,** ἐν τούτῳ can either be anaphoric, pointing back to the preceding discussion, or cataphoric, pointing forward. Here "*by this*" is cataphoric and points forward to the ὅτι clause. The content of the prepositional phrase is found in the ὅτι clause (v. 13b).

γινώσκομεν: The Greek word γινώσκομεν is first person plural present active indicative from the verb γινώσκω meaning "to know" or "to know about" or "to arrive at a knowledge of something" (BDAG, s.v. "γινώσκω" 1, p. 200). **Syntactically,** γινώσκομεν is the main verb of the independent clause. The subject of the verb is an implied "we" embedded in the verb and refers to John and his readers who live in love for other believers. **Semantically,** γινώσκομεν is a customary present: "we know" (cf. KJV NASB ESV NET NIV etc.). It points out that believers have a consistent knowledge (W, 521). It's not a secret knowledge because John provides the content of what all believers know in the next ὅτι clause.

ὅτι: The Greek word ὅτι is a conjunction meaning "that" (BDAG, s.v. "ὅτι" 1c, p. 731). **Syntactically,** ὅτι introduces a dependent conjunctive clause: "*that* we remain in him (=God) and he [remains] in us" (ὅτι ἐν αὐτῷ μένομεν καὶ αὐτὸς ἐν ἡμῖν). It functions substantivally as the direct object of the verb of perception "we know" (γινώσκομεν). The entire ὅτι clause is placed in parentheses in order to visualize its grammatical contribution to the independent clause. **Semantically,** ὅτι is an indirect discourse marker: "that" (cf. KJV NASB ESV NIV NET). It provides the content of the believer's knowledge (W, 456). What a follower of Jesus knows is rather significant and evident in the next verb.

μένομεν: The Greek word μένομεν is first person plural present active indicative from the verb μένω meaning "to remain," "to abide," "to continue," or is used of "someone who does not leave" (BDAG, s.v. "μένω" 1aβ, 631). **Syntactically,** μένομεν is the governing verb of the first part of the compound dependent substantival ὅτι clause. The subject is an implied "we" referring to John and his readers. **Semantically,** μένομεν is a customary present: "remains" or "abides" (ASV NASB ESV CNT) or "lives" (NRSV NIV NLT) or "resides" (NET). The present tense underscores our continual relationship with God (W, 521). Believers can be assured that they have an abiding relationship with God.

καί: The Greek word καί is a conjunction meaning "and" (BDAG, s.v. "καί" 1a, p. 494). **Syntactically,** καί introduces the second part of the substantival conjunctive clause: "*and* he [remains] in us" (καὶ αὐτὸς ἐν ἡμῖν). **Semantically,** καί is a coordinating connector of two clauses within the dependent substantival ὅτι clause: "and" (cf. KJV NASB ESV NIV NET etc.). It introduces some additional information about their relationship (W, 671). John adds more information to the simple fact that his readers have a relationship with God. That information is found in the next verb.

[μένει]: The Greek word μένει is third person singular present active indicative from the verb μένω meaning "to remain," "to abide," "to continue," or is used of "someone who does not leave" (BDAG, s.v. "μένω" 1aβ, 631). **Syntactically,** μένει is an ellipsis and the governing verb of the second part of the dependent substantival ὅτι clause. The subject is the emphatic pronoun "he" (αὐτός = God). **Semantically,** [μένει] is a customary present: "remains" or "abides" (ASV NASB NRSV ESV CNT) or "lives" (NIV; cf. NLT) or "resides" (NET). The present tense underscores God's continual relationship with believers (W, 521). So not only do his readers abide in God, John adds here that God abides in them as well. It is not a one-way relationship.

4:13b ὅτι: The Greek word ὅτι is a conjunction meaning "that" (BDAG, s.v. "ὅτι" 2a, p. 732). **Syntactically,** ὅτι introduces a dependent conjunctive clause: "*that* he has given us of his Spirit" (ὅτι ἐκ τοῦ πνεύματος αὐτοῦ δέδωκεν ἡμῖν). It modifies the demonstrative pronoun, "this" (τοῦτο). **Semantically,** ὅτι is epexegetical: "that" (NET; cf. NLT). It explains or clarifies the demonstrative (W, 459). The evidence of an abiding relationship with Jesus is highlighted in the next verb.

δέδωκεν: The Greek word δέδωκεν is third person singular perfect active indicative from the verb δίδωμι meaning "to give" or "to grant" (BDAG, s.v. "δίδωμι" 17b, p. 243). **Syntactically,** δέδωκεν is the governing verb of the dependent adjectival ὅτι clause. The subject is an implied "he" embedded in the verb and is a reference to God. **Semantically,** δέδωκεν is an extensive perfect: "he *has* given" (cf. KJV NASB ESV NIV NET etc.). It emphasizes the completed action of God's giving of his Spirit (W, 577). John's readers can be assured that they have a relationship with God because he has given them his Spirit (cf. 2:20, 27; 3:24; 4:13). The evidence is the presence of God's Spirit in the lives of the followers of Jesus.

Semantical Nugget: How is the prepositional phrase ἐκ τοῦ πνεύματος αὐτοῦ to be understood? On the one hand, a literal rendering of the phrase "*of* his Spirit" (ἐκ τοῦ πνεύματος αὐτοῦ) seems like a strange way to describe the believer's relationship with Jesus. On the other hand, the preposition ἐκ could be classified as source (*from* the Spirit). However it seems more reasonable to classify ἐκ as partitive (*a portion* of the Spirit). Although it seems strange to think that God has given believers only a portion of his Spirit and not his entire Spirit. Culy, following Fee, argues that this is the best way to understand it (Culy, 112). The idea is not that John's readers were once for all given the Spirit at conversion, but that God constantly provides them with empowerment from the Spirit throughout the course of their daily lives. Therefore, the presence of God's spiritual empowering in the daily lives of believers is evidence that they have an abiding relationship with God.

⁴:¹⁴ καί: The Greek word καί is a conjunction meaning "and" (BDAG, s.v. "καί" 1a, p. 495). **Syntactically,** καί introduces the independent conjunctive clause: "*and* we have seen *and* testify that the Father sent the Son to be the savior of the world" (καὶ ἡμεῖς τεθεάμεθα καὶ μαρτυροῦμεν ὅτι ὁ πατὴρ ἀπέσταλκεν τὸν υἱὸν σωτῆρα τοῦ κόσμου). **Semantically,** καί is a coordinating connector of two independent clauses: "and" (KJV ASV NASB NRSV ESV NIV NET). It introduces additional information about the reader's reciprocated abiding relationship with God (W, 671). There is the sense that John echoes the beginning of the letter where he focused on eyewitness accounts to the life of Jesus. They beheld the selfless love of the Father that was manifested through the sending of his Son into the world in order to save it from sin.

τεθεάμεθα: The Greek word τεθεάμεθα is first person plural perfect middle indicative from the verb θεάομαι meaning "to see" or "to behold" or "to perceive something above and beyond what is merely seen with the eye" (BDAG, s.v. "θεάομαι" 3a, p. 445). **Syntactically,** τεθεάμεθα is the first main verb of a compound independent conjunctive clause. The subject of the verb is the emphatic personal pronoun "we" (ἡμεῖς). It refers to John and his readers. **Semantically,** τεθεάμεθα is an extensive perfect: "we *have* seen" (cf. KJV NASB ESV NIV NET etc.). It emphasizes the completed action of what John saw in the past on which his current message is founded (W, 577). Since John and other eyewitnesses have seen the life, death, and resurrection of Jesus, they are able to testify that God indeed sent his Son, Jesus, into the world to save it.

μαρτυροῦμεν: The Greek word μαρτυροῦμεν is first person plural present active indicative from the verb μαρτυρέω meaning "to bear witness" or "to confirm or attest something to be true based upon personal knowledge" (BDAG, s.v. "μαρτυρέω" 1a, 1b, p. 618). **Syntactically,** μαρτυροῦμεν is the second main verb of the compound independent conjunctive clause joined with a καί. The subject is also the emphatic personal pronoun "we" (ἡμεῖς). It too refers to John and his readers. **Semantically,** μαρτυροῦμεν is a progressive present: "*now* testify" (NLT) or "do testify" (KJV NRSV). It emphasizes John's continuous proclamation (W, 518). John and other eyewitnesses are right now bearing witness to what they have seen (cf. 1:2c). The specifics of their witness are disclosed in the next dependent ὅτι clause.

ὅτι: The Greek word ὅτι is a conjunction meaning "that" (BDAG, s.v. "ὅτι" 1a, p. 731). **Syntactically,** ὅτι introduces a dependent conjunctive clause: "*that* the Father sent his Son to be the savior of the world" (ὅτι ὁ πατὴρ ἀπέσταλκεν τὸν υἱὸν σωτῆρα τοῦ κόσμου). It functions substantivally as the direct object of the compound verbs of perception: "we have seen" (τεθεάμεθα) and "we bear witness" (μαρτυροῦμεν). The entire ὅτι clause is placed in parentheses in order to visualize its contribution to the independent clause. **Semantically,** ὅτι is an indirect discourse marker: "that" (cf. KJV NASB ESV NIV NET etc.). The ὅτι clause provides the content of what John and other eyewitnesses testify (W, 456). The content of their message is evident in the next discussion about ἀπέσταλκεν.

ἀπέσταλκεν: The Greek word ἀπέσταλκεν is third person singular perfect active indicative from the verb ἀποστέλλω meaning "to send" or "to dispatch someone for the achievement of some objective" (BDAG, s.v. "ἀποστέλλω" 1bγ, p. 121). **Syntactically,** ἀπέσταλκεν is the governing verb of the dependent substantival clause. The subject is the proper noun "the Father" (ὁ πατήρ). We have here another double accusative object-complement construction. The direct object of the verb "sent" (ἀπέσταλκεν) is the noun "Son" (τὸν υἱόν). The second accusative functions as a complementary noun, "the savior" (σωτῆρα). This type of construction is often translated with the words "to be." Therefore, we should translate this, "that the Father has sent the Son *to be* the savior of the world" (W, 181–86). **Semantically,** ἀπέσταλκεν is an extensive perfect: "he sent" (KJV ASV NLT) or "has sent" (NASB NRSV ESV NIV NET CNT). It emphasizes a past action from which a present state emerges (W, 577). Since the Father sent the Son into the world, its inhabitants are now able to experience salvation. They saw with their eyes and now bear witness to the fact that Jesus came to save the world (cf. 1:1–3).

Theological Nugget: What is the theological significance of the word "the savior" (σωτῆρα)? The word "the savior" (σωτῆρα) only occurs twice in John's writings (John 4:42; 1 John 4:13). Hellenistic literature mainly uses the term in medical contexts to express healings where people are saved from maladies or diseases (Plutarch, *Adul. am.* 11; Sophocles, *Oed. tyr.*; Philo, *Leg.* 3.129; *Praem.* 145, 170; *Det.* 110; *Ios.* 110). In the LXX, it is used more broadly for any human conqueror or deliverer from oppressive powers (Judg. 3:9, 15), and often of God as the ideal "deliverer" (1 Sam. 10:19; Isa. 45:15, 21; Jdt 9:11; 3 Macc 6:29; Wis 16:7; Sir 51:1). In the New Testament, it is used to describe both God (1 Tim. 4:10; cf. Luke 1:47) and Jesus (Titus 2:13; cf. Luke 2:11) as those who save those who believe in Jesus. In John 4:42, it is the Samaritan woman who calls Jesus "the savior of the world." It seems likely that Jesus's atoning work is in view here. Throughout John's writings God's intention for sending Jesus into the world was to be an atoning sacrifice for the sins of the world (John 3:16; 1 John 2:2). Jesus saves people from their sin.

4:15a ὃς ἐάν: The Greek word ὃς is a nominative singular neuter from the relative pronoun ὅς meaning "who" (BDAG, s.v. "ὅς" 1jα, p. 727). The Greek word ἐάν is a conjunction meaning "when" or "whoever" (BDAG, s.v. "ἐάν" 2, p. 268). It is typically rendered "whoever" (NASB ESV cf. KJV ASV) or "anyone" (NIV NET CNT). **Syntactically,** the Greek construction ὃς ἐάν is an indefinite relative pronoun. It identifies the clause as a dependent pronominal clause. The entire clause "*whoever* professes that Jesus is the Son of God" (ὃς ἐάν ὁμολογήσῃ ὅτι Ἰησοῦς ἐστιν ὁ υἱὸς τοῦ θεοῦ) functions adjectivally. It modifies the personal pronouns "him" (αὐτῷ) and "he" (αὐτός) in the subsequent independent clause (4:15b). The entire ὃς ἐάν clause provides further information about any person within whom God remains.

ὁμολογήσῃ: The Greek word ὁμολογήσῃ is third person singular aorist active subjunctive from the verb ὁμολογέω meaning "to confess" or "to profess" or "to acknowledge something ordinarily in public" (BDAG, s.v. "ὁμολογέω" 4b, p. 708). **Syntactically,** ὁμολογήσῃ is the governing verb of the dependent adjectival indefinite relative ὃς ἐάν clause. The subject is the indefinite relative pronoun "whoever" (ὃς ἐάν). **Semantically,** ὁμολογήσῃ is a gnomic aorist: "professes" or "confesses" (NASB ESV) or "confess" (NRSV NET CNT). It presents a timeless or general fact about anyone who professes Jesus (W, 562). In 1 John 1:9, this particular verb occurs in the present tense "if we confess our sin," while here in 4:15 it appears in the aorist tense. Why the shift in tense? In 1:9 there is the expressed need for every believer to habitually confess their sins, while here John merely describes a generic one-time event. This is a rather significant theological distinction.

ὅτι: The Greek word ὅτι is a conjunction meaning "that" (BDAG, s.v. "ὅτι" 1a, p. 731). **Syntactically,** ὅτι introduces a dependent conjunctive clause: "*that* Jesus is God's Son" (ὅτι Ἰησοῦς ἐστιν ὁ υἱὸς τοῦ θεοῦ). It functions substantivally as the direct object of the verb, "professes" (ὁμολογήσῃ). The entire ὅτι clause is placed in parentheses in order to visualize its contribution as the dependent indefinite relative ὃς ἐάν clause. **Semantically,** ὅτι is an indirect discourse marker: "that" (cf. KJV NASB ESV NIV NET etc.). It provides

the content of the profession or confession (W, 456). The profession is about
Jesus as God's Son (= God's Messiah).

Theological Nugget: What is the theological significance of the word "I confess" or "I profess" (ὁμολογέω)? The content of ὁμολογέω is rather consistent in John's writings. In 1 John 2:23, John underscores that the person who
persists in their confession about *Jesus as Messiah* has a relationship with
God. In 1 John 4:2–3, the emphasis is that the person who repeatedly acknowledges in his or her teaching that *Jesus was human and is God's Messiah*
reveals that their teaching is from God, versus the person who does not profess that *Jesus was human and is God's Messiah*. In 1 John 4:15, there is once
again the emphasis on professing *Jesus as God's Son* (= God's Messiah) and
God's remaining within that person. This confession or profession of Jesus's
identity is very significant in 1 John. It is a must to believe that Jesus is indeed
the Messiah for a relationship with God the Father to exist.

ἐστίν: The Greek word ἐστίν is third person singular present active indicative from the verb εἰμί meaning "to be" or "to be in close connection with"
(BDAG, s.v. "εἰμί" 2a, p. 283). **Syntactically,** ἐστίν is the governing verb of
the dependent substantival ὅτι clause. The subject of the verb is the proper
noun "Jesus" ('Ιησοῦς). This is an example where a proper name assumes the
position of the subject of an εἰμί verb over an articular noun or messianic title, "Son of God" (W, 45). **Semantically,** ἐστίν is an equative present: "is" (cf.
KJV NASB ESV NIV NET etc.). John equates Jesus with God's Son (= Messiah).

4:15b μένει: The Greek word μένει is third person singular present active indicative
from the verb μένω meaning "to remain," "to abide," "to continue," or is used
of "someone who does not leave" (BDAG, s.v. "μένω" 1aβ, p. 631). **Syntactically,** μένει is the first main verb of the compound independent clause: "God
remains in him (or her)" (ὁ θεὸς ἐν αὐτῷ μένει). The subject is the proper
noun "God" (ὁ θεός). **Semantically,** μένει is a customary present: "remains"
or "dwells" (KJV) or "abides" (ASV NASB NRSV ESV CNT) or "lives" (NIV; cf. NLT)
or "resides" (NET). The present tense underscores God's continual relationship
(W, 521). John tells his readers that God has a continual relationship with those
who profess that Jesus is God's Messiah.

4:15c καί: The Greek word καί is a conjunction meaning "and" (BDAG, s.v. "καί"
1bα, p. 494). **Syntactically,** καί introduces another independent conjunctive
clause: "*and* he (or she) [remain] in God" (καὶ αὐτὸς [μένει] ἐν τῷ θεῷ).
Semantically, καί is a coordinating connector: "and" (cf. KJV NASB ESV NIV
NET etc). It links two independent clauses together and provides additional
information (W, 671). More specifically, John expands his previous thoughts
on God's relationship with those who profess Jesus to be Messiah.

[μένει]: The Greek word μένει is third person singular present active indicative from the verb μένω meaning "to remain," "to abide," "to continue," or is said of "someone who does not leave" (BDAG, s.v. "μένω" 1aβ, p. 631). **Syntactically,** μένει is an elliptical verb of the second part of the compound independent clause. The subject is the emphatic personal pronoun "he" (αὐτός). **Semantically,** μένει is a customary present: "remains." Most translations do not indicate the presence of an elliptical [μένει]; it is understood. The present tense underscores for John's readers their continual relationship with God (W, 521). In this additional information (καί), John underscores that the one who confesses that Jesus is God's Son (= Messiah) has an abiding relationship with God.

Theological Nugget: What is the significance of the word "to remain" or "to abide" (μένω)? The Greek word μένω occurs twenty-four times in 1 John. Sometimes it speaks of God who remains or continues in his relationship with believers (3:24; 4:12, 15). Other times it speaks of believers who remain or retain their relationship with God (2:24, 27; 3:6, 24; 4:13). It's an important word because it reveals that a relationship is two-way activity: God's relationship with ordinary people and ordinary people's relationship with God. Loyalty is a two way street in John's writings.

4:16a καί: The Greek word καί is a conjunction meaning "and so" or "indeed" or is used "to introduce a result that comes from what precedes" (BDAG, s.v. "καί" 1bζ, p. 495). **Syntactically,** καί introduces an independent conjunctive clause: "*and* so we have come to know" (καὶ ἡμεῖς ἐγνώκαμεν). **Semantically,** καί is inferential: "and so" (NIV) or "so" (NRSV ESV CNT). While most translations translate καί as "and" (KJV ASV NET), it seems more reasonable to also suggest that καί is inferential. "And so" underscores John's concluding remarks (W, 673).

ἐγνώκαμεν: The Greek word ἐγνώκαμεν is first person plural perfect active indicative from the verb γινώσκω meaning "to know" or "to have come to know" (BDAG, s.v. "γινώσκω" 6aα, p. 200). **Syntactically,** ἐγνώκαμεν is one of two main verbs of an independent conjunctive καί clause. The subject of the verb is the emphatic pronoun, "we" (ἡμεῖς). It refers to John and his readers who have an abiding relationship with God. The accusative, "love" (τὴν ἀγάπην), is an accusative for both "we have come to know" and "we have believed" (ἐγνώκαμεν and ἐγνώκαμεν). **Semantically,** ἐγνώκαμεν is an extensive perfect: "we *have come to* know" (NASB ESV NET) or "we *have* known" (KJV NRSV). It emphasizes a past act of knowledge from which a present state of understanding exists (W, 577). John's readers have come to *know* of God's love.

4:16b πεπιστεύκαμεν: The Greek word πεπιστεύκαμεν is first person plural perfect active indicative from the verb πιστεύω meaning "to believe" or "to consider something to be true and therefore worthy of one's trust" (BDAG, s.v. "πιστεύω" 1bα, p. 816). **Syntactically,** πεπιστεύκαμεν is the second verb of this independent conjunctive καί clause: and we have believed the loved love" (καὶ πεπιστεύκαμεν τὴν γάπην). The subject of the verb is the emphatic pronoun "we" (ἡμεῖς) that refers to John and readers who have a relationship with God. **Semantically,** πεπιστεύκαμεν is an extensive perfect: "*have come to* believe" or "*have* believed" (NASB). It emphasizes a past action from which a present state emerges (W, 577). John's readers have also come to *believe* the message about God's love.

4:16c ἥν: The Greek word ἥν is accusative singular feminine from the relative pronoun ὅς meaning "which" (BDAG, s.v. "ὅς" 1a, p. 725). **Syntactically,** ἥν introduces a relative clause: "*that* God has for us" (ἥν ἔχει ὁ θεὸς ἐν ἡμῖν). It functions adjectivally modifying the noun "love" (ἀγάπην) This relative pronoun is in the accusative case because it is the direct object of the verb "has" (ἔχει). It provides the further information about the love of God.

ἔχει: The Greek word ἔχει is third person singular present active indicative from the verb ἔχω meaning "to have" or "to possess" (BDAG, s.v. "ἔχω" 1a, p. 420). **Syntactically,** ἔχει is the governing verb of the dependent relative clause. The subject is the articular proper noun "God" (ὁ θεός). **Semantically,** ἔχει is a customary present: "has" (cf. KJV NASB ESV NIV NET etc.). It emphasizes an ongoing state for believers (W, 521). God has an ongoing love relationship with believers.

Syntactical Nugget: How is the prepositional phrase ἐν ἡμῖν to be understood? On the one hand, Brown translates it spatially: "in us." He argues that it refers to God's love that is expressed in believers when they love each other (Brown, 525–26). In 4:12, John points out that when the believer shows selfless love, they prove that God abides in them. On the other hand, most translations and commentators translate ἐν ἡμῖν referentially: "for us." Thus John references God's love for us as demonstrated in the selfless sending of Jesus, the Messiah. In 4:9, God's love is revealed among us through the sending of his one and only Son into the world (John 3:16). John's broader context underscores that we have come to know what selfless love is through the example of the Father sending Jesus into the world to save ordinary people from their sin (1 John 2:2). Based upon this selfless example, believers who have a relationship with God should imitate that same selfless love.

1 JOHN 4:16d–21

Big Greek Idea: After asserting that God is love, John now asserts that all those who love have a mutual bond with God that results in confidence before God (rather than fear of punishment), reveals God's initiation of love, speaks of misguided love, and expects anyone who truly loves God to love all others who also have a bond with God.

Structural Overview: Advancing his discussion from a community of believers' duty to love and subsequent proofs of a community's relationship with God (4:11–16c), John returns to his theme of love with a focus on what perfect love looks like (4:16d–21).[1]

John opens with a claim about God's love that serves as the mutual bond between believers with significant results (vv. 16d–18). First, John makes an assertion: God is (ἐστίν) love and identifies that those who live (μένει) lives of love have a mutual connection (μένει) with God (v 16d). In his summary (ἐν τούτῳ) of verse 16, John then describes the mutual bond between God and his followers as perfected (τετελείωται) with an impending result (ἵνα): confidence in the day of God's judgment (v. 17). This feeling of confidence differs from feeling fear. He asserts (ἐστίν) there is (ἐστίν) no fear in God's love. It is gone (βάλλει) because (ὅτι) fear involves punishment (v. 18).

John returns to a reasoned statement of fact with a contradiction (vv. 19–21). First, the reason (ὅτι) followers of Jesus love (ἀγαπῶμεν) is because God loved (ἠγάπησεν) his followers first (v. 19). Second, John draws attention to anyone who says (εἴπῃ) they love and yet detests a fellow follower of Jesus. It reveals (ἐστίν) their misguided understanding of God (v. 20a–c). This is why (γάρ) anyone who refuses to love visible fellow followers of Jesus, cannot love an invisible God (v. 20d–f). God's expectation is that anyone who truly loves God will love others who also have a bond with God (v. 21).

Outline:

> Followers of Jesus Have a Mutual Connection with God (vv. 17–18)
>> God is love (v. 16d)
>> God's love is the mutual bond between believers (v. 17)
>> God's love results in confidence and elimination of fear (v. 18)

---

1.   Once again, there remains a lack of agreement about where to break the verses (see the previous note). Here the challenge is where to end this section. For Brown, the polemical tone against the opponents, which surfaces in verse 20, is sufficient to indicate the start of a new paragraph (Brown, 563 cf. Painter, 277). For Painter, the paragraph begun in verse 16b concludes in verse 21 (Painter, 277; Strecker, 173). We follow Painter.

Love between Believers Demonstrates a Relationship with God (vv. 19–21)
>   Believers love because God loved believers first (v. 19)
>   The absence of love is a misunderstanding of God (v. 20a–c)
>   Believers love God via their love for other believers (v. 20d–f)
>   God expects to be loved and for believers to love others (v. 21)

CLAUSAL OUTLINE FOR 1 JOHN 4:16d–21

4:16d Ὁ θεὸς ἀγάπη **ἐστίν**,
4:16d God **is** love,

4:16e <u>καὶ</u> (ὁ μένων ἐν τῇ ἀγάπῃ) ἐν τῷ θεῷ **μένει**
4:16e <u>and</u> (the one who abides in love) **abides** in God

4:16f <u>καὶ</u> ὁ θεὸς ἐν αὐτῷ **μένει**.
4:1fc <u>and</u> God **abides** in him (or her).

4:17a <u>ἐν τούτῳ</u> **τετελείωται** ἡ ἀγάπη μεθ᾽ ἡμῶν,
4:17a <u>By this</u>, love **is perfected** with us,
      |
    4:17b **ἵνα** παρρησίαν **ἔχωμεν** ἐν τῇ ἡμέρᾳ τῆς κρίσεως,
    4:17b **so that** **we may have** confidence in the day of judgment,
         |
        4:17c **ὅτι** . . . καὶ ἡμεῖς **ἐσμεν** ἐν τῷ κόσμῳ τούτῳ.
        4:17c **because** . . . so also **are we** in this world
            |
           4:17d **καθὼς** ἐκεῖνός **ἐστιν**
           4:17d **just as** that one (= Jesus) **is**

4:18a φόβος οὐκ **ἔστιν** ἐν τῇ ἀγάπῃ,
4:18a There **is** no fear in love,

4:18b <u>ἀλλ</u>᾽ ἡ τελεία ἀγάπη ἔξω **βάλλει** τὸν φόβον,
4:18b <u>but</u> perfect love **expels** fear,
        |
        4:18c **ὅτι** ὁ φόβος κόλασιν **ἔχει**,
        4:18c **because** fear **includes** punishment,

        4:18d ὁ δὲ [ὅτι] φοβούμενος οὐ **τετελείωται**
        ἐν τῇ ἀγάπῃ.
        4:18d <u>and</u> [*because*] the one who fears **has** not
        been perfected in love.

^{4:19a} ἡμεῖς **ἀγαπῶμεν**,
^{4:19a} *As for us* (lit. We) **we** *persist in* **love**

|

       ^{4:19b} **ὅτι** αὐτὸς πρῶτος **ἠγάπησεν** ἡμᾶς.
       ^{4:19b} **because he** (= God) first **loved** us.

      ^{4:20a} **ἐάν** τις **εἴπῃ** (ὅτι Ἀγαπῶ τὸν θεόν),
      ^{4:20a} **If** someone **says,** "I love God,"

      |

     ^{4:20b} καὶ [*ἐάν* τις] τὸν ἀδελφὸν αὐτοῦ **μισῇ**,
     ^{4:20b} **and** [*if that same someone*] **hates** his (or her) brother (or sister)

     |

^{4:20c} ψεύστης **ἐστίν·**
^{4:20c} he (or she) **is** a liar;

^{4:20d} (ὁ γὰρ μὴ ἀγαπῶν τὸν ἀδελφὸν αὐτοῦ) . . . , τὸν θεὸν . . . οὐ δύναται ἀγαπᾶν.
^{4:20d} (for the one who does not love his brother [and sister]) . . . **is unable** to love God.

        ┌──────────┐   ┌──────────┐

      ^{4:20e} **ὃν ἑώρακεν**^{4:20f} **ὃν** οὐχ **ἑώρακεν**
      ^{4:20e} **whom he has seen**   ^{4:20f} **whom he has** not **seen**

^{4:21a} καὶ ταύτην τὴν ἐντολὴν **ἔχομεν** ἀπ᾽ αὐτοῦ,
^{4:21a} **And** this commandment **we have** from him (= God),

|

     ^{4:21b} **ἵνα** (ὁ ἀγαπῶν τὸν θεὸν) **ἀγαπᾷ** καὶ τὸν ἀδελφὸν αὐτοῦ.
     ^{4:21b} *namely* **that** (the one who loves God) **should love** his brother (and sister) also.

Syntax Explained for 1 John 4:16d–21

^{4:16d} ἐστίν: The Greek word ἐστίν is third person singular present active indicative from the verb εἰμί meaning "to be" or "to be in close connection with" (BDAG, s.v. "εἰμί" 2a, p. 283). **Syntactically,** ἐστίν is the main verb of the independent anacoluthon clause: "God *is* love" (Ὁ θεὸς ἀγάπη ἐστίν). The subject of the verb is the articular proper noun "God" (ὁ θεός). **Semantically,** ἐστίν is a gnomic present: "is" (cf. KJV NASB ESV NIV NET etc.). It identifies a timeless fact about God (W, 523). The verb equates God with his abiding character (cf. 1:5d). The equative nature of the verb of being here does not mean that this definition can go both ways (for more information, see note 4:8b).

^{4:16e} καί: The Greek word καί is a conjunction meaning "and" (BDAG, s.v. "καί" 1bα, p. 494). **Syntactically,** καί introduces the independent conjunctive clause: "*and* the one who abides in love abides in God" (καὶ ὁ μένων ἐν τῇ ἀγάπῃ ἐν τῷ θεῷ μένει). **Semantically,** καί is a coordinating connector: "and" (KJV ASV NASB NRSV ESV NIV NET NLT). The entire conjunctive clause links two independent clauses together and provides additional information about those who share God's character (W, 671). That additional information is found in the discussions about the next two Greek terms in the clause.

μένων: The Greek word μένων is a nominative masculine singular present active participle from the verb μένω meaning "to remain," "to abide," "to continue," or is used of "someone who does not leave" (BDAG, s.v. "μένω" 1aβ, p. 631). **Syntactically,** μένων introduces a dependent participle clause. The entire participial clause: "the one who abides in love" (ὁ μένων ἐν τῇ ἀγάπῃ) is functioning as the subject of the verb "abides" (μένει). The entire clause is placed in parentheses to visualize its substantival contribution to the clause. **Semantically,** μένων is a gnomic present: "the one who abides" (NASB) or "the one who remains" or "the one who resides" (NET) or "whoever lives" (NIV; cf. NLT). It describes a timeless fact about a generic believer (W, 523, 615), ordinary people who have a relationship with God.

μένει: The Greek word μένει is third person singular present active indicative from the verb μένω meaning "to remain," "to abide," "to continue," or is used of "someone who does not leave" (BDAG, s.v. "μένω" 1aβ, p. 631). **Syntactically,** μένει is the main verb of the independent conjunctive καί clause. The subject is the participial phrase: "*The one who abides* in love" (ὁ μένων ἐν τῇ ἀγάπῃ). **Semantically,** μένει is a gnomic present: "abides" (ASV NASB NRSV ESV CNT) or "lives" (NIV NLT). It describes a timeless fact (W, 523). Believers who demonstrate love show that they have a relationship with God.

^{4:16f} καί: The Greek word καί is a conjunction meaning "and" (BDAG, s.v. "καί" 1bα, p. 494). **Syntactically,** καί introduces the independent conjunctive clause: "*and* God abides in him (or her)" (καὶ ὁ θεὸς ἐν αὐτῷ μένει). **Semantically,** καί is a coordinating connector: "and" (KJV ASV NASB NRSV ESV NIV NET NLT). The entire conjunctive clause provides additional information about those who have a relationship with God (W, 671).

μένει: The Greek word μένει is third person singular present active indicative from the verb μένω meaning "to remain," "to abide," "to continue," or is used of "someone who does not leave" (BDAG, s.v. "μένω" 1aβ, p. 631). **Syntactically,** μένει is the main verb of the independent conjunctive clause. The subject is the articular proper noun "God" (ὁ θεός). **Semantically,** μένει is a gnomic present: "abides" (ASV NASB NRSV ESV CNT) or "lives" (NIV NLT). It describes a timeless fact (W, 523). The believer who demonstrates selfless love has a continual abiding relationship with God.

4:17a ἐν τούτῳ: The Greek word ἐν is a preposition meaning "by" (BDAG, s.v. "ἐν" 5b, p. 328). The Greek word τούτῳ is a dative singular neuter from the demonstrative pronoun οὗτος meaning "this one" (BDAG, s.v. "οὗτος" 1bβ, p. 741). **Syntactically,** ἐν τούτῳ introduces an independent prepositional clause: "*by this* love is perfected with us" (ἐν τούτῳ τετελείωται ἡ ἀγάπη μεθ᾽ ἡμῶν). "By this" (ἐν τούτῳ) occurs frequently in 1 John (2:3, 4, 5; 3:10, 16, 19, 24; 4:2, 9, 10, 13; 5:2). **Semantically,** ἐν τούτῳ can either be anaphoric, pointing back to the preceding discussion, or cataphoric, pointing forward. Here "by this" (ἐν τούτῳ) points back (anaphoric). It is a summary of the previous material about God's love abiding in believers.

Syntactical Nugget: Is this prepositional phrase ἐν τούτῳ anaphoric or cataphoric? The usual rule is that the prepositional phrase is cataphoric if it is followed by a subordinating conjunction. So some classify the phrase as cataphoric either pointing forward to the ἵνα clause or the subsequent ὅτι clause. If ἐν τούτῳ points forward to the ἵνα clause, then God perfects love in the life of the believer so that they can be confident when they are judged by him. It seems odd though to suggest that a believer's love is perfect (or mature) already in a future event. If ἐν τούτῳ points forward to the ὅτι clause, then love is perfected in us when we love just like Jesus loved when he was in the world. Having a ὅτι clause explicating a demonstrative is common in 1 John, but the intervening ἵνα clause makes this difficult. The best option seems to be that ἐν τούτῳ points back and serves as a summary of the previous material (anaphoric). Thus John summarizes that if believers continue in their abiding relationship with God by imitating his selfless love, then love itself has come to maturity in them (Strecker, 162). This option would seem to fit with the author's emphasis in 4:12 that God's love is perfected in us when we love others (cf. Bateman[1], 488–89; also Culy, 115–16).

τετελείωται: The Greek word τετελείωται is third person singular perfect passive indicative from the verb τελειόω meaning "to perfect" or "to overcome an imperfect state" (BDAG, s.v. "τελειόω" 2eβ, p. 996). **Syntactically,** τετελείωται is the main verb of the independent clause. The subject is the articular noun "love" (ἡ ἀγάπη). **Semantically,** τετελείωται is an intensive perfect: "is perfected" (NASB NET CNT; cf. ESV). It emphasizes the present state of love within the believer that emerges from a past action (W, 574). John's summarized point is that love is being perfected in the believer due to God, who is love, abiding in us.

Syntactical Nugget: What does the prepositional phrase "with us" (μεθ᾽ ἡμῶν) modify, the noun "love" (ἡ ἀγάπη) or the verb "is perfected" (τετελείωται)? On the one hand, if it is modifying the noun "love" (ἡ ἀγάπη), it would be translated: "the love which is with us is perfected" or "our love is made perfect" (seemingly KJV). On the other hand, if it is functioning adverbially modifying the verb "is perfected" (τετελείωται), it would be translated: "the love is perfected for us" (cf. NASB NIV NET). Since there is no article before the prepositional phrase, the best option seems to be that the prepositional phrase is functioning adverbially (Culy, 116). If this is the case the emphasis is on the idea that when believers love one another, God's love in us is brought to maturity.

4:17b ἵνα: The Greek word ἵνα is a conjunction meaning "so that" (BDAG, s.v. "ἵνα" 3, p. 477). **Syntactically,** ἵνα introduces a conjunctive dependent clause: "*so that* we might have confidence in the day of judgment" (ἵνα παρρησίαν ἔχωμεν ἐν τῇ ἡμέρᾳ τῆς κρίσεως). While it is possible to view the ἵνα clause as epexegetical to "this" (τούτῳ; KJV ASV NRSV NET CNT; BDAG, s.v. "οὗτος" 2e, p. 476), it seems the entire ἵνα clause is adverbial. It modifies the verb "is perfected" (τετελείωται) (See the discussion above for 4:17a, ἐν τούτῳ). **Semantically,** ἵνα is a result: "so that" (NASB ESV NIV). It is a substitute for the infinitive of result (BDAG, s.v. "ἵνα" 3, p. 477) and thereby expresses the result of the verb τετελείωται (W, 473). The result of God's love being perfected in the believer is found in their confidence.

ἔχωμεν: The Greek word ἔχωμεν is first person plural present active subjunctive from the verb ἔχω meaning "to have" or "to experience an inner condition" (BDAG, s.v. "ἔχω" 7aβ, p. 421). The verb is in the subjunctive mood because ἵνα takes the subjunctive. **Syntactically,** ἔχωμεν is the governing verb of the dependent ἵνα clause. The subject is the pronoun "we" embedded in the verb and refers to John and his readers. **Semantically,** ἔχωμεν is an ingressive future present: "we may have" (KJV ASV NASB NRSV ESV NET CNT) or "we will have" (NIV; cf. NLT). It describes a condition (e.g., confidence) begun in the present time but that will be experienced fully in the future (W, 537). Believers who exhibit God's love in their lives will have confidence when they stand before him on judgment day (cf. 5:14).

4:17c ὅτι: The Greek word ὅτι is a conjunction meaning "because" (BDAG, s.v. "ὅτι" 4a, p. 732). **Syntactically,** ὅτι introduces a dependent conjunctive clause: "*because* just as he is, so also are we in this world" (ὅτι καθὼς ἐκεῖνός ἐστιν καὶ ἡμεῖς ἐσμεν ἐν τῷ κόσμῳ τούτῳ). The entire clause functions adverbially. It modifies "we may have" (ἔχωμεν). **Semantically,** ὅτι is causal: "because" (cf. KJV NASB ESV NIV NET etc.). It provides the reason (W, 460) why believers can have confidence when we stand before God on judgment day. It is because of Jesus's example.

Syntactical Nugget: How is ὅτι to be understood? Three options exist. First as discussed above, the ὅτι clause could be functioning adjectivally providing us with the content of the demonstrative (for reasons why that does not seem to be the best option, see note 4:17a above). The next two options understand the force of the phrase to be causal. But the question is this: Which main verb does it modify? Is it "is perfected" (τετελείωται) or is it "we have" (ἔχωμεν)? If the ὅτι modifies the verb "is perfected" (τετελείωται), then John would be telling us that the reason why love is perfected in the believer who has an abiding relationship with God is because they are imitating the selfless example of love that Jesus lived out while he was here. If, however, ὅτι modifies the verb, "we have" (ἔχωμεν), then John is providing us with a reason why we can be confident on judgment day. It seems either is possible.

ἐσμέν: The Greek word ἐσμέν is first person plural present active indicative from the verb εἰμί meaning "to be" or "to be in close connection with" (BDAG, s.v. "εἰμί" 2a, p. 283). **Syntactically,** ἐσμέν is the governing verb of the dependent conjunctive ὅτι clause. The subject of the verb is an implied "we" embedded in the verb and refers to John and anyone else who has a relationship with God. The καί in this clause is not a coordinating connector but rather an adjunctive ("so also"; BDAG, s.v. "καί" 2a, p. 495; NASB ESV NET). It adds emphasis to the comparison between the believer who loves and the selfless life of Jesus (W, 671). **Semantically,** ἐσμέν is an equative present: "we are" (cf. KJV NASB ESV NIV NET etc.). It is an identifying statement that underscores the believer's close connection with the world, namely, that believers live in this physical world.

4:17d καθώς: The Greek word καθώς is a conjunction meaning "as" (BDAG, s.v. "καθώς" 493.1). **Syntactically,** καθώς introduces a dependent conjunctive clause. The entire καθώς clause: *just as* that one is" (καθὼς ἐκεῖνός ἐστιν) is functioning adverbially modifying the verb "we *are*" (ἐσμέν). **Semantically,** καθώς is comparative: "just as" (KJV ASV NASB NRSV ESV CNT). It makes a comparison between Jesus and believers (W, 675). Believers who have a relationship with God are similar to Jesus in that they too live in the world, face similar people conflicts, and love other people whether friend or foe.

ἐστίν: The Greek word ἐστίν is third person singular present active indicative from the verb εἰμί meaning "to be" or "to be in close connection with" or "to be in reference to location" (BDAG, s.v. "εἰμί" 2a, p. 283, or 3b, p. 284). **Syntactically,** ἐστίν is the governing verb of the dependent conjunctive καθώς clause. The subject of the verb is the demonstrative pronoun "that one" (ἐκεῖνος). This particular demonstrative is virtually a technical term for Jesus throughout 1 John (2:6; 3:3, 5, 16; 4:17). **Semantically,** ἐστίν is equative: "is" (KJV ASV NASB NRSV ESV NET CNT). It underscores Jesus's historical presence in the world and his interrelationship with people.

Theological Nugget: To whom does "that one" (ἐκεῖνος) refer, God or Jesus? The demonstrative pronoun "that one" (ἐκεῖνος) appears five times in 1 John to speak of Jesus. In 2:6, it is used to speak of Jesus's life on earth. In 3:3, it is used to describe Jesus's purity. In 3:5 it is used of Jesus's appearance on earth followed by "in him" (ἐν αὐτῷ) to describe Jesus's purity. In 3:16, it is used to underscore that Jesus died willingly. In 4:17, it points out that believers are in the world just as Jesus was in the world.

4:18a ἐστίν: The Greek word ἐστίν is third person singular present active indicative from the verb εἰμί meaning "to be" or is used in reference to a person's condition (BDAG, s.v. "εἰμί" 3c, p. 284). **Syntactically,** ἐστίν is the main verb of the independent clause: "no fear *is* in love" (φόβος οὐκ ἔστιν ἐν τῇ ἀγάπῃ). The subject of the verb is the noun "fear" (φόβος). **Semantically,** ἐστίν is gnomic present in that it is part of a generic statement that describes something that is true at any time (W, 523). John underscores that real love does not contain fear.

Lexical Nugget: What does John mean when he speaks of "fear" (φόβος)? This noun and its cognate verb appear three times in 1 John and every instance is in this verse. In the Gospel of John it either refers to the natural human emotion of fear when a person's perceptions of the world are overturned, such as when Jesus was walking out to the disciples on the water (John 6:19–20). It also refers to a preoccupation with one's own reputation or status being threatened, such as when the parents of the man born blind are afraid of getting excommunicated from the synagogue (John 9:22; cf. 7:13; 19:38; 20:19). In a similar way, Pilate feared for his own well-being at the trial of Jesus (19:8). The fear these people experienced was concern for their own welfare. It is this latter usage that appears in 4:18a. What John underscores is that love does not exist in a selfish preoccupation with reputation or status. This sort of fear hinders believers from following Jesus's selfless example of love and puts our relationship with God in doubt. The believer who remains with God and imitates his love has no need to fear (Bateman[1], 491–92).

4:18b ἀλλ': The Greek word ἀλλά is a conjunction meaning "but" (BDAG, s.v. "ἀλλά" 3, p. 43). **Syntactically,** ἀλλά introduces an independent conjunctive clause: "*but* perfect love expels fear" (ἀλλ' ἡ τελεία ἀγάπη ἔξω βάλλει τὸν φόβον). **Semantically,** ἀλλά is contrastive: "but" (cf. KJV NASB ESV NIV NET etc.). It introduces a strong contrast to underscore something that is true all the time. In this case, it contrasts John's depiction about love.

βάλλει: The Greek word βάλλει is third person singular present active indicative from the verb βάλλω meaning "to drive out" or "to expel" or "to force out" (BDAG, s.v. "βάλλω" 2, p. 163). **Syntactically,** βάλλει is the main verb of the independent clause. The subject is the nominal phrase "perfect love" (ἡ τελεία ἀγάπη). **Semantically,** βάλλει is a gnomic present: "expels" (NLT) or "casts out" (KJV ASV NASB NRSV ESV CNT) or "drives out" (NIV NET). It too is part of a generic statement that describes something that is true at any time (W, 523). John is emphasizing a timeless truth about perfect or mature love, namely, that there is no fear in perfect love.

4:18c ὅτι: The Greek word ὅτι is a conjunction meaning "because" (BDAG, s.v. "ὅτι" 4a, p. 732). **Syntactically,** ὅτι introduces two dependent conjunctive clauses: "*because* fear includes punishment and [*because*] the one who fears has not been perfected in love" (ὅτι ὁ φόβος κόλασιν ἔχει [ὅτι] ὁ δὲ φοβούμενος οὐ τετελείωται ἐν τῇ ἀγάπῃ). Both ὅτι clauses function adverbially. They modify the verb "casts out" (βάλλει). **Semantically,** ὅτι is causal: "because" (KJV ASV NASB NIV NET CNT) or "for" (NRSV ESV NLT). It answers the question "why?" (cf. W, 460). John provides the first of two reasons why perfect love drives away fear as evident in the rest of the clause.

ἔχει: The Greek word ἔχει is third person singular present active indicative from the verb ἔχω meaning "to have" or "to bring about" or "to include" (BDAG, s.v. "ἔχω" 8, p. 422). **Syntactically,** ἔχει is the governing verb of the first part of the dependent adverbial ὅτι clause. The subject is "fear" (ὁ φόβος). **Semantically,** ἔχει is a gnomic present: "includes" or "involves" (NASB) or "has to do with" (ASV ESV NIV NET CNT). It too is a generic statement that describes something that is true at any time (W, 523). Behind the idea of fear is the prospect of punishment (κόλασιν).

Lexical Nugget: What does the word "punishment" (κόλασις) mean? The word "punishment" (κόλασις) can either refer to physical torture in this life, such as persecution, or it can refer to eternal punishment. On the one hand, Second Temple literature uses κόλασις to speak of temporal torture inflicted on the Jewish people by both Greeks and Romans (4 Macc 8:9; Josephus *B.J.* 5.9.1 §355; 7.8.1 §272). The Jewish writer Philo describes how the "fear of punishment" caused Jewish women to eat swine flesh (*Flacc.* §96). He also uses the term a bit more generally to speak of the punishment due those who violate the law of God (*Spec.* 1.55). Similarly, in the early second-century church, Ignatius used this term to describe the "cruel tortures" he expected to suffer as a martyr for Christ (Ignatius *Rom.* 5.3). Thus all of these examples give κόλασις a definite association with brutal physical punishment and torture. On the other hand, Second Temple literature also uses κόλασις to speak of punishment that is eternal. For example, it was thought that people who prospered by evil means (T. Gad 7:5) and women who adorned themselves (T. Reu. 5:5) would suffer eternal punishment. In a similar manner, Matthew 25:46 also speaks of eternal punishment. It seems that judgment day is in view (v. 17b; cf. John 5:24). John is envisioning eternal punishment for those who do not have a relationship with God and so do not live out his selfless example of love (Bateman[1], 494–95).

4:18d δέ: The Greek word δέ is a conjunction meaning "but" or "rather" (BDAG, s.v. "δέ" 1, p. 213). **Syntactically,** δέ is in the postpositive position and introduces the second part of the compound dependent adverbial clause: "*and* [because] the one who fears is not perfected in love" (ὁ δὲ φοβούμενος οὐ τετελείωται ἐν τῇ ἀγάπῃ). **Semantically,** δέ is coordinating connective: "and" (ASV NASB NRSV ESV NIV NLT). The entire conjunctive clause provides an additional reason (ὅτι) about those who who fear (W, 671).

φοβούμενος: The Greek word φοβούμενος is a nominative masculine singular present middle participle from the verb φοβέομαι meaning "to fear" or "to be in an apprehensive state" (BDAG, s.v. "φοβέομαι" 1a, p. 1060). **Syntactically,** φοβούμενος is a substantival participle: "the one who fears" (NASB NIV NET) or "whoever" (NRSV ESV) or "he that fears" (KJV ASV). It functions as the subject of the verb "is perfected" (τετελείωται). It is not in parentheses because it is not part of a participial clause. **Semantically,** φοβούμενος is a gnomic present describing a timeless truth due to its generic subject (W, 523, 615). John underscores a timeless truth about anyone who fears.

τετελείωται: The Greek word τετελείωται is third person singular perfect passive indicative from the verb τελειόω meaning "to perfect" or "to overcome an imperfect state" (BDAG, s.v. "τελειόω" 2eα, p. 996). **Syntactically,** τετελείωται is the governing verb of the second part of the compound dependent ὅτι clause. The subject is the substantival participle "the one who fears" (ὁ . . . φοβούμενος). It is not in parentheses because it is not a participial clause. **Semantically,** τετελείωται is a gnomic and extensive perfect negated with οὐ: "*has* not *been* perfected" (ESV NET cf. NRSV). It too speaks of a general truth. Its focus is on the lack of any decisive acts of extending and thereby maturing in God's love (cf. W, 580).

4:19a ἀγαπῶμεν: The Greek word ἀγαπῶμεν is first person plural present active indicative from the verb ἀγαπάω meaning "to cherish," "to have affection for," "to love," or "to have a warm regard for and interest in another" (BDAG, s.v. "ἀγαπάω" 1bα, p. 5). **Syntactically,** ἀγαπῶμεν is the main verb of the independent clause. The subject of the verb is the emphatic personal pronoun "we" (ἡμεῖς). The emphatic pronoun emphasizes the distinction between those who need to fear and those whose love has been brought to maturity. Brown suggests we highlight this contrast by translating it "*as for us*, we love . . ." (Brown, 532). **Semantically,** ἀγαπῶμεν is a customary present: "we *persist* in love" or "we love" (cf. KJV NASB ESV NIV NET etc.). It illustrates an ongoing state (W, 521). Believers persist in or exhibit a pattern of behavior in that they love other believers.

Grammatical Nugget: How is ἀγαπῶμεν to be interpreted? On the one hand, ἀγαπῶμεν could be translated as a subjunctive: "let us love because God first loved us." This is clearly how it is to be understood in 1 John 4:7 (i.e., "let us love one another"). On the other hand, ἀγαπῶμεν could be translated as an indicative because of the lack of an object (cf. 1 John 3:14a). The direct object of this verb is left implicit (explaining why the textual tradition has often supplied objects such as "God" and "him"). Therefore, we have to determine for whom this perfected love is directed. It could be a love for God, a love for other believers, or it could be referring to both. The context of 1 John definitely includes both ideas, so the ambiguity here is most likely intentional (cf. Culy, 117). Because of God's previous love for believers, they should overflow with love toward God and others.

4:19b ὅτι: The Greek word ὅτι is a conjunction meaning "because" (BDAG, s.v. "ὅτι" 4a, p. 732). **Syntactically,** ὅτι serves to introduce the dependent conjunctive clause: "*because* he (= God) first loved us" (ὅτι αὐτὸς πρῶτος ἠγάπησεν ἡμᾶς). The entire ὅτι clause functions adverbially modifying the verb "we love" (ἀγαπῶμεν). **Semantically,** ὅτι is causal: "because" (cf. KJV NASB ESV NIV NET etc.). It answers the question "why?" (cf. W, 460). John provides the reason why believers persist in love.

ἠγάπησεν: The Greek word ἠγάπησεν is third person singular aorist active indicative from the verb ἀγαπάω meaning "to cherish," "to have affection for," "to love," or "to have a warm regard for and interest in another" (BDAG, s.v. "ἀγαπάω" 1bα, p. 5). **Syntactically,** ἠγάπησεν is the governing verb of the dependent adverbial clause. The subject of the verb is an emphatic personal pronoun, "he" (αὐτός), and refers to God. The direct object of the verb is the personal pronoun, "us" (ἡμᾶς), and refers to the believing community. **Semantically,** ἠγάπησεν is a constative aorist qualified with πρῶτος: "he first loved" (cf. KJV NASB ESV NIV NET etc.). It describes a historical act as a whole (W, 557). God loved ordinary people first.

4:20a ἐάν: The Greek word ἐάν is a conjunction meaning "if" (BDAG, s.v. "ἐάν" 1aβ, p. 267). **Syntactically,** ἐάν identifies the clause as a dependent conjunctive clause: "*if* someone says, "I love God," yet hates their brother" (ἐάν τις εἴπῃ ὅτι Ἀγαπῶ τὸν θεόν). The entire ἐάν clause functions adverbially. It modifies the verb "is" (ἐστίν). **Semantically,** ἐάν introduces a third class conditional clause of probability: "if" (cf. KJV NASB ESV NIV NET etc). The condition is uncertain of fulfillment but still likely (W, 696). That uncertain condition is found in the next verb.

εἴπῃ: The Greek word εἴπῃ is third person singular aorist active subjunctive from the verb λέγω meaning "to say" or "to express oneself orally" (BDAG, s.v.

"λέγω" 1aβ, p. 588). The verb is in the subjunctive mood because ἐάν takes the subjunctive mood. **Syntactically,** εἴπῃ is functioning as the governing verb of the first part of the dependent adverbial ἐάν clause. The subject of the verb is the indefinite pronoun "anyone" (τις). **Semantically,** εἴπῃ is a constative aorist: "says" (NASB ESV NIV NET NLT CNT) or "say" (KJV ASV NRSV). It describes a hypothetical event as a whole (W, 557). It underscores a person's assumed claim to love God.

ὅτι: The Greek word ὅτι is a conjunction that is not translated (BDAG, s.v. "ὅτι" 3, p. 732). **Syntactically,** ὅτι introduces the dependent conjunctive clause: "I love God" (ὅτι Ἀγαπῶ τὸν θεόν). The entire clause is functioning substantivally as the direct object of the verb "we love" (ἀγαπῶμεν). The ὅτι clause is placed in parentheses in order to visualize its contribution to the independent clause. **Semantically,** ὅτι is the direct discourse marker. It is not translated in English, but rather quotation marks are used to evidence a quote (cf. KJV NASB ESV NIV NET etc.; cf. W, 454). It provides the words of the hypothetical believer's claim to know God.

ἀγαπῶ: The Greek word ἀγαπῶ is first person singular present active indicative from the verb ἀγαπάω meaning "to love" or "to have a warm regard for and interest in another person" (BDAG, s.v. "ἀγαπάω" 1aα, p. 5). **Syntactically,** ἀγαπῶ is functioning as the main verb of the dependent substantival ὅτι clause. The subject of the verb is the pronoun "I" embedded in the verb and refers to the hypothetical believer who is making a claim to know God. **Semantically,** ἀγαπῶ is a gnomic present: "I love" (cf. KJV NASB ESV NIV NET etc.). John draws attention to a timeless truth about anyone's claim (W, 523). It draws attention to a hypothetical claim of anyone who loves God.

4:20b καί [ἐάν τις]: The Greek word καί is a conjunction meaning "and" (BDAG, s.v. "καί" 1bε, p. 494). **Syntactically,** καί introduces the second part of the compound dependent adverbial clause, "*and* [*that same person*] hates his (or her) brother (or sister)" (καὶ [ἐάν τις] τὸν ἀδελφὸν αὐτοῦ μισῇ). **Semantically,** καί is a coordinating connector: "and" (KJV NASB NRSV ESV CNT etc.). It provides additional information about the hypothetical [ἐάν] believer who claims to know God (W, 671). Even though they say that they love God, they despise their fellow believers. Some translations use a contrastive conjunction "yet" (NIV NET; cf. NLT). It highlights a person's hypocrisy. The contextual idea, however, is connective and thereby rendered "and."

μισῇ: The Greek word μισῇ is third person singular present active subjunctive from the verb μισέω meaning "to hate" " or "to detest" or "to have a strong aversion to" (BDAG, s.v. "μισέω" 1a, p. 652). **Syntactically,** μισῇ is the governing verb of the second part of the compound dependent adverbial clause. The verb is in the subjunctive mood because ἐάν takes the subjunctive. The subject of the verb is an implied pronoun "he (or she)" embedded in the verb and refers to the hypothetical [ἐάν] believer who claims to know God. **Semantically,** μισῇ is a gnomic present: "he (or she) hate" (NASB ESV NIV NET NLT CNT). John draws attention to a timeless truth about anyone's claim whose action does not follow (W, 523). It illustrates a hypothetical claim of any person whose talk does not match their walk.

4:20c ἐστίν: The Greek word ἐστίν is third person singular present active indicative from the verb εἰμί meaning "to be" or "to be in close connection with" (BDAG, s.v. "εἰμί" 2a, p. 283). **Syntactically,** ἐστίν is the main verb of the independent clause, "he (or she) *is* a liar" (ψεύστης ἐστίν). The subject of the verb is an implied "they [singular]" embedded in the verb and refers back to the hypothetical believer who claims to have a relationship with God. **Semantically,** ἐστίν is a gnomic present: "is" (cf. KJV NASB ESV NIV NET etc.). It points out a timeless reality (W, 523). Anyone who claims to love God and hates their follow believer is equated with being a liar. They have no relationship with God (cf. 1:9; 3:10; 4:8).

4:20d γάρ: The Greek word γάρ is a conjunction meaning "for" or "you see" (BDAG, s.v. "γάρ" 2, p. 189). **Syntactically,** γάρ is in the postpositive position that identifies the clause as an independent conjunctive clause: "*for* the one who does not love his (or her) brother (or sister) whom he (or she) has seen is not able to love God whom he (or she) has not seen" (ὁ γὰρ μὴ ἀγαπῶν τὸν ἀδελφὸν αὐτοῦ ὃν ἑώρακεν, τὸν θεὸν ὃν οὐχ ἑώρακεν οὐ δύναται ἀγαπᾶν). **Semantically,** γάρ is a marker of clarification: "for" (KJV ASV NASB NRSV ESV NLT CNT; cf. W, 658). John explains why the believer who claims to know God yet hates their brother is a liar.

ἀγαπῶν: The Greek word ἀγαπῶν is a nominative masculine singular present active participle from the verb ἀγαπάω meaning "to love" or "to have a warm regard for and interest in another person" (BDAG, s.v. "ἀγαπάω" 1aα, p. 5). **Syntactically,** ἀγαπῶν introduces a dependent participle clause. The entire participial clause, "the one who does not love his (or her) brother (or sister)" (ὁ . . . μὴ ἀγαπῶν τὸν ἀδελφὸν αὐτοῦ), is placed in parentheses to visualize its substantival contribution to the independent clause. The participle clause is functioning as the subject of the verb, "is not able" (οὐ δύναται). **Semantically,** ἀγαπῶν is a gnomic present negated with μή: "the one who does not love" (NASB NET; cf. ESV CNT) or "anyone who does not have" (NIV) or "those who do not have" (NRSV). John is presenting a timeless fact about people who refuse to love their brothers and sisters in Christ (cf. 4:8a; W, 521), which is clarified with the next verbal and verb.

δύναται: The Greek word δύναται is third person singular present middle indicative from the verb δύναμαι meaning "can," "to be able," "to be capable," or "to possess capability (whether because of personal or external factors) for experiencing or doing something" (BDAG, s.v. "δύναμαι" aα, p. 262). **Syntactically,** δύναται is the main verb of the independent clause. The subject of the verb is the substantival participial clause, "the one who does not love his (or her) brother (or sister)" (ὁ … μὴ ἀγαπῶν τὸν ἀδελφὸν αὐτοῦ). **Semantically,** δύναται is a gnomic present negated with μὴ. John is explaining a timeless fact about people who refuse to love their brothers and sisters in Christ (cf. 4:8a; W, 521).

ἀγαπᾶν: The Greek word ἀγαπᾶν is a present active infinitive from the verb ἀγαπάω meaning "to love" or "to have a warm regard for and interest in another person" (BDAG, s.v. "ἀγαπάω" 1aα, p. 5). **Syntactically,** ἀγαπᾶν is the complementary infinitive for δύναται negated with μὴ: "cannot love" (ASV NASB NRSB ESV NIV NET CNT). It completes the thought of the verb "is not able" (δύναται; W, 598). The one who does not love their fellow believers cannot possibly love God.

4:20e ὅν: The Greek word ὅν is accusative singular masculine from the relative pronoun ὅς meaning "whom" (BDAG, s.v. "ὅς" 1a, p. 725). **Syntactically,** ὅν introduces a dependent relative clause: "whom he (or she) has seen" (ὅν ἑώρακεν). It is adjectival, modifying the noun "brother (or sister)" (ἀδελφόν). The relative pronoun is in the accusative case because it is the direct object of the verb, "they have seen" (ἑώρακεν). The entire relative clause provides information about the hypothetical follower of Jesus who does not love.

ἑώρακεν: The Greek word ἑώρακεν is third person singular perfect active indicative from the verb ὁράω meaning "to see" or "to notice" or "to perceive by the eye" (BDAG, s.v. "ὁράω" A1b, p. 719). **Syntactically,** ἑώρακεν is the governing verb of the dependent relative clause. The subject of the verb is an implied "he (or she)" embedded in the verb that refers to the hypothetical believer who claims to love God. **Semantically,** ἑώρακεν is a gnomic and extensive perfect: "they *has* seen" (cf. NASB ESV NIV NET CNT). It contributes to John's generic proclamation about many individuals that focuses on the decisive act of noticing another believer (W, 580). If believers do not love fellow followers of Jesus they encounter in their everyday lives, they cannot possibly love God, whom they have not seen.

4:20f ὅν: The Greek word ὅν is accusative singular masculine from the relative pronoun ὅς meaning "whom" (BDAG, s.v. "ὅς" 1a, p. 725). **Syntactically,** ὅν introduces a dependent relative clause: "*whom he (or she) has* not *seen*" (ὅν οὐχ ἑώρακεν). It is adjectival, modifying the noun, "God" (θεόν). The relative pronoun is in the accusative case because it is the direct object of the verb, "they have seen" (ἑώρακεν). The entire relative clause provides information about God whom the hypothetical believer claims to know.

ἑώρακεν: The Greek word ἑώρακεν is third person singular perfect active indicative from the verb ὁράω meaning "to see" or "to notice" or "to perceive by the eye" (BDAG, s.v. "ὁράω" A1b, p. 719). **Syntactically,** ἑώρακεν functions as the governing verb of the dependent relative clause. The subject of the verb is an implied "they [singular]" embedded in the verb and refers to the hypothetical believer who claims to love God. **Semantically,** ἑώρακεν is a gnomic and extensive perfect negated with μὴ: "whom *he (or she) has* not seen" (NASB ESV NIV NET CNT). It contributes to John's generic proclamation about many individuals that focuses on the decisive act of noticing another believer (W, 580). A believer who cannot love fellow believers, whom they have encountered in their everyday life, cannot possibly love God, whom they have not seen.

We have an obvious example of a chiasm in this verse. A chiasm is a figure of speech that inverts ideas in order to emphasize main points.

A ὁ γὰρ μὴ ἀγαπῶν τὸν ἀδελφὸν αὐτοῦ,
For the one who does not loves their brother
B ὃν ἑώρακεν
whom they have seen
B' τὸν θεὸν ὃν οὐχ ἑώρακεν
God whom they have not seen
A' οὐ δύναται ἀγαπᾶν.
they are not able to love

The emphasis of this structure is this: any individual who refuses to love their visible fellow believer cannot possibly love an invisible God.

4:21a καί: The Greek word καί is a conjunction meaning "and" (BDAG, s.v. "καί" 1aα, p.494). **Syntactically,** καί introduces the independent conjunctive clause: "*and* we have this commandment from him (= God)" (καὶ ταύτην τὴν ἐντολὴν ἔχομεν ἀπ᾽ αὐτοῦ). **Semantically,** καί is a coordinating connective: "and" (KJV ASV NASB ESV NIV NET NLT). It provides additional information about the loving lifestyle that God expects from those who claim to have a relationship with him.

4:21b ἔχομεν: The Greek word ἔχομεν is first person plural present active indicative from the verb ἔχω meaning "to have" or "to experience something in the sense of an obligation" (BDAG, s.v. "ἔχω" 7aδ, p. 421). **Syntactically,** ἔχομεν is the main verb of the independent clause. The subject of the verb is an implied "we" embedded in the verb and refers to John and his readers. **Semantically,** ἔχομεν is a customary present: "we have" (NASB NRSV ESV NET CNT). It illustrates that the command to love is something that believers continually possess (cf. W, 521).

Theological Nugget: To whom does "him" (αὐτοῦ) refer, God or Jesus? There is some more Trinitarian ambiguity here concerning the possessive pronoun "him" (αὐτοῦ). Is the love command from Jesus or from God the Father? Brown argues that if Jesus were indeed the referent, then the demonstrative pronoun ἐκεῖνος would be used (Brown, 534). It is also suggested that there is a difference in emphasis between the Gospel of John and 1 John. In the Gospel, Jesus is seen as the issuer of the love command (John 13:34–35), whereas in 1 John, God the Father is seen as the giver of the commands to love (2:3–4; 3:22–24). This marks an interesting change in emphasis from the work and teaching of Jesus in the Gospel to the person and work of God.

4:21b ἵνα: The Greek word ἵνα is a conjunction meaning "that" (BDAG, s.v. "ἵνα" 2e, p. 476). **Syntactically,** ἵνα serves to introduce a conjunctive dependent clause: "*namely, that* the one who loves God lovers his (or her) brother (and sister) also" (ἵνα ὁ ἀγαπῶν τὸν θεὸν ἀγαπᾷ καὶ τὸν ἀδελφὸν αὐτοῦ). The entire ἵνα clause is substantival. It clarifies the demonstrative pronoun, "this" (ταύτην). **Semantically,** ἵνα is an appositional conjunction: "*namely, that*" (KJV ASV NASB NET CNT). It clarifies the demonstrative pronoun, "this" (ταύτην). It is almost idiomatic within John's writings (W, 475). The content of the command is that God expects those who love him to make a lifestyle out of loving fellow believers (cf. 3:11c, ἵνα, 3:23b, ἵνα).

ἀγαπῶν: The Greek word ἀγαπῶν is a nominative masculine singular present active participle from the verb ἀγαπάω meaning "to love" or "to have a warm regard for and interest in another person" (BDAG, s.v. "ἀγαπάω" 1aα, p. 5). **Syntactically,** ἀγαπῶν is a substantival participle that functions as the subject of the verb, "loves" (ἀγαπᾷ). The entire clause is placed in parentheses to visualize its substantival contribution to the ἵνα clause. **Semantically,** ἀγαπῶν is a gnomic present: "the one who loves" (NASB NET), "he who loves" (KJV ASV CNT), "those who love" (NASB NLT), "whoever loves" (ESV NIV). It refers to a general, timeless fact that is universally true and envisioned for many people (W, 523). John describes a universal truth about people who love God.

ἀγαπᾷ: The Greek word ἀγαπᾷ is third person singular present active subjunctive from the verb ἀγαπάω meaning "to love" or "to have a warm regard for and interest in another person" (BDAG, s.v. "ἀγαπάω" 1aα, p. 5). The verb is in the subjunctive mood because ἵνα takes the subjunctive. **Syntactically,** ἀγαπᾷ is the governing verb of the dependent adjectival clause. The subject of the verb is the substantival participial phrase, "the one who loves God" (ὁ ἀγαπῶν τὸν θεὸν). **Semantically,** ἀγαπᾷ is a gnomic present: "loves" (NASB). It illustrates a timeless truth about believers in general who love (W, 523). However, some translations appear to render it as an expectation: "must also love" (ESV NIV NLT) or "should love" (NASB NET).

1 John 5:1–4

Big Greek Idea: John underscores that anyone who believes in Jesus is part of God's family, is aware of their love for God and others, and exhibits their love for God in their persistence in living out God's expectations as victorious people of faith.

Structural Overview: John moves from his theme of love that focuses on what perfect love looks like (4:16d–21) to another favored theme of his: belief in Jesus, what it means, and what it demands. John opens with a proverbial-like statement. Anyone who believes (πᾶς ὁ πιστεύων) is part of God's family (γεγέννηται) in that they share the same spiritual DNA: love for God (ὁ ἀγαπῶν) and love (ἀγαπᾷ) for others in God's family (v. 1).

John then moves to clarify (ἐν τούτῳ) a self-awareness (γινώσκομεν) of Jesus followers about their love for other followers: persistence in loving (ἀγαπῶμεν) God as well as a persistence in living out (ποιῶμεν) God's expectations (v. 2).

John closes with an explanation (γάρ) about loving God. First, love for God is evident in a person's persistence to comply with what God expects. Second, love for God is evident in a person's ability (εἰσίν) to carry out God's expectations because (ὅτι) followers of Jesus can rise above (νικᾷ) the world's practice and system of selfishness. Finally, love for God is evident in a person's faith in Jesus (vv. 3–4).

Outline:

> A Person's Belief in Jesus as Messiah Places Them in God's Family (v. 1)
> Evidences of Being in God's Family Is Loving and Obeying God (v. 2)
> A Family's Member Love for God Is Obedience to God (vv. 3–4)

Clausal Outline for 1 John 5:1–4

> 5:1a (Πᾶς ὁ πιστεύων [ὅτι Ἰησοῦς ἐστιν ὁ Χριστὸς]) ἐκ τοῦ θεοῦ **γεγέννηται,**
> 5:1a (Everyone who *persists in* believing [that Jesus is the Christ]) **has been fathered** by God,
>
> 5:1b καὶ (πᾶς ὁ ἀγαπῶν τὸν γεννήσαντα) **ἀγαπᾷ** [καὶ] (τὸν γεγεννημένον ἐξ αὐτοῦ).
> 5:1b and (everyone who *persists in* loving the Father) **loves** [also] (those who have been fathered by him).

5:2a ἐν τούτῳ **γινώσκομεν** (ὅτι ἀγαπῶμεν τὰ τέκνα τοῦ θεοῦ),
5:2a By this **we know** (that we love the children of God),

    |
    5:2b **ὅταν** τὸν θεὸν **ἀγαπῶμεν**
    5:2b **whenever** we *persist* **in loving** God

    |
    5:2c καὶ [*ὅταν*] τὰς ἐντολὰς αὐτοῦ **ποιῶμεν**.
    5:2c and [*whenever*] **we** *persist* **in carrying out** his (= God's) commandments.

5:3a αὕτη **γάρ ἐστιν** ἡ ἀγάπη τοῦ θεοῦ,
5:3a **For** this **is** the love *for* God,

    |
    5:3b **ἵνα** τὰς ἐντολὰς αὐτοῦ **τηρῶμεν**·
    5:3b *namely* that **we** *persist* **in keeping** his (= God's) commandments;

5:3c καὶ αἱ ἐντολαὶ αὐτοῦ βαρεῖαι οὐκ **εἰσίν**,
5:3c and his (= God's) commandments **are** not difficult to carry out,

                 |
                 5:4a **ὅτι** (πᾶν τὸ γεγεννημένον ἐκ
                      τοῦ θεοῦ) **νικᾷ** τὸν κόσμον·
                 5:4a **because** (everyone who has been
                      fathered by God) **overcomes** the
                      world;

5:4b καὶ αὕτη **ἐστὶν** ἡ νίκη ἡ νικήσασα τὸν κόσμον, ἡ πίστις ἡμῶν.
5:4b and this **is** the victory (that overcame the world), our faith.

SYNTAX EXPLAINED FOR 1 JOHN 5:1–4

5:1a πιστεύων: The Greek word πιστεύων is a nominative masculine singular present active participle from the verb πιστεύω meaning "to believe" or "to consider something to be true and therefore worthy of one's trust" (BDAG, s.v. "πιστεύω" 1aβ, p. 816). **Syntactically,** πιστεύων introduces a dependent participle clause. The entire participial clause, "who *persists in* believing [that Jesus is the Christ])" (ὁ πιστεύων [ὅτι Ἰησοῦς ἐστιν ὁ Χριστὸς]), modifies the adjective (πᾶς). The πᾶς + participial clause is placed in parentheses in order to visualize its contribution to the independent clause. Together they are the subject of the verb "has been fathered" (γεγέννηται). **Semantically,** πιστεύων is a gnomic present with a customary present force: "everyone who *persists in* believing" (cf. NRSV ESV NIV NET CNT NLT) or "whoever believes" (NASB; cf. KJV ASV). It draws attention to a timeless fact about something that is currently happening" (W, 521, 523, 615). John draws attention to a timeless truth about any person who persists in believing that Jesus is the Christ (= Messiah).

ὅτι: The Greek word ὅτι is a conjunction meaning "that" (BDAG, s.v. "ὅτι" 1c, p. 731). **Syntactically,** ὅτι introduces a dependent conjunctive clause: "*that* Jesus is the Christ" (ὅτι Ἰησοῦς ἐστιν ὁ Χριστός). The entire clause functions substantivally as the direct object of the participle "believes" (πιστεύων). The ὅτι clause is placed in parentheses in order to visualize its contribution to the independent clause. **Semantically,** ὅτι is an indirect discourse marker: "that" (cf. KJV NASB ESV NIV NET etc.). It provides the content of what the generic "everyone" *persists in* believing (W, 456).

ἐστίν: The Greek word ἐστίν is third person singular present active indicative from the verb εἰμί meaning "to be" or "to be in close connection with" (BDAG, s.v. "εἰμί" 2a, p. 282). **Syntactically,** ἐστίν is the verb of the dependent ὅτι clause. The subject of the verb is the proper name "Jesus" (Ἰησοῦς). Even though the articular noun is usually the subject in an equative clause, a proper noun normally takes precedence (W, 44–45; Culy, 55). **Semantically,** ἐστίν is an equative present: "is" (cf. KJV NASB ESV NIV NET etc.). It equates or identifies Jesus as the Messiah, the anointed one, or king.

γεγέννηται: The Greek word γεγέννηται is third person singular perfect passive indicative from the verb γεννάω meaning "to become the parent of" or "to exercise the role of a parental figure" (BDAG, s.v. "γεννάω" 1b, p. 193). **Syntactically,** γεγέννηται is the main verb of the independent clause: "everyone who persists in believing that Jesus is the Christ has been fathered by God" (πᾶς ὁ πιστεύων ὅτι Ἰησοῦς ἐστιν ὁ Χριστὸς ἐκ τοῦ θεοῦ γεγέννηται). The subject is the participial phrase "everyone who persists in believing that Jesus is the Christ" (πᾶς ὁ πιστεύων ὅτι Ἰησοῦς ἐστιν ὁ Χριστὸς). **Semantically,** γεγέννηται is both gnomic and an extensive perfect: "*has been* fathered" (NET) or "*has been* born" (NRSV ESV; cf. NLT). It is gnomic because of the generic subject (πᾶς) while extensive in that the focus is on the decisive relationship between God and the believer (W, 580). This generic or proverbial force may also be rendered intensive: "is born" (KJV NASB NIV CNT; cf. ASV) with an emphasis on the results of the present condition of the believer. Regardless of where one places the emphasis of the perfect, John's point is that God has fathered believers in the past and that past event has continuing results in the present (cf. 2:29; 3:9; 5:1, 4, 18). The focus is upon those who practice righteousness: they have an ongoing relationship with God.

Theological Nugget: What was wrong with the theology of the misguided people of John's day? It seems from 1 John 5:1 that part of it concerned their misguided teaching about Jesus's messiahship and their unwillingness to accept that Jesus was the Christ (= Messiah). In 4:2, the concept of Jesus as Messiah is coupled with Jesus coming in the flesh or being a living human being (cf. 2 John 7). In 4:15 and 5:5 those who had left the church had a difficulty with the claim that Jesus is the "Son of God," which possibly could be another messianic title (Bateman[2], 303–25). It appears as if the main theological problem for those who left the church (cf. 2:19) was their refusal to accept that Jesus was the Messiah, the Son of God.

5:1b καί: The Greek word καί is a conjunction meaning "and" (BDAG, s.v. "καί" 1bα, p. 494). **Syntactically,** καί introduces a conjunctive independent clause: "*and* everyone who loves the Father [also] loves the one who has been fathered by him" (καὶ πᾶς ὁ ἀγαπῶν τὸν γεννήσαντα ἀγαπᾷ [καὶ] τὸν γεγεννημένον ἐξ αὐτοῦ). **Semantically,** καί is a coordinating connector: "and" (KJV ASV NASB NRSV ESV NIV NET NLT CNT). It provides additional information about the generic person who is part of God's family (W, 671). The added information is found in the rest of the clause.

ἀγαπῶν: The Greek word ἀγαπῶν is a nominative masculine singular present active participle from the verb ἀγαπάω meaning "to love" or "to cherish" or "to have a warm regard for and interest in another" (BDAG, s.v. "ἀγαπάω" 1aα, p. 5). **Syntactically,** ἀγαπῶν introduces a dependent participle clause. The entire participial clause, "who *persists in* loving the Father" (ὁ ἀγαπῶν τὸν γεννήσαντα), modifies the adjective (πᾶς). The πᾶς + participial clause is placed in parentheses in order to visualize its contribution as the independent clause. Together they are the subject for the verb, "loves" (ἀγαπᾷ). **Semantically,** ἀγαπῶν is a gnomic present with a customary present force: "everyone who *persists in* loving" (cf. NRSV ESV NIV NET NLT CNT) or "whoever loves" (NASB; cf. ASV). It draws attention to a timeless fact about a generic "anyone" who persists in loving God, which in turn translates into loving other people (W, 521, 523, 615).

γεννήσαντα: The Greek word γεννήσαντα is an accusative masculine singular aorist active participle from the verb γεννάω meaning "to become the parent of" or "to exercise the role of a parental figure" (BDAG, s.v. "γεννάω" 1b, p. 193). **Syntactically,** γεννήσαντα is the object of "who loves" (ὁ ἀγαπῶν). **Semantically,** γεννήσαντα is a constative aorist: "*has been* fathered" (NET; cf. NRSV ESV). John draws attention to an example from everyday life (Brown, 566). As a general rule if someone loves the parent, they usually love the children of that parent.

ἀγαπᾷ: The Greek word ἀγαπᾷ is third person singular present active indicative from the verb ἀγαπάω meaning "to love" or "to cherish" or "to have a warm regard for and interest in another" (BDAG, s.v. "ἀγαπάω" 1aα, p. 5). **Syntactically,** ἀγαπᾷ is the main verb of the independent clause: "and everyone who loves the Father [also] *loves* the one who has been fathered by him" (καὶ πᾶς ὁ ἀγαπῶν τὸν γεννήσαντα ἀγαπᾷ [καὶ] τὸν γεγεννημένον ἐξ αὐτοῦ). **Semantically,** ἀγαπᾷ is a gnomic present: "loves" (cf. KJV NASB ESV NIV NET etc.). John draws attention to an example from everyday life (W, 523). As a general rule if someone loves the parent, they usually love the children of that parent (Brown , 566). People who claim God is their father will love him, and they will love other believers whom he has fathered.

Text-Critical Nugget: Why do some Greek texts include the conjunction καί and others do not? It is a structural and syntactical issue. The textual variant [καί] in this clause is not a structural marker, because even if it is original, it is functioning adjunctively ("also") [KJV ASV CNT; cf. "as well," NIV]. Is it original? The UBS committee had some difficulty in deciding in favor of καί (giving it a C rating; Metzger[1], 646). On the one hand, the major Alexandrian witnesses Sinaiticus (ℵ) and Alexandrinus (A), the Byzantine K, and the Coptic, Armenian, and Ethiopic versions include the conjunction. On the other hand, Vaticanus (B) and ψ are two Alexandrian uncials that omit it along with minuscules 048 33 and others. Therefore, the external evidence points to its inclusion due to its widespread geographic distribution. On the other hand, the internal evidence points in a different direction. The omission of the conjunction makes the syntax much more complicated. It seems more likely that a scribe added the conjunction to make the syntax of this difficult sentence more clear. Painter argues that the addition of the καί might be influenced by 4:21 and thus is not original (289; cf. Brown, 535). Most translations do not acknowledge the καί (NASB NRSV ESV NET NLT).

γεγεννημένον: The Greek word γεγεννημένον is an accusative masculine singular perfect passive participle from the verb γεννάω meaning "to become the parent of" or "to exercise the role of a parental figure" (BDAG, s.v. "γεννάω" 1b, p. 193). **Syntactically,** γεγεννημένον introduces a dependent participial clause. The entire clause, "the one who has been fathered by him" (τὸν γεγεννημένον ἐξ αὐτοῦ), is the direct object of the verb "loves" (ἀγαπᾷ). It is placed in parentheses to visualize its contribution to the independent clause. **Semantically,** γεγεννημένον is both gnomic and an extensive perfect: "*has been* fathered" (NET) or "*has been* born" (ESV). It is gnomic because of the generic subject (πᾶς), while extensive in that the focus is on the decisive relationship between God and the believer (W, 580). This generic or proverbial force may also be rendered intensive: "is born" (cf. KJV ASV NASB) with an emphasis on the results of the present condition of the believer. Regardless of where one places the emphasis of the perfect, John's point is simply this: believers have been fathered by God in the past and that past event has continuing results in the present (cf. 2:29; 3:9; 4:7; 5:4, 18). The focus is upon those who practice righteousness: they have an ongoing relationship with God.

5:2a ἐν τούτῳ: The Greek word ἐν is a preposition meaning "by" (BDAG, s.v. "ἐν" 5b, p. 328). The Greek word τούτῳ is declined as a dative singular neuter from the demonstrative pronoun οὗτος meaning "this one" (BDAG, s.v. "οὗτος" 1bβ, p. 741). **Syntactically,** ἐν τούτῳ introduces an independent prepositional clause: "by this we know that we love the children of God" (ἐν τούτῳ γινώσκομεν ὅτι ἀγαπῶμεν τὰ τέκνα τοῦ θεοῦ). "by this" (ἐν τούτῳ) occurs frequently in 1 John (2:3, 4, 5; 3:10, 16, 19, 24; 4:2, 9, 10, 13, 17). **Semantically,** ἐν τούτῳ can either be anaphoric, pointing back to the preceding discussion, or cataphoric, pointing forward. In this instance, the phrase is cataphoric. It points forward to the conjunction ὅταν (5:2b), which provides the content of the test by which believers can know that they really love the children of God.

γινώσκομεν: The Greek word γινώσκομεν is first person plural present active indicative from the verb γινώσκω meaning "to know" or "to know about" or "to arrive at a knowledge of someone or something" (BDAG, s.v. "γινώσκω" 6c, p. 200). **Syntactically,** γινώσκομεν is the main verb of the independent clause. The subject of the verb is an implied "we" embedded in the verb and refers to John and his readers. **Semantically,** γινώσκομεν is a customary present: "we know" (cf. KJV NASB ESV NIV NET etc.). It focuses on the continual knowledge that a believer can possess. The content of that knowledge is found in the following ὅτι clause.

ὅτι: The Greek word ὅτι is a conjunction meaning "that" (BDAG, s.v. "ὅτι" 1c, p. 731). **Syntactically,** ὅτι introduces a substantival dependent clause: "*that* we love the children of God" (ὅτι ἀγαπῶμεν τὰ τέκνα τοῦ θεοῦ). It functions as the direct object of the verb, "we know" (γινώσκομεν). The entire ὅτι clause is placed in parentheses in order to visualize its contribution to the independent clause. **Semantically,** ὅτι completes a verb of cognition and therefore is an indirect discourse conjunction (W, 456). It provides the content of what is known (cf. KJV NASB ESV NIV NET etc.), which is evident in the rest of the clause.

ἀγαπῶμεν: The Greek word ἀγαπῶμεν is first person plural present active indicative from the verb ἀγαπάω meaning "to love" or "to cherish" or "to have a warm regard for and interest in another" (BDAG, s.v. "ἀγαπάω" 1aα, p. 5). **Syntactically,** ἀγαπῶμεν is the governing verb of the dependent ὅτι clause. The subject of the verb is an implied "we" embedded in the verb and refers to John and his readers. **Semantically,** ἀγαπῶμεν is a customary present: "we love" (cf. KJV NASB ESV NIV NET etc.). It points out that the love for God's children that believers should be looking for is a habitual love that is grounded in action (W, 521).

5:2b ὅταν: The Greek word ὅταν is a conjunction meaning "at the time that," "whenever," "when," or "pertaining to an action that is conditional, possible, and, in many instances, repeated" (BDAG, s.v. "ὅταν" 1aα, p. 730). **Syntactically,** ὅταν introduces a dependent conjunctive clause: *"whenever* we *persist in* loving God" (ὅταν τὸν θεὸν ἀγαπῶμεν). The entire ὅταν clause modifies the demonstrative pronoun, "this" (τούτῳ). **Semantically,** ὅταν is temporal: "whenever" (NET) or "when" (KJV ASV NASB NRSV ESV CNT). It tells when a believer knows that he or she has a relationship with God (W, 677), which John makes clear in the next verb.

ἀγαπῶμεν: The Greek word ἀγαπῶμεν is first person plural present active subjunctive from the verb ἀγαπάω meaning "to love" or "to cherish" or "to have a warm regard for and interest in another" (BDAG, s.v. "ἀγαπάω" 1aα, p. 5). **Syntactically,** ἀγαπῶμεν is the governing verb of the dependent conjunctive ὅταν clause. The subject of the verb is an implied "we" embedded in the verb and refers to the readers of the letter. **Semantically,** ἀγαπῶμεν is a customary present: "we *persist in* loving" or "we love" (cf. KJV NASB ESV NIV NET etc.). It points out that continual love for God is evidence of genuine love for his children (W, 521). But it doesn't end there.

5:2c καὶ [ὅταν]: The Greek word καί is a conjunction meaning "and" (BDAG, s.v. "καί" 1bα, p. 494). **Syntactically,** καί introduces the second part of the compound dependent conjunctive ὅταν clause, thus the inclusion of "whenever" [ὅταν] in brackets: *and* practice his commands" (καὶ τὰς ἐντολὰς αὐτοῦ ποιῶμεν). **Semantically,** καὶ is a coordinating connector: "and" (cf. KJV NASB ESV NIV NET etc.). It provides further information about a believer and when they can know that they have genuine love for God's children.

ποιῶμεν: The Greek word ποιῶμεν is first person plural present active subjunctive from the verb ποιέω meaning "to do," "to keep," "to carry out," "to practice," or "to carry out an obligation of a moral or social nature" (BDAG, s.v. "ποιέω" 3a, p. 840). **Syntactically,** ποιῶμεν is the second verb of the dependent conjunctive ὅταν clause. The subject of the verb is an implied "we" embedded in the verb and refers to John and his readers. **Semantically,** ποιῶμεν is a customary present: "we *persist in* carrying out" or "we obey" (NASV ESV NET CNT NLT). It stresses that repeated acts of practicing the love commands of Jesus are evidence that a believer loves God's children (W, 521). The love for God and the practice of his love commands are not necessarily two separate proofs of love for God's children. Most likely this is an example of a figure of speech called a hendiadys where two separate acts form one idea (see Smalley, 268). Thus the evidence for a genuine love of other children of God demonstrates a sincere affection for God that results in repeated acts of obedience to his love commands.

Text-Critical Nugget. Why do some Greek manuscripts read "keep" (τηρῶμεν: KJV) and others read "do" (ποιῶμεν: ASV)? This may be considered a stylistic issue. On the one hand, the external evidence seems to be split. Significant manuscripts, such as Sinaiticus (ℵ) and P support the reading τηρῶμεν, while Vaticanus (B) and ψ support the reading ποιῶμεν. On the other hand, the internal evidence favors the reading ποιῶμεν. The verb τηρέω is used far more often when talking about God's commands. In fact, it is even used in verse 3 for this very purpose. It seems likely that a scribe harmonized the text to agree with the majority of 1 John (2:3, 4, 5; 3:22, 24), or that he accidentally let his eye slip and copied τηρῶμεν from verse 3. The UBS committee had little difficulty in deciding in favor of ποιῶμεν (giving it a B rating; Metzger[1], 646).

5:3a γάρ: The Greek word γάρ is a conjunction meaning "for" or "because" (BDAG, s.v. "γάρ" 1a, p. 189). **Syntactically,** γάρ introduces an independent conjunctive clause: *"for* this is the love for God" (αὕτη γάρ ἐστιν ἡ ἀγάπη τοῦ θεοῦ). **Semantically,** γάρ is explanatory: "for" (KJV NASB NRSV ESV NIV NLT CNT) or "because" (NET). It explains how a believer can determine if they truly love other believers (cf. Culy, 49, 122).

ἐστίν: The Greek word ἐστίν is third person singular present active indicative from the verb εἰμί meaning "to be" or "to be in close connection with" (BDAG, s.v. "εἰμί" 2a, p. 282). **Syntactically,** ἐστίν is the main verb of the independent clause: "for this *is* God's love" (αὕτη γάρ ἐστιν ἡ ἀγάπη τοῦ θεοῦ). The subject of the verb is the demonstrative pronoun, "this" (αὕτη), due to the grammatical priority of pronouns (W, 42–43). **Semantically,** ἐστίν is gnomic: "is" (cf. KJV NASB ESV NIV NET etc.). It is a timeless fact about the one who follows the love commandments of Jesus (W, 523).

Semantical Nugget: How should the genitive phrase "love of God" (ἡ ἀγάπη τοῦ θεοῦ) be understood? On the one hand, it could be a subjective genitive: "God's love" (W, 113). But John is not seeking to explain what God's love for us looks like (subjective genitive). On the other hand, it seems more than likely that John is telling his readers how to demonstrate love for God: "the love *for* God" (objective genitive; W, 116). Followers of Jesus show God and the world their love for him when they obey his love commands.

5:3b ἵνα: The Greek word ἵνα is a conjunction meaning "that" (BDAG, s.v. "ἵνα" 2e, p. 476). **Syntactically,** ἵνα introduces a dependent conjunctive clause: *"namely that* we keep his commandments" (ἵνα τὰς ἐντολὰς αὐτοῦ τηρῶμεν). The ἵνα clause is substantival. It clarifies the demonstrative pronoun, "this" (αὕτη). **Semantically,** ἵνα is an appositional conjunction: *"namely* that" (KJV NASB NRSV ESV NET CNT). It clarifies the demonstrative pronoun, "this" (αὕτη). It is almost idiomatic within John's writings (W, 475). The basis for love is found in the next verb.

τηρῶμεν: The Greek word τηρῶμεν is first person plural present active subjunctive from the verb τηρέω meaning "to keep" or "to observe" or "to persist in obedience" (BDAG, s.v. "τηρέω" 3, p. 1002). It is in the subjunctive mood because it follows ἵνα. **Syntactically,** τηρῶμεν is the governing verb of the dependent conjunctive ἵνα clause. It explains the content of the demonstrative pronoun, "this" (αὕτη). The assumed subject, "we," refers to any believer who desires to demonstrate their love for God. **Semantically,** τηρῶμεν is a customary present: "we *persist in* keeping" or "we keep" (KJV ASV ESV NET; cf. NLT). It describes a pattern of behavior (W, 521). It defines followers of Jesus who persist in keeping God's commands, especially the command to love others (cf. 2:3).

5:3c καί: The Greek word καί is a conjunction meaning "and" (BDAG, s.v. "καί" 1bβ, p. 494). **Syntactically,** καί introduces an independent conjunctive clause: "*And* his (= God's) commandments are not difficult to carry out" (καὶ αἱ ἐντολαὶ αὐτοῦ βαρεῖαι οὐκ εἰσίν). **Semantically,** καί is a connector drawn from Hebrew where καί is used as a *waw* consecutive that begins a new sentence (cf. NRSV ESV NIV NET CNT). It joins two sentences together that expand the information about God's commands to love. These commands are not difficult for the genuine believer to keep because they have conquered the world in their hearts through their faith in the work of Jesus.

εἰσίν: The Greek word εἰσίν is third person plural present active indicative from the verb εἰμί meaning "to be" or "to be in close connection with" (BDAG, s.v. "εἰμί" 2a, p. 283). **Syntactically,** εἰσίν is the main verb of the independent clause. The subject of the verb is the nominal phrase, "his commands" (αἱ ἐντολαὶ αὐτοῦ), referring to the love commands of God given through Jesus. The predicate nominative, βαρεῖαι, pertains to being a source of difficulty (BDAG, s.v. "βαρύς" 2a, p. 167). **Semantically,** εἰσίν is an equative present: "are" (cf. KJV NASB ESV NIV NET etc.). It underscores for John's readers who have God's command to love that such an expectation is not too much to ask of his followers. The reason why the expectation to love is provided in the following clause.

Lexical Nugget: What does βαρύς mean? This adjective appears six times in the New Testament (Matthew [2x], Acts [2x], 2 Corinthians, 1 John). It is often used metaphorically to describe the rules and regulations of the Pharisees as "heavy burdens" (Matt. 23:4). Their expectations were unbearable in the same way that taxes were oppressive (P. Mich. 529, 28, 35–36; Ant. Papyrus 100, 11). At other times, it is used as a description of cruel leadership (Acts 20:29). For instance, the people of Gadara complained that Herod's injunctions were "heavy" (Josephus, *A.J.* 15.10.3 §354). In the same way, Pharaoh published laws that made demands beyond the Jews ability to keep them (Philo, *Mos.* 1.37). John also employs the adjective metaphorically to describe God's command to love as something that is *not heavy or burdensome*. Philo says something similar, he contends, "God asks nothing from you that is heavy [βαρύς], complicated, or difficult, but only something quite simple and easy" (*Spec.* 1.299; cf. Matt. 11:30). God's expectation to love other believers is something that should never be a burden, but something that should come quite easily to those animated by his Spirit. John is telling his readers that God's expectation to love others is not too much to ask.

5:4a ὅτι: The Greek word ὅτι is a conjunction meaning "because" (BDAG, s.v. "ὅτι" 4a, p. 732). **Syntactically,** ὅτι serves to introduce the dependent conjunctive clause: "*because* everyone who has been fathered by overcomes the world" (ὅτι πᾶν τὸ γεγεννημένον ἐκ τοῦ θεοῦ νικᾷ τὸν κόσμον). The entire clause is functioning adverbially, modifying the verb, "carry out" (εἰσίν). **Semantically,** ὅτι is causal: "because" (NET; cf. NRSV NIV), though many translate ὅτι as "for" indicating perhaps a loose connection with the preceding clause (KJV ASV NASB ESV CNT NLT; BDAG, s.v. "ὅτι" 4b, p. 732). It provides the reason why God's love commands are not burdensome for those who believe (W, 460). The reason is pointed out in the next verb.

γεγεννημένον: The Greek word γεγεννημένον is a nominative neuter singular perfect passive participle from the verb γεννάω meaning "to become the parent of" or "to exercise the role of a parental figure" (BDAG, s.v. "γεννάω" 1b, p. 193). **Syntactically,** γεγεννημένον introduces a dependent participial clause. The entire participial clause, "the one who has been fathered by God" (τὸ γεγεννημένον ἐκ τοῦ θεοῦ), modifies the adjective (πᾶν). The πᾶς + participial clause is placed in parentheses in order to visualize its contribution to the independent clause. Together they are the subjects of the verb, "overcomes" (νικᾷ). **Semantically,** γεγεννημένον is both gnomic and an extensive perfect: "*has been* fathered" (NET) or "*has been* born" (ESV). It is gnomic because of the generic subject (πᾶν) while extensive in that the focus is on the decisive relationship between God and the believer (W, 580). This generic or proverbial force may also be rendered as intensive: "is born" (KJV NASB NRSV CNT cf. ASV) with an emphasis on the results of the present condition of the believer. Regardless of where one places the emphasis of the perfect, John's point is simply this: believers have been fathered by God in the past and that past event has continuing results in the present (cf. 2:29; 3:9; 4:7; 5:18). The focus is upon those who practice righteousness: they have had an ongoing relationship with God.

νικᾷ: The Greek word νικᾷ is third person singular present active indicative from the verb νικάω meaning "to vanquish" or "to overcome" or "to overcome someone" (BDAG, s.v. "νικάω" 2a, p. 673). **Syntactically,** νικᾷ is the governing verb of the dependent adverbial ὅτι clause. The subject of the verb is "everyone who is born of God" (πᾶν τὸ γεγεννημένον ἐκ τοῦ θεοῦ). **Semantically,** νικᾷ is a gnomic present: "overcomes" (KJV ASV NASB ESV CNT) or "conquers" (NRSV NET). It emphasizes a timeless reality (W, 523) concerning the believer's victory over the world (cf. NLT).

> **Grammatical Nugget:** Why is the subject of this clause πᾶν τὸ γεγεννημένον neuter? The neuter gender is a challenge to explain. Why refer to a group of individuals by the neuter here? This difficulty is compounded because the masculine πᾶς ὁ πιστεύων is used in 5:1. One of two things could be going on here or both. First, it could refer back to the neuter gender of "children" (τέκνα). Its meaning is not different from the masculine inclusive pronouns elsewhere. Yet, the reference to "children" (τέκνα) is far removed in the context. Second, it could be a collective construction, referring to everyone who is born of God. John could be saying that every believer (πᾶν τὸ γεγεννημένον) is a "conqueror of the world" rather than the individual (cf. BDF §138).

5:4b καί The Greek word καί is a conjunction meaning "and" (BDAG, s.v. "καί" 1bα, p. 494). **Syntactically,** καί introduces a conjunctive independent clause: "*and* this is the victory that overcame the world, our faith" (καὶ αὕτη ἐστὶν ἡ νίκη ἡ νικήσασα τὸν κόσμον, ἡ πίστις ἡμῶν). **Semantically,** καί is a coordinating connector. It provides additional information about the victory that believers have over the world system. While most translations translate καί as "and" (KJV ASV NASB ESV NET NLT), the NIV leaves the καί untranslated, which seems to heighten John's point that it is faith in the work of Jesus that enables the believers to achieve victory.

ἐστίν The Greek word ἐστίν is third person singular present active indicative from the verb εἰμί meaning "to be" or "to be in close connection with" (BDAG, s.v. "εἰμί" 2a, p. 283). **Syntactically,** ἐστίν is the main verb of the independent clause. The subject of the verb is the demonstrative pronoun, "this" (αὕτη), due to the grammatical priority of pronouns (W, 42–43). **Semantically,** ἐστίν is an equative present: "is" (cf. KJV NASB ESV NIV NET etc.). It equates the victory (= success) that believers have over the world (= world system of selfishness) with what is gained through their faith in the work of Jesus.

νικήσασα: The Greek word νικήσασα is a nominative singular feminine aorist active participle from the verb νικάω meaning "to vanquish" or "to overcome" or "to overcome someone" (BDAG, s.v. "νικάω" 2a, p. 673). **Syntactically,** νικήσασα is adjectival in the attributive position with "victory" (ἡ νίκη). The entire participial clause, "that overcame the world" (ἡ νικήσασα τὸν κόσμον), modifies the noun, "victory" (ἡ νίκη). **Semantically,** νικήσασα is a constative aorist: "overcame," though most translations render it as a consummative aorist: "has overcome" (NASB ESV NIV NET, cf. KJV ASV). The constative aorist describes the action as a whole (W, 557). This participial clause echoes the noun that it modifies and is difficult to translate due to John's use of cognates (see also 1 John 2:25). Nevertheless, it emphasizes the power that believers possess to overcome the world. This victory or triumph is further explained with another nominative set in apposition to the demonstrative pronoun, "our faith" (ἡ πίστις ἡμῶν). John points out to his readers that the origin of the believer's victory comes from their faith that Jesus is God's Son (= Messiah).

1 John 5:5–12

Big Greek Idea: Success in this self-centered world system comes to all those who believe in God's Messiah Jesus, whose life and death—along with the Spirit—verifies his messiahship, through whom God has promised an endless relationship for anyone who believes in Jesus.

Structural Overview: This is the fifth and final unit of thought for the second half of 1 John 3:11–5:12. John expands the evidence of a follower's love for God (v. 4), namely, their faith in Jesus provides for success in this world system of selfishness (= overcomes the world). John now (δέ) draws specific attention to those who have *success* in this self-centered world system, through whom that success comes, and about whom there are eyewitnesses (vv. 5–8).

First, John asserts (ἐστίν) that people who believe in Jesus, God's Messiah, have (ἐστίν) success in this world system of selfishness (v. 5). Second, John stresses (ἐστίν) the birth and death (ἦλθεν) of God's Messiah (v. 6a–c). Finally, John identifies (ἐστίν) three eyewitnesses to this historical event: the Spirit of truth, the birth of Jesus, and the death of Jesus (vv. 6d–8).

John then intensifies his discussion about God's testimonies (vv. 9–11). First, he strengthens his own eyewitness (λαμβάνομεν) about Jesus with God's because (ὅτι) *God's statements* about Jesus's birth and his death are (ἐστίν) superior to his own (v. 9). Second, John distinguishes between those who share (ὁ πιστεύων) God's testimony and those who disbelieve (ὁ μὴ πιστεύων) God (vv. 10). Finally, those who share God's testimony have (ἔδωκεν) an endless relationship with God, a perpetual bond that comes through God's Messiah, Jesus (ἐστίν; v. 11).

John closes this unit of thought with a timeless assertion (v. 12). *Anyone who believes* (ὁ ἔχων) that Jesus is God's Messiah who was born and died has (ἔχει) an endless relationship with God (v. 12a). Anyone who refuses (ὁ μὴ ἔχων) to believe these things about Jesus is perpetually separated (ἔχει) from God (v. 12b).

Outline:

> Overcoming the World's System Is Possible (vv. 5–8)
>> Overcoming the world's system comes to those who believe that Jesus is the Messiah (v. 5)
>> Overcoming the world's system comes to those who believes in Jesus's birth, death, and Spirit (vv. 6–8)
> Believing the Testimony about Jesus Is Essential (vv. 9–11)

God's Testimony about Jesus is the ultimate witness (v. 9–10)
Believing God's testimony involves having an endless relationship
with him (v. 11).
Belief or Disbelief in Jesus's Messiahship Has Eternal Consequences (v. 12)

CLAUSAL OUTLINE FOR 1 JOHN 5:5–12

5:5a τίς [δέ] **ἐστιν** (ὁ νικῶν τὸν κόσμον)
5:5a Now who **is** (the one who overcomes the world)

|

5:5b **εἰ μὴ** [ἐστιν] (ὁ πιστεύων [ὅτι Ἰησοῦς **ἐστιν** ὁ υἱὸς τοῦ θεοῦ]);
5:5b **except** [*it is*] (the one who believes [that Jesus **is** the Son of God])?

5:6a Οὗτός **ἐστιν** (ὁ ἐλθὼν δι᾽ ὕδατος καὶ αἵματος), Ἰησοῦς Χριστός·
5:6a "This **is** (the one who came through water and blood), Jesus, *who is
the* Christ";

5:6b οὐκ [ἦλθεν] ἐν τῷ ὕδατι μόνον
5:6b [*he* (=Jesus) *came*] not by water only

5:6c ἀλλ᾽ [ἦλθεν] ἐν τῷ ὕδατι καὶ ἐν τῷ αἵματι·
5:6c but [*he* (= Jesus) *came*] by water and blood;

5:6d καὶ τὸ πνεῦμά **ἐστιν** τὸ μαρτυροῦν,
5:6d and the Spirit **is** the one who testifies,

|

5:6e **ὅτι** τὸ πνεῦμά **ἐστιν** ἡ ἀλήθεια.
5:6e **because** the Spirit **is** the truth.

5:7 ὅτι τρεῖς **εἰσιν** οἱ μαρτυροῦντες,
5:7 For the ones that testify **are** three,

5:8a τὸ πνεῦμα καὶ τὸ ὕδωρ καὶ τὸ αἷμα [εἰσιν],
5:8a [*they are*] the Spirit and the water and the blood,

5:8b καὶ οἱ τρεῖς εἰς τὸ ἕν **εἰσιν**.
5:8b and these three **are** one.

5:9a **εἰ** τὴν μαρτυρίαν τῶν ἀνθρώπων **λαμβάνομεν**,
5:9a **If we receive** the testimony of people,

5:9b ἡ μαρτυρία τοῦ θεοῦ μείζων **ἐστίν**,
5:9b God's testimony **is** greater,

5:9c **ὅτι** αὕτη **ἐστὶν** ἡ μαρτυρία τοῦ θεοῦ,
5:9c **because** this **is** the testimony of God,

5:9d **ὅτι μεμαρτύρηκεν** περὶ τοῦ υἱοῦ αὐτοῦ.
5:9d *namely* **that he** (= God) **has testified** concerning his Son.

5:10a (ὁ πιστεύων εἰς τὸν υἱὸν τοῦ θεοῦ) **ἔχει** τὴν μαρτυρίαν ἐν αὐτῷ·
5:10a (The one who believes in the Son of God) **has** the testimony in himself;

5:10b (ὁ μὴ πιστεύων τῷ θεῷ) ψεύστην **πεποίηκεν** αὐτόν,
5:10b (the one who does not believe God) has made him *to be* a liar,

5:10c **ὅτι** οὐ **πεπίστευκεν** εἰς τὴν μαρτυρίαν
5:10c **because** he **has** not **believed** in the testimony

5:10d **ἣν μεμαρτύρηκεν** ὁ θεὸς περὶ τοῦ υἱοῦ αὐτοῦ.
5:10d **that** God **has testified** concerning his Son (= Jesus).

5:11a καὶ αὕτη **ἐστὶν** ἡ μαρτυρία,
5:11a And this **is** the testimony,

5:11b **ὅτι** ζωὴν αἰώνιον **ἔδωκεν** ἡμῖν ὁ θεός,
5:11b **that** God **granted** us eternal life,

5:11c καὶ [*ὅτι*] αὕτη ἡ ζωὴ ἐν τῷ υἱῷ αὐτοῦ **ἐστιν**.
5:11c and [*that*] this life **is** in his Son.

5:12a (ὁ ἔχων τὸν υἱὸν) **ἔχει** τὴν ζωήν·
5:12a (The one who has the Son) **has** the life;

5:12b (ὁ μὴ ἔχων τὸν υἱὸν τοῦ θεοῦ) τὴν ζωὴν οὐκ **ἔχει**.
5:12b (the one who does not have the Son of God) **does** not **have** the life.

Syntax Explained for 1 John 5:5–12

^{5:5a} [δέ]: The Greek word δέ is a conjunction in the postpositive position meaning "now" (BDAG, s.v. "δέ" 213.2). **Syntactically,** [δέ] introduces an independent conjunctive clause: "[*Now*] who is the one who conquers the world" (τίς [δέ] ἐστιν ὁ νικῶν τὸν κόσμον). **Semantically,** δέ is a transitional conjunction: "now" (NET; cf. CNT), though some translate it as a coordinating connector (ASV NLT). Some translations reject [δέ] as an authentic textual reading (KJV NASB NRSV NIV NLT). Yet, we accept the textual reading [δέ] and render it as "now," indicating a change to a new topic of discussion (W, 674). The new topic is disclosed in the subsequent clauses.

ἐστίν: The Greek word ἐστίν is third person singular present active indicative from the verb εἰμί meaning "to be" or is used "in explanations to show how something is to be understood" (BDAG, s.v. "εἰμί" 2cβ, p. 282). **Syntactically,** ἐστίν is the main verb of the independent clause. The subject of the verb is the interrogative pronoun, "who" (τίς), due to the grammatical priority of pronouns over articular nouns (W, 42–43). **Semantically,** ἐστίν is an equative present demonstrating the close connection between the interrogative pronoun, "who" (τίς), and the following phrase.

νικῶν: The Greek word νικῶν is a nominative singular masculine present active participle from the verb νικάω meaning "to vanquish" or "to overcome" or "to overcome someone" (BDAG, s.v. "νικάω" 2a, p. 673). **Syntactically,** νικῶν introduces a dependent participle clause. The entire clause, "the one who overcomes the world" (ὁ νικῶν τὸν κόσμον), functions as the predicate of the verb, "is" (ἐστίν). It is placed in parentheses to visualize its grammatical contribution to the independent clause. **Semantically,** ὁ νικῶν is a gnomic present: "the one who overcomes" (cf. KJV ASV NASB ESV NIV CNT). The participle makes a generic statement (W, 523, 615). John is presenting a timeless truth about the person who overcomes the world or succeeds within the world's system of self-centeredness. That timeless truth is clarified in the next clause.

^{5:5b} εἰ μή: The Greek construction εἰ + μή is a subcategory of the conditional conjunction meaning "except" or "but" (BDAG, s.v. "εἰ" 6iα, p. 278). **Syntactically,** εἰ μή introduces a dependent conjunctive clause, which is functioning adverbially modifying the verb, "is" (ἐστιν). **Semantically,** εἰ μή expresses a contrast or an exception: "except" (ESV NET) or "but" (KJV ASV NASB NRSV CNT). The exception is clarified in the verbal participle and subsequent ὅτι clause.

πιστεύων: The Greek word πιστεύων is a nominative masculine singular present active participle from the verb πιστεύω meaning "to believe" or "to consider something to be true and therefore worthy of one's trust" (BDAG, s.v. "πιστεύω" 1aβ, p. 816). **Syntactically,** πιστεύων introduces a dependent participial clause. The entire participial clause, "the one who believes (that Jesus is the Son of God)" (ὁ πιστεύων [ὅτι Ἰησοῦς ἐστιν ὁ υἱὸς τοῦ θεοῦ]), is functioning as the subject of the elliptical verb, "[it is]" (cf. Culy, 124; Yarbrough, 269). The participial clause is placed in parentheses along with the ὅτι clause in order to visualize its contribution to the independent clause. **Semantically,** πιστεύων is a gnomic present: "the one who believes" (NRSV ESV NET) or "he who" (NASB NIV CNT). The participle makes a generic statement (W, 523, 615). If anyone has conquered the world, it is definitely the one who believes that Jesus is God's Son.

ὅτι: The Greek word ὅτι is a conjunction meaning "that" (BDAG, s.v. "ὅτι" 1d, p. 731). **Syntactically,** ὅτι introduces a dependent conjunctive clause: "*that* Jesus is the Son of God" (ὅτι Ἰησοῦς ἐστιν ὁ υἱὸς τοῦ θεοῦ). The entire ὅτι clause functions substantivally as the object of the participle, "the one who believes" (ὁ πιστεύων). The clause is placed in brackets in order to visualize its contribution to the dependent participial clause. **Semantically,** ὅτι is an indirect discourse marker: "that" (cf. KJV NASB ESV NIV NET etc.). It provides the content of what the person who overcomes the world believes.

ἐστίν: The Greek word ἐστίν is third person singular present active indicative from the verb εἰμί meaning "to be" or "to be in close connection with" (BDAG, s.v. "εἰμί" 2a, p. 283). **Syntactically,** ἐστίν is the governing verb of the dependent conjunctive ὅτι clause. The subject of the verb is the proper noun, "Jesus" (Ἰησοῦς), even though articular nouns and proper names hold the same weight when it comes to determining which substantive is the subject and which is the predicate nominative. Wallace points out that when two substantives have equal weight, word order should be the determining factor (W, 44). **Semantically,** ἐστίν is an equative present: "is" (cf. KJV NASB ESV NIV NET etc.). It equates Jesus with the demonstrative pronoun, which is clarified in subsequent clauses.

5:6a ἐστίν: The Greek word ἐστίν is third person singular present active indicative from the verb εἰμί meaning "to be" or "to be in close connection with" (BDAG, s.v. "εἰμί" 2a, p. 283). **Syntactically,** ἐστίν is the main verb of the independent clause: "this *is* the one who came through water and blood, Jesus, who is the Christ" (οὗτός ἐστιν ὁ ἐλθὼν δι' ὕδατος καὶ αἵματος, Ἰησοῦς Χριστός). The subject of the verb is the demonstrative pronoun, "this one" (οὗτός), due to the grammatical priority of demonstratives (W, 42–43). The pronoun anaphorically points back to its referent, the proper noun, "Jesus" (Ἰησοῦς), found in verse 5. The demonstrative is also further clarified by a subsequent appositional phrase, "Jesus, who is the Christ" (Ἰησοῦς Χριστός). **Semantically,** ἐστίν is an equative present: "is" (cf. KJV NASB ESV NIV NET etc.). It equates Jesus with being human, more specifically his birth and death (e.g. "by water and blood").

ἐλθών: The Greek word ἐλθών is a nominative masculine singular aorist active participle from the verb ἔρχομαι meaning "to come" or "to make a public appearance" (BDAG, s.v. "ἔρχομαι" 1bα, p. 394). **Syntactically,** ἐλθών introduces a dependent participial clause: "the one who came by water and blood" (ὁ ἐλθὼν δι᾽ ὕδατος καὶ αἵματος). It functions substantivally as the predicate nominative of the verb, "is" (ἐστίν). The entire clause is placed in parentheses in order to visualize its contribution to the independent clause. **Semantically,** ἐλθών is a constative aorist: "the one who came" (NASB NRSV NIV NET). It describes an event as a whole (W, 559). John describes Jesus's historical baptism (or birth) and death (i.e., "by water and by blood").

Syntactical, Lexical, and Theological Nugget: What does the prepositional phrase "through water and blood" (δι᾽ ὕδατος καὶ αἵματος) mean? First there are a variety of textual variants at this point in the text that go beyond the scope of this guide (for a treatment of these variants, see Painter, 300; Culy, 125). Second there is a syntactical issue. How are we to classify and translate διά + genitive? It seems that the best way to classify this usage is means: Jesus came *by means* of water and *by means* of blood (cf. Painter, 300–01). Finally, there is an interpretive issue: What does "by water and blood" (δι᾽ ὕδατος καὶ αἵματος) mean? There are at least four explanations.

(1) The clause "who came through water and blood" refers to the sacraments/ordinances of baptism and the Eucharist. This view is as old as the fourth century (*Works of Saint Augustine*, 1.218). The polemic of 1 John 5:6 and its obscurity within the context of 1 John seem to argue against this view because (a) the two nouns, water and blood, appear to be references to events in Jesus's life, and (b) there is nothing in the context to suggest that the misguided teachers were denying the ordinances. (For other presentations and arguments against this view, see Brown, 575; Kruse 2000, 177; Lieu, 211 #3).

(2) The clause "who came through water and blood" refers to the death of Jesus. Based upon John 19:34, Brown argues that "water and blood" echoes an occurrence during his death. Upon Jesus's death, water and blood flowed from his side. It is the only other passage in John where the two substances are connected. Jesus's death then describes the reason for his advent (John 18:37), and the only other mention of blood in John's Gospel is concerned with Jesus' death (1:7). One weakness is that John 19:34 reads εὐθὺς αἷμα καὶ ὕδωρ, ("immediately blood and water) while 1 John 5:6 reads ἐν τῷ ὕδατι καὶ ἐν τῷ αἵματι ("by water and by blood") reversing the order.

(3) The clause "who came through water and blood" refers to the incarnation of Jesus. This view has more to commend it because it parallels the authentic confession in 1 John 4:2 that Jesus Christ has come in the flesh, which defi-

nitely refers to Jesus's incarnation. It also does justice to the implied participle
"coming" (ἐλθών). If John is dealing with a docetic-like heresy (cf. Irenaeus,
Haer. 1.25.1–2), John may be emphasizing Jesus's incarnation and his salvific
ministry on the cross (Culpepper, 272; cf. Culy , 125–26). (For other presentations and arguments against this view, see Brown, 575–76; Kruse 2000, 176;
Lieu, 209 #1a.)

(4) The clause "who came through water and blood" refers to the baptism
and death of Jesus. In support of this view is John's statement that Jesus
did not come in water only, but in water and blood. This may imply that
the misguided teachers with whom John is disagreeing separated Jesus's
humanity and his deity. They believed it was at Jesus's baptism that a divine
figure separate from Jesus descended on him to empower his ministry, only
to leave Jesus during his crucifixion (Irenaeus, *Haer.* 1:26.1; 3:11.3). In response, John insists on the unity between Jesus and the Son of God/Messi-
ah (1 John 2:22; 4:2–3, 6, 15; 5:1, 5). The link between the Holy Spirit and
baptism in John 1:33 echoes the same link between water and the Spirit in
1 John 5:6, suggesting that baptism should be equated with water. Thus the
phrase "water and blood" might be a merismus (a poetic expression using
two halves to indicate a whole) to describe Jesus's entire human ministry
(Westcott, 181; Schnackenburg, 232–33; cf. Stott, 180–81; Painter, 305; Yarbrough, 282). For further discussion of this view, see Brown, 576–77; Lieu,
209 #1b.

The latter two appear the most feasible. John's emphasis is on the humanity and
messiahship of Jesus. It seems either one of these fits John's argument the best.

5:6b [ἦλθεν]: The implied Greek word ἦλθεν is third person singular aorist active indicative from the verb ἔρχομαι meaning "to come" or "to make a public appearance" (BDAG, s.v. "ἔρχομαι" 1bα, p. 394). **Syntactically,** [ἦλθεν] is an elliptical
verb that governs the independent anacoluthon clause. The subject of [ἦλθεν] is
he (= Jesus): "*Jesus* came not by water only" (οὐκ ἐν τῷ ὕδατι μόνον). **Semantically,** the ellipsis [ἦλθεν] is a constative aorist negated with οὐκ: "[he (= Jesus)
came] not." It points out the general historical act as a whole that Jesus did not
come by water alone (W, 557). These images serve as a metonymy pointing to
events associated with Jesus's ministry (baptism [or birth] and death).

5:6c ἀλλ᾿: The Greek word ἀλλά is a conjunction meaning "but" (BDAG, s.v.
"ἀλλά" 1a, p. 44). **Syntactically,** ἀλλά introduces a dependent conjunctive
clause. **Semantically,** ἀλλά is contrastive: "but" (cf. KJV NASB ESV NIV NET
etc.). It emphasizes a contrast with Jesus coming by water only (= baptism [or
birth]). The content of that contrast is found in the prepositional phrase: "by
water and by blood" (ἐν τῷ ὕδατι καὶ ἐν τῷ αἵματι).

[ἦλθεν]: The implied Greek word ἦλθεν is third person singular aorist active indicative from the verb ἔρχομαι meaning "to come" or "to make a public appearance" (BDAG, s.v. "ἔρχομαι" 1bα, p. 394). **Syntactically,** [ἦλθεν] is an elliptical verb that governs the independent clause. The subject of [ἦλθεν] is he (= Jesus): "but *Jesus* came by water and by blood" (ἀλλ' ἐν τῷ ὕδατι καὶ ἐν τῷ αἵματι). **Semantically,** ἦλθεν is a constative aorist: "[he (= Jesus) came]." It points out the general historical act as a whole, that Jesus did not come by water alone (W, 557). Once again, these images serve as a metonymy pointing to events associated with Jesus's incarnation (baptism [or birth] and death).

5:6d καί: The Greek word καί is a conjunction meaning "and" (BDAG, s.v. "καί" 1bα, p. 494). **Syntactically,** καί introduces a conjunctive independent clause: "*and* the Spirit is the one who testifies" (καὶ τὸ πνεῦμά ἐστιν τὸ μαρτυροῦν). **Semantically,** καί is a coordinating connective: "and" (cf. KJV NASB ESV NIV NET etc.). It provides additional information (W, 671). The additional information is found in the remainder of the clause.

ἐστίν: The Greek word ἐστίν is third person singular present active indicative from the verb εἰμί meaning "to be" or "to be in close connection with" (BDAG, s.v. "εἰμί" 2a, p. 283). **Syntactically,** ἐστίν is the main verb of the independent conjunctive clause. Both the subject and the verb in this clause happen to have an article. The subject is the articular noun "Spirit" (τὸ πνεῦμά). Since it is a proper designation, the participle requires an article to nominalize it, and it is the subject of the next clause as well (Culy, 126; see also W, 42–46). **Semantically,** ἐστίν is an equative present: "is" (cf. KJV NASB ESV NIV NET etc.). It equates the Spirit as the one who bears witness to the coming of Jesus as a human being.

μαρτυροῦν: The Greek word μαρτυροῦν is a neuter nominative singular present active participle from the verb μαρτυρέω meaning "to bear witness" or "to testify" or "to confirm or attest something on the basis of personal knowledge or belief" (BDAG, s.v. "μαρτυρέω" 1aα, p. 617). **Syntactically,** μαρτυροῦν is functioning substantivally as the predicate nominative of the verb, "is" (ἐστίν). **Semantically,** μαρτυροῦν is a customary present: "who testifies" (cf. NASB ESV NIV NET etc.). It illustrates a pattern of behavior (W, 521). The Spirit always bears witness to the incarnation of Jesus.

5:6e ὅτι: The Greek word ὅτι is a conjunction meaning "because" (BDAG, s.v. "ὅτι" 4a, p. 732). **Syntactically,** ὅτι introduces the dependent conjunctive clause: "*because* the Spirit is truth" (ὅτι τὸ πνεῦμά ἐστιν ἡ ἀλήθεια). The entire clause is functioning adverbially, modifying the verb, "is" (ἐστίν). **Semantically,** ὅτι is causal: "because" (KJV NASB ESV NIV NET CNT). It provides the reason why the Spirit's testimony is valid (W, 460). The reason for the Spirit's testimony being valid is evident in the remainder of the clause.

ἐστίν: The Greek word ἐστίν is third person singular present active indicative from the verb εἰμί meaning "to be" or "to be in close connection with" (BDAG, s.v. "εἰμί" 2a, p. 283). **Syntactically,** ἐστίν is the main verb of the dependent conjunctive ὅτι clause. The subject of the verb is the articular noun, "Spirit" (τὸ πνεῦμα). **Semantically,** ἐστίν is an equative present: "is" (cf. KJV NASB ESV NIV NET etc.). It equates the Spirit's identity with truth. The Spirit speaks truth because he is by nature truthful.

5:7 ὅτι: The Greek word ὅτι is a conjunction meaning "for" or "so" (BDAG, s.v. "ὅτι" 4b, p. 732). **Syntactically,** ὅτι introduces the dependent conjunctive clause: "*For* the ones that testify are three" (ὅτι τρεῖς εἰσιν οἱ μαρτυροῦντες). **Semantically,** ὅτι is classified as explanatory: "for" (KJV NASB ESV NIV NET). It explains the previous discussion (W, 673)

> **Semantical Nugget:** How should ὅτι be understood? First, it could be classified as a second causal clause also dependent on the verb, "is" (ἐστίν) (cf. Culy, 127). Thus, it would provide another reason why the Spirit testifies in truth. Second, it could be classified adjectivally as an epexegetical ὅτι clause. Thus, it would explain the nature of the "truth" (ἀλήθεια). Finally, it could be classified as a substantival ὅτι clause. In that case it would point out an inference from the previous discussion: "for." The best option seems to be the third option: a loosely connected conjunction drawing an inference or making a deduction from the previous clauses: "*for* the ones that testify are three" (ὅτι τρεῖς εἰσιν οἱ μαρτυροῦντες).

εἰσιν: The Greek word εἰσίν is third person plural present active indicative from the verb εἰμί meaning "to be" or "to be in close connection with" (BDAG, s.v. "εἰμί" 2a, p. 283). **Syntactically,** εἰσίν is the main verb of the independent clause. The subject of the verb is the articular participle, "the ones that testify" (οἱ μαρτυροῦντες), due to the grammatical priority of articular nouns over adjectives (W, 42–44). **Semantically,** εἰσιν is an equative present: "are" (cf. KJV NASB ESV NIV NET etc.). It equates the substantival participle "the ones that testify" (οἱ μαρτυροῦντες) with "three" (τρεῖς). The significance of this equation is explained in the next word (cf. W, 332 n44).

μαρτυροῦντες: The Greek word μαρτυροῦντες is a nominative plural masculine present active participle from the verb μαρτυρέω meaning "to declare" or "to bear witness to" or "to attest to something based upon personal knowledge" (BDAG, s.v. "μαρτυρέω" 1b, p. 618). **Syntactically,** μαρτυροῦντες is functioning substantivally. It is the subject of the verb, "are" (εἰσίν). **Semantically,** μαρτυροῦντες is a customary present: "the ones who testify" (W, 615). It underscores the existence of three separate witnesses to the incarnation of Jesus. All three witnesses mentioned point to the incarnation of Jesus: the Spirit, the water, and the blood.

Text-Critical Nugget: What is the *Comma Johanneum* (=*Johannine Comma*)? Some New Testament Greek texts (e.g., Holmes 2010, 475) contain an additional reading known as the *Johannine Comma*: "The ones who testify in heaven, the Father, the word, and the Holy Spirit and these three are one. And there are three that testify on earth." This rather lengthy material occurs after the participle "testify" and before the nouns "the Spirit, the water, and the blood." Historically, eclectic texts (e.g., NA[28]) have a shorter reading that does not include the *Johannine Comma*. In spite of the fact that such a passage could be a clear prooftext for the Trinity, it was never cited by the early church fathers as such in their extensive Trinitarian debates. The obvious conclusion is that it was not, at that time, part of the textual tradition. In fact, the *Johannine Comma* does not appear in any Greek text until 1215 c.e. Furthermore, it doesn't fit into the immediate context of 1 John 5. The UBS committee had no difficulty in deciding in eliminating the extensive addition (giving it an A rating; Metzger[1], 647–48; cf. Comfort, 396–97). We agree with the Nestle-Aland traditional rendering (cf. Westcott, 181; NET note on the Comma).[1]

5:8a [ἐισιν]: The Greek word ἐισίν is third person plural present active indicative from the verb ἐιμί meaning "to be" or "to be in close connection with" (BDAG, s.v. "ἐιμί" 2a, p. 283). **Syntactically,** [ἐισιν] is the main verb of the independent clause. The subject of the verb is the implied "they" of [ἐισιν] and the predicate nominative is "Spirit and the water and the blood" (τὸ πνεῦμα καὶ τὸ ὕδωρ καὶ τὸ αἷμα). **Semantically,** the ellipsis [ἐισιν] is an equative present: "are" (cf. KJV NASB ESV NIV NET etc.). It equates the implied subject that refers back to "three" (τρεῖς) in 5:7a with three predicate nominatives: the Spirit, water, and blood.

5:8b καί: The Greek word καί is a conjunction meaning "and" (BDAG, s.v. "καί" 1bα, p. 494). **Syntactically,** καί introduces a conjunctive independent clause: "*and* these three are one" (καὶ οἱ τρεῖς εἰς τὸ ἕν ἐισιν). **Semantically,** καί is a coordinating connection: "and" (KJV ASV NASB NRSV ESV NIV NET NLT CNT). It provides additional information (W, 671) about the three witnesses: the Spirit, the water, and the blood.

ἐισίν: The Greek word ἐισίν is third person plural present active indicative from the verb ἐιμί meaning "to be" or "to be in close connection with" (BDAG, s.v. "ἐιμί" 2a, p. 283). **Syntactically,** ἐισίν is the main verb of the independent clause. The subject of the verb is the substantival adjective, "the three" (οἱ τρεῖς). The prepositional phrase "into one" (εἰς τὸ ἕν) is the predicate nominative due to word order and the contextual clue that "the three"

---

1.   It is worth noting that *The Greek New Testament According to the Majority Text* (MT, 713) does not include the *Johannine Comma*. It too is in agreement with the Nestle-Aland tradition. See earlier critical Greek texts; see also Eberhard Nestle's *Greek New Testament*, 16th edition (1898, 606).

has been the subject of the previous discussion. This type of prepositional construction used as a predicate nominative is rare. It is used most often in Old Testament quotations, which may mean that it reflects Semitic influence. **Semantically,** εἰσίν is an equative present: "are" (cf. KJV NASB ESV NIV NET etc.). It underscores a phenomenon or an event, namely, that the testimony of the Spirit, the baptism (or birth) of Jesus, and the death of Jesus unite together as a powerful witness to the messianic mission of Jesus. The idea behind the phrase is not that the three witnesses are one in identity, but that they are in agreement about Jesus's testimony (Smalley, 282).

Syntactical and Lexical Nugget: What is the significance of the prepositional phrase εἰς τὸ ἕν? On the one hand, the phrase occurs nowhere else in the New Testament. On the other hand, the construction εἰς + accusative can have the force equivalent to a predicate nominative. The use of εἰς as the equivalent to a predicate nominative is especially common in quotations from the Old Testament (W, 47–48n35). For example, ἐγὼ ἔσομαι πατήρ ("I will be a father") could instead become ἐγὼ ἔσομαι εἰς πατέρα (Heb. 1:5). Similar expressions are used in John's Gospel: "that all the scattered children of God might be gathered *as one*" (εἰς ἕν; 11:52), and "that the children of God might be brought *into total unity*" (ἵνα ὦσιν τετελειωμένοι εἰς ἕν; 17:23). Here in 1 John 5:8, John seems to be saying that "the Spirit, water and blood converge on the same point, and work together toward the same result: that of establishing the truth that Jesus is the Messiah and Son of God" (Smalley, 282). So εἰς τὸ ἕν implies that the three witnesses reflect the Mosaic law of testimony (Deut. 17:16; 19:15).

5:9a εἰ: The Greek word εἰ is a conjunction meaning "if" (BDAG, s.v. "εἰ" 1a, p. 277). **Syntactically** εἰ identifies the clause as a dependent conjunctive clause. The entire dependent clause, "*If we receive the testimony of men*" (εἰ τὴν μαρτυρίαν τῶν ἀνθρώπων λαμβάνομεν), is functioning adverbially as the protasis of a conditional clause which modifies the verb, "is" (ἐστίν). **Semantically,** εἰ introduces a first class conditional clause: "if" (KJV ASV NASB NRSV ESV NET CNT). Some translations, however, appear to view the conjunction as an assertion without an apodosis (NIV NLT; BDAG, s.v. "εἰ" 4, p. 278). Nevertheless, the best option is to consider the entire εἰ clause as an assertion for the sake of argument (W, 690–94). John's assumption is identified in the next verb.

λαμβάνομεν: The Greek word λαμβάνομεν is first person plural present active indicative from the verb λαμβάνω meaning "to receive," "to get," "to obtain," or "to be a receiver" (BDAG, s.v. "λαμβάνω" 10b, p. 584). **Syntactically,** λαμβάνομεν is the governing verb of the dependent conditional conjunctive εἰ clause. The subject is an embedded "we." It is a generic reference to anyone. **Semantically,** λαμβάνομεν is a customary present: "we receive"

(KJV ASV NASB NRSV ESV CNT). It expresses an ongoing acceptance (W, 521; cf. NIV NET). John's ongoing assumption is a person's comfort level of accepting the testimony of humans as truth (cf. 1:1–3). Based upon an assumption his readers would agree to be true, John makes a point about God's testimony in the next clause (W, 694; see, e.g., Rom. 8:9).

5:9b ἐστίν: The Greek word ἐστίν is third person singular present active indicative from the verb εἰμί meaning "to be" or "to be in close connection with" (BDAG, s.v. "εἰμί" 2a, p. 283). **Syntactically,** ἐστίν is the main verb of the independent clause "God's testimony *is* greater" (ἡ μαρτυρία τοῦ θεοῦ μείζων ἐστίν). It is the apodosis of the conditional thought. The subject of the verb is the articular noun "testimony" (ἡ μαρτυρία) due to the presence of the article. The genitive "of God" (τοῦ θεοῦ) is subjective: "God's testimony" (W 1996, 115). **Semantically,** ἐστίν is an equative present: "is" (cf. KJV NASB ESV NIV NET etc.). It underscores a phenomenon or an event about God's testimony, namely, that God's testimony is greater and thus more reliable than the testimony of ordinary people.

> **Theological Nugget:** How should the threefold witness of the water, the blood, and the Spirit be understood? On the one hand, some suggest that the three witnesses represent the presence of Jesus and his work through the presence of the Spirit (cf. 3:20; 4:4). On the other hand, others suggest that John is making a comparison between the Spirit and John the Baptist (John 1:32 and 3:31–33). If people believed John the Baptist, why won't they believe the testimony of the Spirit? However, the plural here seems to suggest that mankind in general is in view here rather than an individual like John the Baptist or the Spirit of God. It seems likely that John is pointing out that if people will believe fallible humans, they should believe the Spirit, because the Spirit's testimony about the water and the blood is the testimony of God, which is far more reliable than the testimony of any person (Brown, 586; Smalley, 283). If this is the case then the genitive here should be taken subjectively. The Spirit's testimony is God's testimony, not the testimony about God (Culy, 128; Yarbrough, 285).

5:9c ὅτι: The Greek word ὅτι is a conjunction meaning "because" (BDAG, s.v. "ὅτι" 4a, p. 732). **Syntactically,** ὅτι introduces the dependent conjunctive clause: "*because* this is the testimony of God" (ὅτι αὕτη ἐστὶν ἡ μαρτυρία τοῦ θεοῦ). The entire clause is functioning adverbially, modifying the verb, "is" (ἐστίν). **Semantically,** ὅτι is causal: "because" (KJV NASB ESV NIV NET CNT). It provides the reason why God's testimony is greater than the testimony of any person (W, 460).

ἐστίν: The Greek word ἐστίν is third person singular present active indicative from the verb εἰμί meaning "to be" or "to be in close connection with" (BDAG, s.v. "εἰμί" 2a, p. 282). **Syntactically,** ἐστίν is the governing verb of the dependent adverbial clause. The subject of the verb is the demonstrative pronoun "this" (αὕτη) due to the grammatical priority of demonstratives over articular nouns (W, 42–44). **Semantically,** ἐστίν is an equative present: "is" (cf. KJV NASB ESV NIV NET etc.). It elucidates the idea that the Spirit's testimony is equated with God's testimony.

5:9d ὅτι: The Greek word ὅτι is a conjunction meaning "that" (BDAG, s.v. "ὅτι" 2a, p. 732). **Syntactically,** ὅτι introduces the dependent conjunctive clause: "*namely that* he has testified concerning his Son" (ὅτι μεμαρτύρηκεν περὶ τοῦ υἱοῦ αὐτοῦ). The clause modifies "this" (αὕτη). **Semantically,** ὅτι is epexegetical: "that" (NASB CNT). It explains or clarifies the demonstrative (W, 459). That content is clarified with the next verb.

μεμαρτύρηκεν: The Greek word μεμαρτύρηκεν is third person singular perfect active indicative from the verb μαρτυρέω meaning "to bear witness to" or "to attest to something based upon personal knowledge" (BDAG, s.v. "μαρτυρέω" 1aα, p. 617). **Syntactically,** μεμαρτύρηκεν is the governing verb of the dependent conjunctive ὅτι clause. The subject is an implied "he" embedded in the verb and a reference to God. **Semantically,** μεμαρτύρηκεν is an extensive perfect: "he (= God) has testified" (KJV NASB NRSV NET NLT). It focuses on the past action from which a present state emerges (W, 577). God's past testimony about his Son has certainty in the present. God testified about his Son, namely, that he is the Messiah who has conquered the world.

Syntactical Nugget: How is the ὅτι clause to be understood? There are at least three options. First, the ὅτι clause could be functioning adverbially, modifying the verb "is" (ἐστίν) in the previous ὅτι clause. If so, the ὅτι is causal. It provides a second reason why God's testimony is greater than the testimony of people. Second, the ὅτι could be redivided into an indefinite relative clause "that which" (ὅ τι; cf. KJV NIV NET). This indefinite relative construction is very rare in Johannine literature and the lack of agreement between the neuter ὅ and the feminine "testimony" (ἡ μαρτυρία) seems problematic, even though the NET Bible favors this redivision. Finally, the ὅτι could be considered substantival. It provides the content of either the demonstrative pronoun, "this" (αὕτη), or the noun, "testimony" (ἡ μαρτυρία). This ὅτι clause would then provide us with the content of God's testimony, namely, that he has testified concerning the Son. The best explanation is the last option, that this entire ὅτι clause modifies the demonstrative pronoun, "this" (αὕτη). It is characteristic of John's style in 1 John (cf. 3:1, 5, 16; 4:9, 10, 13).

5:10a πιστεύων: The Greek word πιστεύων is a nominative masculine singular present active participle from the verb πιστεύω meaning "to believe" or "to entrust oneself to an entity in complete confidence" (BDAG, s.v. "πιστεύω" 2aβ, p. 817). **Syntactically,** πιστεύων introduces a dependent participial clause. It is substantival and begins a parenthesis in John's argument (NET). The entire clause, "the one who believes in the Son of God" (ὁ πιστεύων εἰς τὸν υἱὸν τοῦ θεοῦ) is functioning nominally as the subject of the verb "has" (ἔχει). The object of belief is God. **Semantically,** πιστεύων is a gnomic present: "the one who believes" (NASB NET). Some translations reveal the gnomic sense of this singular participle with "those who do not believe" (NRSV) or "anyone" (NIV). It points out a generic truth about anyone who does not believe (W, 523, 615). That gnomic or timeless truth is evident in the next verb.

ἔχει: The Greek word ἔχει is third person singular present active indicative from the verb ἔχω meaning "to have" or "to possess" or "to have within oneself" (BDAG, s.v. "ἔχω" 1d, p. 420). **Syntactically,** ἔχει is the main verb of the independent clause: "The one who believes in the Son of God *has* this testimony in him" (ὁ πιστεύων εἰς τὸν υἱὸν τοῦ θεοῦ ἔχει τὴν μαρτυρίαν ἐν αὐτῷ). The subject is the participial clause, "the one who believes in the Son of God" (ὁ πιστεύων εἰς τὸν υἱὸν τοῦ θεοῦ). **Semantically,** ἔχει is a gnomic present: "has" (KJV NASB ESV NIV NET CNT). It is emphasizing a timeless fact (W, 523). Anyone who believes in Jesus as God's Son (= Messiah) has God's testimony within them and thereby life.

Text-Critical Nugget: What reading is correct "in him" (ἐν αὐτῷ) or "in himself" (ἐν ἑαυτῷ)? This issue has theological significance. The manuscript evidence is split between the third person personal pronoun, "in him" (ἐν αὐτῷ), and the third person reflexive pronoun, "in himself" (ἐν ἑαυτῷ). Perhaps ἑαυτῷ is a secondary development from αὐτῷ. The context, however, demands a reflexive translation, which is why it is likely that a scribe changed to an easier reading at a later date. Either way, the one who believes that Jesus is God's Son has God's testimony in him (Brown, 589). The UBS committee had little difficulty in deciding in favor of "in himself" (ἐν ἑαυτῷ, giving it a B rating; Metzger[1], 649). What does it mean that the believer possesses God's testimony in himself? It seems to suggest a belief that goes beyond just agreeing that the facts are true. It reflects a commitment to the testimony so strong that it affects one's daily life. Surely this inner confidence in Jesus is at least partially a result of the internal anointing that all believers share (1 John 2:20–27).

5:10b πιστεύων: The Greek word πιστεύων is a nominative masculine singular present active participle from the verb πιστεύω meaning "to believe" or "to consider something to be true and therefore worthy of one's trust" (BDAG, s.v. "πιστεύω" 1b, p. 816). **Syntactically,** πιστεύων introduces a dependent participial clause. The entire clause, "the one who does not believe God" (ὁ μὴ πιστεύων τῷ θεῷ), is functioning as the subject of the verb, "makes" (πεποίηκεν). The dative case is used because πιστεύω takes a direct object in the dative. The negative particle, "not" (μή), is used instead of the normal "not" (οὐ) because μή negates non-indicatives, such as participles, infinitives, and verbs that appear in the subjunctive or optative mood. **Semantically,** πιστεύων is a gnomic present negated with μή: "the one who does not believe" (NASB NET). Some translations try to reveal the gnomic sense of the singular participle with "those who do not believe" (NRSV NLT) or "anyone" (NIV). It speaks generically of any person who does not believe (W, 615). It is a timeless truth more pointedly defined with the next verb.

πεποίηκεν: The Greek word πεποίηκεν is third person singular perfect active indicative from the verb ποιέω meaning "to do" or "to bring about" or "to undertake or do something that brings about a state or condition" (BDAG, s.v. "ποιέω" 2nβ, p. 840). **Syntactically,** πεποίηκεν is the main verb of the independent clause: "the one who does not believe God *has made* him (= God) a liar" (ὁ μὴ πιστεύων τῷ θεῷ ψεύστην πεποίηκεν αὐτόν). The subject is the participial clause, "the one who does not believe God" (ὁ μὴ πιστεύων τῷ θεῷ). This is a double accusative object-complement construction. The direct object of the verb, "has made" (πεποίηκεν), is the pronoun, "him (= God)" (αὐτόν). The second accusative, "liar" (ψεύστην), functions as the complement. This type of construction is often translated with the words "to be." Therefore, it is translated "the one who does not believe God has made him *to be* a liar" (W, 181–86). **Semantically,** πεποίηκεν is a gnomic perfect with an extensive sense: "has made" (KJV ASV NASB ESV NIV NET CNT). The generic subject is in view with a focus on the decisive act having been carried out (W, 580). The one who has disbelieved God has labeled him a liar.

Theological Nugget: Who is the liar mentioned throughout 1 John? John has insinuated that anyone who denies God's main claims is a liar. The one who claims that they have never sinned (1:10), the one who says they know God but experiences no life change (2:4), the one who denies that Jesus is the Messiah (2:22), the one who says they love God but refuses to love other believers (4:20), and the one who does not believe in God's testimony about Jesus (5:10) are all called liars. These may be laid out chiastically whereby the ultimate liar is the one who denies that Jesus is the Christ.

1:10	If we say, "We have not sinned," we make God a liar ...
2:4	The one who says, "I have known God," yet does not keep his commandments is a liar ...
2:22	**Who is the liar but the person who denies that Jesus is the Christ?**
4:20	If anyone says, "I love God," but hates their fellow Christian, they are a liar ...
5:10	The one who does not believe God has made [God] a liar ...

5:10c ὅτι: The Greek word ὅτι is a conjunction meaning "because" (BDAG, s.v.

"ὅτι" 4a, p. 732). **Syntactically,** ὅτι introduces the dependent conjunctive clause, "*because* he has not believed in the testimony" (ὅτι οὐ πεπίστευκεν εἰς τὴν μαρτυρίαν). The entire ὅτι clause functions adverbially. It modifies the verb "has made" (πεποίηκεν). **Semantically,** ὅτι is causal: "because" (KJV ASV NASB ESV NIV NET NLT CNT). It provides the reason why the one who does not believe makes God out to be a liar. That reason is found in the next verb.

πεπίστευκεν: The Greek word πεπίστευκεν is third person singular perfect active indicative from the verb πιστεύω meaning "to believe" or "to consider something to be true and therefore worthy of one's trust" (BDAG, s.v. "πιστεύω" 1aε, p. 816). **Syntactically,** πεπίστευκεν is the governing verb of the dependent ὅτι clause. The subject of the verb is an implied "he." It refers to "the one who does not believe God" (ὁ μὴ πιστεύων τῷ θεῷ). **Semantically,** πεπίστευκεν is a gnomic perfect with an extensive perfect negated with οὐ: "he *has* not believed" (cf. KJV NASB ESV NIV NET). It focuses on the past event from which a current state emerges (W, 577). A generic subject is in view with a focus on the decisive act of disbelief (W, 580). Anyone who does not trust what God has said is labeled as a liar.

5:10d ἥν: The Greek word ἥν is accusative singular feminine from the relative pronoun ὅς meaning "that" (BDAG, s.v. "ὅς" 1a, p. 725). **Syntactically,** ἥν introduces a dependent relative clause: "*that* God has testified about his Son" (ἥν μεμαρτύρηκεν ὁ θεὸς περὶ τοῦ υἱοῦ αὐτοῦ). It is an adjectival clause modifying the noun, "testimony" (μαρτυρίαν). This relative pronoun is in the accusative case because it is the direct object of the verb, "has testified" (μεμαρτύρηκεν). The entire relative clause closes John's parenthesis in his argument and provides some concluding information about God's testimony, which is identified in the next verb.

μεμαρτύρηκεν: The Greek word μεμαρτύρηκεν is third person singular perfect active indicative from the verb μαρτυρέω meaning "to bear witness" or "to confirm or attest something on the basis of personal knowledge or belief" (BDAG, s.v. "μαρτυρέω" 1b, p. 618). **Syntactically,** μεμαρτύρηκεν is the governing verb of the dependent relative clause. The subject is the proper noun, "God" (ὁ θεός). **Semantically,** μεμαρτύρηκεν is an extensive perfect: "*has* testified" (KJV ASV NASB NRSV ESV NET CNT). It focuses on a past event from which a current state emerges (W, 577). God has born witness about the identity of his Son and that testimony remains valid.

5:11a καί: The Greek word καί is a conjunction meaning "and" (BDAG, s.v. "καί" 1c, p. 494). **Syntactically,** καί introduces a conjunctive independent clause: "*And* this is the testimony" (καὶ αὕτη ἐστὶν ἡ μαρτυρία). **Semantically,** καί is a coordinating connector: "and" (cf. KJV NASB ESV NIV NET etc.). It is a coordinating explicative that explains God's greater testimony introduced in 5:9b. It provides additional information about God's testimony, which is underscored with the equative verb and subsequent ὅτι clause.

ἐστίν: The Greek word ἐστίν is third person singular present active indicative from the verb εἰμί meaning "is" or "to be in close connection with" (BDAG, s.v. "εἰμί" 2a, p. 283). **Syntactically,** ἐστίν is the main verb of the independent clause. The subject of the verb is the demonstrative pronoun "this" (αὕτη) due to the grammatical priority of pronouns (W, 42–44). **Semantically,** ἐστίν is an equative present: "is" (cf. KJV NASB ESV NIV NET etc.). It equates the demonstrative pronoun "this" (αὕτη) with the testimony. The meaning of the demonstrative pronoun is clarified in the next ὅτι clause.

5:11b ὅτι: The Greek word ὅτι is a conjunction meaning "that" (BDAG, s.v. "ὅτι" 2a, p. 732). **Syntactically,** ὅτι introduces the compound dependent clause: "*that* God granted us eternal life" (ὅτι ζωὴν αἰώνιον ἔδωκεν ἡμῖν ὁ θεός). The entire clause is functioning adjectivally, modifying the demonstrative pronoun, "this" (αὕτη). **Semantically,** ὅτι is epexegetical: "that" (KJV ASV NASB ESV CNT). The ὅτι clause explains or clarifies the demonstrative pronoun, "that" (αὕτη; W, 459). The testimony of God is clearly defined in the remainder of the clause.

ἔδωκεν: The Greek word ἔδωκεν is third person singular aorist active indicative from the verb δίδωμι meaning "to give," "to bestow," "to grant," or "to give something out" (BDAG, s.v. "δίδωμι" 2, p. 242). **Syntactically,** ἔδωκεν is the governing verb of the first part of the compound dependent adjectival clause. The subject of the verb is the proper noun, "God" (ὁ θεός). **Semantically,** ἔδωκεν is a constative aorist: "granted" or "gave" (ASV NRSV ESV). It focuses on the event as a whole (W, 557). God granted eternal life to all those who trust in his testimony about Jesus.

5:11c καί [ὅτι]: The Greek word καί is a conjunction meaning "and" (BDAG, s.v. "καί" 1c, p. 494). **Syntactically,** καί introduces a dependent conjunctive clause: "*and* [that] this life is in his Son" (καὶ αὕτη ἡ ζωὴ ἐν τῷ υἱῷ αὐτοῦ ἐστιν). **Semantically,** καί is a coordinating connector: "and" (cf. NRSV ESV NIV NET CNT). It adds more information [ὅτι] about the testimony (v. 11a), namely, from whence eternal life comes. The expanded information is identified in the remainder of the clause.

ἐστίν: The Greek word ἐστίν is third person singular present active indicative from the verb εἰμί meaning "to be" or "to be in close connection with" (BDAG, s.v. "εἰμί" 2a, p. 283). **Syntactically,** ἐστίν is the governing verb of an independent conjunctive clause. The subject of the verb is the nominal phrase "this life" (αὕτη ἡ ζωή). The demonstrative pronoun, "this" (αὕτη), is anaphoric and refers back to the eternal life mentioned in the previous clause. **Semantically,** ἐστίν is an equative present: "is" (cf. KJV NASB ESV NIV NET etc.). It equates "this life" (αὕτη ἡ ζωή) with being "in Jesus." Naturally, "this life" (αὕτη ἡ ζωή) refers back to "eternal life" (ζωὴν αἰώνιον). It speaks to the endless life in Jesus that, according to the next clause, has already been consummated (cf. John 20:30–31).

5:12a ἔχων: The Greek word ἔχων is a nominative masculine singular present active participle from the verb ἔχω meaning "to have" or "to experience an emotion or inner possession" (BDAG, s.v. "ἔχω" 7aβ, p. 421). **Syntactically,** ἔχων introduces a dependent participle clause. The entire participial clause, "the one who has the Son" (ὁ ἔχων τὸν υἱόν), functions as the subject of the verb, "has" (ἔχει). It is placed in parentheses in order to visualize its contribution to the independent clause. **Semantically,** ἔχων is a gnomic present: "the one who" (NET CNT) or "whoever" (NRSV ESV NLT). The participle is being used in generic utterances (W, 615). John describes a timeless fact about people in general. The timeless fact is described within the remaining portion of the clause beginning with the next verb.

ἔχει: The Greek word ἔχει is third person singular present active indicative from the verb ἔχω meaning "to have" or "to experience an emotion or inner possession" (BDAG, s.v. "ἔχω" 7aβ, p. 421). **Syntactically,** ἔχει is the main verb of the independent asyndeton clause. The subject is the entire participial phrase, "the one who has the Son" (ὁ ἔχων τὸν υἱόν). **Semantically,** ἔχει is a gnomic present: "has" (cf. KJV NASB ESV NIV NET etc.). The verb is part of the generic statement that was introduced with the generic participle (W, 523). John underscores a timeless truth about a person's possession of eternal life in the here and now.

Theological Nugget: What does it mean to "have" the Son? It means that Jesus is present in the life of an individual. The NET Bible points out that this is a similar thought to the famous passage found in John 3:16. The one who believes in the work of God's Son will not perish, but already *possesses* eternal life. Life with Jesus has already begun and it is an endless relationship. The implication is that those who do not hold to the teaching about the nature of Jesus's messiahship do not possess this perpetual life nor can they look forward to being purified (cf. 3:3).

5:12b ἔχων: The Greek word ἔχων is a nominative masculine singular present active participle from the verb ἔχω meaning "to have" or "to experience an emotion or inner possession" (BDAG, s.v. "ἔχω" 7aβ, p. 421). **Syntactically,** ἔχων introduces a dependent participle clause. The entire participial clause, "the one who does not have the Son" (ὁ μὴ ἔχων τὸν υἱὸν τοῦ θεοῦ), is functioning as the subject of the verb, "has" (ἔχει). It is placed in parentheses in order to visualize its contribution to the independent clause. The negative particle, "not" (μή), is used instead of the normal "not" (οὐ) because μή negates non-indicatives, such as participles, infinitives, and verbs that appear in the subjunctive or optative mood. **Semantically,** ἔχων is a gnomic present: "the one who" (NET CNT) or "whoever" (NRSV ESV NLT). The participle is being used in generic utterances (W, 615). John describes a timeless fact about people in general. The specifics of this timeless fact are described within the remaining portion of the clause.

ἔχει: The Greek word ἔχει is third person singular present active indicative from the verb ἔχω meaning "to have" or "to experience an emotion or inner possession" (BDAG, s.v. "ἔχω" 7aβ, p. 421). **Syntactically,** ἔχει is the main verb of the independent asyndeton clause. The subject is the entire participial phrase, "the one who does not have the Son of God does not have this life" (ὁ μὴ ἔχων τὸν υἱὸν τοῦ θεοῦ τὴν ζωὴν οὐκ ἔχει). The NET Bible rightly translates the article here as "this" since it anaphorically points back to the eternal life previously mentioned in 5:12a. **Semantically,** ἔχει with the negated μή is a gnomic present: "has not" or "does not have" (NRSV ESV NIV NET NLT CNT). The verb is part of the generic statement that was introduced with the generic participle (W, 523). With this thought John summarizes what he has been saying in the previous verses. Eternal life is based on receiving, agreeing with, and firmly believing in Jesus's identity as Messiah and ignoring the misguided information that floats around about him.

1 John 5:13–21[1]

Big Greek Idea: Before expressing his exhortation to avoid turning from Jesus, God's Messiah, John closes, in summary fashion, with a restatement about belief in Jesus's messiahship that results in an awareness of an endless relationship with God, a confidence and awareness that God listens to personal needs and the interventions for others, an awareness of God's preservation and protection from the Devil, and an awareness of the bond that exists with God through God's Messiah, Jesus.

Structural Overview: As noted above, 1 John can be divided into two major units, 1:5–3:10 and 3:11–5:12 because they have parallel beginnings: "Now this is the gospel" (καὶ ἔστιν αὕτη ἡ ἀγγελία) and "for this is the gospel" (ὅτι αὕτη ἐστὶν ἡ ἀγγελία). Furthermore, it suggests that 1 John 1:1–4 is the prologue, and that 1 John 5:13–21 concludes the letter.

First John 5:13–17 is the first of two subsections for the epistle's epilogue. In this first subsection, John introduces the theme of "sin not to death." It is key for understanding John's teaching about sin. John reminds believers that based upon the fact that they have eternal life, they can have confidence when they approach God in prayer (5:13–14), even when it concerns praying for other believers who are living in sin (5:15–17).

First John 5:18–21 is the second subsection for the epistle's epilogue. It has three solemn assertions of knowledge, each introduced with οἴδαμεν in verses 18, 19 and 20. Each statement reflects divine privileges granted to true believers, such as being fathered by God (v. 18), belonging to God (v. 19), and knowing the true God (v. 20). Verse 21, then, while admittedly an abrupt ending, serves as the negative counterpart to the three statements in the preceding verses.

Outline:

> Belief in Jesus's Messiahship Creates Confidence (vv. 13–17)
>> Belief in Jesus's Messiahship creates an endless relationship with God (v. 13)
>> Belief in Jesus's Messiahship creates a confidence and awareness that God listens to personal needs (v. 14)

---

1. Commentators disagree about whether the final section of 1 John should begin with 5:13 or 5:14. It seems likely, however, that 5:13 begins the final section of 1 John because of an *inclusio* of similar themes in 5:13 and 5:20 (i.e., Son of God and eternal life). Furthermore, the theme of "knowing" in verse 13 continues throughout the section (vv. 14–20). Thus, 1 John 5:13–21 appears to form a conclusion of sorts to 1 John. While 5:13–21 may not be structured as a logical argument, it revisits some of the main thoughts of the letter (i.e., sin, paternity, the world, the Evil One, Jesus as Messiah, eternal life).

       Belief in Jesus's Messiahship creates a confidence and awareness of
and the interventions for others (v. 15–17)

Belief in Jesus's Messiahship Creates Awareness (vv. 18–20)

      Belief in Jesus's Messiahship creates an awareness of God's preservation and protection from the Devil (v. 18).

      Belief in Jesus's Messiahship creates an awareness of the bond that exists with God through Jesus (vv. 19–20)

Beware of Exchanging Belief in Jesus Messiahship for Something Else (v. 21)

CLAUSAL OUTLINE FOR 1 JOHN 5:13–21

5:13a Ταῦτα **ἔγραψα** ὑμῖν . . . (τοῖς πιστεύουσιν εἰς τὸ ὄνομα τοῦ υἱοῦ τοῦ θεοῦ).

5:13a **I have written** these *things* to you . . . (*namely,* you who believe in the name of the Son of God).

    5:13b **ἵνα εἰδῆτε** (ὅτι ζωὴν ἔχετε αἰώνιον),

    5:13b **so that you may know** (that you have eternal life),

5:14a καὶ αὕτη **ἐστὶν** ἡ παρρησία

5:14a and this **is** the confidence

    5:14b **ἣν ἔχομεν** πρὸς αὐτόν,

    5:14b **that we have** before him (= God):

    5:14c **ὅτι** . . . **ἀκούει** ἡμῶν.

    5:14c **that** . . . **he (= God) listens to** us.

       5:14d **ἐάν** τι **αἰτώμεθα** κατὰ τὸ θέλημα αὐτοῦ

       5:14d **whenever we ask** for anything according to his will

5:15a καὶ **ἐὰν οἴδαμεν** (ὅτι ἀκούει ἡμῶν)

5:15a and **if we know** (that he (= God) listens to us)

       5:15b [**ἀκούει**] (ὃ **ἐὰν αἰτώμεθα**),

       5:15b *namely,* [*he listens to*] (**whatever we ask**),

    5:15c **οἴδαμεν** (ὅτι ἔχομεν τὰ αἰτήματα)

    5:15c **we know** (that we have the requests)

       5:15d **ἃ ᾐτήκαμεν** ἀπ' αὐτοῦ.

       5:15d **that we have asked** from him (= God)

5:16a Ἐάν τις ἴδῃ τὸν ἀδελφὸν αὐτοῦ (ἁμαρτάνοντα ἁμαρτίαν μὴ πρὸς θάνατον),

5:16a **If** anyone **sees** his (or her) brother (or sister) (*to be* committing a sin not *leading* to death),

|
5:16b **αἰτήσει**,
5:16b **they should ask**,

5:16c καὶ **δώσει** αὐτῷ ζωήν, (τοῖς ἁμαρτάνουσιν μὴ πρὸς θάνατον).
5:16c and he (= God) **will grant** to him (or her) life (*namely*, to the one who does not commit a sin *leading* to death).

5:16d **ἔστιν** ἁμαρτία πρὸς θάνατον·
5:16d There **is** a sin *leading* to death;

5:16e οὐ (περὶ ἐκείνης) **λέγω** (ἵνα ἐρωτήσῃ).
5:16e **I do** not **say** (that they should ask) (about that).

5:17a πᾶσα ἀδικία ἁμαρτία **ἐστίν**,
5:17a All unrighteousness **is** sin,

5:17b καὶ **ἔστιν** ἁμαρτία οὐ πρὸς θάνατον.
5:17b and *yet* there **is** a sin not *leading* to death.

5:18a **Οἴδαμεν** (ὅτι πᾶς ὁ γεγεννημένος ἐκ τοῦ θεοῦ οὐχ ἁμαρτάνει,
5:18a **We know** (that everyone who has been fathered by God does not *persist in* sin,

    5:18b ἀλλ᾽ [ὅτι] ὁ γεννηθεὶς ἐκ τοῦ θεοῦ **τηρεῖ** αὐτόν,
    5:18b but the one fathered by God **he preserves** him (or her)

    5:18c καὶ [ὅτι] ὁ πονηρὸς οὐχ **ἅπτεται** αὐτοῦ).
    5:18c and [that] the Evil One cannot **harm** him (or her).

5:19a **οἴδαμεν** (ὅτι ἐκ τοῦ θεοῦ ἐσμεν,
5:19a **We know** (that we are of God,

    |
    5:19b καὶ [*ὅτι*] ὁ κόσμος ὅλος ἐν τῷ πονηρῷ **κεῖται**).
    5:19b and [*that*] the whole world **lies** in the power of the Evil *One*).

5:20a **οἴδαμεν** δὲ (ὅτι ὁ υἱὸς τοῦ θεοῦ ἥκει,
5:20a And **we know** (that the Son of God has come,

^{5:20b} <u>καὶ</u> [<u>ὅτι</u>] **δέδωκεν** ἡμῖν διάνοιαν
^{5:20b} <u>and</u> [*that*] <u>**he (= Jesus) has given**</u> us understanding
                                                           |
       ^{5:20c} **ἵνα γινώσκωμεν** τὸν ἀληθινόν)·
       ^{5:20c} **<u>in order that</u>** <u>we may know</u> the true one);

^{5:20d} <u>καὶ</u> **ἐσμὲν** ἐν τῷ ἀληθινῷ, ἐν τῷ υἱῷ αὐτοῦ Ἰησοῦ Χριστῷ.
^{5:20d} <u>and</u> **<u>we are</u>** in the true one, in his Son Jesus, who is the Christ.

^{5:20e} οὗτός **ἐστιν** ὁ ἀληθινὸς θεὸς καὶ ζωὴ αἰώνιος.
^{5:20e} This one **<u>is</u>** the true God and eternal life.

^{5:21} Τεκνία, **φυλάξατε** ἑαυτὰ ἀπὸ τῶν εἰδώλων.
^{5:21} Children, **<u>guard</u>** yourselves from idols.

SYNTAX EXPLAINED FOR 1 JOHN 5:13–21

^{5:13a} ἔγραψα: The Greek word ἔγραψα is first person singular aorist active indicative from the verb γράφω meaning "to write" or "to compose" with reference to composing a letter (BDAG, s.v. "γράφω" 2d, p. 207). **Syntactically,** ἔγραψα is the main verb of the independent clause "*I have written* these *things* to you" (Ταῦτα ἔγραψα ὑμῖν). The assumed subject, "I," refers to John. **Semantically,** ἔγραψα is an epistolary aorist: "I *have* written" (NASB NET NLT; cf. W, 562).

> **Lexical Nugget:** What does John mean when he says "these *things*" (ταῦτα)? On the one hand, it could simply be a reference to the preceding discussion (5:11–12 or 5:1–12). On the other hand, it seems to be more than that. In a similar way to John 20:31, John appears to be referring to his entire work. Notice the parallel to the ending of the prologue in 1 John 1:4 "and we have written these *things*" (καὶ ταῦτα γράφομεν ἡμεῖς). John is summarizing the intention behind the letter as a whole (Brown, 607).

πιστεύουσιν: The Greek word πιστεύουσιν is a dative masculine plural present active participle from the verb πιστεύω meaning "to believe" or "to trust" or "to entrust oneself to an entity in complete confidence" (BDAG, s.v. "πιστεύω" 2aβ, p. 817). **Syntactically,** πιστεύουσιν introduces a dependent participle clause. It is a substantival participle. The entire clause, "*namely, you who believe* in the name of the Son of God" (τοῖς πιστεύουσιν εἰς τὸ ὄνομα τοῦ υἱοῦ τοῦ θεοῦ), is in apposition to the personal pronoun, "to you" (ὑμῖν), which is the indirect object of the verb, "I wrote" (ἔγραψα). The entire clause is placed in parentheses in order to visualize its contribution to the independent clause. **Semantically,** πιστεύουσιν is a customary present: "who believe" (NASB NRSV ESV NIV NET NLT CNT). Since the participle is substantival, its aspect has less force (W, 527, 615). It describes the one who has eternal life as the one who continually holds to the truth about the true identity of Jesus as God's Son. So John writes to those who believe that Jesus is the Son of God to assure them of their salvation and destiny.

> **Lexical Nugget:** What does τὸ ὄνομα mean? This is the last of three occurrences of this word in 1 John (2:12; 3:23; 5:13). First, τὸ ὄνομα is used as a figure of speech called a metonymy of subject, where one noun is used to reference another noun closely associated with it. Second, "the name" in John's writings may be a reference to God the Father, or Jesus. In every instance in 1 John it is a reference to Jesus (cf. 3 John 7).

5:13b ἵνα: The Greek word ἵνα is a conjunction meaning "that" or "in order that" (BDAG, s.v. "ἵνα" a, p. 475) or "so that" (BDAG, s.v. "ἵνα" 3, p. 477). **Syntactically,** ἵνα introduces a conjunctive dependent clause: "*so that* you might know that you have eternal life" (ἵνα εἰδῆτε ὅτι ζωὴν ἔχετε αἰώνιον). **Syntactically,** the clause is adverbial, modifying the verb "I wrote" (ἔγραψα). **Semantically,** ἵνα is classified as purpose: "in order that" or "that" (KJV ASV ESV; cf. NET note), though some translations seem to indicate result: "so that" (NASB NRSV NIV NLT CNT). However, the ἵνα clause indicates John's purpose for writing.

εἰδῆτε: The Greek word εἰδῆτε is a second person plural perfect active subjunctive from the verb οἶδα meaning "to know" or "to have information about" (BDAG, s.v. "οἶδα" 1e, p. 693). It is in the subjunctive mood because it is part of a ἵνα clause, which requires that the verb is subjunctive. **Syntactically,** εἰδῆτε is the governing verb of the dependent conjunctive ἵνα clause. It functions adverbially modifying the verb, "I wrote" (ἔγραψα). The assumed subject, "you," refers to the recipients of the letter. **Semantically,** εἰδῆτε is a perfect with present force: "you may know" (cf. KJV NASB ESV NIV NET etc.). It is a verb in the "perfect tense without the usual aspectual significance" (W, 579). John's intention for writing this letter to his readers is for them to come to know something. That something is found in the ὅτι clause.

ὅτι: The Greek word ὅτι is a conjunction meaning "that" (BDAG, s.v. "ὅτι" 1c, p. 731). **Syntactically,** ὅτι introduces a dependent conjunctive clause: "*that* you have eternal life" (ὅτι ζωὴν ἔχετε αἰώνιον). The entire clause is functioning substantivally as the direct object of the verb "you may know" (εἰδῆτε). **Semantically,** ὅτι is an indirect discourse marker: "that" (cf. KJV NASB ESV NIV NET etc.). The entire ὅτι clause provides the content of the knowledge (W, 456), which is clearly expressed in the next verb.

ἔχετε: The Greek word ἔχετε is a second person plural present active in-dicative from the verb ἔχω meaning "to have" or "to experience an emotion or inner possession" (BDAG, s.v. "ἔχω" 7aβ, p. 421). **Syntactically,** ἔχετε is the governing verb of the dependent substantival clause. The subject is the implied "you" embedded in the verb and refers to his readers of the letter. **Semantically,** ἔχετε is a customary present: "you have" (cf. KJV NASB ESV NIV NET etc.). It describes an ongoing action (W, 521). John underscores to his readers their possession of eternal life.

5:14a καί: The Greek word καί is a conjunction meaning "and" (BDAG, s.v. "καί" 1b, p. 494). **Syntactically,** καί introduces a conjunctive independent clause: "*and* this is the confidence" (καὶ αὕτη ἐστὶν ἡ παρρησία). **Semantically,** καί is a coordinating connective: "and" (KJV ASV NRSV ESV NET NLT CNT). Two translations, however, do not translate καί (NASB NIV). Nevertheless, we believe it provides additional information (W, 671) about the assurance believers can have about eternal life, which is clarified in the subsequent verb and dependent clauses.

ἐστίν: The Greek word ἐστίν is third person singular present active indic-ative from the verb εἰμί meaning "to be" or "to be in close connection with" (BDAG, s.v. "εἰμί" 2a, p. 283). **Syntactically,** ἐστίν is the main verb of the independent clause: "this *is* the confidence" (καὶ αὕτη ἐστὶν ἡ παρρησία). The subject of the verb is the demonstrative pronoun "this" (αὕτη), due to the grammatical priority of demonstratives (W, 42–43). **Semantically,** ἐστίν is an equative present: "is" (cf. KJV NASB ESV NIV NET etc.). It equates "this" (αὕτη), which is defined in the next two clauses, with confidence.

5:14b ἥν: The Greek word ἥν is accusative singular feminine from the relative pro-noun ὅς meaning "which" (BDAG, s.v. "ὅς" 1a, p. 725). **Syntactically,** ἥν in-troduces a relative clause: "*that* we have from him (= God)" (ἥν ἔχομεν πρὸς αὐτόν). It modifies the predicate nominative, "confidence" (ἡ παρρησία) and is thereby adjectival. This relative pronoun is in the accusative case be-cause is serves as the direct object of the verb "has" (ἔχομεν).

ἔχομεν: The Greek word ἔχομεν is first person plural present active in-dicative from the verb ἔχω meaning "to have" or "to experience an inner condition" (BDAG, s.v. "ἔχω" 7aβ, p. 421). **Syntactically,** ἔχομεν is the gov-erning verb of the dependent relative clause. The subject of the verb is an implied "we" embedded in the verb and refers to John and his readers who have placed their faith in Jesus as the Son of God. **Semantically,** ἔχομεν is a customary present: "we have" (cf. KJV NASB ESV NIV NET etc.). It points out a continual state of being (W, 521). Believers have their confidence bestowed on them by God himself (cf. 4:17).

Theological Nugget: To whom does "him" (αὐτόν) refer, is it God, the Father, or Jesus? There is some more Trinitarian ambiguity here. Throughout the epistle John has used the remote demonstrative "that one" (ἐκεῖνος) to refer to Jesus (2:6; 3:3, 5, 7, 16; 4:17; 5:16). While it does seem like every instance of the remote demonstrative is a reference to Jesus, it does not logically follow that every other pronoun is a reference to God the Father. Most likely God the Father is in mind, but this could just be another example of the Trinitarian ambiguity found throughout the letter. Nevertheless, it is our view that John is referring to God the Father.

5:14c ὅτι: The Greek word ὅτι is a conjunction meaning "that" (BDAG, s.v. "ὅτι" 2a, p. 732). **Syntactically,** ὅτι introduces the dependent conjunctive clause: "*that* he listens to us" (ὅτι ἀκούει ἡμῶν). The entire ὅτι clause functions adjectivally, modifying the demonstrative pronoun "this" (αὕτη). **Semantically,** ὅτι is expexegetical: "that" (cf. KJV NASB ESV NIV NET etc.). It clarifies or completes the demonstrative pronoun "this" (αὕτη; cf. W, 459). The details of that clarification are found in the next verb and the subsequent ἐάν clause.

ἀκούει: The Greek word ἀκούει is third person singular present active indicative from the verb ἀκούω meaning "to listen" or "to pay attention to by listening" (BDAG, s.v. "ἀκούω" 5, p. 38). **Syntactically,** ἀκούει is the main verb of the independent clause. It is the apodosis of the conditional idea: "*he (= God) listens* to us" (ἀκούει ἡμῶν). The subject of the verb is an implied "he" embedded in the verb and refers to God. The pronoun is genitive because ἀκούω takes an object in the genitive case. **Semantically,** ἀκούει is a customary present: "he listens" or "he hears" (seemingly BDAG, s.v. "ἀκούω" 1c, p. 38). It stresses the continual nature of God's desire to listen to believers (W, 521). Yet what is to be asked is qualified in the next ἐάν clause.

5:14d ἐάν: The Greek word ἐάν is a conjunction meaning "whenever" (BDAG, s.v. "ἐάν" 2, p. 268). **Syntactically,** ἐάν identifies the clause as a dependent conjunctive clause. The entire dependent clause: "*whenever* we ask for anything according to his will" (ἐάν τι αἰτώμεθα κατὰ τὸ θέλημα αὐτοῦ) functions adverbially, modifying the verb, "he listens" (ἀκούει). **Semantically,** ἐάν introduces a third class conditional clause: "whenever" (NET), though a popular alternative is "if" (seemingly BDAG, s.v. "ἐάν" 1aα, p. 267). It presents a condition as uncertain of fulfillment, but still likely (W, 696). The conjunction ἐάν is a marker that coordinates the likelihood of God's listening as long as it occurs with the action presented in the next verb.

αἰτώμεθα: The Greek word αἰτώμεθα is first person plural present middle subjunctive from the verb αἰτέω meaning "to ask" or "to ask for, with a claim on receipt of an answer" (BDAG, s.v. "αἰτέω," p. 30). It is in the subjunctive mood because it follows ἐάν. **Syntactically,** αἰτώμεθα is the governing verb of the dependent conditional clause. **Semantically,** αἰτώμεθα is an iterative present: "we ask" (cf. KJV NASB ESV NIV NET etc.). It describes an event that repeatedly happens (W, 520). John underscores that whenever a believer asks God for something that is in agreement with his will, God will hear them. The believer is to talk with God in ways that correspond with God's will, namely, keeping his commands (Culy, 133).

> **Syntactical Nugget:** Why is αἰτώμεθα in the middle voice? John has previously used the same verb in the active voice, so there must be a special nuance in this context. The classical middle voice is normally used when the action is both performed by the subject and the subject receives some sort of benefit from that action. We can see both apects here in this passage. The petitioner is the one making the request from God, but is also the beneficiary of God's sympathetic audience (cf. Culy, 133).

5:15a καί: The Greek word καί is a conjunction meaning "and" (BDAG, s.v. "καί" 1bβ, p. 494). **Syntactically,** καί introduces an independent conjunctive clause: "*and* if we know that he (= God) listens to us" (καὶ ἐὰν οἴδαμεν ὅτι ἀκούει ἡμῶν). **Semantically,** καί is a coordinating connective: "and" (NIV NET NLT CNT). It is a common feature drawn from Hebrew. Many translations do not translate καί (KJV ASV NASB NRSV ESV). Nevertheless it provides additional comments on the confidence evident in the ἐάν clause.

ἐάν: The Greek word ἐάν is a conjunction meaning "if" (BDAG, s.v. "ἐάν" 1bβ, p. 267). **Syntactically,** ἐάν identifies the clause as a dependent conjunctive clause. The entire ἐάν clause: "*if* we know that he (= God) listens to us" (ἐὰν οἴδαμεν ὅτι ἀκούει ἡμῶν) functions adverbially, modifying the verb, "we know" (οἴδαμεν). **Semantically,** ἐάν introduces a third class conditional clause of probability: "if" (cf. KJV NASB ESV NIV NET etc.). The condition is uncertain of fulfillment but still likely (W, 696). That uncertain condition is made evident in the next verb.

οἴδαμεν: The Greek word οἴδαμεν is first person plural perfect active indicative from the verb οἶδα meaning "to know" or "to have information about" (BDAG, s.v. "οἶδα" 1e, p. 693). **Syntactically,** οἴδαμεν is the governing verb of the dependent conditional clause. The assumed subject, "we," refers to John and the readers of the letter. The appearance of οἴδαμεν in the indicative mood is rare after the conjunction ἐάν. Perhaps a first class condition is intended with an anomalous switch in conjunction from εἰ to ἐάν. If so, then instead of a hypothetical, John is assuming for the sake of argument that God does listen and that believers have whatever we ask (NET note). Culy calls this strange usage of ἐάν + indicative solecistic, but the usage is not unheard of (Culy, 134; Zerwick, §330–331; Brown, 609–10). **Semantically,** οἴδαμεν is a perfect with present force: "we know" (cf. KJV NASB ESV NIV NET etc.). It is a verb in the "perfect tense without the usual aspectual significance" (W, 579). What John means by what is known is found in the ὅτι clause.

ὅτι: The Greek word ὅτι is a conjunction meaning "that" (BDAG, s.v. "ὅτι" 1c, p. 731). **Syntactically,** ὅτι introduces a dependent conjunctive clause: "*that* he (= God) listens to us" (ὅτι ἀκούει ἡμῶν). The entire clause is functioning substantivally as the direct object of the verb "know" (οἴδαμεν). The "us" refers to those who talk with God. The clause is placed in parentheses in order to visualize its contribution to the independent clause. **Semantically,** ὅτι is an indirect discourse marker: "that" (cf. KJV NASB ESV NIV NET etc.). The entire ὅτι clause provides the content of a believer's knowledge (W, 456), which is clearly expressed in the next verb.

ἀκούει: The Greek word ἀκούει is third person singular present active indicative from the verb ἀκούω meaning "to listen" or "to pay attention to by listening" (BDAG, s.v. "ἀκούω" 5, p. 38). **Syntactically,** ἀκούει is the governing verb of the dependent ὅτι clause. The assumed subject, "we," refers to John and the readers of the letter. **Semantically,** ἀκούει is a customary present: "he listens" or "he hears" (seemingly BDAG, s.v. "ἀκούω" 1c, p. 38). It stresses the continual nature of God's listening to believers (W, 521). John's assurance that God listens is underscored in the next clause.

5:15b ὃ ἐάν: The Greek word ὃ is a neuter singular accusative from the relative pronoun ὅς meaning "what" (BDAG, s.v. "ὅς" 1jα, p. 727). The Greek word ἐάν is a conjunction meaning "ever" (BDAG, s.v. "ἐάν" 3, p. 268). Together ὃ ἐάν is translated "whatever" (see previous occurrence in 3:22): "*namely,* [he listens to] whatever we ask" **Syntactically,** the Greek construction ὃ ἐάν is an indefinite relative pronoun that is classified as a dependent pronominal clause. The entire clause "whatever we ask" (ὃ ἐάν αἰτῶμεν) most likely functions as the direct object of an elliptical verb "he listens" ([ἀκούει]). The entire thought is in apposition (namely) to the previous clause "he listens to us" (ἀκούει ἡμῶν; cf. Culy, 134). The relative pronoun itself is in the accusative case because it is functioning as the direct object of the verb "we ask" (αἰτώμεθα).

αἰτώμεθα: The Greek word αἰτώμεθα is first person plural present middle subjunctive from the verb αἰτέω meaning "to ask" or "to ask for, with a claim on receipt of an answer" (BDAG, s.v. "αἰτέω," p. 30). It is in the subjunctive mood because it follows ἐάν. **Syntactically,** αἰτώμεθα is the governing verb of the dependent indefinite relative ὃ ἐάν clause. **Semantically,** αἰτώμεθα is an iterative present: "we ask" (cf. KJV NASB ESV NIV NET etc.). It describes an event that repeatedly happens (W, 521). John points out that whenever a believer asks God for anything, God considers it.

5:15c οἴδαμεν: The Greek word οἴδαμεν is first person plural perfect active indicative from the verb οἶδα meaning "to know" or "to have information about" (BDAG, s.v. "οἶδα" 1e, p. 693). **Syntactically,** οἴδαμεν is the main verb of the independent clause: "*we know* that we have the requests" (οἴδαμεν ὅτι ἔχομεν τὰ αἰτήματα). The assumed subject, "we," refers to John and the readers of the letter who believe in Jesus. This clause is the apodosis of the conditional phrase. **Semantically,** οἴδαμεν is a perfect with present force: "know" (cf. KJV NASB ESV NIV NET etc.). It is in the "perfect tense without the usual aspectual significance" (W, 579). The content of what John's readers know appears in the ὅτι clause.

ὅτι: The Greek word ὅτι is a conjunction meaning "that" (BDAG, s.v. "ὅτι" 1c, p. 731). **Syntactically,** ὅτι introduces the dependent clause: "*that* we have the requests" (ὅτι ἔχομεν τὰ αἰτήματα). The entire clause is functioning substantivally. It is the direct object of the verb "we know" (οἴδαμεν). The clause is placed in parentheses in order to visualize its contribution to the independent clause. **Semantically,** ὅτι is an indirect discourse marker: "that" (cf. KJV NASB ESV NIV NET etc.). The entire ὅτι clause provides the content of the knowledge (W, 456), which is clearly expressed in the next verb.

ἔχομεν: The Greek word ἔχομεν is first person plural present active indicative from the verb ἔχω meaning "to have" or "to experience a benefit" (BDAG, s.v. "ἔχω" 7aγ, p. 421). **Syntactically,** ἔχομεν is the governing verb of the dependent substantival clause. The subject of the verb is an implied "we" embedded in the verb and refers to John and his readers who believe that Jesus is God's Son. **Semantically,** ἔχομεν is a customary present: "we have" (cf. KJV NASB ESV NIV NET etc.). It describes an event that occurs regularly (W, 521). Believers always and repeatedly receive answers to their requests.

5:15d ἅ: The Greek word ἅ is accusative plural neuter from the relative pronoun ὅς meaning "that" (BDAG, s.v. "ὅς" 1a, p. 725). **Syntactically,** ἅ introduces a dependent relative clause: "*that* we have asked from him" (ἅ ᾐτήκαμεν ἀπ᾽ αὐτοῦ). It is an adjectival clause in that the entire clause modifies the noun "requests" (αἰτήματα). This relative pronoun is in the accusative case because it is the direct object of the verb "we have asked" (ᾐτήκαμεν). The clause provides more information about a believer's continual request.

ᾐτήκαμεν: The Greek word ᾐτήκαμεν is first person plural perfect active indicative from the verb αἰτέω meaning "to ask" or "to ask for, with a claim on receipt of an answer" (BDAG, s.v. "αἰτέω." p. 30). **Syntactically,** ᾐτήκαμεν functions as the governing verb of the dependent relative clause. The subject of the verb is an implied "we" embedded in the verb, which refers to John and his readers who believe that Jesus is God's Son. **Semantically,** ἠτήκαμεν is an extensive perfect: "we *have* asked" (ASV NASB NET CNT). It emphasizes the completed action from which a present state emerges (W, 577). When believers ask God for things in accordance with his will, they can expect that they will receive them.

5:16a ἐάν: The Greek word ἐάν is a conjunction meaning "if" (BDAG, s.v. "ἐάν" 1ab, p. 267). **Syntactically,** ἐάν identifies the clause as a dependent conjunctive clause. The entire dependent clause: "*if* anyone sees his (or her) brother (or sister) to be committing a sin not leading to death" (ἐάν τις ἴδη τὸν ἀδελφὸν αὐτοῦ ἁμαρτάνοντα ἁμαρτίαν μὴ πρὸς θάνατον) functions adverbially. It modifies the verbs "they should ask" (αἰτήσει) and "he will give" (δώσει). **Semantically,** ἐάν introduces a third class conditional clause: "if" (cf. KJV NASB ESV NIV NET etc.). It presents a condition as uncertain of fulfillment, but still likely (W, 696). That uncertain condition appears in the next verb.

ἴδη: The Greek word ἴδη is third person singular aorist active subjunctive from the verb ὁράω meaning "to see" or "to be mentally or spiritually perceptive" (BDAG, s.v. "ὁράω" 4b, p. 720). It is in the subjunctive mood because it follows ἐάν. **Syntactically,** ἴδη is the governing verb of the dependent conditional ἐάν clause. The subject of the verb is the indefinite pronoun "anyone" (τις). **Semantically,** ἴδη is a gnomic aorist: "sees" (cf. KJV NASB ESV NIV NET etc.). It presents a timeless fact about a generic person (τις; W, 562). The general fact of which John speaks is clarified with the next verb.

ἁμαρτάνοντα: The Greek word ἁμαρτάνοντα is an accusative singular masculine present active participle from the verb ἁμαρτάνω meaning "to sin" or "to commit a wrong" (BDAG, s.v. "ἁμαρτάνω," p. 50). **Syntactically,** ἁμαρτάνοντα introduces a dependent participial clause: "to be committing a sin not *leading* to death" (ἁμαρτάνοντα ἁμαρτίαν μὴ πρὸς θάνατον). It is a complement to the noun "brother" (ἀδελφόν). This is a double accusative object-complement construction (W, 182–86). The direct object of the verb "sees" (ἴδη) is "his (or her) brother (or sister)" (τὸν ἀδελφὸν αὐτοῦ). The second accusative, which functions as the complement, is the participial clause "sinning a sin not leading to death" (ἁμαρτάνοντα ἁμαρτίαν μὴ πρὸς θάνατον). This type of construction is often translated with the words "to be." Therefore, we should translate it like this, "if anyone sees his (or her) brother (or sister) *to be* committing a sin not leading to death." **Semantically,** ἁμαρτάνοντα is a progressive present: "sinning" (NLT) or "sin" (KJV). It describes an event in progress (W, 518). When believers see a fellow follower of Jesus in the process of sinning a sin that is not the outright denial of Jesus and his messiahship, they should pray for that individual and God will listen.

Theological Nugget: How does "a sin *not leading* to death" differ from "a sin *leading* to death"? Several suggestions exist. On the one hand, death could refer to actual physical death, not some sort of spiritual atrophy or separation from God. If true, it speaks of suicide. However, those committing the sin of suicide would need no prayer. This doesn't seem to fit with the theology of loving our brothers and sisters in Christ as this letter teaches very clearly. Some Second Temple texts seem to suggest a similar view (Jub. 21:22; 26:34; 33:13, 18; T. Isaac 7:1; cf. Num. 18:22; Deut. 22:15; Isa. 22:14). On the other hand, John could be distinguishing between serious sins and less serious sins. Prayer is to be offered for those who commit lesser sins against God, not for those whose sins are more egregious or serious. Many Christian traditions have distinguished between the seriousness of sins, most notably the distinction between what are called venial sins and mortal sins. Jesus himself even suggests that there is a sin that leads to death in Mark 3:29 and its parallel passages in Matthew 12:32 and Luke 12:1. The Didache, however, places wrong speech and murder alongside each other, refusing to distinguish between the seriousness of each sin. Finally, throughout his letter, John addresses the sin of unbelief in Jesus's humanity and his messiahship. In 1 John, the sin that leads to spiritual death is the rejection of God's Messiah, Jesus. When Jesus himself talks about the sin leading to death, it is in the context of confronting the Pharisees who were rejecting him by attributing his miraculous ministry to the work of Satan (Mark 3:29). The rejection of the incarnation of Jesus and his work on the cross brings spiritual death by definition. Therefore, John is urging us to pray for those who are caught in sin, but for those who are so far gone that they have rejected the person and work of Jesus, prayer for them is not required, but voluntary (Bateman[1], 569; Brown, 613–19).

5:16b αἰτήσει: The Greek word αἰτήσει is third person singular future active indicative from the verb αἰτέω meaning "to ask" or "to ask for, with a claim on receipt of an answer" (BDAG, s.v. "αἰτέω," p. 30). **Syntactically,** αἰτήσει is the main verb of the independent clause "they *should* ask" (αἰτήσει). It is the first part of the compound apodosis of the conditional ἐάν clause. The subject of the verb is an implied "he or she" embedded in the verb and refers to the one in the protasis who sees a fellow believer caught in sin. **Semantically,** αἰτήσει is an imperative future: "they should ask" (NET; cf. NLT) or "they shall ask" (KJV ASV NASB ESV). While not common outside of Matthew, "they should ask" issues an indirect command (W, 569). The believer, who sees a brother or sister caught in sin, has a moral obligation to offer prayers on their behalf (Culy, 135).

5:16c καί: The Greek word καί is a conjunction meaning "and" (BDAG, s.v. "καί" 1b, p. 494). **Syntactically,** καί introduces the independent conjunctive clause: "*and* he (= God) will grant him (or her) them life" (καὶ δώσει αὐτῷ ζωήν).

It serves as the second part of the compound apodosis. **Semantically,** καί is a coordinating connective: "and" (cf. KJV NASB ESV NIV NET etc.). It provides additional information (W, 671) about the prayer offered on behalf of the erring believer. That additional information is found in the rest of the clause.

δώσει: The Greek word δώσει is third person singular future active indicative from the verb δίδωμι meaning "to give" or "to grant" or "to give something out" (BDAG, s.v. "δίδωμι" 2, p. 242). The verb is in the subjunctive mood because it is the second part of a compound ἐάν clause. **Syntactically,** δώσει is the main verb of the independent conjunctive καί clause. It is the second part of the compound apodosis of the conditional ἐάν clause. The subject of the verb is an implied "God" assumed from context. We've chosen to interpret the singular "to him" (αὐτῷ) as "to him (or her)" to reflect a more inclusive understanding of John's congregation made up of both men and women. **Semantically,** δώσει is a predictive future: "God will grant" (NET) or "God will give" (KJV ASV NRSV ESV NIV NLT CNT). It describes something that will take place (W, 568). God will grant life, but to whom? The next verbal is important in answering this question.

Grammatical and Theological Nugget: Who are the subjects of "he should ask" (αἰτήσει) and "he will be granted" (δώσει)? At least three options exist. First, the most natural reading is to assume that the subject is the believer. It assumes that the referent of the indirect object "to him [singular]" (αὐτῷ) is a sinner. If true, then the one who grants life to the sinner is the one who asks God for help. Although grammatically possible, theologically it is suspect. How can a believer grant life to another? God grants life. Second, the implied subject of δώσει is God. In this case God would grant the petitioner of 5:16b life for praying for the sinner. Yet, it is strange to think that the recipient of life would be the petitioner when they are praying for "life" to be bestowed on a sinner. Finally, God is the implied subject of the verb and the sinner as the referent of the pronoun (αὐτῷ). This is perhaps the most grammatically awkward, since it sets a singular noun and a plural participial phrase in apposition to each other, but it makes the best contextual sense. In this case, God promises to grant life to the sinner for whom the caring Christan of 5:16b is praying. Therefore, the subject of the verb is an implied "God" assumed from context (NET Bible note; cf. Brown, 611–12).

ἁμαρτάνουσιν: The Greek word ἁμαρτάνουσιν is a dative masculine plural active participle from the verb ἁμαρτάνω meaning "to sin" or "to commit a wrong" (BDAG, s.v. "ἁμαρτάνω," p. 50). **Syntactically,** ἁμαρτάνουσιν is a substantival participle. The entire phrase: "*namely, to the one who does not commit a sin* leading to death" (τοῖς ἁμαρτάνουσιν μὴ πρὸς θάνατον) is set in apposition (*namely*) to the pronoun "them [singular]" (αὐτῷ). **Semantically,** ἁμαρτάνουσιν is a gnomic present negated with μή: "to the one who does not commit a sin" or "to those who commit a sin not" (NASB ESV NIV CNT). It is another generic utterance (W, 615). The phrase is placed in parentheses in order to visualize its contribution to the independent clause. John presents a timeless truth about a petitioner who prays for a person who is caught in the middle of a sin, which does not lead to spiritual separation from God.

5:16d ἐστίν: The Greek word ἐστίν is third person singular present active indicative from the verb εἰμί meaning "to be" or "to exist" or "to be on hand" (BDAG, s.v. "εἰμί" 1, p. 283). **Syntactically,** ἐστίν is the main verb of the independent clause "there is a sin leading to death" (ἔστιν ἁμαρτία πρὸς θάνατον). The subject of the verb is the nominal phrase "a sin leading to death" (ἁμαρτία πρὸς θάνατον). **Semantically,** ἐστίν is a gnomic present: "is" (cf. KJV NASB ESV NIV NET etc.). It presents a gnomic truth about sin, more specifically a sin exists that leads to a separation from God.

5:16e λέγω: The Greek word λέγω is first person singular present active indicative from the verb λέγω meaning "to say" or "to express oneself in a specific way" (BDAG, s.v. "λέγω" 2c, p. 589). **Syntactically,** λέγω is the main verb of the independent clause: "*I do* not *say* that they should ask about that" (οὐ περὶ ἐκείνης λέγω ἵνα ἐρωτήσῃ). The subject of the verb is an implied "I" embedded in the verbal ending and refers to John. **Semantically,** λέγω is an instantaneous present negated with οὐ: "I do not say" (KJV NASB NRSV ESV NET CNT). It indicates that John's statement is completed at the moment of writing (W, 517). John is clarifying what he means or what he is saying. That clarity appears in the ἵνα clause.

ἵνα: The Greek word ἵνα is a conjunction meaning "that" (BDAG, s.v. "ἵνα" 2aα, p. 476). **Syntactically,** ἵνα introduces a conjunctive dependent clause: "*that* he (or she) should ask" (ἵνα ἐρωτήσῃ). **Syntactically,** the ἵνα clause is substantival functioning as the direct object of the verb "I am saying" (λέγω). The clause is placed in parentheses in order to visualize its contribution to the independent clause. **Semantically,** ἵνα is an indirect discourse marker: "that" (cf. KJV NASB ESV NIV NET etc.). It provides the content of John's clarified saying, which is evident in the verb of the ἵνα clause.

ἐρωτήσῃ: The Greek word ἐρωτήσῃ is third person singular aorist active subjunctive from the verb ἐρωτάω meaning "to ask" or "to request" or "to ask for something" (BDAG, s.v. "ἐρωτάω" 2, p. 395). It is in the subjunctive mood because it follows a ἵνα. **Syntactically,** ἐρωτήσῃ is the governing verb of the dependent substantival clause. The subject of the verb is an implied "he" (or she) embedded in the verb and refers to the one who is petitioning God for life for the sinner. The object of ἐρωτήσῃ is the prepositional phrase, "about that" (περὶ ἐκείνης). **Semantically,** ἐρωτήσῃ is a constative aorist: "he (or she) should ask" (NET) or "he (or she) should pray" (NIV CNT). It describes an action as a whole (W, 557). It focuses attention on what ought not be requested in a prayer.

5:17a ἐστίν: The Greek word ἐστίν is third person singular present active indicative from the verb εἰμί meaning "to be" or "to be in close connection with" (BDAG, s.v. "εἰμί" 2a, p. 282). **Syntactically,** ἐστίν is the main verb of the independent asyndeton clause: "all unrighteousness *is* sin" (πᾶσα ἀδικία ἁμαρτία ἐστίν). The subject of the verb is the nominal phrase "all unrighteousness" (πᾶσα ἀδικία). Although both the subject and the predicate nominative in this clause are anarthrous, "unrighteousness" (ἀδικία) is clearly the subject because of the presence of the adjectival qualifier (W, 42–44). **Semantically,** ἐστίν is a gnomic present: "is" (cf. KJV NASB ESV NIV NET etc.). It points out the timeless principle (W, 523): unrighteousness is sin.

> **Lexical Nugget:** What does ἀδικία mean? This noun occurs twenty-five times in the New Testament, yet only appears in John's letters three times. In John 7:18, ἀδικία is used to describe Jesus in whom no "unrighteousness" exists. In 1 John 1:9, believers are told that when they confess their sins, that God will cleanse them from all "unrighteousness." Here John makes a simple statement of fact: all sin is "unrighteousness." The alpha privative (ἀ) affixed to the beginning of the root word "righteous" (δίκαιον) creates a negation. This means that ἀδικία is the opposite of that which is righteous or what is right in God's eyes. In 1 John, sin or "the quality of injustice" is equated with unrighteousness, which means that it is unjust and goes against what God has determined to be right (BDAG, s.v. "ἀδικία" 2, p. 20).

5:17b καί: The Greek word καί is a conjunction meaning "and yet" (BDAG, s.v. "καί" 1bη, p. 495). **Syntactically,** καί introduces a coordinating independent clause: "*and yet* there is sin not leading to death" (καὶ ἔστιν ἁμαρτία οὐ πρὸς θάνατον). **Semantically,** καί is adversative: "and yet" or "but" (NRSV NET ESV NLT). It emphasizes an unexpected fact, identified in the rest of the clause.

ἐστίν: The Greek word ἐστίν is third person singular present active indicative from the verb εἰμί meaning "to be" or "to exist" or "to be on hand" (BDAG, s.v. "εἰμί" 1, p. 283). **Syntactically,** ἐστίν is the main verb of the independent clause. The subject of the verb is the nominal phrase "a sin not leading to death" (ἁμαρτία οὐ πρὸς θάνατον). **Semantically,** ἐστίν is a gnomic present: "is" (cf. KJV NASB ESV NIV NET etc.). It presents a gnomic truth about sin (W, 523). There is a sin that does not lead to a separation from God.

5:18a Οἴδαμεν: The Greek word οἴδαμεν is first person plural perfect active indicative from the verb οἶδα meaning "to know" or "to have information about"

(BDAG, s.v. "οἶδα" 1e, p. 693). **Syntactically,** οἴδαμεν is the main verb of the independent clause: "*We know* that everyone who has been fathered by God does not *persist in* sin" (οἴδαμεν ὅτι πᾶς ὁ γεγεννημένος ἐκ τοῦ θεοῦ οὐχ ἁμαρτάνει). The subject of the verb is an implied "we" embedded in the verb. It refers to John and his readers. **Semantically,** οἴδαμεν is a perfect with present force: "we know" (cf. KJV NASB ESV NIV NET etc.). It is a verb in the "perfect tense without the usual aspectual significance" (W, 579). What we know is found in the ὅτι clause.

ὅτι: The Greek word ὅτι is a conjunction meaning "that" (BDAG, s.v. "ὅτι" 1c, p. 731). **Syntactically,** ὅτι introduces a dependent conjunctive clause: "*that* everyone who has been fathered by God does not *persist in* sin" (ὅτι πᾶς ὁ γεγεννημένος ἐκ τοῦ θεοῦ οὐχ ἁμαρτάνει). The entire ὅτι clause is functioning substantivally as the direct object of the verb "we know" (οἴδαμεν). It is placed in parentheses in order to visualize its contribution to the independent clause. **Semantically,** ὅτι is an indirect discourse marker: "that" (cf. KJV NASB ESV NIV NET etc.). The entire ὅτι clause provides the content of the knowledge (W, 456), which is clearly expressed in the next verb.

γεγεννημένος: The Greek word γεγεννημένος is a nominative masculine singular perfect passive participle from the verb γεννάω meaning "to become the parent of" or "to exercise the role of a parental figure" (BDAG, s.v. "γεννάω" 1b, p. 193). **Syntactically,** γεγεννημένος introduces a dependent participle clause. The entire participial clause, "who has been fathered by God" (ὁ γεγεννημένος ἐκ τοῦ θεοῦ), modifies the adjective (πᾶς). The πᾶς + participial clause is placed in parentheses in order to visualize its contribution to the independent clause. Together they are the subject of the verb "sins" (ἁμαρτάνει). **Semantically,** γεγέννηται is both a gnomic and extensive perfect: "has been fathered" (cf. NET) or "has been born" (ESV). It is gnomic because of the generic subject (πᾶς) while extensive in that the focus is on the decisive relationship between God and the believer (W, 580). This generic or proverbial force may also be rendered intensively: "is born" (KJV NASB; cf. ASV NRSV) with an emphasis on the results of the present condition of the believer. Regardless of where one places the emphasis of the perfect, John's point is that God has brought followers of Jesus into his family in the past and that reality has continuing results in the present (cf. 2:29; 3:9; 4:7; 5:1, 4). The focus is upon those who practice righteousness: they have had an ongoing relationship with God.

ἁμαρτάνει: The Greek word ἁμαρτάνει is third person singular present active indicative from the verb ἁμαρτάνω meaning "to sin" or "to commit a wrong" (BDAG, s.v. "ἁμαρτάνω" a, p. 49). **Syntactically,** ἁμαρτάνει is the governing verb of the dependent substantival clause. The subject is the substantival adjective πᾶς plus the entire participial phrase that modifies it, "*everyone* who is born of God" (πᾶς ὁ γεγεννημένος ἐκ τοῦ θεοῦ). **Semantically,** ἁμαρτάνει negated with οὐχ is a customary present: "does not *persist* in sin" or "does not keep on sinning" (ESV) or "does not continue to sin" (NIV) or "does not sin" (NET CNT). It speaks of something that occurs regularly (W, 521). John says the one who has God as their Father is unable to sin (= deny Jesus).

Theological Nugget: In what way is someone who has been born of God free from sin? A couple of options exist. On the one hand, the ones who place their faith in Jesus are capable of not sinning anymore (cf. 1 John 3:6–10). Throughout the entire letter John repeatedly makes contrasts between the righteous character of those who believe in Jesus versus the unrighteousness of nonbelievers. On the other hand, he also makes an issue of the fact that no believer should claim that they have no sin in a list of hypothetical statements in the first chapter of the book (1:8–10). The second option focuses on the immediate context where John is distinguishing between the sin that leads to death and the sin that doesn't. If that is the case then John could be suggesting that it is impossible for the true believer to commit the sin that leads to death, which is an outright rejection of Jesus. John is returning to the idea that the believer's paternity must affect their behavior.

5:18b ἀλλ' [ὅτι]: The Greek word ἀλλά is a conjunction meaning "but" (BDAG, s.v. "ἀλλά" 1a, p. 44). **Syntactically,** ἀλλά identifies a dependent conjunctive clause: "*but* [that] the one fathered by God he preserves him (or her) (ἀλλ' [ὅτι] ὁ γεννηθεὶς ἐκ τοῦ θεοῦ τηρεῖ αὐτόν). It is also part of the direct object of "we know" (οἴδαμεν) in 5:18a. We've chosen to interpret the singular "him" (αὐτόν) as "them" to reflect a more inclusive understanding of John's congregation made up of both men and women. **Semantically,** ἀλλά is contrastive: "but" (KJV ASV NASB NRSV ESV NET CNT). It introduces a contrast to the previous οὐχ clause (W, 671). The significance of the contrast is evident in next verb.

γεννηθείς: The Greek word γεννηθείς is a nominative masculine singular aorist passive participle from the verb γεννάω meaning "to beget" or "to become the parent of" (BDAG, s.v. "γεννάω" 1b, p. 193). **Syntactically,** γεννηθείς is functioning as a pendant nominative that further describes the direct object of the clause "him" (αὐτόν). It is the logical rather than the syntactical subject (W, 51–53). Once again, we've chosen to interpret the singular "him" (αὐτόν) as "them" to reflect a more inclusive understanding of John's congregation made up of both men and women. **Semantically,** γεννηθείς is a gnomic aorist: "the one fathered" or "the one who was born" (NRSV NIV). It presents a generic statement that reflects a timeless truth (W, 615). John focuses on a general fact about the one whom God has fathered. The specifics are found in the next verb.

τηρεῖ: The Greek word τηρεῖ is third person singular present active indic-ative from the verb τηρέω meaning "to keep" or "to preserve" or "to cause a condition or activity to continue" (BDAG, s.v. "τηρέω" 2b, p. 1002). **Syntac-tically,** τηρεῖ is the main verb of the independent clause. The subject of the verb is an implied "he" embedded in the verbal ending that refers to God. **Semantically,** τηρεῖ is a customary present: "he preserves" or "keeps" (NASB CNT) or "he protects" (NRSV ESV NET). It is an action that happens regularly (W, 521). God *continually* preserves or protects those whom he has fathered.

Text-Critical and Theological Nugget: Which textual variant best explains, "the one fathered by God" (ὁ γεννηθείς)? If the participle refers to Jesus, the third person pronoun "him" (αὐτόν) is adopted as the direct object of the clause. This a theological issue: is it Jesus, the one fathered by God who pre-serves the believer or is the one fathered by God the believer who preserves other believers? While the UBS committee had limited difficulty about this variant (giving it a B rating; Metzger[1], 647–48; cf. Comfort, 398), the NET Bible note points out four options.

(1) First, the one fathered by God is Jesus and the pronoun "him" (αὐτόν) is an individual Christian. Therefore, Jesus is the one who protects those who follow him keeping them from denying their faith and from the attacks of the Evil One. However, the immediate context indicates that the one fathered by God is a reference to followers of Jesus and that Jesus is the Son of God.

(2) Second, the phrase "the one fathered by God" is a reference to believers and the pronoun is referring to the believers themselves. In this case the be-lievers would be protecting themselves from failure by their own faith in God's Son. Here is where the textual tradition provides the third person reflexive pro-noun "himself" (ἑαυτόν) instead of the third person pronoun "him [singular]" (αὐτόν). In this case, John is pointing to the believers protection of themselves through their faith in Jesus. If the text-critical principle that says the harder reading is more accurate, then the third person pronoun is most likely the orig-inal reading. Yet this doesn't preclude the fact that the third person pronoun can often be used reflexively. The immediate context is focused on the protec-tion of God and not on the protection of the individual believer.

(3) Third, the "one fathered by God" is a reference to followers of Jesus, and the pronoun as a reference to God. In this case, believers guard God or "hold on" to God. But this is not a common lexical usage of the verb "guard" (τηρέω).

(4) The best option, though admittedly awkward, is to take this as a pendant nominative construction. A pendant nominative is grammatically independent of the rest of the clause, but it functions as the logical rather than the gram-

matical subject of the sentence (W, 51). In the clause that follows a pronoun is placed almost in apposition to the thought included in the phrase. The reason it has been moved up is for emphasis. Thus, the words "the one fathered by God" (ὁ γεννηθεὶς ἐκ τοῦ θεοῦ) is the pendant nominative and is related to the third person pronoun, which is the direct object of the verb within the clause. The idea is that God protects followers of Jesus, namely, the one fathered by God (see the full discussion in the NET Bible notes; Culy, 137; Metzger[1], 650).

5:18c καὶ [ὅτι]: The Greek word καί is a conjunction meaning "and" (BDAG, s.v. "καί" 1bα, p. 494). **Syntactically,** καί introduces another dependent conjunctive clause: "*and* [that] the Evil One cannot touch him" (καὶ [ὅτι] ὁ πονηρὸς οὐχ ἅπτεται αὐτοῦ). It also is part of the direct object of "we know" (οἴδαμεν) in 5:18a. **Semantically,** καί is a coordinating connective: "and" (KJV ASV NASB NRSV ESV NIV NET NLT CNT). The conjunctive καί clause provides more information about the one whom God protects, which is clearly stated in the next verb.

ἅπτεται: The Greek word ἅπτεται is third person singular present middle indicative from the verb ἅπτω meaning "to harm" or "to make contact with a view to causing harm" (BDAG, s.v. "ἅπτω" 5, p. 126). **Syntactically,** ἅπτεται is the main verb of the independent clause. The subject is the substantival adjective, is "the Evil One" (ὁ πονηρός). **Semantically,** ἅπτεται negated with οὐχ is a customary present: "cannot harm" (NIV) or "cannot touch" (KJV ASV NASB NRSV ESV NET NLT CNT). It presents an ongoing or habitual action (W, 521). The Devil is not able to harm the true believer because God himself protects him (or her). As you will see throughout our interpretive translation at the end of our analysis, we've chosen to interpret the singular "him" (αὐτοῦ) as "them" to reflect a more inclusive understanding of John's congregation made up of both men and women.

Lexical Nugget: What does ἅπτω mean? The verb occurs thirty-nine times in the New Testament, but only twice in John's writings (John 20:17; 1 John 5:18). The overwhelming usage of ἅπτω in the New Testament occurs in the Synoptic Gospels. It is used thirty times to describe Jesus and his healing ministry. Jesus "touches" people and they are healed (e.g., a man with leprosy, Matt. 8:3; Peter's mother-in-law, Matt. 8:15) or people touch Jesus with the intention that they be healed (i.e., a woman subject to bleeding for twelve years, Mark 5:27, 28, 30, 31). In John 20:17, Jesus commands Mary not to "touch" him. The great majority of the occurrences also refer to physical touch of some kind. Less frequent, however, is the use of the term to describe sexual intimacy (1 Cor. 7:1), cultic impurity (2 Cor. 6:17; Col. 2:21), and contact with the intent to "harm" someone (1 John 5:18). So John's use of ἅπτω to speak of harming someone is unique in the

New Testament. Nevertheless, it is not unique in extrabiblical works. In the Psalms of Solomon, the righteous are comforted to know that though destruction comes to the sinner, nothing "will harm" the righteous (13:6; cf. 15:4). Here in 1 John 5:18, the Devil is not able to "touch" a believer "with the intent to harm," because God protects them.

5:19a οἴδαμεν: The Greek word οἴδαμεν is first person plural perfect active indicative from the verb οἶδα meaning "to know" or "to have information about" (BDAG, s.v. "οἶδα" 1e, p. 693). **Syntactically,** οἴδαμεν is the main verb of the independent clause: "*we know* that we are of God" (οἴδαμεν ὅτι ἐκ τοῦ θεοῦ ἐσμεν). The assumed subject, "we," refers to John and his readers. **Semantically,** οἴδαμεν is a perfect with present force: "we know" (cf. KJV NASB ESV NIV NET etc.). It is a verb in the "perfect tense without the usual aspectual significance" (W, 579). What we know is found in the ὅτι clause.

ὅτι: The Greek word ὅτι is a conjunction meaning "that" (BDAG, s.v. "ὅτι" 1c, p. 731). **Syntactically,** ὅτι introduces a dependent conjunctive clause: "*that* we are of God" (ὅτι ἐκ τοῦ θεοῦ ἐσμεν). The entire clause is functioning substantivally as the direct object of the verb "we know" (οἴδαμεν) and is placed in parentheses in order to visualize its contribution to the independent clause. **Semantically,** ὅτι is an indirect discourse marker: "that" (cf. KJV NASB ESV NIV NET etc.). The entire ὅτι clause provides the content of the knowledge (W, 456), which is clearly expressed in the next verb.

ἐσμέν: The Greek word ἐσμέν is first person plural present active indicative from the verb εἰμί meaning "to be" or "to be in close connection (with)" (BDAG, s.v. "εἰμί" 283.2b). **Syntactically,** ἐσμέν is the governing verb of the dependent substantival clause. The subject of the verb is an implied "we" and refers to John and his readers. **Semantically,** ἐσμέν is an equative present: "is" (cf. KJV NASB ESV NIV NET etc.). It describes a special connection between the subject (e.g. the readers) and the predicate (e.g. God), pointing out that the person who believes that Jesus is God's Son can have assurance that they have been fathered by God.

5:19b καὶ [ὅτι]: The Greek word καί is a conjunction meaning "and" (BDAG, s.v. "καί" 1e, p. 494). **Syntactically,** καί introduces a dependent conjunctive clause: "*and* [that] the whole world is under the control of the Evil One" (καὶ [ὅτι] ὁ κόσμος ὅλος ἐν τῷ πονηρῷ κεῖται). It is also part of the direct object of "we know" (οἴδαμεν). **Semantically,** καί is a coordinating conjunction: "and" (cf. KJV NASB ESV NIV NET etc.). It introduces something new with a loose connection to the previous ὅτι clause (BDAG, "καί" 1e, p. 495; W, 671). The conjunctive καὶ [ὅτι] clause then provides more information about what is known by the reader.

κεῖται: The Greek word κεῖται is third person singular present middle indicative from the verb κεῖμαι meaning "to exist," "to be there," "to find oneself," or "to be in a certain state or condition" (BDAG, s.v. "κεῖμαι" 3d, p. 537). **Syntactically,** κεῖται is the governing verb of the second dependent [ὅτι] clause. The subject of the nominal phrase, "the whole world" (ὁ κόσμος ὅλος) and refers to the world system in opposition to God and his values (cf. 2:15–17). **Semantically,** κεῖται is a customary present: "lies or *continually* lies *in the power of*" (NASB NRSV ESV NET) or "under the control of" (NIV NLT; cf. CNT). It describes an ongoing occurrence (W, 521): the world system continually lies under Satan's power.

> **Lexical and Theological Nugget:** What does it mean that "the whole world lies in the power of the Evil One" (ὁ κόσμος ὅλος ἐν τῷ πονηρῷ κεῖται)? This is another example of a figure of speech called a metonymy of subject, where the subject is stated for an attribute of it. Here the "world" (subject) is put in place of "its inhabitants" or "value system" (attribute). The expression "lies in" (κεῖται ἐν) is only used in the New Testament elsewhere to describe Jesus literally lying in a manger (Luke 2:12, 16). It is used, however, in a figurative sense in 2 Maccabees. Whereas Hyracanus is said to possess a prominent place of authority (2 Macc 3:11), Andronicus is said to be a man of high rank (4:31). In 1 John 5:19, we see this same kind of figurative usage. The inhabitants and value system of the world are under the control of one who possesses a prominent place of authority, even if that person is evil. There is a sharp dualism between the state of the secessionists who are controlled by the Evil One and the orthodox community's existence in the true one in verse 20. Even though the Evil One sits in a place of power over the world, believers are free from his power because of the protection of God.

5:20a οἴδαμεν: The Greek word οἴδαμεν is first person plural perfect active indicative from the verb οἶδα meaning "to know" or "to have information about" (BDAG, s.v. "οἶδα" 1e, p. 693). **Syntactically,** οἴδαμεν is the main verb of the independent clause: "and *we know* that the Son of God has come" (οἴδαμεν δὲ ὅτι ὁ υἱὸς τοῦ θεοῦ ἥκει). The assumed subject, "we," refers to John and his readers. **Semantically,** οἴδαμεν is a perfect with present force: "we know" (cf. KJV NASB ESV NIV NET etc.). It is a verb in the "perfect tense without the usual aspectual significance" (W, 579). What we know is found in the ὅτι clause.

δέ: The Greek word δέ is a conjunction in the postpositive position meaning "and" (BDAG, s.v. "δέ" 1, p. 213). **Syntactically,** δέ introduces an independent conjunctive clause. **Semantically,** δέ is a coordinating connective: "and" (cf. KJV NASB ESV NIV NET etc.). It connects yet another clause about what John claims his readers know (W, 671).

ὅτι: The Greek word ὅτι is a conjunction meaning "that" (BDAG, s.v. "ὅτι" 1c, p. 731). **Syntactically,** ὅτι introduces a dependent conjunctive clause: "*that the Son of God comes*" (ὅτι ὁ υἱὸς τοῦ θεοῦ ἥκει). The entire clause is functioning substantivally as the direct object of the verb "we know" (οἴδαμεν). It is placed in parentheses in order to visualize its contribution to the independent clause. **Semantically,** ὅτι is an indirect discourse marker: "that" (cf. KJV NASB ESV NIV NET etc.). The entire ὅτι clause provides the content of the knowledge (W, 456), which is clearly expressed in the next verb.

ἥκει: The Greek word ἥκει is third person singular present active indicative from the verb ἥκω meaning "to have come" or "to be in a place as the result of movement" (BDAG, s.v. "ἥκω" 1c, p. 435). **Syntactically,** ἥκει is the governing verb of the dependent [ὅτι] clause. The subject of the verb is the nominal phrase "the Son of God" (ὁ υἱὸς τοῦ θεοῦ) and is a reference to Jesus. **Semantically,** ἥκει is a perfective present: "*has* come" (NASB NRSV ESV NIV NET NLT CNT). It emphasizes the results of a past action that are still continuing (W, 532). Jesus the Messiah has come, and yet there is more that is known by John's readers, which is evident in the next clause.

5:20b καὶ [ὅτι]: The Greek word καί is a conjunction meaning "and" (BDAG, s.v. "καί" 1bα, p. 494). **Syntactically,** καί introduces a dependent clause: "*and* [that] he (= Jesus) has given to us insight" (καὶ [ὅτι] δέδωκεν ἡμῖν διάνοιαν). It is also part of the direct object of "we know" (οἴδαμεν) in 5:20a. **Semantically,** καί is a coordinating conjunction: "and" (cf. KJV NASB ESV NIV NET etc.). It introduces something new with a loose connection to the previous ὅτι clause (BDAG, s.v. "καί" 1e, p. 494; W, 671). The conjunctive καὶ [ὅτι] clause once again provides more information about what is known by the reader.

δέδωκεν: The Greek word δέδωκεν is third person singular perfect active indicative from the verb δίδωμι meaning "to give" or "to give something out" (BDAG, s.v. "δίδωμι" 2, p. 242). **Syntactically,** δέδωκεν is the governing verb of the second part of the compound dependent clause. The subject of the verb is an implied "he" and refers back to the Son of God. **Semantically,** δέδωκεν is an extensive perfect: "he *has* given" (cf. KJV NASB ESV NIV NET etc.). It emphasizes a past event from which a present state emerges (W, 577). Since Jesus came as a living person, we have gained insight. God's intention for revealing insight is clarified in the next clause.

Lexical Nugget: What does διάνοια mean? This noun occurs twelve times in the New Testament, but only once in John. In Classical Greek, διάνοια could mean *intention* (Plato, *Euthyd.* 275b), the *process of thinking* (Plato, *Soph.* 263d), or the intelligence or *understanding* of an individual (Plato, *Resp.* 511d). In the LXX, διάνοια is used to describe the *inclination* of the human heart, generally toward evil (Gen. 8:21), someone who *understands* (is skilled in) artistic crafting (Exod. 28:3), and of the mind, as a place into which wisdom can come (Prov. 2:10), as the seat of reasoning (Jdt 8:14), or as the seat of the emotions (1 Macc 10:74; 11:49). In 4 Maccabees 2:2, διανοία is used to describe the mental energy by which Joseph overcame sexual desire. In the New Testament, διανοία is used to describe the center of human understanding, which is also capable of being darkened (Eph. 4:28), although it can also be focused on loving God and one's neighbor (Mark 12:30; Matt. 22:37; Luke 10:27). The term can also be used to describe the process of thinking (2 Peter 3:1) or one's attitude (Col. 1:21; Luke 1:51). Often the term is placed in quotations placing διανοία in parallel with the term καρδία (Jer. 31:33; Heb. 8:10; 10:16), describing the inward seat of intellect or emotion. Here in 1 John 5:20, the idea is perceptibility. Philo uses the term to refer to the divine portion of humanity, which enables people to see God (*Det.* §20; *Virt.* §57). The idea is that the Son has improved the believer's reasoning ability, so that we can discern what and who is true.

5:20c ἵνα: The Greek word ἵνα is a conjunction meaning "that" or "in order that" (BDAG, s.v. "ἵνα" 1c, p. 475). **Syntactically,** ἵνα introduces the dependent conjunctive clause: "*in order that* we may know the true one" (ἵνα γινώσκωμεν τὸν ἀληθινόν). **Syntactically,** the clause is adverbial modifying the verb "he has given" (δέδωκεν). **Semantically,** ἵνα denotes purpose: "in order that" or "that" (KJV ASV). It indicates John's intention (W, 472). That intention is clearly provided in the next verb.

γινώσκωμεν: The Greek word γινώσκωμεν is first person plural present active subjunctive from the verb γινώσκω meaning "to know" or "to arrive at a knowledge of someone or something" (BDAG, s.v. "γινώσκω" 1b, p. 199). It is in the subjunctive mood because it follows ἵνα. **Syntactically,** γινώσκωμεν is the governing verb of the dependent clause. The subject of the verb is an implied "we" embedded in the verb and refers to John and his readers. **Semantically,** γινώσκομεν is a customary present: "we may know" (KJV NASB NRSV ESV NIV CNT). It signals something that occurs regularly. John's intention for writing this letter is in order that believers may know the truth, ultimately the truth about Jesus as the human Messiah and God's expectation to love other believers.

5:20d καί: The Greek word καί is a conjunction meaning "and" (BDAG, s.v. "καί" 1aα, p. 494). **Syntactically,** καί introduces a conjunctive independent clause: "*and* we are in the true one, in his Son, Jesus Christ" (καὶ ἐσμὲν ἐν τῷ ἀληθινῷ, ἐν τῷ υἱῷ αὐτοῦ Ἰησοῦ Χριστῷ). **Semantically,** καί is a coordinating connective: "and" (cf. KJV NASB ESV NIV NET etc.). It adds additional information about what believers know (W, 671). That additional information is evident in the rest of the conjunctive καί clause.

ἐσμέν: The Greek word ἐσμέν is first person plural present active indicative from the verb εἰμί meaning "to be" or "to be in reference to a person" (BDAG, s.v. "εἰμί" 3b, p. 284). **Syntactically,** ἐσμέν is the main verb of the independent clause. The subject of the verb is an implied "we" embedded in the verb and refers back to John and his readers. **Semantically,** ἐσμέν is a gnomic present: "we are" (cf. KJV NASB ESV NIV NET etc.). It reveals something that is completed (W, 517). Believers have a relationship with Jesus who is the Christ.

5:20e ἐστίν: The Greek word ἐστίν is third person singular present active indicative from the verb εἰμί meaning "to be" or "to be in close connection with" (BDAG, s.v. "εἰμί" 1aα, p. 494). **Syntactically,** ἐστίν is the main verb of the independent clause "this one *is* the true God and eternal life": (οὗτός ἐστιν ὁ ἀληθινὸς θεὸς καὶ ζωὴ αἰώνιος). The subject is the demonstrative pronoun "this one" (οὗτός) and refers back to Jesus, God's Son. **Semantically,** ἐστίν is an equative present pointing out that Jesus, the Messiah, God's Son, is also God himself and eternal life personified.

Theological Nugget: To whom does "this one" (οὗτός) refer, God the Father or Jesus? We have here one final example of Trinitarian ambiguity. The demonstrative most likely refers to Jesus, but it could just as easily refer to God the Father. The title "the true one" is used by Jesus of the Father in John 17:3 and is also used of God the Father in the previous verse. The second phrase "eternal life," however, exclusively refers to Jesus (John 11:25; 14:6; also see 1 John 1:2). Also, the nearest previous antecedent is also Jesus Christ. Therefore, this is one final reference to the person and nature of Jesus, the very one that the misguided were denying. One last time John wants his readers to know exactly who Jesus is. He is truly God and is eternal life itself. This is a striking Christological statement. Jesus is a divine Messiah who came in the flesh (cf. Phil. 2:5–11; Heb. 1:2–13).

5:21 φυλάξατε: The Greek word φυλάξατε is a second person plural aorist active imperative from the verb φυλάσσω meaning "to guard" or "to protect" or "to protect by taking careful measures" (BDAG, s.v. "φυλάσσω" 2b, p. 1068). **Syntactically,** φυλάξατε is the main verb of the independent clause: "children, *keep* yourselves from idols" (τεκνία, φυλάξατε ἑαυτὰ ἀπὸ τῶν εἰδώλων). The subject of the verb is an implied "you" hidden in the verb and refers to John's readers. **Semantically,** φυλάξατε is an imperative of request with the personal pronoun, ἑαυτά: "guard yourselves" (NASB ESV NET). It is an imperative from a leader to his readers (W, 488). John admonishes his readers to avoid following after idolatrous views of God, namely, heterodox teachings about the nature of Jesus.

Lexical Nugget: What does it means "to keep yourselves from idols" (φυλάξατε ἑαυτὰ ἀπὸ τῶν εἰδώλων)? The verb φυλάσσω means "to guard."

In its literal usage it can refer to guarding the king's palace or temple from attack (2 Kings 11:5–6; 1 Macc 12:34), prisoners from escape (Acts 12:4; 28:16), or garments from theft (Acts 22:20). It can also be used figuratively to describe protection (John 17:12), perseverance (John 12:25; cf. 2 Thess. 3:3; 2 Tim. 1:12), and, when used with a reflexive pronoun, of guarding yourself against something. The objects to guard oneself against include a person (Timothy against Alexander, the coppersmith, 2 Tim. 4:15), an error (2 Peter 3:17), a religious vice (Acts 21:25), or idolatry (1 John 5:21). John closes his letter by encouraging his readers to protect themselves from idols. The word idols can literally refer to an object of wood or stone that serves as a symbol for a pagan god (Rev. 9:20; Rom. 2:22; 1 Cor. 8:4, 7), but it can also be used with a wider range of meaning. In the Qumran scrolls we read, "Cursed be the man who enters this Covenant while walking among the idols of his heart, who sets up before himself his stumbling-block of sin so that he may backslide (1Q28 II, 11–12; cf. CD XX, 8–10; 1Q36 IV, 9–15; Rom. 1:18–32). For John, it seems he is using εἰδώλων to refer to following after the teachings of the misguided who have left the church. John ends his letter with a warning against leaving the community and joining those who have already left. This warning is not a new idea in 1 John. Instead, it sums up the main ideas of the letter. John wants them to guard themselves against any teaching that counters Jesus's messiahship and humanity. They are idolatrous.

Second John

Like 1 John, 2 John is a letter written to a community of believers in the midst of a crisis. Misguided and fraudulent teachers (or secessionists) had risen up within the church and were causing confusion. The letter *opens* with John's declared love for the church and his joy for their commitment to the teachings of Jesus (vv. 1–3). The focus of the letter is twofold: a polite request (ἐρωτῶ) to continue living in accordance with God's expectation, namely, to love one another (vv. 4–6) and then a warning (βλέπετε) about false teachers (vv. 7–11). The letter *concludes* with an expressed desire to speak with the church in person (vv. 12–13).

Big Greek Idea: Due to John's affection for his readers, he asks them to comply with God's expectation to love fellow believers and beware of false teachers.

2 John 1–3

Big Greek Idea: John writes to fellow followers of Jesus whom he loves deeply, and offers a greeting of grace, mercy, and peace.

Structural Overview: In keeping with a typical Greco-Roman style of letter writing, 2 John *opens* with a threefold salutation: it identifies the sender, addresses the recipients, and offers a greeting (vv. 1–3).[1]

Outline:

> John Expresses His Heartfelt Feelings for Followers of Jesus (vv. 1–2)
> John Greets His Readers (v. 3)

CLAUSAL OUTLINE FOR 2 JOHN 1–3

[1a] Ὁ πρεσβύτερος ἐκλεκτῇ κυρίᾳ καὶ τοῖς τέκνοις αὐτῆς,
[1a] The Elder, to the elect lady and her children

> [1b] **οὓς** ἐγὼ **ἀγαπῶ** ἐν ἀληθείᾳ καὶ οὐκ ἐγὼ μόνος
> [1b] whom I love in truth and not I alone,

> > [1c] ἀλλὰ καὶ [οὓς](πάντες οἱ ἐγνωκότες τὴν ἀλήθειαν) [ἀγαπῶσιν]
> > [1c] but also [whom] (all *those* who have known the truth) [*love*],

> [2a] διὰ τὴν ἀλήθειαν τὴν μένουσαν ἐν ἡμῖν,
> [2a] because the truth which remains in us,

> [2b] καὶ [διὰ τὴν ἀλήθειαν] μεθ᾽ ἡμῶν **ἔσται** εἰς τὸν αἰῶνα.
> [2b] and [*because the truth*] **will be** with us forever.

[3] **ἔσται** μεθ᾽ ἡμῶν χάρις ἔλεος εἰρήνη παρὰ θεοῦ πατρός,
[3] Grace, mercy, and peace **will be** with us from God, *who is* the Father,

> > καὶ παρὰ Ἰησοῦ Χριστοῦ τοῦ υἱοῦ τοῦ πατρός,
> > and from Jesus Christ, *who is* the Son of the Father,
> > ἐν ἀληθείᾳ καὶ ἀγάπῃ.
> > in truth and love.

---

1. For a fuller discussion on letter writing during the time of John, see Bateman[4], 19–56.

Syntax Explained for 2 John 1–3

¹ᵃ ὁ πρεσβύτερος: The letter begins with the verbless opening salutation, "*The elder*, to the elect lady and her children" (ὁ πρεσβύτερος ἐκλεκτῇ κυρίᾳ καὶ τοῖς τέκνοις αὐτῆς). The proper noun, the elder (ὁ πρεσβύτερος; BDAG s.v. πρεσβύτερος 2bβ, p. 862) functions as a nominative absolute and does not require a verb. This common phenomenon appears throughout the New Testament. For example, "the elder (ὁ πρεσβύτερος) in 3 John 1; "Paul" (Παῦλος) in Romans 1:1, 1 Corinthians 1:1, 2 Corinthians 1:1, and "Peter" (Πέτρος) in 1 Peter 1:1 are also all nominative absolutes (cf. W, 49–51; Culy, 141). For a lexical discussion for ὁ πρεσβύτερος see the "Lexical Nugget: Who is "the elder" (ὁ πρεσβύτερος)?" below (3 John 1:1; p. 379).

> **Lexical and Semantical Nugget**: Who is "the elect lady and her children" (ἐκλεκτῇ κυρίᾳ καὶ τοῖς τέκνοις αὐτῆς)? The noun, κυρία, is declined as feminine singular dative from κυρία meaning "lady" or figuratively it can mean "congregation" (BDAG, s.v. "κυρία" 1, 2, p. 576). The noun τέκνοις is neuter plural dative from τέκνον meaning "child" (BDAG, s.v. "τέκνον" 3c, p. 995). Both κυρία and τοῖς τέκνοις are datives of recipient, which appear in verbless constructions and serve to identify the recipient of the letter. The elder is writing to the "elect lady" (KJV ASV ESV NRSV NET) and "her children" (cf. KJV ASV etc.), which is a reference to either (1) a woman named Electa and her physical children, (2) a woman named Kuria and her physical children, or most likely (3) a church and its members (cf. Brown, 652–55). It is most commonly agreed that the "elect lady" is a metaphor. Although some see the reference to the church at large (Lieu, 67), others see it as a reference to a specific church located at some distance from the community where John was living (Painter, 341; Stott, 203–4). John seems to be writing this letter to warn a "sister" church about the missionary efforts of a group of false teachers or secessionists and the dangers of welcoming them if and when they should arrive. Thus the "elect lady" is a personified reference to an associated local church at some distance from the community where John is living (D. Guthrie, 886–89; NET). The dative of recipient appears to be a semantic classification unique to Wallace (W, 148–49).

¹ᵇ οὕς: The Greek word οὕς is a neuter plural accusative from the relative pronoun ὅς meaning "who, which, that" (BDAG, s.v. "ὅς" 1cβ, p. 726). **Syntactically**, οὕς introduces the first part of a compound dependent relative clause, "whom I love in truth and not I alone" (οὕς ἐγὼ ἀγαπῶ ἐν ἀληθείᾳ καὶ οὐκ ἐγὼ μόνος). It is an adjectival clause that clarifies information about the recipient. In this case John *clarifies* that the elect lady and her children are individuals that he loves in the truth, as do all who love the truth. Thus the entire relative clause functions adjectivally and modifies "lady and her children" (κυρίᾳ καὶ τοῖς τέκνοις αὐτῆς). Often relative pronouns break the basic rules of agree-

ment as they do here, because sense agreement (*constructio ad sensum*) supersedes syntactical agreement. Therefore, the elder uses a plural neuter pronoun to reference a group of people, the "lady and her children," which is feminine (κυρία) and neuter (τοῖς τέκνοις) and plural, rather than just to her children, as syntactical agreement would suggest (cf. W, 333).

ἀγαπῶ: The Greek word ἀγαπῶ is first person singular present active indicative from the verb ἀγαπάω meaning "to love" or "to have affection for" (BDAG, s.v. "ἀγαπάω" 1a, p. 5). **Syntactically,** ἀγαπῶ is the governing verb of the relative clause "whom *I love* in truth." The subject of the verb is ἐγώ and refers back to the author of the letter, the elder, John. **Semantically,** ἀγαπῶ is a customary present indicating the elder's continued state of affection for his recipients to "continually love" or simply "love" (KJV ASV etc.)

[1c]ἀλλὰ καὶ [οὕς]: The Greek word ἀλλά is a conjunction meaning "but" or "rather" (BDAG, s.v. "ἀλλά" 1a, p. 44). The Greek word καί is a conjunction that means "also" (BDAG, s.v. "καί" 2c, p. 495). **Syntactically,** ἀλλὰ καί introduces the second part of the dependent adjectival relative [οὕς] clause: "*but also* [whom] all those who have known the truth [love]" (ἀλλὰ καὶ [οὕς]πάντες οἱ ἐγνωκότες τὴν ἀλήθειαν [ἀγαπῶσιν]). The relative pronoun "whom" [οὕς] is elliptical. **Semantically,** ἀλλά is contrastive (KJV NASB ESV NIV NET etc.), while the καί is functioning adjunctivally, "also" (KJV NASB ESV NIV NET etc.), modifying the elliptical verb "love" ([ἀγαπῶσιν]) that appears at the very end of the clause. John is providing additional information about his recipients. The church is not only loved by John, *but also* by anyone who knows the truth.

οἱ ἐγνωκότες: The Greek word ἐγνωκότες is a nominative plural masculine perfect active participle from the verb γινώσκω meaning "to know" or "to come to the knowledge of" (BDAG, s.v. "γινώσκω" 6aα, p. 200). **Syntactically,** ἐγνωκότες is a substantival participle functioning as the subject of an implied verb, "love" [ἀγαπῶσιν]. Thus, there are two parallel dependent pronominal clauses: "whom I love in truth and not I alone [love] but also *all those who have known the truth* [love]" (Culy, 142). **Semantically,** ἐγνωκότες is an extensive perfect "*have* known" (KJV) emphasizing the completed action with present results (W, 521–22). The past action of coming to understand the truth has placed them into a group that now feels affection for the church to which the elder is writing. John's style is to frequently use the substantival participle; this is just one of many instances (see the introduction).

[ἀγαπῶσιν]: The Greek word ἀγαπῶσιν is third person plural present active indicative from the verb ἀγαπάω meaning "to love" or "to have affection for" (BDAG, s.v. "ἀγαπάω" 1a, p. 5). **Syntactically,** ἀγαπῶσιν is elliptical and serves as the governing verb of the second part of the compound adjectival relative clause. The subject of the verb is the participial phrase "all those who have known the truth" (πάντες οἱ ἐγνωκότες τὴν ἀλήθειαν). **Semantically,** ἀγαπῶσιν is a customary present: "love," pointing out the *continual love* that both the elder and anyone who loves the truth have for the congregation.

> **Lexical Nugget:** Who are "the ones who have come to know the truth" (οἱ ἐγνωκότες τὴν ἀλήθειαν)? The referent is discernable from the context of 2 John. The group of people to whom John writes are the true followers of Jesus. They are also members of the church from which "the elder" is writing. They are all people who have stood firm in correct Christological confession, despite the false ministry and opposition of the secessionists (cf. 1 John 2:3, 13; and 4:16).

2a δία: The Greek word δία is a preposition that, when followed by an object in the accusative, means "because of" or "for the sake of" (BDAG, s.v. "δία" 2a, p. 225). **Syntactically,** it introduces the dependent adverbial prepositional phrase "*because the truth which remains in us*" (δια τὴν ἀλήθειαν τὴν μένουσαν ἐν ἡμῖν). **Semantically,** δία expresses the reason or cause of the love felt by the elder and his associates (cf. Culy, 142). They love the church "because" (NIV ESV NRSV NET NLT) it is evident that they also hold the truths of the gospel close to their hearts.

τὴν μένουσαν: The Greek word μένουσαν is an accusative singular feminine present active participle from the verb μένω meaning "to remain" or "to continue to exist" or is used "of someone who does not leave a certain realm or sphere" (BDAG, s.v. "μένω" 1aβ, p. 631). **Syntactically,** μένουσαν is an adjectival participle in the attributive position that describes the realm or sphere in which the readers remain. The elder, his church, and his recipients hold firmly to the truth. **Semantically,** μένουσαν is a customary present indicating the continual nature of this *hold* on the truth (W, 521–22). This phrase is alternatively translated as "lives" (NIV NLT), "dwelleth" (KJV), "abideth" (ASV), "abides" (NASB NRSV ESV), and "resides" (NET).

> **Lexical Nugget:** What does ἀλήθεια mean? Although it appears that in this context the term has a doctrinal aspect to it, the adjectival phrase that qualifies it here, "which remains in us" (τὴν μένουσαν ἐν ἡμῖν), suggests *more than* mere doctrine. In John 14:16–17, Jesus promised the disciples, "I will ask the Father, and he will give you another 'helper,' in order that he might be with you forever, [namely] the Spirit of Truth. You know him, because he remains with you and shall be in you." So perhaps, "the truth" (ἀλήθεια) in 2 John may be something that is doctrinal as well as some manifestation of the Spirit of Truth, which takes up permanent residence in the life of the believer.

2b ἔσται: The Greek word ἔσται is third person singular future active indicative from the verb εἰμί meaning "to be" or "to be in close connection (with)"

(BDAG, s.v. "εἰμί" 2, p. 283). **Syntactically,** ἔσται is the governing verb of another adjectival dependent clause, "and [because the truth] *will be* with us forever" (καὶ [διὰ τὴν ἀλήθειαν] μεθ᾽ ἡμῶν ἔσται εἰς τὸν αἰῶνα), which is parallel to the previous participial phrase "which remains in us" (τὴν μένουσαν ἐν ἡμῖν). This clause adds a second description to the truth that is the cause of the author's love. Not only does this truth persist in them, but it will persist in them forever. **Semantically,** ἔσται is a predictive future: "*will* be" (NASB NRSV ESV NIV NET NLT; cf. W, 568). John indicates that the readers will have a close connection with the truth of the gospel and the Spirit of Truth for all eternity.

> **Lexical and Theological Nugget**: What does εἰς τὸν αἰῶνα mean? The Greek phrase εἰς τὸν αἰῶνα is a temporal idiom that refers to a time to come that has no end. It is best translated as "forever" (KJV NIV etc.; cf. John 2:17; for another type of temporal idiom in John's writings, see 1 John 1:6). This particular idiom denotes an "unlimited duration of time, with particular focus upon the future" (Culy, 142). The phrase occurs twenty-six times in the New Testament, fourteen of which occur in Johannine literature. In the Gospel of John, the phrase occurs in Jesus's promises to his followers: the one who drinks living water will never thirst and will have eternal life (4:14), the one who eats the bread of heaven will live forever (6:58), Jesus will send another Advocate to be with us forever (14:16), and no one will snatch the one that has eternal life out of Jesus's hand (10:28). Here in 2 John the phrase occurs with the verb "remains" (μένω). We find this same combination throughout the LXX. When εἰς τὸν αἰῶνα and μένω appear together it frequently involves God. God remains forever (Ps. 9:8[ET 7]; 111[ET 112]:3; Dan. 6:26), as does his justice (Ps. 110[ET 111]:3), his truth (Ps. 116[ET 117]:2), his Word (Isa. 40:8), and his will (Prov. 19:21). John uses the phrase in a similar way here in 2 John. The Spirit of Truth is permanent and has a permanent presence in the life of the believer (John 14:6; Brown, 315; Painter, 338).

3   ἔσται: The Greek word ἔσται is third person singular present active indicative from the verb εἰμι meaning "to be" or "to be in close connection (with)" (BDAG, s.v. "εἰμι" 2, p. 283). Codex Alexandrinus (A), perhaps seeking to harmonize this greeting in 2 John with common convention, or just trying to avoid redundancy by not repeating the verb from verse 2, omits ἔσται. If this were the correct reading, we would then imply an optative "*let there be* grace, mercy, and peace" (BDF 183 §362; see also Brown, 659). The indicative, however, is the preferred reading (cf. KJV ASV etc.). **Syntactically,** ἔσται is the main verb of the independent clause "grace, mercy, and peace will be with us from God, the Father, and from Jesus Christ, the Son of the Father, in truth and love" (ἔσται μεθ᾽ ἡμῶν χάρις ἔλεος εἰρήνη παρὰ θεοῦ πατρός καὶ παρὰ Ἰησοῦ Χριστοῦ τοῦ υἱοῦ τοῦ πατρός ἐν ἀληθείᾳ καὶ ἀγάπῃ). The subject of ἔσται is a compound one: "grace, mercy and peace" (χάρις ἔλεος εἰρήνη). **Semantically,** ἔσται is a predictive future that points out that grace, mercy, and peace

are abiding virtues that will be constant companions to the believer that come straight from the Father and the Son (W, 568).

Semantical Nugget: What is the semantical relationship between (1) "Father" (πατρός) and "God" (θεοῦ) and (2) "Son" (τοῦ υἱοῦ) and "Jesus Christ" (Ἰησοῦ Χριστοῦ)? Notice that each noun is in the genitive case. This is a clear example of a genitive noun functioning appositionally, where one noun in the same case clarifies another. "The Father" (appositive) clarifies "God" (the proper noun) and "the Son" (appositive) clarifies "Jesus Christ" (the proper noun). Translating the appositive as a relative pronoun can help emphasize this appositional connection. "Grace, mercy, and peace from God *who is* the Father, and from Jesus Christ *who is* the Son of the Father will be with us in truth and love."

2 John 4–6

Big Greek Idea: Since living a life of obedience to God brings joy, followers of Jesus are asked to observe God's fundamental command to love other believers and live a life in compliance with that divine expectation.

Structural Overview: After his salutation (vv. 1–3), John moves from an expression of joy to a request (vv. 4–6). John first conveys his delight or his joy (Ἐχάρην) for the church because of their lifestyle of obedience to God's command (v. 4). He then transitions to a polite request (ἐρωτῶ): remain faithful to God's fundamental command, which is to love other followers of Jesus (vv. 5–6).

Outline:

> John Finds Happiness in People Following Jesus (v. 4)
> John Requests a Sister Church to Love One Another (v. 5)
> John Defines Love (v. 6)

CLAUSAL OUTLINE FOR 2 JOHN 4–6

4a **Ἐχάρην** λίαν
4a **I rejoiced** greatly,

> 4b **ὅτι εὕρηκα** [τινας] ἐκ τῶν τέκνων σου <u>περιπατοῦντας</u> ἐν ἀληθείᾳ,
> 4b because <u>I have found</u> [*some*] of your children <u>walking in truth</u>,

>> 4c **καθὼς** ἐντολὴν **ἐλάβομεν** παρὰ τοῦ πατρός
>> 4c **just as we received** the commandment from the Father.

5a <u>καὶ</u> νῦν **ἐρωτῶ** σε, κυρία
5a <u>And</u> now **I ask** you, lady

> 5b οὐχ **ὡς** ἐντολὴν <u>γράφων</u> σοι καινὴν
> 5b not **as** one writing to you a new commandment,

> 5c <u>ἀλλὰ</u> [ὡς ἐντολὴν <u>γράφων</u> σοι]
> 5c <u>but</u> [*as one writing to you a commandment*]

>> 5d **ἣν εἴχομεν** ἀπ᾽ ἀρχῆς
>> 5d <u>that we have had</u> since the beginning,

>> 5e **ἵνα ἀγαπῶμεν** ἀλλήλους.
>> 5e *namely* that <u>we *persist in* loving</u> one another.

^{6a} <u>καὶ</u> αὕτη **ἐστὶν** ἡ ἀγάπη,
^{6a} <u>And</u> this **is** love:

    |
    ^{6b}**ἵνα περιπατῶμεν** κατὰ τὰς ἐντολὰς αὐτοῦ·
    ^{6b}*namely* **that** **we walk** according to his commands.

^{6c} αὕτη ἡ ἐντολή **ἐστιν**,
^{6c} This **is** the command,

      |
      ^{6d}**καθὼς ἠκούσατε** ἀπ᾽ ἀρχῆς,
      ^{6d}**just as** you **have heard** from the beginning,

|
^{6e}**ἵνα** ἐν αὐτῇ **περιπατῆτε**.
^{6e}*namely* **that you walk** in it.

SYNTAX EXPLAINED FOR 2 JOHN 4–6

^{4a} ἐχάρην: The Greek word ἐχάρην is first person singular aorist passive indicative from the verb χαίρω meaning "to rejoice" or "to be in a state of happiness" or "to be glad" (BDAG, s.v. "χαίρω" 1, p. 1074). **Syntactically,** ἐχάρην is the main verb of the independent clause, "*I rejoiced* greatly" (ἐχάρην λίαν). The subject of the verb is an assumed "I" and refers back to "the elder," John. The voice of χαίρω is always active in the present tense, middle in the future tense, and passive in the aorist tense, which is why ἐχάρην is translated with an active meaning, "I rejoiced" (KJV ESV NET CNT cf. ASV), "I was overjoyed" (NRSV), "I was very glad" (NASB), or "how happy" (NLT), even though the form is actually passive (for a fuller discussion see Culy, 143–44). **Semantically,** ἐχάρην is an ingressive aorist indicating the entrance of the elder into a state of joy (W, 558–59; see also Brown, 660). When John heard about the community's continuing faith, he *began* to rejoice.

^{4b} ὅτι: The Greek word ὅτι is a conjunction that in this context should be translated as "because" (BDAG, s.v. "ὅτι" 4a, p. 732). **Syntactically,** the conjunction ὅτι identifies the clause as a conjunctive dependent clause. The entire dependent clause, "*because* I have found some of your children walking in truth" (ὅτι εὕρηκα ἐκ τῶν τέκνων σου περιπατοῦντας), is functioning adverbially, modifying the verb, "I began rejoicing" (ἐχάρην). **Semantically,** ὅτι is causal: "because" (NET). Thus, John provides the reason for his own entrance into a state of happiness. He began to rejoice *because* he found that many in the congregation were living what they believed.

εὕρηκα: The Greek word εὕρηκα is first person singular perfect active indicative from the verb εὑρίσκω meaning "to find" or "to discover intellectu-

ally through investigation" (BDAG, s.v. "εὑρίσκω" 2, p. 412). **Syntactically,**
εὕρηκα is the governing verb of the dependent adverbial clause: "because *I
have found* [*some*] of your children walking in truth" (ὅτι εὕρηκα [τινας]
ἐκ τῶν τέκνων σου περιπατοῦντας ἐν ἀληθείᾳ), modifying the verb, "I
began rejoicing" (ἐχάρην). The subject of the verb is an implied "I" and refers back to the elder, John. **Semantically,** εὕρηκα is an extensive perfect: "I
have found" (ASV NET). The extensive perfect references the elder's current
state of happiness that has resulted from the report he had heard about their
faithfulness.

> **Grammatical Nugget**: How should the prepositional phrase "[*some*] of your
> children" ([τινας] ἐκ τῶν τέκνων) be understood? The phrase "[*some*] of
> your children" is partitive (BDF 90–91 §164; NASB NRSV ESV NIV NET NLT; W,
> 371). This kind of construction, literally "of your children," is an example of
> the Semitic style of the Johannine literature. On the one hand, this partitive
> construction has an accusative indefinite pronoun that is implicitly under-
> stood (an ellipsis): "*some*" (τινας). On the other hand, the subsequent parti-
> cipial phrase, "walking in truth" (περιπατοῦντας ἐν ἀληθείᾳ) is function-
> ing adjectivally as an object complement double accusative to the understood
> partitive phrase: "*some* of your children walking in truth." Such expressions
> were uncommon in Classical Greek, but fairly common in Semitic languages
> (Culy, 144; W, 182–83).

4c καθώς: The Greek word καθώς is a conjunction meaning, "as" or "just as" or
"in so far as" (BDAG, s.v. "καθώς" 41, p. 493). **Syntactically,** καθώς identifies
this dependent clause as conjunctive. The entire dependent clause, "*just as* we
have received the commandment from the Father" (καθὼς ἐντολὴν ἐλάβομεν
παρὰ τοῦ πατρός) is functioning adverbially, modifying the participle "walking" (περιπατοῦντας). **Semantically,** καθώς is a comparative conjunction:
"just as" (NASB NRSV ESV NIV NET NLT; cf. KJV ASV). It describes the manner in
which they are walking or living: they are living according to the commandment that they had received from God (W, 675).

ἐλάβομεν: The Greek word ἐλάβομεν is first person plural aorist active indicative from the verb λαμβάνω meaning "to receive" or "to be a receiver" (BDAG,
s.v. "λαμβάνω" 10c, p. 584). **Syntactically,** ἐλάβομεν is the governing verb of the
conjunctive dependent clause, "just as *we received* the commandment from the
Father" (καθὼς ἐντολὴν ἐλάβομεν παρὰ τοῦ πατρός), which is functioning adverbially (comparatively), modifying the participle "walking" (περιπατοῦντας).
The subject of the verb is an implied "we" referencing John and his readers. **Semantically,** ἐλάβομεν is a constative aorist: "we received" (ASV; cf. NASB). Yet
"we received" is somewhat idiomatic and means, "God gave a commandment" or
"the Father commanded" (cf. NIV NET NLT). John speaks of the act of God giving

his command as a whole (W, 557). John draws attention to the idea that his readers had received the commandment from God in the past and were expected to comply with his expectation.

⁵ᵃ καὶ νῦν: The Greek word καί is a conjunction meaning "and" that introduces something new with a somewhat loose connection with the previous clause (BDAG, s.v. "καί" 1e, p. 495). The Greek word νῦν is an adverb meaning "now" (BDAG, s.v. "νῦν" 1a, p.681). **Syntactically,** καὶ νῦν introduces a conjunctive independent clause, *"and now* I ask you, lady" (καὶ νῦν ἐρωτῶ σε, κυρία). **Semantically,** καὶ νῦν is a temporal connective that reveals John's transitioning to the heart of his letter (Culy, 145; BDAG, s.v. "νῦν" 2a, p. 681): "and now" (see also KJV ASV ESV NIV). Brown gives this καί a slight adversative force, "but now" (see also NRSV NET), because despite the good behavior of some of their congregation, there is danger on the horizon for those who aren't walking in truth (Brown, 663).

ἐρωτῶ: The Greek word ἐρωτῶ is first person singular present active indicative from the verb ἐρωτάω meaning "to request" or "to ask for something" (BDAG, s.v. "ἐρωτάω" 2, p. 395). **Syntactically,** ἐρωτῶ is the main verb of the independent clause. The subject of the verb is an implied "I" and refers back to the elder, John. **Semantically,** ἐρωτῶ is an instantaneous present: "I *now* ask" or "I ask" (NASB NRSV ESV NIV NET; cf. W, 517–18). The elder is right now asking them to love one another.

> **Syntactical and Theological Nugget**: How should "but now" (καὶ νῦν) be understood? How should it be interpreted? In this context, it serves as a polite and personal way of introducing the heart of the letter. Its slight adversative force gives readers a warning. Even though this sister church is presently living according to the truth (v. 4), a threat is on the horizon. Fraudulent believers and misguided teachers are trying to lead John's readers astray (1 John 2:18; 4:1; 2 John 7). Yet the true followers of Jesus must stay true to the love commands of Jesus (Brown, 663).

⁵ᵇ ὡς: The Greek word ὡς is a conjunction meaning "as" (BDAG, s.v. "ὡς" 13a, p. 1104). **Syntactically,** ὡς identifies the clause as a dependent conjunctive clause. The entire dependent clause, "not *as* one writing to you a new commandment" (οὐχ ὡς ἐντολὴν γράφων σοι καινήν), is functioning adverbially modifying the verb "I ask" (ἐρωτῶ). **Semantically,** ὡς is comparative and should be translated "as" (KJV ASV etc.). The conjunction is describing the type of command the author is issuing to them. This love commandment is not new, but one that they have had since they first heard the message about Jesus (W, 675).

⁵ᶜ ἀλλά: The Greek word ἀλλά is a conjunction meaning "but" (BDAG, s.v. "ἀλλά" 1a, p. 44). **Syntactically,** ἀλλά identifies the clause as a conjunctive dependent

clause. Most of the ἀλλά clause is missing (ellipsis). In order to make sense of John's thought, we must insert his understood parallel "[as one writing to you a commandment] (ὡς ἐντολὴν γράφων σοι). **Semantically,** ἀλλά is contrastive: "but" (KJV ASV etc.). It describes the true nature of the love command. The commandment to love is not a new one, *but* one that his readers have had since they first heard the message about Jesus (W, 671).

5d ἥν: The Greek word ἥν is a feminine singular accusative from the relative pronoun ὅς meaning "who, which, that" (BDAG, s.v. "ὅς" 1a, p. 725). **Syntactically,** ἥν modifies "commandment" (ἐντολήν) because it agrees in number and gender. It provides information about the "command" ([ἐντολήν]), namely, that the commandment is not new, but rather something his readers have known since they began following Jesus.

εἴχομεν: The Greek word εἴχομεν is first person plural imperfect active indicative from the verb ἔχω meaning "to have" or "to possess" (BDAG, s.v. "ἔχω" 1a, p. 420). **Syntactically,** εἴχομεν serves as the governing verb of the dependent relative clause. The assumed subject, "we," refers to the elder, his associates, and his readers. **Semantically,** εἴχομεν is a pluperfective imperfect: "we have had" (NIV ESV NET NLT; cf. W, 549). John is indicating that God's commandment was given previously, prior to the time of his writing this short letter.

5e ἵνα: The Greek word ἵνα is a conjunction that means "in order that" or "that" denoting purpose in this context (BDAG, s.v. "ἵνα" 1a, p. 475). **Syntactically,** ἵνα identifies the clause as a conjunctive dependent clause. This entire ἵνα clause, "*namely, that* we *persist in* loving one another" (ἵνα ἀγαπῶμεν ἀλλήλους), could be functioning adverbially modifying the verb "we have had" (εἴχομεν), adjectivally explaining the content of the "command" (ἐντολήν), or substantivally as the direct object of the verb "I ask" (ἐρωτῶ). **Semantically,** if the ἵνα clause is adverbial it describes the intention for the command: to lead believers to love one another. If the ἵνα clause is functioning substantivally, it underscores the request, that they love one another. It is more likely that the clause is functioning adjectivally, explaining the content of the command, and rendered "namely that" or "that" (KJV ASV NASB ESV NET CNT). John underscores a simple fact: his readers—from the very beginning—have had God's command: "love one another" (Culy, 145–46; Bateman[1], 113–14).

ἀγαπῶμεν: The Greek word ἀγαπῶμεν is first person plural present active subjunctive from the verb ἀγαπάω meaning "to love" or "to have a warm regard for and interest in another" person (BDAG, s.v. "ἀγαπάω" 1aα, p. 5). The verb is in the subjunctive mood because ἵνα clauses take the subjunctive. **Syntactically,** ἀγαπῶμεν is the governing verb of the dependent adjectival ἵνα clause. The assumed subject, "we," refers to the elder, his associates, and his readers. **Semantically,** ἀγαπῶμεν is a customary present: "we *persist in* loving" or "we love" (KJV ASV etc.). John is indicating that the type of love that God wants is a love that is ongoing (W, 521–22).

> **Theological Nugget**: When was God's commandment to love issued? John informs his readers that this command is not new, but that they have been in possession of it "from the beginning" (ἀπ᾽ ἀρχῆς). The parallel verse in 1 John 2:7 says virtually the same thing. John is telling his readers that this command did not originate with him, but came from Jesus during his earthly ministry (John 13:34–35; cf. 15:12, 17; Painter, 348). The misguided teaching was novel and had "gone ahead" of John's teaching (2 John 9) and reflected errors about Jesus. Yet we must ask, the beginning of what? Some seek extreme specificity when it comes to finding a temporal referent for this phrase. Others say that "from the beginning" (ἀπ᾽ ἀρχῆς) refers to the beginning of each individual's relationship with Jesus. Still others insist that "from the beginning" (ἀπ᾽ ἀρχῆς) refers back to the teachings of Jesus at the beginning of the Christian era. It seems that since John addresses individuals, then their acquaintance with this command would have come at the beginning of their initial journey as followers of Jesus.

⁶ᵃ καί: The Greek word καί is a conjunction meaning "and" (BDAG, s.v. "καί" 1, p. 494). **Syntactically,** καί introduces a conjunctive independent clause: "*and* this is love" (καὶ αὕτη ἐστὶν ἡ ἀγάπη). **Semantically,** καί is a coordinating connective: "and" (KJV NIV ASV NASB ESV NRSV). John adds an additional thought about the nature of the love command.

ἐστίν: The Greek word ἐστίν is third person singular present active indicative from the verb εἰμί meaning "to be" and has an equative function of identifying one thing with another (BDAG, s.v. "εἰμί" 2, p. 283). **Syntactically,** ἐστίν serves as the main verb of the independent clause. The subject of the verb is the demonstrative "this" (αὕτη). **Semantically,** ἐστίν is a gnomic present: 'is'. It points to a timeless definition of love (W, 523–25).

> **Lexical Nugget**: What does ἀγάπη mean? Although many have erroneously taught and preached that ἀγάπη is a unique kind of *Christian* love, it is nevertheless a significant type of love. In Classical Greek, there are four terms used for expressing love; (1) στέργω, which describes familial affection (BDAG, s.v. "στέργω," p. 943); (2) ἔρος, which is reserved for sexual expression and passion (TLNT 1:9n13); (3) φιλέω, which is indicative of a reciprocal friendship among equals, marked by goodwill and kindness (TLNT 1:10n16; BDAG, s.v. "φιλέω" 1, p. 1056); and (4) ἀγάπη, which also expresses reciprocal friendship, but unlike φιλέω, it also links together people of different social classes and conditions. In Classical Greek, ἀγάπη love is expressed by superiors for infe-

riors, as well as inferiors for their superiors (*TLNT* 1:13nn30–31). The word is used rarely in the LXX, but when it is used, it often speaks of the love that exists between a man and a woman (cf. Song 2:4, 5, 7; 3:10; 5:8; 7:6; 8:4, 6, 7; cf. Jer. 2:2). In the New Testament, ἀγάπη is used to describe God's love for the world (a superior for an inferior; cf. John 3:16). In the Gospel of John, it is also used to emphasize the mutual care of believer's for one another as a response to Jesus's love for them (John 13:35; 15:9, 10, 13; 17:26). In the Johannine letters, ἀγάπη is used to express God's love for his creatures and followers (1 John 3:1; 4:7–21; 2 John 3), the believer's love for God (1 John 2:5, 15; 3:17; 4:10, 12, 20; 5:1–3), the believer's love for Jesus (1 John 5:1), and the believer's love or lack of love for their fellow believers (1 John 2:10; 3:10, 11, 23; 4:7, 11, 20; 2 John 5). This term is used to describe a type of love and affection that knows no racial, social, or cultural boundaries.

[6b] ἵνα: The Greek word ἵνα is a conjunction meaning "that" as part of a fixed expression (BDAG, s.v. "ἵνα" 2e, p. 476). **Syntactically,** ἵνα introduces a conjunctive dependent clause: "*namely, that* we walk according to his commandment" (ἵνα περιπατῶμεν κατὰ τὰς ἐντολὰς αὐτοῦ). The entire ἵνα clause is functioning adjectivally, modifying either the subject "this" (αὕτη; Culy, 146) or the predicate nominative "love" (ἀγάπη; Brown, 665). **Semantically,** the use of ἵνα after "this" (αὕτη) warrants the ἵνα clause being rendered appositionally: "*namely,* that" or "that" is almost idiomatic within Johannine literature (W, 475) even though English translations render ἵνα as "that" (KJV NIV etc.). The type of love that God wants is that we live according to his commands.

περιπατῶμεν: The Greek word περιπατῶμεν is first person plural present active subjunctive from the verb περιπατέω meaning "to walk" or "to conduct one's life" (BDAG, s.v. "περιπατέω" 2a, p. 803). The verb is in the subjunctive mood because ἵνα takes its verb in the subjunctive. **Syntactically,** περιπατῶμεν is the governing verb of the dependent conjunctive ἵνα clause. The assumed subject, "we," refers to the elder, his associates, and his readers. **Semantically,** περιπατῶμεν is a customary present: "we walk" (KJV NASB NRSV ESV NIV NET). The English translation "walk" is a figure of speech for a person's lifestyle. John encourages followers of Jesus to pursue a persistent lifestyle of love (W, 521–22; cf. 1 John 3:22–23; John 15:10–12).

[6c] ἐστίν: The Greek word ἐστίν is third person singular present active indicative from the verb εἰμί meaning "to be" and has an equative function of identifying one thing with another (BDAG, s.v. "εἰμί" 2, p. 283). **Syntactically,** ἐστίν serves as the main verb of the independent clause. The subject of the verb is the demonstrative pronoun "this" (αὕτη), due to the grammatical priority of pronouns (W, 42–43). **Semantically,** ἐστίν is equative: 'is'. It sets the stage for the content of the commandment.

6d κᾰθώς: The Greek word κᾰθώς is a conjunction meaning "as" or "just as" (BDAG, s.v. "κᾰθώς," p. 493). **Syntactically,** κᾰθώς identifies this dependent clause as conjunctive. The entire dependent clause, *"just as you have heard from the beginning"* (κᾰθώς ἠκούσᾰτε ἀπ' ἀρχῆς) is functioning adverbially modifying the verb of being "is" (ἐστίν). **Semantically,** κᾰθώς is comparative and parenthetically describes when they had received the love command: "just as" (NASB ESV NRSV NET NLT). John once again underscores the fact that his readers did not receive the command recently, but that they have had it since the beginning of their faith journey.

ἠκούσᾰτε: The Greek word ἠκούσᾰτε is a second person plural aorist active indicative from the verb ἀκούω meaning "to hear" or "to receive news" (BDAG, s.v. "ἀκούω" 37.1bβ, p. 37; cf. 3d, p. 38). **Syntactically,** ἠκούσᾰτε is the governing verb of the conjunctive adverbial dependent clause. The assumed subject, "you," refers to the readers. **Semantically,** ἠκούσᾰτε is a consummative aorist: "you *have* heard" (KJV NASB NRSV ESV NIV NET). It stresses the cessation of an act (W, 559–61). The congregation had already heard about this commandment in the past, and they were still in possession of it in the present.

6e ἵνα: The Greek word ἵνα is a conjunction meaning "that" as part of a fixed expression (BDAG, s.v. "ἵνα" 2e, p. 476). **Syntactically,** ἵνα serves to introduce a conjunctive dependent clause: *"namely, that you might walk in it"* (ἵνα ἐν αὐτῇ περιπατῆτε). This entire ἵνα clause can either be functioning adverbially, modifying the verb "heard" (ἠκούσᾰτε; "so that" ESV; "thus" NET) or adjectivally, explaining the content of the demonstrative pronoun: "this" (αὕτη; Culy, 146). **Semantically,** the idiomatic use of ἵνα after "this" (αὕτη) warrants the ἵνα clause being rendered appositionally: *"namely, that"*. This is almost idiomatic within Johannine literature (W, 475) even though ἵνα is rendered as "that" (KJV ASV NASB CNT). The original command was to persist in living a lifestyle of love.

περιπατῆτε: The Greek word περιπατῆτε is a second person plural present active subjunctive from the verb περιπατέω meaning "to walk" or "to conduct one's life" (BDAG, s.v. "περιπατέω" 2a, p. 803). The verb is in the subjunctive mood because ἵνα clauses take the subjunctive. **Syntactically,** it is the governing verb of the dependent clause. The assumed subject, "you," refers to the readers. **Semantically,** περιπατῆτε is a customary present: "you walk" or you *continually* walk (KJV ASV NASB ESV NET CNT). Once again, the English translation "walk" is a figure of speech for a person's lifestyle. John expects his readers to persist in living a lifestyle of love (W, 521–22).

Grammatical Nugget: What is the antecedent of the personal pronoun αὐτῇ in the prepositional phrase "in it" (ἐν αὐτῇ)? The referent is hard to locate precisely because there are three feminine nouns in the context that are possible grammatical antecedents. (1) The first one is the noun "truth" (ἀληθείᾳ) from verse 4, which also occurs as the object of the preposition "in" (ἐν). This would make good sense in the context, but this would separate the pronoun from its antecedent by forty-six words! (2) The second option is the noun "love" (ἀγάπη) found at the beginning of verse 6. This seems to be the majority opinion of many commentators. It also makes good sense from the context, but it still separates the pronoun from its antecedent by sixteen words. (3) The last option is that the antecedent of the personal pronoun αὐτῇ is the noun "command" (ἐντολάς), which occurs in the second part of verse 6. Although one objection might be that this particular noun occurs with a different preposition (κατά), John tends to vary his style and so it wouldn't be out of character. It seems most natural to understand the nearest of the three possibilities as the most likely antecedent. John is reminding his readers that the reason that they heard the love commands when they first came to the faith was so that they would obey them. For John, there might not have been a big difference between any of these ideas. To walk in the commandment would also be to love other believers and to walk in the truth.

2 JOHN 7–11

Big Greek Idea: Due to the number of misguided people who deny the humanity of Jesus, followers of Jesus are advised to be alert to impostors so as to guard against harming any future or present relationships, and are expected to ignore any solicitation of such people so as not to appear to endorse, support, and encourage association with them.

Structural Overview: John draws an inference (ὅτι) from verses 4–6, namely, that the love command is necessary due to the many people who have left (ἐξῆλθον) the fellowship, who are frauds, and who refute the humanity of Jesus (v. 7). He then advises his reader to "beware" (βλέπετε) the dangers these fraudulent people pose to the church, namely, that believers could lose their future reward (v. 8) and perhaps even harm their current relationship with God (v. 9).

John offers a strategy for dealing with any potential misguided teachers from infiltrating the church (εἴ τις ἔρχεται and φέρει; v. 10a–b). He quite pointedly tells his readers: "Don't give itinerant teachers who teach contrary to the humanity, messiahship, and love of Jesus an opportunity to explain their positions (μὴ λαμβάνετε and λέγετε; v. 10c–d). Then John provides his reasoning (γάρ). If true believers entertain such misguided people, they are in essence endorsing their teaching, supporting their ministry, and becoming partners in their evil work (κοινωνεῖ; v. 11).

Outline:

John Draws Attention to Misguided People Who Have Left the Church (v. 7)
John's Warning about the Misguided (v. 8)
John Distinguishes the True Followers from the Misguided (v. 9)
John Addresses Unwelcome Solicitors (v. 10–11)

CLAUSAL OUTLINE FOR 2 JOHN 7–11

⁷ᵃ **ὅτι** πολλοὶ πλάνοι **ἐξῆλθον** εἰς τὸν κόσμον,
⁷ᵃ **For** many deceivers **have gone out** into the world,

|

⁷ᵇ οἱ μὴ ὁμολογοῦντες (Ἰησοῦν Χριστὸν ἐρχόμενον ἐν σαρκί·)
⁷ᵇ the ones who do not confess (Jesus, who is the Christ has come in the flesh;)

⁷ᶜ οὗτός **ἐστιν** ὁ πλάνος καὶ ὁ ἀντίχριστος.
⁷ᶜ this one **is** the deceiver and the Antichrist.

⁸ᵃ **βλέπετε** ἑαυτούς
⁸ᵃ **Watch** yourselves,

    |

    ⁸ᵇ **ἵνα** μὴ **ἀπολέσητε** (ἃ εἰργασάμεθα)
    ⁸ᵇ **in order that** **you do** not **lose** (<u>what we have worked for</u>),

    ⁸ᶜ <u>ἀλλὰ</u> [*ἵνα*] μισθὸν πλήρη **ἀπολάβητε**
    ⁸ᶜ <u>but</u> [*in order that*] **you may receive** *your* full reward.

⁹ᵃ (πᾶς ὁ προάγων καὶ μὴ μένων ἐν τῇ διδαχῇ τοῦ Χριστοῦ) θεὸν οὐκ
ἔχει·
⁹ᵃ (Everyone who goes on ahead and does not remain in the teaching about
Christ) **does** not **have** God.

⁹ᵇ (ὁ μένων ἐν τῇ διδαχῇ) οὗτος καὶ τὸν πατέρα καὶ τὸν υἱὸν **ἔχει.**
⁹ᵇ (the one who remains in the teaching,) this one **has** both the father and
the son.

    ¹⁰ᵃ **εἴ** τις **ἔρχεται** πρὸς ὑμᾶς
    ¹⁰ᵃ **If** anyone **comes** to you

    ¹⁰ᵇ <u>καὶ</u> [*εἰ*] ταύτην τὴν διδαχὴν οὐ **φέρει**,
    ¹⁰ᵇ <u>and</u> [*if*] he **does** not **carry** this teaching,

¹⁰ᶜ μὴ **λαμβάνετε** αὐτὸν εἰς οἰκίαν
¹⁰ᶜ **do** not **welcome** him (or her) into your home

¹⁰ᵈ <u>καὶ</u> (χαίρειν) αὐτῷ μὴ **λέγετε·**
¹⁰ᵈ <u>and</u> **do** not **say** to him (or her): (Greetings!)

      |

      ¹¹ (ὁ λέγων <u>γὰρ</u> αὐτῷ χαίρειν) **κοινωνεῖ** τοῖς
      ἔργοις αὐτοῦ τοῖς πονηροῖς.
      ¹¹ (<u>for</u> the one who says to him [or her]) "Greetings,"
      he (or she) **shares** in his (or her) evil works.

SYNTAX EXPLAINED FOR 2 JOHN 7–11

⁷ᵃ ὅτι: The Greek word ὅτι is a conjunction meaning "because" or "for" (BDAG,
s.v. "ὅτι" 4b, p. 732). **Syntactically,** ὅτι introduces an independent conjunctive
clause: "*For* many deceivers have gone out into the world" (ὅτι πολλοὶ πλάνοι
ἐξῆλθον εἰς τὸν κόσμον). Although Culy classifies this ὅτι clause as causal
(NIV NLT) and thereby adverbially dependent on the verb περιπατῆτε, Brown
points out that often the subordination of a ὅτι clause is very loose (Culy, 147;

Brown, 668). Therefore, this particular ὅτι clause assumes a mediatory role between two thoughts (Bateman[1], 123; see also the notes in the NET Bible). Thus John is drawing an inference based on the entire discussion that has already unfolded. **Semantically,** ὅτι is an explanatory conjunction: "for" (KJV ASV NASB ESV NET). In the clauses that follow, John will infer a conclusion about God's command and the importance of complying with it.

ἐξῆλθον: The Greek word ἐξῆλθον is third person plural aorist active indicative from the verb ἐξέρχομαι meaning "to depart" or "to discontinue an association" (BDAG, s.v. "ἐξέρχομαι" 1aα, p. 348). **Syntactically,** ἐξῆλθον is the governing verb of the conjunctive independent clause. The subject of the verb is the "deceivers" (πλάνοι) who have gone out into the world. **Semantically,** ἐξῆλθον is a consummative aorist and focuses on the cessation of an act (W, 559–61) and should be translated "*have* gone out" (NASB NRSV ESV NIV NET NLT). The action describes that the world (= world system; cf. 1 John 2:15–17) is full of frauds, some of whom have departed from their own community of followers of Jesus (1 John 2:18–21; 2 John 9).

Lexical Nugget: Who are the ones who "have gone out" into the world? They are described here as "deceivers" (πλάνοι). This word is used only three other times in the New Testament. First, the scribes and Pharisees call Jesus a "deceiver" (Matt. 27:63). Second, some described Paul as an "impostor" (2 Cor. 6:8). Finally, the term is used as an adjective to describe evil spirits and demons (1 Tim. 4:1). Here in verse 7, John identifies a group of people who left the community due to a disbelief in the humanity of Jesus. This group is the same one that is described in 1 John 2:18–19 and 4:1. These deceivers are fraudulent people who are animated by the spirit of the Antichrist and whose teaching about Jesus's humanity and messiahship is corrupt.

7b ὁμολογοῦντες: The Greek word ὁμολογοῦντες is a nominative masculine plural present active participle from the verb ὁμολογογέω meaning "to confess" or is used "of a profession of allegiance" (BDAG, s.v. "ὁμολογογέω" 4b, p. 708). **Syntactically,** ὁμολογοῦντες introduces the dependent participial clause "the ones who do not confess that Jesus, who is the Christ, has come in the flesh" (οἱ μὴ ὁμολογοῦντες Ἰησοῦν Χριστὸν ἐρχόμενον ἐν σαρκί). The entire clause functions as an appositive, further defining the "deceivers" (πλάνοι). **Semantically,** ὁμολογοῦντες is a progressive present: "confess" (KJV ASV NRSV ESV NET) or "acknowledge" (NASB NIV). It describes the ongoing belief that Jesus did not come in the flesh (W, 518–19). Their confession was not just something they said, but something they believed in their heart.

ἐρχόμενον: The Greek word ἐρχόμενον is an accusative masculine singular present active participle from the verb ἔρχομαι meaning "to come" or "to ap-

proach from the narrator's perspective" (BDAG, s.v. "ἔρχομαι" 1bα, p. 394).
Syntactically, ἐρχόμενον is an indirect discourse participle completing the
idea of the verbal of communication, "the ones confessing" (ὁμολογοῦντες).
John discloses to his readers that deceivers are people who promote the idea
that Jesus did not have a flesh and blood body. **Semantically,** ἐρχόμενον is a
perfective present: "has come" (NRSV). John, however, emphasizes that Jesus
did have a human body and that it has results in our theological beliefs (W,
532–33; see also the perfect participle in the parallel thought in 1 John 4:2;
Bateman[1], 125). The emphasis here is that Jesus did come in the flesh, and that
those who do not hold to this belief are false teachers.

7c ἐστίν: The Greek word ἐστίν is third person singular present active indicative
from the verb εἰμί meaning "to be" and has an equative function of identifying one thing with another (BDAG, s.v. "εἰμί" 2, p. 283). **Syntactically,** ἐστίν
serves as the main verb of the independent clause: "this one *is* the deceiver and
the Antichrist" (οὗτός ἐστιν ὁ πλάνος καὶ ὁ ἀντίχριστος). The subject of
the verb is the demonstrative pronoun "this one" (οὗτος), due to the grammatical priority of pronouns (W, 42–43). **Semantically,** ἐστίν is a gnomic present,
pointing to the timeless fact that any person who denies that Jesus came in the
flesh is against Jesus (W, 523–25).

Lexical and Theological Nugget: What does "Jesus Christ coming in the flesh"
mean? This confession is the same confession found in 1 John 4:2, except that the
perfect participle found in 1 John 4:2 (ἐληλυθότα) has been replaced here in 2
John 7 with a present participle (ἐρχόμενον). It seems reasonable to understand
the phrase the same way that we interpreted it in 1 John 4:2. The word "flesh"
is being used as a figure of speech called a synecdoche, where a part is used in
place of the whole. The idea that Jesus came in the flesh is a reference to his full
humanity at his incarnation—a truth that was being denied by fraudulent people.

8a βλέπετε: The Greek word βλέπετε is a second person plural present active imperative from the verb βλέπω meaning "to watch" or "to beware of" or "be ready
to learn about something that is hazardous" (BDAG, s.v. "βλέπω" 5, p. 179). **Syntactically,** βλέπετε is the main verb of the independent clause: "*watch* yourselves"
(βλέπετε ἑαυτούς). The assumed subject, "you," refers to the readers. The direct
object of the imperative is the reflexive pronoun "yourselves" (ἑαυτούς). **Semantically,** βλέπετε is a customary imperative of request: "watch yourselves" (NASB
ESV CNT; cf. W, 487–88). John is warning his readers to beware continually of the
danger of fraudulent people.

8b ἵνα: The Greek word ἵνα is a conjunction that means "in order that" or "that"
denoting purpose (BDAG, s.v. "ἵνα" 1a, p. 475). **Syntactically,** ἵνα introduces
a conjunctive dependent clause: "*in order that* you do not lose what we worked

for" (ἵνα μὴ ἀπολέσητε ἃ εἰργασάμεθα). The entire ἵνα clause functions adverbially modifying "watch" (βλέπετε). **Semantically,** the ἵνα is a purpose clause: "in order that" or "that" (KJV ASV NASB NIV NLT). John's intention behind his warning against frauds or misguided teachers is that his readers might not miss out on the rewards for their pastoral and missionary efforts. If they allow fraudulent teaching to take root in their community, all their progress and effort could come to nothing.

ἀπολέσητε: The Greek word ἀπολέσητε is a second person plural aorist active subjunctive from the verb ἀπόλλυμι meaning "to lose" or "to fail to obtain what one expects" (BDAG, s.v. "ἀπόλλυμι" 2, p. 116). The verb is in the subjunctive mood because ἵνα clauses take their verb in the subjunctive. **Syntactically,** ἀπολέσητε is the main verb of the adverbial dependent ἵνα clause. The assumed subject, "you," refers to the readers. **Semantically,** ἀπολέσητε negated with μή is a constative aorist: "you do not lose" (NASB NRSV NIV NET NLT). It looks at the action of losing something as a whole (W, 557–58). John expresses concern about his readers losing their missionary efforts if they allow fraudulent teaching to take root.

ἃ: The Greek word ἃ is accusative neuter plural from the relative pronoun ὅς meaning "who, which, that" (BDAG, s.v. "ὅς" 1a, p. 725). **Syntactically,** ἃ introduces a relative clause that functions as the direct object of the verb, "might not lose" (ἀπολέσητε). The entire relative clause is placed in parentheses alongside ἀπολέσητε. Since this is a substantival use of the relative pronoun there is no antecedent. John is referring to the work which his readers have done building their Christian community. If they allow fraudulent teaching to be interspersed with their teachings, they could unravel "the things" for which they have worked so hard.

εἰργασάμεθα: The Greek word εἰργασάμεθα is first person plural aorist middle (= deponent) indicative from the verb ἐργάζομαι meaning "to do" or "to accomplish something through work" (BDAG, s.v. "ἐργάζομαι" 2a, p. 389). The textual tradition is divided over whether the original reading was first person plural ("*we* have worked for"; KJV) or second person plural ("*you* have worked for"; ASV NASB NIV NLT CNT). It seems safe to assume that the second person plural is most likely secondary. Perhaps an editor wanted to smooth the thought out by making it parallel to the second person plural ἀπολέσητε above (Brown, 671–72; Culy, 149). **Syntactically,** εἰργασάμεθα is the main verb of the dependent relative clause. The entire clause functions as the direct object of the verb "might not lose" (ἀπολέσητε) and is placed in parentheses to visualize that though a dependent clause it functions as part of the independent clause. The assumed subject, "we," refers to the readers to whom John was writing, namely, those who put a great deal of effort into their missionary activities, as well as John himself. **Semantically,** εἰργασάμεθα is a constative aorist: "we *have* worked for" (NRSV ESV NIV NET). John focuses attention on the action as a whole (W, 559–61). If they allow this heterodox teaching to spread, the efforts and achievements the followers of Jesus have made in their mission's work and their building of their ministry could come to nothing.

Theological Nugget: How do we interpret the relative clause, "what we worked for" (ἃ εἰργασάμεθα)? Two options exist. On the one hand, Brown suggests John is teaching that if they follow after the fraudulent teachings of the misguided, then his readers might lose their faith or salvation (Brown, 672). The assumption is that they have been working to maintain their faith in the face of being tempted to accept the false teachings of those who have left the church. This presupposes a certain view of salvation and the possibility of apostasy, which doesn't appear elsewhere in John (cf. 1 John 5:16–17). It also presupposes that those who have left the church may have "lost their salvation," even though John presents them as having never been believers (1 John 2:19). Finally, in John 10:28–29, genuine believers cannot be snatched away, not even by the heretical teaching of the opponents in view here. On the other hand, John is referring to the pastoral and missionary efforts of the readers, especially in their surrounding geographic area (Smalley, 330; Painter, 353; NET). This might also explain the awkward "you, we, you" sequence: "*You* do not lose what *we* have worked for; *you* must receive your reward." If the false Christology gets a hold in the community, then all the prior effort to establish a church might be in jeopardy, including the efforts of John himself. This view also explains the following clause about receiving their "reward" for their faithful Christian service.

[8c] ἀλλά: The Greek word ἀλλά is a coordinating conjunction that means "but" or "rather" (BDAG, s.v. "ἀλλά" 1a, p. 44). **Syntactically,** ἀλλά introduces a conjunctive dependent implied ἵνα clause: "but [in order that] you may receive *your* full reward" (ἀλλὰ [ἵνα] μισθὸν πλήρη ἀπολάβητε). **Semantically,** ἀλλά is contrastive (KJV ASV etc.) and introduces his second intention for warning them, which is clearly stated in the ἵνα clause.

[ἵνα]: The Greek word ἵνα is a conjunction that means "in order that" or "that" (BDAG, s.v. "ἵνα" 1a, p. 475). **Syntactically,** this implied [ἵνα] serves to introduce a conjunctive dependent clause. The support for an assumed ἵνα is evident in the next verb: it is in the subjunctive mood. **Semantically,** this implied ἵνα introduces another adverbial purpose clause parallel to "in order that you might not lose that for which you have worked" ([ἵνα] μὴ ἀπολέσητε ἃ εἰργάσασθε). John's intention for his readers to beware of fraudulent teachers is to insure that his readers might receive their full reward for their pastoral and missionary efforts. If they allow false teaching to take root in their community, all of their progress and effort could come to nothing, and they would lose their future reward.

ἀπολάβητε: The Greek word ἀπολάβητε is a second person plural aorist active subjunctive from the verb ἀπολαμβάνω meaning "to receive" or "to obtain something from a source" (BDAG, s.v. "ἀπολαμβάνω" 1, p. 115). The verb is in the subjunctive mood because ἵνα clauses take the subjunctive. **Syntactically,** ἀπολάβητε serves as the main verb of the adverbial dependent and implied ἵνα clause. The assumed subject, "you," refers to the readers. **Semantically,** ἀπολάβητε is a constative aorist: "you may receive" (NASB NRSV CNT). It views the action as a whole (W, 559–61). John points out that his readers might lose their full reward if they allow this false teaching to take root.

Lexical Nugget: What is the "reward" (μισθόν) that John does not want the community to lose? The term μισθός normally refers to a workman's wage, which he is due in exchange for his labor (Matt. 20:8; James 5:4; cf. BDAG, s.v. "μισθός," p. 653). Throughout the New Testament, rewards are promised and given to Christians who serve faithfully (1 Cor. 3:8–10; Matt. 5:12; 10:22; Mark 9:41; 13:13; Luke 19:11–27). Although rewards are not a typical theme in Johannine literature, the idea is found in John 4:36 (cf. Rev. 11:18; 22:12). Here in this context, reward appears to be halting the growth of their ministry and destroying the basis for a future reward. John earnestly desires for his readers to hold fast to a correct confession about Jesus and thereby keep the ministry alive, validating their missionary efforts, and leading to some sort of future reward from God.

9a προάγων: The Greek word προάγων is a nominative masculine singular present active participle from the verb προάγω meaning "to go before" or "to move ahead of" (BDAG, s.v. "προάγω" 2a, p. 864). **Syntactically,** προάγων introduces a dependent participle clause. It is one of two participles that make up a compound subject: "Everyone who goes on ahead and does not remain in the teaching about Christ" (πᾶς ὁ προάγων καὶ μὴ μένων ἐν τῇ διδαχῇ τοῦ Χριστοῦ), The entire participial clause modifies the adjective (πᾶς). The πᾶς + participial clause is placed in parentheses in order to visualize its contribution to the independent clause. **Semantically,** προάγων is a gnomic present: "who runs ahead" (NIV) or "goes on ahead" (ESV NET). John presents a timeless truth (W, 523, 615). Anyone who leads others to accept teachings against Jesus's incarnation, has a problem. That problem is evident in the next verb.

μένων: The Greek word μένων is a nominative masculine singular present active participle from the verb μένω meaning "to remain" "to continue," "to abide," or is used to describe someone who does not leave a certain realm or sphere" (BDAG, s.v. "μένω" 1aβ, p. 631). **Syntactically,** μένων is a participle functioning substantivally as the second participle of a compound subject for the verb "have" (ἔχει). The entire participle clause is placed in parentheses to visualize its function within the independent clause. John is speaking of any person (πᾶς) who does not continue to hold to the correct teaching about the humanity of

Jesus (Culy, 150; Brown, 673). **Semantically,** μένων is a gnomic present: "does not remain" (NET, "does not continue" (NIV), or "does not abide" (KJV NASB NRSV ESV). The misguided, who go ahead and do not maintain the teaching of Jesus's incarnation, do not have a right relationship with God.

Semantical Nugget: How is the genitive Χριστοῦ to be understood? This noun modifies the noun, "teaching" (τῇ διδαχῇ). Although most translations render it simply "the teaching of Christ" (KJV NASB NRSV NIV NLT), the genitive "of Christ" (Χριστοῦ) can be rendered subjectively ("Christ's teaching"), objectively ("the teaching *about* Christ"), or as a plenary genitive with Christ as both the object of the teaching and the one who teaches it. The objective genitive seems like the best option because the specific teachings being denied were those about the humanity of Jesus rather than a specific teaching of his from his earthly ministry (Culy, 150).

ἔχει: The Greek word ἔχει is third person singular present active indicative from the verb ἔχω meaning "to have" or "to have a close relationship with someone" (BDAG, s.v. "ἔχω" 2b, p. 420; cf. 1 John 2:23). **Syntactically,** ἔχει serves as the main verb of the independent clause, "everyone who goes on ahead and does not remain in the teaching about Christ does not *have* God" (πᾶς ὁ προάγων καὶ μὴ μένων ἐν τῇ διδαχῇ τοῦ Χριστοῦ θεὸν οὐκ ἔχει). The subject of ἔχει is "Everyone who goes ahead and does not remain in the teaching about Christ" (πᾶς ὁ προάγων καὶ μὴ μένων ἐν τῇ διδαχῇ τοῦ Χριστοῦ). **Semantically,** ἔχει is a gnomic present: "have" (KJV NASB ESV NIV NET etc.). It describes a general theological principle that anyone who does not continue to hold to teachings about Jesus's humanity and his messiahship does not have a right relationship with God (W, 523, 615). The NLT captures John's point best: "Anyone who wanders away from this teaching has no relationship with God.

Lexical Nugget: What does the verb μένω mean and what does it say about the misguided? The verb is used twenty-four times in 1 John. Fourteen times the term is used to refer to the permanence of a relationship: between (1) God and the believer (2:6, 17; 3:24 [2x]; 4:12, 13, 15, 16 [2x]), (2) Jesus and the believer (2:27, 28; 3:6), (3) both God and Jesus and the believer (2:24), and (4) between believers (2:19). The word is also used five times to refer to other realities residing in the believer, such as the word of God (2:14), the gospel message (2:24 [2x]), the anointing (2:27), and God's seed (3:9), and twice to refer to realities not residing in the opponents, such as eternal life (3:15) and the love of God (3:17). Finally, it is used three times in a varied manner: the one who loves his brother *resides* in the light (2:10), the one who does not love *resides* in death (3:14), and the one who resides in love *resides* in God (4:16). In this context, John charges the secessionists with not *remaining* in the correct teaching about the nature of Jesus. They have gone ahead or beyond the teaching of the apostolic eyewitnesses. John is teaching that anyone who refuses to *remain* in the teaching about Jesus's humanity is not a genuine Christian. John goes on to make this explicit in the rest of the clause when he claims that the fraudulent teachers about Jesus's humanity "do not have God" (= no relationship with God).

⁹ᵇ μένων: The Greek word μένων is a nominative masculine singular present active participle from the verb μένω meaning "to remain" "to continue," "to abide," or is used to describe someone who does not leave a certain realm or sphere (BDAG, s.v. "μένω" 1aβ, p. 631). **Syntactically,** μένων is a participle functioning substantivally in apposition to the demonstrative pronoun "this one" (οὗτος), clarifying that the one who does have a right relationship with God is the one who continues to believe in the teachings about the incarnation of Jesus. **Semantically,** μένων is a gnomic present: "remains" (NET NLT, "does not abide" (KJV NASB NRSV ESV) or "continues" (NIV). It describes a general theological principle about anyone who persists in their belief about the humanity of Jesus and his messiahship which is fully developed with the next verb (W, 523, 615).

ἔχει: The Greek word ἔχει is third person singular present active indicative from the verb ἔχω meaning "to have" or "to have a close relationship with someone" (BDAG, s.v. "ἔχω" 2b, p. 420). **Syntactically,** ἔχει serves as the main verb of the independent clause, "the one who remains in the teaching has both the Father and the Son" (ὁ μένων ἐν τῇ διδαχῇ οὗτος καὶ τὸν πατέρα καὶ τὸν υἱὸν ἔχει). The subject of ἔχει is the demonstrative pronoun "this one" (οὗτος). **Semantically,** ἔχει is a gnomic present: "has" (KJV NASB ESV NIV NET etc.). It describes the general theological principle that those who continue to hold to teaching about Jesus's humanity have a right relationship with God (1 John 2:24; cf. Brown, 676; NET).

¹⁰ᵃ εἰ: The Greek word εἰ is a conjunction that means "if" (BDAG, s.v. "εἰ" 7, p. 279). **Syntactically,** the conjunction εἰ identifies the clause as a dependent adverbial clause. The entire dependent clause, "*if* anyone comes to you" (εἴ τις ἔρχεται πρὸς ὑμᾶς), is functioning adverbially. It modifies the verb, "receive" (λαμβάνετε), which is idiomatic for offering hospitality. **Semantically,** εἰ introduces a first class conditional clause: "if" (KJV NASB ESV NIV NET etc.). John provides a probable condition for offering hospitality (Culy, 151; see also 2 Cor. 11:4 for a similar condition). It was not uncommon for strangers to appear at one's door and to offer hospitality to strangers. In fact, it tends to be a cultural expectation (cf. Lexical Nugget on 3 John 3a). So in all probability John foresaw false teachers coming and soliciting hospitality.

ἔρχεται: The Greek word ἔρχεται is third person singular present middle (= deponent) indicative from the verb ἔρχομαι meaning "to come" or "to approach from the narrator's perspective (BDAG, s.v. "ἔρχομαι" 1aβ, p. 393).

Syntactically, ἔρχεται is one of the main verbs of the dependent adverbial conditional clause. The subject is the pronoun, "anyone" (τις). **Semantically,** ἔρχεται is a gnomic present: "comes" (KJV NASB ESV NIV NET etc.). John is about to offer a general practice for people who request hospitality (W, 523), which is clarified in the independent clause.

^{10b} καὶ [εἴ] The Greek word καί is a conjunction meaning "and" (BDAG, s.v. "καί" 1, p. 494). **Syntactically,** καί introduces a conjunctive independent clause: "and (if) he (or she) does not carry this teaching" (καὶ [εἴ] ταύτην τὴν διδαχὴν οὐ φέρει). **Semantically,** καί is a coordinating connective that expands the conditional thought that began in verse 10a. φέρει: The Greek word φέρει is third person singular present active indicative from the verb φέρω meaning "to carry" or "to bring with" (BDAG, s.v. "φέρω" 1aβ, p. 1051). **Syntactically,** φέρει is the main verbs of the elliptical [εἴ], which introduces a dependent adverbial conditional clause. The subject is the pronoun, "anyone" (τις). **Semantically,** φέρει is a gnomic present: "carry" or "bring" (KJV NASB ESV NIV NET etc.). John specifies a general principle and targets misguided teachers (W, 523).

^{10c} λαμβάνετε: The Greek word λαμβάνετε is a second person plural present active imperative from the verb λαμβάνω meaning "to receive" or "to include in an experience" (BDAG, s.v. "λαμβάνω" 5, p. 584). **Syntactically,** λαμβάνετε is the main verb of the independent clause, "*do* not *welcome* him (or her) into your home" (μὴ λαμβάνετε αὐτὸν εἰς οἰκίαν). The assumed subject, "you," refers to John's readers. **Semantically,** the negated μὴ λαμβάνετε is an imperative of request: "do not receive" (NASB ESV NET CNT) or "do not welcome" (cf. NRSV) or "do not invite" (NLT). John exhorts his readers not to welcome solicitors who promote false teaching about Jesus. But John gives another exhortation in the next clause.

> **Lexical Nugget:** What does εἰς οἰκίαν mean? John tells his readers not to welcome any false teachers "into the house." Brown is correct in his suggestion that John is not referring to a private residence, but rather to the meetings of the "Johannine house-church in the area" (Brown, 676; Smalley, 333). "Solicitors are not welcome." John is seeking to take away an opportunity for the opponents to spread their false Christology among the churches that he helped establish. Although the masculine form for "house" (οἶκος) is normally used in the New Testament to refer to house churches (Rom. 16:5; 1 Cor. 16:19; Col. 4:15; Philem. 1:2), the feminine form for "house" (οἰκίαν) is used here. John could simply have used the feminine to correspond to the feminine form of ἐκλεκτῇ κυρίᾳ found in the greeting to a sister church in the area that opens John's letter: "to the elect lady and her children" (ἐκλεκτῇ κυρίᾳ καὶ τοῖς τέκνοις αὐτῆς; v. 1).

^{10d} καί: The Greek word καί is a coordinating conjunction meaning "and" (BDAG, s.v. "καί" 1b, p. 494). **Syntactically,** καί introduces a conjunctive independent clause, "do not say to him (or her): Greetings!" (καὶ χαίρειν αὐτῷ μὴ λέγετε). **Semantically,** καί is a coordinating connective: "and" (NASB NET) or simply "or" (ESV NIV NLT CNT). It connects John's first expectation with his second.

λέγετε: The Greek word λέγετε is a second person plural present active imperative from the verb λέγω meaning "to say" or "to order, command, direct, enjoin" (BDAG, s.v. "λέγω" 2c, p. 589). **Syntactically,** λέγετε is the main verb of the independent clause. The assumed subject, "you," refers to the community to which the elder was writing. **Semantically,** λαμβάνετε is an imperative of request: "do not say to him (or her): Greetings!" "do not give him any greeting" (ASV NASB ESV NET). John expects his readers to close the door to solicitors who promote unacceptable teaching about Jesus.

χαίρειν: The Greek word χαίρειν is a present active infinitive from the verb χαίρω meaning "to rejoice" or "to wish one well"; it was a "formalized greeting wishing one well" (BDAG, s.v. "χαίρω" 2a, p. 1075). **Syntactically,** χαίρειν is functioning as the direct object of "do not say" (μὴ λέγετε). **Semantically,** χαίρειν is an idiomatic phrase meaning "Greetings." It is variously translated as "do not welcome them" (NIV), "neither bid him speed" (KJV), "do not give him any greeting" (NET), or "give any kind of encouragement" (NLT). Brown suggests that this phrase and the preceding one about not welcoming false teachers into your house are related. The two actions together (not accepting them into your home and not even offering them a greeting) form one thought, teaching that believers should never show any type of hospitality to those carrying heterodox teaching (Brown, 676; see also Culy, 151).

11 γάρ: The Greek word γάρ is a conjunction in the postpositive position meaning "for" (BDAG, s.v. "γάρ" 2, p. 189). **Syntactically,** the conjunction γάρ identifies the clause as a conjunctive dependent clause. The entire dependent clause, "*for* the one who says to him (or her), 'Greetings,' shares in his (or her) evil works" (ὁ λέγων γὰρ αὐτῷ χαίρειν κοινωνεῖ τοῖς ἔργοις αὐτοῦ τοῖς πονηροῖς), functions adverbially. It modifies the verb, "says" (λέγετε). **Semantically,** γάρ is a marker for clarification: "for" (KJV ASV NASB NRSV ESV), though a case could be made for cause: "because" (NET; BDAG, s.v. "γάρ" 1, p. 189). John is about to clarify himself concerning his expectation to reject solicitors.

λέγων: The Greek word λέγων is a nominative masculine singular present active participle from the verb λέγω meaning "to say" or "to express oneself orally" (BDAG, s.v. "λέγω" 1aβ, p. 588). **Syntactically,** λέγων is a participle functioning substantivally as the subject of the verb, "shares" (κοινωνεῖ). The entire participial clause appears in parentheses to visualize its contribution to the dependent γάρ clause. **Semantically,** λέγων is a gnomic present: "the one who says." John is speaking of anyone; it is a generic reference (W, 523, 615). Specifics about this generic person are made known with the next verb.

κοινωνεῖ: The Greek word κοινωνεῖ is third person singular present active indicative from the verb κοινωνέω meaning "to share" or "to participate in the deeds of others and thereby sharing responsibility with them" (BDAG, s.v. "κοινωνέω" 1bβ, p. 552). **Syntactically,** κοινωνεῖ serves as the main verb of the adverbial dependent clause. The subject is "the one who gives him (or her) a greeting" (ὁ λέγων . . . αὐτῷ χαίρειν). **Semantically,** κοινωνεῖ is a gnomic present: "shares" (NIV NET) or "participates" (NASB NRSV). Anyone, according to John, who accepts the solicitation of a false teacher endorses, supports, and enters into a partnership with them in their evil work.

Lexical Nugget: What does John mean when he speaks of "evil deeds" (τοῖς ἔργοις αὐτοῦ τοῖς πονηροῖς)? In 2 John, the deeds may be spreading a false Christology (vv. 7–10) or denying the importance of love (vv. 5–6), or perhaps even both, doctrinal and ethical. Since the immediate context is about refusing hospitality to the opponents, it would seem that the evil deeds involve willfully deceiving others about the nature of Jesus (Smalley, 334). If any reader welcomes and aids those who promote a false Christology, they themselves take part in their deception and share equal responsibility (NET; BDAG, s.v. "κοινωνέω" 1bβ, p. 552).

2 John 12–13

Big Greek Idea: John's intention for cutting short his letter and waiting until he and his readers can meet together is so that they may anticipate a pleasurable reunion, and thereby he ends the letter courteously.

Structural Overview: John brings closure to his letter with a bit of suspense. He concedes (ἔχων) that he has more to say, but choses not (οὐκ ἐβουλήθην) to write about those things in this letter. So rather than writing any more (ἀλλά), he'll wait until he can come (γενέσθαι) and speak (λαλῆσαι) with them face-to-face. John's intention (ἵνα) for meeting with his readers, however, is for mutual enjoyment (πεπληρωμένη ᾖ) of each other's company. John then closes with greetings (ἀσπάζεται) from the sister church where he currently abides.

Outline:

>   John's Desire to Write More Is Curtailed (v. 12)
>   John's Closing Greetings (v. 13)

CLAUSAL OUTLINE FOR 2 JOHN 12–13

> ¹²ᵃ Πολλὰ **ἔχων** (ὑμῖν γράφειν)
> ¹²ᵃ *Although* **I have** many things to write to you,
>
> |
>
> ¹²ᵇ οὐκ **ἐβουλήθην** [*γράφειν*] διὰ χάρτου καὶ μέλανος
> ¹²ᵇ **I do** not **wish** (*to write*) by means of pen and ink,
>
> ¹²ᶜ ἀλλὰ **ἐλπίζω γενέσθαι** πρὸς ὑμᾶς καὶ στόμα πρὸς στόμα λαλῆσαι,
> ¹²ᶜ **but I hope to come** to you and to speak face-to-face,
>
> > |
> >
> > ¹²ᵈ **ἵνα** ἡ χαρὰ ἡμῶν **ᾖ πεπληρωμένη**.
> > ¹²ᵈ **in order that** our joy **might be complete**.
>
> ¹³ **Ἀσπάζεταί** σε τὰ τέκνα τῆς ἀδελφῆς σου τῆς ἐκλεκτῆς.
> ¹³ The children of your elect sister **greet** you.

SYNTAX EXPLAINED FOR 2 JOHN 12–13

¹²ᵃ ἔχων: The Greek word ἔχων is a nominative masculine singular present active participle from the verb ἔχω meaning "to have" or "to experience something" with "a sense of inevitability" (BDAG, s.v. "ἔχω" 7aε, p. 421). **Syntactically,** ἔχων introduces a dependent participial clause: "*although I have* many things to write to you" (πολλὰ ἔχων ὑμῖν γράφειν). The entire clause is adverbial,

modifying the verb "to wish" (ἐβουλήθην). **Semantically,** ἔχων is a concessive participle: "*although* I have" (NRSV) or "though" (NASB ESV NET). Some translations simply translate it as simple participle: "having" (KJV ASV) while others translate it as a finite verb, "to have" (NIV NLT). The concessive participle communicates that John is conceding to not writing any more—even though there is much more he would like to write.

γράφειν: The Greek word γράφειν is an aorist active infinitive from the verb γράφω meaning "to write" or "to correspond with someone" (BDAG, s.v. "γράφω" 2c, p. 207). **Syntactically,** γράφειν is a substantival infinitive modifying "the many *more things*" (πολλά). **Semantically,** γράφειν is seemingly an epexegetical infinitive that clarifies, explains, or qualifies a noun or adjective (cf. 3 John 13a; W, 607). Yet, Culy suggests γράφειν is a complementary infinitive to ἔχων. Thus, πολλά is the direct object of both ἔχων and γράφειν (Culy, 152; cf. BDAG, s.v. "ἔχω" 7e, p. 421). However, the clausal outline above has placed parentheses around ὑμῖν γράφειν as a way to visualize the infinitive clause as substantive and thereby modifying "the many *more things*" (πολλά). Thus, the elder wishes to write about many more things to this sister church.

12b ἐβουλήθην: The Greek word ἐβουλήθην is first person singular aorist passive indicative from the verb βούλομαι meaning "to wish" or "to desire to experience something" (BDAG, s.v. "βούλομαι" 2aζ, p. 182). **Syntactically,** ἐβουλήθην is the main verb of the independent clause, "*I do* not *wish* [to write] by means of pen and ink" (οὐκ ἐβουλήθην [γράφειν] διὰ χάρτου καὶ μέλανος). The assumed subject, "I," refers to John. **Semantically,** the negated (οὐκ) ἐβουλήθην is a constative aorist: "do not want to do so" (NASB NET). Many translations opt for a more dynamic translation of this clause, such as, "I would rather not use paper and ink" (NRSV ESV) or "but I don't want to do it with paper and ink" (NLT). The aorist tense views the act of writing as a whole (W, 557). John's desire to write any more in this letter has ended.

[γράφειν]: The Greek word γράφειν is an aorist active infinitive from the verb γράφω meaning "to write" or "to correspond with" (BDAG, s.v. "γράφω" 2c, p. 207). The infinitive is placed in [brackets] to visualize that the word is an ellipsis. **Syntactically,** [γράφειν] is part of the verb "I desire" (ἐβουλήθην). **Semantically,** γράφειν is a complementary infinitive. It completes the thought of what John "desires" (ἐβουλήθην).

Lexical Nugget: What does διὰ μέλανος καὶ καλάμου mean? The prepositional phrase "by means [διά] of paper and ink" simply means "by letter." A similar phrase appears in 3 John 13. Perhaps it is merely a standard way to close a Hellenistic letter (Painter, 356). Rather than by letter, the author wishes to communicate with the church in a more personal way, "face-to-face" or in person (στόμα πρὸς στόμα lit. means "mouth-to-mouth"). (See also Culy, 153; 3 John 13 and 1 Cor. 13:12; Brown, 678.) This underscores John's anticipation of a personal appearance at a sister church in the very near future.

12c ἀλλά: The Greek word ἀλλά is a conjunction meaning "but" (BDAG, s.v. "ἀλλά" 3, p. 44). **Syntactically,** ἀλλά introduces a conjunctive independent clause: "*but* I hope to come to you and to speak face-to-face" (ἀλλὰ ἐλπίζω γενέσθαι πρὸς ὑμᾶς καὶ στόμα πρὸς στόμα λαλῆσαι). **Semantically,** ἀλλά is contrastive: "but" (KJV ASV NASB NET NLT CNT) or "instead" (NRSV ESV NIV). John is about to contrast his desire with his hope.

ἐλπίζω: The Greek word ἐλπίζω is first person singular present active indicative from the verb ἐλπίζω meaning "to hope" or "to expect" or "to look forward to something" (BDAG, s.v. "ἐλπίζω" 2, p. 319). **Syntactically,** ἐλπίζω is the main verb of the independent clause. The assumed subject, "I," refers to John. **Semantically,** ἐλπίζω is a progressive present: "I hope" (ASV NASB ESV NIV NET etc), or "I trust" (KJV). John *right* now is hoping (W, 518). What he is hoping for is found in the rest of the clause.

γενέσθαι: The Greek word γενέσθαι is an aorist middle (= deponent) infinitive from the verb γίνομαι meaning "to move" or "to come" or "to make a change of location in space" (BDAG, s.v. "γίνομαι" 6e, p. 199). **Syntactically,** γενέσθαι is part of the verb "I hope" (ἐλπίζω). **Semantically,** γενέσθαι is a complimentary infinitive: "to come" (KJV ASV NASB NRSV ESV NET) or "visit" (NIV NLT). It completes the thought of what John "hopes" (ἐλπίζω). He hopes that he will be able to come and pay them a personal visit. But yet there's more in the next verbal.

λαλῆσαι: The Greek word λαλῆσαι is an aorist active infinitive from the verb λαλέω meaning "to speak" or "to utter words" (BDAG, s.v. "λαλέω" 2aδ, p. 582). **Syntactically,** λαλῆσαι is also part of the verb "I hope" (ἐλπίζω). **Semantically,** λαλῆσαι is a complimentary infinitive: "to speak" (KJV ASV NASB NET) or "talk" (NRSV ESV NIV NLT CNT). The elder hopes that not only will he be able to come, but that he might speak in person. In all probability, "to come" and "speak" is a figure of speech known as a hendiadys where two words are used to communicate one idea.

Lexical Nugget: What does στόμα πρὸς στόμα mean? The Greek phrase στόμα πρὸς στόμα is idiomatic. Literally the phrase means "mouth-to-mouth," but a translation of "face-to-face" (KJV ASV etc.) makes more sense in English (see also 3 John 13 and 1 Cor. 13:12; Brown, 678).

¹²ᵈ ἵνα: The Greek word ἵνα is a conjunction meaning "in order that" or "that" (BDAG, s.v. "ἵνα" 1a, p. 475). **Syntactically,** ἵνα introduces a conjunctive dependent clause, "*in order that* our joy might be complete" (ἵνα ἡ χαρὰ ἡμῶν ᾖ πεπληρωμένη), The entire clause is functioning adverbially. It modifies the verb "hope" (ἐλπίζω). **Semantically,** ἵνα is a purpose clause: "in order that" or "that" (KJV ASV; cf. NET). Other translations seem to classify the conjunction as result or purpose-result: "so that" (NASB NRSV ESV NIV; cf. NET). John's intentions are clearly stated and apparent in the next verb.

ᾖ πεπληρωμένη: The Greek word πεπληρωμένη is a nominative feminine singular perfect passive participle from the verb πληρόω meaning "to complete" or "to finish" or "to bring to completion that which was already begun" (BDAG, s.v. "πληρόω" 3, p. 828). The Greek word ᾖ is third person singular present active subjunctive from the verb εἰμί meaning "to be" (BDAG, s.v. "εἰμί" 11a, p. 285). **Syntactically,** ᾖ πεπληρωμένη is a periphrastic construction functioning as the main verbal idea of the dependent adverbial ἵνα clause (W, 647–49). The subject of the periphrastic construction is "joy" (χαρά). **Semantically,** ᾖ πεπληρωμένη is an extensive perfect: "may be complete" (NIV ESV NRSV NET), "may be full" (KJV) or even "will be full" (NLT). John believes that when they have an in-person encounter, they would enter into a state of mutual joy, a pleasurable reunion.

Text-Critical Nugget: What reading, "our" (ἡμῶν) or "your" (ὑμῶν), is the best supported reading? Why do some translations have "your joy" (NASB; Painter, 356), while others have "our joy" (KJV NRSV NIV NET NLT; Brown, 678). This is because some manuscripts support ἡμῶν (Sinaiticus and Byzantine), while others support ὑμῶν (Alexandrinus and Vaticanus). Modern translations, like the external evidence, are split over the original reading (the UBS Committee had a hard time deciding, giving it a C rating; Metzger[1], 720). Brown suggests that the original is ἡμῶν due to the parallel phrase in 1 John 1:4, "so that our joy may be complete" (Brown, 678). It seems likely that this is a reference to John and the readers of the letter. A face-to-face meeting would bring all of them great happiness.

¹³ Ἀσπάζεται: The Greek word ἀσπάζεται is third person singular present middle (= deponent) indicative from the verb ἀσπάζομαι meaning "to greet" or "to engage in hospitable recognition of another" (BDAG, s.v. "ἀσπάζομαι" 1a, p. 144). **Syntactically,** ἀσπάζεται serves as the main verb of the independent clause: "the children of your elect sister *greet* you" (ἀσπάζεταί σε τὰ τέκνα τῆς ἀδελφῆς σου τῆς ἐκλεκτῆς). The subject is "the children of your elect sister" (τὰ τέκνα τῆς ἀδελφῆς σου τῆς ἐκλεκτῆς). **Semantically,** ἀσπάζεται is an instantaneous present: "greet" (KJV NASB ESV NET CNT) or "send their greetings" (NIV NRSV). John is describing the greeting sent to the readers by his sister church.

Lexical Nugget: Who are "the children" (τὰ τέκνα) of the elect sister that are sending a greeting? Is it significant that the sister herself does not send greetings? We concluded in verse 1 that the "lady and her children" was most likely a reference to a local body of believers that existed at some distance from the author's home church. If this is true, then it is clear that the sister's children are indeed another local body of believers, perhaps John's own community of believers. This would explain why the children send their greetings but not the sister herself. John's church is sending a greeting to the recipients as well.

Third John[1]

Unlike 1 and 2 John, 3 John is a letter of commendation directed to an individual, Gaius.[2] The letter opens with Gaius receiving the elder's greeting, prayer, and applause for his living a life of love and kindness (vv. 1–4). The letter moves quickly from salutation to the elder's full disclosure for writing, which can be divided into three sections: the solicitation of all Christians to support God's vocational servants (vv. 5–8), the stubbornness of Diotrephes, who refuses to support God's vocationally called servants (vv. 9–10), and the request for sponsoring Demetrius, who is a good servant (vv. 11–12). The letter *concludes* with an expressed desire to speak with the church in person (vv. 14–15).

Big Greek Idea: In contrast to John's prayer, love, praise, and reasoned expectation of Gaius to support lavishly worthy preachers and teachers (like Demetrius), John sternly scorns Diotrephes's refusal to support God's servants.

---

1. For suggestions for how to outline and preach a sermon on 3 John, see Bateman[4] (2013), 209–47.
2. For commentators who consider 3 John to be a letter of commendation see Strecker, 253–54; Yarbrough, 363; Kim, 1972.

3 John 1–4

Big Greek Idea: In a typical first-century manner, John greets his beloved friend Gaius, which discloses both his prayer for and joy about Gaius's faithfulness in supporting God's servants.

Structural Overview: Following a typical first-century letter formula, John *greets* his beloved friend, Gaius. After John *greets* and expresses his love for Gaius (v. 1), he transitions (ἀγαπητέ) to his prayer (εὔχομαι) for Gaius. The *content* of the author's *prayer is that* Gaius might prosper and experience physical health (εὐοδοῦσθαι καὶ ὑγιαίνειν) that mirrors his spiritual health (v. 2). He then closes with an expression of joy (ἐχάρην) for Gaius. The *basis* for the elder's *joy* about Gaius *is founded* (γάρ) upon *reports* (μαρτυρούντων) about the manner in which Gaius is living for God (vv. 3–4). The big idea of these verses is simply this: John discloses both his *prayer* for and *joy* about Gaius's *faithfulness in supporting God's servants*.

Outline:

> John Greets Gaius (v. 1)
> John Prays for Gaius (v. 2)
> John Expresses His Joy for Gaius (vv. 3–4)

CLAUSAL OUTLINE FOR 3 JOHN 1–4

1a Ὁ πρεσβύτερος Γαΐῳ τῷ ἀγαπητῷ,
1a The Elder, to Gaius the beloved,

> |
> 1b **ὃν** ἐγὼ **ἀγαπῶ** ἐν ἀληθείᾳ.
> 1b **whom** **I love** in truth.

2a Ἀγαπητέ, περὶ πάντων **εὔχομαί** (σε εὐοδοῦσθαι καὶ ὑγιαίνειν),
2a Beloved, in all respects **I pray** (that you are prospering and that you are well),

> > |
> > 2b **καθὼς** **εὐοδοῦταί** σου ἡ ψυχή.
> > 2b **just as** your soul **is prospering**.

³ᵃ **ἐχάρην** γὰρ λίαν
³ᵃ <u>For</u> **I rejoiced** greatly

|

³ᵇ λίαν **ἐρχομένων** ἀδελφῶν καὶ **μαρτυρούντων** σου τῇ ἀληθείᾳ,
³ᵇ <u>when</u> the brothers **came** and **testified** to your truth,

³ᶜ **καθὼς** σὺ ἐν ἀληθείᾳ **περιπατεῖς**.
³ᶜ <u>namely</u>, <u>how</u> **you are walking** in truth

⁴ᵃ μειζοτέραν τούτων οὐκ **ἔχω** χαράν,
⁴ᵃ **I have** no greater joy than this,

|

⁴ᵇ **ἵνα ἀκούω** τὰ ἐμὰ τέκνα ἐν τῇ ἀληθείᾳ
περιπατοῦντα.
⁴ᵇ <u>namely</u> **that I hear** my children are *continually* walking in
the truth.

SYNTAX EXPLAINED FOR 3 JOHN 1–4

¹ᵃ ὁ πρεσβύτερος: The letter begins just like 2 John with a verbless opening salutation, "The elder, to Gaius the beloved" (ὁ πρεσβύτερος Γαΐῳ τῷ ἀγαπητῷ). Once again, the proper noun, "the elder" (ὁ πρεσβύτερος; BDAG s.v. πρεσβύτερος 2bβ, p. 862) functions as a nominative absolute and does not require a verb (cf. W, 49–51; Culy, 141). The use of the article, ὁ, points out that the πρεσβύτερος is a well-known person.

Lexical Nugget: Who is "the elder" (ὁ πρεσβύτερος)? Although little evidence exists that *demands* authorship to be by someone other than the apostle John, some suggest the author to be an unnamed elder, John the Elder, a group of church elders, or John and a second-generation redactor. Tradition, however, points to John, the apostle. Perhaps John adopted the designation of "elder" as a reference to his old age and leadership within the Christian community. Perhaps the term πρεσβύτερος is an alternative designation for the apostles. Peter refers to himself as a "fellow elder" (1 Peter 5:1) as well as "an apostle" (1 Peter 1:1). More convincingly, a statement by Papias as recorded by Eusebius may suggest that "apostle" and "elder" could be used interchangeably (*Hist. eccl.* 3.39). In the Gospel of John, however, there is a noticeable reticence to identify himself as the apostle John. He consistently refers to himself as "the apostle whom Jesus loved." Perhaps using the term "elder" instead of his name or title "apostle" was a sort of first-century humility. Regardless, original readers would have known his exact identity and credentials. While there may be some debate, we will refer to the author as "John."

1a ὅν: The Greek word ὅν is a masculine singular accusative from the relative pronoun ὅς meaning "whom" (BDAG, s.v. "ὅς" 1bα, p. 725). **Syntactically,** ὅν introduces a dependent relative clause: *"whom I love"* (ὅν ἐγὼ ἀγαπῶ). It is functioning adjectivally, modifying Gaius (Γαΐῳ), because it agrees in number (singular) and gender (masculine). The entire relative clause reveals personal information about Gaius.

ἀγαπῶ: The Greek word ἀγαπῶ is first person singular present active indicative from ἀγαπάω meaning "to love," generally "to have a warm regard for and interest in another person" (BDAG, s.v. "ἀγαπάω" 1aα, p. 5). **Syntactically,** ἀγαπῶ is the governing verb of the relative clause "whom *I love*" (ὅν ἐγὼ ἀγαπῶ). The presence of "I" (ἐγώ) gives emphasis to John's love for Gaius (Culy, 155). The accusative case of the relative pronoun ὅν determines the pronoun's grammatical function in the clause. It is the direct object of ἀγαπῶ. **Semantically,** ἀγαπῶ is a customary present: "I love" (KJV NASB ESV NIV NET etc.). It expresses John's sincere emotional regard for Gaius.

> **Lexical Nugget:** Who is Γαΐῳ, the recipient of the letter? Gaius is well-known to the author (vv. 1–2), he is a valuable ally in providing support for traveling Christian workers (vv. 3, 5–8), and he is apparently a friend to the author. Although the Apostolic Constitutions 7.46.9 (ca. 370 C.E.) states that John the apostle ordained a person by the name of Gaius as bishop of Pergamum, the connection with the Gaius of 3 John seems dubious. Furthermore, the commonality of the name makes it unlikely that he was associated with Paul (1 Cor. 1:14, Rom. 16:23; Acts 19:29; 20:4). So Gaius remains an unknown figure to interpreters of 3 John.

2a εὔχομαι: The Greek word εὔχομαι is first person singular present middle indicative from εὔχομαι meaning "to pray" or "to make a request of God" (BDAG, s.v. "εὔχομαι" 1, p. 417). The term occurs often in the context of speaking or making a request of God (i.e., Acts 26:29; 2 Cor. 13:7, 9). An alternative is "I wish" (KJV; BDAG, s.v. "εὔχομαί" 2, p. 417). **Syntactically,** εὔχομαι is the main verb of the independent clause: "Beloved, in all respects *I pray* that you are prospering and that you are well" (Ἀγαπητέ, περὶ πάντων εὔχομαί σε εὐοδοῦσθαι καὶ ὑγιαίνειν). The subject of the clause is "I," which is embedded in the verb εὔχομαι and refers to John. **Semantically,** εὔχομαι is a customary present or perhaps an iterative present: "I pray" (ASV NASB NRSV ESV NIV NET). John makes it a point to pray for Gaius on a regular basis, but not necessarily every time he prays (W, 521). Thus, John prays for Gaius quite often.

εὐοδοῦσθαι and ὑγιαίνειν: These two Greek words are present active infinitives: εὐοδοῦσθαι is a present middle infinitive from εὐοδόω meaning "to prosper" or having the sense that "things turn out well" (BDAG, s.v. "εὐοδόω," p. 410), and ὑγιαίνειν is a present active infinitive from ὑγιαίνω meaning "to be well" more specifically "to be in good physical health" (BDAG, s.v. "ὑγιαίνω" 1, p. 1023). **Syntactically,** the infinitives introduce an infinitival clause. They are substantival infinitives in that they function as the direct object of "he prays" (εὔχομαι). **Semantically,** they are infinitives of indirect discourse (W, 603–5; Culy, 157). In other words, the author shares the specific content of his prayer with Gaius, namely, that Gaius prospers financially (εὐοδοῦσθαι) and physically (ὑγιαίνειν). The entire infinitival clause is placed in parentheses to draw attention to the content of the author's prayer: that Gaius might continue to experience prosperity comparable to his spiritual well-being.

Semantical and Lexical Nugget: How should we translate the word εὔχομαί, which can be rendered as "I wish" (KJV) or "I pray" (NASB, NRSV, NIV, NET)? How we translate this word is important, because it has implications for how we understand the infinitives εὐοδοῦσθαι and ὑγιαίνειν. On the one hand, the term could simply be translated as "I wish." The word εὔχομαι was often used in first-century letters to convey the writer's general wish for the welfare of the recipient in a completely nonreligious sense (Brown, 730). If translated "wish" the infinitives would be complementary infinitives. On the other hand, εὔχομαι is also typical in New Testament letters (2 Cor. 13:7–9; Rom. 9:3; Acts 26:29), where the term expresses the writer's specific prayer to God on behalf of others. In this case, John would be praying for Gaius to prosper financially and physically, rather than merely wishing it to be true. In this case the infinitives provide the contents of John's prayer on behalf of Gaius.

²ᵇ καθώς: The Greek word καθώς is a conjunction meaning "as" or "just as" (BDAG, s.v. "καθώς" 1, p. 494). **Syntactically,** καθώς introduces the dependent conjunctive clause, "*just as* your soul is prospering" (καθὼς εὐοδοῦταί σου ἡ ψυχή). The entire clause is functioning adverbially modifying the infinitive, "are prospering" (εὐοδοῦσθαι). **Semantically,** καθώς is comparative: "just as" (NASB NRSV NET) or "even as" (KJV ASV NIV). John is asking God that Gaius's physical health might be reflective of his spiritual health.

εὐοδοῦται: The Greek word εὐοδοῦται is third person singular present middle/passive indicative from εὐοδόω meaning "to prosper" or "to turn out well" (BDAG, s.v. "εὐοδόω," p. 410). **Syntactically,** εὐοδοῦται is the main verb of the dependent καθώς clause. The subject of the clause is "soul" (ἡ ψυχή). **Semantically,** εὐοδοῦται is a customary present: "prospers" (NASB) or "goes well with" (ESV). It signals a continuous and ongoing state (W, 521). Thus, John appears to equate Gaius's physical health with the regular prosperity of his soul.

Lexical Nugget: What does ἡ ψυχή mean? The word appears ten times in the Gospel of John and twice in 1 John. Half of these occurrences refer to a person's "life," which could be laid down or sacrificed for someone or something else. In John 10:24 and 12:27, ἡ ψυχή is used to refer to the part of a person that experiences emotion. A person's ἡ ψυχή can be held in suspense or even deeply troubled. It refers to the immaterial part of a person as opposed to the material/ physical part. A close parallel is found in Philo, "Nourished with peace, he will depart having gained a calm, unclouded life . . . welfare in the body . . . welfare in the soul [ἡ ψυχή], health and strength . . . delight in virtues" (*Her.* 285). A modern equivalent might be "spiritual health" as opposed to "physical health." Thus the phrase "your soul prospers" (εὐοδοῦταί σου ἡ ψυχή) is most likely being used as a figure of speech called a metonymy where a noun is named by another noun closely associated with it. John is praying for Gaius's physical health and prosperity to match his "spiritual maturity" (εὐοδοῦταί σου ἡ ψυχή).

³ᵃ ἐχάρην: The Greek word ἐχάρην is first person singular aorist passive indicative from χαίρω meaning "to rejoice" or "to be in a state of happiness and well-being" (BDAG, s.v. "χαίρω" 1, p. 1075). **Syntactically,** ἐχάρην is the main verb of the independent clause: "for *I rejoiced* greatly" (ἐχάρην γὰρ λίαν). The subject of the clause is "I," which is embedded in the verb and is a reference to John. **Semantically,** ἐχάρην is a constative aorist: "I rejoiced" (KJV ASV ESV NET). It describes the act of rejoicing as a whole (W, 557). Thus John was very happy or glad concerning Gaius.

γάρ: The Greek word γάρ is a conjunction in the postpositive position meaning "for" or "you see" (BDAG, s.v. "γάρ" 2, p. 189). Syntacically, γάρ introduces an independent conjunctive clause. **Semantically,** γάρ is a marker of clarification: "for" (KJV ASV NASB ESV NET), even though some translations leave it untranslated (NRSV NIV NLT). John is clarifying or expressing his reasoning for his happiness that is more clearly articulated in the next clause.

³ᵇ ἐρχομένων and μαρτυρούντων: These two Greek words are genitive participles: ἐρχομένων is a genitive masculine plural present middle (deponent) participle from ἔρχομαι meaning "to come" or "to approach" (BDAG, s.v. "ἔρχομαι" 1αζ, p. 394), and μαρτυρούντων is a genitive masculine plural present active participle from μαρτυρέω meaning "to testify" or "to affirm a person in a supportive manner" (BDAG, s.v. "μαρτυρέω" 1αα, p. 618). **Syntactically,** ἐρχομένων and μαρτυρούντων introduce a dependent participial clause. Consequently, the ἐρχομένων and μαρτυρούντων clause is indented and placed under the verb "to rejoice" (ἐχάρην) in the independent clause. **Semantically,** ἐρχομένων and μαρτυρούντων are genitive absolute participles with a temporal force in that they answer the question, *when.* Nevertheless, the temporal nuance may convey a secondary notion indicating why. Thus, they may describe both *when* (primary notion) and *why* (secondary notion) John rejoiced (cf. W, 654–55; Culy, 157–58). Together ἐρχομένων and

μαρτυρούντων tell us that John was very happy when itinerant preachers returned to his church and told John about Gaius's support.

Lexical Nugget: Who are the "brothers" (ἀδελφῶν)? The term is often used in the New Testament to refer to Christian believers in general (esp. in Paul). In this context, it is being used to refer to a specific group of believers. The word "of the brothers" (ἀδελφῶν) refers to a group of traveling or itinerant Christian workers who have made their way to Gaius's church. This view is supported by the use of "send" (προπέμψας) and "on behalf of 'the Name'" (ὑπὲρ ... τοῦ ὀνόματος) in 3 John 6–7. This means that a majority of the instances of this word in 3 John (3, 5, 6, 7, 8, and possibly 12) reference a group of itinerant Christian workers who proclaim the message about Jesus.

3c καθώς: The Greek word καθώς is a conjunction meaning "namely, how" (BDAG, s.v. "καθώς" 3, p. 494). **Syntactically,** καθώς introduces a dependent conjunctive clause. The entire dependent clause, *"namely, how* you are walking in truth" (καθὼς σὺ ἐν ἀληθείᾳ περιπατεῖς) is functioning adverbially, The entire clause modifies the participle "testifying" (μαρτυρούντων). **Semantically,** καθώς generally indicates a comparison and therefore is translated "*as indeed* you do follow the truth" (NRSV ESV; Culy, 158) or "just as" (NET). However, when following verbs of saying like μαρτυρούντων ("testifying"), καθώς introduces indirect discourse and thereby expresses "how." Thus, καθώς may be translated "*namely, how* you walk in the truth" (NRSV; Acts 15:14; cf. BDAG, s.v. "καθώς" 5, p. 493), or "*that is, how* you walk in the truth" (NASB), or "as exemplified by the fact that" (Brown, 706).

περιπατεῖς: The Greek word περιπατεῖς is a second person singular present active indicative from περιπατέω meaning "to live" as it pertains to how a person conducts their life or more specifically how they behave (cf. 2 John 4, 6; BDAG, s.v. "περιπατέω" 2δ, p. 803). **Syntactically,** περιπατεῖς is the governing verb of the dependent καθώς clause. The subject of the καθώς clause is "you," which is embedded in the verb, περιπατεῖς. **Semantically,** περιπατεῖς is a customary present tense: "continue to walk" (NIV), "are walking" (NASB ESV), or "are living" (NET NLT). It indicates a pattern of behavior. John essentially speaks of the enjoyment he gets out of hearing of believers making it a practice to live according to God's expectations.

Lexical Nugget: What does ἀληθείᾳ mean? The phrase ἐν ἀληθείᾳ περιπατεῖς literally means, "walking in truth." The term appears twice in 3 John 3. In Johannine literature, the term can either refer to correct Christological belief (1 John 2:21–23; 4:2, 6; 5:10, 20; 2 John 7) or to ethical behavior (1 John 1:6; 2:4; 3:18–19; 4:20). Here the emphasis is on ethical behavior since the noun is used in conjunction with the verb "walk" (περιπατέω). This word is typically used metaphorically for a lifestyle throughout the New Testament (cf. 1 John 2:6). "Walking in truth" references behavior that is in accordance with God's desire and in close relationship with God (1 John 1:6). In this context, itinerant preachers commend Gaius for "living the truth," particularly his provision of hospitality on their behalf (v. 5).

4a ἔχω: The Greek word ἔχω is first person singular present active indicative from the verb ἔχω meaning, "to have" in the sense of one's inner emotion (BDAG, s.v. "ἔχω" 7aβ, p. 421). **Syntactically,** ἔχω is the main verb of the independent clause, "*I have* no greater joy than this" (μειζοτέραν τούτων οὐκ ἔχω χαράν). The subject of ἔχω is "I," which is embedded in the verb and refers to John. The direct object of ἔχω is "joy" (χαράν). **Semantically,** ἔχω would appear to be an iterative present: "I have" (KJV NASB etc.). John is elated *every time* he hears good reports about people supporting God's workers.

Syntactical Nugget: How should the demonstrative pronoun τούτων be interpreted? First of all, it is a genitive noun and is classified as a genitive of comparison because of the presence of the comparative adjective "greater" (μειζοτέραν). Determining the referent of the demonstrative pronoun is a bit more difficult. On the one hand, it could be anaphoric pointing back to the reports about Gaius and his spiritual life. If that is the case, then we would translate this phrase as "I have no greater joy than [hearing] *these things.*" On the other hand, it could be cataphoric pointing forward to the ἵνα clause (cf. John 15:13). In that case we would translate the phrase: "I have no greater joy than this, *namely,* that I hear that my children are walking in truth." Typically, when the demonstrative occurs it points forward to a following dependent clause (cf. 1 John 2:3; 3:16, 24; 4:9, 10, 13; 5:2). It seems likely that this is the case here. This means that the demonstrative is clarified by the following ἵνα clause.

4b ἵνα: The Greek word ἵνα is a conjunction meaning "that" as part of a fixed expression (BDAG, s.v. "ἵνα" 2e, p. 476). **Syntactically,** ἵνα identifies the clause as a conjunctive dependent clause: "*namely, that* I hear my children are continually walking in truth" (ἵνα ἀκούω τὰ ἐμὰ τέκνα ἐν τῇ ἀληθείᾳ περιπατοῦντα). The entire clause modifies "this" (τούτων) and is thereby substantival. **Semantically,** this substantival ἵνα clause is in apposition: "namely, that" or "namely, how" (NRSV). Many translations don't translate the demonstrative or the conjunction and move straight to the explanation: "than to hear" (ASV ESV NLT). Others readily agree that ἵνα is epexegetical to "these" (τούτων) (Brown, 706–7). Such occurrences of the demonstrative + conjunction are idiomatic within John's literature (cf. John 17:3; 1 John 3:11, 23; 4:21; 5:3; 2 John 6; W, 475). Culy does not distinguish between an appositional and epexegetical ἵνα. In his evaluations of ἵνα, they appear to be one and the same (Culy, 159). Nevertheless, the ἵνα clause is idiomatic within Johannine literature (W, 475) and rendered "namely, that."

ἀκούω: The Greek word ἀκούω is first person singular present active subjunctive from the verb ἀκούω meaning, "to hear" or "to receive news or information about" (BDAG, s.v. "ἀκούω" 3f, p. 38). The verb is in the subjunctive because verbs in ἵνα clauses are in the subjunctive mood. **Syntactically,** ἀκούω is the governing verb of the conjunctive dependent ἵνα clause. The assumed subject, "I," refers to John. **Semantically,** ἀκούω is an iterative present: "I hear" or "to hear" (KJV ASV etc.). John repeatedly hears of people providing for God's vocational works.

Τὰ . . . περιπατοῦντα: The Greek word τὰ . . . περιπατοῦντα is a neuter accusative plural present active participle from περιπατέω meaning literally "walking" but figuratively "behaving" or "conducting one's life" (BDAG, s.v. "περιπατέω" 2, p. 803; cf. 2 John 4). **Syntactically,** τὰ . . . περιπατοῦντα functions as a double accusative object complement construction (W, 182–89; Culy, 159). **Semantically,** it is a customary present indicating a habit or a pattern of behavior. Gaius regularly behaves in a manner that reveals correct behavior, particularly as it pertains to Gaius's support of God's vocationally called believers (vv. 3b, 5–7).

3 JOHN 5-8

The Big Greek Idea: While commending Gaius about his faithful support of God's servants, John exhorts him to lavish support upon God's workers because their livelihood depends upon God's people, and thereby the expectation is expanded to include all believers.

Structural Overview: John transitions (ἀγαπητέ) from his opening wholehearted approval for Gaius to a commendation, exhortation, and expectation of him. *The basis* (γάρ) for John's *commendation* (ποιεῖς) for Gaius *is founded* upon the *testimony* of itinerant preachers and teachers who recalled the support Gaius extended to them (vv. 5–6a). The *reason* Gaius is *exhorted* to support (ποιήσεις προπέμψας) Christian workers lavishly *is because* (γάρ) they have given their lives to God's service and accept (λαμβάνοντες) nothing from nonbelievers (vv. 6b–7). John's *intention* for *expecting* (ὀφείλομεν) all followers of Jesus to be in the habit of supporting lavishly itinerant preachers and teachers *is in order that* (ἵνα) everyone can become coworkers with Jesus (v. 8).

Outline:

> John Affirms Gaius for Supporting God's Workers (vv. 5–6a)
> John Exhorts Gaius to Continue Supporting God's Workers (vv. 6b–7)
> John Expects All Followers of Jesus to Support God's Workers (v. 8)

CLAUSAL OUTLINE FOR 3 JOHN 5–8

5a Ἀγαπητέ, πιστὸν **ποιεῖς**
5a Beloved, you *continually* **demonstrate** faithfulness
 |
5b **ὃ ἐὰν ἐργάσῃ** εἰς τοὺς ἀδελφοὺς καὶ τοῦτο ξένους,
5b **in whatever you do** for the brothers, and strangers at that,

6a **οἳ ἐμαρτύρησάν** σου τῇ ἀγάπῃ ἐνώπιον ἐκκλησίας,
6a **who have testified** to your love before the church,
 |
6b **οὓς** καλῶς **ποιήσεις προπέμψας** ἀξίως τοῦ θεοῦ·
6b **whom you will do well to send** *them* on their way in a manner worthy of God;
 |
7a ὑπὲρ γὰρ τοῦ ὀνόματος **ἐξῆλθον**
7a for **they have gone** forth on behalf of 'The Name' (= Jesus)

7b μηδὲν **λαμβάνοντες** ἀπὸ τῶν ἐθνικῶν.
7b *while* **accepting** nothing from the pagans.

8a ἡμεῖς **οὖν ὀφείλομεν ὑπολαμβάνειν** τοὺς τοιούτους,
8a **We**, therefore, **are obligated to support** such people,
 |
8b **ἵνα** συνεργοὶ **γινώμεθα** τῇ ἀληθείᾳ.
8b *so that* **we become** coworkers in cooperation with *the truth* (= Jesus).

Syntax Explained for 3 John 5–8

5a ποιεῖς: The Greek word ποιεῖς is a second person singular present active indicative from ποιέω that means "to do" or "to undertake or do something that brings about a condition" (BDAG, s.v. "ποιέω" 2e, p. 840). **Syntactically,** ποιεῖς is the main verb of the independent clause: "Beloved, you *continually demonstrate* faithfulness" (ἀγαπητέ, πιστὸν ποιεῖς). What is done is indicated with the adjective πιστόν, which is the direct object of ποιεῖς. **Semantically,** ποιεῖς is a customary present: "you *continually* do" or "you *continually* demonstrate" (cf. NET). It communicates a lifestyle of a consistent pattern of social behavior, namely, that of hospitality.

> **Lexical Nugget:** What does the phrase πιστὸν ποιεῖς mean? The translation of ποιεῖς is seemingly dependent on how πιστόν is understood. On the one hand, ποιεῖς could convey the idea of carrying out an obligation of a moral or social nature (BDAG, s.v. "ποιέω" 3b, p. 840). Thus Gaius acts faithfully. The elder could be saying that Gaius is "acting faithfully" (NASB; cf. KJV, NRSV). In this case, πιστόν is an adverbial accusative: "you act loyally" (BDAG, s.v. "πιστός" 1b, p. 821) or "you act faithfully" (Culy, 160). On the other hand, πιστόν could be a direct object of ποιεῖς: "you demonstrate fidelity" or "faithfulness" (BDAG, s.v. "ποιέω" 2e, p. 840; Brown, 708; see W, 179). Gaius "demonstrates faithfulness" (NET).

5b ὃ ἐάν: The Greek word ὅ is a neuter singular accusative from the relative pronoun ὅς joined with ἐάν (BDAG, s.v. "ὅς" 1jα, p. 727). The Greek word ἐάν is a conjunction that follows a relative pronoun (BDAG, s.v. "ἐάν" 3, p. 268) and is indefinite. **Syntactically,** ὃ ἐάν identifies the dependent clause as an indefinite relative clause "in whatever you do for the brothers, and strangers at that" (ὃ ἐὰν ἐργάσῃ εἰς τοὺς ἀδελφοὺς καὶ τοῦτο ξένους). The entire ὃ ἐάν clause modifies "faithfulness" (πιστόν; contra Culy, 160), and thereby refers to the faithful service Gaius offered. Apparently, there were a variety of things Gaius did and was doing for the itinerant preachers: "in whatever you do" (KJV ASV NRSV NET) or "in all your efforts" (ESV).

ἐργάσῃ: The Greek word ἐργάσῃ is a second person singular aorist middle (deponent) subjunctive from ἐργάζομαι meaning "to work" or in this case "to do a fine thing to someone" (BDAG, s.v. "ἐργάζομαι" 2a, p. 389). **Syntactically,** ἐργάσῃ is the controlling verb of the dependent ὃ ἐάν indefinite relative clause. It is in the subjunctive mood because ἐάν clauses take their verb in the subjunctive. **Semantically,** ἐργάσῃ is a constative aorist: "you do" (NRSV ESV NET) or "complexive aorist" (BDF §332). It speaks of a collection of activities and is regarded as a whole (W, 557–58). Gaius has done, is doing, and will do a number of things to support God's vocationally called servants.

Lexical Nugget: What does the phrase καὶ τοῦτο ξένους mean? The conclud-ing phrase καὶ τοῦτο ξένους (lit. "and this strangers") is an unusual expression. In fact, some witnesses read καὶ ξένους τοῦτο in an attempt to ease the diffi-culty of the phrase. However, the better reading, καὶ τοῦτο, may be translated as "and at that," "and especially," (NASB) or "even though they are" (NRSV NET NLT) (BDF §290 [5]; §442 [9]; cf. 1 Cor. 6:6). Thus, Gaius's faithfulness is elevat-ed because those whom he helped (and those in v. 3 as well) were strangers to him; he did not know them personally and yet he assisted them.

^{6a} οἵ: The Greek word οἵ is a masculine nominative plural from the relative pro-noun ὅς meaning, "who" (BDAG, s.v. "ὅς" 1a, p. 725). **Syntactically,** οἵ iden-tifies the clause as a relative dependent clause: "*who* have testified to your love before the church" (οἳ ἐμαρτύρησάν σου τῇ ἀγάπῃ ἐνώπιον ἐκκλησίας). Because οἵ agrees in number and gender with τοὺς ἀδελφούς, the entire clause modifies "the brothers" (τοὺς ἀδελφούς). Since οἵ is nominative, it is the subject of "they have testified" (ἐμαρτύρησαν).

ἐμαρτύρησαν: The Greek word ἐμαρτύρησαν is third person plural aorist ac-tive indicative from μαρτυρέω meaning "to testify" or "to confirm or attest to something based upon personal experience" (BDAG, s.v. "μαρτυρέω" 1aα, p. 618). **Syntactically,** ἐμαρτύρησαν is the governing verb of the relative clause. The entire relative clause is adjectival, modifying "faithfulness" (πιστόν). **Se-mantically,** ἐμαρτύρησαν is a consummative aorist: "have testified" (NASB NRSV NET) or "have told" (NIV NLT). The stress is on the cessation or the com-pletion of the testimony (W, 559–61). People have returned from Gaius's church and have given a report or testimony about Gaius and his support (cf. v. 3b).

Lexical Nugget: Which "church" (ἐκκλησίας) is John referring to in this clause? Where did these traveling preachers testify about Gaius's acts of love? The church could be the church where Gaius is, the church where John is, a different local church where the "brothers" are, or the universal church at large. It seems from context that the "brothers" or traveling preachers had moved on from Gaius's church and gave their report to a church in a different location. The most likely scenario is that these traveling missionary preachers eventually made their way to John's church and told him and his community about Gaius. Other scenarios are possible but many that some commentaries offer seem un-necessarily complicated.

^{6b} οὕς: The Greek word οὕς is a masculine plural accusative from the relative pronoun ὅς meaning "who, which, that" (BDAG, s.v. "ὅς" 1a, p. 725). **Syntac-tically,** οὕς identifies the clause as a dependent relative clause: "*whom* you will do well to send them on their way in a manner worthy of God" (οὓς καλῶς ποιήσεις προπέμψας ἀξίως τοῦ θεοῦ). Because οὕς agrees in number and

gender with τοὺς ἀδελφούς, the entire clause also modifies "the brothers" (τοὺς ἀδελφούς). However, οὕς is the direct object of "you will do well to send" (ποιήσεις προπέμψας) because οὕς is accusative. Thus the relative clause clarifies John's expectation of Gaius, which is evident in the next verb.

ποιήσεις: The Greek word ποιήσεις is a second person singular future active indicative from ποιέω meaning "to do," or "to make" but here it is more of a formula "do well if," "do well to," or simply "please" (BDAG, s.v. "ποιέω" 5d, p. 841). **Syntactically,** ποιήσεις is the main verb for the relative clause: "whom you will *do well to send* them on their way in a manner worthy of God" (οὓς καλῶς ποιήσεις προπέμψας ἀξίως τοῦ θεοῦ). **Semantically,** ποιήσεις is a predictive future: "you will do" (NASB NRSV ESV NET). John is assuming that another group of itinerant preachers will arrive at Gaius's home. Gaius is expected to send God's servants on their way.

προπέμψας: This Greek word προπέμψας is a nominative masculine singular aorist active participle from προπέμπω meaning "to send on one's way" or "to assist someone in making a journey and thereby supply food, money, arranging for companions, means of travel etc." (BDAG, s.v. "προπέμπω" 2, p. 873). **Syntactically,** προπέμψας is an adverbial complementary participle that helps complete the thought of verb ποιήσεις: "to send on their way" (NASB NRSV ESV NET). Lexically, προπέμψας is frequently used in the New Testament in the sense of providing Christian workers with supplies to enable them to continue their journey to the next stopping place (Acts 15:3; Rom. 15:24; 1 Cor. 16:6, 11; 2 Cor. 1:16; and Titus 3:13). Thus, προπέμψας is virtually a technical term for supporting Christian workers.

Grammatical and Semantical Nugget: Why do some translators render this dependent relative clause as an independent thought: "You will do well to send them on their way in a manner worthy of God" (KJV, NASB, NRSV, NIV, NET)? This is because the phrase "you will do well" (καλῶς ποιήσεις) is a mitigated exhortation. These types of exhortations are polite ways to give commands (Culy, xvii–xx, 161). Such words soften a command and make it more likely that the reader will respond. Brown identifies καλῶς ποιήσεις "as a standard way in Epistolary Format for introducing the request that embodies the whole purpose of the letter" (Brown, 710). If Brown is correct, then this clause is key to understanding the main purpose of John's letter. John wants to ensure proper treatment of traveling missionary pastors. He wants Gaius to continue to provide them with supplies for their journey (for similar uses of προπέμπω, see Acts 15:3; Rom. 15:24; 1 Cor. 16:6, 11; 2 Cor. 1:16; Titus 3:13). For this reason, many translations opt to render it as an independent thought. John *clarifies* further when he tells Gaius to provide for God's itinerant servants in a manner worthy of God.

7a γάρ: The Greek word γάρ is a conjunction in the postpositive position meaning "for" or "you see" (BDAG, s.v. "γάρ" 2, p. 189). **Syntactically,** the conjunction γάρ could be identifying the clause as a conjunctive dependent clause:
"for they have gone forth on behalf of 'The Name'" (ὑπὲρ γὰρ τοῦ ὀνόματος
ἐξῆλθον). It is adverbial, modifying "you will do well to send them" (ποιήσεις
προπέμψας; Culy, 161). **Semantically,** γάρ is explanatory: "for" (NASB NRSV
ESV NET NLT). John clarifies why Gaius is to send out itinerant preachers with
provisions in a manner worthy of God. John's reasoning is spelled out in the
rest of the γάρ clause and the subsequent participial clause.

ἐξῆλθον: The Greek word ἐξῆλθον is third person plural aorist active indicative from the verb ἐξέρχομαι meaning, "to depart" or "to discontinue an association" (BDAG, s.v. "ἐξέρχομαι" 1a⊃. 348, p. 348). **Syntactically,** ἐξῆλθον
is the governing verb of the conjunctive independent clause. The subject of
ἐξῆλθον is "they" assumed in the verb ἐξῆλθον and refers to itinerant preachers. The implied starting point was probably a sending church (cf. Acts 13:3).
Semantically, ἐξῆλθον is a consummative aorist, "*have* gone forth" (NET) or
"*have* gone out" (ESV). The stress is on their past activity and not merely describing the event as a whole (W, 559). John's clarification explains the reason
for providing for the needs of God's servants. They have gone out on behalf of
Jesus, who is the Christ.

Lexical Nugget: What does it mean to say that the missionaries "have gone out
on behalf of the name" (ἐξῆλθον ὑπὲρ γὰρ τοῦ ὀνόματος)? First, the verb
ἐξέρχομαι is used of Paul's missionary travels in Acts 14:20 and 15:40. So here,
too, it supports missionary activity. Second, "The Name" on behalf of which
these missionaries set out on their journey is a figure of speech called a metonymy of adjunct. This is when an attribute or adjunct of a subject "The Name"
appears rather than clearly stating the subject. So, what does this metonymy
reference? (1) It could be a reference to God (Ps. 124:8; Isa. 30:27). This would
make good sense here in 3 John 7. In the previous verse, John just instructed
Gaius to send the missionaries on their way "in a manner worthy of God." (2) It
could also be a reference to Jesus. A similar phrase occurs in 1 John 2:12, "Your
sins are forgiven on account of his [Jesus's] name" (NRSV). The Gospel of John
also makes references to believing in the "name of Jesus (1:12; 3:18; cf. Rom.
1:5). It seems in the New Testament the common usage for "name" is as a reference to Jesus, which is also likely the case here.

7b λαμβάνοντες: The Greek word λαμβάνοντες is nominative plural masculine
present active participle from λαμβάνω meaning "to take" or "to receive in the
sense that they take, receive, or accept payment" (BDAG, s.v. "λαμβάνω" 4, p.
584). **Syntactically,** λαμβάνοντες introduces a dependent participial clause:
"*while accepting* nothing from the pagans" (μηδὲν λαμβάνοντες ἀπὸ τῶν

ἐθνικῶν). The entire clause is adverbial, modifying the verb "they have gone forth" (ἐξῆλθον). **Semantically,** λαμβάνοντες is translated in the clausal outline above with temporal force: "while." But others render it as means or manner ("by accepting"; Culy, 161; Painter, 370). Attendant circumstance is another alternative because it coordinates with the finite verb, ἐξῆλθον (cf. W, 640–46). Brown argues that λαμβάνοντες serves to "confirm" the finite verb (Brown, 712; NLT) and is thereby translated as a finite verb, connected to the main verb by "and". It then provides a second reason why traveling Christian workers merit support. To avoid making a decision, most translations merely provide a generic translation (KJV NASB NRSV NIV NET). The translation above considers λαμβάνοντες to be an adverbial temporal participle of time. While these itinerant preachers move from place to place, they accept no help from nonbelievers.

> **Lexical Nugget:** Who are the ἐθνικόι? Although the word ἔθνος is used in the Gospel of John to describe the Jewish leaders as unbelievers (John 11:48, 50–52; 18:35), the similar word "pagan" or "Gentile" (ἐθνικοί) only occurs four times in the New Testament (3 John 7; Matt. 5:47; 6:7; 18:17). Here ἐθνικοί is being used as a synonym for the more common ἔθνος (used 162 times in the New Testament). John, then, is referring to unbelievers. John is not using the term strictly to refer to "Gentiles" or "non-Jews." It seems unlikely that John would forbid missionaries from receiving support from Gentile converts (cf. Paul's reception of support from Gentile converts in 1 Cor. 9:14; Phil. 4:10–18). John uses ἐθνικοί to refer to unbelievers that were both Gentile and Jewish. These traveling missionaries have been completely supported by followers of Jesus and have taken nothing from nonfollowers.

⁸ᵃ ἡμεῖς: The Greek word ἡμεῖς is a pronoun. The author's placement of ἡμεῖς gives emphasis to his expectation with the presence of "we" (ἡμεῖς) at the very beginning of the clause. John's use of ἡμεῖς is inclusive of all Christians (W, 321–23, 393–99).

οὖν: The Greek word οὖν is a conjunction in the postpositive position meaning "therefore" (BDAG, s.v. "οὖν" 1a, p. 736). **Syntactically,** οὖν identifies the clause as a conjunctive independent clause, "we, *therefore*, ought to support such people" (ἡμεῖς οὖν ὀφείλομεν ὑπολαμβάνειν τοὺς τοιούτους). **Semantically,** οὖν is an inferential conjunction that introduces the result or deduction for what was said previously: "therefore" (KJV NASB ESV NIV NET etc.). John is drawing a deduction, conclusion, or summary for verses 5–7 about the faithfulness of Gaius who provided abundantly for God's servants, even when he was unacquainted with them.

ὀφείλομεν: The Greek word ὀφείλομεν is first person plural present active indicative from ὀφείλω meaning "to be obligated" or "to be under obligation to meet certain social and moral expectations" (BDAG, s.v. "ὀφείλω" 2αβ, p. 743). Culy rightly avers, "this verb, which implies a degree of obligation, moves the level of urging closer to a direct command" (Culy, 30; cf. Brown, 713). Thus ὀφείλομεν carries with it the idea of a person's social or moral expectation. Believers are both socially and morally obligated to support God's vocationally called servants. **Syntactically,** ὀφείλομεν is the main verb of the clause but it is one of those verbs that needs another verb (e.g., an infinitive) to complete its thought (W, 598–99). **Semantically,** ὀφείλομεν is a customary present tense verb: "we are obligated" or "we must" or "we ought" (cf. KJV NASB ESV NIV NET etc.). While the word "ought" indicates the believer's obligation, the customary present indicates an ongoing action (W, 521). John underscores that all followers of Jesus have an ongoing obligation. That obligation is revealed in the infinitive (ὑπολαμβάνειν).

ὑπολαμβάνειν: The Greek word ὑπολαμβάνειν is a present active infinitive from ὑπολαμβάνω meaning "to lift up" or "to take someone under one's care, *receive as a guest, support*" (BDAG, s.v. "ὑπολαμβάνω" 2, p. 1038). **Syntactically,** ὑπολαμβάνειν is a complementary infinitive: "to support" (NASB NRSV ESV NET CNT). It is part of the main verb of the clause because it completes the thought of ὀφείλομεν (W, 598–99; Culy, 162). While the NIV renders ὀφείλομεν ὑπολαμβάνειν as "show hospitality," it is a rather poor rendering because hospitality of John's day differs greatly from the twenty-first century. **Semantically,** ὑπολαμβάνειν is a customary present infinitive that emphasizes a pattern of behavior: believers ought (ὀφείλομεν) to *make it a practice* to support or care for God's vocational servants, to take responsibility to provide for their physical needs.

Lexical Nugget: What did hospitality mean in John's culture? According to Delling, the idea of supporting someone is not limited to hospitality but extends to even protecting those who are persecuted (*TDNT* 4:15 s.v. "ὑπολαμβάνω"; cf. BDAG, s.v. "ὑπολαμβάνω" 1, p. 1038). This is a clear and substantial shift in John's letter that moves a directive from only Gaius to all those who claim to follow Jesus. All followers of Jesus are obligated or *expected* to offer various kinds of support to those whose vocation it is to proclaim Jesus, the Messiah. No pastor or missionary should be living in a state of poverty. They should be provided for in a manner worthy of God.

8b ἵνα: The Greek word ἵνα is a conjunction meaning "in order that" or "that" (BDAG, s.v. "ἵνα" 3, p. 477). **Syntactically,** ἵνα introduces a conjunctive dependent clause: "*so that* we become coworkers in cooperation with the truth" (ἵνα συνεργοὶ γινώμεθα τῇ ἀληθείᾳ). The entire clause is functioning adverbially and modifies the verb "hope" (ἐλπίζω). **Semantically,** the ἵνα is a purpose-result ἵνα providing both John's intention and result: "so that" (NIV NASB NRSV NET

NLT). "In many cases purpose and result cannot be clearly differentiated, and hence is used for the result that follows according to the purpose" (BDAG, s.v. "ἵνα" 3, p. 477; cf. W, 473). The ἵνα clause, then, reflects John's theology: what God purposes, happens. Thus, ἵνα is used to express both the divine purpose and the result (John 4:36; 12:36; 19:28; 1 John 1:9). God's divine purpose in supporting his servants has a result evident in the next verb.

γινώμεθα: The Greek word γινώμεθα is first person present middle (deponent) subjunctive from γίνομαι meaning "to become" or "to be" or "to experience a change in nature and so indicate entry into a new condition, to become something" whether that something be a fisher of people (Mark 1:17), children of God (John 1:12), or as used here in 3 John 8 a coworker with God's vocationally called (BDAG, s.v. "γίνομαι" 5a, p. 198). The verb is in the subjunctive mood because governing verbs in a ἵνα clause are always subjunctive. **Syntactically,** γινώμεθα is the main verb of the dependent ἵνα clause. **Semantically,** γινώμεθα is a gnomic present tense: "become" (NRSV NET) or "we may be" (ASV NASB ESV CNT). John reveals a timeless fact (W, 523). The moment someone supports God's vocational servants something happens: they join as coworkers with Jesus.

Syntactical and Lexical Nugget: How is τῇ ἀληθείᾳ to be interpreted? The dative could be classified in two different ways. On the one hand, it could be a dative of reference with τῇ ἀληθείᾳ serving as a complement to the noun "fellow workers" (συνεργοί) with an implied pronoun and translated as "fellow workers *with them* in the truth" or "partners *with them* for the truth" (NLT). In this case the truth would be the *true* message (Culy, 162). On the other hand, it could be classified as a dative of association and translated, "with the truth" (NASB NRSV NET). This is the preferred understanding taken in the clausal outline above. But what does John mean when he says, "coworkers . . . with the truth" (συνεργοὶ . . . τῇ ἀληθείᾳ)? Obviously, a believer cannot become a coworker (corresponding to the συν- prefix of the noun modified) with an abstract concept like "truth." In John's writings, "truth" is often personified as either a reference to God's Spirit or to Jesus. Truth is God's Spirit in John 8:32, "the truth will make you free" and in 1 John 4:6 "the Spirit of Truth," a characterization repeated in 1 John 5:6. (NET). So if the Spirit is what John means in 3 John 8b, then John teaches that when believers support the work of itinerant preachers, they become a coworker with the Spirit of God (Brown, 714). Yet in John 14:6, Jesus describes himself as "the truth." So if the "the truth" (τῇ ἀληθείᾳ) is Jesus, John teaches that support of itinerant workers results in becoming coworkers with Jesus. Context seems to favor Jesus due the previous understanding of "the name" (v. 7). Thus, John's theological understanding is that support of a traveling Christian worker results in becoming a coworker with Jesus. Either way the bottom line is simple. When communities support God's workers, they participate with God either by associating with his Spirit or his Messiah, Jesus.

3 John 9–10

Big Greek Idea: The basis for John's concern about a church leader is founded upon the rejection of John's authority, refusal to support God's workers, and the obstacles he creates to prevent others from helping itinerant preachers.

Structural Overview: John now shifts to an unpleasant incident and legitimate charge against a sister church leader, Diotrephes. The *basis* for John's concern *is founded* upon Diotrephes's rejection of a letter John had written and sent (Ἔγραψά . . . ἀλλ᾽ . . . ἐπιδέχεται) concerning the support of God's workers (v. 9). John's initial *basis* is compounded with charges (ὑπομνήσω) against Diotrephes for his slander (φλυαρῶν) of John, his refusal (ἐπιδέχεται) to support workers, his hindering (κωλύει) others who support workers, and his excommunication (ἐκβάλλει) of people who support God's workers (v. 10).

Outline:

> John Is Concerned about Believers Who Reject Him (v. 9)
> John Is Concerned about Believers Who Reject God's Workers (v. 10)

CLAUSAL OUTLINE FOR 3 JOHN 9–10

9a **Ἔγραψά** τι τῇ ἐκκλησίᾳ·
9a **I wrote** something to the church;

9b ἀλλ᾽ (ὁ φιλοπρωτεύων) αὐτῶν Διοτρέφης οὐκ **ἐπιδέχεται** ἡμᾶς.
9b **but** Diotrephes, (*namely*, the one who loves to be first) among them, **does** not **acknowledge** us.

10a διὰ τοῦτο, **ἐὰν ἔλθω,**
10a Therefore, **if I come,**

10b **ὑπομνήσω** αὐτοῦ τὰ ἔργα
10b **I will bring up** his deeds,

10c **ἃ ποιεῖ,**
10c **which he is** *continually* **doing,**

10d λόγοις πονηροῖς **φλυαρῶν** ἡμᾶς·
10d *by* **talking nonsense** about us with evil words (= slander);

^{10e} καὶ μὴ **ἀρκούμενος** ἐπὶ τούτοις

^{10e} and *because* **he is** not **content** with that (lit. "these things"),

^{10f} τούτοις οὔτε αὐτὸς **ἐπιδέχεται** τοὺς ἀδελφοὺς

^{10f} **he** himself *continually* **refuses** to welcome the traveling servants of God,

^{10g} καὶ τοὺς βουλομένους **κωλύει**

^{10g} and **he** *continually* **hinders** the people who want *to welcome these servants*

^{10h} καὶ ἐκ τῆς ἐκκλησίας **ἐκβάλλει.**

^{10h} and **he** *continually* **throws** them out of the church.

SYNTAX EXPLAINED FOR 3 JOHN 9–10

^{9a} Ἔγραψα: The Greek word ἔγραψα is first person singular aorist active indicative from γράφω meaning "to write" as the author's form of correspondence (BDAG, s.v. "γράφω" 2c, p. 207). **Syntactically,** ἔγραψα is the governing verb of the independent clause, "*I wrote* something to the church" (ἔγραψά τι τῇ ἐκκλησίᾳ). **Semantically,** ἔγραψα is a constative aorist: "I wrote" (KJV ASV NASB NIV NET NLT). It views the author's correspondence as a whole (e.g., the writing, the sending etc.; W, 562): So John recalls his former correspondence with Diotrephes.

> **Lexical Nugget:** Which church did John write to in 3 John 9? Is the church mentioned here in verse 9 (Diotrephes's church) the same church mentioned in verse 6 (John's church)? It seems safe to answer negatively. John mentions that he may visit this church of verse 9 in the future (v. 10), indicating that this is a different church than his. Also, it seems unlikely that Gaius belonged to Diotrephes's church because John uses a third person pronoun (αὐτῶν) to refer to the other members of the church (v. 9). If Gaius were indeed a member of that church, wouldn't John have used a second person pronoun instead? Furthermore, Gaius has been praised for his support of itinerant preachers with no repercussion (vv. 5–7). Therefore, there appear to be several churches involved: John's church (v. 6), Diotrephes's church (v. 9), and possibly Gaius's church (vv. 5–7).

^{9b} ἀλλ': The Greek word ἀλλά is a coordinating conjunction meaning "but" or "rather" (BDAG, s.v. "ἀλλά" 1a, p. 44). **Syntactically,** ἀλλά introduces a conjunctive independent clause, "*but* Diotrephes, (namely, the one who loves to be first) among them, does not acknowledge us" (ἀλλ' ὁ φιλοπρωτεύων αὐτῶν Διοτρέφης οὐκ ἐπιδέχεται ἡμᾶς). **Semantically,** ἀλλά is contrastive: "but" (KJV NASB ESV NIV NET etc.). Even though the apostle John has corresponded with Diotrephes, there's a problem evident and clearly noted in the rest of the clause.

ὁ φιλοπρωτεύων: The Greek word ὁ φιλοπρωτεύων is a nominative singular masculine active participle from φιλοπρωτεύω that conveys the idea to have a special interest in being in the leading position with a focus on controlling others and may be translated "wish to be first" or "like a leader" or "to have a special interest in being in the leading position" (BDAG, s.v. "φιλοπρωτεύω," p. 1058). **Syntactically,** ὁ φιλοπρωτεύων is a substantival participle. **Semantically,** ὁ φιλοπρωτεύων is in apposition to Diotrephes, "*namely,* the one who wishes to place himself first." Thus, the point is simply this: Diotrephes appears to be in a place of leadership and able to execute resistance against those who wish to support itinerant teachers and preachers (cf. NET). Perhaps he may have looked upon John's letter and its contents as interference in the church of which he was leader.

Lexical Nugget: What does φιλοπρωτεύων mean? The word is a *hapax legomenon*, but it appears in subsequent church literature. Contra Moulton and Milligan's definition, "I love the chief place," Brown suggests the elder may have coined the participle (ὁ φιλοπρωτεύων) to discredit Diotrephes (Brown, 717, 743). Others render the term as though it were a relative pronoun: "wish to be first" or "who loves to be first" (KJV NASB NRSV NIV NET NLT). Perhaps John desires to paint Diotrephes as an arrogant leader, one who was rising to prominence.

ἐπιδέχεται: The Greek word ἐπιδέχεται is third person singular present middle (= deponent) indicative from ἐπιδέχομαι meaning "to welcome" or "to acknowledge receptively" (BDAG, s.v. "ἐπιδέχομαι" 2, p. 370). **Syntactically,** ἐπιδέχεται is the main verb of the independent clause. **Semantically,** the negated οὐκ ἐπιδέχεται is a constative aorist: "does not acknowledge" (NRSV ESV NET). It views the action as a whole (W, 557). While some translations render ἐπιδέχεται as "welcome" (NIV; BDAG, s.v. "ἐπιδέχομαι" 1, p. 270) or "reception" (KJV ASV NASB), "does not acknowledge" seems to be a better contextual fit. It is not John's physical presence that Diotrephes is shunning, but his confrontation. Diotrephes refuses to accept John's authority and has chosen to ignore John's written correspondence.

καί: The Greek word καί is a conjunction meaning "and" (BDAG, s.v. "καί" 1, p. 494). **Syntactically,** καί introduces a dependent conjunctive clause: "*and* because he is not content with that (lit. "these things")." **Semantically,** καί is a coordinating connective: "and" providing additional information.

10a διὰ τοῦτο: The prepositional phrase διὰ τοῦτο is a frequent structural marker in John's writings that usually refers to what precedes (John 1:31; 6:65; 7:21–22; 9:23; 12:27; 13:11; 15:19; 16:15; 19:11; 1 John 4:5; 3 John 10; Brown, 391–92; BDAG, s.v. "οὗτος" 1aα, p. 740). **Syntactically,** διὰ τοῦτο introduces an independent prepositional clause. It is anaphoric, pointing back to opening comments about "Diotrephes" (Διοτρέφης) and his disregard for John and his authority. **Semantically,** διὰ τοῦτο is causal: "for this reason" (NASB), "therefore" (ASV NET), or "so" (NRSV ESV NIV CNT). It explains why John is about to do something. That something is found in the rest of the clause.

ἐάν: The Greek word ἐάν is a conjunction meaning "if" to denote what is expected to occur under certain circumstances (BDAG, s.v. "ἐάν" 1aß, p. 267; BDF §371). **Syntactically,** ἐάν identifies the clause as a dependent conjunctive clause: "*if* I come" (ἐὰν ἔλθω). The entire clause is functioning adverbially. It modifies the verb "I will bring up" (ὑπομνήσω) in the subsequent independent clause "I will bring up his deeds" (ὑπομνήσω αὐτοῦ τὰ ἔργα). The deeds are of an immoral character (cf. BDAG, s.v. "ἔργον" 1cß, p. 390). **Semantically,** ἐάν is a marker of condition: "if" (KJV ASV NASB NRSV ESV NET). It indicates the probability of an activity expressed (W, 696). In this case, John makes a statement about his probable visit to Gaius. Some English translations capture this sense with "when I come" (NIV GNT NLT).

ἔλθω: The Greek word ἔλθω is first person singular aorist active subjunctive from ἔρχομαι meaning "to come" or "to approach from the narrator's perspective" (BDAG, s.v. "ἔρχομαι" 1aα, p. 393). The verb is in the subjunctive because it is the verb of an ἐάν clause. **Syntactically,** "I come" (ἔλθω) is the governing verb for the dependent conditional clause. The assumed subject of ἔλθω, "I," refers to John. The combination of ἐάν with ἔλθω occurs in Paul's letters to the Corinthians (1 Cor. 14:6; 2 Cor. 9:4; 31:2) as well as in his letter to the Colossians (4:10) about an anticipated visit. Here, too, the combination of ἐάν with ἔλθω gives the impression that John anticipates (with some degree of certainty) a visit to Gaius (cf. Brown, 718). What John will do during his visit is clearly noted in the next independent clause.

10b ὑπομνήσω: The Greek word ὑπομνήσω is first person singular future active indicative from ὑπομιμνήσκω meaning "to call to mind" or "to bring up" (BDAG, s.v. "ὑπομιμνήσκω" 1bα, p. 1039). **Syntactically,** ὑπομνήσω is the main verb of the independent clause: "*I will bring up* what he is doing" (ὑπομνήσω αὐτοῦ τὰ ἔργα). **Semantically,** ὑπομνήσω is a predictive future: "I will bring up" (ESV) or "I will call attention to" (NASB NRSV NET). It articulates John's future action. John will confront Diotrephes's actions; he's not blowing smoke.

Lexical Nugget: What does ὑπομιμνήσκω mean? The verb may indicate positive (of Herod before the Roman Senate, Josephus *A.J.* 14.14.4) or negative (of Cretans in Herodotus *Hist.* 7.171; Wis 12:2; 2 Tim. 2:14) reports or confrontations. Here in 3 John 10, ὑπομνήσω is negative. John intends to expose Diotrephes's malicious acts publicly that may require disciplinary action (perhaps expulsion—certainly removal from leadership).

10c ἅ: The Greek word ἅ is accusative neuter plural from the relative pronoun ὅς meaning, "which" or "what" (BDAG, s.v. "ὅς" 1a, p. 725). **Syntactically,** ἅ introduces a dependent relative clause: *which he is continually doing* (ἅ ποιεῖ). The pronoun agrees in number (plural) and gender (neuter) with "the works" (τὰ ἔργα). Thus, the entire relative clause is adjectival to "the works" (τὰ ἔργα) in the independent clause. Grammatically, ἅ is in the accusative: "which" (KJV ASV NASB) or "what" (NRSV ESV NIV CNT). It indicates that ἅ is the direct object of "deeds" (ποιεῖ).

ποιεῖ: The Greek word ποιεῖ is third person singular present active indicative from ποιέω meaning, "to work" or "to be active" in some way (BDAG, s.v. "ποιέω" 3c, p. 840). **Syntactically,** "is doing" (ποιεῖ) is the controlling verb of the relative clause. **Semantically,** "is doing" (ποιεῖ) is a customary present indicating a pattern of behavior (W, 521). Structurally and lexically, the "deeds" (ποιεῖ) of Diotrephes are in contrast to the "deeds" (ποιεῖς) of Gaius (v. 5; cf. BDAG, s.v. "ποιέω" 3b, p. 840).

10d φλυαρῶν: The Greek word φλυαρῶν is a nominative singular masculine present active participle from φλυαρέω meaning "to indulge in utterance that makes no sense" or "to talk nonsense" or "to talk disparagingly about someone" (BDAG, s.v. "φλυαρέω," p. 1060). **Syntactically,** φλυαρῶν introduces a dependent participial clause: *by talking nonsense about us with evil words* (λόγοις πονηροῖς φλυαρῶν ἡμᾶς). The entire clause is functioning adverbially and modifies the verb ποιεῖ in the preceding relative clause. **Semantically,** φλυαρῶν is a participle of means: "by talking nonsense." John explains the means by which Diotrephes carries out his evil deeds. He does it with his disparaging comments about John.

Lexical Nugget: What does φλυαρέω mean? The word is a *hapax legomena*, and is generally translated as "talk nonsense (about)" or may speak of one who is "an idle babbler" or of one who "brings unjustified charges against" another. The noun occurs in 1 Timothy 5:13 and is translated "gossipy" or "foolish" (cf. MM, 673). Thus, John tells how it is that Diotrephes has rejected him: by talking nonsense or by gossiping about him. Apparently Diotrephes does so with hostility ("evil words," λόγοις πονηροῖς) or as Smalley translates it, "with a malicious tongue" (Smalley, 356) or "gossiping maliciously" (NIV). Thus, the relative clause can be translated "which he is doing, by talking nonsense about us maliciously," or perhaps "gossiping maliciously about us." However it is understood, this much can be said: his words are poison.

¹⁰ᵉ καί: The Greek word καί is a conjunction meaning "and" (BDAG, s.v. "καί" 1, p. 494). Syntactically, καί introduces a dependent conjunctive clause: "and because he is not content with that (lit. "these things")." Semantically, καί is a coordinating connective: "and" providing additional information.

ἀρκούμενος: The Greek word ἀρκούμενος is a nominative singular masculine present middle participle from ἀρκέω meaning "to be content" or "to be satisfied with something" (BDAG, s.v. "ἀρκέω" 2, p. 132). **Syntactically,** ἀρκούμενος introduces a dependent participial clause: "and *because he is not content* with that" (καὶ μὴ ἀρκούμενος ἐπὶ τούτοις). The entire clause is functioning adverbially. It modifies the verb "refuses" (ἐπιδέχεται) in the clause that follows. **Semantically,** the negated μὴ ἀρκούμενος is a causal: "because he is not content" (cf. KJV ASV NRSV ESV NET). More specifically, this causative middle (W, 423, 631) reveals that Diotrephes "can't get no satisfaction" from his rejection of John's authority and malevolent slander. His discontentment is reason for other dysfunctional behavior evident in the next three independent clauses.

¹⁰ᶠ ἐπιδέχεται: The Greek word ἐπιδέχεται is third person singular present middle indicative from ἐπιδέχομαι meaning "to welcome" or "to receive into one's presence in a friendly manner" (BDAG, s.v. "ἐπιδέχομαι" 1, p. 370). **Syntactically,** ἐπιδέχεται is the main verb of the independent clause: "he himself *refuses to welcome* the traveling servants of God" (τούτοις οὔτε αὐτὸς ἐπιδέχεται τοὺς ἀδελφούς). **Semantically,** ἐπιδέχεται is a customary present: "he continually he continually refuses," "refuses to welcome" (NRSV ESV NIV NET CNT cf. NLT). It views the action as a whole (W, 557). Diotrephes's lack of satisfaction with insubordination and slander is the reason for his own refusal to support itinerant preachers. But wait, there is more.

¹⁰ᵍ καί: The Greek word καί is a conjunction meaning "and" (BDAG, s.v. "καί" 1, p. 494). **Syntactically,** καί introduces an independent conjunctive clause: "*and* he hinders the people who want to welcome" (καὶ τοὺς βουλομένους κωλύει). **Semantically,** καί is a coordinating connective: "and" (KJV NASB ESV NIV NET etc.). John adds another dysfunctional behavior to Diotrephes's lack of satisfaction with insubordination, slander, and his own refusal to welcome missionaries, which is clearly evident in the next verb.

κωλύει: The Greek word κωλύει is third person singular present active indicative from κωλύω meaning "to hinder" or "to forbid" or "to keep something from happening" (BDAG, s.v. "κωλύω" 1a, p. 580). **Syntactically,** κωλύει is the main verb of the independent clause. The assumed subject of κωλύει, "he," refers to Diotrephes. **Semantically,** κωλύει is a customary present: "he continually hinders," "he hinders" (NET), "stops" (ESV NIV CNT), "forbids" (KJV ASV

NASB). It indicates a pattern of behavior, in this case an unbecoming pattern of behavior (W, 521). Diotrephes is preventing people from supporting God's vocationally called servants. So, Diotrephes's lack of satisfaction with insubordination, slander, his own refusal to support itinerant preachers, includes preventing others from supporting itinerant preachers. But wait, there is more.

[10h] καί: The Greek word καί is a conjunction meaning "and" (BDAG, s.v. "καί" 1, p. 494). **Syntactically,** καί introduces an independent conjunctive clause: "*and* he throws them out of the church" (καὶ ἐκ τῆς ἐκκλησίας ἐκβάλλει). **Semantically,** καί is a coordinating connective: "and" (KJV NASB ESV NIV NET etc.). John adds another dysfunctional behavior to Diotrephes's lack of satisfaction with insubordination, slander, his own refusal to welcome missionaries, and hindering of others. Diotrephes's additional dysfunction is clearly evident in the next verb.

ἐκβάλλει: The Greek word ἐκβάλλει is third person singular present active indicative from ἐκβάλλω meaning "to cast out." The term is a rather strong one for forcing, driving out, or compelling someone to leave (BDAG, s.v. "ἐκβάλλω" 1, p. 299). **Syntactically,** ἐκβάλλει serves as the main verb of the independent clause. The assumed subject of ἐκβάλλει, "he," once again refers to Diotrephes. **Semantically,** ἐκβάλλει is a customary present indicating another unbecoming pattern of behavior: "he continually throws them out" (NET) or "expels them" (NRSV). Diotrephes is forcefully expelling people who support God's servant.

Lexical Nugget: What does ἐκβάλλω mean? This term is typically used in cases of divorce ("nor to put her away," MM, 1050.15), in cases of the Essenes who expelled people from their community ("those who are convicted of serious crimes they *expel* from the order," Josephus, *B.J.* 2.8.8 §143), and in cases of expulsion from the synagogue (John 9:34–35). In 3 John 10, it seems that Diotrephes, as a leader in his local church, instigated the creation of a policy that forbade people from supporting traveling Christian workers and of expelling those who disobeyed his church policy. All three of these verbs in the latter part of verse 10 (ἐπιδέχεται, κωλύει, ἐκβάλλει) are customary present tense verbs. This indicates that Diotrephes had a pattern of behavior that John has deemed to be unacceptable.

3 John 11–12

Big Greek Idea: The basis for John's exhortation to imitate people who have a relationship with God, like Demetrius, is founded on Demetrius's relationship with God and his reputation with God's people.

Structural Overview: John shifts (ἀγαπητέ) attention from Diotrephes to one final expectation coupled with an endorsement. John exhorts (μιμοῦ) Gaius to imitate followers who are saved. He then contrasts two types of people, those who have a saving relationship with God (ὁ ἀγαθοποιῶν), and those who do not (ὁ κακοποιῶν). One person who knows God is Demetrius who is endorsed with having a good reputation (μεμαρτύρηται) from many people, including John and his church (μαρτυροῦμεν).

Outline:

> Followers of Jesus Are Expected to Imitate Other Believers (v. 11)
> Followers of Jesus Are Expected to Endorse Other Believers (v. 12)

CLAUSAL OUTLINE 3 JOHN 11–12

11a Ἀγαπητέ, μὴ **μιμοῦ** τὸ κακὸν ἀλλὰ τὸ ἀγαθόν.
11a Beloved, **do** not **imitate** that which is bad (behavior), but (imitate) that which is good.

11b ὁ ἀγαθοποιῶν ἐκ τοῦ θεοῦ **ἐστιν·**
11b The (one who does what is good) **is** of God;

11c ὁ κακοποιῶν οὐχ **ἑώρακεν** τὸν θεόν.
11c the one who does what is bad **has** not **seen** God.

12a Δημητρίῳ **μεμαρτύρηται** ὑπὸ πάντων καὶ ὑπὸ αὐτῆς τῆς ἀληθείας·
12a Demetrius **has been testified to** by all, even by the truth itself;

12b καὶ ἡμεῖς δὲ **μαρτυροῦμεν**,
12b and we also **testify** to him,

12c καὶ **οἶδας** (ὅτι ἡ μαρτυρία ἡμῶν ἀληθής ἐστιν).
12c and **you know** (that our testimony **is** true).

Syntax Explained for 3 John 11–12

^{11a} μιμοῦ: The Greek word μιμοῦ is second person singular present middle (deponent) imperative from μιμέομαι meaning "to use as a model," "to imitate," "to emulate," or "to follow" (BDAG, s.v. "μιμέομαι," p. 651). **Syntactically,** μιμοῦ is the main verb for the independent asyndeton clause: "Beloved, *do* not *imitate* that which is bad but that which is good" (ἀγαπητέ, μὴ μιμοῦ τὸ κακὸν ἀλλὰ τὸ ἀγαθόν). The subject, "you," is assumed in the imperative. **Semantically,** the negated μὴ μιμοῦ is a customary imperative of command: "do not imitate" (NASB NRSV ESV NIV NET) or "don't let this bad example influence you" (NLT). John expects Gaius and his community of followers to realize that Diotrephes's behavior is evil and should not be replicated.

> **Lexical Nugget:** What does John mean when he writes "Do not imitate the evil but the good" (τὸ κακὸν ἀλλὰ τὸ ἀγαθόν)? The brevity of this group of words is difficult to translate. A wooden word-for-word rendering is "the bad but the good." Thus, there are some interpretive liberties taken in order to make sense out of the author's point: "*that which is* bad but *that which is* good." There is the added challenge of determining to whom "*that which is* good" refers? On the one hand, "*that which is good*" may be a reference to the reputation or behavior of John. Thus, Gaius is called to choose between John and Diotrephes. On the other hand, "*that which is good*" could be a reference to the reputation or behavior of Demetrius. The latter seems to be true because of the chiastic structure of verses 11 and 12 (see Stylistic Nugget below) supporting the contrast (ἀλλά) between the bad behavior of Diotrephes and good of Demetrius (Brown, 720; NET). Thus, Gaius is expected to imitate the godly behavior of Demetrius.

^{11b} ἐστίν: The Greek word ἐστίν is third person singular present active indicative from the verb εἰμί meaning, "is" or "to be in close connection (with)" (BDAG, s.v. "εἰμί" 22b, p. 282). **Syntactically,** ἐστίν is the main verb for the independent asyndeton clause: "The one who does what is good *is* of God" (ὁ ἀγαθοποιῶν ἐκ τοῦ θεοῦ ἐστιν). The subject of the independent clause is the substantival participial phrase, "The one who does what is good" (ὁ ἀγαθοποιῶν). **Semantically,** ἐστίν is a gnomic present: "is" (KJV NASB ESV NIV NET etc.). John provides a matter-of-fact, proverbial-like statement about people who live good lives: what a person does or how he lives is equated with or evidence of their relationship with God. Assuming that the one who does what is good refers to Demetrius, John points to him as a good example to imitate.

^{11c} ἑώρακεν: The Greek word ἑώρακεν is third person singular perfect active indicative from ὁράω meaning "to perceive," in this case "to be mentally or spiritually perceptive" with a focus on the cognitive (cf. 1 John 3:6; BDAG, s.v. "ὁράω" 4b, p. 720). **Syntactically,** ἑώρακεν is the main verb for the asyn-

deton independent clause, "the one who does what is bad has not seen God" (ὁ κακοποιῶν οὐχ ἑώρακεν τὸν θεόν). The subject of ἑώρακεν is the substantival participle "the one who does what is bad" (ὁ κακοποιῶν). **Semantically,** ἑώρακεν is an extensive perfect: "*has* not seen" (NASB NIV etc.). It emphasizes a completed action from which a present state emerges (W, 577–78). John provides a matter-of-fact, proverbial-like statement about people who live bad lives: that person has not seen God (a past action), nor does that person have a relationship with God (a present state). Assuming that the one who does what is bad refers to Diotrephes, John identifies him to be mentally or spiritually blind and not an example to follow.

Syntactical Nugget: What is the significance of the repetitious use of "evil" and "good" in verse 11? Brown views the good/bad parallels in verse 11 as reflecting a chiastic Semitic literary pattern (Brown, 720). A chiasmus is generally recognized as a Semitic literary pattern A B B' A'. It is a form of parallelism in which there is the inversion of terms in the second half of the verse. In verse 11, the chiastic relationship is as follows:

A   μὴ μιμοῦ τὸ κακόν (11a)
  B   ἀλλὰ (μιμοῦ) τὸ ἀγαθόν (11b)
  B'   ὁ ἀγαθοποιῶν ἐκ τοῦ θεοῦ ἐστιν· (11c)
A'   ὁ κακοποιῶν οὐχ ἑώρακεν τὸν θεόν (11d)

The emphasis, then, is on 11b and 11c. The structure reiterates the common Johannine theme of behavior as an indication of genuine faith (cf. John 3:17–21; 1 John 2:6; 3:10; 4:7, 20). Thus the use of the phrase "has not seen God" calls into question the genuineness of a person's faith, perhaps Diotrephes's faith, because he has obviously done "what is bad" (vv. 9–10). Granted, John does not describe Diotrephes as an antichrist, a misguided person who has left the church, or a fraudulent teacher who denies that Jesus Christ has come in the flesh (cf. 1 John 2:18–23; 4:1–2; 2 John 7), but the genuineness of Diotrephes's faith is questioned because he does not and will not support God's itinerant preachers.

[12a] μεμαρτύρηται: The Greek word μεμαρτύρηται is third person, singular, perfect, passive, indicative from μαρτυρέω meaning "to testify" or "to affirm in a supportive manner" and thereby approve (BDAG, s.v. "μαρτυρέω" 2, p. 618). **Syntactically,** μεμαρτύρηται is the main verb for the independent asyndeton clause, "Demetrius has been testified to by all, even by the truth itself" (Δημητρίῳ μεμαρτύρηται ὑπὸ πάντων καὶ ὑπὸ αὐτῆς τῆς ἀληθείας). Although "Demetrius" (Δημητρίῳ) appears to be the subject in the above translation (cf. KJV NASB NIV), in actuality the assumed "it" in the verb is the actual subject. Thus "it is affirmed by everyone" (Culy, 166–67). Demetrius

(Δημητρίῳ) is a dative of reference. Thus a more literal rendering is "about Demetrius, it has been testified by all" or "Everyone has testified about Demetrius" (NRSV). **Semantically,** μεμαρτύρηται is an extensive perfect: "*has been* testified" (NET) or "has received" (NASB NRSV ESV CNT). It emphasizes the completed action of a past action from which a present state emerges (W, 577–78). Affirmations about Demetrius (a past action) confirm the current affirmation given by John. In essence, the testimonies about Demetrius are in concord: Demetrius is a good man in a good relationship with God.

Lexical Nugget: Who is "Demetrius" (Δημητρίῳ)? In the New Testament, there are two men by the name of Demetrius. One was a silversmith in Ephesus who led a demonstration against Paul (Acts 19:24, 38). The other is the one mentioned in 3 John. Demetrius may have been the leader of a delegation of traveling Christian workers and may even have been the bearer of this letter to Gaius and his congregation, supporting the view that this is a letter of recommendation. Letters of introduction are well attested in Pauline literature (1 Cor. 16:3; 2 Cor. 3:1; Col. 4:7–9; perhaps Rom. 16:1–2). While little is known about Demetrius, it is clear that John thought very highly of him.

12b καί ... δέ: The Greek word καί is a conjunction meaning "and also" (BDAG, s.v. "καί" 496.2iγ, p. 496). The Greek word δέ is also a conjunction in the postpositive position meaning "and" (BDAG, s.v. "δέ" 5b, p. 213). **Syntactically,** δέ introduces a conjunctive independent clause, "*and* we also testify to him" (καὶ ἡμεῖς δὲ μαρτυροῦμεν). **Semantically,** δέ are coordinating connectors that when taken together function as a marker of heightened emphasis: "and also" (KJV) or "also add" (ESV). The good testimony about Demetrius isn't just from nameless people: John and his church vouch for his goodness as well.

μαρτυροῦμεν: The Greek word μαρτυροῦμεν is first person, plural, present, active, indicative from μαρτυρέω meaning "to testify" or "to affirm in a supportive manner" and thereby approve (BDAG, s.v. "μαρτυρέω" 2a, p. 618). **Syntactically,** μαρτυροῦμεν is the main verb for the independent conjunctive clause. The subject of μαρτυροῦμεν is the pronoun ἡμεῖς. The presence of "we" (ἡμεῖς) is emphatic and shifts the emphasis from the testimony of the others to John's testimony (Culy, 167). **Semantically,** μαρτυροῦμεν is an instantaneous present: "we testify" (NRSV NET) or "speak well of" (NIV). It emphasizes John's current recommendation (W, 517–18). John provides Gaius with a rather strong recommendation on behalf of Demetrius.

12c καί: The Greek word καί is a conjunction meaning "and" (BDAG, s.v. "καί" 1, p. 494). **Syntactically,** καί introduces an independent conjunctive clause: "*and* you know (that our testimony is true)" (καὶ οἶδας ὅτι ἡ μαρτυρία ἡμῶν ἀληθής ἐστιν). **Semantically,** καί is a coordinating connective: "and" (BDAG, s.v. "καί" 1, p. 494). It introduces additional information about John and his associates, which is noted in the next verb.

οἶδας: The Greek word οἶδας is second person singular perfect active indicative from οἶδα meaning "to know" in this case "to have information about the author." The formula οἶδας plus ὅτι is frequently used in the New Testament to introduce a well-known fact (BDAG, s.v. "οἶδα" 1e, p. 693). **Syntactically,** οἶδας is the verb for the independent clause. The subject of the clause is "you" embedded in the verb, οἶδας and refers to Gaius. **Semantically,** οἶδας is a perfect with present force: "you know" (KJV NASB ESV NIV NET etc.). Some verbs like οἶδα always appear in the perfect tense without the perfect's aspectual significance (W, 579). Gaius knows John. What is known is specified in the ὅτι clause.

ὅτι: The Greek word ὅτι is a conjunction meaning "that" (BDAG, s.v. "ὅτι" 1a, p. 731). **Syntactically,** ὅτι introduces a dependent conjunctive clause: "*that* our testimony is true" (ὅτι ἡ μαρτυρία ἡμῶν ἀληθής ἐστιν). The entire clause functions as the direct object of the verb "you know" (οἶδας). The entire ὅτι clause is placed in parentheses to mark the clause's contribution to the independent clause. **Semantically,** ὅτι is an indirect discourse marker: "that" (KJV NASB ESV NIV NET etc.). It provides the content of what Gaius knows (W, 454–58). Gaius knows that John speaks the truth.

ἐστίν: The Greek word ἐστίν is third person singular present active indicative from the verb εἰμί meaning, "is" or "to be in close connection (with)" (BDAG, s.v. "εἰμί" 2b, p. 283). **Syntactically,** ἐστίν is the governing verb for the dependent ὅτι clause. **Semantically,** ἐστίν is an equative present: "is" (KJV NASB ESV NIV NET etc.). John's recommendation has a special connection with truth.

3 John 13–15

Big Greek Idea: John ends his letter with expressed unwillingness to discuss the issue of supporting itinerant preachers in writing, an expressed desire to visit Gaius and speak with him in person, and closing greetings.

Structural Overview: John closes his letter with an expressed desire to write more (εἶχον) but states he'd rather not (οὐ θέλω; v. 13). He'd rather (δέ) come to visit (ἐλπίζω ... ἰδεῖν) Gaius and (καί) speak with him in person (λαλήσομεν; v. 14). He ends with a statement of peace, greetings (ἀσπάζονταί) from others, and a request to greet (ἀσπάζου) others (v. 15).

Outline:

> John Desires to Write More (v. 13)
> John Desires to Visit (v. 14)
> John Closes His Letter with a Greeting (v. 15)

CLAUSAL OUTLINE FOR 3 JOHN 13–15

13a Πολλὰ **εἶχον** (γράψαι σοι),
13a **I had** many *more things* (to write to you),

13b ἀλλ᾽ οὐ **θέλω** διὰ μέλανος καὶ καλάμου σοι **γράφειν**·
13b but I do not **wish to write** *them out* to you by means of ink and pen;

14a **ἐλπίζω** δὲ εὐθέως σε **ἰδεῖν**,
14a Rather, **I hope to see** you immediately,

14b καὶ στόμα πρὸς στόμα **λαλήσομεν**.
14b and **we will speak** face-to-face.

15a εἰρήνη σοι.
15a Peace *be* to you.

15b **ἀσπάζονταί** σε οἱ φίλοι.
15b The friends [here] **greet** you.

15c **ἀσπάζου** τοὺς φίλους κατ᾽ ὄνομα.
15c **Greet** the friends [there] by name.

Syntax Explained for 3 John 13–15

^{13a} εἶχον: The Greek word εἶχον is first person singular imperfect active indicative from the verb ἔχω meaning, "to have" "to be in a position to do something" (BDAG, s.v. "ἔχω" 5, p. 421) or perhaps "to experience something" (BDAG, s.v. "ἔχω" 7aδ, p. 421). **Syntactically,** εἶχον is the main verb of the independent asyndeton clause, "*I had* many things (to write to you)" (πολλὰ εἶχον γράψαι σοι). The subject of the clause is "I," which is embedded in the verb, εἶχον. The direct object of the verb is "the many *more things*" (πολλά). **Semantically,** εἶχον is a progressive imperfect: "I had" (KJV ASV NASB ESV CNT). It describes John's actions as in progress at the time (W, 543). John was in the process of writing.

γράψαι: The Greek word γράψαι is an aorist active infinitive from the verb γράφω meaning, "to write" or "to express thought in writing" of written correspondence to someone (BDAG, s.v. "γράφω" 2c, p. 207). **Syntactically,** γράψαι is a substantival infinitive modifying "the many *more things*" (πολλά). **Semantically,** γράψαι is seemingly an epexegetical infinitive that clarifies, explains, or qualifies a noun or adjective (cf. 2 John 12a; W, 607). Culy suggests γράψαι is a complementary infinitive to εἶχον (Culy, 167; cf. BDAG, s.v. "ἔχω" 7aε, p. 421). However, in the clausal outline above we have placed parentheses around γράψαι σοι as a way to visualize the infinitive clause as substantive and thereby modifying "the many *more things*" (πολλά). Here in 3 John, γράψαι clarifies "the many *more things*" (πολλά). John wants to include more in his letter.

^{13b} ἀλλ᾽: The Greek word ἀλλά is a coordinating conjunction meaning "but" or "rather" (BDAG, s.v. "ἀλλά" 1a, p. 44). **Syntactically,** ἀλλά introduces an independent conjunctive clause: "*but* I do not wish to write it out to you by means of ink and pen" (ἀλλ᾽ οὐ θέλω διὰ μέλανος καὶ καλάμου σοι γράφειν). **Semantically,** ἀλλά is contrastive: "but" (KJV ASV etc.). It offers a distinct contrast. John has shared one desire. He's about to offer a different desire.

θέλω: The Greek word θέλω is first person singular present active indicative from the verb θέλω meaning "to wish," in this case to have a resolve about any further writing (BDAG, s.v. "θέλω" 2, p. 448). **Syntactically,** θέλω is the main verb of the independent conjunctive clause. The subject of the clause is "I," which is embedded in the verb and refers to John. **Semantically,** the negated οὐ θέλω is an instantaneous present: "I do not wish" (NET) or "I do not want" (NIV NLT CNT). It describes intentions at that present moment (W, 517). John at that present moment did not desire or want to write anymore,

γράφειν: The Greek word γράφειν is a present active infinitive from the verb γράφω meaning, "to write" or "to express thought in writing (BDAG, s.v. "γράφω" 2c, p. 207). **Syntactically,** γράφειν is a complementary infinitive completing the thought of what the author "wishes" (θέλω). **Semantically,** γράφειν is seemingly an instantaneous present like its helper verb θέλω (W, 517). John expresses his desire not to do something at that moment, in this case, to write more to Gaius.

> **Lexical and Syntactical Nugget:** What does μέλανος mean, and how should we interpret the phrase "I do not wish to write it out to you 'by means of ink and pen'" (διὰ μέλανος καὶ καλάμου)? The word μέλανος can be used in different ways. (1) Its most basic use is simply as an adjective, "black." It describes clothing used in mourning (Rev. 6:12) and the color of an eschatological horse (Rev. 6:5). (2) In the Apostolic Fathers, the term is used as a figure of speech to describe the Devil (Barn. 4.9; 20.1). (3) It is also used to describe black beans and black olives (MM, 395). (4) In the neuter, it often refers to ink. Paul writes to the Corinthians that they are a living letter, not a letter written in ink (3:3). In 2 John 12, it is a reference to "ink." Due to its similarity to 2 John, "by means of ink and pen" (διὰ μέλανος καὶ καλάμου), it seems to be just a common way to close Hellenistic letters (Painter, 356). So John is merely saying that he has nothing more that he desires to write. He considers it prudent to wait and speak with Gaius "face-to-face" or in person (στόμα πρὸς στόμα; lit. "mouth-to-mouth"). The phrase οὐ θέλω διὰ μέλανος καὶ καλάμου σοι γράφειν parallels 2 John 12, where it is a bit more elegantly stated (Brown, 725).

¹⁴ᵃ ἐλπίζω: The Greek word ἐλπίζω is first person singular present active indicative from the verb ἐλπίζω meaning, "to hope" or "to look forward to something" (BDAG, s.v. "ἐλπίζω" 2, p. 319). **Syntactically,** ἐλπίζω is the main verb of the independent conjunctive clause: "rather, *I hope* to see you immediately" (ἐλπίζω δὲ εὐθέως σε ἰδεῖν). The subject of the clause is the embedded "I" in ἐλπίζω that refers to John. **Semantically,** ἐλπίζω is an instantaneous present: "I hope" (NASB NRSV ESV NIV NET NLT). John is describing his current expectation. Thus the point is simply this: the elder currently expects to visit Gaius soon.

δέ: The Greek word δέ is a conjunction meaning "but" or "rather" (BDAG, s.v. "δέ" 4a, p. 44). **Syntactically,** δέ is in the postpositive position that identifies the clause as an independent conjunctive clause. **Semantically,** δέ is a contrastive coordinating connector: "but" (KJV ASV NASB NET) or "instead" (NRSV). Some translations leave δέ untranslated (ESV NIV), while one seems to classify it as explanatory, "for" (NLT). It seems, however, that John has another aspiration evident in the next verb.

ἰδεῖν: The Greek word ἰδεῖν is an aorist active infinitive from ὁράω meaning "to see" in the sense of making a friendly call or visit (cf. Heb. 13:23; BDAG, s.v. "ὁράω" A2, p. 719). This second aorist verb is spelled ἰδεῖν without the augment because it originally came from a different verbal root. **Syntactically,** ἰδεῖν is part of the main verb of the clause, completing the thought of "hope" (ἐλπίζω). Thus it is a complementary infinitive. **Semantically,** ἰδεῖν is an instantaneous aorist with the same force as ἐλπίζω: "to visit" or "to see" (ASV NASB NRSV ESV NIV NET NLT CNT), thereby emphasizing the elder's current expectation to visit Gaius soon.

Lexical Nugget: What does ἐλπίζω mean? There are two main meanings for this term. On the one hand, ἐλπίζω can refer to hope as a virtue, especially when used to describe a certain confidence in something, such as in God, Jesus, or in eternal life. For example, in the Epistle of Barnabas 1.3, the author rejoices in his certain *expectation* of salvation (cf. 1 Thess. 5:8). In a similar way, it can also be used to describe the object in which one puts one's hope: the temple (Barn. 16.1), God (1 Peter 3:5; 1 Tim. 4:10; 5:5; 6:17), or the root of Jesse (Rom. 15:12). Or, it can indicate what one expects to receive in the future: eternal life (Titus 1:2), grace (1 Peter 1:13), or deliverance (2 Cor. 1:10). On the other hand, ἐλπίζω can speak of hope more generally in the sense of wishful thinking. For instance, Herod *hoped* to see Jesus perform a miracle (Luke 23:8). The wicked rich person may give (deceptive) *hope* to the poor (Sir 13:6). Here in 3 John 14, John uses the term in the second sense as expressing a wish or a desire to visit Gaius if he is able (cf. Rom. 15:24; 1 Cor. 16:7; Phil. 2:19, 23; 2 John 12).

14b καί: The Greek word καί is a conjunction meaning "and" (BDAG, s.v. "καί" 1, p. 494). **Syntactically,** καί introduces an independent conjunctive clause: "*and* we will speak face-to-face" (καὶ στόμα πρὸς στόμα λαλήσομεν). **Semantically,** καί is a coordinating connective "and" (KJV NASB ESV NIV NET etc.). It provides additional information about John's impending visit with Gaius. That additional information is evident in the next verb.

λαλήσομεν: The Greek word λαλήσομεν is first person plural future active indicative from the verb λαλέω meaning, "to speak" in the sense of uttering words or "to talk with personally" (BDAG, s.v. "λαλέω" 2aγ, p. 582). **Syntactically,** λαλέω is the main verb of the independent conjunctive clause. The subject of the clause is an embedded "we" in the verb and refers to John and Gaius. **Semantically,** λαλέω is a predictive future: "we will speak" (KJV NASB NET) or "we will talk" (NRSV ESV NIV NLT CNT). It describes John's intentions to visit and talk with Gaius soon. It is on his "to-do list."

Lexical Nugget: What does στόμα πρὸς στόμα mean? The Greek phrase στόμα πρὸς στόμα is idiomatic. Literally, the phrase means "mouth-to-mouth," but a translation of "face-to-face" (KJV NASB ESV NIV NET etc.)

makes more sense in English. (See also 2 John 12 and 1 Cor. 13:12; Num. 12:8 [LXX] Brown, 678.)

¹⁵ᵃ εἰρήνη σοι: The Greek word εἰρήνη is a nominative absolute that expresses a state of well-being or peace like the Hebrew word *shalom* (cf. 2 John 3; Jude 2; BDAG, s.v. "εἰρήνη" 2a, p. 288). In Paul's letters, it is characteristically used with "grace" (Rom. 1:7; 1 Cor. 1:3; 2 Cor. 1:2; Gal. 1:3; Eph. 1:2; Phil. 1:2; Col. 1:2; 1 Thess. 1:1; 2 Thess. 1:2; Titus 1:4; Philem. 3). It is also fairly frequent in the conclusions of early Christian letters (Gal. 6:16; Eph. 6:23; 2 Thess. 3:16; 1 Peter 5:14; Ignatius, *Smyrn.* 12.2). John extends a typical cultural greeting of well-being to Gaius: "peace to you" (NIV) or "peace *be* to you" (NASB ESV).

¹⁵ᵇ ἀσπάζονται: The Greek word ἀσπάζονται is third person singular present middle (deponent) indicative from the verb ἀσπάζομαι meaning, "to greet" or "to welcome" in the hospitable recognition of another person or persons (BDAG, s.v. "ἀσπάζομαι" 1a, p. 144). **Syntactically,** ἀσπάζονται is the main verb of the independent asyndeton clause: "the friends [here] greet you" (ἀσπάζονταί σε οἱ φίλοι). The subject is those members of a sister church, who are currently with the elder (οἱ φίλοι). **Semantically,** ἀσπάζονται is an instantaneous present: "greet" (ESV NIV etc.). John is sending a greeting to Gaius and the readers from members of a sister church.

Lexical Nugget: Who are οἱ φίλοι? On the one hand, οἱ φίλοι may indicate that these are personal friends of Gaius. But if this is the case it is somewhat surprising that their names are not mentioned. On the other hand, οἱ φίλοι may be an alternative to ἀδελφοί, especially within the Johannine community. It may have arisen in the Johannine community from Jesus's teaching in the Gospel of John 15:13–15, "you are my friends if you do what I command you" (Brown, 726; cf. Culy, 168). If true, then the articles that accompany φίλοι (οἱ φίλοι and τοὺς φίλους) are perhaps individualizing articles that highlight a strong personal bond between the author's church and Gaius due to the support he and his church have extended to God's servants (cf. W, 216–31)

¹⁵ᶜ ἀσπάζου: The Greek word ἀσπάζου is a second person singular middle (deponent) imperative from ἀσπάζομαι meaning "to greet" or "to welcome" in the hospitable recognition of another person (BDAG, s.v. "ἀσπάζομαι" 1a, p. 144). **Syntactically,** ἀσπάζου is the main verb of the independent asyndeton clause: "Greet the friends [there] by name" (ἀσπάζου τοὺς φίλους κατ᾽ ὄνομα). The subject assumed in the verb is "you": "you greet." **Semantically,** ἀσπάζου is seemingly a command from a superior (ὁ πρεσβύτερος) to an inferior (Γαΐῳ; cf. W, 485–86). John expects Gaius to extend to his church a hospitable greeting from him and his church.

First John: Interpretive Translation[1]

Eyewitness Testimony

1: [1]That which was from the beginning, which we have heard, which we have seen with our eyes, which we have looked at, and which our hands have touched about Jesus, which is life—[2]for the life was revealed, and we have seen, and we now testify and we now proclaim to you eternal life, which was with the Father and was revealed to us—[3]that which we have seen and heard we now proclaim to you also in order that even you may have fellowship with us. And indeed our fellowship is with the Father and with his Son, Jesus, who is the Christ. [4]Therefore we are writing these things in order that our joy may be complete.

The Gospel Lifestyle

[5]Now this is the gospel message, which we have heard from Jesus and which we now proclaim to you, namely, that God is light and that in him there is no darkness at all. [6]If we say, "We have fellowship with God"[2] yet if we persist on living in the darkness, we lie and we are not practicing the truth; [7] but if we make it a point to live in the light as God is in the light, we have fellowship with one another and the blood of Jesus, his Son, cleanses us from all sins.

[8]If we say, "We have no sin", we deceive ourselves and the truth is not in us. [9]But if we confess our sins, God is faithful and righteous to pardon our sins and to declare us purified from all unrighteousness. [10]If we say "We have not sinned," we make God a liar and his word is not in us.

2: [1]My children, I now write these things to you in order that you may not sin. But if anyone does sin, we have an advocate with the Father, Jesus who is the Christ, the righteous one; and he himself is the atoning sacrifice for our sins, and he is the atoning sacrifice not only for our sins, but also, he is the atoning sacrifice for the whole world.

[3]Now by this we know that we have known God, if we persist in keeping his commandments. [4]The one who says, "I know God," but does not persist in keeping his commands, is a liar, and the truth is not in this person; [5]but whoever persists in keeping God's word, truly, in this person, love for God has been perfected. By

---

1. While all English translations of scripture are interpretive, the following translations for John's letters are no exception and each letter will evidence our interpretations.
2. Wherever "he" or "him" appears in the clausal outline that is a reference to "God," the pronouns are rendered "God" throughout this translation.

this, we know that we are in God; [6]the one who says that God abides in them is obligated also to persist in living just as Jesus lived.

COMMAND TO LOVE

[7]Beloved, I write no new commandment to you, but I now write an old commandment, which you have had as an obligation from the beginning; the old commandment is the word, which you have heard, which is true in Jesus[3] and in you. [8]On the other hand, I now write to you a new commandment because the darkness is passing away right now and true light is already shining. [9]Those who claim to be in the light and yet persist in hating because their[4] brother and sister are still in the darkness until now. [10] In contrast, the one who persists in loving his brother and sister abides in the light, and in that person, there is no cause for stumbling. [11]But those who persist in hating their brother and sister are in the darkness and so they are walking in the darkness and they do not know where they are going because the darkness has blinded their eyes.

ASSURANCES GIVEN

[12] I now write to you, children, that for your benefit your sins have been pardoned because of Jesus's name. [13]I now write to you, fathers, that you have known him who is from the beginning. I now write to you, young people, that you have overcome the Evil One. [14]I have written to you, children, that you have known the Father. I have written to you, fathers, that you have known the Father from the beginning. I have written to you, young people, that you are strong, and that the word of God abides in you, and that you have conquered the Evil One.

WARNINGS ABOUT THE WORLD

[15]Do not love the world nor the things in the world. If anyone persists in loving the world, the love of the Father is not in them; [16]for this reason all that is in the world, the flesh that desires and the eyes that desire and the boastful pride about one's life, is not from God, but all that is in the world is from the world. [17]And the world is now passing away, and also its lusts, but the one who does the will of God remains forever.

END-TIME SIGNS

[18]Children, it is the last hour, and as you heard that the Antichrist is coming, even now many antichrists have appeared; whereby we now know that it is the

---

3.   Wherever "he" or "him" appears in the clausal outline that is a reference to "Jesus," those pronouns are rendered "Jesus" throughout this translation.

4.   Wherever "he (or she)," "his (or her)," "him (or her)," "himself (or herself)" appears in the clausal outline, the translation provides the more generic rendering "their," "they," "them," "themselves," etc.

last hour. [19]They went out from us, but they were not of us; for you see if they had been of us, they would have remained with us; but they did go out, so that it would be shown that they all are not of us. [20]But you have an anointing from the Holy One, and you know all things. [21]I have not written to you because you do not know the truth, but rather I have written to you because you know it, and because you know that no lie is of the truth. [22]Who is the liar except the one who persists in denying that Jesus is the Christ; this is the Antichrist, namely, the one who persists in denying the Father and the Son. [23]Everyone who persists in denying the Son does not have the Father; the one who persists in their confession of the Son has the Father also.

GOD'S PROMISE

[24]Let what you yourselves have heard from the beginning remain in you; if what you have heard from the beginning remains in you, you also will remain in Jesus the Son and in God the Father. [25]Now this is the promise that God himself made to us: eternal life. [26]I have written these things to you concerning those who persist in their attempt to mislead you.

GOD'S ANOINTING

[27]Now as for you, the anointing that you have received from God remains continually in you. And you have no need that anyone teach you; but now the anointing is true and it is not a lie, as God's anointing continually teaches you about all things—and just as his Spirit has taught you, make it a practice to remain in Jesus. [28]Even now, children, make it a practice to remain in Jesus, so that we may have confidence when Jesus appears and so that we may not shrink away from Jesus at his coming. [29]If you know that Jesus is righteous, you also know that everyone who practices righteousness has been fathered by God.

IDENTITY AFFIRMED

3: [1]Consider what sort of love the Father has granted to us that we should be called children of God; and so we really are called children of God. For this reason, the world does not know us: the world did not know Jesus. Beloved, we are God's children, [2]and what we will be, whenever Jesus comes, has not been revealed. We know that we will be like Jesus when he appears, because we will see Jesus as he is. [3]And so everyone who has this hope in them purifies themselves even as Jesus is pure. [4]Everyone who practices sin also practices lawlessness, indeed sin is lawlessness. [5]And you know that Jesus appeared in order to take away sin, and you know that in Jesus there is no sin. [6]Everyone who makes it a practice to abide in Jesus does not persist in sin; everyone who makes it a practice to sin has neither seen Jesus nor known Jesus.

DIRECTIONS TO LOVE

[7]Children, let no one mislead you; the one who practices righteousness is righteous, even as Jesus is righteous; [8]the one who practices sin comes from the Devil, because the Devil persists in sinning from the very beginning. For this purpose the Son of God appeared, namely, that he might destroy the works of the Devil. [9]Everyone who has been fathered by God does not practice sin, because God's seed remains in him; and he is not able to persist in sin, because he has been fathered by God. [10]By this the children of God and the children of the Devil are made clear; everyone who does not practice righteousness is not of God, that is the one who does not persist in loving his brother and sister.

THE GOSPEL LIFESTYLE

[11]For this is the gospel message that you heard from the beginning, namely, that we should love one another; [12]not as Cain who was of the Evil One [12]and who brutally murdered his brother, Abel; and for what reason did he brutally murder Abel? because Cain's deeds were evil, but Abel's deeds were righteous. [13]And so, do not be surprised, brothers and sisters, that the world persists in hating you. [14]We know that we have passed out of death into life, because we persistently love our brothers and sisters. The one who does not persist in love abides in death. [15]Everyone who persists in hating his brother and sister is a murderer, and you know that no murderer possesses eternal life abiding in him or her. [16]By this we know love, that Jesus gave up his life for us; and that we are obligated to give up our lives for our brothers and sisters. [17]But whoever possesses the resources of the world and whoever perceives his brother or sister with a need and whoever shuts off their heart against them, how does the love of God remain in those who claim to follow Jesus? [18]Little children, let us not love with word or with tongue, but let us love in deed and truth.

ASSURANCE CONFIRMED

[19]And so by this we will know that we are of the truth, and that we will convince our heart before God [20]that whenever our heart condemns us, that God is greater than our heart and that he knows all things. [21]Beloved, if our heart does not condemn us, we feel confident before God, [22]and so whatever we ask for we will receive from God, because we persist in keeping his commandments and because we persist in doing the things that are pleasing in his sight. [23]And this is God's commandment, namely, that we believe in the name of his Son Jesus, who is the Christ and that we persist in loving one another, just as Jesus gave God's commandment to us. [24]And the one who persists in keeping God's commandments abides with God and God abides with followers of Jesus; and by this we know that God abides in us, by the Spirit whom he has given us.

DISCERNMENT EXPECTED

4: [1]Beloved, do not believe every spirit, but test every spirit to determine whether they are from God, because many false prophets have gone out into the world. [2]By this you know the Spirit of God; every spirit, who repeatedly acknowledges Jesus to be the Christ who has come in flesh, is from God, [3]but every spirit, who does not repeatedly claim Jesus has come in the flesh, is not from God; and this is the spirit of the Antichrist, about which you have heard that it is coming, and which is now in the world already. [4]You yourselves are from God, little children, and you have overcome these antichrists, because the Spirit of God who is in you is greater than the spirit of the Antichrist who is in the world. [5]These antichrists are from the world; therefore they speak regularly from the world's perspective and the world listens regularly to them. [6]We are from God; the person who knows God listens to us, whoever is not from God does not listen to us. From this we know the spirit of truth and the spirit of deceit.

MUTUAL LOVE EXPECTED

[7]Beloved, let us persist in love for one another, because love is from God, and because everyone who loves has been fathered by God and everyone who loves knows God. [8]The person who does not love does not know God, because God is love. [9]By this the love of God was made known among us, that God sent his one and only Son into the world in order that we may live through Jesus. [10]By this is love, not that we loved God, but that he loved us and that he sent his Son to be the atoning sacrifice for our sins.

OBLIGATIONS TO LOVE

[11]Beloved, if God so loved us, then we ourselves are obligated to love one another. [12]No one has seen God at any time; if we persist in loving one another, God abides in us, and his love is perfected in us. [13]By this we know that we remain in God and he remains in us, that God has given us a portion of his Spirit. [14]And we have seen and we now testify that the Father sent the Son to be the savior of the world. [15]Whoever professes that Jesus is the Son of God, God remains in them, and they remain in God. [16]And so we have come to know and we have come to believe the love that God has for us.

VERIFICATIONS OF GOD'S LOVE

God is love, and the one who abides in love abides in God and God abides in them. [17]By this, love is perfected with us, so that we may have confidence in the day of judgment, because just as Jesus is so also are we in this world. [18]There is no fear in love, but perfect love expels fear, because fear includes punishment and because the one who fears is not perfected in love. [19]As for us, we persist in love because he first loved us. [20]If someone says, "I love God," and that same someone hates his brother or sister, he is a liar; for the one, who does not love his brother or sister whom he has seen, is unable to love God whom they have not seen. [21]And this commandment we have from God, namely, that the one who loves God should love his brother and sister also.

GOD'S FAMILY

5: [1]Everyone who persists in believing that Jesus is the Christ has been fathered by God, and everyone who persists in loving the Father loves those who have been fathered by him also. [2]By this we know that we love the children of God, whenever we persist in loving God and whenever we persist in carrying out God's commandments. [3]For this is the love for God, namely, that we persist in keeping God's commandments; and God's commandments are not difficult to carry out, [4]because everyone who has been fathered by God overcomes the world; and this is the victory that overcame the world, our faith.

OVERCOMING THE WORLD'S SYSTEM

[5]Now who is the one who overcomes the world except it is the one who believes that Jesus is the Son of God? [6]This is the one who came through water and blood, Jesus, who is the Christ. Jesus came not by water only but Jesus came by the water and the blood; and the Spirit is the one who testifies, because the Spirit is the truth. [7]For the ones that testify are three, [8]they are the Spirit and the water and the blood, and these three are one. [9]If we receive the testimony of men, God's testimony is greater, because this is the testimony of God, namely that God has testified concerning his Son.

[10]The one who believes in the Son of God has the testimony in himself; [10]the one who does not believe God has made God to be a liar, [10]because he has not believed in the testimony that God has testified concerning his Son, Jesus.

[11]And this is the testimony, that God granted us eternal life, and that this life is in his Son. [12]The one who has the Son has the life; the one who does not have the Son of God does not have the life.

CREATING CONFIDENCE

[13]I have written these things to you, namely, you who believe in the name of the Son of God, so that you may know that you have eternal life. [14]And this is the confidence that we have before God: that whatever we ask for according to his will, God listens to us. [15]And if we know that God listens to us, namely, he lis-

tens to whatever we ask, we know that we have the requests that we have asked from God. [16]If anyone sees their brother or sister committing a sin not leading to death, they should ask God, and God will grant to them life, namely, to the one who does not commit a sin leading to death. There is a sin leading to death; I do not say that he should ask about that. [17]All unrighteousness is sin, and yet there is a sin not leading in death. [18]We know that everyone fathered by God does not persist in sin, but the one fathered by God he preserves them and the Evil One cannot harm them. [19]We know that we are of God, and that the whole world lies in the power of the Evil One. [20]And we know that the Son of God has come, and that he has given us understanding in order that we may know the true one; and we are in the true one, in his Son Jesus, who is the Christ. This one is the true God and eternal life. [21]Children, guard yourselves from idols.

Second John: Interpretive Translation

John's Heartfelt Greeting

[1]The Elder, to the elect lady and her children, whom I love in truth and not I alone, but also whom all those who have known the truth love, [2]because the truth remains in us, and because the truth will be with us forever. [3] Grace, mercy, and peace will be with us from God, the father, and from Jesus Christ, who is the son of the Father, and in truth and love.

John's Expectation

[4]I rejoiced greatly, because I have found some of your children walking in truth, just as we received the commandment from the Father. [5]And now I ask you, lady, not as one writing to you a new commandment, but as one writing to you a commandment that we have had since the beginning, namely that we persist in loving one another. [6]And this is love: that we walk according to his commandments. This is the commandment, just as you have heard from the beginning, namely, that you walk in it.

John's Warning

[7]For many deceivers have gone out into the world, the ones who do not confess Jesus Christ has come in the flesh. This one is the deceiver and the Antichrist. [8]Watch yourselves, in order that you do not lose what you worked for, but in order that you might receive *your* full reward. [9]Everyone who goes on ahead and does not remain in the teaching about Christ does not have God; the one who remains in the teaching, this one has both the Father and the Son. [10]If anyone comes to you if they do not carry this teaching, do not welcome them into your home and do not say to them, "Greetings." [11]For the one who says to them, "Greetings," shares in her evil works.

John's Desire

[12]Although I have many things to write to you, I do not wish to do so through pen and ink, but I hope to come to you and to speak face-to-face, in order that our joy might be complete. [13]The children of your elect sister greet you.

Third John: Interpretive Translation

JOHN'S GREETING AND PRAYER

[1]The elder, to Gaius the beloved, whom I love in truth.

[2]Beloved, in all respects I pray that you are prospering and that you are well, just as your soul is prospering. [3]For I rejoiced greatly when our delegation of preachers and teachers came and testified to your faithfulness to the truth, just as I know you are living with respect to the truth. [4]I have no greater joy than this, namely, that I hear my children are continually living in the truth.

JOHN'S EXHORTATION

[5]Beloved, you continually demonstrate faithfulness, in whatever you do for the brothers (and strangers at that), [6]who have testified to your love before the church, whom will do well to send them on their way in a manner worthy of God; [7]for they have gone forth on behalf of 'The Name' (of Jesus) and while accepting nothing from pagans. [8]We therefore are obligated to support such people, so that we become co-workers in cooperation with the truth.

JOHN'S CONCERN

[9]I wrote a similar letter to a sister church; but Diotrephes, namely, the one who loves to be first among them, does not acknowledge us. [10]Therefore, if I come, I will bring up his deeds, which he is continually doing, by talking slanderous nonsense about us; and because he is not being content with these things, he himself continually refuses to welcome the traveling servants of God, he continually hinders the people who want to welcome these servants, and he continually throws them out of the church.

JOHN'S EXPECTATION

[11]Beloved, do not imitate that which is bad behavior, but imitate behavior which is good behavior. The one who does what is good has a relationship with God; the one who does what is bad has no relationship with God. [12]Demetrius has received a good report by all, even by the truth itself; and we also testify to him, and you know that our testimony is true.

John's Desire

[13]I had many more things to write to you, but I do not wish to write them out to you by means of ink and pen. [14]Rather, I hope to see you immediately, and we will speak face-to-face. [15]Peace be to you. The friends here greet you. Greet the friends there by name.

Figures of Speech in John's Writings

FIGURES OF SPEECH INVOLVING COMPARISON

1. Simile, or Resemblance: a declaration that one thing explicitly (by the presence of "like or "as") resembles another.

   John 1:14 "And we saw his glory, the glory as of the only begotten of the Father." (NIV)

2. Metaphor, or Representation: a declaration that one thing is or represents another.

   John 8:12 "I am the light of the world." (NASB NIV NET, etc.)

3. Hypocatastasis, or Implication: a declaration that implies the comparison.

   John 2:19 "Destroy this temple and in three days I will raise it up again." (Cf. 2:21) (NET)

4. Allegory, or Continued Metaphor and Hypocatastasis: a continued comparison by representation or implication.

   John 4:35 (possible) "Don't you say, 'There are four more months and then comes the harvest'? I tell you, look up and see that the fields are already white for harvest!" (NET)

5. Proverb: a wayside saying in common use, a specific illustration to signify a truth of life.

   John 4:37 "For in this instance the saying is true, 'One sows and another reaps.'" (NET cf. NASB)

   (Perhaps 1 John 5:1 "everyone who persists in loving the Father, loves also those who have been fathered by him.")

6. Personification: the giving of human characteristics to inanimate objects, ideas, or animals.

   1 John 2:16 ". . . the flesh that desires and the eyes that desire . . ."

7. Anthropomorphism: the representation of God in the form of, or with the attributes of man.

   1 John 5:14–15a "Whenever we ask anything according to his will . . . he (=God) listens to us."

8. Zoomorphism: the representation of God (or man) in the form of, or with the attributes of, the lower animals:

    John 1:29 "Look, the Lamb of God who takes away the sin of the world!"

9. Idiom: a fixed expression that cannot be understood grammatically from its component parts, but it has an understood and set meaning.

    Bullinger offers many examples of idiomatic expressions such as "my soul," "lift up your eyes," "the sons of God," "breaking bread," "the Son of Man," and "turn to ashes."

    1 John 3:22 (possible) "and so whatever we ask for, we will receive from him (= God)"

    2 John 12c "we will speak face-to-face" (lit. "mouth to mouth")

    3 John 14b "we will speak face-to-face" (lit. "mouth to mouth")

FIGURES OF SPEECH INVOLVING SUBSTITUTION

1. Metonymy, or Change of Noun: the change of a word naming an object for another word closely associated with it.

    a. When the cause is stated but the effect is intended (instrument for product):

        3 John 2 "I pray (that you are prospering ... just as your soul is prospering"

    b. When the effect is stated but the cause is intended (reverse of the above):

        1 John. 3:15 "Everyone who persists in hating his brother is a murderer."

    c. When the subject is stated for an attribute or adjunct of it (metonymy of subject):

        1 John. 2:15 "Do not love the world" ("world" = people; cf. 2:2; 3:1; 4:1; 5:19)

        1 John 2:16 "... the flesh that desires and the eyes that desire ..."

        1 John 3:12 "if our heart condemns us" ("heart" = conscience)

        1 John 3:17 "whoever shuts off his (or her) heart" ("heart" = "compassion").

    d. When the attribute or adjunct that pertains to the subject is put for the subject (metonymy of adjunct; opposite of the previous):

        1 John 5:13a "I have written these things to you ... namely, you who believe in the name of the Son of God ..." (cf. 1 John 2:12; 3:23; 3 John 7)

2. Synecdoche, or Transfer: the exchange of one idea for another associated idea (the metonymy deals with nouns, the synecdoche with closely related ideas).

    a. The genus is put for the species (general for specific):

        1 John 3:6 "Everyone who makes it a practice to abide in him (= Jesus) does not persist in sin"

b. The species is put for the genus (specific for the general): (NET)
    John 13:14 "…you too ought to <u>wash one another's feet</u>." (idea of service)
    1 John 3:16 Jesus gave up his life . . . "<u>we are obligated to give</u> up our lives
    for our brothers (and sisters)"
    1 John 3:19c "we will convince our <u>hearts</u> before him (= God)" ("hearts"
    represents the whole person)

c. The whole is put for the part (this may be a lexical consideration):
    1 John. 3:16 "By this we have come to know love: that one (= Jesus) <u>gave
    up his life</u> for us" (Idea of service)

d. The part is put for the whole:
    1 John 2:18 "that it is the last <u>hour</u>." (hour = time period)
    1 John 4:2 "Jesus to be the Christ who has come in <u>flesh</u>" (flesh = physical
    body)

3. <u>Hendiadys</u>, or Two for One: two formally coordinate terms express a single
    concept in which one of the components defines the other (see also verbal
    hendiadys in Lambdin).
        John 4:23 "The true worshipers will worship the Father in <u>spirit and truth</u>."
        (NASB ESV NET etc.)
        1 John 3:18a "let us not love with <u>word</u> or with <u>tongue</u>"
        1 John 5:2 (possible) "whenever we persist <u>in loving</u> God and whenever]
        we persist <u>in carrying out</u> his commandments"; cf. 3:22)

4. <u>Euphemism</u>: the substitution of an inoffensive or mild expression for an of-
    fensive one:
        1 John 3:16 "By this we have come to know love: that one (= Jesus) <u>gave
        up his life</u> for us"
        (gave up his life = violent crucifixion death)

5. <u>Apostrophe</u>: a turning aside from the direct matter to address others (who or
    which may not actually be present):
        1 John 2:4 (possible) "The one who says ("I know him [= God]"), and who
        does not persist in keeping his commands, is a liar"
        1 John 3:18b (possible) "but [let us love] <u>in deed and truth</u>"

6. <u>Hyperbaton</u>, or Transposition: the placing of a word out of its usual order in
    the sentence for the sake of emphasis.
        1 John 2:24 "Let what you <u>yourselves</u> have heard from the beginning re-
        main in you" (see the Greek clausal outline)

7. <u>Antimereia</u>: the use of one part of speech for another.

    Perhaps 1 John 1:1 "and which our hands have touched about the word, which is <u>life</u>"

    (Noun used adjectivally = life)

8. <u>Type</u>: a divinely prefigured illustration of a corresponding reality (called the antitype):

    1 John 3:11a–12b (possible) "namely that we should love one another; not as <u>Cain</u> who was of the Evil One and who brutally murdered his brother (= Abel)"

9. <u>Symbol</u>: a material object substituted for a moral or spiritual truth.

    1 John 1:5 "namely that God is <u>light</u> and [that] in him there is no darkness at all" (light = morally pure)

10. <u>Irony</u>: the expression of thought in a form that conveys its opposite.

    John 3:10 "Jesus answered, 'Are you the teacher of Israel, and yet you don't understand these things?'" (NET)

FIGURES OF SPEECH INVOLVING ADDITION OR AMPLIFICATION

1. <u>Chiasm</u>: a form of parallelism in which there is the inversion of terms in the second half of the verse.

    3 John 11 "Beloved, do not imitate that which is bad (behavior),

    but (imitate) that which is good.

    The (one who does what is good) is of God;

    the one who does what is bad has not seen God.

    1 John 4:20b (possible)

    "If someone says, "I <u>love God,</u>

    and [that same someone] <u>hates</u> his brother and sister

    he is a liar

    or the one who <u>does not love</u> his or her brother or sister

    is unable to <u>love God</u> . . . whom he has not seen

    1 John 5:14b–15a

    whatever <u>we ask</u> anything according to his will

    and if we know (that <u>he listens</u> to us)

    namely, [<u>he listens</u> to] (whatever we ask),

    we know . . . the requests that <u>we have asked</u> from him (= God)

2. <u>Repetition</u>: the repetition of the same word or words in a passage (many varieties).

    1 John 3:20 "that whenever our heart <u>condemns</u> us, that God is greater than our heart and [that] he <u>knows</u> all things." (Two different words from the same Greek root)

3. <u>Anaphora</u>, or Like Sentence Beginnings: the repetition of key words or lines at the beginning of successive predications.

> 1 John 1:1, 3 "That which was from the beginning,
>> which we have heard,
>> which we have seen with our eyes,
>> which we have looked at . . .
>> that which we have seen and heard we announce to you too."

4. <u>Inclusio</u>: the rhetorical device in which a literary unit begins and ends with the same (or similar) word, phrase, or clause. It is a framing device, stressing the theme.

> 1 John 2:18 "Children, it is the <u>last hour</u> . . . many antichrists have appeared, whereby we now know it is the <u>last hour</u>."

5. <u>Polysyndeton</u>, or Many Ands: the repetition of the conjunction.

> John 10:27–28 "My sheep listen to my voice,
>> and I know them,
>> and they follow me.
>> (and) I give them eternal life,
>> and they will never perish;
>> (and) no one will snatch them from my hand." (Parentheses represent conjunctions in the Greek text.) (NASB cf. KJV)

6. <u>Anabasis</u>, or Gradual Ascent: an increase of sense in successive lines.

> 1 John 1:1 "That which was from the beginning,
>> which we have heard,
>> which we have seen with our eyes,
>> which we have looked at
>> and which our hands have touched (concerning the word of life)."

7. <u>Hyperbole</u>: exaggerated theme for the purpose of emphasis or heightened effect (more is said than is literally meant).

> John 12:19 "Look, the <u>world</u> has run off after him!" (NET cf. NASB NRSV)
> 1 John 5:19 "and that the <u>whole world</u> lies in the power of the Evil One"

FIGURES OF SPEECH INVOLVING OMISSION OR SUPPRESSION

1. Ellipsis: the omission of any element of language that technically renders a sentence to be "ungrammatical," yet the sentence is usually understood in context.
   > 1 John 2:7 "Beloved, I write no new commandment to you, but [I now write] an old commandment"
   > (perhaps: 1 John 1:3; 3:20; 2 John 5, 8)

2. Aposiopesis, or Sudden Silence: the breaking off from what is being said (in anger, grief, deprecation, promise etc.) with sudden silence.
   > John 6:62 "Then what if you see the Son of Man ascending to where he was before?" (NET) (implying "would you believe then?")

3. Erotesis, or Rhetorical Questions: the asking of questions without expecting an answer (to express affirmation, demonstration, wonder, exultation, wishes, denials, doubts, admonitions, expostulations, prohibitions, pity, disparagements, reproaches, lamentation, indignation or absurdities).
   > 1 John 2:22 "Who is the liar except the one who persists in denying that Jesus is the Christ?"
   > 1 John 3:17 "and whoever shuts off their heart against him (or her), how does the love of God remain in him (or her)?"

4. Meiosis, or Belittling: a belittling of one thing to magnify another (also called litotes or understatement).
   > 1 John 3:17 "and whoever shuts off their heart against him (or her), how does the love of God remain in him (or her)?"

5. Tapeinosis, or Demeaning: a lessening of a thing in order to increase it.
   > John 6:37 "... the one who comes to me I will never send away" (Implying that he will by all means receive that one). (NIV NET)

6. Anacoluthon, or Non-sequence: a breaking off of the sequence of thought, a change from a construction which has been begun already, to one of a different kind (especially after a long parenthesis).
   > 1 John 1:9 "if we confess our sins, he is faithful and righteous to pardon our sins..."
   > 3 John 11b (possible) "Beloved, do not imitate that which is bad (behavior), but (imitate) that which is good."

Bibliography

Aland, Kurt, et al. 1979. *Novum Testamenum Graece.* 26th ed. Stuttgart: Deutsche Bibelgesellschaft.

———. 1993. *Novum Testamenum Graece.* 27th ed. Stuttgart: Deutsche Bibelgesellschaft.

———. 2012. *Novum Testamenum Graece.* 28th ed. Stuttgart: Deutsche Bibelgesellschaft.

Apostolic Fathers. 1912–1913, 1914–1917. Translated by Kirsopp et al. 2 vols. LCL. Cambridge: Harvard University Press.

Bateman IV, Herbert W. 2006. "3 John: Tracing the Flow of Thought." Pages 449–61 in *Interpreting the New Testament Text: Introduction to the Art and Science of Biblical Study.* Edited by Darrell L. Bock and Buist Fanning. Wheaton, IL: Crossway.

———. 2008. *A Workbook for Intermediate Greek: Grammar, Exegesis, and Commentary on 1–3 John.* Grand Rapids: Kregel.

———. 2013. *Interpreting the General Letters.* HNTE. Grand Rapids: Kregel.

———. 2015. *Jude.* EEC. Bellingham, WA: Lexham.

Bateman IV, Herbert W., Darrell L. Bock, and Gordon H. Johnston. 2012. *Jesus the Messiah: Tracing the Promises, Expectations, and Coming of Israel's King.* Grand Rapids: Kregel.

Bateman IV, Herbert W., and Aaron C. Peer. 2017. *Translating 1 John Clause by Clause: An Exegetical Guide.* Leesburg, IN: Cyber-Center for Biblical Studies.

Balz, Horst and Gerhard Schneider. 1990–1993. *Exegetical Dictionary of the New Testament.* 3 vols. Grand Rapids: Eerdmans.

Baugh, S. M. 1999. *A First John Reader: Intermediate Greek Reading Notes and Grammar.* Phillipsburg: NJ: P&R Publishing.

Blass, Frederich, Albert Debrunner, and Robert W. Funk. 1961. *A Greek Grammar of the New Testament and Other Early Christian Literature.* Chicago: University of Chicago Press.

Brown, Raymond E. 1982. *The Epistles of John.* AB 30. Garden City, NY: Doubleday.

Bock, Darrell L., and Buist M. Fanning, eds. 2006. *Interpreting the New Testament Text: Introduction to the Art and Science of Exegesis.* Wheaton, IL: Crossway.

Bullinger, E. W. 1898, 1986. *Figures of Speech Used in the Bible: Explained and Illustrated.* Grand Rapids: Baker.

Burer, Michael H., and Jeffery E. Miller. 2008. *A New Reader's Lexicon of the Greek New Testament.* Grand Rapids: Kregel.

Campbell, Constantine R. 2008. *Basics of Verbal Aspect in Biblical Greek.* Grand Rapids: Zondervan.

Carson, D. A. 1996. *Exegetical Fallacies.* 2nd ed. Grand Rapids: Baker.

Charlesworth, James H., ed. 1985. *The Old Testament Pseudepigrapha.* 2 vols. New York: Doubleday.

Comfort, Philip Wesley. 2015. *A Commentary on the Manuscripts of the New Testament.* Grand Rapids: Kregel.

Culpepper, R. Alan. 1998. *The Gospel and Letters of John.* Nashville: Abingdon.

Culy, Martin M. 2004. *I, II, III John: A Handbook on the Greek Text.* BHGNT. Waco, TX: Baylor University Press.

Danker, Frederick W., Walter Bauer, William F. Arndt, and F. Wilbur Gingrich. 2000. *A Greek–English Lexicon of the New Testament and Other Early Christian Literature.* 3rd ed. Chicago: University of Chicago Press.

Eusebius. 1926–1938. *Ecclesiastical History.* Translated by Kirsopp Lake and J. E. L. Oulton et al. 2 vols. LCL. Cambridge: Harvard University Press.

Fanning, Buist. 1990. *Verbal Aspect in the New Testament.* OTM. Oxford: Clarendon.

Funk, Robert W. 1967. "Form and Structure of II John and III John." *JBL* 86:424–30.

Guthrie, Donald. 1990. *Introduction to the New Testament.* Downers Grove, IL: Intervarsity Press.

Guthrie, George H., and J. Scott Duvall. 1988. *Biblical Greek Exegesis: A Guided Approach to Learning Intermediate and Advanced Greek.* Grand Rapids: Zondervan.

Hass, C., Marinus de Jonge, and Jan L. Swellengrebal. 1972. *A Translator's Handbook on the Letters of John.* HeTr 13. London: United Bible Societies.

Herodotus. 1921–1928. *The History of Herodotus.* Translated by A. D. Godley et al. 4 vols. LCL. Cambridge: Harvard University Press.

Hodges, Zane C., and Arthur L. Farstad. 1985. *The Greek New Testament According to the Majority Text.* 2nd ed. Nashville: Nelson.

Holmes, Michael W. 2010. *The Greek New Testament SBL Edition*, Atlanta, GA: Society of Biblical Literature; Bellingham, WA: Logos Bible Software.

Josephus. 1926–1965. Translated by H. St. J. Thackeray et al. 10 vols. LCL. Cambridge: Harvard University Press.

Kim, Chan-Hie. 1972. *Form and Structure of the Familiar Greek Letter of Recommendation.* SBLDS 4. Missoula, MT: Scholars.

Kittel, Gerhard, and Gerhard Friedrich, eds. 1964–1976. *Theological Dictionary of the New Testament.* Translated by Geoffrey W. Bromiley. 10 vols. Grand Rapids: Eerdmans.

Kruse, Colin G. 2000. *The Letters of John.* PNTC. Grand Rapids: Eerdmans.

Lieu, Judith M. 2008. *I, II, III John: A Commentary.* NTL. Louisville: Westminster John Knox.

Louw, Johannes P., and Eugene A. Nida, eds. 1989. *Greek-English Lexicon of the New Testament: Based on Semantic Domains.* 2nd ed. New York: United Bible Societies.

MacDonald, William G. 1986. *Greek Enchiridion: A Concise Handbook of Grammar for Translation and Exegesis.* Peabody, MA: Hendrickson.

Metzger, Bruce M. 1992. *The Text of the New Testament: Its Transmission, Corruption, and Restoration.* 3rd enlarged ed. New York: Oxford University Press.

———. 1994. *A Textual Commentary on the Greek New Testament.* 2nd ed. Stuttgart: Deutsches Bibelgesellschaft.

Moule, C. F. D. 1959. *An Idiom Book of the Greek New Testament.* 2nd ed. Cambridge: Cambridge University Press.

Moulton, James Hope, and George Milligan. 1930. *The Vocabulary of the Greek Testament: Illustrated from the Papyri and Other Non-literary Sources.* Grand Rapids: Eerdmans.

Mounce, William D. 1996. *A Graded Reader of Biblical Greek.* Grand Rapids: Zondervan.

———. 2009. *Basics of Biblical Greek Grammar.* 3rd ed. Grand Rapids: Zondervan.

Nestle, Eberhard. 1898. *Greek New Testament.* New York: American Bible Society.

The Oxyrhynchus Papyri. Translated by Bernard P. Grenfell and Arthur S. Hunt, 15 vols. Cornell University Library Historical Monographs Collection. Reprinted by Cornell University Library Digital Collections.

Painter, John. 2002. *1, 2, and 3 John.* SP 18. Collegeville, MN: Liturgical.

Peer, Aaron C., and Herbert W. Bateman IV. 2015. *Translating 2 and 3 John Clause by Clause: An Exegetical Guide*. Leesburg, IN: Cyber-Center for Biblical Studies.

Philo. 1929–1962. Translated by F. H. Colson and G. H. Whitaker et al. 10 vols. LCL. Cambridge: Harvard University Press.

Porter, Stanley E. 1994. *Idioms of the Greek New Testament*. 2nd ed. BLG 2. Sheffield: JSOT Press.

Robertson, A. T. 1934. *A Grammar of the Greek New Testament in the Light of Historical Research*. Nashville: Broadman.

Robinson, Maurice A., and William G. Pierpont. 2005. *The New Testament in the Original Greek: Byzantine Textform, 2005*. Southborough, MA: Chilton.

Rogers, Cleon L., Jr., and Cleon L. Rogers III. 1998. *The New Linguistic and Exegetical Key to the Greek New Testament*. Grand Rapids: Zondervan.

Rotelle, John E. editor. 1990. *The Works of Saint Augustine: A Translation for the 21st Century*. Translated by Edmund Hill. Brooklyn, NY: New City Press.

Schnackenburg, Rudolf. 1979. *Die Johannesbriefe*. 6th ed. HTKNT 13, no. 3. Freiburg in Breisgau: Herder.

Smalley, Stephen S. 1984. *1, 2, 3 John*. WBC 51. Waco, TX: Word.

Spiq, Ceslas. 1996. *Theological Lexicon of the New Testament*. Translated by James Ernest. 3 vols. Peabody, MA: Hendrickson.

Stott, John R. W. 1988. *The Letters of John: An Introduction and Commentary*. 2nd ed. TNTC. Grand Rapids: Eerdmans. First edition 1964.

Stowers, Stanley K. 1986. *Letter Writing in Greco-Roman Antiquity*. LEC. Philadelphia: Westminster.

Strecker, Georg. 1996. *The Johannine Letters*. Edited by Harold Attridge. Translated by Linda M. Maloney. Hermeneia. Minneapolis: Fortress.

Turner, Nigel. 1963. *A Grammar of New Testament Greek: Volume 3 Syntax*. Edinburgh: T&T Clark.

_____. 1976. *A Grammar of New Testament Greek: Volume 4 Style*. Edinburgh: T&T Clark.

Wallace, Daniel B. 1996. *Greek Grammar Beyond the Basics: An Exegetical Syntax of the New Testament*. Grand Rapids: Zondervan.

Wenham, J. W. 1991. *The Elements of New Testament Greek*. Repr. with corrections. New York: Cambridge University Press.

Westcott, Brooke Foss. 1966. *The Epistles of St. John: The Greek Text.* 3rd ed. 1892. Repr. Grand Rapids: Eerdmans.

Wise, Michael, Martin Abegg, and Edward Cook. 1996. *The Dead Sea Scrolls: A New Translation.* New York: HarperSanFrancisco.

Yarbrough, Robert W. 2008. *1–3 John.* BECNT. Grand Rapids: Baker Academic.

Zerwick, Maximilian. 1963. *Biblical Greek: Illustrated by Examples.* Translated by Joseph Smith. SubBi 41. Rome: Pontifical Biblical Institute.

Nugget Index

GRAMMATICAL NUGGETS

Syntactical Nuggets

SEMANTICAL NUGGETS

1 JOHN

2 JOHN

3 JOHN

LEXICAL NUGGETS

1 JOHN

2 John

3 JOHN

THEOLOGICAL NUGGETS

1 JOHN

TEXT-CRITICAL NUGGETS

1 JOHN

2 JOHN